Beginning C# 2008 Objects

From Concept to Code

Grant Palmer and Jacquie Barker

Apress®

Beginning C# 2008 Objects: From Concept to Code

Copyright © 2008 by Grant Palmer and Jacquie Barker

ISBN-13 (pbk): 978-1-4302-1088-7

ISBN-13 (electronic): 978-1-4302-1087-0

Printed and bound in the United States of America 9 8 7 6 5 4 3 2 1

Trademarked names may appear in this book. Rather than use a trademark symbol with every occurrence of a trademarked name, we use the names only in an editorial fashion and to the benefit of the trademark owner, with no intention of infringement of the trademark.

Lead Editors: Joohn Choe, Dominic Shakeshaft
Technical Reviewer: Andy Olsen
Editorial Board: Clay Andres, Steve Anglin, Mark Beckner, Ewan Buckingham, Tony Campbell,
    Gary Cornell, Jonathan Gennick, Michelle Lowman, Matthew Moodie, Jeffrey Pepper,
    Frank Pohlmann, Ben Renow-Clarke, Dominic Shakeshaft, Matt Wade, Tom Welsh
Project Manager: Beth Christmas
Copy Editor: Nancy Sixsmith
Associate Production Director: Kari Brooks-Copony
Production Editor: Elizabeth Berry
Compositor: Diana Van Winkle
Proofreader: Linda Seifert
Indexer: John Collin
Artist: April Milne
Cover Designer: Kurt Krames
Manufacturing Director: Tom Debolski

Distributed to the book trade worldwide by Springer-Verlag New York, Inc., 233 Spring Street, 6th Floor, New York, NY 10013. Phone 1-800-SPRINGER, fax 201-348-4505, e-mail orders-ny@springer-sbm.com, or visit http://www.springeronline.com.

For information on translations, please contact Apress directly at 2855 Telegraph Avenue, Suite 600, Berkeley, CA 94705. Phone 510-549-5930, fax 510-549-5939, e-mail info@apress.com, or visit http://www.apress.com.

Apress and friends of ED books may be purchased in bulk for academic, corporate, or promotional use. eBook versions and licenses are also available for most titles. For more information, reference our Special Bulk Sales–eBook Licensing web page at http://www.apress.com/info/bulksales.

The source code for this book is available to readers at http://www.apress.com.

In loving memory of my wonderful parents, Bill and Dorothy Jost
—Jacquie Barker

To Lisa, Zachary, and Jackson, oh my!
—Grant Palmer

Contents at a Glance

PART ONE ▪▪▪ The ABCs of Objects

PART TWO ▪▪▪ Object Modeling 101

PART THREE ■■■ Translating a UML "Blueprint" into C# Code

Contents

PART ONE ■■■ The ABCs of Objects

PART TWO ■■■ Object Modeling 101

About the Authors

 **GRANT PALMER** has worked in the Space Technology Division at NASA Ames Research Center in Moffett Field, CA for the past 23 years. Grant was a NASA engineer for 15 years and currently works as a scientific programmer with the ELORET Corporation, developing computer applications that help design the thermal protection systems of spacecraft reentering the Earth's atmosphere.

Grant earned a Bachelor of Science degree in mechanical engineering from the University of California, Berkeley. He later received a Master of Science degree in aerospace engineering from Stanford University. Grant is an expert in FORTRAN, C, C++, and Perl, but now does most of his programming in the more modern languages of Java and C#. He has authored or coauthored seven books on computer programming, including *Physics for Game Programmers* (Apress) and *C# Programmer's Reference* (Wrox).

Grant lives in Bothell, Washington, with his wife, Lisa; his two sons, Jackson and Zachary; and various members of the animal kingdom.

 **JACQUIE BARKER** is a professional software engineer, author, and adjunct faculty member at George Mason University (GMU) in Fairfax, Virginia and The George Washington University (GWU) in Washington, D.C. With more than 25 years of experience as a hands-on software engineer and project manager, Jacquie has spent the past 12 years focusing on object technology, becoming proficient as an object modeler and Sun Microsystems–certified Java developer. She is currently employed as a senior member of the technical staff at Technology Associates, Inc. in Herndon, Virginia, and is also the founder of ObjectStart LLC, an object technology mentorship and training firm.

Jacquie earned a Bachelor of Science degree in computer engineering with highest honors from Case Western Reserve University in Cleveland, Ohio. She later received a Master of Science degree in computer science from UCLA, focusing on software systems engineering, and has subsequently pursued post-graduate studies in information technology at GMU.

The first edition of *Beginning C# Objects* was adapted from Jacquie's bestselling book, *Beginning Java Objects: From Concepts to Code*, published originally by the former Wrox Press, Ltd. and now by Apress. Jacquie's winning formula for teaching object fundamentals continues to receive praise from readers around the world, and *Beginning Java Objects: From Concepts to Code* has been adopted by many universities as a key textbook in their core IT curricula. Her latest book, *Taming the Technology Tidal Wave: Practical Career Advice for Technical Professionals*, is now available through ObjectStart Press.

Please visit Jacquie's web sites, `http://objectstart.com` and `http://techtidalwave.com`, for more information on her various publications and service offerings.

On a personal note, Jacquie's passions include her husband, Steve; their four pet cats, Kwiddie, Tiffie, Walter, and Wynxie; and her work as an animal rescue volunteer (please visit `http://petsbringjoy.org`). When not engaged in computer-related pursuits, Jacquie and Steve enjoy motorcycle road trips through the Virginia countryside on their Gold Wing, tandem bicycling, and spending quality time with family and friends.

About the Technical Reviewer

ANDY OLSEN is a freelance developer and consultant based in the UK. He has been working with .NET since the Beta 1 days and has authored and reviewed several books for Apress, covering C#, Visual Basic, ASP.NET, and other topics. Andy is a keen football and rugby fan, and enjoys running and skiing (badly). He lives by the seaside in Swansea with his wife, Jayne, and children, Emily and Thomas, who have just discovered the thrills of surfing and look much cooler than he ever will!

Acknowledgments

We'd like to offer sincere, heartfelt thanks to everyone who helped us produce this book:

- To Andy Olsen, who served as our primary technical reviewer. He's like an all-knowing kung fu master, except he knows everything about .NET instead of kung fu. Thanks also to Damien Foggon who gave the book an extra set of expert eyes during the reviews of the chapters in Part 3 of the book.

- To Dominic Shakeshaft, our editor, for his dedication to ensuring the clarity of our book's message.

- To Gary Cornell, Apress publisher, for suggesting a Java-to-C# "port" of *Beginning Java Objects*.

- To *all* the folks at Apress—especially Beth Christmas, Joohn Choe, Nancy Sixsmith, Laura Cheu, and Elizabeth Berry—for their superb editorial/production/marketing support.

- To our spouses, children, and assorted other family members and friends, for once again being patient as we became temporarily consumed with the "writing biz."

Grant Palmer and Jacquie Barker

Preface

As a Java developer and instructor, Jacquie Barker wrote her first book, *Beginning Java Objects,* to communicate her passionate belief that learning objects thoroughly is an essential first step in mastering an object-oriented programming language (OOPL). Since *Beginning Java Objects* was first published in November 2000, we've heard from countless readers who agree wholeheartedly!

We were therefore delighted when Gary Cornell, the publisher of Apress, and Dominic Shakeshaft, Apress editorial director, approached us about producing a C# version of *Beginning Java Objects*. It's indeed true that basic object concepts are "language neutral." What you'll learn conceptually about objects in Part One of this book, and about object modeling in Part Two, could apply equally well to any OOPL.

But our goal for this book is twofold: not only do we want to teach you about objects and object modeling, but we also want to get you properly jump-started with the C# programming language by showing you how such concepts translate into C# syntax specifically. Hence, *Beginning C# Objects* was born!

The first edition of *Beginning C# Objects* came out in the spring of 2004. Since that time, C# and the .NET platform have grown by leaps and bounds. Several new releases of the .NET Framework have come out, and many exciting new features have been added to the C# programming language. This second edition of the book captures the "latest and greatest" of .NET and C# for beginning programmers and should get you well on your way to becoming an expert C# programmer.

Grant Palmer and Jacquie Barker

Introduction

First and foremost, *Beginning C# 2008 Objects: From Concept to Code* is a book about software objects: what they are, why they are so "magical" and yet so straightforward, and how one goes about structuring a software application to use objects appropriately.

This is also a book about C#: not a hard-core, "everything-there-is-to-know-about-C#" book; it's a gentle, yet comprehensive, introduction to the language, with special emphasis on how to transition from an object model to a fully functional C# application (which few, if any, other books provide).

Goals for this Book

Our goals in writing this book (and, hopefully, yours for buying it) are the following:

- Make you comfortable with fundamental object-oriented (OO) terminology and concepts

- Give you hands-on, practical experience with object modeling; that is, with developing a "blueprint" that can be used as the basis for subsequently building an OO software system

- Illustrate the basics of how such an object model is translated into a working software application—a C# application, to be specific, although the techniques that you'll learn for object modeling apply equally well to any object-oriented programming language (OOPL)

If you're already experienced with the C# language (but not with object fundamentals), this book will provide you with critical knowledge about the language's OO roots. On the other hand, if you're a newcomer to C#, this book will get you properly "jump-started." Either way, this book is a "must-read" for anyone who wants to become proficient with an OOPL like C#.

Just as importantly, this book is *not* meant to do the following:

- *Turn you into an overnight "pro" in object modeling.* Like all advanced skills, becoming totally comfortable with object modeling takes two things: a good theoretical foundation and a lot of practice. We give you the foundation in this book, along with suggestions for projects and exercises that will enable you to apply and practice your newfound knowledge. But the only way you'll really get to be proficient with object modeling is by participating in OO modeling and development projects over time. This book will give you the skills—and hopefully the confidence—to begin to apply object techniques in a professional setting, which is where your real learning will take place, particularly if you have an OO-experienced mentor to guide you through your first "industrial-strength" project.

- *Make you an expert in any particular OO methodology*: There are dozens of different formal methods for OO software development; new variations continue to emerge, and no one methodology is necessarily better than another. For example, UML (Unified Modeling Language) notation is one of the newest, and OMT (Object Modeling Technique) notation is one of the oldest, yet the two are remarkably similar because UML is based to a great extent on OMT. By making sure that you understand the generic *process* of object modeling along with the specifics of the UML, you'll be armed with the knowledge you need to read about, evaluate, and select a specific methodology—or craft your own. (Who knows? Maybe someday you'll even write a book yourself on the methodology that you invent!)

- *Teach you everything you'll ever need to know about C#*: C# is a very rich language, consisting of dozens of core classes, hundreds of classes available from the Framework Class Library, and literally thousands of operations that can be performed with and by these classes. If C# provides a dozen alternative ways to do something in particular, we'll explain the one or two ways that we feel best suit the problem at hand, to give you an appreciation for how things are done. Nonetheless, you'll definitely see enough of the C# language in this book to be able to build a complete application.

Armed with the foundation you gain from this book, you'll be poised and ready to appreciate a more thorough treatment of C# such as that offered by one of the many other C# references that are presently on the market or an in-depth UML reference.

Why Is Understanding Objects So Critical to Being a Successful OO Programmer?

Time and again, we meet software developers—at our places of employment, at clients' offices, at professional conferences, on college campuses—who have attempted to master an OOPL like C# by taking a course in C#, reading a book about C#, or installing and using a C# integrated development environment (IDE) such as Visual Studio .NET. However, there is something fundamentally missing: a basic understanding of what objects are all about and, more importantly, knowledge of how to structure a software application from the ground up to make the most of objects.

Imagine that you know the basics of home construction and you're asked to build a house. In fact, you're a world-renowned home builder whose services are in high demand! Your client tells you that all the materials you'll need for building this home will be delivered to you. On the day construction is to begin, a truck pulls up at the building site and unloads a large pile of strange blue, star-shaped blocks with holes in the middle. You're totally baffled! You've built countless homes using materials like lumber, brick, and stone, and you know how to approach a building project using these familiar materials; but you haven't got a clue about how to assemble a house using blue stars.

Scratching your head, you pull out a hammer and some nails and try to nail the blue stars together as if you were working with lumber, but the stars don't fit together very well. You then try to fill in the gaps with the same mortar that you would use to make bricks adhere to one another, but the mortar doesn't stick to these blue stars very well. Because you're working under tight cost and schedule constraints (and because you're too embarrassed to admit that you, as an "expert" builder, don't know how to work with these modern materials), you press on. Eventually, you wind up with something that looks (on the outside, at least) like a house.

Your client comes to inspect the work and is terribly disappointed. One of the reasons he had selected blue stars as a construction material was that they are extremely energy efficient, but because you have used nails and mortar to assemble the stars, they have lost a great deal of their inherent ability to insulate the home. To compensate, your client asks you to replace all the windows in the home with thermal glass windows so that they will allow less heat to escape. You're panicking at this point! Swapping out the windows will take as long, if not longer, than it has taken to build the house in the first place, not to mention the cost of replacing stars that will be damaged in the renovation process. When you tell your customer this, he goes ballistic! Another reason why he selected blue stars as the construction material was because of their recognized flexibility and ease of accommodating design changes, but because of the ineffective way in which you assembled these stars, you'll have to literally rip them apart and replace a great many of them.

Sad to say, this is the way many programmers wind up building an OO application when they don't have appropriate training in how to approach the project from the perspective of objects. Worse yet, the vast majority of would-be OO programmers are blissfully ignorant of the need to understand objects in order to program in an OO language. So they take off programming with a language such as C# and wind up with a far-from-ideal result: a program that lacks flexibility when an inevitable "mid-course correction" is required (for example, when new functionality needs to be introduced after an application has been deployed).

Who Is This Book Written For?

Anyone who wants to get the most out of an OOPL such as C#! It also was written for the following people:

- Anyone who has yet to tackle C#, but wants to get off on the right foot with the language

- Anyone who has ever purchased a book on C# and read it faithfully; who understands the "bits and bytes" of the language, but doesn't quite know how to structure an application to best take advantage of the OO features of the language

- Anyone who has purchased a C# IDE software tool, but really only knows how to drag and drop graphical user interface (GUI) components and add a little bit of logic behind buttons, menus, and so on without any real sense of how to properly structure the core of the application around objects

- Anyone who has built a C# application, but was disappointed with how difficult it was to maintain or modify it when new requirements were presented later in the application's life cycle

- Anyone who has previously learned something about object modeling, but is "fuzzy" on how to transition from an object model to real live code (C# or otherwise)

The bottom line is that anyone who really wants to master an OO language such as C# *must* become an expert in objects first!

To gain the most value from this book, you should have some programming experience under your belt; virtually any language will do. You should understand simple programming concepts such as the following:

- Simple data types (integer, floating point, and so on)

- Variables and their scope (including the notion of global data)

- Control flow (if-then-else statements, for/do/while loops, and so on)

- Arrays: what they are and how to use them

- The notion of a function/subroutine/method: how to pass data in and get results back out

You don't need any prior exposure to C# (we'll give you a taste of the language at the beginning of Part One and will go into the language in depth in Part Three). And you needn't have ever been exposed to objects, either—in the software sense, at least! As you'll learn in Chapter 2, human beings naturally view the entire world from the perspective of objects.

Even if you've already developed a full-fledged C# application, it's certainly not too late to read this book if you still feel "unclear" about the object aspects of structuring an application. Universities often offer separate courses in object modeling and C# programming. Although they would ideally take both courses in sequence, students often arrive at an object modeling course having already taken a stab at learning C#. Even for folks who will see some familiar landmarks (in the form of C# code examples) in this book, many new insights will be gained as they learn the rationale for why we do many of the things that we do when programming in C# (or any other OOPL, for that matter).

It ultimately makes someone a better C# programmer to know the "whys" of object orientation instead of just the mechanics of the language. If you have had prior experience with C#, you may find that you can quickly skim those chapters that provide an introduction to the language—namely, Chapter 1 in Part One and Chapter 13 in Part Three.

Because this book has its roots in courses that the authors teach, it's ideally suited for use as a textbook for a semester-long graduate or upper-division undergraduate course in either object modeling or C# programming.

What If You're Interested in Object Modeling, but Not Necessarily in C# Programming?

Will this book still be of value to you? Definitely! Even if you don't plan on making a career of programming (as is true of many of our object modeling students), we've found that being exposed to a smattering of code examples written in an OOL such as C# really helps to cement object concepts. So, you're encouraged to read Part Three—at least through Chapter 14—even if you never intend to set your hands to the keyboard for purposes of C# programming.

How This Book Is Organized

The book is structured around three major topics, as follows:

Part One: The ABCs of Objects

Before we dive into the how-to's of object modeling and the details of OO programming in C#, it's important that we all speak the same language with respect to objects. Part One, consisting of Chapters 1–7, starts out slowly by defining basic concepts that underlie all software development approaches, OO or otherwise. But the chapters quickly ramp up to a discussion of advanced object concepts so that, by the end of Part One, you should be "object-savvy."

Part Two: Object Modeling 101

In Part Two—Chapters 8–12 of the book—we focus on the underlying principles of how and (more importantly) why we do the things we do when we develop an object model of an application—principles that are common to all object modeling techniques. It's important to be conversant in UML notation because it is an industry standard and is most likely what the majority of your colleagues/clients will be using. So we'll teach you the basics of the UML and use the UML for all our concrete modeling examples. Using the modeling techniques presented in these chapters, we'll develop an object model "blueprint" for a Student Registration System (SRS), the requirements specification for which is presented at the end of this introduction.

Part Three: Translating an Object "Blueprint" into C# Code

In Part Three of the book—Chapters 13–17—we illustrate how to render the SRS object model that we've developed in Part Two into a fully functioning C# application, complete with a GUI and a way to persist data from one user logon to the next. All the code examples that we present in this section are available for download from the Apress web site (www.apress.com), and we strongly encourage you to download and experiment with this code. In fact, we provide exercises at the end of each chapter that encourage such experimentation. The requirements specification for the SRS is written in the narrative style with which software system requirements are often expressed. You might feel confident that you could build an application today to solve this problem, but by the end of this book you should feel much more confident in your ability to build it as an OO application.

To round out the book, we've included a final chapter, "Next Steps," which provides suggestions for how you might wish to continue your OO discovery process after finishing this book. We furnish you with a list of recommended books that will take you to the next level of proficiency, depending on what your intention is for applying what you've learned in this book.

Conventions

To help you get the most from the text and keep track of what's happening, we've used a number of conventions throughout the book.

For instance:

Note Note and Tip boxes reflect important background information and advice.

As for styles in the text:

- When we introduce important words, we *italicize* them.

- Terms that you should type in or significant new additions to code samples are shown in **boldface**.

- File names, URLs, and code within the text are in a `special code font`.

Example code is shown as follows:

```
// Bolding is used to call attention to new or significant code:
Student s = new Student();
// whereas unbolded code is code that's less important in the
// present context, or perhaps has been seen before.
int x = 3;
```

Which Version of C# Is This Book Based On?

As with any programming language, from time to time new versions of C# will be released by Microsoft. At the time the second edition of this book was published (fall 2008), the latest version of .NET was 3.5, and we do use some of the "latest and greatest" C# language features in this book such as auto-implemented properties and object initializers. However, the insights into proper OO programming that you will gain after reading this book aren't tied to any version of .NET and will serve you equally well when new versions of C# appear.

A Final Thought Before We Get Started

A lot of the material in this book—particularly at the beginning of Part One—might seem overly simplistic to experienced programmers. This is because much of object technology is founded on basic software engineering principles that have been in practice for many years and—in many cases—just repackaged slightly differently. There are indeed a few new tricks that make OOPLs extremely powerful and virtually impossible to achieve with non-OO languages—inheritance and polymorphism, for example, which you'll learn more about in Chapters 5 and 7, respectively. (Such techniques can be simulated by hand in a non-OOPL, just as programmers could program their own database management system [DBMS] from scratch instead of using a commercial product such as Oracle, Sybase, or MS SQL Server—but who'd want to?)

The biggest challenge for experienced programmers in becoming proficient with objects is to reorient the way they think about the problem they will be automating:

- Software engineers/programmers who have developed applications using non-OO methods often have to "unlearn" certain approaches used in the traditional methods of software analysis and design.

- Paradoxically, people just starting out as programmers (or as OO modelers) sometimes have an easier time when learning the OO approach to software development as their only approach.

Fortunately, the way we need to think about objects when developing software turns out to be the natural way that people think about the world in general. So, learning to "think" objects—and to program them in C#—is as easy as 1, 2, 3!

Tell Us What You Think

We've worked hard to make this book as useful to you as possible, so we want to know what you think. We're always keen to know what it is you want and need to know.

We appreciate feedback on our efforts and take both criticism and praise to heart in our future editorial efforts. If you have anything to say, please let us know at info@apress.com or www.apress.com, or contact the authors at grantepalmer@gmail.com, jacquie@objectstart.com, or http://objectstart.com.

STUDENT REGISTRATION SYSTEM (SRS) CASE STUDY: STUDENT REGISTRATION SYSTEM REQUIREMENTS SPECIFICATION

We have been asked to develop an automated Student Registration System (SRS) that will enable students to register online for courses each semester, as well as track a student's progress toward completion of his or her degree.

When a student first enrolls at the university, he or she uses the SRS to set forth a plan of study about which courses he or she plans to take to satisfy a particular degree program, and chooses a faculty advisor. The SRS will verify whether the proposed plan of study satisfies the requirements of the degree the student is seeking. Once a plan of study is established, students are can view the schedule of classes online during the registration period preceding each semester and then choose whichever classes they wish to attend, indicating the preferred section (day of the week and time of day) if the class is offered by more than one professor. The SRS will verify whether the student has satisfied the necessary prerequisites for each requested course by referring to the student's online transcript of courses completed and grades received (the student can review his or her transcript online at any time).

Assuming that (a) the prerequisites for the requested course(s) are satisfied, (b) the course(s) meets one of the student's plan-of-study requirements, and (c) there is room available in each of the class(es), the student is enrolled in the class(es).

If (a) and (b) are satisfied, but (c) is not, the student is placed on a first-come, first-served waiting list. If a class/section that he or she was previously waitlisted for becomes available (either because some other student has dropped the class or because the seating capacity for the class has been increased), the student is automatically enrolled in the waitlisted class, and an email message to that effect is sent to the student. It is his or her responsibility to drop the class if it is no longer desired; otherwise, he or she will be billed for the course.

Students can drop a class up to the end of the first week of the semester in which the class is being taught.

The ABCs of Objects

CHAPTER 1

■■■

A Little Taste of C#

If the first part of this book is supposed to be about general object concepts, then why on earth are we starting out with an introductory chapter on C#?

- It's indeed true that objects are "language neutral," so what you'll learn conceptually about objects in Part One of this book, and about object modeling in Part Two, could apply equally well to any object-oriented programming language (OOPL).

- We've found that seeing a sprinkling of code examples helps to cement object concepts; but we *could* have simply used language-neutral *pseudocode*—a natural-language way of expressing computer logic without worrying about the syntax of a specific language such as C#—for all our code examples in Parts One and Two.

This brings us back to our initial question: *why are we diving into C# syntax so soon?* Our reason for doing so is that we want you to become comfortable with C# syntax from the start because our goal for this book is not only to teach you about objects and object modeling but also to ultimately show you how objects translate into C# code. So although we do indeed use a bit of pseudocode to hide some of the more complex logic of our code examples throughout Parts One and Two, we focus for the most part on real C# syntax. Just remember that the object concepts you'll learn in Parts One and Two are equally applicable to other OOPLs unless otherwise noted.

In this chapter, you'll learn about the following:

- The many strengths of the C# programming language

- Predefined C# types, operators on those types, and expressions formed with those types

- The anatomy of a simple C# program

- The C# block structured nature

- Various types of C# expressions

- Loops and other control flow structures

- Printing messages to the screen, primarily for use in testing code as it evolves

- Elements of C# programming style

If you're a proficient C, C++, or Java programmer, you'll find much of C# syntax to be very familiar and should be able to breeze through this chapter fairly quickly.

If you've already been exposed to C# language basics, please feel free to skip to Chapter 2.

Getting Hands-On with C#

You're probably eager to get started writing, compiling, and running C# programs. But we're purposely not going to get into the details of downloading and installing C# and the .NET Framework on your computer, the mechanics of compiling programs, or any of that just yet. Here is a roadmap of the way this book is organized:

- Part One of the book focuses on object concepts—in other words, the "what" of objects; we don't want you to be distracted from learning these basic concepts by the bits and bytes of getting the C# environment up and running on your machine.

- Part Two of the book focuses on object modeling—that is, the "how" of designing an application to make the best use of objects. We don't want you to be trying to program without an appropriate OO "blueprint" to work from.

- You'll then be ready for the "grand finale"—rendering the object model in C# code to produce a working Student Registration System (SRS) application—in Part Three.

We'll be showing C# code throughout the book, but in Parts One and Two it will mostly be code snippets and simple examples. We'll wait until Part Three, when you have a good grounding in OO programming concepts, before we really dive into developing a complete C# application.

Why C#?

We *could* walk you through building the SRS using any OOPL. Why might we want to use C#? Read on and you'll quickly see why!

Practice Makes Perfect

The designers of C# were able to draw upon the lessons learned from other OOPLs that preceded it. They borrowed the best features of C++, Java, Eiffel, and Smalltalk, and then added some capabilities and features not found in those languages. Conversely, the features that proved to be most troublesome in earlier languages were eliminated. As a result, C# is a powerful programming language that is also easy to learn.

This is not to say that C# is a perfect language—no language is!—but simply that it has made some significant improvements over many of the languages that have preceded it.

C# Is Part of an Integrated Application Development Framework

The C# language is integrated into Microsoft's *.NET Framework*—Microsoft's powerful, comprehensive platform for developing applications and managing their runtime environment. The .NET Framework primarily supports the C#, C++, J#, and Visual Basic programming languages, but also provides a functionality called *cross-language interoperability* that allows objects created in different programming languages to work with each other. A core element of the .NET Framework is the *common language runtime (CLR)* that is responsible for the runtime management of any .NET Framework program. The CLR takes care of loading, running, and providing support services for the .NET Framework program.

The .NET Framework provides a high degree of interoperability between the languages it supports—C#, C++, Visual Basic, and JScript—through a *Common Language Specification (CLS)* that defines a common set of types and behaviors that every .NET language is guaranteed to recognize. The CLS allows developers to seamlessly integrate C# code with code written in any of the other .NET languages.

The .NET Framework also contains a vast collection of libraries called the *.NET Framework Class Library (FCL)* that provides almost all the common functionality needed to develop applications on the Windows platform. You'll find that with the FCL a lot of programming work has already been done for you on topics ranging from file access to mathematical functions to database connectivity. The C# language and the .NET Framework provide one-stop shopping for all your programming needs.

You can find out more about the .NET Framework here: `http://msdn.microsoft.com/en-us/library/default.aspx`.

C# Is Object-Oriented from the Ground Up

Before newer OOPLs such as C# and Java arrived on the scene, one of the most widely used OOPLs was C++, which is actually an object-oriented extension of the non-OOPL C. As such, C++ provides a lot of "back doors" that make it very easy to write decidedly "un-OO" code. In fact, many proficient C programmers transitioned to C++ as a better C without properly learning how to design an object-oriented application, and hence wound up using C++ for the most part as a procedural (non-OO) language.

In contrast, C# was built from the ground up to be a purely OOPL. As we'll discuss in more detail in the chapters that follow, *everything* in C# is an object:

- Primitive value types, such as `int` and `double`, inherit from the `Object` class.

- All the graphical user interface (GUI) building blocks—windows, buttons, text input fields, scroll bars, lists, menus, and so on—are objects.

- All functions are attached to objects and are known as *methods*—there can be no free-floating functions as there are in C/C++.

- Even the entry point for a C# program (now called the `Main` method) no longer stands alone, but is instead bundled within a *class*, the reasons for which we'll explore in depth in chapters to come.

Because of this, C# lends itself particularly well to writing applications that uphold the object-oriented paradigm. Yet, as we pointed out in the introduction to this book, merely using such an object-oriented language doesn't *guarantee* that the applications you produce will be *true* to this paradigm! You must be knowledgeable in *both* (a) how to design an application from the ground up to make the best use of objects and (b) how to apply the language correctly, our two primary intents of this book.

C# Is Free

One last valuable feature of C# that we'll mention is that it's *free*! You can download the C# compiler and all other libraries and utilities you'll need from the Microsoft Developer Network (MSDN) web site at no cost. We go into the details of setting up C# on your machine in Appendix A.

C# Language Basics

For those readers who have never seen C# code before, the rest of this chapter will present an introduction to the basic syntax of the C# programming language. Keep in mind that this is only a taste of C#, enough to help you understand the coding examples in Parts One and Two of this book. We'll revisit C# in substantially more depth in Part Three (Chapters 13 through 16), in which we'll delve much more deeply into the language in building a fully functional SRS application.

Note If you haven't taken the time to read the introduction to this book, now is a good time to do so! The SRS application requirements are introduced as a case study there.

A Reminder About Pseudocode vs. Real C# Code

As mentioned in the beginning of this chapter, we occasionally use little bits of pseudocode in our code examples throughout Parts One and Two of the book to hide irrelevant logic details. To make it clear when we're using pseudocode versus real code, we used *italic* versus regular code font:
This is real C# syntax:

```
for (int i = 0; i <= 10; i++) {
```

This is pseudocode:

```
    compute the grade for the ith Student
}
```

We'll remind you of this fact a few more times, so that you don't forget and accidentally try to type in and compile pseudocode somewhere along the way.

Anatomy of a Simple C# Program

One of the simplest of all C# applications, the classic "Hello" program, is shown in Figure 1-1.

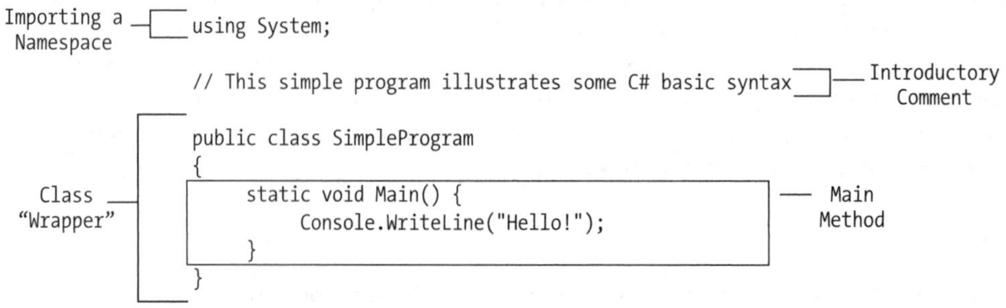

Figure 1-1. *Anatomy of a simple C# program*

Let's go over the key elements of our simple program.

The using System; Statement

The first line of the program is required for our program to compile and run properly, by providing the compiler with knowledge of the types in the System *namespace*, which is a logical grouping of predefined C# programming elements (in the case of C#, part of the FCL mentioned earlier):

```
using System;
```

We'll defer a detailed explanation of namespaces until Chapter 13; for now, simply realize that the using System; statement is required for this program to compile properly—specifically, for the line Console.WriteLine("Hello!"); to compile properly.

using is a C# *keyword*. Keywords, also known as *reserved words*, are tokens that have special meaning in a language, so they cannot be used by programmers as the names of variables, functions, or any of the other C# building blocks that you'll be learning about. We'll encounter many more C# keywords throughout the book.

Comments

The next line of our program is a *single-line* comment:

```
// This simple program illustrates some basic C# syntax.
```

In addition to single-line comments, the C# language also supports the C language style of *delimited comments*, which can span multiple lines. Delimited comments begin with a forward slash followed by an asterisk (/*) and end with an asterisk followed by a forward slash (*/). Everything enclosed between these delimiters is treated as a comment and is therefore ignored by the compiler, no matter how many lines the comment spans:

```
/* This is a single line C-style comment. */
```

```
/* This is a multiline C-style comment. This is a handy way to temporarily
   comment out entire sections of code without having to delete them.
   From the time that the compiler encounters the first 'slash asterisk'
   above, it doesn't care what we type here; even legitimate lines of code,
   as shown below, are treated as comment lines and thus ignored by the
   compiler until the first 'asterisk slash' combination is encountered.
x = y + z;
a = b / c;
j = s + c + f;
*/
```

■**Note** There is also a third type of C# comment that is used within XML document files. XML documentation comments are denoted by three slashes (///).

Note that comments can't be nested; that is, the following will *not* compile:

```
/* This starts a comment...
x = 3;

/* Whoops!  We are mistakenly trying to nest a SECOND comment
before terminating the FIRST!
This is going to cause us compilation problems, because the
compiler is going to IGNORE the start of this second/inner comment - we're IN
a comment already, after all! - and so as soon as we try to terminate
this SECOND/inner comment, the compiler will think that we've terminated the
FIRST/outer comment instead... */
z = 2;
 */ ...then, when we try to terminate the FIRST/outer comment,
           the compiler will inform us that THIS line of code is invalid.
```

When the compiler reaches what we intended to be the terminating */ of the "outer" comment in the last line of code, the following compiler error will be reported:

```
error: Invalid expression term '/'
error: ; expected
```

Class Declaration/"Wrapper"

Next comes a class "wrapper"—more properly termed a *class declaration*—of the following form where braces, {...}, enclose the main logic to be performed by the class, as well as enclosing other building blocks of a class:

```
class name

{...}
```

e.g.,

```
class SimpleProgram
{...}
```

In later chapters, you'll learn all about classes, how to name them, and in particular why you even need a class wrapper in the first place. For now, simply note that the token class is another one of C#'s keywords, whereas SimpleProgram is a name that we invented.

Main Method

Within the SimpleProgram class declaration, we find the starting function for the program, called the Main method in C#. The Main method serves as the entry point for a C# program. When the program executable is invoked, the system will call the Main method to launch our application.

Note With trivial applications such as this simple example, all logic can be contained within this single method. For more complex applications, on the other hand, the Main method can't possibly contain all the logic for the entire system. You'll learn how to construct an application that transcends the boundaries of the Main method later in the book.

The first line of the method, shown here, defines what is known as the Main method's *header*, and must appear exactly as shown (with one minor exception that we'll explain in Chapter 13 having to do with optionally receiving arguments from the command line):

```
static void Main() {
```

Our Main *method body*, enclosed in braces, {...}, consists of a single statement:

```
Console.WriteLine("Hello!");
```

This statement prints the following message to the screen:

```
Hello!
```

We'll talk more about this statement's syntax in a bit, but for now note the use of a semicolon at the end of the statement. As in C, C++, and Java, semicolons are placed at the end of individual C# statements. Braces {...} delimit *blocks* of code, the significance of which we'll discuss in more detail later in this chapter, in the section entitled "Code Blocks and Variable Scope."

Other things that we'd typically do inside of the Main method of a more elaborate program include declaring variables, creating objects, and calling other methods.

Now that we've looked at a simple C# program, let's explore some of the basic syntax features of C# in more detail.

Predefined Types

Generally speaking, C# is said to be a *strongly typed* programming language in that when a variable is declared, its type must also be declared. Among other things, declaring a variable's type tells the compiler how much memory to allocate for the variable.

The C# language and .NET Framework make use of the CTS, a specification that defines a set of types as well as the behavior of those types. The CTS defines a wide variety of types in two main families: *value types* and *reference types*. Both value types and reference types can also be declared to be *generic types*, which means that they can represent more than one type. In this chapter, we'll focus on C#'s *predefined value types*, also known as *simple types*, along with the string type, which happens to be a reference type.

The C# language supports a variety of simple types. The most commonly used types are as follows (all of them are C# keywords):

- bool: Boolean true or false value

- char: 16-bit Unicode character

- byte: 8-bit unsigned integer

- short: 16-bit signed integer

- int: 32-bit signed integer

- long: 64-bit signed integer

- float: 32-bit single-precision floating point

- double: 64-bit double-precision floating point

Each variable declared to be of a simple type represents a *single* integer, floating point, Boolean, byte, or character value.

Variables

As previously stated, before a variable can be used in a program, the type and name of the variable must be declared. An initial value can be supplied when a variable is first declared, or the variable can be assigned a value later in the program. For example, the following code snippet declares two simple type variables. The first variable, of type int, is given an initial value when the variable is declared. The second variable, of type double, is declared and then assigned a value on a subsequent line of code.

```
int count = 3;

double total;
// intervening code...details omitted
total = 34.3;
```

A value can be assigned to a bool variable using the true or false keywords:

```
bool blah;
blah = true;
```

Boolean variables are often used as flags to signal whether some code should be conditionally performed. An example follows:

```
bool error = false;  // Initialize the flag.
//...

// Later in the program (pseudocode):
if (some error situation arises) {
  // Set the flag to true to signal that an error has occurred.
  error = true;
}
//...

// Still later in the program:
if (error == true) {
    // Pseudocode.
    take corrective action
}
```

Note We'll talk specifically about the syntax of the `if` statement, one of several different kinds of C# flow control statements, a bit later.

A literal value can be assigned to a variable of type `char` by surrounding the value (a single Unicode character) in *single* quotes as follows:

```
char c = 'A';
```

Variable Naming Conventions

Most variable names use what is known as *Camel casing*, wherein the first letter of the name is in lowercase, the first letter of each subsequent concatenated word in the variable name is in uppercase, and the rest of the characters are in lowercase.

Note In subsequent chapters, we'll refine the rules for naming variables as we introduce additional object concepts.

For example, the following variable names follow the C# variable naming conventions:

```
int grade;
double averageGrade;
string myPetRat;
bool weAreFinished;
```

Recall that, as mentioned earlier, a C# keyword can't be used as a variable name:

```
int float;  // this won't compile—"float" is a keyword
```

Variable Initialization and Value Assignment

There are different types of variables in C# based on how and where the variables are declared in the program. Some variable types are *initialized* with a default value when they are declared. Local variables, those that are declared inside a method or other block of code, are given no default value when they are declared, so we must explicitly *assign* a value to a variable before the variable's value is accessed in a statement. For example, in the following code snippet, two local integer variables are declared: `foo` and `bar`. A value is assigned to the variable `foo`, but not to variable `bar`, and an attempt is made to add the two variables together:

```
static void Main() {
        int foo;    // local variable
        int bar;    // another local variable

        foo = 3;    // We're assigning a value to foo, but not bar.
        foo = foo + bar;    // this line won't compile
```

If we were to try to compile this code snippet, we would get the following compilation error message regarding the last line of the preceding code example:

```
error: use of unassigned local variable 'bar'
```

The compiler is telling us that the local variable bar has been declared, but its value is undefined. To correct this error, we need to assign an explicit value to bar before trying to add its value to foo:

```
int foo;
int bar;

foo = 3;
bar = 7;   // We're now assigning values to BOTH variables.

foo = foo + bar;   // This line will now compile properly.
```

Note As it turns out, the story with respect to variable initialization is a bit more complex than what we've discussed here. You'll learn in Chapter 13 that the rules of automatic initialization are somewhat different when dealing with the inner workings of objects.

Strings

We'll discuss one more important predefined type in this chapter: the string type.

Note Just a reminder: unlike the other C# types introduced in this chapter, string isn't a value type; it's a reference type, as we mentioned earlier. For purposes of this introductory discussion of strings, this observation isn't important; the significance of the string type's being a reference type will be discussed in Chapter 13.

A string represents a sequence of Unicode characters. There are several ways to create and initialize a string variable. The easiest and most commonly used way is to declare a variable of type string and to assign the variable a value using a *string literal*, which is any text enclosed in double quotes:

```
string name = "Zachary";
```

Note that we use double quotes, not single quotes, to surround a string literal when assigning it to a string variable, even if it consists of only a single character:

```
string shortString = "A";      // Use DOUBLE quotes when assigning a literal
                               // value to a string...
```

```
string longString = "supercalifragilisticexpialadocious";  // (ditto)

char c = 'A';                    //...and SINGLE quotes when assigning a
                                 // literal value to a char.
```

Two commonly used approaches for assigning an initial value to a string variable as a placeholder are as follows:

- Setting it equal to an empty string, represented by two consecutive double quote marks:

```
string s = "";
```

- Setting it equal to the reserved word null, which is the "zero equivalent" value for the string type (and, as you'll learn later on, for reference types/objects in general):

```
string s = null;
```

The plus sign (+) operator is normally used for addition, but when used with string variables, it represents *string concatenation*. Any number of string variables or string literals can be concatenated together with the + operator:

```
string x = "foo";
string y = "bar";
string z = x + y + "!";  // z now equals "foobar!"; x and y are unchanged
```

You'll learn about some of the many other operations that can be performed with or on strings, along with gaining insights into their object-oriented nature, in Chapter 13.

Case Sensitivity

C# is a *case-sensitive* language. That is, the use of uppercase versus lowercase in C# is deliberate and mandatory. For example:

- Variable names that are spelled the same way but that differ in their use of case; e.g., x (lowercase) versus X (uppercase) represent *different* variables.

- All keywords are expressed in all lowercase: public, class, int, bool, and so forth. Don't get "creative" about capitalizing them because the compiler will complain!

- Capitalization of the name of the Main method is mandatory.

C# Expressions

A *simple expression* in C# is the following (plus a few more expression types having to do with objects that you'll learn about in Chapter 13):

- A constant: 7, false

- A char(acter) literal: 'A', '&'

- A string literal: "foo"

- The name of any variable declared to be of one of the predefined types that we've discussed so far: myString, x

- Any *two* of the preceding items that are combined with one of the C# *binary operators* (discussed in detail later in this chapter): x + 2

- Any *one* of the preceding items that is modified by one of the C# *unary operators* (discussed in detail later in this chapter): i++

- Any of the preceding simple expressions enclosed in parentheses: (x + 2)

Assignment Statements

Assigning a value to a variable is accomplished by using the assignment operator =. An *assignment statement* consists of a (previously declared) variable name to the left of the =, and an expression that evaluates to the appropriate type to the right of the =; for example:

```
count = 1;

total = total + 4.0;  // assuming that total was declared to be a double variable

price = cost + (a + b)/length;  // assuming all variables properly declared
```

Arithmetic Operators

The C# language provides a number of basic arithmetic operators, as follows:

+	Addition
–	Subtraction
*	Multiplication
/	Division
%	Modulus (the remainder when the operand to the left of the % operator is divided by the operand to the right)

The + and – operators can also be used in prefix fashion to indicate positive or negative numbers: -3.7, +42.

In addition to the simple assignment operator, =, there are a number of specialized *compound assignment operators*, which combine variable assignments with an operation. The compound assignment operators for arithmetic operations are as follows:

+=	a += b is equivalent to a = a + b
-=	a -= b is equivalent to a = a - b
*=	a *= b is equivalent to a = a * b
/=	a /= b is equivalent to a = a / b
%=	a %= b is equivalent to a = a % b

■Note The compound assignment operators don't add any new functionality; they are simply provided as a convenience to simplify code. For example, the statement

```
total = total + 4.0;
```

can be alternatively written as

```
total += 4.0;
```

The final two arithmetic operators that we'll introduce are the *increment* (++) and *decrement* (--) operators, which are used to increase or decrease the value of an integer variable by 1 or of a floating point value by 1.0. The increment and decrement operators can also be used on char variables. For example, consider the following code snippet:

```
char c = 'e';
c++;
```

When the code snippet is executed, the variable c will have the value 'f', which is the next character in the Unicode sorting sequence.

The increment and decrement operators can be used in either a *prefix* or *postfix* manner.

If the operator is placed *before* the variable it's operating on (*prefix* mode), the increment or decrement of that variable is performed *before* the variable's value is used in any assignments made via that statement.

If the operator is placed *after* the variable it's operating on (*postfix* mode), the increment or decrement occurs *after* the variable's value is used in any assignments made via that statement.

For example, consider the following code snippet, which uses the prefix increment (++) operator:

```
int a = 1;
int b = ++a;  // a will be incremented to 2, then b will be assigned the
              // value 2
```

After both lines of code have executed, the value of variable a will be 2 (as will the value of variable b) because in the second line of code, the increment of variable a (from 1 to 2) occurs *before* the value of a is assigned to variable b. The preceding two lines of code are logically equivalent to the following three lines:

```
int a = 1;
a = a + 1;
int b = a;
```

Now let's look at the same code snippet with the increment operator written in a postfix manner:

```
int a = 1;
int b = a++;  // b will be assigned the value 1, then a will be incremented
              // to 2
```

After both lines of code have executed, the value of variable b will be 1, whereas the value of variable a will be 2 because in the second line of code, the increment of variable a (from 1 to 2) occurs *after* the (old) value of a is assigned to variable b. The preceding two lines of code are logically equivalent to the following three lines:

```
int a = 1;
int b = a;
a = a + 1;
```

Here is a slightly more complex example:

```
int y = 1;
int z = 2;
int x = y++ * ++z;   // x will be assigned the value 3, because z will be
                     // incremented from 2 to 3 before its value is used in
                     // the multiplication, whereas y will remain at 1 until
                     // AFTER its value is used.
```

As you'll see in a bit, the increment and decrement operators are commonly used in loops and other flow of control structures.

Evaluating Expressions and Operator Precedence

Expressions of arbitrary complexity can be built up around the various different simple expression types by nesting parentheses; for example, $((((4/x) + y) * 7) + z)$. The compiler evaluates such expressions from innermost to outermost parentheses, left to right. Assuming that x, y, and z are declared and initialized as shown here:

```
int x = 1;
int y = 2;
int z = 3;
```

then the expression on the right side of the following assignment statement

```
int answer = ((8 * (y + z)) + y) * x;
```

would be evaluated piece by piece as follows:

$$((8 * \underline{(y + z)}) + y) * x$$
$$(\underline{(8 * 5)} + y) * x$$
$$\underline{(40 + y)} * x$$
$$\underline{42 * x}$$
$$42$$

In the absence of parentheses, certain operators take precedence over others in terms of when they will be applied in evaluating an expression. For example, multiplication or division is by default performed before addition or subtraction. The automatic precedence of one operator over another can be explicitly altered through the use of parentheses; operations inside parentheses will be performed before operations outside of them. Consider the following code snippet:

```
int j = 2 + 3 * 4;   // j will be assigned the value 14
int k = (2 + 3) * 4;    // k will be assigned the value 20
```

In the first line of code, which uses no parentheses, the multiplication operation takes precedence over the addition operation, so the overall expression evaluates to the value 2 + 12 = 14; it's as if we've explicitly written "2 + (3 * 4)" without having to do so.

In the second line of code, parentheses are explicitly placed around the operation 2 + 3 so that the addition operation will be performed first, and the resultant sum will then be multiplied by 4 for an overall expression value of 5 * 4 = 20.

Logical Operators

A *logical expression* compares two (simple or complex) expressions *exp1* and *exp2*, in a specified way, and evaluates to a Boolean value of true or false.

To create logical expressions, C# provides the following *relational operators*:

exp1 == *exp2*	true if *exp1* equals *exp2* (note use of a double equal sign)
exp1 > *exp2*	true if *exp1* is greater than *exp2*
exp1 >= *exp2*	true if *exp1* is greater or equal to *exp2*
exp1 < *exp2*	true if *exp1* is less than *exp2*
exp1 <= *exp2*	true if *exp1* is less than or equal to *exp2*
exp1 != *exp2*	true if *exp1* isn't equal to *exp2* (! is read as "not")
!*exp*	true if *exp* is false, and false if *exp* is true

In addition to the relational operators, C# provides *logical operators* that can be used in combination with the relational operators to create complex logical expressions that involve more than one comparison.

&&	Logical "and"
||	Logical "or"
!	Logical "not" (the ! operator toggles the value of a logical expression from true to false and vice versa)

The logical "and" and "or" operators are binary operators; their left and right operands must both be valid logical expressions so that they evaluate to Boolean values. If the && operator is used, both the left and right operands must be true for the compound logical expression to be true. With the || operator, the compound logical expression will be true if either the left or right operand is true.

Here is an example that uses the logical "and" operator to program the compound logical expression "if x is greater than 2.0 and y isn't equal to 4.0":

```
if (x > 2.0 && y != 4.0) {
  // Pseudocode.
  do some stuff...
}
```

Note that because the > and != operators take precedence over the && operator, we don't need to insert extra parentheses as shown here:

```
if ((x > 2.0) && (y != 4.0)) {
  // Pseudocode.
  do some stuff...
}
```

Logical expressions are most commonly seen in flow of control structures, discussed later in this chapter.

Implicit Type Conversions and Explicit Casting

C# supports *implicit type conversions*. For example, we try to assign the value of some variable y to another variable x, as shown here:

```
x = y;
```

The two variables were originally declared to be of different types; then C# will attempt to perform the assignment, automatically converting the type of the value of y to the type of x, but only if precision won't be lost in doing so. (C# differs from C and C++ in this regard because the latter two perform automatic type conversions even if precision is lost.) This is best understood by looking at an example:

```
int x;
double y;
y = 2.7;
x = y;  // Trying to assign a double value to an int variable; this line
        // will compile in C and C++, but not in C#.
```

In the preceding code snippet, we're attempting to copy the double value of y, 2.7, into x, which is declared to be an int. If this assignment were to take place, the fractional part of y would be truncated, and x would wind up with an integer value of 2. This represents a loss in precision, also known as a *narrowing conversion*. A C or C++ compiler will permit this assignment, thereby truncating the value; instead of assuming that this is what we intended to do, however, the C# compiler will generate an error on the last line:

```
Error::  Cannot implicitly convert type 'double' to type 'int'
```

To signal to the C# compiler that we're willing to accept the loss of precision, we must perform an *explicit cast*, which involves preceding the expression whose value is to be converted with the desired target type enclosed in parentheses. In other words, we'd have to rewrite the last line of the preceding example as follows for the C# compiler to accept it:

```
int x;
double y;
y = 2.7;
x = (int) y;  // This will compile now. The C# compiler 'relaxes',
              // because we have explicitly told it that we WANT the
              // narrowing conversion to occur.
```

Of course, if we were to reverse the direction of the assignment, as follows, the C# compiler would have no problem with the last statement, because in this particular case, we're assigning a value of less precision—2—to a variable capable of more precision; y will wind up with the value of 2.0:

```
int x;
double y;
x = 2;
y = x;          // Assign an int value to a double variable; y will assume
                // the value 2.0.
```

This is known as a *widening conversion*; such conversions are performed automatically in C#, and need not be explicitly cast.

Note that there is an idiosyncrasy with regard to assigning constant values to a float in C#; the following statement will generate a compiler error because a numeric constant value with a fractional component such as 3.5 is automatically treated by C# as a more precise double value, so the compiler will once again refuse to make a transfer that causes precision to be lost:

```
float y = 3.5;    // won't compile!
```

To make such an assignment, we must explicitly cast the floating point constant into a float:

```
float y = (float)3.5;    // OK; we're using a cast here.
```

Alternatively, few can force the constant on the right side of the assignment statement to be treated as a float by using the suffix F, as shown here:

```
float y = 3.5F;    // OK, because we're indicating that the constant is to be
            // treated as a float, not as a double.
```

Tip Yet another option is to simply use double instead of float variables to represent floating point numeric values. We'll typically use a double instead of a float whenever we need to declare floating point variables in our SRS application, just to avoid these hassles of type conversion.

There are no implicit conversions to the char type, and the bool type can't be cast, either implicitly or explicitly, into another type.

You'll see other applications of casting that involve objects later in the book.

Loops and Other Flow of Control Structures

Very rarely will a program execute sequentially, line by line, from start to finish. Instead, the execution flow of the program will be conditional. It might be necessary to have the program execute a certain block of code if a condition is met or another block of code if the condition isn't met. A program might have to repeatedly execute the same block of code. The C# language provides a number of different types of loops and other flow of control structures to take care of these situations.

if Statements

The if statement is a basic conditional branch statement that executes one or more lines of code if a condition, represented as a logical expression, is satisfied. Alternatively, one or more lines of code can be executed if the condition is *not* satisfied by placing that code after the keyword else. The use of an else clause within an if statement is optional.

The basic syntax of the if statement is as follows:

```
if (condition) {
  execute whatever code is contained within the braces if condition is met
}
```

Or add an optional else clause:

```
if (condition) {
  execute whatever code is contained within the braces if condition is met
}
else {
  execute whatever code is contained within the braces if condition is NOT met
}
```

If only one executable statement follows either the if or (optional) else keyword, the braces can be omitted as shown here, but it's generally considered good practice to always use braces:

```
// Pseudocode.
if (condition)
    single statement to execute if true;
else

    single statement to execute if false;
```

A single Boolean variable as a simple form of Boolean expression can, of course, serve as the logical expression/condition of an if statement. For example, it's perfectly acceptable to write the following:

```
// Use this bool variable as a 'flag' that gets set to true when
// some particular operation is completed.
bool finished;

// Initialize it to false.
finished = false;

// Intervening code, in which the flag may get set to true...details omitted.

// Test the flag. This next line is equivalent to: if (finished == true) {
if (finished) {
    Console.WriteLine("we are finished");
}
```

In this case, the logical expression serving as the condition for the if statement corresponds to "if finished" or "if finished equals true".

The ! operator can be used to negate a logical expression, so that the block of code associated with an if statement is executed when the expression is false:

```
// equivalent to: if (finished == false)
if (!finished) {
    // If the finished variable is set to false, this code will execute.
    Console.WriteLine("we are not finished");
}
```

In this case, the logical expression serving as the condition for the if statement corresponds to "if *not* finished" or "if finished equals false".

When testing for equality, remember that we must use two consecutive equal signs, not just one:

```
// Note use of double equal signs (==) to test for equality.
if (x == 3) {
  y = x;
}
```

Note A common mistake made by beginning C# programmers is to try to use a *single* equal sign to test for equality as in this example:

```
    if (x = 3) {...}
```

In C#, an if test must be based on a valid logical expression; x = 3 isn't a *logical* expression; it's an *assignment* expression.

Although the preceding if statement doesn't even compile in C#, it does compile in the C and C++ programming languages because in those languages, if tests are based on evaluating expressions to either the integer value 0 (equivalent to false) or nonzero (equivalent to true).

It's possible to nest if-else constructs to test more than one condition. If nested, an inner if (plus optional else) statement is placed within the else part of an outer if.

A basic syntax for a two-level nested if-else construct is shown here:

```
if (condition1) {
  // execute this code
}
else {
  if (condition2) {
    // execute this alternate code
  }
  else {
    // execute this code if none of the conditions are met
  }
}
```

There is no limit to how many nested if-else constructs can be used, but try not to go too crazy with nesting.

The nested if statement shown in the preceding example may alternatively be written without using nesting as follows:

```
if (condition1) {
  // execute this code
}
else if (condition2) {
    // execute this alternate code
}
else {
    // execute this code if none of the conditions are met
}
```

The two forms are logically equivalent.

Here is an example that uses a nested if-else construct to determine the size of an employee's bonus based on the employee's sales and length of service:

```
using System;

public class IfDemo
{
  static void Main() {
    double sales = 40000.0;
    int lengthOfService = 12;
    double bonus;

    if (sales > 30000.0 && lengthOfService >= 10) {
      bonus = 2000.0;
    }
    else if (sales > 20000.0) {
      bonus = 1000.0;
    }
    else {
      bonus = 0.0;
    }

    Console.WriteLine("Bonus = " + bonus);
  }
}
```

Here's the output generated by this example code:

```
Bonus = 2000.0
```

switch Statements

A switch statement is similar to an if-else construct in that it allows the conditional execution of one or more lines of code. However, instead of evaluating a logical expression as an if-else construct does, a switch statement compares the value of an integer, char, enum, or string expression against values defined by one or more case labels. If a match is found, the code following the matching case label is executed. An optional default label can be included to define code that is to be executed if the integer, char, enum, or string expression matches none of the case labels.

The general syntax of a switch statement is as follows:

```
switch (expression) {
    case value1:
      // code to execute if expression matches value1
      break;
    case value2:
      // code to execute if expression matches value2
      break;
  // more case labels, as needed...
    case valueN:
      // code to execute if expression matches valueN
      break;
    default:
      // default code if no case matches
      break;
}
```

For example:

```
int x;

// x is assigned a value somewhere along the line...details omitted.

switch (x) {
    case 1:
      // Pseudocode.
      do something based on the fact that x equals 1
      break;
    case 2:
      // Pseudocode.
      do something based on the fact that x equals 2
      break;
    default:
      // Pseudocode.
      do something if x equals something other than 1 or 2
      break;
}
```

Note the following:

- The expression in parentheses following the switch keyword must be an expression that evaluates to a string or integer value.

- The values following the case labels must be constant values (a "hard-wired" integer constant, character literal, or a string literal).

- Colons, not semicolons, terminate the case and default labels.

- The statements following a given case label do not have to be enclosed in braces. They constitute a *statement list* rather instead of a code block.

Unlike an if statement, a switch statement isn't automatically terminated when a match is found and the code following the matching case label is executed. To exit a switch statement, a *jump statement* must be used—typically, a break statement. If a jump statement isn't included following a given case label, the execution will "fall through" to the next case or default label. This behavior can be used to our advantage: when the same logic is to be executed for more than one case label, two or more case labels can be stacked up back to back as shown here:

```
// x is assumed to have been previously declared as an int
switch (x) {
    case 1:
    case 2:
    case 3:
        // code to be executed if x equals 1, 2, or 3
        break;
    case 4:
        // code to be executed if x equals 4
        break;
}
```

A switch statement is useful for making a selection between a series of mutually exclusive choices. In the following example, a switch statement is used to assign a value to a variable named capital based on the value of a variable named country. If a match isn't found, the capital variable is assigned the value "not in the database".

```
using System;

public class SwitchDemo
{
    static void Main() {
        string country;
        string capital;
        country = "India";

        // This switch statement compares the value of the variable "country"
        // against the value of three case labels. If no match is found,
        // the code after the default label is executed.
```

```
    switch (country) {
      case "England":
        capital = "London";
        break;
      case "India":
        capital = "New Delhi";
        break;
      case "USA":
        capital = "Washington D.C.";
        break;
      default:
        capital = "not in the database";
        break;
    }

    Console.WriteLine("The capital of " + country + " is " + capital);
  }
}
```

Here's the output for the preceding code example:

```
The capital of India is New Delhi
```

for Statements

A for statement is a programming construct that is used to execute one or more statements a certain number of times. The general syntax of the for statement is as follows:

```
for (initializer; condition; iterator) {
  // code to execute while condition is true
}
```

A for statement defines three elements that are separated by semicolons and placed in parentheses after the for keyword.

The *initializer* is typically used to provide an initial value for a *loop control variable*. The variable can be declared as part of the initializer or it can be declared earlier in the code, ahead of the for statement. For example:

```
// The loop control variable 'i' is declared within the for statement:
  for (int i = 0; condition; iterator) {
    // code to execute while condition is true
}
  // Note that i goes out of scope when the 'for' loop exits.
```

or:

```
// The loop control variable 'i' is declared earlier in the program:
  int i;

for (i = 0; condition; iterator) {
    // code to execute while condition is true
```

```
    }
    // Note that because i is declared before the for loop begins in this
    // case, i remains in scope when the 'for' loop exits.
```

The *condition* is a logical expression that typically involves the loop control variable:

```
for (int i = 0; i < 5; iterator) {
    // code to execute as long as i is less than 5
}
```

The *iterator* typically increments or decrements the loop control variable:

```
for (int i = 0; i < 5; i++) {
    // code to execute as long as i is less than 5
}
```

Again, note the use of a semicolon (;) after the initializer and condition, but *not* after the iterator.

Here's a breakdown of how a for loop operates:

- When program execution reaches a for statement, the initializer is executed first (and only once).

- The condition is then evaluated. If the condition evaluates to true, the block of code following the parentheses is executed.

- After the block of code finishes, the iterator is executed.

- The condition is then reevaluated. If the condition is still true, the block of code and update statement are executed again.

This process repeats until the condition becomes false, at which point the for loop exits.

Here is a simple example of using nested for statements to generate a simple multiplication table. The loop control variables j and k are declared inside their respective for statements. As long as the conditions in the respective for statements are met, the block of code following the for statement is executed. The ++ operator is used to increment the values of j and k after each time the respective block of code is executed.

```
using System;

public class ForDemo
{
    static void Main() {
        // Compute a simple multiplication table.

        for (int j = 1; j <= 4; j++) {
            for (int k = 1; k <= 4; k++) {
                Console.WriteLine(j + " * " + k + " = " + (j * k));
            }
        }
    }
}
```

Here's the output:

```
1 * 1 = 1
1 * 2 = 2
1 * 3 = 3
1 * 4 = 4
2 * 1 = 2
2 * 2 = 4
2 * 3 = 6
2 * 4 = 8
```

■**Note** Note the use of the `string` concatenation operator + in the `ForDemo` example; `string` representations of the value of `int` variables j and k are concatenated to the `string` literals " * ", and " = ".

Each of the three elements inside the parentheses of a `for` statement is optional (although the two separating semicolons are mandatory).

If the initializer is omitted, the loop control variable must have been declared and initialized before the `for` statement is encountered:

```
int i = 0;
for (; i < 5; i++) {
    // do some stuff as long as i is less than 5
}
```

If the iterator is omitted, we must make sure to take care of explicitly updating the loop control variable within the body of the `for` loop to avoid an infinite loop:

```
for (int i = 0; i < 5; ) {
    // do some stuff as long as i is less than 5

    // Explicitly increment i.
    i++;
}
```

If the condition is omitted, it will always be evaluated as being true, and the result is a potentially infinite loop:

```
for (;;) {
    // infinite loop!
}
```

■**Note** In the section titled "Jump Statements" later in this chapter, you'll see that jump statements can be used to break out of a loop.

As with other flow of control structures, if only one statement is specified after the `for` condition, the braces can be omitted (but it is considered good programming practice to use braces regardless):

```
for (int i = 0; i < 3; i++)
    sum = sum + i;
```

while Statements

A `while` statement is similar in function to a `for` statement, in that both are used to repeatedly execute an associated block of code. However, if the number of times that the code is to be executed is unknown when the loop first begins, a `while` statement is the preferred choice because a `while` statement continues to execute as long as a specified condition is met.

The general syntax for the `while` statement is as follows:

```
while (condition) {
    // code to execute while condition is true
}
```

The condition can be either a simple or complex logical expression that evaluates to a `true` or `false` value; for example:

```
int x = 1;
int y = 1;

while (x < 20 || y < 10) {
    // Pseudocode.
    presumably do something that affects the value of either x or y
}
```

When program execution reaches a `while` statement, the condition is evaluated first. If `true`, the block of code following the condition is executed. When the block of code is finished, the condition is evaluated again; if it is still `true`, the process repeats itself until the condition evaluates to `false`, at which point the `while` loop exits.

Here is a simple example illustrating the use of a `while` loop. A `bool` variable named `finished` is initially set to `false`. The `finished` variable is used as a flag: as long as `finished` is `false`, the block of code following the `while` loop will continue to execute. Presumably, there will be a statement inside the block of code that will eventually set `finished` to `true`, at which point the `while` loop will exit the next time the condition is retested.

```
using System;

public class WhileDemo
{
    static void Main() {
        bool finished = false;
        int i = 0;
```

```
    while (!finished) {
      Console.WriteLine(i);
      i++;
      if (i == 3)
        finished = true; // toggle the flag value
    }
  }
}
```

Here's the output:

```
0
1
2
```

As with the other flow of control structures, if only one statement is specified after the condition, the braces can be omitted (but it is considered good programming practice to use braces regardless):

```
while (x < 20)
  x = x * 2;
```

do Statements

With a while loop, the condition is evaluated before the code block following it is (conditionally) executed. Thus, it is possible that the code inside the loop body will never be run if the condition is false from the start. A do loop is similar to a while loop, except that the block of code is executed *before* the condition is evaluated. Therefore, we are guaranteed that the code block of the loop will be executed at least once.

The general syntax of a do statement is as follows:

```
do {
  // code to execute
} while (condition);
```

As was the case with the while statement, the condition of a do statement is a logical expression that evaluates to a Boolean value. A semicolon is placed after the parentheses surrounding the condition to signal the end of the do statement. We typically use a do loop when we know that we need to perform at least one iteration of a loop for initialization purposes.

```
bool flag;

do {
  // perform some code regardless of initial setting of 'flag', then
  // evaluate whether the loop should iterate again based on the value
  // of 'flag'. The value of 'flag' can be set to true or false within
  // the loop to indicate whether the loop should execute again.
} while (flag);
```

Jump Statements

Some of the loops and flow of control structures we have discussed will exit automatically when a condition is met (or not met), and some of them will not. The C# language defines a number of jump statements that are used to redirect program execution to another statement elsewhere in the code. The two types of jump statements that we will discuss in this section are the break and continue statements. Another jump statement, the return statement, is used to exit a method. We will defer our discussion of the return statement until Chapter 4.

You have already seen break statements in action earlier in this chapter, when they were used in conjunction with a switch statement. A break statement can also be used to abruptly terminate a do, for, or while loop. When a break statement is encountered during loop execution, the loop immediately terminates, and program execution is transferred to the line of code immediately after the loop or flow of control structure.

```
// This loop is intended to execute four times...
for (int j = 1; j <= 4; j++) {
  //...but, as soon as j attains a value of 3, the following 'if'
  // test passes, the break statement that it controls executes, and we
  // 'break out of' the loop.
  if (j == 3)
    break;

  // If, on the other hand, the 'if' test fails, we skip over the
  // 'break' statement, print the value of j, and keep on looping
  Console.WriteLine(j);
}

// The break statement, if/when executed, takes us to this line of code
// immediately after the loop.
Console.WriteLine("Loop finished");
```

The output produced by the preceding code snippet would be as follows:

```
1
2
Loop finished
```

A continue statement, on the other hand, is used to exit from the current iteration of a loop without terminating overall loop execution. A continue statement transfers program execution back up to the top of the loop (to the iterator part of a for loop) without finishing the particular iteration that is already in progress.

```
// This loop is intended to execute four times...
for (int j = 1; j <= 4; j++) {
  //...but, as soon as j attains a value of 3, the following 'if' test
  // passes and we 'jump' back to the j++ part of the for statement,
  // with j being incremented to 4...
  if (j == 3)
    continue;
```

```
  //...and so the following line doesn't get executed when j equals 3,
  // but DOES get executed when j equals 1, 2, and 4.
    Console.WriteLine(j);
  }
  Console.WriteLine("Loop finished");
```

The output produced by this code would be as follows:

```
1
2
4
Loop finished
```

Excessive use of break and continue statements in loops can result in code that is difficult to follow and maintain, so it's best to use these statements only when you have to use them.

Code Blocks and Variable Scope

C# (like C, C++, and Java) is a *block structured language*. As mentioned earlier in the chapter, a "block" of code is a series of zero or more lines of code enclosed within braces, like so: {...}.

- A method declaration, like the Main method of our SimpleProgram, defines a block.

- A class declaration, like the SimpleProgram class as a whole, also defines a block.

- As you have seen, many *control flow statements* also involve defining blocks of code.

Blocks can be nested inside one another to any arbitrary depth:

```
public class SimpleProgram
{
  // We're inside of the 'class' block (one level deep).
  static void Main() {
    // We're inside of the 'Main method' block (two levels deep).
    int x = 3;
    int y = 4;
    int z = 5;

    if (x > 2) {
      // We're now one level deeper (level 3), in a nested block.
      if (y > 3) {
        // We're one level deeper still (level 4), in yet another
        // nested block.
        // (We could go on and on!)
      } // We've just ended the level 4 block.
      // (We could have additional code here, at level 3.)
    } // Level 3 is done!
    // (We could have additional code here, at level 2.)
  } // That's it for level 2!
  // (We could have additional code here, at level 1.)
} // Adios, amigos! Level 1 has just ended.
```

The *scope* of a variable name is defined as that portion of code in which a name remains defined to the compiler, typically from the point where it is first declared down to the closing (right) brace for the block of code that it was declared in. A variable is said to be *in scope* only inside the block of code in which it is declared. Once program execution exits a block of code, any variables that were declared inside that block go out of scope and will be inaccessible to the program.

As an example of the consequences of variable scope, let's write a program called ScopeDemo, shown next. The ScopeDemo class declares three nested code blocks: one for the ScopeDemo class declaration, one for the Main method, and one as part of an if statement inside the body of the Main method.

```
public class ScopeDemo
{
  static void Main() {
    double cost = 2.65;

    if (cost < 5.0) {
      double discount = 0.05;  // declare a variable inside the 'if' block
      // other details omitted...
    }

    // When the 'if' block exits, the variable 'discount' goes out of scope,
    // and is no longer recognized by the compiler. If we try to use it
    // in a subsequent statement, the compiler will generate an error.

    double refund = cost * discount;   // this won't compile - discount is
  }                                    // no longer in scope
}
```

In the preceding example, a variable named cost is declared inside the block of code comprising the Main method body. Another variable named discount is declared inside the block of code associated with the if statement. When the if statement block of code exits, the discount variable goes out of scope. If we try to access it later in the program, as we do in the following line of code:

```
double refund = cost*discount;
```

The compiler will generate the following error:

```
error:: The name 'discount' does not exist in the current context
```

Note that a variable declared in an *outer* code block *is* accessible to any *inner* code blocks that follow the declaration. For example, in the preceding ScopeDemo example, the variable cost is accessible inside the nested if statement code block that follows its declaration.

Printing to the Screen

Most applications communicate information to users by displaying messages via the application's GUI. However, it is also useful at times to be able to display simple text messages to the command-line window from which we are running a program as a "quick and dirty" way of verifying that a program is working properly (you'll learn how to run C# programs from the command line in Chapter 13). Until we discuss how to craft a C# GUI in Chapter 16, this will be our program's primary way of communicating with the "outside world."

To print text messages to the screen, we use the following syntax:

```
Console.WriteLine(expression to be printed);
```

The Console.WriteLine method can accept very complex expressions and does its best to ultimately turn them into a single string value, which then gets displayed on the screen. Here are a few examples:

```
Console.WriteLine("Hi!");    // Printing a string literal/constant.

string greeting = "Hi!";
Console.WriteLine(greeting);    // Printing the value of a string variable.

string s = "foo";
string t = "bar";
Console.WriteLine(s + t);    // Using the string concatenation operator (+)
                             // to print "foobar".

int x = 3;
int y = 4;

Console.WriteLine(x);        // Converts x's int value into a string and
                             // prints the value "3" to the screen.

Console.WriteLine(x + y);    // Computes the sum of x and y, then
                             // prints the value "7" to the screen.
```

Note in the last line of code that the plus sign (+) is interpreted as the *integer* addition operator, not as the string concatenation operator, because it separates two variables that are both declared to be of type int. So, the sum of 3 + 4 is computed to be 7, which is then printed. In the next example, however, we get different (and arguably undesired) behavior:

```
Console.WriteLine("The sum of x plus y is:   " + x + y);
```

The preceding line of code causes the following to be printed:

```
The sum of x plus y is:   34
```

Why is this?

We evaluate most expressions from left to right, so because the first of the two plus signs separates a string literal and an int, it is interpreted as a string concatenation operator, and the value of x is thus converted into a string, producing the intermediate string value "The sum of x plus y is: 3".

The second plus sign separates this intermediate string value from an int as well (y), so it is also interpreted as a string concatenation operator, and the value of y is thus converted into a string, producing the final string value "The sum of x plus y is: 34", which is what finally gets printed.

To print the correct sum of x and y, we must force the second plus sign to be interpreted as an integer addition operator by enclosing the addition expression in nested parentheses:

```
Console.WriteLine("The sum of x plus y is: " + (x + y));
```

The nested parentheses cause the innermost expression to be evaluated first; the second plus sign is now seen by the compiler as separating two int values, and will thus serve as the integer addition operator. Then the first plus sign is seen as separating a string from an int, and is thus treated as a string concatenation operator, ultimately causing this print statement to display the correct message on the screen:

```
The sum of x plus y is: 7
```

When writing code that involves complex expressions, it is a good idea to use parentheses liberally to make our intentions clear to the compiler. Extra parentheses never hurt!

Write versus WriteLine

When we use Console.WriteLine(...), whatever expression is enclosed inside the parentheses will be printed, followed by a *line terminator*. The following code snippet:

```
Console.WriteLine("First line.");
Console.WriteLine("Second line.");
Console.WriteLine("Third line.");
```

produces this as output:

```
First line.
Second line.
Third line.
```

By contrast, the following statement causes whatever expression is enclosed in parentheses to be printed *without* a line terminator:

```
Console.Write(expression to be printed);
```

Using Write in combination with WriteLine allows us to build up a single line of output with a series of Write statements, as shown by the following example:

```
Console.Write("C");      // Using Write here.
Console.Write("SHA");    // Using Write here.
Console.WriteLine("RP"); // Note use of WriteLine as the last statement.
```

This code snippet produces the single line of output:

```
CSHARP
```

We can make a program listing more readable by breaking up the contents of a long print statement into multiple concatenated strings, and then breaking the statement along plus-sign boundaries:

```
    statement;
    another statement;
```

```
Console.WriteLine("Here is an example of how " +
                  "to break up a long print statement " +
                  "with plus signs.");
```

```
yet another statement;
```

Even though the preceding statement is broken across three lines of code, it will be printed as a single line of output:

```
Here is an example of how to break up a long print statement with plus signs.
```

Note that without the + signs in the preceding example, the code would not compile because a string literal won't automatically carry over onto the next line.

Escape Sequences

C# defines a number of *escape sequences* so that we can represent special characters, such as newline and tab characters, in string expressions. The most commonly used escape sequences are listed here:

\n	Newline
\b	Backspace
\t	Tab
\v	Vertical tab
\\	Backslash
\'	Single quote
\"	Double quote

One or more escape sequences can be included in the expression that is passed to the Write and WriteLine methods. For example, consider the following code snippet:

```
Console.WriteLine("Presenting...");
Console.WriteLine("\n...for a limited \"time\" only...\n");
Console.WriteLine("\tBailey the Wonder Dog!");
```

When the preceding code is executed, the following output is displayed:

```
Presenting...

...for a limited "time" only...

        Bailey the Wonder Dog!
```

There is a blank line before and after the second line of output because we inserted extra \n escape sequences in the second statement, the word "time" is quoted because of our use of the \" escape sequences in that same statement, and the third line of output has been tabbed over one position to the right by virtue of our use of \t.

Elements of C# Style

One of the trademarks of good programmers is that they produce readable code. Your professional life will probably not involve generating code by yourself on a mountaintop, so your colleagues will need to be able to work with and modify your programs. Here are some guidelines and conventions that will help you to produce clear, readable C# programs.

Proper Use of Indentation

One of the best ways to make C# programs readable is through proper use of indentation to clearly delineate statement hierarchies. Statements within a block of code should be indented relative to the starting/end line of the enclosing block (that is, indented relative to the lines carrying the braces). The examples in the MSDN web pages use four spaces, but some programmers use two spaces and others prefer three. The examples in this book use a two-space indentation convention.

Tip If you are using Visual Studio, you can configure the indentation spacing as one of the VS options.

To see how indentation can make a program readable, consider the following two programs. In the first program, no indentation is used:

```csharp
using System;

public class StyleDemo
{
static void Main() {
string name = "cheryl";
for (int i = 0; i < 4; i++) {
if (i != 2) {
Console.WriteLine(name + " " + i);
}
}
Console.WriteLine("what's next");
}
}
```

It is easy to see how someone would have to go through this program very carefully to figure out what it is trying to accomplish; it's not very readable code.

Now let's look at the same program when proper indentation is applied. Each statement within a block is indented two spaces relative to its enclosing block. It's much easier now to see what the code is doing. It is clear, for example, that the if statement is inside of the for statement's code block. If the if statement condition is true, the WriteLine method is called. It is also obvious that the last WriteLine method call is outside of the for loop. Both versions of this program produce the same result when executed, but the second version is much more readable.

```
using System;

public class StyleDemo
{
  static void Main() {
    string name = "Cheryl";
    for (int i = 0; i < 4; i++) {
      if (i != 2) {
        Console.WriteLine(name + " " + i);
      }
    }
    Console.WriteLine("What's next");
  }
}
```

This code's output is shown here:

```
Cheryl 0
Cheryl 1
Cheryl 3
What's next
```

Failure to properly indent makes programs unreadable and hence harder to debug—if a compilation error arises because of imbalanced braces, for example, the error message often occurs much later in the program than where the problem exists. For example, the following program is missing an opening brace on line 11, but the compiler doesn't report an error until line 25!

```
using System;
public class Indent2
{
  static void Main() {
    int x = 2;
    int y = 3;
    int z = 1;

    if (x >= 0) {
      if (y > x) {
        if (y > 2) // missing opening brace here on line 11, but...
          Console.WriteLine("A");
          z = x + y;
        }
        else {
          Console.WriteLine("B");
          z = x - y;
        }
      }
      else {
        Console.WriteLine("C");
```

```
         z = y - x;
      }
    }
    else Console.WriteLine("D");  // compiler first complains here!(line 25)
  }
}
```

The error message that the compiler generates in such a situation is rather cryptic; it points to line 25 as the problem and doesn't really help us much in locating the real problem on line 11:

```
IndentDemo.cs (25,5) error:
Invalid token 'else' in class, struct, or interface member declaration.
```

However, at least we've properly indented, so it will likely be easier to hunt down the missing brace than it would be if our indentation were sloppy.

Sometimes we have so many levels of nested indentation, or individual statements are so long, that lines "wrap" when viewed in an editor or printed as hardcopy:

```
while (a < b) {
    while (c > d) {
       for (int j = 0; j < 29; j++) {
          x = y + z + a + b - 125*
(c * (d / e) + f) - g + h + j - 1 - m - n + o +
p * q / r + s;
       }
    }
}
```

To avoid this, it is best to break the line in question along white space or punctuation boundaries:

```
while (a < b) {
  while (c > d) {
    for (int j = 0; j < 29; j++) {
      // This is cosmetically preferred.
      x = y + z + a + b - 125*(c * (d / e) + f) - g +
          h + j - 1 - m - n + o + p * q / r + s;
    }
  }
}
```

Use Comments Wisely

Another important feature that makes code more readable is the liberal use of meaningful comments. Always keep in mind when writing code that you know what you are trying to do, but someone else trying to read your code may not. (We sometimes even need to remind *ourselves* of why we did what we did if we haven't looked at code that *we've* written in awhile!)

If there can be any doubt as to what a section of code does, add a comment:

- Include enough detail in the comment to clearly explain what you mean.

- Make sure that the comment adds value; don't state the obvious. The following is a fairly useless comment because it states the obvious:

```
// Declare x as an integer, and assign it an initial value of 3.
int x = 3;
```

- Indent each comment to the same level as the block of code or statement to which it applies.

For an example of how comments are important in making code readable, let's revisit an example from earlier in the chapter:

```
using System;

public class IfDemo
{
  static void Main() {
    double sales = 40000.0;
    int lengthOfService = 12;
    double bonus;

    if (sales > 30000.0 && lengthOfService >= 10) {
      bonus = 2000.0;
    }
    else {
      if (sales > 20000.0) {
        bonus = 1000.0;
      }
      else {
        bonus = 0.0;
      }
    }

    Console.WriteLine("Bonus = " + bonus);
  }
}
```

Because of the lack of comments, someone trying to read the code might have difficulty figuring out what business logic this program is trying to apply. Now let's look at the same program when clear, descriptive comments have been included in the code listing:

```
using System;

// This program computes the size of an employee's bonus.
//
// Written on March 5, 2008 by Jacquie Barker and Grant Palmer.         ·
```

```
public class IfDemo
{
  static void Main() {
    // Quarterly sales in dollars.
    double sales = 40000.0;

    // Length of employment in months.
    int lengthOfService = 12;

    // Amount of bonus to be awarded in dollars.
    double bonus;

    // An employee gets a $2K bonus if (a) they've sold more than $30K this
    //quarter and (b) they've worked for the company for 10 months or more.
    if (sales > 30000.0 && lengthOfService >= 10) {
      bonus = 2000.0;
    }
    else {
      // Otherwise, ANY employee who has sold more than $20K this quarter
      // earns a bonus of $1K, regardless of how long they've worked for
      // the company.
      if (sales > 20000.0) {
        bonus = 1000.0;
      }
      // Employees who have sold less than $20K earn no bonus.
      else {
        bonus = 0.0;
      }
    }

    Console.WriteLine("Bonus = " + bonus);
  }
}
```

The program is now much more understandable because the comments explain what each section of the code is intended to accomplish.

Placement of Braces

For block structured languages that use braces, {...}, to delineate the start/end of blocks (for example, C, C++, Java, C#), there are two general schools of thought as to where the left/opening brace of a code block should be placed.

The first style is to place the left brace at the end of the line of code that starts the block and the matching right/closing brace on a line by itself:

```
public class Test { //  Left brace on same line as class declaration

    static void Main() {  //  Ditto for method headers
```

```
      for (int i = 0; i < 3; i++) { //  And again for control flow blocks
        Console.WriteLine(i);

      //  Each closing brace goes on its own line:
      }
    }
  }
```

An alternative opening brace placement style is to place every opening brace on a line by itself:

```
public class Test
{
    static void Main()
    {
        for (int i = 0; i < 3; i++)
        {
          Console.WriteLine("i");
        }
    }
}
```

Another possibility is a hybrid of these two approaches: the second style (brace on a separate line) is used for class declarations, and the first style (brace on the same line) is used for virtually everything else:

```
//  Left brace for class declaration on its own line:
public class Test
{
  //  but all others are on the same line as the initial line of code.
  static void Main() {

      for (int i = 0; i < 3; i++) {
        Console.WriteLine(i);

      //  Each closing brace goes on its own line:
      }
    }
  }
```

There is no absolute right or wrong style because the compiler doesn't care one way or the other. It is a good practice to maintain consistency in your code, however, so pick a brace placement style and stick with it.

Either way, it is important that the closing brace for a given block be indented the same number of spaces as the first line of code in the block so that they visually line up, as was discussed earlier.

Self-Documenting Variable Names

As with indentation and comments, the goal when choosing variable names is to make a program as readable, and hence self-documenting, as possible. Avoid using single letters as variable names, except for loop control variables. Abbreviations should be used sparingly, and only when the abbreviation is commonly used and widely understood by developers. Consider the following variable declaration:

```
int grd;
```

It's not completely clear what the variable name grd is supposed to represent. Is the variable supposed to represent a grid, a grade, or a gourd? A better practice is to spell the entire word out:

```
int grade;
```

At the other end of the spectrum, names that are too long, such as the following example, can make a code listing overwhelming to anyone trying to read it:

```
double averageThirdQuarterReturnOnInvestment;
```

It can sometimes be challenging to reduce the size of a variable name and still keep it descriptive, but do try to keep the length of your variable names within reason.

Note We'll talk about naming conventions for other OO building blocks, such as methods and classes, as we introduce these topics later in the book.

The .NET Framework provides a series of naming guidelines to promote a uniform style across C# programs. If you want to read the complete details on the C# naming conventions, the guidelines can be found at the following site: http://msdn.microsoft.com/en-us/library/ms229045.aspx.

Summary

In this chapter, we discussed some of the advantages of C#, including the following:

- C# is an intuitive OOPL that improves upon many languages that preceded it.

- C# was designed from the ground up to be fully object-oriented.

- C# is part of (and thus has access to the power of) Microsoft's .NET Framework.

- C# can be downloaded for free from the MSDN web site.

Note Of course, we haven't sung *all* of C#'s praises in this chapter; there are many other features that make C# a powerful OOPL that we'll cover in subsequent chapters.

In addition to exploring some of the advantages of C#, we also introduced you to some basic elements of C# syntax. In particular, we did the following in this chapter:

- Presented the anatomy of a simple C# program

- Discussed the predefined simple types and the `string` type

- Examined how value type variables are declared and initialized

- Introduced how a value of one type can be cast into a different type

- Discussed arithmetic, assignment, and logical expressions

- Presented loops and other flow of control structures available with C#

- Explored how to define blocks of code and the concept of variable scope

- Learned how to print text messages to the console with the `Write` and `WriteLine` methods

- Discussed some basic elements of good C# programming style

There's a lot more to learn about C#—things you'll need to know in building the SRS application in Part Three of the book—but we need to explain a number of basic object concepts first. So, on to Chapter 2!

Exercises

1. Research Microsoft's C# Language Tour web site at `http://msdn.microsoft.com/en-us/library/67ef8sbd.aspx`.

   Cite any advantages or features of C# not mentioned in this chapter.

2. Explore the Microsoft .NET Framework home page at `http://msdn.microsoft.com/en-us/library/w0x726c2.aspx`.

   Remember that C# can make use of all the libraries and other capabilities provided by the .NET Framework.

3. Using a `for` loop and a `continue` statement, create a code snippet that will write the even numbers from 1 to 10 to the console.

4. Using what you know about defining blocks of code and proper indentation technique, make the following code snippet more readable:

```
int count = 0;
for (int j = 0; j < 2; j++) {
count = j;
for (int k = 0; k < 3; k++)
count++;
Console.WriteLine("count = " + count);
}
```

5. Compare what you've learned about C# so far to another programming language that you are already familiar with. What is similar about the two languages? What is different?

6. Given these initial variable declarations and value assignments:

```
int a = 1;
int b = 1;
int c = 1;
```

evaluate the following expression:

```
((((c++ + --a) * b) != 2) && true)
```

CHAPTER 2
■ ■ ■

Abstraction and Modeling

As human beings, we're flooded with information every day of our lives. Even if we could temporarily turn off all of the sources of "e-information" that are constantly bombarding us—email, voicemail, news broadcasts, and the like—our five senses alone collect millions of bits of information per day just from our surroundings. Yet we manage to make sense out of all of this information, typically without getting overwhelmed. Our brains naturally simplify the details of all that we observe so that these details are manageable through a process known as *abstraction*.

In this chapter, you'll learn the following:

- How abstraction serves to simplify our view of the world

- How we organize our knowledge hierarchically to minimize the amount of information that we have to mentally juggle at any given time

- The relevance of abstraction to software development

- The inherent challenges that we face as software developers when attempting to model a real-word situation in software

Simplification Through Abstraction

Take a moment to look around the room in which you're reading this book. At first, you may think that there really aren't that many things to observe: some furniture, light fixtures, perhaps some plants, artwork, even some other people or pets. Maybe there is a window to gaze out of that opens up the outside world to observation.

Now look again: for each thing that you see, there are a myriad of details to observe: its size, its color, its intended purpose, the components from which it's assembled (the legs on a table, the light bulbs in a lamp), and so on. In addition, each one of these components in turn has details associated with it: the type of material used to make the legs of the table (wood or metal), the wattage of the light bulbs, and so on. Now factor in your other senses: the sound of someone snoring (hopefully not while reading this book!), the smell of popcorn coming from the microwave oven down the hall, and so forth. Finally, think about all the unseen details of these objects—who they were manufactured by or what their chemical, molecular, or genetic composition is.

It's clear that the amount of information to be processed by our brains is truly overwhelming! For the vast majority of people, this doesn't pose a problem, however, because we're innately skilled at *abstraction*: a process that involves recognizing and focusing on the important characteristics of a situation or object, and filtering out or ignoring all the unessential details.

One familiar example of an abstraction is a roadmap. As an abstraction, a roadmap represents those features of a given geographic area relevant to someone trying to navigate with the map, perhaps by car: major roads and places of interest, obstacles such as major bodies of water, and so on. Of necessity, a roadmap can't include every building, tree, street sign, billboard, traffic light, fast food restaurant, and so on that physically exists in the real world. If it did, it would be so cluttered as to be virtually unusable; none of the important features would stand out.

Compare a roadmap with a topographical map, a climatological map, and a population density map of the same region: each abstracts out different features of the real world—namely, those relevant to the intended user of the map in question.

As another example, consider a landscape. An artist may look at the landscape from the perspective of colors, textures, and shapes as a prospective subject for a painting. A home-builder may look at the same landscape from the perspective of where the best building site may be on the property, assessing how many trees will need to be cleared to make way for a construction project. An ecologist may closely study the individual species of trees and other plant/animal life for their biodiversity, with an eye toward preserving and protecting them. A child may simply be looking at all of the trees in search of the best site for a tree house! Some elements are common to all these four observers' abstractions of the landscape—the types, sizes, and locations of trees, for example—while others aren't relevant to all the abstractions.

Generalization Through Abstraction

If we eliminate enough detail from an abstraction, it becomes generic enough to apply to a wide range of specific situations or instances. Such generic abstractions can often be quite useful. For example, a diagram of a generic cell in the human body, such as the one in Figure 2-1, might include only a few features of the structures that are found in an actual cell.

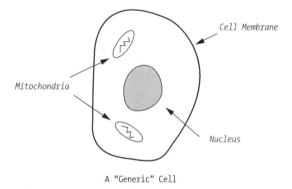

Figure 2-1. *A generic abstraction of a cell*

This overly simplified diagram doesn't look like a real nerve cell, or a real muscle cell, or a real blood cell; and yet, it can still be used in an educational setting to describe certain aspects of the structure and function of all of these cell types—namely, those features that the various cell types have in common.

The simpler an abstraction—that is, the fewer features it presents—the more general it is and the more versatile it is in describing a variety of real-world situations. The more complex an abstraction, the more restrictive it is, and thus the fewer situations it is useful in describing.

Organizing Abstractions into Classification Hierarchies

Even though our brains are adept at abstracting concepts such as roadmaps and landscapes, that still leaves us with hundreds of thousands, if not millions, of separate abstractions to deal with over our lifetimes. To cope with this aspect of complexity, human beings systematically arrange information into categories according to established criteria; this process is known as *classification.*

For example, science categorizes all natural objects as belonging to the animal, plant, or mineral kingdom. In order for a natural object to be classified as an animal, it must satisfy the following rules:

- It must be a living being.

- It must be capable of spontaneous movement.

- It must be capable of rapid motor response to stimulation.

The rules for what constitute a plant, on the other hand, are different:

- It must be a living being (same as for an animal).

- It must lack an obvious nervous system.

- It must possess cellulose cell walls.

Given clear-cut rules such as these, placing an object into the appropriate category, or *class*, is rather straightforward. We can then "drill down," specifying additional rules that differentiate various types of animal, for example, until we've built up a hierarchy of increasingly more complex abstractions from top to bottom. A simple example of an *abstraction hierarchy* is shown in Figure 2-2.

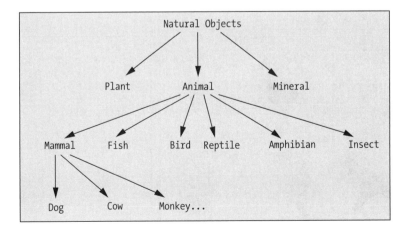

Figure 2-2. *A simple abstraction hierarchy of natural objects*

When thinking about an abstraction hierarchy such as the one shown in Figure 2-2, we mentally step up and down the hierarchy, automatically zeroing in on only the single layer or subset of the hierarchy (known as a *subtree*) that is important to us at a given point in time. For example, we may be concerned only with mammals, and so can focus on the mammalian subtree, shown in Figure 2-3, temporarily ignoring the rest of the hierarchy.

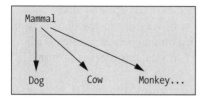

Figure 2-3. *Focusing on a small subset of the hierarchy is less overwhelming.*

By doing so, we automatically reduce the number of concepts that we mentally need to juggle at any one time to a manageable subset of the overall abstraction hierarchy; in our simplistic example, we're now dealing with only 4 concepts instead of the original 13. No matter how complex an abstraction hierarchy grows to be, it needn't overwhelm us if it's properly organized.

Coming up with precisely which rules are necessary to properly classify an object within an abstraction hierarchy isn't always easy. Take, for example, the rules we might define for what constitutes a bird: namely, something that

- Has feathers

- Has wings

- Lays eggs

- Is capable of flying

Given these rules, neither an ostrich nor a penguin could be classified as a bird because neither can fly (see Figure 2-4).

Figure 2-4. *Deriving the correct classification rules can be difficult.*

If we attempt to make the rule set less restrictive by eliminating the "flight" rule, we're left with

- Has feathers

- Has wings

- Lays eggs

According to this rule set, we now may properly classify both the ostrich and the penguin as birds, as shown in Figure 2-5.

Figure 2-5. *Proper classification rules have been established.*

This rule set is still unnecessarily complicated because as it turns out, the "lays eggs" rule is redundant; whether we keep it or eliminate it, it doesn't change our decision of what constitutes a bird versus a non-bird. Therefore, we simplify the rule set once again:

- Has feathers

- Has wings

Feeling particularly daring (!), we try to take our simplification process one step further by eliminating yet another rule, defining a bird as something that

- Has wings

As Figure 2-6 shows, we've gone too far this time: the abstraction of a bird is now so general that we'd include airplanes, insects, and all sorts of other non-birds in the mix!

Figure 2-6. *A rule set that is too relaxed is as much of a problem as an overly restrictive rule set.*

The process of rule definition for purposes of categorization involves "dialing in" just the right set of rules—not too general, not too restrictive, and containing no redundancies—to define the correct membership in a particular class.

Abstraction As the Basis for Software Development

When pinning down the requirements for an information systems development project, we typically start by gathering details about the real-world situation on which the system is to be based. These details are usually a combination of

- Those that are explicitly offered to us as we interview the intended users of the system, plus

- Those that we otherwise observe

We must make a judgment call as to which of these details are relevant to the system's ultimate purpose. This is essential, because we can't automate them all! To include too much detail is to overly complicate the resultant system, making it that much more difficult to design, program, test, debug, document, maintain, and extend in the future.

As with all abstractions, all our decisions of inclusion versus elimination when building a software system must be made within the context of the overall purpose and *domain*, or subject matter focus, of the future system. When representing a person in a software system, for example, is the eye color important? How about the genetic profile? Salary? Hobbies? The answer is this: *any* of these features of a person can be relevant or irrelevant, depending on whether the system to be developed is a

- Payroll system

- Marketing demographics system

- Optometrist's patient database

- FBI's "most-wanted" tracking system

- Public library

Once we've determined the essential aspects of a situation—something that we'll show you how to do in Part Two of this book—we can prepare a *model* of that situation. *Modeling* is the process by which we develop a pattern for something to be made. A blueprint for a custom home, a schematic diagram of a printed circuit, and a cookie cutter are all examples of such patterns. As you'll see in Parts Two and Three, an *object model* of a software system is such a pattern. Modeling and abstraction go hand in hand because a model is essentially a physical or graphical portrayal of an abstraction; before we can model something effectively, we must have determined the essential details of the subject to be modeled.

Reuse of Abstractions

When learning about something new, we automatically search our mental archive for other abstractions/models that we've previously built and mastered to look for similarities that we can build upon. When learning to ride a two-wheeled bicycle for the first time, for example, you may have drawn upon lessons that you learned about riding a tricycle as a child (see Figure 2-7). Both have handlebars that are used to steer; both have pedals that are used to propel the bike forward. Although the abstractions didn't match perfectly—a two-wheeled bicycle introduced the new challenge of having to balance oneself—there was enough of a similarity to allow you to draw upon the steering and pedaling expertise you already had mastered and to focus on learning the new skill of how to balance on two wheels.

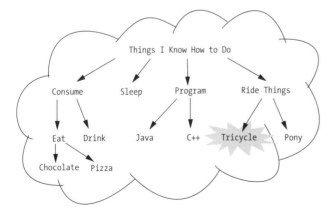

Figure 2-7. *The human brain is adept at learning by building upon already-established abstractions.*

This technique of comparing features to find an abstraction that is similar enough to be reused successfully is known as *pattern matching and reuse*. As you'll see in Chapter 12, pattern reuse is also an important technique for object-oriented software development because it spares us from having to reinvent the wheel with each new project. If we can reuse an abstraction or model from a previous project, we can focus on those aspects of the new project that differ from the old, gaining a tremendous amount of productivity in the process.

Inherent Challenges

Despite the fact that abstraction is such a natural process for human beings, developing an appropriate model for a software system is perhaps the most difficult aspect of software engineering because

- There are an unlimited number of possibilities. Abstraction is in the eye of the beholder to a certain extent: several different observers working independently are almost guaranteed to arrive at different models. Whose is the best? Passionate arguments have ensued!

- To further complicate matters, there is virtually never only one "best" or "correct" model, only "better" or "worse" models relative to the problem to be solved. The same situation can be modeled in a variety of different, equally valid ways. As you'll see when we get into actually doing some modeling in Part Two of this book, you'll look at a number of valid alternative abstractions for our Student Registration System (SRS) case study that was presented at the end of the Introduction.

- Note, however, that there *is* such a thing as an incorrect model: namely, one that misrepresents the real-world situation (for example, modeling a person as having two different blood types).

- There is no acid test to determine whether a model has adequately captured all of a user's requirements. The ultimate evidence of whether or not an abstraction was appropriate is in how successful the resultant software system turns out to be. We don't want to wait until the end of a project before finding out that we've gone astray. Because of this, it's critical that we learn ways of communicating our model concisely and unambiguously to the following people:

  - The intended future users of our application, so that they may sanity-check our understanding of the problem to be solved before we embark upon software development

  - Our fellow software engineers, so that team members share a common vision of what we're to build collaboratively

Despite all these challenges, it's critical to get the up-front abstraction "right" before beginning to build a system. Fixing mistakes in the abstraction once a system is modeled, designed, coded, documented, and undergoing acceptance testing is much more costly (by orders of magnitude) than correcting the abstraction when it's still a gleam in the project team's eye. This isn't to imply that an abstraction should be rigid—quite the contrary! The art and science of object modeling, when properly applied, yields a model that is flexible enough to withstand a wide variety of functional changes. In addition, the special properties of objects further lend themselves to flexible software solutions, as you'll learn throughout the rest of the book. However, all things being equal, we'd like to harness this flexibility in expanding a system's capabilities over time instead of in repairing mistakes.

What Does It Take to Be a Successful Object Modeler?

Coming up with an appropriate abstraction as the basis for a software system model requires the following:

- *Insight into the problem domain*: Ideally, you'll be able to draw upon your own real-world experience, such as your former or current experience as a student, which will come in handy when determining the requirements for the SRS.

- *Creativity*: To enable us to think "outside the box," in case the future users that we're interviewing have been immersed in the problem area for so long that they fail to see innovations that might be made.

- *Good listening skills*: These will come in handy as future users of the system describe how they do their jobs currently, or how they envision doing their jobs in the future, with the aid of the system that we're about to develop.

- *Good observational skills*: Actions often speak louder than words; just by observing users going about their daily business, we may pick up an essential detail that they have neglected to mention because they do it so routinely that it has become a habit.

But all this isn't enough, we also need

- An organized *process* for determining what the abstraction should be. If we follow a proven checklist of steps for producing a model, then we greatly reduce the probability that we'll omit some important feature or neglect a critical requirement.

- A way to *communicate* the resultant model concisely and unambiguously to our fellow software developers and to the intended users of our application. Although it's certainly possible to describe an abstraction in narrative text, a picture is worth 1,000 words, so the language with which we communicate a model is often a *graphical notation*. In several chapters of this book, we'll make use of Unified Modeling Language ((UML) notation as our model communication language (see Figure 2-8). (A brief introduction to UML will be provided in Chapters 9 and 10.) Think of a graphical model as a blueprint of the software application to be built.

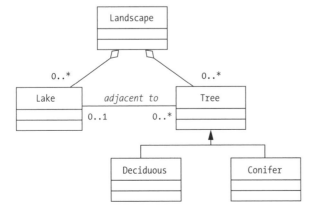

Figure 2-8. *Describing a landscape in UML notation*

■**Note** You'll learn how to interpret UML diagrams in Part Two of the book.

- Ideally, we'll also have a *software tool* to help us automate the process of producing such a blueprint.

Part Two of this book covers these three aspects of modeling—process, notation, and tool—in detail. For starters, however, we'll make sure that you understand the basics of objects, which is the focus of the remainder of Part One.

Summary

In this chapter, you learned that

- Abstraction is a fundamental technique that people use to perceive the world and is a necessary first step of all software development.

- We naturally organize information into classification hierarchies based upon rules that we carefully structure, so that they are neither too general nor too restrictive.

- We often reuse abstractions when attempting to model a new concept.

- Producing an abstraction of a system to be built, known as a model, is in some senses second nature to us, yet paradoxically is one of the hardest things that software developers have to do in the life cycle of an information systems project. It's also one of the most important.

Exercises

1. Sketch an abstraction hierarchy that relates all the following classes in a reasonable manner:

Apple

Banana

Beef

Beverage

Cheese

Consumable

Dairy Product

Food

Fruit

Green Bean

Meat

Milk

Pork

Spinach

Vegetable

Note any challenges you faced in doing so.

2. What aspects of a television set would be important to abstract from the perspective of

- A consumer wishing to buy one?

- An engineer responsible for designing one?

- A retailer who sells them?

- The manufacturer?

3. Select a problem area that you want to model from an object-oriented perspective. Ideally, this will be a problem that you're actually going to be working on at your place of employment or that you have a keen interest in. Assume that you're going to write a program to automate some aspect of this problem area. Write a one-page overview of the requirements for this program, patterned after the Student Registration System case study.

Make certain that your first paragraph summarizes the intent of the system, as the first paragraph in the SRS case study does. Also, emphasize the *functional requirements*— that is, those that a nontechnical end user might state as to how the system should behave—and avoid stating *technical requirements* (for example, "This system must run on a Windows Vista platform, and must use the TCP/IP protocol to . . .").

CHAPTER 3

■■■

Objects and Classes

Objects are the fundamental building blocks of an object-oriented (OO) system. Just as you learned in Chapter 2 that abstraction involves producing a model of the real world, you'll see in this chapter that objects are "mini-abstractions" of the various real-world components that comprise such a model.

In this chapter, you'll learn:

- What a software object is made of

- How we use classes to specify an object's data and behavior

- How we create objects based on a class definition

- How objects keep track of one another

What Is an Object?

Before we talk about software objects, let's talk about real-world objects in general. According to *Merriam-Webster's Collegiate Dictionary*, an object is

(1) Something material that may be perceived by the senses; (2) something mental or physical toward which thought, feeling, or action is directed.

The first part of this definition refers to objects as we typically think of them: as physical "things" that we can see and touch, and that occupy space. Because we intend to use the Student Registration System (SRS) case study as the basis for learning about objects throughout this book, let's think of some examples of *physical objects* that make sense in the general context of an academic setting:

- The *students* who attend classes

- The *professors* who teach them

- The *classrooms* in which class meetings take place

- The *furniture* in these classrooms

- The *buildings* in which the classrooms are located

- The *textbooks* students use

And on and on. Of course, although all these types of objects are commonly found on a typical college campus, not all of them are relevant to registering students for courses, nor are they all necessarily called out by the SRS case study, but we won't worry about that for the time being. In Part Two of this book, you'll learn a technique for using a requirements specification as the basis for identifying which types of objects are relevant to a particular abstraction.

Now, let's focus on the second half of the definition, particularly on the phrase *"something mental ...toward which thought, feeling, or action is directed."* There are a great many *conceptual objects* that play important roles in an academic setting; some of these are

- The *courses* that students attend

- The *departments* that faculty work for

- The *degrees* that students receive

And, of course, many others. Even though we can't see, hear, touch, taste, or smell them, conceptual objects are every bit as important as physical objects are in describing an abstraction.

Let's now get a bit more formal and define a *software object*:

- A (software) *object* is a software construct that bundles together *state* (*data*) and *behavior* (*operations*) that, taken together, represent an abstraction of a "real-world" (physical or conceptual) object.

Let's explore the two sides of objects—*state* and *behavior*—separately and in more depth.

State/Fields/Data

If we want to record information about a student, what data might we require? Some examples might include the following:

- The student's name

- His or her student ID number

- The student's birth date

- His or her address

- The student's designated major field of study, if the student has declared one yet

- His or her cumulative grade point average (GPA)

- The name of the student's faculty advisor

- A list of the courses that the student is currently enrolled in this semester (that is, the student's current course load)

- A history of all courses that the student has taken to date, the semester/year in which each was taken, and the grade that was earned for each: in other words, the student's transcript

And so on. Now, how about for an academic course? Perhaps you want to record the following information:

- The course number (for example, "ART 101")

- The course name (for example, "Ballroom Dancing")

- A list of all the courses that must have been successfully completed by a student prior to allowing that student to register for *this* course (that is, the course's prerequisites)

- The number of credit hours the course is worth

- A list of the professors who have been approved to teach the course

And so on. In object nomenclature, the data elements used to describe an object are referred to as the object's *fields*.

■**Note** The convention for .NET languages is to use the term *field* to describe the data elements of an object. Sometimes other OO references might use the term *attribute* instead, but all .NET languages (including C#) have a specific *programming construct* called an attribute, which has a more complex purpose than simply referring to a data element of an object. It's important not to confuse the two uses of the term *attribute*, so the term *field* will be used for object data elements throughout this book. We'll explain what an attribute (in the C# [.NET]–specific sense) is all about in Chapter 13.

An object's field values, when taken collectively, are said to define the *state*, or condition, of the object. For example, if we want to determine whether or not a student is "eligible to graduate," we might look at a combination of the following to see whether the student indeed is expected to have satisfied the course requirements for their chosen major field of study (a third field) by the end of the current academic year:

- The student's transcript (a field)

- The list of courses they are currently enrolled in (a second field)

A given field can be simple (for example, "GPA" can be represented as a simple floating point number) or complex (for example, "transcript" represents a rather extensive collection of information with no simple representation).

Behavior/Operations/Methods

Now let's revisit the same two types of objects—a student and a course—and talk about these objects' respective behaviors. A student's behaviors (relevant to academic matters, that is!) might include these:

- Enrolling in a course

- Dropping a course

- Choosing a major field of study

- Selecting a faculty advisor

- Telling you his or her GPA

- Telling you whether or not he or she has taken a particular course; if so, when the course was taken, which professor taught it, and what grade the student received

It's a bit harder to think of an inanimate, conceptual object such as a course as having behaviors, but if we were to imagine a course to be a living thing, we can imagine that a course's behaviors might include the following:

- Permitting a student to register

- Determining whether or not a given student is *already* registered

- Telling you how many students have registered so far or, conversely, how many seats remain before the course is full

- Telling you what its prerequisite courses are

- Telling you how many credit hours it's worth

- Telling you which professor is assigned to teach the course this semester

And so on.

When we talk about software objects specifically, we define an object's behaviors, also known as its *operations*, as both the processes an object uses to *access* its fields (data) and the processes that an object uses to *modify/maintain* its field values.

If we take a moment to reflect on the behaviors we expect of a student as listed previously, we see that each operation involves one or more of the student's fields. For example:

- Telling you his or her GPA involves *accessing* the value of the student's "GPA" field.

- Choosing a major field of study involves *modifying* the value of the student's "major" field.

- Enrolling in a course involves *modifying* the value of the student's "course load" field.

Because we recently learned that the collective set of field values for an object defines its state, we now can see that operations are capable of *changing an object's state*. Let's say that we refer to a student who hasn't yet selected a major field of study as an "undeclared" student. Asking such a Student object to perform its "choosing a major field of study" method will cause that object to update the value of its "major field of study" field to reflect the newly selected major field. This then changes the student's condition from "undeclared" to "declared".

Yet another way to think of an object's operations are as *services* that can be requested of the object. For example, one service that we might call upon a Course object to perform is to provide us with a list of all the students who are currently registered for the course (that is, a student roster).

When we actually get around to programming an object in a language such as C#, we refer to the programming language representation of an operation as a *method*, whereas, strictly speaking, the term "operation" is typically used to refer to a behavior conceptually.

Classes

A *class* is an abstraction describing the common features of all objects in a group of similar objects. For example, a class called Student could be created to describe all Student objects recognized by the SRS.

A class defines the following:

- The data structure (names and types of fields) needed to define an object belonging to that class

- The operations to be performed by such objects: specifically, what these operations are, how an object belonging to that class is formally called upon to perform them, and what "behind the scenes" things an object has to do to actually carry them out

For example, the Student class might be defined to have the nine fields described in Table 3-1.

Table 3-1. *Proposed Fields of the Student Class*

Field	Type
name	string
studentId	string
birthdate	DateTime
address	string
major	string
gpa	double
advisor	???
courseLoad	???
transcript	???

This means each and every Student object will have these *same* nine fields. Note that many of the fields can be represented by predefined C# types (for example, string, double, and Date-Time), but that a few of the fields (for example, advisor, courseLoad, and transcript) are too complex for built-in types to handle; you'll learn how to tackle such fields a bit later on.

In terms of operations, the Student class might define five methods as follows:

- RegisterForCourse

- DropCourse

- ChooseMajor

- ChangeAdvisor

- PrintTranscript

Note that an object can do only those things for which methods have been defined by the object's class. In that respect, an object is like an appliance: it can do whatever it was designed to do (a DVD player provides buttons to play, pause, stop, and seek a particular movie scene) and nothing more (you can't ask a DVD to toast a bagel—at least not with much chance of success!). So an important aspect of successfully designing an object is making sure to anticipate all the behaviors it will need to carry out its "mission" within the system. You'll see how to determine what an object's mission, data structure, and behaviors should be, based on the requirements for a system, in Part Two of the book.

Note The term *member* is used to refer to both fields and methods of a class. That is, a class definition that includes three field declarations and five method declarations is said to have eight members. When talking specifically about C# fields, we sometimes refer to them as *instance variables* or *class variables*.

Members are the building blocks of a class: virtually everything found within a class definition is either a field or a method of the class.

A Note Regarding Naming Conventions

It is recommended practice to name classes starting with an *uppercase* letter, but to use mixed case for the name overall: Student, Course, Professor, and so on. When the name of a class would ideally be stated as a multiword phrase, such as "course catalog", start each word with a capital letter and concatenate the words without using spaces, dashes, or underscores to separate them; for example, CourseCatalog. This style is known as *Pascal casing*.

For method names, the C# convention is to use Pascal casing as well. Typical method names might thus be Main, GetName, or RegisterForCourse.

Note In contrast, the C# convention for field names is to start with a *lowercase* letter, but to capitalize the first letter of any subsequent words in the field name. Typical field names might thus be name, studentId, or courseLoad. This style is known as Camel casing. In subsequent chapters, we'll refine the rules for how Pascal and Camel casing are to be used.

Instantiation

A class definition may be thought of as a template for creating software objects—a "pattern" used to do the following:

- Stamp out a prescribed data area in memory to house the fields of a new object

- Associate a certain set of behaviors with that object

The term *instantiation* is used to refer to the process by which an object is created (constructed) based upon a class definition. From a single class definition (Student, for example) we can create many objects, in the same way that we use a single cookie cutter to make many cookies. Another way to refer to an object, then, is as an *instance* of a particular class; for example, a Student object is an instance of the Student class, and each Student object will contain values relevant for a particular student (for example his or her name, student ID, and so on). We'll talk about the physical process of *instantiating* objects as it occurs in C# in a bit more detail later in this chapter.

Classes may be differentiated from objects as follows:

- A *class* defines the members—fields, methods, and so on—that all objects belonging to the class possess, and can be thought of as serving as an object *template*, as illustrated in Figure 3-1.

- An *object*, on the other hand, is a unique instance of a *filled-in* template for which field values have been provided, and on which methods may be called, as illustrated in Figure 3-2.

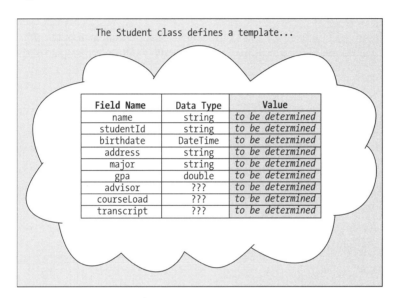

Figure 3-1. *A class defines field names, field types, and methods.*

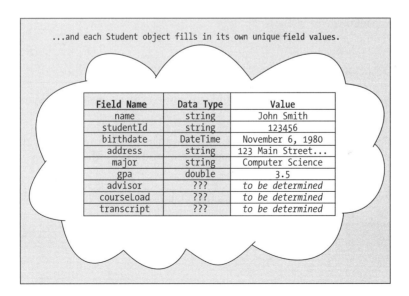

Figure 3-2. *An object provides field values*

Encapsulation

Encapsulation is a formal term referring to the mechanism that bundles together the state and behavior of an object into a single logical unit. Everything that we need to know about a given student is, in theory, contained within the "walls" of the Student object, either directly as fields of that object or indirectly through methods that can answer a question or make a determination about the object's state.

User-Defined Types and Reference Variables

In a non-OO programming language such as C, the following statement is a *declaration* that variable x is an int(eger), one of several simple, *predefined types* defined to be part of the C language:

```
int x;
```

What does this *really* mean? It means the following:

- x is a symbolic name that represents a location in memory that stores an integer value.

- The "thing" that we named x understands how to respond to a number of different operations, such as addition (+), subtraction (-), multiplication (*), division (/), logical comparisons (>, <, =), and so on that have been defined for the int type.

- Whenever we want to operate on this particular integer value in our program, we refer to it via its symbolic name x:

```
if (x > 17) {
    x = x + 5;
}
```

In an object-oriented language such as C#, we can define a class such as Student and then declare a variable as follows:

```
Student y;
```

What does this mean? It means that

- y is a symbolic name that can serve as a reference to a Student object (an instance of the Student class).

- The "thing" that we have named y understands how to respond to a number of different requests—how to register for a course, drop a course, and so on—that have been defined by the Student class.

- Whenever we want to operate on this particular object, we refer to y:

```
// Pseudocode.
  if (y hasn't chosen an advisor yet) {
     Console.WriteLine("Uh oh ...");
}
```

Note the parallels between y as a Student in the preceding example and x as an int earlier. Just as int is a predefined type (in both C and C#), the Student class is a *user-defined type*. And because y in the preceding example is a variable that *refers to a* instance (object) of class Student, y is informally known as a *reference variable*.

Instantiating Objects: A Closer Look

Different OO languages differ in terms of when an object is actually instantiated (created). In C#, when we declare a variable to be of a user-defined type, such as the following, we haven't actually created an object in memory yet:

```
Student y;
```

Instead we simply declared a reference variable of type Student named y. This reference variable has the *potential* to refer to a Student object, but it doesn't refer to one just yet. We have to take the distinct step of using a special C# operator, the new operator, to actually carve out a brand-new Student object in memory and to then associate the new object with the reference variable y, as follows:

```
y = new Student();
```

■**Note** Behind the scenes, what we're actually doing is associating the value of the *physical memory address* at which this object was created—known as a *reference*—to variable y. Don't worry about the parentheses at the end of the preceding statement; we'll talk about their significance in Chapter 4, when we discuss the notion of *constructors*.

Think of the newly created object as a helium balloon, as shown in Figure 3-3, and a reference variable as the hand that holds a string tied to the balloon so that you can access the object whenever you want.

Figure 3-3. *Using a reference variable to keep track of an object in memory*

We can also create a new object without immediately assigning it to a reference variable, as in the following line of code:

```
new Student();
```

Such an object would be like a helium balloon without a string, however. It would indeed exist, but we'd never be able to access this object in our program. It would, in essence, "float away" from us in memory.

Note that we can combine the two steps—declaring a reference variable and actually instantiating an object for that variable to refer to—into a single line of code:

```
Student y = new Student();
```

Another way to initialize a reference variable is to hand it a *preexisting* object: that is, an object ("helium balloon") that is already being referenced ("held onto") by a *different* reference variable ("hand"). Let's look at an example:

```
// We declare a reference variable, and instantiate our first
// Student object.
Student x = new Student();

// We declare a second reference variable, but do not instantiate a
// second object.
Student y;

// We pass y a reference to the same object that x is holding onto
// (x continues to hold onto it, too).  We now, in essence,
// have two "strings" tied to the same "balloon".
y = x;
```

The conceptual outcome of the preceding code is illustrated in Figure 3-4: two "strings" being held by two different "hands" and tied to the same "balloon"—that is, two *different* reference variables referring to the *same* physical object in memory.

Figure 3-4. *Maintaining multiple references on the same object*

We therefore see that the same object can have many reference variables simultaneously referring to it; but, as it turns out, any *one* reference variable can hold on to/refer to only *one* object at a time. To grab on to a new object requires that a reference variable let go of the object that it was previously holding on to, if any.

If there comes a time when *all* references for a particular object have been let go of, then (as we discussed earlier) the object is no longer accessible to our program, like a helium balloon that has been let loose. (See Figures 3-5, 3-6, and 3-7). We continue with our previous example (note highlighted code):

```
// We instantiate our first Student object.
Student x = new Student();

// We declare a second reference variable, but do not instantiate a
// second object.
Student y;

// We pass y a reference to the same object that x is holding onto
// (x continues to hold onto it, too).  We now, in essence,
// have TWO 'strings' tied to the same 'balloon'.
y = x;

// We now declare a third reference variable and instantiate a
// second Student object.
Student z = new Student();
```

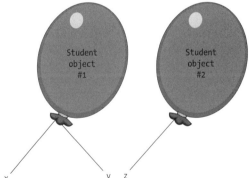

Figure 3-5. *A second object comes into existence.*

```
// y lets go of the first Student object and grabs onto the second.
y = z;
```

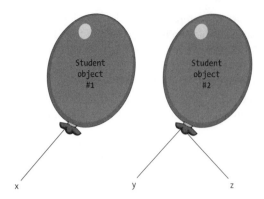

Figure 3-6. *Transferring object references*

```
// Finally, x lets go of the first Student object, and grabs onto
// the second, as well; the first Student object is now lost to
// the program because we no longer have any reference variables
// maintaining a reference to it!
x = z;
```

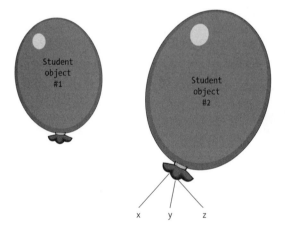

Figure 3-7. *The first object is now lost to our program.*

As it turns out, if all the references to an object are lost, it might seem as if the memory that the object occupies is permanently wasted. (In a language such as C++, this is indeed the case, and programmers have to explicitly take care to "reclaim" the memory of an object that is no longer needed before all its references are lost. Failure to do so is a chronic source of problems in C++ programs.) In C# (and all other .NET languages), the *common language run-time (CLR)* periodically performs *garbage collection*, a process that automatically reclaims the memory of "lost" objects for us. We'll revisit this topic in Chapter 13.

Objects As Fields

When we first discussed the fields and methods associated with the Student class, we stated that some of the fields could be represented by predefined types provided by the C# language, whereas the types of a few others (advisor, courseLoad, and transcript) were left undefined. Let's now put what we learned about user-defined types to good use.

Instead of declaring the Student class's advisor field as simply a string representing the advisor's name, we'll declare it to be a user-defined type—namely, type Professor, another class that we invented (see Table 3-2).

Table 3-2. *Student Class Fields, Revisited*

Field	Type
name	string
studentId	string
birthdate	DateTime
address	string
major	string
gpa	double
advisor	Professor
courseLoad	???
transcript	???

By having declared the advisor field to be of type Professor—that is, by making the advisor field a reference variable—we just enabled a Student object to maintain a reference to the actual Professor object that is advising the student. We'll still leave the courseLoad and transcript types unspecified for the time being; you'll see how to handle these a bit later.

The Professor class, in turn, might be defined to have the fields listed in Table 3-3.

Table 3-3. *Professor Class Fields*

Field	Type
name	string
employeeId	string
birthdate	DateTime
address	string
worksFor	string (or Department)
studentAdvisee	Student
teachingAssignments	???

Again, by having declared the studentAdvisee field to be of type Student—that is, by making the studentAdvisee field a reference variable—we just gave a Professor object a way to hold on to/refer to the actual Student object that the professor is advising. We'll leave the type of teachingAssignments undefined for the time being.

The methods of the `Professor` class might be as follows:

- `TransferToDepartment`

- `AdviseStudent`

- `AgreeToTeachCourse`

- `AssignGrades`

A few noteworthy points about the `Professor` class:

- It's likely that a professor will be advising several students simultaneously, so having a field such as `studentAdvisee` that can track only a single `Student` object is not terribly useful. We'll discuss techniques for handling this in Chapter 6, when we talk about *collections*, which we'll also see as being useful for defining the `teachingAssignments` field of `Professor`, and the `courseLoad` and `transcript` fields of `Student`.

- The `worksFor` field represents the department to which a professor is assigned. We can choose to represent this as either a simple `string` representing the department name— for example, `MATH`—or as a reference variable that maintains a reference to a `Department` object—specifically, the `Department` object representing the "real-world" Math Department. Of course, to do so would require defining the fields and methods for a new class called `Department`. As we'll see in Part Two of this book, the decision of whether we need to invent a new user-defined type/class to represent a particular real-world concept/abstraction isn't always clear-cut.

Association

Whenever we create a class, such as `Student` or `Professor`, in which one or more of the fields are themselves references to other objects, we are employing an OO technique known as *association*. The number of levels to which objects can be conceptually bundled inside one another is endless, so association enables us to model very sophisticated real-world concepts. As it turns out, most "interesting" classes employ association.

With association, it may seem as if we're nesting objects one inside the other, as depicted in Figure 3-8.

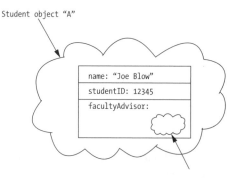

Figure 3-8. *Conceptual object "nesting"*

Actual object nesting (that is, declaring one class inside of another) is possible in C# and does indeed sometimes make sense—namely, if an object A doesn't need to have a life of its own from the standpoint of an OO application, and exists only for the purpose of serving enclosing object B.

- Think of your brain, for example, as an object that exists only within the context of your body (another object).

- As an example of object nesting relevant to the SRS, let's consider a grade book used to track student performance in a particular course. If we were to define a GradeBook class and then create GradeBook objects as fields—one per Course object—then it might be reasonable for each GradeBook object to exist wholly within the context of its associated Course object. No other objects would need to communicate with the GradeBook directly; if a Student object wanted to ask a Course object what grade the Student has earned, the Course object might internally consult its embedded GradeBook object and simply hand a letter grade back to the Student.

However, we often encounter the situation—as with the sample Student and Professor classes—in which an object A needs to refer to an object B, object B needs to refer back to A, and *both* objects need to be able to respond to requests independently of each other as made by the application as a whole. In such a case, object references come to the rescue! In reality, we are *not* storing whole objects as fields inside of other objects; instead we are storing *references* to objects. When a field of an object A is defined in terms of an object reference B, the two objects exist separately in memory and simply have a convenient way of finding one another whenever it's necessary for them to interact. Think of yourself as an object and your cellular phone number as your reference. Other people—"objects"—can reach you to speak with you whenever they need to, even though they don't know where you're physically located, using your cell phone number.

Memory allocation using object references might look something like Figure 3-9 conceptually.

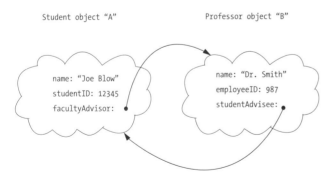

Figure 3-9. *Objects exist separately in memory and maintain references to one another.*

With this approach, each object is allocated in memory only once; the Student object knows how to find and communicate with its advisor (Professor) object whenever it needs to through its reference, and vice versa.

What do we gain by defining the Student's advisor field as a reference to a Professor object instead of merely storing the name of the advisor as a string field of the Student object?

For one thing, we can ask the Professor object its name whenever we need it (through a technique that we'll discuss in Chapter 4). Why is this important? *To avoid data redundancy and the potential for loss of data integrity.*

If the Professor object's name changes for some reason, the name will be stored only in one place: encapsulated as a field within the Professor object that "owns" the name, which is precisely where it belongs.

If we instead were to redundantly store the name of the Professor both as a string field of the Professor object and as a string field of the Student object, we'd have to remember to update the name in two places any time the name changed (or three, or four, or however many places this Professor's name is referenced as an advisor of countless Students). If we were to forget to do so, then the name of the Professor would be "out of synch" from one instance to another.

Just as importantly, by maintaining a reference to the Professor object via the advisor field of Student, the Student object can also *request other services* of this Professor object via whatever methods are defined for the Professor class. A Student object can, for example, ask its advisor (Professor) object where the office of the Professor is located, or what classes the Professor is teaching so that the Student can sign up for one of them.

Another advantage of using object references from an implementation standpoint is that they also reduce memory overhead. Storing a reference to (aka memory address of) an object requires only 4 bytes (on 32-bit machines) or 8 bytes (on 64-bit machines) of memory, instead of however many bytes of storage the referenced object as a whole occupies in memory. If we were to have to make a copy of an entire object every place we needed to refer to it in our application, we could quickly exhaust the total memory available to our application.

Three Distinguishing Features of an Object-Oriented Programming Language

In order to be considered truly object oriented, a programming language must provide support for three key mechanisms:

- (Programmer creation of) User-defined types

- Inheritance

- Polymorphism

You've just learned about the first of these mechanisms, and we'll discuss the other two in chapters to follow.

Summary

In this chapter, you've learned the following:

- An object is a software abstraction of a physical or conceptual real-world object.

- A class serves as a template for defining objects; specifically, a class defines the following:

  - What data the object will house, known as an object's fields

  - What behaviors an object will be able to perform, known as an object's operations (methods)

- An object can then be thought of as a filled-in template.

- Just as we can declare variables to be of simple predefined types such as `int`, `double`, and `bool`, we can also declare variables to be of user-defined types such as `Student` and `Professor`.

- When we create a new object (a process known as instantiation), we typically store a reference to that object in a reference variable. We can then use that reference to communicate with the object.

- We can define fields of a class A to serve as references to objects of another class B. In doing so, we allow each object to encapsulate the information that rightfully belongs to that object, but enable objects to share information by contacting one another whenever necessary.

Exercises

1. From the perspective of an academic setting (but not necessarily the SRS case study specifically), think about what the appropriate fields and methods of the following classes might be:

   - `Classroom`

   - `Department`

   - `Degree`

   Which of the fields of each of these classes should be declared using predefined C# types, and which should be declared using user-defined types? Explain your rationale.

2. For the problem area whose requirements you defined for exercise 3 in Chapter 2, list the classes that you might need to create in order to model it properly.

3. Would `Color` be a good candidate for a user-defined type/class? Why or why not?

CHAPTER 4

■■■

Object Interactions

As you learned in Chapter 3, objects are the building blocks of an object-oriented (OO) software system. In such a system, objects collaborate with one another to accomplish common system goals, similar to ants in an anthill, employees of a corporation, or cells in your body. Each object has a specific structure and "mission"; these respective missions complement one another in accomplishing the mission of the system as a whole.

In this chapter, you'll learn:

- How external events set the objects within an OO application in motion.

- How methods can be used to specify an object's behaviors. We'll talk about the various code elements that make up a method and how methods are invoked.

- How objects publicize their methods as services to one another.

- How objects communicate with one another to request one another's services.

- How objects maintain their data and how they "guard" their data to ensure its integrity.

- About the power of encapsulation and how it can be used to limit "ripple effects" when the private implementation details of a class change.

- How constructors can be used to initialize field values when an object is instantiated.

Events Drive Object Collaboration

At its simplest, the process of OO software development involves the following:

- Properly establishing the functional requirements for, and overall mission of, an application

- Designing the appropriate classes necessary to fulfill the requirements and mission

- Instantiating the classes to create objects

- Setting the objects in motion through internal and/or external triggering events

Think of an anthill: at first glance, you may see no apparent activity taking place. But if you drop an ice cream cone nearby, a flurry of activity suddenly begins as ants rush around to gather up the "goodies," as well as to repair any damage that may have been caused if you dropped the ice cream cone *too close* to the anthill!

Within an OO application (the "anthill"), the objects ("ants") may be set in motion by an external event such as

- The click of a button on the Student Registration System (SRS) graphical user interface (GUI), indicating a student's desire to register for a particular course.

- The receipt of information from some other automated system, such as when the SRS receives a list of all students who have paid their tuition from the university's billing system.

As soon as such a triggering event has been noted by an OO system, the appropriate objects react, performing services themselves or requesting services of other objects in chain-reaction fashion, until some overall system goal has been accomplished. For example, the request to register for a course as made by a student user via the SRS application's GUI may involve the collaboration of many different objects (see Figure 4-1):

- A Student object (an abstraction of the *real* student user)

- A DegreeProgram object to ensure that the requested course is truly required for the student to graduate

- The appropriate Course object to make sure that there is a seat available in the course for the student

- A Classroom object representing the room in which the course will be meeting, to verify its seating capacity

- A Transcript object—specifically, the Transcript of the Student of interest—to ensure that the student has met all prerequisites for the course

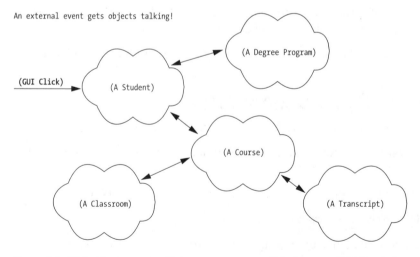

Figure 4-1. *SRS objects must collaborate to accomplish the overall SRS mission.*

Meanwhile, the user of the SRS is blissfully ignorant of all the objects that are "scurrying around" behind the scenes to accomplish the student's goal; the student merely fills in a few fields and clicks a button on the SRS GUI and a few moments later sees a message that either confirms or rejects the student's registration request.

Once the ultimate goal of an event chain has been achieved (for example, registering a student for a course), an application's objects may effectively become idle, and may remain so until the next such triggering event occurs. An OO application is in some ways similar to a game of billiards: hit the cue ball with your cue stick, and it (hopefully!) hits another ball, which might collide with three other balls, and so on. Eventually, however, all balls will come to a standstill until the cue ball is hit again.

Declaring Methods

Let's talk in a bit more detail about how we specify an object's behaviors. Recall from Chapter 3 that an object's methods may be thought of as operations that the object can perform. In order for an object **A** to request some operation of an object **B**, **A** needs to know the specific language with which to communicate with **B**. That is:

- Object **A** needs to be clear as to exactly which of **B**'s methods/operations **A** wants **B** to perform. Think of yourself as object **A** and a pet dog as object **B**. Do you want your dog to sit? Stay? Heel? Fetch?

- Depending on the method request, object **A** may need to give **B** some additional information so that **B** knows exactly how to proceed. If you tell your dog to fetch, the dog needs to know *what* to fetch: A ball? A stick? The neighbor's cat?

- Object **A** also needs to know how or whether **B** will report back the outcome of what it has been asked to do. In the case of a command to fetch something, your dog will hopefully bring the requested item to you as an outcome. However, if your dog is in another room and you call out the command "sit," you won't see the result of your command; you have to trust that the dog has done what you have asked it to do.

We take care of communicating these three aspects of each method by defining a *method header*. We must then program the behind-the-scenes logic for *how* B will perform the requested operation, also known as the *method body*. In the case of our dog fetch example, the method header might be the following:

```
bool Fetch(string item)
```

Let's look a little more closely at method headers.

Method Headers

A method header is a formal specification (from a programming standpoint) of how that method is to be invoked. A method header includes the following:

- The method's *name*

- An optional list of comma-separated *formal parameters* (specifying their names and types) to be passed to the method enclosed in parentheses

- A method's *return type*—that is, the data type of the information that will be passed back by object **B** to object **A**, if any, when the method is finished executing

As an example, here is a typical method header that we might define for the Student class:

```
bool    RegisterForCourse (string courseID, int secNo)
return type   method name    comma-separated list of formal parameters,
                             enclosed in parentheses
                             (parentheses may be left empty)
```

■**Note** When casually referring to a method such as RegisterForCourse in narrative text, many authors attach an empty set of parentheses, (), to the method name; for example, RegisterForCourse(). This doesn't necessarily imply that the formal header has no arguments, however.

Passing Arguments to Methods

The purpose of passing arguments into a method is twofold:

- To provide the object receiving the request with some (optional) additional information necessary to do its job

- To (optionally) guide its behavior in some fashion

In the RegisterForCourse method shown previously, for example, it's necessary to tell the method which course we want it to register for by passing in the course ID (for example, MATH 101) and the section number (for example, 10, which happens to meet Monday nights from 8–10 p.m.

Had we instead declared the RegisterForCourse method header with an *empty* parameter list, the method (presumably) would already have all the information it needed to register a course:

```
bool RegisterForCourse()
```

In fact, it is quite common for methods to produce results solely based on the information stored internally within an object, in which case no additional guidance is needed in the form of arguments. For example, the following method is designed to be *parameterless* (that is, it takes no arguments) because a Student object can presumably tell us its age (based on its birthDate field, perhaps) without having to be given any qualifying information:

```
int GetAge()
```

Let's say, however, that we wanted a Student object to be able to report its age expressed either in years (rounded to the nearest year) or in months; in such a case, we might want to declare the GetAge method as follows:

```
int GetAge(string ageType)
```

We would pass in an string argument to serve as a control flag for informing the Student object of how we want the answer to be returned; that is, we might program the GetAge method to ensure the following:

- If we pass in a value of IN_YEARS, it means that we want the answer to be returned in terms of years (for example, 30).

- If we pass in a value of IN_MONTHS, we want the answer to be returned in terms of months (for example, 30 × 12 = 360).

Using string parameters instead of, say, an integer parameter can make the code listing easier to read and understand.

■**Note** An alternative way of handling the requirement to retrieve the age of a Student object in two different formats would be to define two separate methods, such as the following:

```
int GetAgeInYears()
    int GetAgeInMonths()
```

Method Return Types

The RegisterForCourse method as previously declared is shown to have a *return type* of bool, which implies that this method will return one of the following two values:

- A value of true to signal "mission accomplished"—namely, that the Student object has successfully registered for the course that it was instructed to register for

- A value of false, to signal that the mission has failed for some reason; perhaps the desired section was full, or the student didn't meet the prerequisites of the course, or the requested course/section was cancelled, and so on

---

■**Note** In Part Three of the book, you'll learn techniques for communicating and determining precisely why the mission has failed when we discuss *exception handling*.

Note that a method need not return anything—that is, it may go about its business silently, without reporting the outcome of its efforts. If so, it is declared to have a return type of void (another C# keyword).

Here are several additional examples of method headers that we might define for the Student class:

- void SetName(string newName)

  This method requires one argument—a string representing the new name that we want this Student to assume—and performs "silently" by setting the internal name field of the Student to whatever value is being passed into the method, returning no answer (a return type of void) in response.

- void SwitchMajor(string newDepartment, Professor newAdvisor)

  This method represents a request for a Student to change the major field of study, which involves designating both a new academic department (for example, BIOLOGY) as well as a reference to the Professor object that is to serve as the student's advisor in this new department.

The preceding example demonstrates that we can declare parameters to be of any type, including user-defined types; the same is true for the *return type* of a method:

- Professor GetAdvisor()

  This method is used to ask a Student object who the advisor is. Rather than merely returning the name of the advisor, the Student object returns a reference to the Professor object as a whole (as recorded in Student field facultyAdvisor).

  You'll see a need for returning references to objects in this fashion shortly, when we explore how objects interact.

Note that a method can return only one result or answer, which may seem limiting. What if, for example, we want to ask a Student object for a list of all the courses that the student has ever taken? Must we ask for them one by one through multiple method calls? Fortunately not; the result handed back by a method can actually be a reference to an object of arbitrary complexity, including a special type of object called a *collection* that can contain multiple other objects. We'll talk about collections in more depth in Chapter 6.

Method Bodies

When we design and program a class in an OO language, we must not only provide headers for all of its methods but also program the internal details of how each method should behave when it is invoked. These internal programming details, known as the *method body*, are enclosed within braces, {...}, immediately following the method header, as follows:

```
public class Student
{
  // Fields.
  double gpa;
  // other fields omitted from this snippet...

  // Here is a full-blown method, complete with a block of code to be
  // executed when the method is invoked.
  bool IsHonorsStudent() {
    // The programming details of what this method is to do
    // go between the braces...this is the method body.

    // "gpa" is a field of the Student class, declared above.
    if (gpa >= 3.5) {
      return true;   // true means "yes, this is an honors student"
    }
    else {
```

```
      return false;  // false means "no, this isn't an honors student"
    }
  } // end of the method body

// etc.
}
```

Methods Implement Business Rules

The logic contained within a method body defines the *business logic*, also known as *business rules*, for an abstraction. In the preceding IsHonorsStudent method, for example, there is a single business rule for determining whether or not a student is an honors student:

> "If a student has a grade point average (GPA) of 3.5 or higher, then he/she is an honors student."

This rule is implemented in the preceding method through the use of a simple if test. Suppose that the business rules underlying this method were more complex—say, the rules were as follows:

> "In order for a student to be considered an honors student, the student must:
>
> (a) Have a grade point average (GPA) of 3.5 or higher;
>
> (b) Have taken at least three courses;
>
> (c) Have received no grade lower than 'B' in any of these courses."

Our method logic would then of necessity be more complex:

```
bool IsHonorsStudent() {
    // Pseudocode.
    if ((gpa >= 3.5) &&
        (number of courses taken >= 3) &&
        (no grades lower than a B have been received)) {
      return true;
    }
    else {
      return false;
    }
  }
```

The return Statement

A return statement is a jump statement that is used to exit a method and to send whatever information is returned by the method:

```
public int GetAge() {

    return age;
}
```

In the preceding example, the GetAge method has a return type of int, and the age field is placed after the return keyword to indicate that the value of the age field will be returned when the method exits. Whenever a return statement is executed, the method containing that return statement stops executing, and execution control returns to the code that invoked the method in the first place.

For methods with a return type of void, the return keyword can be used by itself, as a complete statement:

```
return;
```

However, it turns out that for methods with a return type of void, the use of a return statement is *optional*. If omitted, a return; statement is implied as the last line of the method. That is, the following two versions of method DoSomething are equivalent:

```
public void DoSomething() {
    int x = 3;
    int y = 4;
    int z = x + y;
}
```

And:

```
public void DoSomething() {
    int x = 3;
    int y = 4;
    int z = x + y;
    return;
}
```

The bodies of methods with a non-void return type *must* include at least one explicit return statement. The return keyword in such a case must be followed by an expression that evaluates to the proper type to match the method's return type:

```
return expression;
```

For example, if a method is defined to have a return type of int, any of the following return statements would be acceptable:

```
return 13;      // returning a constant integer value

return x;       // assuming x is declared to be an int

return x + y;  // assuming both x and y are declared to be ints
```

And so forth.

A method body is permitted to include more than one return statement if desired. For an example of a method containing multiple return statements, let's look once again at the IsHonorsStudent method discussed previously:

```
bool IsHonorsStudent() {
    if (gpa >= 3.5) {
        return true;    // first return statement
```

```
    }
    else {
      return false;  // second return statement
    }
  }
```

Good programming practice, however, is to have only one `return` statement in a method and to use a locally declared variable to capture the result that is to ultimately be returned. Having only a single `return` statement can make it easier to follow the execution flow of a complicated method. Although it is not a particularly complicated method, here is an alternative version of the `IsHonorsStudent` method that observes this practice:

```
bool IsHonorsStudent() {
  // Declare a local variable to keep track of the outcome;
  // arbitrarily initialize it to false.
  bool honors = false;

  if (gpa >= 3.5) {
    honors = true;
  }
  else {
    honors = false;
  }

  // We now have a single return statement at the end of our method.
  return honors;
}
```

Naming Suggestions

Inventing descriptive names for both methods and parameters help to make methods self-documenting. For example, the following method header:

```
void SwitchMajor(string newDepartment, Professor newAdvisor)
```

is much more self-explanatory than this alternative version:

```
void Switch(string d, Professor p)
```

In the latter case, we don't know what is being "switched," or what values for d and p would be relevant, without referring to the documentation for this method. Yet, to the compiler, both versions of the header are equally acceptable.

■**Note** Of course, one could argue that we'd always want to look at the documentation of a method anyway to determine its intended purpose and proper usage; but making the header self-documenting is even better.

C# method names are crafted using a style known as *Pascal casing*, wherein the first letter of the name is in *uppercase*; the *first* letter of each subsequent concatenated word in the variable name is in *uppercase*; and the rest of the characters are in *lowercase*. As an example, `SwitchMajor` is an appropriate method name, whereas neither `Switchmajor` (lowercase *m*) nor `switchMajor` (lowercase *s*) would be appropriate.

■Note Recall from Chapter 1 that most variable names use what is known as Camel casing, which is the same as Pascal casing except that the first letter is lowercase with Camel casing, whereas the first letter is capitalized with Pascal casing.

Method Invocation and Dot Notation

Now that you understand how methods are formally specified, how do we represent in code that a method is being invoked on an object? The name of the reference variable representing the object that the method is called on is followed with a dot (period) and then the method (function) call. For example:

```
// Instantiate a Student object.
Student x = new Student();

// A method is called on Student object x, asking it to
// register for course MATH 101, section 10.
x.RegisterForCourse("MATH 101", 10);  // This is a method call
```

Because we are using a dot to "glue" the reference variable to the method name, this is informally known as *dot notation*. And, in referring to the following logic, we can describe this process as "calling a method on object x":

```
x.RegisterForCourse("MATH 101", 10);
```

Arguments vs. Parameters

A bit of terminology: to make sure that everyone understands the difference between parameters and arguments, both of which are programming language terms. Let's define both terms here.

A *parameter* is a locally scoped variable, declared in a method header, which temporarily comes into existence while a method is executing. An *argument* is a value (or reference) that is passed to the method. For example, when the following method is invoked:

```
public void Foo(int bar) {...}
```

a variable named bar of type int temporarily comes into existence and is initialized with the value of the *argument* that is passed in when the method is invoked from client code:

```
// Here, we're invoking the Foo method, passing in an argument value
// of 3.
x.Foo(3);
```

In this case, *parameter* bar assumes the *argument* value 3.

While the method is executing, it can then use the parameter as a variable as it sees fit:

```
public void Foo(int bar) {.
  // Use the value of bar as appropriate.
  if (bar > 17) {
    // Pseudocode.
    Do something nifty!
}
// "bar" goes out of scope here...it's only defined within the Foo
// method.
```

The parameter bar ceases to exist—that is, goes out of scope (a concept we discussed in Chapter 1)—when the method exits.

Although the terms *parameter* and *argument* are frequently and casually used interchangeably, the bottom line is that they are different concepts: arguments are values; parameters are variables.

Objects As the Context for Method Invocation

In an object-oriented programming language (OOPL), an object serves as the context for a method call. We can thus think of the notation "x.*method_call(...)*" as "*talking to object x*"; specifically, "*talking to object x to request it to perform a particular method.*" Let's use a simple example to illustrate this point.

With respect to household chores, a person is capable of

- Mowing the lawn

- Taking out the trash

- Washing the dishes

Expressing this abstraction as C# code:

```
public class Person {
  // Fields omitted from this example.

  // Methods:

  public bool TakeOutTheTrash() {...}
  public bool MowTheLawn() {...}
  public bool WashTheDishes()  {...}
}
```

We decide that we want our teenaged sons Larry, Moe, and Curley to each do one of these three chores. How would we ask them to do this? If we were to say the following, chances are that *none* of the chores would get done, because we haven't tasked a *specific* son with fulfilling any of these requests:

- "Please wash the dishes."

- "Please take out the trash."

- "Please mow the lawn."

Larry, Moe, and Curley will probably all stay glued to the TV, because although any of them could fulfill the requests, none will acknowledge that a request has been directed toward them.

On the other hand, if we were to instead say the following, we'd be assigning each task to a *specific* son:

- "*Larry*, please wash the dishes."

- "*Moe*, please take out the trash."

- "*Curley*, please mow the lawn."

Again, using C# syntax, this might be expressed as follows:

```
// We create three Person objects/instances:
Person larry = new Person();
Person moe = new Person();
Person curley = new Person();

// We call a method on each, indicating the operation that we wish
// each of them to perform:
larry.WashTheDishes();
moe.TakeOutTheTrash();
curley.MowTheLawn();
```

By applying each method call to a different "son" (`Person` object reference), there is no ambiguity as to which object is being asked to perform which operation.

Tip We'll learn in Chapter 7 that a *class* can also be the target of a method call for a special type of method known as a *static method*.

Assuming that `WashTheDishes` is a `Person` method as defined previously, the following code won't compile in C# (or, for that matter, in any OOPL).

```
public class BadCode
{
  static void Main() {
    // This next line won't compile -- where's the "dot"?
```

```
    WashTheDishes();
  }
}
```

Because the compiler would expect such a method call to be associated with a particular Person object via dot notation; the following error message would result:

```
error: An object reference is required for the non-static field,
method, or property 'Person.WashTheDishes()'
```

C# Expressions, Revisited

When we defined the term *simple expression* in Chapter 1, there was one form of expression that we omitted because we hadn't yet talked about objects: method calls. We repeated our list of what constitutes C# expressions here, adding method calls to the mix:

- A constant: 7, false

- A char(acter) literal: 'A', '&'

- A string literal: "foo"

- The name of any variable declared to be of one of the predefined types that we've seen so far: myString, x

- A *method call*: z.length()

- Any two of the preceding expressions combined with one of the C# *binary operators*: x + 2

- Any one of the preceding expressions that is modified by one of the C# *unary operators*: i++

- Any of the preceding simple expressions enclosed in parentheses: (x + 2)

Tip In Chapter 13, you'll learn about one more type of expression: a *chain* of two or more methods, concatenated by dots (.); for example, x.GetAdvisor().GetName();.

The type of a "method call expression" is, by definition, the type of result that the method returns when executed. For example, if RegisterForCourse is a method with a return type of bool, then the expression s.RegisterForCourse(...) is said to be an expression of type bool.

Capturing the Return Value from a Method Call

In an earlier example, although we declared the Student class's RegisterForCourse method to have a return type of bool:

```
bool RegisterForCourse(string courseId, int sectionNumber)
```

we didn't capture the returned bool value when we invoked the method:

```
x.RegisterForCourse("MATH 101", 10);
```

Whenever we invoke a non-void method, it's up to us whether to ignore or respond to the value that it returns. If we want to respond to the returned value, we can optionally capture the result in a specific variable:

```
bool outcome;
outcome = x.registerForCourse("MATH 101", 10);

if (!outcome) {
  action to be taken if registration failed...
}
```

If we plan to use only the returned value once, however, then going to the trouble of declaring an explicit variable such as outcome to capture the result is overkill. We can instead react to the result simply by *nesting* a method call, which you learned a moment ago is considered to be a valid expression within a more complex statement. For example, we can rewrite the preceding code snippet to eliminate the variable outcome as follows:

```
// An if expression must evaluate to a Boolean result; the
// RegisterForCourse method does indeed return a Boolean value,
// however, and so the expression (method call) enclosed within
// parentheses represents valid syntax.
if (!(x.RegisterForCourse("MATH 101", 10))) {
  action to be taken if registration failed...
}
```

■**Note** In fact, we use the "method-call-as-expression" syntax liberally when developing OO applications; for example, when returning values from methods:

```
public string GetAdvisorName() {
  return advisor.GetName();
}
```

or printing to the console:

```
Console.WriteLine("The student's gpa is:  " + s.GetGPA());
```

The resulting code is more compact, and it eliminates the need to create objects that are used for one line of code only. However, "method-call-as-expression" syntax is one of the aspects of OOP that seems to take the most getting used to for folks who are just getting started with learning the OO paradigm.

Method Signatures

You already learned that a method header consists of the method's return type, name, and formal parameter list:

```
void SwitchMajor(string newDepartment, Professor newAdvisor)
```

From the standpoint of the *code used to invoke a method on an object*, however, the return type and parameter names aren't immediately evident upon inspection:

```
Student s = new Student();
Professor p = new Professor();

// Details omitted...

s.SwitchMajor("MATH", p);
```

We can infer the following from inspecting the line of code that invokes the method:

- SwitchMajor is a method defined for the Student class because s is a Student and we're invoking SwitchMajor on s.

- The SwitchMajor method requires two arguments of type string and Professor, respectively, because that's what we're passing in.

However, we can't see how the formal parameters were named in the corresponding method header, nor can we tell whether the method returns a result or not and, if so, what type of result it returns because we may simply be ignoring the result.

For this reason, we refer to a *method signature* as those aspects of a method header that are "discoverable" from the perspective of the code used to invoke the method: namely, the method's name, and the order, types, and number of arguments being passed into the method, but *excluding* the parameter names and method return type.

- Method header: int GetAge(int ageType)

    - Method signature: GetAge(int)

- Method header: void SwitchMajor(string newDepartment, Professor newAdvisor)

    - Method signature: SwitchMajor(string, Professor)

- Method header: string GetName()

    - Method signature: GetName()

Object Interaction via Methods

Let's now look at an example of two objects interacting with each other. Assume that we have two classes defined—Student and Course—and that the methods listed in Table 4-1 are defined on each.

Table 4-1. *Student and Course Class Methods*

Student Method:	
`bool SuccessfullyCompleted(Course c)`	Given a reference c to a particular Course object, we're asking the Student object to confirm that they have indeed taken the course in question and received a passing grade.
Course Method:	
`bool Register(Student s)`	Given a reference s to a particular Student object, we are asking the Course method to do whatever is necessary to register the student. In this case, we expect the Course to ultimately respond `true` or `false` to indicate success or failure of the registration request.

Figure 4-2 reflects one possible sequence of method calls between a Course object c and a Student object s; each numbered step in the diagram is narrated in the text that follows.

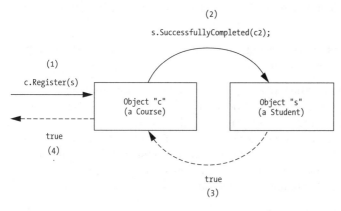

Figure 4-2. *Method calls on a Student and Course object*

(Please refer to this diagram when reading through steps 1 through 4.)

1. We register a student with a course by invoking the following method where s represents a particular Student object:

   ```
   c.Register(s);
   ```

   For now, we won't worry about where in the code this statement came from; it was most likely triggered by a user's interaction with the SRS GUI. You'll see the complete code context of how all of these methods are called later in this chapter, in the section entitled "Objects as Clients and Suppliers."

2. In order for Course object c to officially determine whether or not s should be permitted to register, c invokes the following method:

   ```
   s.SuccessfullyCompleted(c2);
   ```

on Student s, where c2 represents a reference to a *different* Course object that happens to be a prerequisite of Course c. (Don't worry about how Course c knows that c2 is one of its prerequisites; this involves interacting with c's internal prerequisites field, which we haven't talked about. Also, Course c2 isn't depicted in Figure 4-2 because, strictly speaking, c2 isn't engaged in this "discussion" between objects c and s; c2 is being talked about, but is not doing any talking itself!)

3. If the SuccessfullyCompleted method returns the value true to c, indicating that s has successfully completed the prerequisite course. (For the time being, we will ignore the details as to how s determines this; it involves interacting with s's internal transcript field, which we haven't fully explained the structure of just yet.)

4. Convinced that the student has complied with the prerequisite requirements for the course, Course object c finishes the job of registering the student (internal details omitted for now) and confirms the registration by responding with a value of true to the originator of the method call.

This example was overly simplistic; in reality, Course c may have had to interact with numerous other objects:

- A Classroom object (the room in which the course is to be held, to make sure that it has sufficient room for another student)

- A DegreeProgram object (the degree sought by the student, to make sure that the requested course is indeed required for the degree that the student is pursuing)

and so forth—before sending a true response to indicate that the request to register Student s had been fulfilled. We'll see a slightly more complicated version of interactions between objects later in the chapter.

Accessing Fields via Dot Notation

Just as we use dot notation to call methods on objects, we can also use dot notation to refer to an object's accessible fields. For example, if we declare a reference variable x to be of type Student, we can potentially refer to any of Student x's fields via the following notation:

x.field_name

where the dot is used to qualify the name of the *field* of interest with the name of the reference variable representing the *object* of interest: x.name, x.gpa, and so forth.

Here are a few additional examples:

```
// Instantiate three objects.
Student x = new Student();
Student y = new Student();
Professor z = new Professor();

// We may use dot notation to access the value of accessible fields.

// Set student x's name...
x.name = "John Smith";
```

```
//...and student y's name.
y.name = "Joe Blow";

// Set professor z's name to be the same as student x's name.
z.name = x.name;

// Compute the total of the two students' ages.
int i = x.age + y.age;


// Set the professor's age to be 40.
z.age = 40;
```

However, we'll see later in this chapter that just because we *can* access fields this way doesn't mean that we *should*. There are many reasons why we'll want to restrict access to an object's data to give the object complete control over when and how its data is altered, and several mechanisms for how we can do so.

Delegation

If a request is made of an object A and, in fulfilling the request, A in turn requests assistance from another object B, this is known as *delegation* by A to B. The concept of delegation among objects is exactly the same as delegation between people in the real world: if your "significant other" asks you to mow the lawn while they are out running errands, and you in turn hire a neighborhood teenager to mow the lawn, then, as far as your partner is concerned, the lawn has been mowed. The fact that you delegated the activity to someone else is (hopefully!) irrelevant.

The fact that delegation has occurred between objects is often transparent to the initiator of a method call as well. In our previous message passing example, Course c delegated part of the work of registering Student s *back to* s when c asked s to verify a prerequisite course. However, from the perspective of the originator of the registration request—c.Register(s);—this seems like a simple interaction: namely, the requestor asked c to register a student, and it did so! All the "behind the scenes" details of what c had to do to accomplish this are hidden from the requestor (see Figure 4-3).

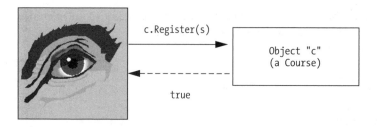

Figure 4-3. *A requestor sees only the external details of a method call.*

Access to Objects

The only way that an object A can call a method on an object B is if A has access to an object reference to B. This can happen in several different ways:

- Object A might maintain a reference to B as one of A's fields; for example, here's the example from Chapter 3 of a Student object having a Professor reference as a field:

```
public class Student
{
  // Fields.
  string name;
  Professor facultyAdvisor;
  // etc.
```

- Object A may be handed a reference to B as an argument of one of A's methods. This is how Course object c obtained access to Student object s in the preceding method calling example, when c's Register method was called:

```
c.Register(s);
```

- A reference to object B may be made "globally available" to the entire application, such that all other objects can access it. We'll discuss techniques for doing so when we construct the SRS in Part Three of the book.

- Object A may have to explicitly request a reference to B by calling a method on some third object C. Because this is potentially the most complex way for A to obtain a reference to B, we'll illustrate this with an example.

Going back to the example interaction between Course object c and Student object s from a few pages ago, let's complicate the interaction a bit:

- First, we introduce a third object: a Transcript object t, which represents a record of all courses taken by Student object s.

- Furthermore, we assume that Student s maintains a reference to Transcript t as one of s's fields (specifically, the transcript field), and conversely that Transcript t maintains a reference back to its "owner," Student s, as one of t's fields (see Figure 4-4).

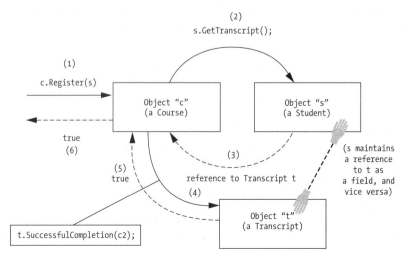

Figure 4-4. *A more complex method calling example involving three objects*

1. In this enhanced object interaction, the first step is exactly as previously described: namely, the `Register` method is invoked on `Course` object c where s represents a `Student` object:

   ```
   c.Register(s);
   ```

2. Now, instead of `Course` c invoking the method s.`SuccessfullyCompleted(c2)` on `Student` s as before, where c2 represents a prerequisite `Course`, the `GetTranscript` method is invoked on `Student` object s because c wants to check s's transcript firsthand:

   ```
   s.GetTranscript();
   ```

   This method is declared in the `Student` class with a header defined as follows:

   ```
   Transcript GetTranscript()
   ```

   Note that this method is defined to return a `Transcript` object reference: specifically, a reference to the `Transcript` object t belonging to this student.

3. Because `Student` s maintains a reference to its `Transcript` object as a field, it's a snap for the `GetTranscript` method to return a reference to the student's `Transcript` object.

4. Now that `Course` c has its *own* temporary reference to `Transcript` t, object c can talk directly to t. Object c proceeds to ask t whether t has any record of c's prerequisite course c2 having successfully been completed by `Student` s by invoking the method:

   ```
   t.SuccessfulCompletion(c2);
   ```

   This implies that there is a method declared in the `Transcript` class with the following header:

   ```
   bool SuccessfulCompletion(Course c)
   ```

5. `Transcript` object t answers back with a response of true, indicating that `Student` s has indeed successfully completed the prerequisite course in question. (Note that `Student` s is unaware that c is talking to t; object s knows that it was asked by c to return a reference to t in an earlier message, but s has no insights as to *why* c asked for the reference.)

■**Note** This is not unlike the real-world situation in which person A asks person B for person C's phone number, without telling B why they want to call C.

---

6. Satisfied that `Student` s has complied with its prerequisite requirements, `Course` object c finishes the job of registering the student (internal details omitted for now) and confirms the registration by responding with a value of true to the originator of the registration request that first arose in step 1. Now that c has finished with this transaction, it discards its (temporary) reference to t.

   Note that from the perspective of whoever invoked the original method on `Course` c, this more complicated interaction appears *identical* to the earlier, simpler interaction, (see Figure 4-5):

   ```
   c.Register(s);
   ```

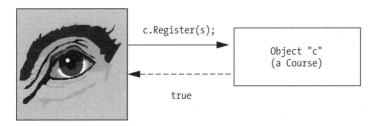

Figure 4-5. *The external details of this more complex interaction appear identical from the requestor's standpoint.*

All the caller of the original method knows is that the Register method call eventually responded with a value of true.

Objects As Clients and Suppliers

In the preceding example of object interaction between a Course object and a Student object, we can consider Course object c to be a *client* of Student object s because c is requesting that s perform one of its methods—namely, GetTranscript—as a *service* to c. This is analogous to the real-world concept of *you*, as a client, requesting the services of an accountant, or an attorney, or an architect. Similarly, c is a client of Transcript t when c asks t to perform its Successful-Completion method. We therefore refer to code that invokes a method on an object A as *client code* relative to A because the code benefits from the service(s) performed by A.

Let's look at a few examples of client code. The following code corresponds to the object interaction example involving a Course, Student, and Transcript object from a few pages back, and as promised earlier, provides the context for the methods that were called in that example.

The following code snippet, taken from the Main method of an application, instantiates two objects and invokes a method on one of them, which gets them "talking":

```
static void Main() {
  Course c = new Course();
  Student s = new Student();

  // Details omitted.

  // Invoke a method on Course object c.

  c.Register(s);

  // etc.
}
```

In this example, the Main method is considered to be client code relative to Course object c because it calls upon c to perform its Register method.

Let's now look at the code that implements the body of the Register method, inside of the Course class:

```
public class Course
```

```
{
  // details omitted...

  public bool Register(Student s) {
    bool outcome = false;

    // Get a reference to Student s's Transcript object.

    Transcript t = s.GetTranscript();


    // Now, invoke a method on that Transcript object.
    // (Assume that c2 is a reference to a prerequisite Course)

    if (t.SuccessfulCompletion(c2)) {

      outcome = true;
    }
    else {
      outcome = false;
    }

    return outcome;
  }

  // etc.
}
```

We see that the Register method body is considered to be client code relative to *both*
Student object s and Transcript object t because this code calls upon s and t to each perform
an operation.

Whenever an object A is a client of object B, object B in turn can be thought of as a *supplier*
to A.

Note that the roles of client and supplier are not absolute between two objects; such roles
are only relevant for the duration of a particular method call event. Similarly, if I ask you to
pass me the butter, I am your client, and you are my supplier; and if a moment later you ask
me to pass you the bread, then you are my client, and I am your supplier.

■Note The notion of clients and suppliers is discussed further in *Object-Oriented Software Construction* by
Bertrand Meyer (Prentice Hall).

Information Hiding/Accessibility

As we discussed earlier in this chapter, dot notation can potentially be used to access an object's field values, as in the following simple example:

```
Student x = new Student();

// Set the value of the name field of Student x.
x.name = "Fred Schnurd";

// Retrieve the value of x's name so as to print it.
Console.WriteLine(x.name);
```

There is an obvious danger with giving all the data stored by a class public access. For example, if a student's GPA field was publicly accessible, an enterprising student could change his GPA simply by typing the following:

```
bob.gpa = 4.0;
```

In reality, therefore, objects often restrict access to some of their members (fields in particular). Such restriction is known as *information hiding*. In a well-designed object-oriented application, an object publicizes *what* it can do—that is, the operations it is capable of providing, or its method headers—but *hides* the internal details both of *how* it performs these operations and of the data (fields) that it maintains in order to *support* these operations.

We use the term *accessibility* to refer to whether or not a particular member of an object (field or method) can be accessed outside of the class in which it is declared. The accessibility of a member is established by placing an *access modifier keyword* at the beginning of its declaration:

```
public class ClassName
{
    private string name;
    protected Professor adviser;
    // etc.

    public bool printClassSchedule(string Semester) {
        ...
    }
    // etc.
}
```

Types of Accessibility

C# defines five different access modifier keywords: public, private, protected, internal, and protected internal.

When a member is declared to have *public accessibility*, it's freely accessible by the method code in any other class; that is, we can access public fields from client code using dot notation.

For example, suppose that we declare that the name field of the Student class is public, which we do by placing the keyword public just ahead of the field's type declaration:

```
public class Student
{
  public string name;
  // etc.
```

It would then be perfectly acceptable to write client code as follows:

```
using System;

public class MyProgram
{
  static void Main() {
    Student x = new Student();

    // Because name is a public field, we may access it via dot
    // notation from client code.
    x.name = "Fred Schnurd";
    // or:
    Console.WriteLine(x.name);

    // etc.
  }
}
```

Note Because we first introduced the notion of a class wrapper in Chapter 1, recall that we've also been using the *public* access modifier on all of our *class* declaration examples:

```
public class Student {...
public class SimpleProgram {...
```

We'll discuss what it means to define a *class's* accessibility, and in particular, what other accessibility modifiers make sense for a class besides *public*, in Chapter 13.

Similarly, if we were to declare the IsHonorsStudent method of Student to be public, which we do by again inserting the keyword public into the method header:

```
public class Student
{
  // Fields omitted.

  // Methods.
  public bool IsHonorsStudent() {
    // details omitted.
```

```
  }

  // etc.
}
```

it would then be perfectly acceptable to invoke the IsHonorsStudent method from client code as follows:

```
public class MyProgram
{
  static void Main() {
    Student x = new Student();

    // Because IsHonorsStudent() is a public method, we may access
    // it via dot notation from client code.
    if (x.IsHonorsStudent()) {
      // details omitted.
    }

    // etc.
```

As you'll learn a little later in this chapter, it's quite common to give methods public accessibility, but it's usually undesirable to give fields (that is, the data) of a class public accessibility.

When a member is declared to have *private* accessibility, it's *not* accessible outside of the class in which it's declared.

For example, suppose that we declare that the id field of the Student class is private:

```
public class Student
{
  public string name;
  private string id;
  // etc.
```

Then we are *not* permitted to access it directly via dot notation from client code, as illustrated here:

```
public class MyProgram
{
  static void Main() {
    Student x = new Student();

    // Not permitted from client code!  id is private to the
    // Student class, and so this will not compile.
    x.id = "123-45-6789";
```

The following compilation error will result:

```
error: 'Student.id' is inaccessible due to its protection level
```

Fields are often given private accessibility to give the class complete control of how or if the data can be accessed outside of the class.

Private access works the same way for methods: that is, they can't be invoked from client code. (We'll discuss *why* we'd ever want to declare a method as private a bit later in this chapter.) For example, if we were to declare the PrintInfo method of Student to be private:

```
public class Student
{
  // Fields omitted.

  // Methods.
  private void PrintInfo() {
    // details omitted.
  }

  // etc.
}
```

then it would *not* be possible to invoke the PrintInfo method from client code:

```
public class MyProgram
{
  static void Main() {
    Student x = new Student();

    // Because PrintInfo() is a private method, we may not access
    // it via dot notation from client code; this won't compile:
    x.PrintInfo();

    // etc.
```

The following compiler error would result:

```
error: 'Student.PrintInfo()' is inaccessible due to its protection level
```

The other C# access modifiers are *protected, internal,* and *protected internal*—but we'll defer a discussion of these until Chapter 13 because there are a few more object concepts that we have to cover first. For now, it's perfectly appropriate to think of accessibility as coming in only two "flavors": public and private.

If we don't explicitly specify the accessibility of a member when we declare it, it will be private by default:

```
public class Student
{
  private string age;
  string name;  // Since accessibility is not explicitly specified for
                // the "name" field, it will be private by default.

  // The same is true for this method.
  void DoSomething() {
```

```
    // details omitted
  }

  // etc.
}
```

Accessing Members of a Class from Within Its Own Methods

Note that we can access all of a given class's members, regardless of their accessibility, from *within* any of that class's *own* method bodies; that is, public/private designations affect only access to a member *from outside the class itself*; that is, *from client code*.

In the following example, the Student class's PrintAllFields method is accessing the private name and id fields of the Student class:

```
using System;

public class Student
{
  private string name;
  private string id;
  // etc.

  public void PrintAllFields() {
    Console.WriteLine(name);
    Console.WriteLine(id);

    // etc.

  }


  // etc.
}
```

Furthermore, note that we needn't use dot notation to access a member of a class when we're inside the body of one of the class's own methods; it's automatically understood that the class is accessing one of its own members when a *simple name*—that is, a name without a dot notation prefix—is used. This language member is illustrated by the following (abbreviated) Student class code:

```
public class Student
{
  // A few private fields.
  private double totalLoans;
  private double tuitionOwed;
  // other fields omitted

  public bool AllBillsPaid() {
    // We can call upon another method that is defined within this
```

```
    // SAME class (see declaration of MoneyOwed() below) without using
    // dot notation.
    double amt = MoneyOwed();
    if (amt == 0.0) {
      return true;
    }
    else {
      return false;
    }
  }

  public double MoneyOwed() {
    // We can access members of this class (totalLoans and
    // tuitionOwed) -- even though they are declared to be private! --
    // without using dot notation.
    return totalLoans + tuitionOwed;
  }
}
```

■Note The order in which methods are declared within a C# class doesn't matter; that is, we're permitted to call a method B from within method A even though the definition of method B comes after/below A in the class declaration. In particular, in the preceding code example, we call MoneyOwed from within AllBillsPaid despite the fact that MoneyOwed is declared *after* AllBillsPaid.

Camel vs. Pascal Casing, Revisited

Previously in the book, we introduced the Camel and Pascal capitalization styles and discussed how they are applied to C# programming elements. Now that we touched on accessibility, let's refine our understanding of when to use these two alternate styles.

- **Pascal casing** (uppercase starting letter) is used for all class and method names regardless of their accessibility. It's also used for the names of *public* fields.

- **Camel casing** (lowercase starting letter) is used for the names of *nonpublic* fields.

Here is an example class to illustrate these rules:

```
public class Student // uppercase S for class name
{
  private string name;  // lowercase n for private field
  public string Major;   // uppercase M for public field
  // etc.
```

```
public void DoSomething() { // uppercase D for method name
  // A local variable; while not explicitly private, it is not
  // accessible from outside this method, and so begins with a
  // lowercase letter.
  int x = 0;

  // details omitted...
}

// Uppercase D for this method name even though it has
// private access because ALL methods use Pascal casing
// regardless of their accessibility.
private void DoSomethingElse() {
  // details omitted...
}

// etc.
}
```

Method Headers, Revisited

Going back to our definition of method header from a bit earlier in the chapter, let's amend that definition to also include the accessibility modifier for a method. That is, a *method header* actually consists of the following:

- A method's (accessibility) modifier(s)

- A method's return type—that is, the data type of the information that will be returned from the method, if any, when the method is finished executing

---

▉Note There are also other types of modifiers on methods besides accessibility modifiers. We'll talk about some of the other modifiers that can be applied to methods in Chapters 7 and 13.

- A method's *name*.

- An optional list of comma-separated *formal parameters* (specifying their names and types) to be passed to the method enclosed in parentheses.

As an example, here is a typical method header that we might define for the RegisterForCourse method:

```
    public        bool      RegisterForCourse (string courseID, int secNo)
accessibility   return type  method name     comma-separated list of formal
  modifier                                   parameters, enclosed in parentheses
                                             (parentheses may be left empty)
```

■**Note** There is actually one more aspect to a method's header, having to do with what are referred to as *modifiers* on individual parameters, which is beyond the scope of this book to address. If you want more information, consult the section "Statements, Expressions, and Operators" from the "C# Programming Guide" at the MSDN web site.

Accessing Private Members from Client Code

If private members can't be accessed outside of an object's own methods, how does client code ever manipulate them? Through *public* members, of course! Good OO programming practice calls for providing public *accessors* by which clients of an object can effectively manipulate selected private fields to read or modify their values. Why is this? *So that we may empower an object to have the "final say" in whether or not what client code is trying to do to its fields is "okay."* That is, letting an object determine whether or not any of the business rules defined by its class are being violated. Before we go into an in-depth discussion of why this is so important, we'd like to first discuss the "mechanics" of how we create accessors.

Two General Approaches

There are two general approaches to providing accessors:

- The *generic OOPL approach* is to provide what are known informally as "get" and *"set"* methods (or, collectively, *accessor methods*) for reading/modifying fields, respectively.

- The *C# preferred approach* is to use a language construct called a *property* for accessing (reading/modifying) fields. A property defines what are known as *get* and *set accessors* (note that these are *not* methods, despite the similarity of their names) that can return the value of a field to client code or modify the value of a field value at the request of client code, respectively.

Because our goals in this book are twofold—namely, to introduce you to general object concepts as well as to teach you basic C# syntax—and because *both* of these goals are equally important in our opinion, we'll cover both of these approaches—conventional OOPL "get"/"set" methods and properties—in this section. Please realize, however, that the .NET programming community favors the use of properties over "get"/"set" methods for reasons that will become clear a bit later.

"Get"/"Set" Methods

The following code, excerpted from the Student class, illustrates the conventional "get" and "set" methods that we might write for a private field called name:

```
public class Student
{
  // Fields are typically declared to be private.
  private string name;
  // other fields omitted...

  // Provide public accessor methods for reading/modifying
```

```
  // the private "name" field from client code.

  // Read ("get") the value of the name field.
  public string GetName() {
    return name;
  }

  // Modify ("set") the value of the name field.
  public void SetName(string newName) {
    name = newName;
  }

  // etc.
}
```

The nomenclature "get" and "set" is stated from the standpoint of *client code*: think of a "set" method as the way that *client code* stuffs a value *into* an object's field (see Figure 4-6).

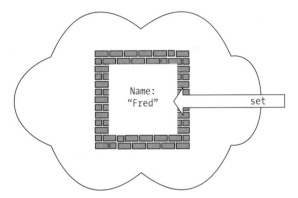

Figure 4-6. *A "set" method is used to pass data into an object.*

And the "get" method as the way that *client code* retrieves a field value *from* an object (see Figure 4-7).

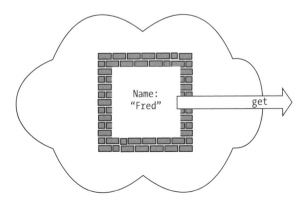

Figure 4-7. *A "get" method is used to retrieve data out of an object.*

Declaring "Get"/"Set" Methods

For a field declaration of the form

```
accessibility*  field-type  fieldName;
```

```
* typically, but not always, private
```

for example:

```
    private string major;
```

the recommended accessor method headers are as follows:

- "get" method: `public  field-type  GetFieldName()`

    For example, `public string GetMajor()`

   Note that we don't pass any arguments into a "get" method because all we want an object to do is to hand us back the value of one of its fields; we don't typically need to tell the object anything more for it to know how to do this.

   Also, because we're expecting an object to hand back the value of a specific field, the return type of the "get" method must match the type of the field of interest. If we're "getting" the value of an `int` field, then the return type of the method must be `int`; if we're "getting" the value of a `string` field, then the return type of the method must be `string`; and so forth.

- "set" method: `public void SetFieldName(field-type parameterName)`

    For example, `public void SetMajor(string newValue)`

   In the case of a "set" method, we must pass in the value that we want the object to use when setting its corresponding field value, and the type of the value that we're passing in must match the type of the field being set. If we're "setting" the value of an `int` field, then the argument that is passed in must be an `int`; if we're "setting" the value of a string field, then the argument that is passed in must be a string; and so forth.

   However, since most "set" methods perform their mission silently, without returning a value to the client, we typically declare "set" methods to have a return type of `void`.

   Note that we devise the names for both types of method by capitalizing the first letter of the field name and sticking either Get or Set in front of it. There is one exception to this method naming convention: when a field is of type `bool`, it's recommended that we name the "get" method starting with the verb Is instead of with Get. The "set" method for a `bool` field would still follow the standard naming convention. For example:

```
public class Student
{
  private bool honorsStudent;
  // other fields omitted...

  // Get method.
  public bool IsHonorsStudent() {
    return honorsStudent;
```

```
    }

    // Set method.
    public void SetHonorsStudent(bool x) {
      honorsStudent = x;
    }

// etc.
}
```

All of the "get"/"set" method bodies that we've seen thus far are simple "one liners": we're either returning the value of the field of interest with a simple `return` statement in a "get" method, or copying the value of the passed-in argument to the internal field in a "set" method so as to store it. This isn't to imply that all "get"/"set" methods need be this simple; in fact, there are endless possibilities for what actually gets coded in accessor methods because as we discussed earlier, methods must implement business rules, not only about how an object behaves but also what valid states its data can assume.

Utilizing "Get"/"Set" Methods from Client Code

We already know how to utilize dot notation to invoke methods on objects from client code:

```
    Student s = new Student();

    // Modify ("set") the field value.
    s.SetName("Joe");

    // Read ("get") the field value.
    Console.WriteLine("Name: " +  s.GetName());
```

Properties

As mentioned earlier, C# also provides a programming construct for accessing fields called a *property*. In a nutshell, a property is a way of "disguising" accessor logic so that, from the perspective of client code, it appears that we're accessing a public field:

```
// Client code for setting Student s's name via a property it APPEARS as though
// we're accessing a public field, but we are not!
s.Name = "Melbito";

// or, for getting s's name via a property:
Console.WriteLine(s.Name);
```

In fact we are invoking *behind-the-scenes* accessor code, albeit not in the explicit "get"/"set" method-calling sense.

Let's learn how to declare and use properties.

Declaring Properties

We use the following general syntax for declaring a property:

```
access_modifier type propertyName {
  get {
    // code body of get accessor
  }

  set {
    // code body of set accessor
  }
}
```

For example, if we want to declare a property associated with the private field name in lieu of "get"/"set" methods in our Student class, we might write the following code:

```
public class Student
{
  // We're still declaring the name field the same as we did before.
  private string name;
  // etc.

  // However, we're now defining a property called "Name" in lieu of
  // writing "get"/"set" methods for the "name" field.
  public string Name {
    // This takes the place of a "get" method.
    get {
      return name;
    }

    // This takes the place of a "set" method.
    set {
      // "value" is an implicit input parameter that is automatically
      // passed to the set accessor.
      name = value;
    }

    // etc.
  }
}
```

Some noteworthy features about properties include the following:

- The convention for a property name is that it should match the name of its associated field, but should begin with a capital letter (property names use the Pascal capitalization style). Because C# is a case-sensitive language, name and Name are treated as different symbols by the compiler.

- The type of a property must match the type of its associated field. Our Name property is defined to be of type string, which indeed is the type of the name field.

- A property defines *get* and *set accessors*, which work very much like "get"/"set" methods, but are syntactically quite different, both in terms of how they are declared and how they are invoked from client code (the latter of which we'll see in a moment).

- Analogous to a "get" method, a get accessor is used to return the value of the corresponding field to client code.

- Note that there is no need to declare a return type for a get accessor as we must do for a "get" method, because a get accessor *implicitly* returns the same type as the property in which it is defined.

```
get {
    return name;
}
```

- Analogous to a "set" method, a set accessor is used to change the value of the corresponding field at the request of client code.

Note that there is no need to declare a parameter list for a set accessor as we must do for a "set" method because a set accessor *implicitly* takes a single parameter named value that represents the new value being suggested for the field by client code:

```
set {
    name = value; // value is implicitly declared
}
```

There is also no need to declare a return type for a set accessor because it implicitly has a return type of void.

The preceding example featured a property with simple, "one-liner" get and set accessors. Of course, as we mentioned for "get"/"set" methods earlier, there are endless possibilities for what actually gets coded in get and set accessors because they must implement the appropriate business logic for the field that they control. We'll see more complex examples of property accessors later in the chapter.

Let's place the code used in the two different approaches to declaring accessors—"get"/"set" methods vs. properties—side by side to emphasize the differences in their syntax:

Student Version with "Get"/"Set" Methods	Equivalent Student Version Using a Property
```public class Student { private string name;```	```public class Student { private string name;```
```public string GetName() { return name; }```	```public string Name { get { return name; }```
```public void SetName(string n) { name = n; }```	```set { name = value; } }```
```}```	```}```

Property syntax is a bit more streamlined, as follows:

- By declaring a type for the property as a whole—string—we don't have to redundantly declare the return type of the get accessor or the type of the value being handed in to the set accessor: they will automatically derive the string type from the property.

- By declaring accessibility of the property—public—we don't have to redundantly declare the accessibility of the get accessor or set accessor; both will derive public accessibility from the property.

Accessing Properties from Client Code

Now, let's take a look at how we access a property from client code. We'll continue our example using the Name property defined earlier:

```
// Client code:
Student s = new Student();

// Modify ("set") the field value.
// Note that it LOOKS LIKE we're accessing a public field.
s.Name = "Joe";

// Read ("get") the field value.
// Again, it LOOKS LIKE we're accessing a public field.
Console.WriteLine("Name is " + s.Name);
```

From the standpoint of client code, properties are accessed via dot notation *as if they were declared to be public fields*. That is, from client code, when we see an expression such as the following, we can't tell whether Name represents a property or a public field:

```
s.Name = "Joe";
```

But behind the scenes, there is quite a difference, in that with public fields, no code is being executed beyond the direct assignment . . . whereas with property accessors, whatever code we've written is transparently executed behind the scenes. We'll return to this critical distinction later in the chapter when we discuss pseudo-attributes.

Let's place the code used in the two different approaches to accessing fields from client code—"get"/"set" methods vs. properties—side by side to emphasize the differences in their syntax:

Client Code Version Utilizing "Get"/"Set" Methods	Equivalent Client Code Utilizing a Property

`Student s = new Student();`
 	
`// Modify ('set') the field value.`
`s.SetName("Joe");`
 	
`// Read ('get') the field value.`
`Console.WriteLine("Name: " +`
`s.GetName());`
	`Student s = new Student();`
	
	`// Modify ('set') the field value.`
	`s.Name = "Joe";`
	
	`// Read ('get') the field value.`
	`Console.WriteLine("Name is " +`
	`s.Name);`

Client code is simpler when properties are used.

Singing the Praises of Properties

In a sense, properties give programmers the best of both worlds. They look and act like fields, and code written using properties is more compact than code that uses "get"/"set" methods. At the same time, properties can provide the same programmatic control over data integrity that we get with private fields and "get"/"set"methods.

Note When working with OOPLs that don't support the notion of properties—for example, C++ and Java—one *must* be savvy in the use of "get"/"set" method syntax to reap all the benefits of encapsulation and information hiding—benefits that we'll cover in depth a bit later in this chapter. Because of the "favored status" of properties when programming in C#, however, we'll illustrate all remaining OO principles throughout the book in detail using properties, but will remind you that many of the *same* benefits can be achieved using "get"/"set" method syntax.

The "Persistence" of Field Values

Because we haven't explicitly stated so before, and because it may not be obvious to everyone, let's call attention now to the fact that an object's field values persist as long as the object itself persists in memory. That is, once we instantiate a Student object in our application:

```
Student s = new Student();
```

then any values that we assign to s's fields, whether via "set" methods or properties:

```
s.Name = "Fred";
```

will persist until either

- such time as the value is explicitly changed:

```
// Renaming Student s.
s.Name = "Mel";
```

- such time as the object is destroyed and its memory is recycled (we'll talk about ways of destroying an object and recycling its memory in Chapter 13).

So, as long as the memory allocated to Student object s stays around (or to return to our analogy from Chapter 3, as long as the "helium balloon" representing s stays "inflated"), whenever we ask s for its name, it will remember whatever value we've *last* assigned to its name field.

Exceptions to the Public/Private Rule

Even though it's generally true that

- Fields are declared to be private;

- Methods are declared to be public; and

- Private fields are accessed through either public properties or methods;

there are numerous exceptions to this rule.

1. A field may be used by a class strictly for internal housekeeping purposes. (Like the dishwashing detergent you keep under the sink, guests needn't know about it!) For such fields, we needn't bother to provide public accessors. One example for the Student class might be a field:

   ```
   private int countOfDsAndFs;
   ```

   This field might be used to keep track of how many poor grades a student has received in order to determine whether or not the student is on academic probation. We may provide a Student class method as follows:

   ```
   public bool OnAcademicProbation() {
     // If the student received more than three substandard grades,
     // they will be put on academic probation.
     if (countOfDsAndFs > 3) {
       return true;
     }
     else {
       return false;
     }
   }
   ```

   This method uses the value of private field countOfDsAndFs to determine whether a student is on academic probation, but no *client code* need ever know that there is such a field as countOfDsAndFs, and so no explicit public accessors are provided for this field. Such fields are instead set as a "side effect" of performing some *other* method, as in the following example, also taken from the Student class:

   ```
   public void CompleteCourse(string courseName,
                              int creditHours,
                              char grade) {
     // Updating the count of D's and F's is considered to be a
     // "side effect" of completing a course.
     if (grade == 'D' || grade == 'F') countOfDsAndFs++;

     // Other processing details omitted.
   }
   ```

2. Some methods/properties may be used strictly for internal housekeeping, as well, in which case they may also be declared private rather than public. An example of such a Student class method might be UpdateGpa, which recomputes the value of the gpa field each time a student completes another course and receives a grade. The only time this method may ever need to be called is perhaps from within another method of Student—for example, the public CompleteCourse method—as follows:

```
public class Student
{
  private double gpa;
  private int totalCoursesTaken;
  private int totalQualityPointsEarned;
  private int countOfDsAndFs;
  // other details omitted...

  public void CompleteCourse(string courseName,
                             int creditHours,
                             char grade) {
    if (grade == 'D' || grade == 'F') {
      countOfDsAndFs++;
    }

    // Record grade in transcript.
    // details omitted...

    // Update a field...
    ++totalCoursesTaken;

    //...and call a PRIVATE housekeeping method from within this
    // public method to adjust the student's GPA accordingly.
    UpdateGpa(creditHours, grade);
  }

  // The details of HOW the GPA gets updated are a deep, dark
  // secret. Even the EXISTENCE of this next method is hidden from
  // the "outside world" (i.e., inaccessible from client code) by
  // virtue of its having been declared to be PRIVATE.
  private void UpdateGpa(int creditHours, char grade) {
    int letterGradeValue = 0;

    if (grade == 'A') letterGradeValue = 4;
    if (grade == 'B') letterGradeValue = 3;
    if (grade == 'C') letterGradeValue = 2;
    if (grade == 'D') letterGradeValue = 1;
    // For an 'F', it remains 0.

    int qualityPoints = creditHours * letterGradeValue;

    // Update two fields.
    totalQualityPointsEarned += qualityPoints;
    gpa = totalQualityPointsEarned/totalCoursesTaken;
  }
}
```

Client code shouldn't be able to directly cause a Student object's GPA to be updated; this should occur only as a side effect of completing a course. By making the UpdateGpa method private, we've prevented any client code from explicitly invoking this method to manipulate this field's value out of context.

3. We needn't always provide both a "getter" and a "setter" for private fields.

    If we provide only a "getter" for a field, then that field is rendered effectively read-only. We might do so, for example, with a student's GPA that, once set, should remain unchanged as far as the client code is concerned:

```
public class Student
{
  string gpa;
  // details omitted

  // We define a read-only property by only writing a get accessor
  public string Gpa {
    get {
      return gpa;
    }

    // The set accessor is omitted.
  }
}
```

By the same token, we can provide only a "setter" for a field, in which case the field would be write-only from the point of view of client code.

If we provide *neither* a "getter" nor "setter," we've effectively rendered the field as a private "housekeeping" data item that can be accessed only from members in that class, as previously discussed.

The Power of Encapsulation

You learned earlier that encapsulation is the mechanism that bundles together the state information (fields) and behavior (methods) of an object. Now that you've gained some insights into public/private accessibility, encapsulation warrants a more in-depth discussion.

It's useful to think of an object as a "fortress" that "guards" data—namely, the values of all its fields. Rather than trying to march straight through the walls of a fortress, which typically results in death and destruction (!), we ideally would approach the guard at the gate to ask permission to enter. Generally speaking, the same is true for objects; we can't directly access the values of an object's privately declared fields without an object's permission and knowledge, that is, without using one of an object's publicly accessible methods/properties to access the field's value.

Assume that you've just met someone for the first time and want to know his name. One way to determine his name would be to reach into his pocket, pull out his wallet, and look at his driver's license—essentially, accessing his private field values without his permission! The more "socially acceptable" way would be to simply ask him for his name—akin to using his

CHAPTER 4 ■ OBJECT INTERACTIONS   115

GetName method or Name property—and to allow him to respond accordingly. He may respond with his formal name, or a nickname, or an alias, or may say "It's none of your business!"—but the important point is that you're giving the person (object) control over his response.

By restricting access to an object's private fields through public accessors, we derive three benefits:

- Preventing unauthorized access to encapsulated data

- Helping to ensure data integrity

- Limiting "ripple effects" that can otherwise occur throughout an application when the private implementation details of a class must change.

Let's discuss each of these benefits in detail.

Preventing Unauthorized Access to Encapsulated Data

Some of the information that a Student object maintains about itself—say, the student's identification number—may be highly confidential. A Student object may choose to selectively pass along this information when necessary—for example, when registering for a course—but may not want to hand out this information to any object that happens to casually ask for it. Simply by making the field private, and intentionally omitting a public "getter" with which to request the field's value, there would be no way for another object to request the Student object's identification number.

Helping to Ensure Data Integrity

As mentioned previously, one of the arguments against declaring public fields is that the object loses control over its data. As we saw earlier, a public field's value can be changed by client code without regard to any business rules that the object's class may want to impose. On the other hand, when an accessor is used to change the value of a private field, value checking can be built into the set method or set accessor of a property to ensure that the field value won't be set to an "improper" value.

As an example, let's say that we've declared a Student field as follows:

```
private string birthDate;
```

Our intention is to record birth dates in the format *mm/dd/yyyy*. By providing accessors with which to manipulate the birthDate field (instead of permitting direct public access to the field), we can provide logic to validate the format of any newly proposed date and reject those that are invalid. We'll illustrate this concept by declaring a property called BirthDate for the student class as illustrated in the following code; but again, keep in mind that we could accomplish essentially the same "bulletproofing" through the creation of a SetBirthDate method:

```
public class Student
{
  private string birthDate;
  // Details omitted.

  // Properties.
```

```
public string BirthDate {
  get {
    return birthDate;
  }
  set {
    // Perform appropriate validations.
    // Remember, italics represent pseudocode!
    if (date is not in the format mm/dd/yyyy) {
      do not update the birthDate field
    }
    else if (mm not in the range 01 to 12) {
      do not update the birthDate field
    }
    else if (the day number isn't valid for the selected month) {
      do not update the birthDate field
    }
    else if (the year is NOT a leap year, but 2/29 was specified) {
      // details omitted...
    }
    // etc. for other validation tests.
    else {
      // All is well with what was passed in as a value to this
      // set accessor, and so we can go ahead and update the value
      // of the birthDate field with this value.
      birthDate = value;
    }
  }
}

// etc.
}
```

If an attempt is made to pass an invalid birth date to the property from client code, as in the following, the change will be rejected and the value of the birthDate field will be unchanged:

```
s.BirthDate = "foo";
```

On the other hand, if birthDate had been declared to be a *public* field:

```
public class Student
{
  public string birthDate;
  // etc.
```

then setting the field directly, thus bypassing the property (note *lowercase* 'b') as follows would corrupt the field's value:

```
s.birthDate = "foo";
```

■**Note** In the previous example, for simplicity, we used a string to represent a date. The C# FCL has a pre-defined type called `DateTime` that can store date and time information.

Limiting "Ripple Effects" When Private Members Change

Despite our best attempts, we often have a need to go back and modify code after an application has been deployed, either when an inevitable change in requirements occurs or if we unfortunately discover a design flaw that needs attention. Unfortunately, this can often open us up to "ripple effects," wherein dozens, or hundreds, or *thousands* of lines of code throughout an application have to be changed, retested, and so on. One of the most dramatic examples of the impact of ripple effects was the notorious "Y2K" problem: when the need to change date formats to accommodate a four-digit year arose, the burden to hunt through *millions* of lines of code in *millions* of applications worldwide to find all such cases—and to *fix* them without *breaking* anything!—was mind boggling.

Perhaps the most dramatic benefit of encapsulation combined with information hiding, therefore, is that the hidden implementation details of a class—that is, its private data structure and/or its (effectively private) accessor code—can change without affecting how an object belonging to that class is used in client code. To illustrate this principle, we'll craft an example using properties; but again, realize that the same power of encapsulation can be achieved through the appropriate use of "get"/"set" methods.

Let's say that a field is declared in the Student class as follows:

```
private int age;
```

and that we craft a corresponding Age property as follows:

```
public int Age {
  get {
    return age;
  }
  // will be read-only -- no set accessor provided.
}
```

We then proceed to use our Student class in countless applications; so, in thousands of places within the client code of these applications, we write statements such as the following, relying on the get accessor to provide us with a student's age as an int value:

```
if (s.Age <= 21)  {...}
// or:
int retirementAge = s.Age + 20;
// etc.
```

A few years later, we decide to change the data structure of a Student so that, instead of maintaining an age field explicitly, we instead use the student's birthDate field to compute a student's age whenever it's needed. We thus modify our Student class code as follows:

The "Before" Code	The "After" Code
```public class Student { // We have an explicit age field. private int age; public int Age { get { return age; } } // etc. }```	```public class Student { // We replace age with birthDate. private DateTime birthDate; public int Age { get { // Compute the age on demand // (pseudocode). return (system date - birthDate); } } // etc. }```

In the "after" version of Student, we're computing the student's age by subtracting the birth date (a field) from today's date. This is an example of what we informally refer to as a *pseudoattribute*—to client code, the presence of an Age property implies that there is a field by the name of age, when in fact there may not be!

Note The same effect can be achieved with "get" and "set" methods; that is, the availability of a getXxx() method signature for a class doesn't guarantee that there is actually an explicit field by the name of *xxx* in that class.

The beauty is that *we don't care that the* private *details of the* Student *class design have changed!* In all of the thousands of places within the client code of countless applications in which we've used an expression, such as the following, to retrieve a student's age as an int value, this code will continue to work *as-is, without any changes being necessary*:

```
// This client code is unaffected by the private details of how age
// is computed internally to the Student class. Such details can in
// fact change after this client code is written, and the client
// code still won't "break"!
if (s.Age <= 21) {...}
// or:
int retirementAge = s.Age + 20;
```

Hence, we avoided the "dreaded" ripple effect and have *dramatically* reduced the amount of effort necessary to accommodate a design change. Such changes are said to be *encapsulated*, or limited to the internal code of the Student class only.

Of course, all bets are off if the developer of a class changes one of its *public* method or property headers because then all the client code that invokes the method or accesses the property will potentially have to change. For example, if we were to change the Student class design as follows:

```
public class Student
{
  // We've changed the type of the age field from int to float...
  private float age;

  //...and the type of the Age property accordingly.
  public float Age {
    get {
      // details omitted.
    }
  }

      // etc.
    }
```

then much our client code would indeed "break," as in the following example:

```
// This will no longer compile!
int currentAge = s.Age;
```

This client code will "break" because we now have a type mismatch: we're getting back a float value, but are trying to assign it to an int variable, which (as you learned in Chapter 1) will generate a compiler error as follows:

```
  error: Cannot implicitly convert type 'float' to 'int'
```

We'd have to hunt for all of the thousands of places in our countless applications where we are using the Age get accessor and modify our code, such as the following, which is indeed a major ripple effect:

```
// We're now using a cast.
int currentAge = (int) s.Age;
```

But again, this ripple effect is due to the fact that we changed a *public* member of our class—a public property header, to be precise. As long as we restrict our changes to private members of a class—private field and accessor code bodies, but not public method/property header(s)—ripple effects are not an issue. Any client code that was previously written to utilize Student accessors will continue to work as intended; the client code will be blissfully ignorant that the internal details of the Student class have changed.

Using Accessors from Within a Class's Own Methods

As you saw earlier in the chapter, there are no restrictions on directly accessing a class's members from within that class's own methods. Both public and private members may be manipulated at will, using simple names, as the following code example illustrates:

```
using System;

public class Student
```

```
{
  private string name;
  private string studentID;
  // etc.

  // Properties.

  public string Name {
    get {
      return name;
    }
    set {
      name = value;
    }
  }

  // etc.

  public void PrintAllField() {
    // We're directly accessing the values of fields, simply because
    // we CAN!  We're not using the properties declared above.
    Console.WriteLine(name);
    // etc.
  }

  // etc.
}
```

However, it's considered a best practice to get into the habit of invoking a class's accessors, when available, even from within that class's *own* methods, instead of directly accessing fields "just because we can," as a convenience. The reason for this is as follows: just because a field may be simple today, there's no guarantee that it won't become complicated down the road.

As an example, let's say that after we program the Student class—including the PrintAllFields method shown previously—we decide that we want a student's name to always appear with the first name abbreviated as a single letter followed by a period; for example, "John Smith" should always appear as "J. Smith". So, we change the internal logic of the Name property's get accessor to make it a bit more sophisticated, as follows:

```
public class Student
{
  private string name;
  private string studentID;
  // etc.

  public string Name {
  // This version of the get accessor does more work.
    get {
```

```
    // Declare a few temporary variables.
    string firstInitial;
    string lastName;

    // Extract the first letter of the first name from the "name"
    // field, and store the result in variable "firstInitial".
    // (Details omitted.)

    // Extract the last name from the "name" field, and store
    // the result in variable "lastName".
    // (Details omitted.)

    return firstInitial + ". " + lastName;
  }
  set {
    name = value;
  }
}

// etc.
}
```

No longer does the Name get accessor simply return the value of the name field unaltered, as it used to. But, if from within our PrintAllFields method we're still directly accessing the values of the fields via dot notation, we wind up circumventing the Name property, which means that all of our hard work to restructure the student's name in the Name get accessor is being ignored:

```
public void PrintAllFields() {
  // We're still directly accessing the values of the fields, and
  // so we're losing out on the logic of the newly crafted Name
  // property's get accessor.
  Console.WriteLine(name);  //  name field rather than Name property
  // etc.
}

// etc.
}
```

Hence, client code such as the following:

```
Student s = new Student();
s.Name = "Cynthia Coleman";
// details omitted.
s.PrintAllFields();
```

produces incorrect results:

```
Output:
Cynthia Coleman
```

On the other hand, if we had recrafted the PrintAllFields method to utilize the Name get accessor:

```
public void PrintAllFields() {
  // We're now using our own get accessors.
  Console.WriteLine(Name);  //  Name property rather than name field
  // etc.
```

then we'd have automatically benefited from the change that we made to Name, and our client code would now produce correct results, again without having to have modified the client code:

```
Student s = new Student();
s.Name = "Cynthia Coleman";
// details omitted.
s.PrintAllFields();
Output:
C. Coleman
```

Constructors

When we talked about instantiating objects in the previous chapter, you may have been curious about the interesting syntax involved with the new operator:

```
Student x = new Student();
```

In particular, you may have wondered why there were parentheses tacked onto the end of the statement. It turns out that when we instantiate an object via the new operator, we're actually invoking a special type of function member called a *constructor*. The new operator is used to allocate the memory needed to store the data of the object. The job of the constructor is to initialize the instance variables of the object.

Default Constructors

It turns out that if we don't explicitly declare any constructors for a class, C# automatically provides a default parameterless constructor for that class. The default constructor will initialize any fields of the class to their zero-equivalent values. So, even though we may have designed a class with no constructors whatsoever:

```
public class Student
{
  // Fields.

  private int age;
  // other details omitted

  // Properties/methods (but NO EXPLICIT CONSTRUCTORS!).

  public string Age {
    get {
```

```
    return age;
  }
  set {
    age = value;
  }
}

// etc.
}
```

we are still able to write client code as follows:

```
Student s1 = new Student();  // We're calling the default constructor.
```

because we are using the *default* parameterless instance constructor. The age field will initialized with the value of 0 by default.

Writing Our Own Constructors

We needn't merely rely on C# to provide us with a default constructor; we can also write constructors of our own design. When writing our own constructors, note that the header for a constructor is a bit different from that of methods:

public	Student	()
Accessibility modifier, but **no return type!**	Constructor name **must** match the class name	Comma-separated list of formal parameters, enclosed in parentheses parentheses may be left empty)

Points to note:

- A constructor's name must be exactly the same as the name of the class for which we're writing the constructor—we have no choice in the matter.

- We *can't* specify a return type for a constructor because by definition a constructor returns a reference to a newly created object of the type represented by the class.

- A parameter list, enclosed in parentheses, is provided for a constructor header as with method headers; and, as with method headers, it may be left empty if appropriate.

Another oddity with respect to constructors, as compared with methods, is that invoking them does *not* involve dot notation:

```
// We are invoking the Professor class's constructor method from
// client code without using dot notation.

Professor p = new Professor();
```

This is because we aren't requesting a service of a particular object, but instead are requesting that a new object be crafted from "thin air" by the programming environment; the use of the new operator emphasizes this difference syntactically. For this reason, constructors aren't considered to be methods because (as you learned earlier) methods are invoked in the context of a particular object using dot notation.

If we want, we can *explicitly* program a parameterless instance constructor for our classes to do something more interesting than merely instantiating a "bare bones" object, in which case the default parameterless constructor is *not* automatically created for us:

```
public class Student
{
  // Fields.
  private string name;
  // etc.

  // We've explicitly programmed a parameterless constructor, thus
  // REPLACING the default.
  public Student() {
    // Perhaps we wish to initialize the field values to something OTHER THAN
    // their zero equivalents.
    name = "?";

    // etc. -- we can do whatever makes sense in constructing a new
    // Student: creating additional objects; accessing a database;
    // communicating with other preexisting objects; whatever is
    // required!
  }
  // Other methods omitted from this example.
}
```

Passing Arguments to Constructors

Constructors can be used to pass in initial values for an object's fields at the time when an object is being instantiated. Instead of creating an object whose fields are all initialized to zero-equivalent values, and then utilizing the property accessors provided by that class to assign values one by one to the fields, as illustrated by this next snippet:

```
// Create a bare bones Student object.
Student s = new Student();

// Assign values to the fields one-by-one.
s.Name = "Fred Schnurd";
s.Id = "123-45-6789";
s.Major = "MATH";
// etc.
```

the initial values for selected fields can all be passed in as a single step when the constructor is called, if desired:

```
Student s = new Student("Fred Schnurd", "123-45-6789", "MATH");
```

In order to accommodate this, we'd have to define a Student constructor with an appropriate header, as shown here:

```
public class Student
{
  // Fields.
  private string name;
  private string id;
  private string major;
  // etc.

  // We've programmed a constructor with three parameters to
  // accommodate passing in argument values.
  public Student(string id, string n, string m) {
    Name = n;
    Id = id;
    Major = m;
  }
```

Note that we're using the Name, Id, and Major properties in the previous constructor to set the values of the associated name, id, and major fields. As we discussed earlier in this chapter, using set accessors to set the value of fields rather than manipulating field values directly allows us to make use of whatever value checking or other operations are performed inside the set accessor.

As with methods, constructor arguments can also be used to provide general "fuel" for controlling how a constructor behaves, as illustrated in the next example:

```
public Student(string name, bool assignDefaults) {
  Name = n;
  if (assignDefaults) {
    Id = "?";
    Major = "undeclared";
  }
}
```

Constructors can be declared with any one of the five previously mentioned C# accessibility types. They are most often given public accessibility so as to enable other classes to freely instantiate objects of the constructor's type.

Note We'll revisit constructors twice more in this book—in our discussion of *overloading* in Chapter 5, and again with respect to inheritance in Chapter 13.

Summary

In this chapter, you've learned

- How to formally specify method headers, the "language" with which operations may be requested of an object, and how to call methods and properties—using dot notation—to actually get an object to perform such operations

- That multiple objects often have to collaborate in carrying out a particular system function, such as registering a student for a course

- That an object A can communicate with another object B only if A has a reference to B, and the various ways that such a reference can be obtained

- How classes designate the public/private accessibility of their members (fields, properties, methods)

- How powerful a mechanism information hiding is, both in terms of protecting the integrity of an object's data and in preventing "ripple effects" in client code when private implementation details of an application inevitably change

- How to declare and use accessors—either accessor ("get"/"set") methods or properties—to gracefully access private fields, and that using properties is the preferred approach with C#

- How to harness the power of encapsulation

- How an instance constructor is specified and used to initialize new objects

Exercises

1. Given a class Book defined as having the following fields:

```
Author author;

string title;

int noOfPages;

bool fiction;
```

Write a set of properties for these fields with simple, one-line get and set accessors.

What would the recommended headers be if we were to write "get" and "set" methods for all of these fields?

2. It's often possible to discern something about a class's design based on the method calls on objects in client code. Consider the following client code "snippet:"

```
Student s;
Professor p;
bool b;
string x = "Math";

s.Major = x;
if (!s.HasAdvisor())

    b = s.DesignateAdvisor(p);
```

What members—fields, methods, properties—are implied for the Student and Professor classes by virtue of how this client code is structured? Be as specific as possible with respect to the following:

- The accessibility of each member

- How each member would be declared; for example, the details (to the extent that you can "discover" them) of a method or property's header

3. What's wrong with the following code? Point out things that go against OO convention based on what you've learned in this chapter, regardless of whether or not the C# compiler would "complain" about them.

First, an example using "get"/"set" methods:

```
public class Building
{
  private string address;
  public int numberOfFloors;

  void GetnumberOfFloors() {
    return numberOfFloors;
  }

  private void SetNoOfFloors(float n) {
    NumberOfFloors = n;
  }
}
```

Next, an example using properties:

```
public class Building
{
  private string address;
  public int numberOfFloors

  public long NumberOfFloors {
    int get {
```

```
            return numberOfFloors;
        }
        private set {
            numberOfFloors = value;
        }
    }
}
```

CHAPTER 5

■■■

Relationships Between Objects

As you saw in Chapter 4, any two objects can have a "fleeting relationship" based on the fact that they invoke methods on each other, in the same way that two strangers passing on the street might say "Hello!" to one another. We call such relationships between objects *behavioral relationships* because they arise out of the behaviors, or actions, taken by one object X relative to another object Y. With behavioral relationships, object X is either temporarily handed a reference to object Y as an argument in a method call or temporarily requests a reference to Y from another object Z. However, the emphasis is on *temporary*; when X is finished communicating with Y, object X often discards the reference to Y.

In the same way that you have significant and more lasting relationships with some people (family members, friends, colleagues, and so forth), there is also the notion of a more permanent relationship between objects. We refer to such relationships as *structural relationships* because in order to keep track of such relationships, an object actually maintains lasting references to its related objects in the form of fields, a technique that we discussed in Chapter 3.

In this chapter, you'll learn

- The various kinds of structural relationships that may exist between classes and between individual objects, and how we characterize them

- How through a powerful mechanism called *inheritance* we can derive new classes by describing only how they differ from existing classes

- The rules for what we can and can't do when deriving classes through inheritance

Associations and Links

The formal name for a structural relationship that exists between objects is an *association*. With respect to the Student Registration System (SRS), some sample associations might be as follows:

- A Student *is enrolled in* a Course.

- A Professor *teaches* a Course.

- A DegreeProgram *requires* a Course.

Whereas an association refers to a relationship between *classes*, the term *link* can be used to refer to a structural relationship that exists between two specific *objects* (*instances*). Given the association "a Student *is enrolled in* a Course," we might have the following links:

- Jackson Palmer (a particular Student object) is enrolled in Math 101 (a particular Course object).

- Helmut Schmidt (a particular Student object) is enrolled in Basketweaving 972 (a particular Course object).

- Mary Smith (a particular Student object) is enrolled in Basketweaving 972 (a particular Course object; as it turns out, the *same* Course object that Fred Schnurd is linked to).

Given any Student object X and any Course object Y, there is the *potential* for a link of type "is enrolled in" to exist between those two objects *precisely because* there is an "is enrolled in" association defined between the two classes that those objects belong to. In other words, associations enable links.

Most of the time, we define associations between two different classes; such associations are known as *binary associations*. The "is enrolled in" association, for example, is a binary association because it interrelates two different classes: Student and Course. A *unary*, or *reflexive, association*, on the other hand, is between two instances of the same class; for example:

- A Course *is a prerequisite for* (another) Course.

- A Professor *supervises* (other) Professor(s).

Even though the two classes at either end of a reflexive association are the same, the objects are typically different instances of that class:

- Math 101 (a Course object) is a prerequisite for Math 202 (a different Course object).

- Professor Gupta (a Professor object) supervises Professors Jones and Green (other Professor objects).

And so forth. However, although somewhat rare, there can be situations in which the same object can serve in both roles of a reflexive relationship.

Higher-order associations are possible, but rare. A *ternary association* involves three classes; for example, a Student takes a Course from a particular Professor, as shown in Figure 5-1.

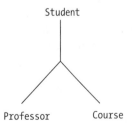

Figure 5-1. *A ternary association*

When describing associations, however, we usually decompose higher-order associations into an appropriate number of binary associations. We can, for example, represent the preceding three-way association as three binary associations instead (see Figure 5-2):

- A Student *attends* a Course.

- A Professor *teaches* a Course.

- A Professor *instructs* a Student.

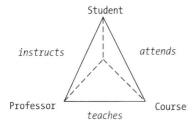

Figure 5-2. *An equivalent representation using three binary associations*

Within a given association, each participant class is said to have a *role*. In the *instructs* association (a Professor *instructs* a Student), the role of the Professor might be said to be *instructor*, and the role of the Student might be said to be *instructee*. We bother to assign names to the roles at either end of an association only if it helps to clarify the model. In the *attends* association (a Student *attends* a Course), there is probably no need to invent role names for the Student and Course ends of the association because they wouldn't add significantly to the clarity of the abstraction of which this association is a part.

Multiplicity

For a given association type X between classes A and B, the term *multiplicity* refers to the number of objects of type A that may be associated with a given instance of type B. For example, a Student attends multiple Courses, but a Student has only one Professor in the role of advisor.

There are three basic categories of multiplicity, which we'll take a closer look at next: one-to-one, one-to-many, and many-to-many.

One-to-One (1:1)

Exactly one instance of class A is related to exactly one instance of class B, no fewer, no more, and vice versa. For example:

- A Student has exactly one Transcript (a multiplicity of one), and a Transcript belongs to exactly one Student.

- A Professor chairs exactly one Department, and a Department has exactly one Professor in the role of chairperson.

We can further constrain an association by stating whether the participation of the class at either end is optional or mandatory. For example, we can change the preceding association to read as follows:

- A given `Professor` *might* chair exactly one `Department`, but it is *mandatory* that a `Department` has exactly one `Professor` in the role of chairperson.

This revised version of the association is a more realistic portrayal of real-world circumstances than the previous version because although every department in a university typically does indeed have a chairperson, not every professor is a chairperson of a department—there aren't enough departments to go around! However, it's true that *if* a professor happens to be a chairperson of a department, the professor is a chairperson of only *one* department.

One-to-Many (1:m)

For a given single instance of class A, there can be many instances of class B related to it in a particular fashion; but from the perspective of an object of type B, there can only be one instance of class A that is so related. For example:

- A `Department` employs many `Professor`s (a multiplicity of many), but a `Professor` (usually) works for exactly one `Department` (a multiplicity of one).

- A `Professor` advises many `Student`s, but a given `Student` has exactly one `Professor` as an advisor.

Note that "many" in this case can be interpreted as either "zero or more (optional)" or as "one or more (mandatory)." To be a bit more specific, we can refine the previous one-to-many associations as follows:

- A `Department` employs *one or more* ("many"; *mandatory*) `Professor`s, but a `Professor` (usually) works for exactly one `Department`.

- A `Professor` advises *zero or more* ("many"; *optional*) `Student`s, but a given `Student` has exactly one `Professor` as an advisor.

In addition, as with one-to-one relationships, the "one" end of a one-to-many association may also be designated as mandatory or as optional. We may, for example, wish to "fine-tune" the previous association as follows, if we are modeling a university setting in which students aren't required to select an advisor:

- A `Professor` advises many (zero or more; *optional*) students, but a given `Student` may *optionally* have at most one advisor.

Many-to-Many (m:m)

For a given single instance of class A, there can be many instances of class B related to it, and vice versa. For example:

- A Student enrolls in many Courses, and a Course has many Students enrolled in it.

- A given Course can have many prerequisite Courses, and a given Course can in turn be a prerequisite for many other Courses. (This is an example of a many-to-many reflexive association.)

As with one-to-many associations, "many" can be interpreted as *zero* or more (*optional*) or as *one* or more (*mandatory*); for example:

- A Student enrolls in *zero or more* ("many"; *optional*) Courses, and a Course has *one or more* ("many"; *mandatory*) Students enrolled in it.

Of course, the validity of a particular association—the classes that are involved, its multiplicity, and the optional or mandatory nature of participation in the association—is wholly dependent on the real-world circumstances being modeled. If you were modeling a university in which departments could have more than one chairperson or where students could have more than one advisor, your choice of multiplicities would differ from those used in our preceding examples.

Multiplicity and Links

Note that the concept of multiplicity pertains to associations, but not to links. *Links always exist in a pairwise fashion between two objects (or, in rare cases, between an object and itself).* Therefore, multiplicity in essence defines how many links of a certain association type can originate from a given object. This is best illustrated with an example.

Consider once again the many-to-many association:

"A Student enrolls in zero or more Courses, and a Course has one or more Students enrolled in it."

A *specific* Student object X can have zero, one, or more *links* to Course objects, but any *one* of those links is between exactly *two* objects—Student X and a single Course object. In Figure 5-3, for example:

- Student X has one link (to Course A).

- Student Y has four links (to Courses A, B, C, and D).

- Student Z has no links to any Course objects whatsoever (Z is taking the semester off!).

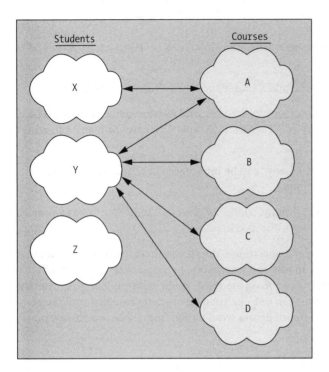

Figure 5-3. *A many-to-many association between classes; links are always pairwise between objects.*

Conversely, a *specific* Course object A must have one or more links to Student objects to satisfy the mandatory nature and multiplicity of the association, but again, any *one* of those links is between exactly *two* objects (a binary linkage): Course A and a single Student object. In Figure 5-2, for example:

- Course A has two links (to Students X and Y).

- Courses B, C, and D each have one link (to the same Student, Y).

Note, however, that once again every link is between precisely two objects: a Student and a Course. This example scenario does indeed uphold the many-to-many "is enrolled in" association between Student and Course; it's but one of a vast number of possible scenarios that may exist between the classes in question.

Just to make sure that this concept is clear, let's look at another example, this time using the one-to-one association.

"A Professor *optionally* chairs exactly one Department, and it is *mandatory* that a Department has exactly one Professor in the role of chairman. As illustrated in Figure 5-4:

- Professor objects 1 and 4 each have one link—to Department objects A and B, respectively.

- Professor objects 2 and 3 have no such links.

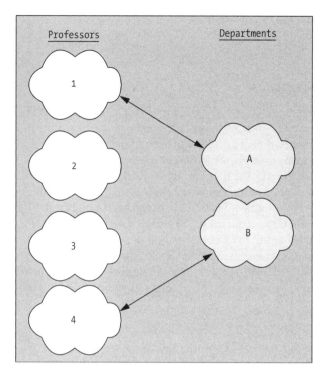

Figure 5-4. *A one-to-one association between classes; links are always pairwise between objects.*

Moreover, from the Department objects' perspective, each Department does indeed have exactly one link to a Professor. Therefore, this example upholds the one-to-one "chairs" association between Professor and Department, while further illustrating the optional nature of the Professor class's participation in such links. Again, it's but one of a number of possible scenarios that may exist between the classes in question.

Aggregation

Aggregation is a special form of association, alternatively referred to as the "consists of," "is composed of," or "has a" relationship. Like an association, an aggregation is used to represent a relationship between two classes A and B. But with an aggregation, we're representing more than mere relationship: we're stating that an object belonging to a class A, known as an *aggregate class*, is composed of, or contains, one or more *component objects* belonging to a class B.

For example, a car is composed of an engine, a transmission, four wheels, and so on; so if Car, Engine, Transmission, and Wheel were all classes, we could form the following aggregations:

- A Car *contains* one Engine.

- A Car *contains* one Transmission.

- A Car *is composed of* many (in this case, four) Wheels.

Or, as an example related to the SRS, we can say that

- A University *is composed of* many Schools (the School of Engineering, the School of Law, etc.).

- A School *is composed of* many Departments.

One wouldn't typically say, however, that a Department is *composed of* many Professors; instead, we'd probably state that a Department *employs* many Professors.

Note that these aggregation statements appear awfully similar to associations, where the name of the association just so happens to be "is composed of" or "contains." That's because an aggregation *is* an association! So why the fuss over trying to differentiate between aggregation and association? Do we even need to recognize that there is such a thing as an aggregation? It turns out that there are some subtle differences between aggregation and association that affect how an abstraction is rendered in code. Therefore, we'll defer further discussion of aggregation for now, but will return to discuss these subtleties in Chapter 14.

For now, use this simple rule of thumb: when you detect a relationship between two classes A and B, and the name you're inclined to give that association implies containment—"contains," "is composed of," "comprises," "consists of," and so forth—then it's probably really an aggregation that you're dealing with.

Inheritance

Let's assume that we've accurately and thoroughly modeled all the essential features of students via our Student class, and that we've actually programmed the class in C# (as you'll learn to do in Part Three). A simplified version of the Student class is shown here:

```
using System;

public class Student
{
  private string name;
  private string studentId;
  // etc.

  public string Name {
    get {
      return name;
    }
    set {
      name = value;
    }
  }

  public string StudentId {
    get {
      return studentId;
    }
    set {
```

```
            studentId = value;
        }
    }

    // etc.
}
```

In fact, let's further assume that our Student class code has been rigorously tested, found to be bug-free, and is actually being used in a number of applications: our SRS, for example, as well as perhaps a student billing system and an alumni relations system for the same university.

A new requirement has just arisen for modeling graduate students as a special type of student. As it turns out, the only features of a graduate student that we need to track above and beyond those that we've already modeled for a "generic student" are

- What undergraduate degree the student previously received before entering their graduate program of study

- What institution they received the undergraduate degree from

All the other features necessary to describe a graduate student—fields name, studentId, and so forth, along with properties to access them—are the same as those that we've already programmed for the Student class because a graduate student *is* a student, after all.

How might we approach this new requirement for a GraduateStudent class? If we weren't well-versed in object-oriented concepts, we might try one of the following approaches:

- Modify the Student class to do "double duty."

- "Clone" the Student class.

- Use *Inheritance* to extend the existing Student class.

Let's talk about each of the three possible approaches in more detail.

Approach #1: Modify the Student Class to Do Double Duty

We could add fields to reflect undergraduate degree information to our definition of a Student, along with properties to access them, and simply leave these fields empty when they are non-applicable; that is, for an undergraduate student who hadn't yet graduated:

```
public class Student
{
  private string name;
  private string studentId;
  private string undergraduateDegree;
  private string undergraduateInstitution;
  // etc.
```

Then, to keep track of whether these fields were supposed to contain values or not for a given Student object, we'd probably also want to add a bool field to note whether a particular student is a graduate student:

```
public class Student
{
  private string name;
  private string studentId;
  private string undergraduateDegree;
  private string undergraduateInstitution;
  private bool isGraduateStudent;
  // etc.
```

In any new methods that we subsequently write for this class, we'll have to take the value of this bool field into account:

```
public void DisplayAllFields() {
  Console.WriteLine(name);
  Console.WriteLine(studentId);

  // If a particular student is NOT a graduate student, then the
  // values of the fields "'undergraduateDegree" and
  // "undergraduateInstitution" would be undefined, and so we would
  // only wish to print them if we are dealing with a graduate
  // student.
  if (isGraduateStudent) {
    Console.WriteLine(undergraduateDegree);
    Console.WriteLine(undergraduateInstitution);
  }
  // etc.
}
```

This results in convoluted code, which is difficult to debug and maintain.

Approach #2: Clone the Student Class

We could instead create a new GraduateStudent class by (a) making a duplicate copy of the Student class, (b) renaming the copy to be the GraduateStudent class, and (c) adding the extra features required of a graduate student to the copy.

```
public class Student {

  // Fields.


  private string name;

  private string studentId;

  private string birthDate;

  // etc.
```

```
public class GraduateStudent {

    // Student fields DUPLICATED!


    private string name;

    private string studentId;

    private string birthDate;

    // etc.



    // Add the two new fields.

    private string undergraduateDegree;

    private string
            undergraduateInstitution;
```

```

  // Properties.


  public string Name {

    get {

      return name;

    }

    set {

      name = value;

    }

  }


  // etc.
```

```

  // Student properties DUPLICATED!


    public string Name {

      get {

        return name;

      }

      set {

        name = value;

      }

    }


    // etc.



    // Add properties for the two

    // new fields.

    // details omitted ...
```

This would be awfully inefficient because we'd then have much of the same code in two places, and if we wanted to change how a particular method worked or how a field was defined later on—say, a change of the type of the `birthDate` field from `string` to `DateTime`, with a corresponding change to the properties for that field—then we'd have to make the same changes in both classes.

Strictly speaking, either of the preceding two approaches would work, but the inherent redundancy in the code would make the application difficult to maintain. In addition, where these approaches both really break down is when we have to add a third, a fourth, or a fifth type of "special" student. For example, consider how complicated the `DisplayAllFields` method introduced in approach #1 would become if we wanted to use it to represent a third type of student: namely, continuing education students, who don't seek a degree, but instead are just taking courses for continuing professional enrichment.

- We'd most likely need to add yet another bool flag to keep track of whether or not a degree was being sought:

```
public class Student
{
  private string name;
  private string studentId;
  private string undergraduateDegree;
  private string undergraduateInstitution;
  private string degreeSought;
  private bool isGraduateStudent;
  private bool seekingDegree;
  // etc.

  //  We'd also have to now take the value of this bool field
  //  into account in the DisplayAllFields method:
  public void DisplayAllFields() {
    Console.WriteLine(name);
    Console.WriteLine(studentId);

    if (isGraduateStudent) {
      Console.WriteLine(undergraduateDegree);
      Console.WriteLine(undergraduateInstitution);
    }

    // If a particular student is NOT seeking a degree, then the value
    // of the field 'degreeSought' would be undefined, and so we
    // would only wish to print it if we are dealing with a degree-
    // seeking student.
    if (seekingDegree) {
      Console.WriteLine(degreeSought);
    } else {
      Console.WriteLine("NONE");
    }

    // etc.
  }
```

This worsens the complexity issue!

We've had to introduce a lot of complexity in the logic of this one method to handle the various types of student; think of how much more "spaghetti-like" the code might become if we had *dozens* of different student types to accommodate! Unfortunately, with non-OO languages, these convoluted approaches would typically be our only options for handling the requirement for a new type of object. It's no wonder that applications have become so complicated and expensive to maintain as requirements inevitably evolve over time!

Fortunately, we do have yet another alternative!

Approach #3: Use Inheritance to Extend the Existing Student Class

With an object-oriented programming language (OOPL), we can solve this problem by taking advantage of *inheritance*, a powerful mechanism for defining a new class by stating only the differences (in terms of members) between the new class and another class that we've already established. Using inheritance, we can declare a new class named GraduateStudent that inherits all of the members of the Student class. The GraduateStudent class would then only have to take care of the two extra fields associated with a graduate student: undergraduateDegree and undergraduateInstitution. Inheritance is indicated in a C# class declaration using a colon followed by the name of the base class being extended.

```
public class GraduateStudent : Student {
  // Declare two new fields above and beyond
  // what the Student class declares...

  private string undergraduateDegree;
  private string undergraduateInstitution;

  //...and properties for each of these new fields.

  public string UndergraduateDegree {
    get {
      return undergraduateDegree;
    }
    set {
      undergraduateDegree = value;
    }
  }

  public string UndergraduateInstitution {
    get {
      return undergraduateInstitution;
    }
    set {
      undergraduateInstitution = value;
    }
  }
}
```

That's all we need to declare in our new GraduateStudent class: two fields plus their associated properties! There is no need to duplicate any of the members of the Student class because we're automatically inheriting them. It's as if we had "borrowed" the code for the fields, properties, and methods from the Student class, and inserted it into GraduateStudent, but without the fuss of actually having done so.

When we take advantage of inheritance, the original class that we're starting from—Student, in this case—is called the *base class*. The new class—GraduateStudent—is called a *derived class.* A derived class is said to extend a base class. An alternative terminology is to say that a *subclass* inherits from (or extends) a *superclass*.

Inheritance is often referred to as the "is a" relationship between two classes because if a class B (GraduateStudent) is derived from a class A (Student), then B truly is a special case of A. Anything that we can say about a base class must also be true about all of its derived classes; that is:

- A Student attends classes, so a GraduateStudent attends classes.

- A Student has an advisor, so a GraduateStudent has an advisor.

- A Student pursues a degree, so a GraduateStudent pursues a degree.

In fact, an "acid test" for the legitimate use of inheritance is as follows: if there is something that can be said about a base class A that can't be said about a proposed derived class B, then B really isn't a valid derived class of A.

Note, however, that the converse isn't true: because a derived class is a special case of its base class, it's possible to say things about the derived class that can't be said about the base class; for example:

- A GraduateStudent has already attended an undergraduate institution, whereas a "general-purpose" Student might *not* have done so.

- A GraduateStudent has already received an undergraduate degree, whereas a "general-purpose" Student might *not* have done so.

Because derived classes are special cases of their base classes, the term *specialization* is used to refer to the process of deriving one class from another. *Generalization,* on the other hand, is a term used to refer to the opposite process: namely, recognizing the common features of several existing classes and creating a new common base class for them all. Let's say we now wish to create the Professor class. Students and Professors have some fields in common (such as name, birthDate, and so on), and the methods that manipulate them. Yet they each have unique fields as well; the Professor class might require the fields title (a string) and worksFor (a reference to a Department), while the Student class's studentID, degreeSought, and majorField fields are irrelevant for a Professor. Because each class has fields that the other would find useless, neither class can be derived from the other. Nonetheless, to duplicate their shared field declarations and method code in two places would be horribly inefficient.

In such a circumstance, we may want to invent a new base class called Person, consolidate the member common to both Students and Professors in that class, and then have Student and Professor inherit these common members from Person. The resultant code in this situation appears here:

```
// Defining the base class:
public class Person
{
    // Fields common to Students and Professors.
    private string name;    // See note about use of private accessibility
    private string address; // with inheritance after this code example.
    private string birthDate;
```

```csharp
  // Common properties.
  public string Name {
    get {
      return name;
    }
    set {
      name = value;
    }
  }

  // etc.
}

// Defining one derived class of Person...
public class Student : Person
{
  // Fields specific only to a Student.
  private string studentId;
  private string majorField;
  private string degreeSought;

  // Student-specific properties.
  public string StudentId {
    get {
      return studentId;
    }
    set {
      studentId = value;
    }
  }

  // etc.
}

//...and another derived class of Person!
public class Professor : Person
{
  // Fields specific only to a Professor.
  private string title;
  private Department worksFor;

  // Professor-specific properties.
  public string Title {
    get {
      return title;
    }
    set {
```

```
        title = value;
      }
    }

    // etc.
}
```

■Note You'll learn in Chapter 13 that there are a few extra complexities about inheriting private members, and how the "protected" accessibility level comes into play, which we aren't tackling just yet because we haven't covered enough ground to do them justice at this point.

Benefits of Inheritance

Inheritance is perhaps one of the most powerful and unique aspects of an OOPL because

- *Derived classes are much more succinct than they would be without inheritance.* Derived classes contain only the "essence" of what makes them different from their base classes. We know from looking at the GraduateStudent class definition, for example, that a graduate student is "a student who already holds an undergraduate degree from an educational institution." As a result, the total body of code for a given application is significantly reduced as compared with the traditional non-OO approach to developing the same application.

- *Through inheritance, we can reuse and extend code that has already been thoroughly tested without modifying it.* As we saw, we were able to invent a new class— GraduateStudent—without disturbing the Student class code in any way. So, we can rest assured that any client code that relies on instantiating Student objects and invoking methods on them will be unaffected by the creation of derived class GraduateStudent, and thus we avoid having to retest huge portions of our existing application. (Had we used a non-OO approach of "tinkering" with the Student class code to try to accommo- date graduate student fields, we would have had to retest our entire existing application to make sure that nothing had broken!)

- *Best of all, you can derive a new derived class from an existing class even if you don't own the source code for the latter!* As long as you have the compiled version of a class, the inheritance mechanism works just fine; you don't need the original source code of a class in order to extend it. This is one of the most useful ways to achieve productivity with an OOPL: find a class (either written by someone else or one that is built into the language) that does much of what you need and create a derived class of that class, adding just those members that you need for your own purposes; or buy a third-party library of classes written by someone else, and do the same.

- Finally, as you saw in Chapter 2, *classification is the natural way that humans organize information;* so, it only makes sense that we'd organize our software along the same lines, making it much more intuitive and hence easier to maintain and extend.

One Drawback of Inheritance

Inheritance is a powerful concept that is used throughout OO programming, but the coupling between base and derived classes can make it tricky to make any modifications to the base class because any changes made to the base class will "trickle down" to any and all derived classes. Potential problems can be avoided or minimized with careful design of a class hierarchy (a concept discussed in the next section and in more detail in Part Two of this book).

Class Hierarchy

Over time, we build up an inverted tree of classes that are interrelated through inheritance; such a tree is called a *class hierarchy*. One such class hierarchy example is shown in Figure 5-5.

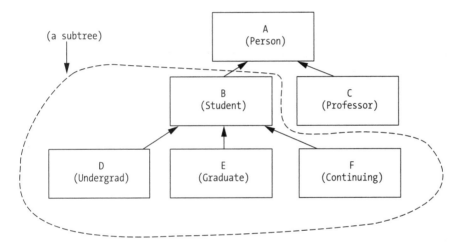

Figure 5-5. *A sample class hierarchy*

A bit of nomenclature:

- We may refer to each class as a *node* in the hierarchy.

- Any given node in the hierarchy is said to be derived (directly or indirectly) from all the nodes above it in the hierarchy, known collectively as its *ancestors*.

- The ancestor that is immediately above a given node in the hierarchy is considered to be that node's *direct base class*.

- Conversely, all nodes below a given node in the hierarchy are said to be its *descendants*.

- The node that sits at the top of the hierarchy is referred to as the *root node*.

- A *terminal*, or *leaf*, *node* is one that has no descendants.

- Two nodes that are derived from the same direct base class are known as *siblings*.

- Note that arrows are used to point *upward* from each derived class to its direct base class.

Applying this terminology to the example hierarchy in Figure 5-5:

- Class A (Person) is the root node of the entire hierarchy.

- Classes B, C, D, E, and F are all said to be derived from class A, and are thus descendants of A.

- Classes D, E, and F can be said to be derived from class B.

- Classes D, E, and F are siblings; so are classes B and C.

- Class D has two ancestors: A and B.

- Classes C, D, E, and F are terminal nodes, in that they don't have any classes derived from them (as of yet, at any rate).

■**Note** In the C# language, the Object class (of the System namespace) serves as the ultimate base class for all other types, both user-defined as well as those built into the language. We'll talk about the Object class in more depth in Part Three of the book.

As with any hierarchy, this one may evolve over time:

- It may *widen* with the addition of new siblings/branches in the tree.

- It may *expand downward* as a result of future specialization.

- It may *expand upward* as a result of future generalization.

Such changes to the hierarchy are made as new requirements emerge, or as our understanding of the existing requirements improves. For example, we may determine the need for MastersStudent and PhDStudent classes (as specializations of GraduateStudent) or of an Administrator class as a sibling to Student and Professor. This would yield the revised hierarchy shown in Figure 5-6.

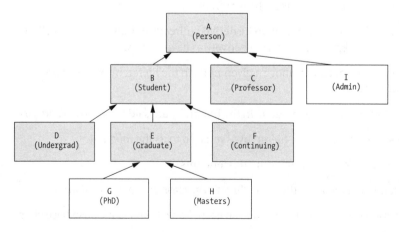

Figure 5-6. *Class hierarchies almost always expand over time.*

Is Inheritance Really a Relationship?

As you've seen earlier in this chapter, association and aggregation (as a special form of association) are object relationships because they are implemented as object references. Two different objects are linked to one another by virtue of the existence of an association between their respective classes. Inheritance, on the other hand, is a class relationship because it's defined statically (that is, before the program is compiled) in the class definition. With inheritance, an object is simultaneously an instance of a derived class and all its base classes: a GraduateStudent is a Student that is a Person, all wrapped into one!

So, in looking once again at the hierarchy shown in Figure 5-6, we see that

- All classes in the Person class hierarchy—Student, Professor, Graduate, and so on—share the qualities of, and are compatible with, the Person class. An array that is declared to hold Person references, for instance, can hold references to Professor, Continuing, and Student objects as well as Person references.

- Subhierarchies work in the same manner; the Undergrad, GraduateStudent, and PhDStudent classes, for example, share the qualities of, and are compatible with, the Student class.

This notion of an object sharing the qualities of its base classes is a significant one that we'll revisit again and again throughout the book.

Avoiding "Ripple Effects"

Once a class hierarchy is established and an application has been coded, changes to nonleaf classes (that is, those classes that have descendants) will introduce "ripple effects" down the hierarchy. For example, if after we establish the GraduateStudent class we go back and add a minorField field to the Student class, then GraduateStudent will inherit this new field once it has been recompiled. Perhaps this is what we want; on the other hand, we may not have anticipated the derivation of a GraduateStudent class when we first conceived of Student, and so this may *not* be what we want!

In an ideal world, developers of the Student class would speak with the developers of all derived classes—GraduateStudent, MastersStudent, and PhDStudent—to obtain their approval for any proposed changes to Student. But this isn't an ideal world, and often we may not even know that our class has been extended if, for example, our code is being distributed and reused on other projects or is being sold to clients. This evokes a general rule of thumb:

> *Whenever possible, avoid adding publicly accessible members to nonleaf classes once they have been established in code in an application to avoid "ripple effects" throughout an inheritance hierarchy.*

This is easier said than done! However, it reinforces the importance of spending as much time as possible on requirements analysis before diving into the coding stage of an application development project. This won't prevent new requirements from emerging over time, but we should avoid oversights regarding the current requirements.

Rules for Deriving Classes: The "Do's"

When deriving a new class, we can do several things to specialize the base class that we are starting out with:

- We can extend the base class by adding members. In our GraduateStudent example, we added four members: two fields—undergraduateDegree and undergraduateInstitution —and two properties—UndergraduateDegree and UndergraduateInstitution.

- We can *specialize* the way that a derived class performs one or more of the methods inherited from its base class. For example, when "general" students enroll for a course, the students may first need to ensure that

    - They have taken the necessary prerequisite courses.

    - The course is required for the degree that the student is seeking.

    - When graduate students enroll for a course, on the other hand, they may need to do both of these things as well as to ensure that their graduate committee feels that the course is appropriate.

Specializing the way that a derived class implements a particular method—as compared with the way that its base class implemented the method—is accomplished via a technique known as overriding.

Overriding

Overriding involves "rewiring" how a method or property works internally in a derived class, without changing the interface to/signature of that method as declared in the base class. For example, suppose that in a simple Student class a Print method were declared to print out the values of all of a student's fields:

```
public class Student
{
  // Fields.
  private string name;
  private string studentId;
  private string majorField;
  private double gpa;
  // etc.

  // Properties for each field would also be provided; details omitted.

  public void Print() {
    // Print the values of all of the fields that the Student class
    // knows about; note use of get accessors.
    Console.WriteLine("Student Name:  " + Name + "\n" +
                  "Student No.:   " + StudentId + "\n" +
                  "Major Field:   " + MajorField + "\n" +
                  "GPA:   " + Gpa);
  }
}
```

The Print method shown in the preceding code assumes that properties have been written for all the Student class fields. The Print method uses a property to access the value of the associated field, instead of accessing the fields directly:

```
// This example accesses fields directly by name, bypassing the
// associated properties; this approach is discouraged.
Console.WriteLine("Student Name:   " + name + "\n" +
                  "Student No.:   " + studentId + "\n" +
                  "Major Field:   " + majorField + "\n" +
                  "GPA:   " + gpa);
```

Using get accessors within a class's own methods reflects a "best practice" discussion that we had in Chapter 4; it allows us to take advantage of any value checking or other operations that the get accessor may provide.

By virtue of inheritance, all the derived classes of Student will inherit this method. However, there is a problem: we added two new fields to the GraduateStudent-derived class: undergraduateDegree and undergraduateInstitution. If we take the "lazy" approach of just letting GraduateStudent inherit the Print method of Student as is, then whenever we invoke the Print method for a GraduateStudent, all that will be printed are the values of the four fields inherited from Student—name, studentId, majorField, and gpa—because these are the only fields that the Print method has been explicitly programmed to print the values of. Ideally, we would like the Print method, when invoked for a GraduateStudent, to print these same four fields *plus* the two additional fields of undergraduateDegree and undergraduateInstitution.

With an OOPL, we are able to override, or supersede, the Student version of the Print method that the GraduateStudent class has inherited. In order to override a base class's method in C#, the method to be overridden first has to be declared to be a *virtual* method in the base class using the virtual keyword. Declaring a method to be virtual means that it *may* be (but doesn't *have to* be) overridden by a derived class.

The derived class can then override the method by reimplementing the method with the override keyword in the derived class's method declaration. The overridden method in the derived class must have the same accessibility, return type, name, and parameter list as the base class method it's overriding.

Let's look at how the GraduateStudent class would go about overriding the Print method of the Student class:

```
public class Student
{
  // Fields.
  private string name;
  private string studentId;
  private string majorField;
  private double gpa;
  // etc.

  // Properties for each field would also be provided; details omitted.

  //  The Student class Print method is declared to be virtual
  public virtual void Print() {
    // Print the values of all the fields that the Student class
```

```
        // knows about; again, note the use of get accessors.
        Console.WriteLine("Student Name:   " + Name + "\n" +
                          "Student No.:   " + StudentId + "\n" +
                          "Major Field:   " + MajorField + "\n" +
                          "GPA:  " + Gpa);
  }
}


public class GraduateStudent : Student
{
  private string undergraduateDegree;
  private string undergraduateInstitution;

  // Properties for each newly added field would also be provided;
  // details omitted.
  // We are overriding the Student class's Print method.
  public override void Print() {
    // We print the values of all the fields that the
    // GraduateStudent class knows about:  namely, those that it
    // inherited from Student plus those that it explicitly declares.
    Console.WriteLine("Student Name:   " + Name + "\n" +
                      "Student No.:   " + StudentId + "\n" +
                      "Major Field:   " + MajorField + "\n" +
                      "GPA:  " + Gpa + "\n" +
                      "Undergrad. Deg.:   " + UndergraduateDegree + "\n" +
                      "Undergrad. Inst.:   " + UndergraduateInstitution);
  }
}
```

The GraduateStudent class's version of Print thus overrides, or supersedes, the version that would otherwise have been inherited from the Student class.

The preceding example is less than ideal because the first four lines of the Print method of GraduateStudent duplicate the code from the Student class's version of Print. You've probably started to sense that redundancy in an application is to be avoided because redundant code represents a maintenance nightmare: when we have to change code in one place in an application, we don't want to have to remember to change it in countless other places or, worse yet, forget to do so and wind up with inconsistency in our logic. We like to avoid code duplication and encourage code reuse in an application whenever possible, so our Print method for the GraduateStudent class would actually be written as follows:

```
public class GraduateStudent : Student
{
  // details omitted...

  public override void Print() {
    // Reuse code by calling the Print method defined by the Student
    // base class...
    base.Print();
```

```
    //...and then go on to print this derived class's specific fields.
    Console.WriteLine("Undergrad. Deg.:  " + UndergraduateDegree + "\n" +
                      "Undergrad. Inst.:  " + UndergraduateInstitution);
  }
}
```

We use a C# keyword, base, as the qualifier for the method name when we want to invoke a version of a method that was defined in a base class:

base.methodName(arguments);

Sometimes, in a complex inheritance hierarchy, we have occasion to override a method multiple times. In the hierarchy shown in Figure 5-6

- Root class A (Person) declares a method with the following header that prints out all of the fields declared for the Person class:

  public virtual void Print()

- Derived class B (Student) overrides this method, changing the internal logic of the method body to print not only the fields inherited from Person, but also those that were added by the Student class itself. The overridden method would have the following header:

  public override void Print()

- Derived class E (GraduateStudent) overrides this method again, to print not only the fields inherited from Student (which include those inherited from Person) but also those that were added by the GraduateStudent class itself. The GraduateStudent version of the Print method would also use the override keyword:

  public override void Print()

Note that, in all cases, the accessibility, return type, and method signature *must* remain the same—public void Print()—for overriding to take place.

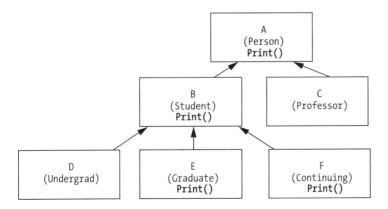

Figure 5-7. *A method may be overridden multiple times within a class hierarchy.*

- Under such circumstances, any class not specifically overriding a given method itself will inherit the definition of that method used by its most immediate ancestor.

Rules for Deriving Classes: The "Don'ts"

When deriving a new class, there are some things that we should *not* attempt to do. (And, as it turns out, OOPLs will actually prevent us from successfully compiling programs that attempt to do most of these things.)

Don't Change the Semantics of a Member

We shouldn't change the semantics—that is, the intention, or meaning—of a member. For example:

- If the Print method of a base class such as Student is intended to display the values of all of an object's fields on the computer screen, then the Print method of a derived class such as GraduateStudent shouldn't, for example, be overridden so that it directs all of its output to a file instead.

- If the name field of a base class such as Person is intended to store a person's name in "last name, first name" order, then the name field of a derived class such as Student should be used in the same fashion.

Don't Eliminate Members

We shouldn't try to effectively eliminate members inherited from base classes by ignoring them in derived classes. To attempt to do so would break the spirit of the "is a" hierarchy. By definition, inheritance requires that all members of all base classes of a class A must also apply to class A itself in order for A to truly be a proper base class. If a GraduateStudent could eliminate the degreeSought field that it inherits from Student, for example, is a GraduateStudent *really* a Student after all?

Don't Change the Type of a Property

A derived class can override a base class property, but the type of the property must remain the same as the base class version of that property. For example, if the Person class declared a Birthdate property of type string:

```
public class Person
{
  // Details omitted.

  // Base class introduces a property.
  public virtual string Birthdate {
    get {
      // details omitted.
    }
  }
}
```

then a Student class that derives from Person could *not*, in overriding the Birthdate property, change its type to, say, DateTime:

```
public class Student : Person
{
  // Details omitted.

  // Derived class overrides property, attempting to modify its type in the
  // process.
  public override DateTime Birthdate {  // this won't compile
    get {
      // details omitted.
    }
  }
}
```

If we tried to compile the Student class, the following compiler error would occur:

```
error:  'Student.Birthdate' type must be 'string' to match overridden
member 'Person.Birthdate'
```

Note It turns out that a derived class can change the type of a base class property by *hiding* the base class property. We'll discuss property and method hiding in Chapter 13.

Don't Attempt to Change a Method Header

For example, if the Print method inherited by the Student class from the Person class has the header public void Print(), where the method takes no arguments, then the Student class can't change this method to require an argument, say, public void Print(int noOfCopies). To do so is to create a different method entirely, due to another C# language feature known as *overloading*, discussed next.

Overloading

Overloading allows two or more *different* methods belonging to the *same* class to have the *same* name as long as they have *different* argument signatures (as defined in Chapter 4). An overloaded method is thus a different concept from an overridden method in which a derived class reimplements a method with the same header declared in a base class. As an example of overloaded methods, the Student class may legitimately define the following five different Print methods:

```
void Print(string fileName) -  a single parameter
void Print(int detailLevel) -  a different parameter type from above
void Print(int detailLevel, string fileName) -  two parameters
int Print(string reportTitle, int maxPages) -  different parameter types
bool Print()- no parameters
```

Hence the `Print` method is said to be overloaded. Note that all five of the signatures differ in terms of their argument signatures:

- The first takes a single `string` as an argument.

- The second takes a single `int`.

- The third takes two arguments: an `int` and a `string`.

- The fourth takes two arguments: a `string` and an `int` (although these are the same parameter types as in the previous signature, they are in a different order).

- The fifth takes no arguments at all.

So all five of these headers represent valid different methods, and all can coexist happily within the `Student` class without any complaints from the compiler! We can pick and choose among which of these five "flavors" of `Print` method we'd like a `Student` object to perform based on what form of method is invoked on the `Student` object:

```
Student s = new Student();

// Calling the version that takes a single string argument.
s.Print("output.rpt");

// Calling the version that takes a single int argument.
s.Print(2);

// Calling the version that takes two arguments, an int and a string.
s.Print(2, "output.rpt");

// etc.
```

The compiler is able to unambiguously match up which version of the `Print` method is being called in each instance based on the argument signatures.

This example hints at something significant; only the parameter types and their order matter when determining when a new method can be added because the *names* of the parameters and the *return type* of the method aren't evident in a method call. For example:

- We already know that we can't introduce the following additional method as a sixth method of `Student`:

  ```
  bool Print(int levelOfDetail)
  ```

  Its argument signature—a single `int`—duplicates the argument signature of an existing method despite the fact that both the return type (`bool` vs. `int`) and the parameter names are different in the two headers:

  ```
  int Print(int detailLevel)
  ```

- Let's suppose for a moment that we *could* introduce the bool Print(int levelOfDetail) header as a sixth "flavor" of the Print method for the Student class. If the compiler were to then see a method call in client code of the following form, it couldn't sort out which of these two methods were to be invoked because all we see in a method call like this is (a) the method name and (b) the argument type (an integer literal, in this case):

```
s.Print(3);
```

So, to make life simple, the compiler prevents this type of ambiguity from arising by preventing classes from declaring methods with identical signatures in the first place.

Constructors, which as we learned in Chapter 4 are a special type of function member used to initialize objects, are commonly overloaded. Here is an example of a class that provides several overloaded constructors:

```
public class Student
{
  private string name;
  private string id;
  private int age;
  // etc.

  // Constructor #1.
  public Student() {
    // Assign default values to selected fields, if desired.
    id = "?";
    // Those which aren't explicitly initialized in the constructor
    // will automatically assume
    // the zero-equivalent value for their respective type.
  }

  // Constructor #2.
  public Student(string s) {
    id = s;
  }

  // Constructor #3.
  public Student(string s, string n, int i) {
    id = s;
    name = n;
    age = i;
  }

  // etc. -- other methods omitted from this example
}
```

By providing different "flavors" of constructor, we made this class more flexible by giving client code a variety of constructors to choose from.

The ability to overload methods allows us to create an entire family of similarly named methods that do essentially the same job, but which accept different types of arguments. Think back to Chapter 1, where we introduced the Write method, which is used to display printed output to the console. As it turns out, there is not one, but *many* Write methods; each one accepts a different argument type (Write(int), Write(string), Write(double), and so on). Using a set of overloaded methods named Write is much simpler and neater than having to use differently named methods such as WriteString, WriteInt, WriteDouble, and so on.

Note that there is no such thing as "field overloading"; that is, if a class tries to declare two fields with the same name:

```
public class SomeClass
{
  private string foo;
  private int foo;
  // etc.
```

the compiler will generate an error message:

```
SomeClass.cs(5,15): error: The type 'SomeClass' already contains
a definition for 'foo'
```

A Few Words About Multiple Inheritance

So far, the inheritance hierarchies we looked at are known informally as "single inheritance" hierarchies because any particular class in the hierarchy may only have a single direct base class (immediate ancestor). In the hierarchy shown in Figure 5-8, for example, classes marked B, C, and I all have the single direct base class A; D, E, and F have the single direct base B; and G and H have the single direct base E.

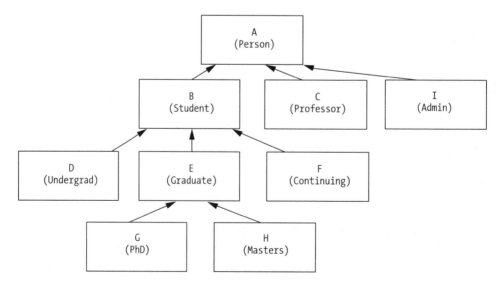

Figure 5-8. *A sample single inheritance hierarchy*

If we for some reason find ourselves needing to meld together the characteristics of two different base classes to create a hybrid third class, *multiple inheritance* may seem to be the answer. While not permitted in C#, multiple (as opposed to single) inheritance allows any given class in a class hierarchy to have two or more classes as immediate ancestors.

For example, we have a Professor class representing people who teach classes and a Student class representing people who take classes. What might we do if we have a professor who wants to enroll in a class via the SRS? Or, a student—most likely a graduate student—who has been asked to teach an undergraduate-level course? In order to accurately represent either of these two people as objects, we would need to be able to combine the members of the Professor class with those of the Student class: a hybrid ProfessorStudent. This might be portrayed in our class hierarchy, as shown in Figure 5-9.

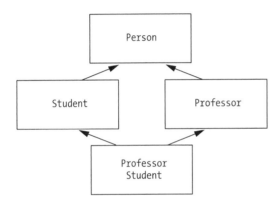

Figure 5-9. *Multiple inheritance permits a derived class to have multiple immediate ancestors.*

On the surface, this seems quite handy. However, there are many complications inherent with multiple inheritance; so many, in fact, that the C# language designers chose not to support multiple inheritance. Instead, they provided an alternative mechanism for handling the requirement of creating an object with a "split personality" (one that can behave like two or more different real-world entities). This mechanism involves the notion of *interfaces* and will be explored in detail in Chapter 7. Therefore, if you are primarily interested in object concepts only as they pertain to the C# language, you may wish to skip the rest of this section. If, on the other hand, you're curious as to why multiple inheritance is so tricky, then please read on.

Here's the problem with what we've done in the previous example. We learned that with inheritance a derived class automatically inherits the fields and methods of its base. What about when we have two or more direct base classes? If these base classes have no overlaps in terms of their field names or method signatures, we are fine. But what if the direct base classes in question

- Have methods with the same signature, but with different code body implementations?

- Have identical fields (name and type the same)?

- Have fields with identical names, but with *different* types?

Let's explore these situations with a simple example.

First, say that we created a trivially simple Person class that declares one field and one method, GetDescription, as shown here:

```
public class Person
{
  private string name;

  //  public Name property syntax not shown.

  public virtual string GetDescription() {
    return name;
    // e.g., "John Doe"
  }
}
```

Later on, we decide to specialize Person by creating two derived classes—Professor and Student—which each add a few fields as well as overriding the GetDescription method to take advantage of their newly added fields, as follows:

```
public class Student : Person
{
  // We add two fields.
  string major;
  int id;  // a unique Student ID number

  // Override this method as inherited from Person.
  public override string GetDescription() {
    return Name + " [" + major + "; " + id + "]";
    // e.g., "Mary Smith [Math; 10273]"
  }
}

public class Professor : Person
{
  // We add two fields; note that one has the same name, but a
  // different data type, as a field of Student.
  string title;
  string id;  // a unique Employee ID number

  // Override this method as inherited from Person.
  public override string GetDescription() {
    return Name + " [" + title + "; " + id + "]";
    // e.g., "Harry Henderson [Chairman; A723]"
  }
}
```

Note that both derived classes happen to have added a field named id, but that in the case of the Student class, it's declared to be of type int; and in Professor, of type string. Also, note that both classes have overridden the GetDescription method differently, to take advantage of each class's own unique fields.

At some future point in the evolution of this system, we determine the need to represent a single object as both a `Student` and a `Professor` simultaneously, and so we create the hybrid class `ProfessorStudent` as a derived class of both `Student` and `Professor`. We don't particularly want to add any fields or methods; we just want to meld together the characteristics of both base classes, so we'd ideally like to declare `ProfessorStudent` as follows:

```
// * * * Important Note:  this is not permitted in C#!!! * * *
class ProfessorStudent : Professor and Student
{
  // It's OK to leave a class body empty; the class itself is not
  // really 'empty', because it inherits the members of its
  // base classes.
}
```

But we encounter several roadblocks to doing so.

First, we have a field name clash. If we were to simple-mindedly inherit all the fields of both `Professor` and `Student`, we'll wind up with the items shown in Table 5-1.

Table 5-1. *Multiple Inheritance Introduces Many Ambiguities with Respect to Derived Class Members*

Field	Notes
`string name;`	Inherited from `Student`, this in turn inherited it from `Person`.
`string major;`	Inherited from `Student`.
`int id;`	Inherited from `Student`; this conflicts with the `string id` field inherited from `Professor` (the compiler won't allow both to coexist).
`string name;`	Inherited from `Professor`, which in turn inherited it from `Person`; a duplicate—the compiler won't allow this.
`string title;`	Inherited from `Professor`.
`string id;`	Inherited from `Professor`; this conflicts with the `int id` field inherited from `Student` (the compiler won't allow both to coexist).

Making a compiler intelligent enough to automatically resolve and eliminate true duplicates, such as the second copy of the `name` field wouldn't be too difficult a task, but what about `int id` vs. `string id`? There's no way for the compiler to know which one to eliminate; indeed, we really shouldn't eliminate either one because they represent different information items. Our only choice would be to go back to either the `Student` class or the `Professor` class (or both), and rename their respective id fields to be perhaps `studentId` and/or `employeeId` to make it clear that the fields represent different information items. Then `ProfessorStudent` could inherit both without any problems. If we don't have control over the source code for at least one of these base classes, however, we're in trouble.

Another problem we face is that the compiler will be confused as to which version of the `GetDescription` method we should inherit. Chances are that we'll want neither because neither one takes full advantage of the other class's fields; but even if we wanted to use one of the base class's versions of the method versus the other, we'd have to invent some way of informing the compiler which one we wanted to inherit, or else we'd be forced to override `GetDescription` in the `ProfessorStudent` class.

This is just a simple example, but it nonetheless illustrates why multiple inheritance can be so cumbersome to take advantage of in an OOPL.

Three Distinguishing Features of an Object-Oriented Programming Language, Revisited

In Chapter 3, we called out three key mechanisms that are required of a programming language in order to be considered truly object-oriented. We've now defined *two* of the three features required of a true OOPL:

- (Programmer creation of) User-defined types—discussed in Chapter 3

- Inheritance—discussed in this chapter

- Polymorphism

All that remains is to discuss *polymorphism*, one of the subjects of an upcoming chapter (Chapter 7, to be precise!). We're going to take a bit of a detour first, however, to discuss what we can do to gather up and organize groups of objects as we create them through the use of a special type of object called a *collection*.

Summary

In this chapter, you learned

- That an association describes a relationship between classes—that is, a potential relationship between objects of two particular types/classes.

- That we define the multiplicity of an association between classes X and Y in terms of how many objects of type X can be linked to a given object of type Y, and vice versa. Possible multiplicities are one-to-one (1:1), one-to-many (1:m), and many-to-many (m:m). In all these cases, the involvement of the objects at either end of the relationship may be optional or mandatory.

- That an aggregation is a special type of association that implies containment.

- How to derive new classes based on existing classes through inheritance and what the do's and don'ts are when deriving these new classes. Specifically, how we can extend a base class by adding members or specialize a base class by overriding methods.

- How class hierarchies develop over time, and what we can do to try to avoid "ripple effects" to our application as the class hierarchy changes with evolving requirements.

- How overloading can be used to create multiple methods with the same name but with different argument signatures.

- Why multiple inheritance can be so troublesome to implement in an OOPL.

Exercises

1. Go back to your solution for exercise No. 3 at the end of Chapter 2. For all the classes you suggested, list the pairwise associations that you might envision occurring between them.

2. If the class `FeatureFilm` were defined to have the following methods:

```
public void Update(Actor a, string title);
public void Update(Actor a, Actor b, string title);
public void Update(string topic, string title);
```

which of the following additional headers would be allowed by the compiler?

```
public bool Update(string category, string theater);
public bool Update(string title, Actor a);
public void Update(Actor b, Actor a, string title);
public void Update(Actor a, Actor b);
```

3. Given the following simplistic code, which illustrates overloading, overriding, and straight inheritance of methods, how many different `Fuel` method signatures would each of the four classes recognize?

```
class Vehicle
{
  string name;

  public virtual void Fuel(string fuelType) {
    // details omitted...
  }

  public virtual bool Fuel(string fuelType, int amount) {
    // details omitted...
  }
}


class Automobile : Vehicle
{
  public virtual void Fuel(string fuelType, string timeFueled) {
    // details omitted...
  }

  public override bool Fuel(string fuelType, int amount) {
    //...
  }
}
```

```
class Truck : Vehicle
{
  public override void Fuel(string fuelType) {
    //...
  }
}

class SportsCar : Automobile
{
  public override void Fuel(string fuelType) {
    //...
  }

  public override void Fuel(string fuelType, string timeFueled) {
    //...
  }
}

// Client code:

Truck t = new Truck();
SportsCar sc = new SportsCar();
```

4. Given the following simplistic classes:

```
class FarmAnimal
{
  string name;

  public virtual string Name {
    get {
      return name;
    }
    set {
      name = value;
    }
  }

  public virtual void MakeSound() {
    Console.WriteLine(Name + " makes a sound...");
  }
}

class Cow : FarmAnimal
{
  public override void MakeSound() {
    Console.WriteLine(Name + " goes Moooooo...");
  }
}
```

```
class Horse : FarmAnimal
{
  public override string Name {
    set {
      base.Name = value + " [a Horse]";
    }
  }
}
```

what would be printed by the following client code?

```
Cow c = new Cow();
Horse h = new Horse();
c.Name = "Elsie";
h.Name = "Mr. Ed";
c.MakeSound();
h.MakeSound();
```

CHAPTER 6

■ ■ ■

Collections of Objects

You learned about the process of creating objects based on class definitions, a process known as instantiation, in Chapter 3. When we're creating only a few objects or declaring a few value-type variables, it's fairly simple to declare individualized variables for these elements: Students s1, s2, s3, perhaps; or Professors profA, profB, profC. But, at other times, individualized variables are impractical.

- Sometimes, there will be too many objects or value types, as when creating Course objects to represent the hundreds of courses in a university's course catalog.

- Worse yet, we may not even *know* how many objects or values of a particular type there will be in advance. With our Student Registration System (SRS), for example, we can create a new Student object each time a new student logs on for the first time.

Fortunately, object-oriented programming languages (OOPLs) solve this problem by providing a special category of object called a *collection* that is used to hold and organize other objects or value types.

In this chapter, you'll learn about the following:

- Arrays as simple collections

- The properties and behaviors of some other common collection types

- How collections enable us to model very sophisticated real-world concepts or situations

- How we can use generic collection types as a type-safe collection

What Are Collections?

We'd like a way to gather up objects or value types as they are created so that they can be managed as a group and operated on collectively, along with referring to them individually when necessary. For example:

- A Professor object may wish to step through all Student objects registered for a particular Course that the professor is teaching in order to compute their grades.

- The SRS application as a whole may need to step through all the Course objects in the current schedule of classes to determine which of them don't yet have any students registered for them, possibly to cancel these courses.

We use a special type of object called a *collection* to group other objects or value types. A collection object can hold/contain multiple references to some other type of element. Think of a collection as an egg carton, and the objects or value types it holds as the eggs. There are different types of collections as well. Some collections store their elements as a list, whereas other types of collections store their elements as a set of key-value pairs.

The original C# collection classes stored their elements as type Object, and the "true nature" of an element extracted from such a collection could be obtained only by casting the extracted element back to its original type. More recent additions to the C# language are generic collections that are declared to hold a specific type of element. (Generic collections will be discussed in more detail later in this chapter as well as in Chapter 13.)

Because collections are implemented as objects, this implies three things:

- Collections must be instantiated before they can first be used.

- Collections are defined by classes that in turn define methods for "getting" and "adding to" their contents.

- By virtue of being objects, OO collections are encapsulated, and hence take full advantage of information hiding.

Let's discuss each of these three matters in turn.

Collections Must Be Instantiated Before They Can First Be Used

We can't merely declare a collection:

```
CollectionType c;
```

For example:

```
ArrayList c;
```

■**Note** ArrayList is one of C#'s predefined collection types, defined by the .NET Framework Class Library (FCL). We'll introduce the ArrayList class in this chapter and then will go into greater detail about several other collection types, in Chapter 13.

All this does is declare a reference variable of type *CollectionType*. We have to take the distinct step of using the new operator to actually create an empty *CollectionType* object in memory, as follows:

```
c = new CollectionType();
```

For example:

```
c = new ArrayList();
```

Think of the `CollectionType` object created in this manner as an *empty* egg carton, and the variable c as the reference that allows us to locate and access this egg carton whenever we want.

Then, as we instantiate objects ("eggs"), we place *their* references into the various egg carton compartments. So, instead of thinking of the objects as eggs placed inside the egg carton compartments, we should really think of the objects as balloons whose strings are tied inside the egg carton compartments, as illustrated in Figure 6-1.The balloons can be thought of as objects "holding in" data. The strings represent references to locations in memory.

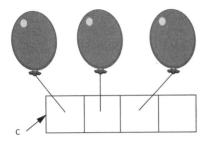

Figure 6-1. *A collection organizes object references.*

When a collection stores object references, the objects themselves live physically *outside* of the collection, but can be located through their references, which are stored *within* the collection. Thus, instead of an egg carton, a more appropriate analogy for a collection might be an address book: we make an entry in the address book (collection) for each of the persons (objects) that we want to contact, but the actual persons themselves are physically remote (see Figure 6-2).

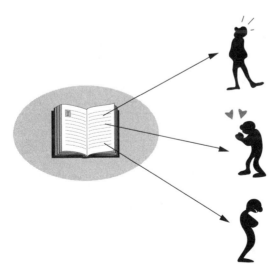

Figure 6-2. *A collection references objects, which live separately in memory.*

■**Note** C# collections can also hold the values of value-type variables (int, float, and so on) because in the C# language, value-type variables are actually implemented as objects. This is in contrast with Java, where simple data types (int, float, and so on) are *not* objects, and hence cannot be stored "as is" in Java collections.

Collections Are Defined by Classes

Here is a code snippet that illustrates the use of a collection in C#; we use a bit of pseudocode here to emphasize the common features of collections:

```
// Instantiate a collection object (pseudocode).
CollectionType collection = new CollectionType();
// Create a few Student objects.
Student a = new Student();
Student b = new Student();
Student c = new Student();

// Store all three students in the collection by calling the appropriate
// method for adding objects to the collection...
collection.Add(a);
collection.Add(b);
collection.Add(c);

//...and then retrieve the first one.
Student studentA = collection[0]; // element indices start at 0.
```

■**Note** Most C# collections declare an Item property that lets you get or set elements of the collection. The syntax collection[0]; looks like we're accessing the elements of an array, but we're really using the Item property.

OO Collections Are Encapsulated

We don't need to know the private details of how object references are stored internally to a specific type of collection to use the collection properly; we only need to know a collection's public members—in particular, its method headers and properties—to choose an appropriate collection type for a particular situation and to use it effectively.

■**Tip** This is a tiny bit misleading: in the case of *huge* collections, it *is* helpful to know a little bit about the inner workings of various collection types to be able to choose the one that is most efficient. We'll consider this matter further in Chapter 13.

Virtually all collections, regardless of type and regardless of the programming language in which they are implemented, provide, at a minimum, methods for the following:

- Adding elements to the collection

- Removing elements from the collection

- Retrieving specific individual collection elements

- Iterating through the collection elements in some predetermined order

- Getting a count of the number of elements stored in the collection

- Answering a true/false question about whether a particular element is referenced by the container or not

Arrays As Simple Collections

One simple type of collection that you may already be familiar with from your work with other programming languages is the *array*. We can think of an array as an egg carton that is sized appropriately for whatever data type the array as a whole is intended to hold. Arrays typically hold items of like type: for example, int(eger)s, or char(acter)s, Student objects, or Course objects, and so on.

Declaring and Instantiating Arrays

As is the case with all C# collections, arrays are objects. The Array class of the System namespace is the basis for all C# arrays. The official C# syntax for declaring that a variable x will serve as a reference to an array containing items of a particular data type is as follows:

```
datatype[] x;
```

For example, the following is to be read "int(eger) array x" (or, alternatively, "x is an array of ints"):

```
int[] x;
```

Because C# arrays are objects, they must be instantiated using the new operator; we also specify how many items the array is capable of holding; that is, its size in terms of its number of compartments, when we first instantiate the array. For example, the following code snippet declares an array named x that is sized to hold 20 Student object references:

```
// Here, we are instantiating an array object that will be used to
// store 20 Student object references, and are keeping a reference to
// the array object via reference variable x.
Student[] x = new Student[20];
```

This use of the new operator is unusual, in that we don't see a typical constructor call (with optional arguments being passed in via parentheses) following the new keyword, the way we do when we're constructing other types of objects. Despite its unconventional appearance, however, this line of code is indeed instantiating a new Array object, just the same.

Accessing Individual Array Elements

Individual array elements are accessed by appending square brackets enclosing the index of the element to be accessed at the end of the array name. This syntax is known as an *element access expression*. Note that when we refer to individual items in an array based on their position, or *index*, relative to the beginning of the array, we start counting at 0. (As it turns out, the vast majority of collection types in C# as well as in other languages are *zero-based*.) So, the items stored in array Student[] x in our previous example would be referenced as x[0], x[1], ..., x[19].

Consider the following code snippet:

```
int[] data = new int[3];
data[0] = 4; // setting an element's value
int temp = data[0]; // getting an element's value
```

In the first line of code, we're declaring and instantiating an int(eger) array of size 3. In the second line of code, we're assigning the int value 4 to the first element (index 0) of the array. In the last line of code, we're obtaining the value of the first element of the array and assigning it to an int variable named temp.

Initializing Array Contents

Values can be assigned to individual elements of an array using indexes as shown earlier, or we can initialize an array with a complete set of values when the array is first instantiated. In the latter case, initial values are provided as a comma-separated list enclosed in braces. This syntax replaces the normal right side of the array instantiation statement. For example, the following code creates and initializes a three-element string array:

```
string[] names = { "Lisa", "Jackson", "Zachary" };
```

Note that C# automatically counts the number of initial values that we're providing, and sizes the array appropriately. The preceding approach is much more concise than the equivalent alternative shown here:

```
string[] names = new string[3];
names[0] = "Lisa";
names[1] = "Jackson";
names[2] = "Zachary";
```

The result in both cases is the same, however: the zeroeth (first) element of the array will reference the string "Lisa", the next element will reference "Jackson", and so on.

Note that it isn't possible to "bulk load" an array in this fashion *after* the array has been instantiated, as a separate line of code; that is, the following won't work:

```
string[] names = new string[5];
// This next line won't compile.
names = {"Steve", "Jacquie", "Chloe", "Shylow", "Baby Grode" };
```

To fix the preceding example so it would compile, you could rewrite it as follows:

```
string[] names;
names = new string[] {"Steve", "Jacquie", "Chloe", "Shylow", "Baby Grode" };
```

If a set of comma-separated initial values aren't provided when an array is first instantiated, the elements of the array are automatically initialized to their zero-equivalent values. For example, `int[] data`, as declared earlier, would be initialized to contain 3 integer zeroes (0s), and a `double[]`array would be initialized to contain floating point zeroes (0.0s) . If we declare and instantiate an array intended to hold references to objects, as in the following, then we'd wind up with an Array object containing 100 null values (recall that `null`, a C# keyword, is the zero equivalent value for an object reference):

```
Student[] studentBody = new Student[100];
```

If we think of an array as a simple type of collection, and we in turn think of a collection as an egg carton, then we've just created an empty egg carton with 100 egg compartments sized to hold Student objects, but no eggs (objects).

Manipulating Arrays of Objects

To fill our Student array with values other than null, we'd have to individually store Student object references in each cell of the array. For example, if we wanted to create brand new Student objects to store in our array, we can write code as follows:

```
studentBody[0] = new Student();
studentBody[1] = new Student();
// etc.
```

Or alternatively:

```
Student s;
s = new Student("Zachary Palmer");
studentBody[0] = s;
// Reuse s!
s = new Student("Maria Lopez");
studentBody[1] = s;
```

In the latter example, note that we're recycling the same reference variable, s, to create many different Student objects. This works because we store a reference to the newly created object in an array compartment after each instantiation, thus allowing s to let go of its reference to that same object, as depicted in Figure 6-3. This technique is used frequently, with *all* collection types, in virtually all OOPLs.

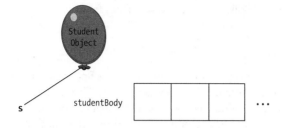

A Student object is created and handed to s ...

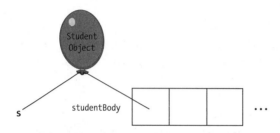

... s hands the object's handle off to the array ...

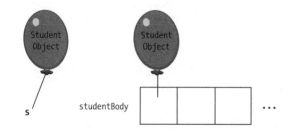

... thus freeing up s to take hold of another new Student!

Figure 6-3. *Handing new objects one by one into a collection.*

After we create an array to hold objects, as we did for the studentBody array, an element accessed using the element access expression is an object reference and methods can be called on it. For example, to call the GetName method on the first element in the studentBody array we could do the following:

```
studentBody[0].GetName();  // We're using dot notation to call a
                           // method on studentBody[0], the first
                           // Student object reference in the array.
```

The syntax of this statement might seem a bit peculiar at first, so let's study it a bit more carefully. Because studentBody is declared to be an array capable of holding Student object references, studentBody[n] represents the contents of the nth compartment of the array—namely, a reference to a Student object! So, the dot in the preceding statement is separating an expression representing an object reference from the method call being made on that object, and is no different than any of the other dot notation syntax that you've seen up until now.

By using a collection such as an array, we don't have to invent a different variable name for each Student object, which means we can step through them all quite easily using a for loop. Here is the syntax for doing so with an array:

```
// Step through all 100 compartments of the array.
for (int i = 0; i < 100; i++) {
  // Access the "ith" element of the array -- a Student object
  // (reference) -- so that we may print each student's name in turn;
  // in effect, we're printing a student roster.
  Console.WriteLine(studentBody[i].GetName());
}
```

■**Tip** You'll learn a more sophisticated way of stepping through collections in general, using the foreach statement, in Chapter 13.

Note that we have to take care when stepping through an array to avoid "land mines" because of empty compartments. That is, if we're executing the preceding for loop, but the array isn't completely filled with Student objects, our invocation of the GetName method would fail as soon as we hit the first empty/null compartment because in essence we'd be trying to talk to an object that wasn't there! If we modify our code by inserting an if test to guard against null values, however, we'd be okay:

```
// Step through all 100 compartments of the array.
for (int i = 0; i < 100; i++) {
  // Avoiding "land mines"!
  if ( studentBody[i] != null ) {
    Console.WriteLine(studentBody[i].GetName());
  }
}
```

■**Note** You'll learn in Chapter 13 that this type of failure—namely, attempting to talk to a nonexistent object, or *null reference*—results in an *exception* being thrown.

Other Array Considerations

Some other facts concerning C# arrays include the following:

- *Once the size of an array has been declared, its size can't be changed.* This can become an issue if we don't know what the size of an array should be at the time that we're declaring it. For this reason, arrays aren't always the best choice of collection type for a given application, as we'll discuss later in this chapter.

- *We can't mix and match incompatible data types in an array.* We're constrained to inserting values whose data type matches the type with which the array was first declared. For instance, we can't assign a string as an element of an integer array.

- *Type mixing is permitted if one type can be cast into another.* If we can cast some value of type A into type B, we can place elements of type A into an array declared to hold type B. For example, if we want to assign the value of a double variable to an element of a float array, we would cast the variable into a float and then assign it to the array element, as shown here:

```
float[] a = new float[10];
double d = 10.37;
a[0] = (float) d;   // note cast
```

Multidimensional Arrays

So far we've been discussing one-dimensional arrays. It's also possible to declare and use arrays of two or more dimensions. For the purposes of this discussion, two types of multidimensional arrays are included here: *rectangular* and *jagged*.

Rectangular Arrays

A rectangular array is one in which every row has the same number of columns:

3	2	37	8	4
7	4	9	0	3
1	11	99	13	5

This represents a three row by five column, two-dimensional rectangular integer array.

The syntax for declaring and instantiating a two-dimensional rectangular array is as follows:

```
ArrayType[,] arrayName = new ArrayType[numRows, numCols];
```

For example:

```
double[,] values = new double[3, 5];   // three rows of five columns each
```

We place one comma between the brackets on the left side to signal that the array will have two dimensions, and must then specify the size of each of the two dimensions, separated by a comma, on the right side. For a three-dimensional rectangular array, we would use two commas between the brackets on the left side and would specify the sizes of three dimensions on the right side (and so forth):

```
ArrayType[,,] arrayName = new ArrayType[dim1, dim2, dim3];
```

To access the elements of a multidimensional rectangular array, we use indexes, but now must specify an index for each dimension of the element to be accessed. For example, consider the following code snippet, in which we instantiate a two-dimensional array of type `double`:

```
double[,] data = new double[2, 3];
data[0, 1] = 23.4;  // insert value into the FIRST row, SECOND column

double temp = data[1, 2]; // retrieve value from the SECOND row, THIRD column
```

The array has two rows and three columns. In the second line of code, the element in the *first* row (index 0) and *second* column (index 1) of the array is assigned the value 23.4. In the third line, we're accessing the value of the element in the second row (index 1) and third column (index 2) of the array, and assigning that value to a `double` variable named `temp`.

The elements of a multidimensional rectangular array can be initialized at the time that the array is declared by placing the initial values in braces, with one set of braces for each dimension of the array. For example, the following syntax would create and initialize a two-row, three-column array of integer values:

```
int[,] data = { {7, 22, 3},
                {48, 5, 10} };
```

Jagged Arrays

A jagged array is one where each row can have a different number of entries:

14	3	85	2
100	11		
3	24	106	

This represents a three-row, two-dimensional jagged integer array.

The syntax for declaring a jagged multidimensional array is different from that of a rectangular array.

- A separate set of empty square brackets is provided in the declaration for every dimension in the array: for a two-dimensional jagged array, we use two sets of square brackets; for a three-dimensional jagged array, we use three; etc. For example, the following syntax would declare a two-dimensional jagged `string` array:

  ```
  string[][] names;  // note two sets of empty square brackets
  ```

- In the array instantiation statement, we specify only the size of the first dimension of such an array. For example, the following syntax would instantiate a two-dimensional jagged `string` array with three rows, allowing for a variable number of columns per row:

  ```
  string[][] names = new string[3][];
  ```

In effect, when we create a two-dimensional jagged array, we create an array of one-dimensional arrays of varying sizes, as illustrated in Figure 6-4.

A two-dimensional
jagged array ...

... can be thought of as an
array of one-dimensional
arrays.

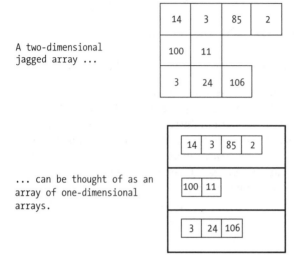

Figure 6-4. *A jagged two-dimensional array as an array of one-dimensional arrays*

The next step in the process is to initialize the length of each row in the array; for example:

```
names[0] = new string[4];  // first row has 4 columns (numbered 0...3)
names[1] = new string[2];  // second row has 2 columns (numbered 0...1)
names[2] = new string[3];  // third row has 3 columns (numbered 0...2)
```

To access the elements of a multidimensional jagged array, we use indexes with a separate set of brackets to specify each dimension. For example, to assign a value to the element in the second row and second column of the names array, we'd use the following syntax:

```
names[1][1] = "Mel";
```

It's possible to initialize the elements of a multidimensional jagged array when the array is first declared, but the syntax is a bit complicated. The elements of every one-dimensional array within the multidimensional array can be initialized by placing the initial values inside braces when the one-dimensional array is declared. The new keyword must be used and the array type must also be specified. For example, the following code creates and initializes a two-dimensional jagged integer array that has three columns in its first row and four columns in the second row:

```
int[][] data = new int[2][];
data[0] = new int[] { 17, 3, 24 };
data[1] = new int[] { 6, 37, 108, 99 };
```

More Sophisticated Collection Types

An OOPL typically offers many different types of collections for programmers, arrays being arguably the most primitive. There are several problems with using an array to hold a collection of objects:

- It's often hard for us to predict in advance the number of objects that a collection will need to hold. (For example, how many students will enroll this semester?) However, as mentioned earlier, arrays require that such a determination be made at the time they are first instantiated and, once sized, can't be expanded. So to use an array in such a situation, we'd have to make it big enough to handle the worst-case scenario, which isn't very efficient. On the other hand, when we do know how many items we're going to need to store—say, the abbreviated names of the 12 months in a year—an array might be a fine choice.

- We also talked earlier about the land mine issues inherent in arrays.

Fortunately, OOPLs provide a wide variety of collection types besides arrays for us to choose from, each of which has its own unique properties and advantages. Let's talk about the general properties of three basic collection types found in most OOPL:

- Ordered lists

- Sets

- Dictionaries

Then, in Chapter 13, we'll illustrate some specific C# implementations of these collection types. One thing to note is that all the more sophisticated collection classes from the C# FCL discussed in this book can be found in the System.Collections and System.Collections. Generic namespaces.

Ordered Lists

An ordered list is similar to an array, in that items can be placed in the collection in a particular order and later retrieved in that same order. Specific objects can also be retrieved based on their position in the list; for example, retrieve the second item. One advantage of an ordered list over an array, however, is that its size doesn't have to be specified when the collection object is first created; an ordered list will automatically grow in size as new items are added (see Figure 6-5). In fact, virtually all collections besides arrays have this advantage!

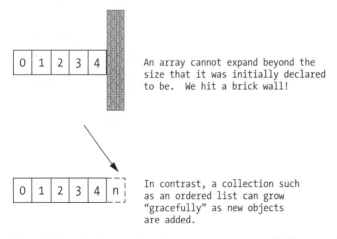

Figure 6-5. *Collections other than arrays grow gracefully as needed.*

When an item is removed from an ordered list, the "hole" that would have been left behind is automatically closed up, as shown in Figure 6-6. This behavior is actually true of most collection types other than arrays, and so we don't generally speaking encounter the land mine problem with non–array collections.

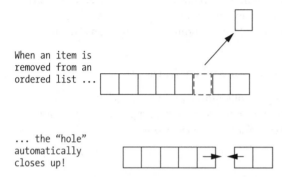

When an item is
removed from an
ordered list ...

... the "hole"
automatically
closes up!

Figure 6-6. *Collections other than arrays automatically shrink as items are removed.*

An example using an ordered list in building our SRS is when managing a wait list for a course that has become full. Because the order with which Student objects are added to the list is preserved, we can be fair about selecting students from the wait list in first-come, first-served fashion if seats later become available in the course.

The C# ArrayList and List classes are specific examples of an ordered list implementation.

Sorted Ordered Lists

A *sorted ordered list* is special type of ordered list. When we add an object to a sorted ordered list, the list automatically inserts the object at the appropriate location in the list to maintain sorted order, instead of automatically adding the new object at the end of the list as with a generic ordered list.

With a sorted ordered list, we have to define on what basis the objects will be sorted (that is, we must define a *sort key*). For example, we may wish to maintain a list of Course objects sorted by the value of each Course's courseNumber field for purposes of displaying the SRS course catalog.

Note that we could accomplish the same goal using a plain ordered list, but then the burden of keeping things sorted properly is on us, the programmers, instead of on the collection object! That is, we'd have to step through the (unsorted) list, comparing a newly added item's value to the value of each object already in the list until we found the correct insertion point to preserve sorted order.

The C# SortedList class is a specific example of a sorted ordered list implementation.

Sets

A set is an *unordered* collection, which means that there is no way to ask for a particular item by number once it has been inserted. Using a set is like throwing an assortment of differently colored marbles into a bag: we can reach into the bag to pull the marbles out one by one, but there is no predictability as to the order with which we pull them out. Similarly, with a set, we can step through the entire collection of objects one by one to perform some operation on them; we just can't guarantee in what order the objects will be processed. We can also perform tests to determine whether a given specific object has been previously added to a set or not, just as we can answer the question "Is the blue marble in the bag?" (See Figure 6-7.)

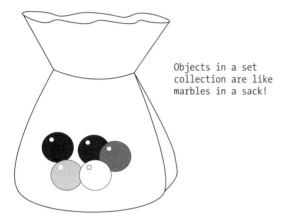

Objects in a set
collection are like
marbles in a sack!

Figure 6-7. *A set is an unordered collection.*

Note that duplicates aren't allowed in a set. If we were to create a set of Student object references, and a particular Student object reference was already placed in that set, the same Student object couldn't be referenced by the same set a second time—the set would reject it. This isn't true of collections in general: if we wanted to, we could add a reference to the same Student object to an ordered list; for example, multiple times (see Figure 6-8).

The same object may be
referenced in multiple
"compartments" within
a single collection ...

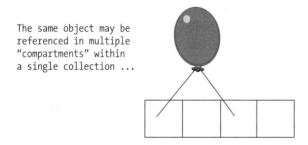

... UNLESS the collection is a set!

Figure 6-8. *Collections other than sets accommodate mutiple references to the same object.*

An example of using sets in building our SRS is to group students according to the academic departments that they are majoring in. Then, if a particular course—say, Biology 216—requires that a student be a Biology major in order to register, it would be a trivial matter to determine whether a particular student is a member of the Biology Department set or not.

Dictionaries

A *dictionary* provides a means for storing each object reference, along with a unique look-up key that can later be used to retrieve the object (see Figure 6-9). The key is typically contrived based on one or more of the object's field values. For example, in our SRS a Student object's ID number would make an excellent key because it's inherently unique for each student. Items in a dictionary can then be quickly retrieved based on this key. In some dictionary implementations, items can also be retrieved one by one in ascending key order.

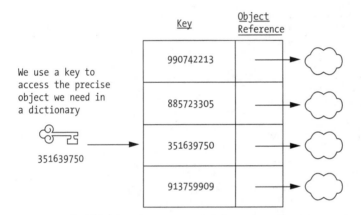

Figure 6-9. *Dictionary collections accommodate direct access by key.*

The SRS might use a dictionary, indexed on a unique combination of course number plus section number, to manage its course catalog. With so many courses to keep track of, being able to "pluck" the appropriate Course object from a collection directly (instead of having to step through an ordered list one by one to find it) adds greatly to the efficiency of the application.

The C# Hashtable and Dictionary classes are examples of a specific implementation of a dictionary.

Generic Collections

The original C# collection classes, such as the ArrayList and Hashtable classes, store all their elements as the most general type possible: Object. These collections make no attempt to keep track of what specific type (int, string, and so on) each element of the collection might be. Similarly, when elements are extracted from a collection, they are always returned as type Object. It is up to the programmer to cast the extracted element to its proper specific type. An example of such a casting operation is shown in the following code snippet:

```
ArrayList list = new ArrayList();
Student s1 = new Student("Frank");
Student s2 = new Student("Rameesh");

list.Add(s1);
list.Add(s2);

Student s3 = (Student)list[1];
Console.WriteLine("name = "+s3.Name);
```

If the cast to the Student were not performed:

```
Student s3 = list[1];
```

the code would not compile and the following error message would result:

```
error: Cannot implicitly convert type 'object' to 'Student'.
An explicit conversion exists (are you missing a cast?)
```

There are several drawbacks of collections storing their elements as type Object. For one thing, the type casting when elements are added or extracted to the collection decreases the performance of the code. It's also perfectly permissible to mix and match types that are added to a collection. For example, the following code will compile:

```
ArrayList list = new ArrayList();
list.Add("Elvis");
list.Add(3);
```

However, it is up to the programmer to remember that the first element of the ArrayList is of type string, and the second element is an integer.

Version 2.0 of the C# language introduced *generics*, which are general classes that can be assigned a specific data type. For example, the generic List collection class can be specified to contain only string objects. Generic collection classes eliminate the need for casting collection elements when they are added or extracted from the collection. Generic collections give better performance, and the compiler will perform type-checking to prevent elements of different types from being added to a generic collection.

When you declare a generic collection, you must specify a type parameter that specifies the type of elements the collection will hold. The general syntax for declaring a generic collection is as follows:

```
Collection_type<element_type> name = new Collection_type<element_type>();
```

For example, the following code declares a generic List collection, specifies that it will hold Student objects, adds some Student object references to the collection, and then extracts one of them:

```
List<Student> students = new List<Student>();
Student s1 = new Student("Frank");
Student s2 = new Student("Rameesh");
```

```
students.Add(s1);
students.Add(s2);

// The students List knows it stores Student objects, so no cast is required.
Student s3 = students[1];
Console.WriteLine("name = "+s3.Name);
```

The students List declared in the code snippet knows that it holds Student objects, so no cast is required when one of the collection elements is accessed. Suppose we try to add a non-Student object to the collection, as follows:

```
students.Add(2);
```

The code will not compile:

```
error: Argument '1': cannot convert from 'int' to 'Student'.
```

Generic classes combine powerful features of reusability, type safety, and efficiency. It is recommended that developers use generic collection classes, such as List whenever possible, instead of the older non–generic collection classes, such as ArrayList. You'll learn more about generics and specific generic collection classes in Chapter 13.

Referencing the Same Object Simultaneously from Multiple Collections

As we mentioned earlier, when we talk about inserting an object into a collection, what we really mean is that we're inserting a reference to the object, not the object itself. This implies that the same object can be referenced by multiple collections simultaneously. Think of a person as an object, and his or her telephone number as a reference for reaching that person. Now, as we proposed earlier in this chapter, think of an address book as a collection: it's easy to see that the same person's phone number (reference) can be recorded in many different address books (collections) simultaneously.

Now, for an example relevant to the SRS: given the students who are registered to attend a particular course, we may simultaneously maintain the following:

- A dictionary that allows us to retrieve a given Student object based on their name

- An ordered list of these students for purposes of knowing who registered first for a follow-on course

- Perhaps even a second SRS-wide dictionary that organizes *all* students at the university based on their student ID numbers

This is depicted conceptually in Figure 6-10. One of the consequences of different collections referring to a single object is that any changes made to the fields of the object will be reflected in all the collections that reference it. This feature is usually a good thing in that it prevents the programmer from having to update the object's fields in every list that contains it.

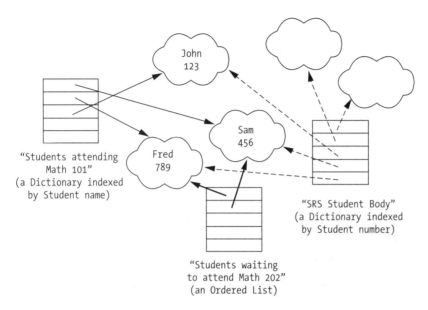

Figure 6-10. *A given object may be referenced by multiple collections simultaneously.*

Collections As Method Return Types

Collections provide a way to overcome the limitation that we noted in Chapter 4 about methods being able to return only a single result. If we define a method as having a return type that is a collection type, we can hand back an arbitrary-sized collection to the client code that invokes the method.

In the code snippet shown next for the Course class, we provide a GetRegisteredStudents method to enable client code to request an object reference to the entire collection of Student objects that are registered for a particular course:

```
public class Course
{
  private List<Student> enrolledStudents;

  // Other details omitted...

  // The following method returns a reference to an entire collection
  // containing however many students are registered for the course in question.
  public List<Student> GetRegisteredStudents() {
    return enrolledStudents;
  }
}
```

An example of how client code would then use such a method is as follows:

```
// Instantiate a course and several students.
Course c = new Course();
Student s1 = new Student();
Student s2 = new Student();
Student s3 = new Student();

// Enroll the students in the course.
c.Enroll(s1);
c.Enroll(s2);
c.Enroll(s3);

// Now, ask the course to give us a reference to the collection of
// all of its registered students...
List<Student> students = c.GetRegisteredStudents();

//...and iterate through the collection, printing out a grade report
// for each Student (pseudocode).
for (each Student in students) {
  s.PrintGradeReport();
}
```

Of course, if we return a direct reference to a collection such as enrolledStudents to client code, we are giving client code the capability to modify that collection (for example, removing a Student reference). Design considerations might warrant that we create a copy of the collection before returning it, so that the original collection is not modified:

```
public class Course
{
  private List<Student> enrolledStudents;

  // Other details omitted...

  // The following method returns a COPY of the Student's enrolledStudents
  // collection, so that client code cannot modify the OFFICIAL version.
  public List<Student> GetRegisteredStudents() {
    List<Student> temp = new List<Student>();

    // Pseudocode.
    copy contents of enrolledStudents to temp

    return temp;
  }
}
```

Collections of Supertypes

We said earlier that arrays, as simple collections, contain items (either simple types or objects) that are all of the same type: all int(egers), for example, or all (references to) Student objects. However, the power of inheritance can be used to make arrays more versatile in the types of objects that they can hold.

If we declare an array to hold objects of a given type (for example, Person), we're free to insert objects explicitly declared to be of type Person *or of any types derived from* Person (for example, UndergraduateStudent, GraduateStudent, and Professor). This is because of the "is a" nature of inheritance; UndergraduateStudent, GraduateStudent, and Professor objects, as sub-classes of Person, are simply special cases of Person objects. The C# compiler would therefore be perfectly happy to see the following code:

```
Person[] people = new Person[100];  // of Person object references

Professor p = new Professor();
UndergraduateStudent s1 = new UndergraduateStudent();
GraduateStudent s2 = new GraduateStudent();

// Add a mixture of professors and students in random order to the array.

people[0] = s1;
people[1] = p;
people[2] = s2;
// etc.
```

Objects of any type can be added to non–generic collections (excluding arrays), but this flexibility can lead to problems down the road. Generic collection classes automatically provide type-checking when elements are added, but this feature seemingly restricts them to store references of only a given type. Luckily, the power of inheritance can be used to make generic collections more versatile as well. For example, here is the preceding code snippet rewritten to use a generic List collection declared to hold Person references; then a variety of Professor, GraduateStudent, and UndergraduateStudent references are added to the List:

```
List<Person> people = new List<Person>();  // of Person object references

Professor p = new Professor();
UndergraduateStudent s1 = new UndergraduateStudent();
GraduateStudent s2 = new GraduateStudent();

// Add a mixture of professors and students in random order to the array.

people.add(s1);
people.add(p);
people.add(s2);
// etc.
```

Composite Classes, Revisited

You might recall that when we talked about the fields of the Student class back in Chapter 3, we held off on assigning types to a few of the items shown in Table 6-1.

Table 6-1. *Proposed Data Structure for the* Student *Class*

Field Name	Data Type
name	string
studentID	string
birthdate	System.DateTime
address	string
major	string
gpa	double
advisor	Professor
courseLoad	???
transcript	???

Armed with what we now know about collections, we can go back and assign types to the courseLoad and transcript fields.

courseLoad

The courseLoad field is meant to represent a list of all Course objects that the Student is presently enrolled in. So, it makes perfect sense that this field be declared to be simply a standard collection of Course objects!

```
public class Student
{
  private string name;
  private string studentId;
  // etc.
  private CollectionType courseLoad; // of Course objects

// etc.
```

transcript

The transcript field is a bit more challenging. What is a transcript in real-world terms? It's a report of all of the courses that students have taken since they were first admitted to this school, along with the semester in which each course was taken, the number of credit hours that each course was worth, and the letter grade received for the course. If we think of each entry in this list as an object, we can define them via a TranscriptEntry class, representing an abstraction of a single-line item on the transcript report, as follows:

```
public class TranscriptEntry
{
  // One TranscriptEntry represents a single line item on a transcript report.
```

```
private Course courseTaken;
private string semesterTaken;  // e.g., "Spring 2009"
private string gradeReceived;  // e.g., "B+"

// Details omitted ...

// Note how we "talk to" the courseTaken object via its methods
// to retrieve some of this information (delegation once again!).
public void PrintTranscriptEntry() {
  // Reminder:  \t is a tab character.
  Console.WriteLine(courseTaken.GetCourseNumber() + "\t" +
    courseTaken.GetTitle() + "\t" +
    courseTaken.GetCreditHours() + "\t" +
    gradeReceived);
}

// other methods TBD
}
```

Note that we're declaring one of the fields of TranscriptEntry to be of type Course, which means that each TranscriptEntry object will maintain a reference to its corresponding Course object. By doing this, the TranscriptEntry object can avail itself of the Course object's title, course number, or credit hour value (needed for computing the GPA)—all privately encapsulated in the Course object as fields—by calling the appropriate methods on that Course object as needed.

Back in the Student class, we can now define the Student's transcript field to be a collection of TranscriptEntry objects. We can then add a PrintTranscript method on the Student class, the code for which is highlighted here:

```
public class Student
{
  private string name;
  private string studentId;
  // etc.
  private CollectionType transcript; // of TranscriptEntry objects

  // Details omitted ...

  public void PrintTranscript() {
    // Pseudocode.
    for (each TranscriptEntry t in transcript) {
      t.PrintTranscriptEntry();
    }
  }
}
```

transcript, Take 2

Alternatively, we can use the technique of creating a wrapper class called `Transcript` to house some standard collection type:

```
public class Transcript
{
    private List<TranscriptEntry> transcriptEntries; // of TranscriptEntry objects
    // other fields omitted from this example

    // Pseudocode.
    public void AddTranscriptEntry(arglist) {
      insert new entry into List -- details omitted
    }

    // We've transferred the logic of the Student class's
    // PrintTranscript method into THIS class instead.
    public void Print(string filename) {
      // Pseudocode.
      for (each TranscriptEntry t in transcript) {
        t.PrintTranscriptEntry();
      }
    }

    // etc.
  }
```

We then can go back to the `Student` class and change our declaration of the `transcript` field from being a standard collection type to being of type `Transcript`:

```
public class Student
{
  private string name;
  private string studentId;
  // etc.
  private Transcript transcript;   // an ENCAPSULATED collection of
                                   // TranscriptEntry objects
  // etc.
```

We can then turn around and simplify the `PrintTranscript` method of the `Student` class accordingly:

```
public class Student
{
  // Details omitted.

  public void PrintTranscript() {
    // We now delegate the work to the Transcript field
    transcript.Print();
  }

  // etc.
```

This "take two" approach of introducing *two* new classes/abstractions—TranscriptEntry and Transcript—is a bit more sophisticated than the first approach, in which we introduced TranscriptEntry only as an abstraction. Also, this second approach is "truer" to the object paradigm, because the Student class needn't be complicated by the details of how Transcripts are represented or managed internally—those details are hidden inside of the Transcript class, as they should be.

Our Completed Student Data Structure

Table 6-2 illustrates how we've taken full advantage of collections to round out our Student class definition.

Table 6-2. *Rounding out the Student Class' Data Structure with Collections*

Field Name	Data Type
name	string
studentID	string
birthdate	System.DateTime
address	string
major	string
gpa	double
advisor	Professor
courseLoad	Standard type collection of Course objects
transcript	Either a standard type collection of TranscriptEntry objects or (preferred) Transcript

Summary

In this chapter, you learned the following:

- Collections are special types of objects used to gather up and manage references to other objects.

- An array is a simple, fixed-length collection type that stores elements of a single type.

- In addition to arrays, the .NET FCL provides other more powerful collection types to draw upon with OOPL, such as the following:

  - Ordered lists

  - Sets

  - Dictionaries

- Generic collection classes can be used to achieve reusability, type-safety, and efficiency when working with collections.

- We can work around the limitation that a method can only return one result by having that result be a collection of objects.

- Declaring a collection of supertypes can be used to make arrays and generic collections more versatile.

- We can create very sophisticated composite classes through the use of collections as fields.

Exercises

1. Given the following abstraction:

    A book is a collection of chapters, which are each collections of pages.

    sketch out the code for the Book, Chapter, and Page classes:

    - Invent whatever fields you think would be relevant, taking advantage of collections as fields where appropriate.

    - Include methods on the Chapter class for adding pages and for determining how many pages a chapter contains.

    - Include methods on the Book class for adding chapters, for determining how many chapters the book contains, for determining how many pages the book contains (hint: use delegation!), and for printing out a book's table of contents.

2. What general type(s) of collection(s)—ordered list, sorted ordered list, set, dictionary—might you use to represent each of the following abstractions? Explain your choices.

    - A computer parts catalog

    - A poker hand

    - Trouble calls logged by a technical help desk

3. What collections do you think it would be important to maintain for the SRS, based on the requirements presented in the introduction to this book?

4. What collections do you think it would be important to maintain for the problem area that you described for exercise 3 in Chapter 2?

CHAPTER 7

■■■

Polymorphism and Some Final Object Concepts

Earlier in this book, we introduced three key mechanisms that are required of an object-oriented programming language (OOPL). We already discussed how the C# language implements two of these concepts.
By way of review:

- We can create our own user-defined types, also known as classes, to model objects of arbitrary complexity, as we discussed in Chapter 3.

- We can arrange these types into class hierarchies to take advantage of the inheritance mechanism of OO languages, as we discussed in Chapter 5.

This chapter introduces the third essential OOPL feature, known as *polymorphism*, which simplifies code maintenance by allowing different objects belonging to different calls to respond to the same method call in different ways.

In addition to polymorphism, this chapter wraps up our initial discussions of OO concepts with a few "special topics"—things that you don't necessarily need to know when you're first setting out to use the technology, but are valuable to know as you become adept with the basics.

Some of the topics covered include the following:

- How programming constructs known as *abstract classes* and *interfaces* can be used to specify *what* an object's mission should be without going to the trouble of specifying the details of *how* the object is to carry out that mission, and also why we'd want to be able to do so

- How an object can have a "split personality" by exhibiting the behaviors of two or more different types of objects

- Creative ways for an entire class of objects to easily and efficiently share data without breaking the spirit of encapsulation

- How *static members* can be defined that are associated with a class instead of with an instance of a class

- How to define a constant whose value can't be changed once it's initially set

What Is Polymorphism?

Polymorphism refers to the capability of two or more objects belonging to different classes to respond to exactly the same method call in different class-specific ways.

As an example, suppose that we instruct three different people—a surgeon, a hair stylist, and an actor—to "cut":

- The surgeon would begin to make an incision.

- The hair stylist would begin to cut someone's hair.

- The actor would abruptly stop acting out the current scene, awaiting directorial guidance.

These three different professionals can be thought of as objects belonging to different professional classes. Each was given the same message—"cut"—but knew the specific details of what this message meant to him or her by virtue of knowing the profession (class) that he or she is associated with.

Turning to a software example relevant to the Student Registration System (SRS), assume that we' defined a Student base class and two derived classes named GraduateStudent and UndergraduateStudent.

In Chapter 5, we discussed the fact that a Print method intended to print the values of all of a Student's fields wouldn't necessarily suffice for printing the field values for a derived class such as GraduateStudent because the code as written for the Student class wouldn't know about any fields that may have been added to the derived class. The method call Print means something different to each Student-derived class, just as "cut" meant something different to the people in the previous example. We would therefore override the Print method of Student to create specialized versions of the method for all of its derived classes. The code for doing so, which was first introduced in Chapter 5, is repeated again here for you to review; we've added the UndergraduateStudent class code and have also made a few minor enhancements to the Print method for the other two classes:

```
// Student.cs

using System;

public class Student
{
  private string name;
  private string studentId;
  private string major;
  private double gpa;

  // Public properties also provided (details omitted)...

  public virtual void Print() {
    // We can only print the fields that the Student class
    // knows about.
    Console.Write("Student Name:  " + Name);
    Console.Write("  Student ID:  " + StudentId);
    Console.Write("  Major Field: " + Major);
```

```
      Console.WriteLine("  GPA:     " + Gpa
  }
}


// GraduateStudent.cs

using System;

public class GraduateStudent : Student
{
  // Adding several fields.
  private string undergraduateDegree;
  private String undergraduateInstitution;

  // Public properties also provided (details omitted)...

  // Overriding the Print method.
  public override void Print() {
    // Reuse code by performing the Print method of the
    // Student base class...
    base.Print();

    //...and then go on to print this derived class's specific fields.
    Console.Write("Undergrad. Deg.:  " + UndergraduateDegree);
    Console.Write("  Undergrad. Inst: " + UndergraduateInstitution);
    Console.WriteLine("  THIS IS A GRADUATE STUDENT");
  }
}


// UndergraduateStudent.cs

using System;

public class UndergraduateStudent : Student
{
  // Adding a field.
  private string highSchool;

  // Public property also provided (details omitted)...

  // Overriding the Print method.
  public override void Print() {
    // Reuse code from the Student base class...
    base.Print();
```

```
  //...and then go on to print this derived class's specific fields.
  Console.Write("High School Attended:  " + HighSchool);
  Console.WriteLine("THIS IS AN UNDERGRADUATE STUDENT...");
 }
}
```

In our main SRS application, we might declare an array called studentBody designed to hold references to Student objects. We then populate the array with Student object references—some graduate students and some undergraduate students, randomly mixed—as shown here:

```
// Declare and instantiate an array.
Student[] studentBody = new Student[4];

// Instantiate various types of Student object.
UndergraduateStudent u1 = new UndergraduateStudent();
UndergraduateStudent u2 = new UndergraduateStudent();
GraduateStudent g1 = new GraduateStudent();
GraduateStudent g2 = new GraduateStudent();
// etc.

// "Stuff" them into the array in random order.
studentBody[0] = u1;
studentBody[1] = g1;
studentBody[2] = g2;
studentBody[3] = u2;
// etc.
```

Because we're storing both GraduateStudent and UndergraduateStudent objects in this array, we declared the array to be of a base type common to all objects that the array is intended to contain, namely, Student. By virtue of the "is a" nature of inheritance, an UndergraduateStudent object *is a* Student, and a GraduateStudent object *is a* Student, so the compiler won't complain when we insert either type of object into the array.

Note The compiler would object, however, if we tried to insert a Professor object into the same array, because a Professor isn't a Student, at least not in terms of the class hierarchy that we've defined for the SRS. If we wanted to include Professors in our array along with various types of Students, we'd have to declare the array as holding a base type common to both the Student and Professor classes, namely, Person.

Perhaps we'd like to print the field values of all of the students in our studentBody array. We'd want each Student object—whether it is a graduate student or an undergraduate student—to use the version of the Print method appropriate for its class. The following code will accomplish this nicely:

```
// Step through the array (collection)...
```

```
for (int i = 0; i < studentBody.Length i++) {
  //...invoking the Print method of the ith student object.
  studentBody[i].Print();
  Console.WriteLine();
}
```

As we step through this collection of Student objects (assuming that their fields were assigned values), processing them one by one, each object will *automatically* know which version of the Print method it should execute, based on its own internal knowledge of its type/class (GraduateStudent versus UndergraduateStudent in this example). We'd wind up with a report similar to the following, in which the highlighted lines emphasize the differences in output between the GraduateStudent and UndergraduateStudent versions of the Print method:

```
Student Name:  John Smith
Student No.:  12345
Major Field:  Biology
GPA:  2.7
High School Attended:  Rocky Mountain High
THIS IS AN UNDERGRADUATE STUDENT...

Student Name:  Paula Prabhu
Student No.:  34567
Major Field:  Education
GPA:  3.6
Undergrad. Deg.:  B.S. English
Undergrad. Inst.:  UCLA
THIS IS A GRADUATE STUDENT...

Student Name:  Romeo Cardiz
Student No.:  98765
Major Field:  Computer Science
GPA:  4.0
Undergrad. Deg.:  B.S. Computer Engineering
Undergrad. Inst.:  Case Western Reserve University
THIS IS A GRADUATE STUDENT...

Student Name:  James Roberts
Student No.:  82640
Major Field:  Math
GPA:  3.1
High School Attended:  James Ford Rhodes High
THIS IS AN UNDERGRADUATE STUDENT...
```

The term *polymorphism* is defined in Merriam-Webster's dictionary as

"The quality or state of being able to assume different forms."

The following line of code is said to be *polymorphic* because the code performed in response to the method call can take many different forms, depending on the class identity of the object:

```
studentBody[i].Print();
```

Of course, this approach of iterating through a collection to ask objects one by one to each do something in its own class-specific way won't work unless all objects in the collection understand the message being sent. That is, all objects in the studentBody array must have defined a method with the signature: Print(). However, we've *guaranteed* that every object in the studentBody array *will* have such a method:

- First of all, we declared the array to hold objects of type Student (or derived classes thereof).

- Secondly, we provided the Student base class with a parameterless Print method. Had we not done so, the compiler would have objected to the following line of code because it would have checked the Student class for the presence of a Print method:

  ```
  studentBody[i].Print();
  ```

- Then, by virtue of inheritance, any derived class of Student is *guaranteed* to either inherit the Student version of the Print method or to optionally override it with one of its own. As you learned in Chapter 5, there is no way for a derived class to "uninherit" a method defined for any of its ancestor classes. The bottom line is that all objects declared to be of type Student are *guaranteed* to be Print savvy!

Reflecting for a moment, you can now see that you've previously learned everything that you need to know about C# objects to facilitate polymorphism—namely, inheritance plus overriding—before this discussion of polymorphism even began. *Inheritance combined with overriding makes polymorphism possible.*

Polymorphism Simplifies Code Maintenance

To appreciate the power of polymorphism, let's look at how we might have to approach this same challenge—handling different objects in different type-specific ways—with a programming language that doesn't support polymorphism.

In the absence of polymorphism, we'd typically handle scenarios having to do with a variety of different kinds of students using a series of if tests:

```
for (int i = 0; i < studentBody.Length; i++) {
  // Process the ith student.
  // Pseudocode.
  if (studentBody[i] is an undergraduate student)
    studentBody[i].PrintAsUndergraduateStudent();
  else if (studentBody[i] is a graduate student)
    studentBody[i].PrintAsGraduateStudent();
  else if...
}
```

As the number of cases grows, so too does the "spaghetti" nature of the resultant code! And, keep in mind that this sort of if test can occur in countless places throughout an application. Maintenance of such code quickly becomes a nightmare.

Let's now contrast this with our polymorphic iteration through the studentBody array:

```
// Step through the array (collection)...
for (int i = 0; i < studentBody.Length; i++) {
  //...invoking the Print method of the ith student object.
  studentBody[i].Print();
}
```

Because client code can be written to operate on a variety of objects without knowing specifically what *type* of object is involved, such client code is robust to change. For example, let's say that long after our SRS application has been coded and tested, we derive classes called MastersStudent and PhDStudent from GraduateStudent, each of which in turn overrides the Print method to provide its own "flavor" of printing, as shown in Figure 7-1.

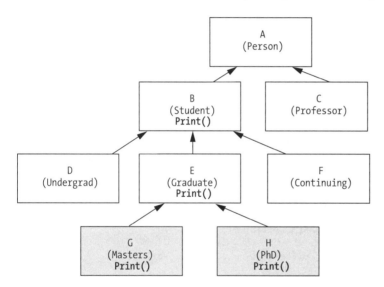

Figure 7-1. *Subsequent overriding of* Print *by newly derived classes*

We are now free to randomly insert MastersStudent and PhDStudent objects into the mix of GraduateStudents and UndergraduateStudents in the array, and our polymorphic array iteration code *doesn't have to change!*

```
// Declare and instantiate an array.
Student[] studentBody = new Student[4];
```

```
// Instantiate various types of Student object. We're now dealing with four
// different derived types.
UndergraduateStudent u1 = new UndergraduateStudent();
PhDStudent p1 = new PhDStudent();
GraduateStudent g1 = new GraduateStudent();
```

```
MastersStudent m1 = new MastersStudent();
// etc.

// Insert them into the array in random order.
studentBody[0] = u1;
studentBody[1] = p1;
studentBody[2] = g1;
studentBody[3] = m1;
// etc.

// Then, later in our application...

// This is the exact same code that we've seen before!
// Step through the array (collection)...
for (int i = 0; i < studentBody.Length; i++) {
  //...and invoke the Print method of the ith student object.
  // Because of the polymorphic nature of C#, this next line didn't
  // require any changes!
  studentBody[i].Print();
}
```

This is because the newly derived types (MastersStudent and PhDStudent) are, as extensions of Student, once again guaranteed to understand the same Print method call by virtue of inheritance plus optional overriding.

The story is quite different, however, with the nonpolymorphic example we crafted earlier. That version of client code would indeed have to change to accommodate these new student types; specifically, we'd have to hunt through our application to find every situation in which we're trying to sort out types of Student and complicate our if tests even further by adding additional cases as shown here, causing the "spaghetti piles" to grow ever taller:

```
for (int i = 0; i < studentBody.Length; i++) {
  // Process the ith student.
  // Pseudocode.
  if (studentBody[i] is an undergraduate student)
    studentBody[i].PrintAsUndergraduateStudent();
  else if (studentBody[i] is a masters student)
    studentBody[i].PrintAsMastersStudent();
  else if (studentBody[i] is a PhD student)
    studentBody[i].PrintAsPhDStudent();
  else if (studentBody[i] is a general graduate student)
    studentBody[i].PrintAsGraduateStudent();
  else if...
}
```

As we saw with encapsulation and information hiding earlier, polymorphism is another extremely powerful feature of OOPLs that can simplify method calls and minimize "ripple effects" on existing applications when requirements inevitably change after an application has been deployed.

Three Distinguishing Features of an OOPL

We now defined all three of the features required to make a language truly object-oriented:

- (Programmer creation of) User-defined types

- Inheritance

- Polymorphism

By way of review, here is a summary of the benefits of each of these language features.

Programmer creation of user-defined types

- Provides an intuitive way to represent real-world objects, resulting in *easier-to-verify requirements.*

- Classes are convenient units of reusable code, which means *less code to write when building an application.*

- Through encapsulation, we minimize data redundancy—each item of data is stored once, in the object to which it belongs—and therefore lessen the chance of data integrity errors.

- Through information hiding, we insulate our application against ripple effects if private details of a class must change after deployment, thereby *dramatically reducing maintenance costs.*

- Objects are responsible for ensuring the integrity of their own data, making it *easier to debug data integrity problems.*

Inheritance

- Can extend deployed code without having to change it, resulting in *dramatically reduced maintenance costs.*

- Derived classes are much more succinct, which means *less code overall to write/maintain.*

Polymorphism

- Causes virtually no "ripple effects" on client code when new subclasses are invented, resulting in *dramatically reduced maintenance costs.*

■**Note** A common misconception, held by many, is that switching from a non-OOPL to an OOPL will dramatically speed up the development time of a given application. Anecdotes abound of managers who have expected that a team utilizing OO approaches should be able to craft an application in a fraction of the time that it would have taken them to build its non-OO counterpart—despite the fact that team in question might be utilizing object-oriented techniques for the first time ever!

Unfortunately, because of the learning curve involved in switching to the OO paradigm—particularly for software developers who've been entrenched in non-OOPL techniques for many years—it actually can take *longer* for a team to build its first OO application.

Where economies of scale *do* come into play, however, is during the *maintenance stage* of an application's life cycle. The maintenance stage of an application—OO or otherwise—is typically much longer/more costly than the development stage. So by dramatically reducing ripple effects through the thoughtful use of encapsulation/information hiding and inheritance/overriding/polymorphism, we stand to reduce maintenance costs significantly.

Once we become adept with the OO paradigm, we should indeed be able to shorten application *development* time, as well, by virtue of the fact that we'll have less code to write overall through reuse via inheritance. And in transitioning from one project to the next, if we embrace the philosophy of code sharing and reuse across projects, we can gain significant productivity during the development stage of the life cycle.

Abstract Classes

You learned in Chapter 5 how useful it can be to consolidate shared features—fields and behaviors—of two or more classes into a common base class, a process known as *generalization*. We did this when we created the Person class as a generalization of Student and Professor and then moved the declarations of all their common fields methods and properties into this base class. By doing so, the Student- and Professor-derived classes both became simpler, and we eliminated a lot of redundancy that would otherwise have made maintenance of the SRS much more cumbersome.

The preceding example involved a situation in which the need for generalization arose after the fact; now let's look at this problem from another perspective. Suppose that we have the foresight at the very outset of our project that we'll need various types of Course objects in our SRS: lecture courses, lab courses, independent study courses, and so on. We therefore want to start out on the right foot by designing a Course base class to be as versatile as possible to facilitate *future* specialization.

We might determine up front that all Courses, regardless of type, are going to need to share a few common methods:

- EstablishCourseSchedule

- EnrollStudent

- AssignInstructor

We also need a few common fields:

- `string courseName;`

- `string courseNumber;`

- `int creditValue;`

- `CollectionType enrolledStudents;`

- `Professor instructor;`

Some of these behaviors might be generic enough so that we can afford to program them in detail for the Course class, knowing that it's a pretty safe bet that any future derived classes of Course will inherit these methods as is, without needing to override them; for example:

```
public class Course
{
  private string courseName;
  private string courseNumber;
  private int creditValue;
  // Pseudocode.
  private Collection enrolledStudents;
  private Professor instructor;

  // Properties provided; details omitted...

  public bool EnrollStudent(Student s) {
    // Pseudocode.
    if (we haven't exceeded the maximum allowed enrollment yet)
      enrolledStudents.Add(s);
  }

  public void AssignInstructor(Professor p) {
    Instructor = p;
  }
}
```

However, other behaviors (for example, EstablishCourseSchedule) might be too specialized for a given derived type to enable us to come up with a useful generic version. For example, the business rules governing how to schedule class meetings might differ for different types of courses:

- A lecture course may only meet once a week for 3 hours at a time.

- A lab course may meet twice a week for 2 hours each time.

- An independent study course may meet on a custom schedule that has been jointly negotiated by a given student and professor.

It would therefore seem to be a waste of time for us to bother trying to program a general-purpose version of the EstablishCourseSchedule method for the Course class because one size simply can't fit all in this situation; all three types would have to override such logic to make it meaningful for them.

Can we just omit the EstablishCourseSchedule method from the Course class entirely, adding such a method to each of the derived classes of Course as a new member instead? Part of our decision has to do with whether we ever plan to instantiate "general" Course objects in our application.

- If we do, the Course class would need an EstablishCourseSchedule method of its own.

- Even if we don't plan to instantiate the Course class directly, however, we still need to define an EstablishCourseSchedule method at the Course class level if we want to enable polymorphic behavior for this method.

Let's assume that we *don't* want to instantiate general Course objects, but *do* want to take advantage of polymorphism. We're faced with a dilemma! We know that we'll need a type-specific EstablishCourseSchedule method to be programmed for all derived classes of Course, but we don't want to go to the trouble of programming code in the parent class that will never serve a useful purpose. How do we communicate the requirement for such a behavior in all derived classes of Course and, more importantly, enforce its future implementation?

OOPLs such as C# come to the rescue with the concept of *abstract classes*. An abstract class is used to specify the required behaviors of a class *without* having to provide an explicit implementation of each and every such behavior. We program an abstract class in much the same way that we program a nonabstract class (also known informally as a *concrete class*), with one exception: for those behaviors for which we can't (or care not to) devise a generic implementation (for example, the EstablishCourseSchedule method in the preceding example), we're permitted to specify method *headers* without having to program the corresponding method *bodies*. We refer to a "bodiless," or header-only, method specification as an *abstract method*.

Let's go back to our Course class definition to add an abstract method, as highlighted in the following code:

```
// Note the use of the "abstract" keyword
public abstract class Course
{
  private string courseName;
  private string courseNumber;
  private int creditValue;
  private List<Student> enrolledStudents;
  private Professor instructor;

  // Other details omitted.

  public bool EnrollStudent(Student s) {
    // Pseudocode.
    if (we haven't exceeded the maximum allowed enrollment yet) {
      enrolledStudents.Add(s);
    }
  }
}
```

```
  public void AssignInstructor(Professor p) {
    Instructor = p;
  }

  // Note the use of the "abstract" keyword and the terminating semicolon.
  public abstract void EstablishCourseSchedule (DateTime startDate,
                                                DateTime endDate);
}
```

The EstablishCourseSchedule method is declared to be abstract by adding the abstract keyword to its header. Note that the header of an abstract method has no braces following the closing parenthesis of the parameter list. Instead, the header is followed by a semicolon (;)—that is, it's missing its code body, which normally contains the detailed logic of how the method is to be performed. The method must therefore be explicitly labeled as abstract to notify the compiler that we didn't accidentally forget to program this method, but instead we knew what we were doing when we intentionally omitted the body.

By specifying an abstract method, we accomplished several very important goals:

- We specified a capability that objects of various Course types must be able to perform.

- We detailed the means by which we'll ask such objects to perform this operation by defining a method header, which (as you learned in Chapter 4) controls the format of the method call that we'll pass to such objects when we want them to perform the operation.

- Furthermore, we facilitated polymorphism—at least with respect to the method in question—by ensuring that all derived classes of Course will indeed recognize a method call involving this method signature.

However, we've done so without pinning down the private details of how the method will accomplish this task (that is, the business rules that apply for a given derived class). In essence, we specified *what* a Course type object needs to be able to do without constraining *how* it must be done. This gives each derived type of Course—LectureCourse, LabCourse, IndependentStudyCourse—the freedom to define the inner workings of the method to reflect the business rules specific to that particular derived type by overriding the abstract method with a concrete version.

Whenever a class contains one or more abstract methods, the class as a whole must be designated to be an abstract class through inclusion of the abstract keyword in the class declaration:

```
public abstract class Course
{
  // details omitted
}
```

Note that it isn't necessary for all methods in an abstract class to be abstract; an abstract class can (and almost always does) contain methods that have a body, known as *concrete methods*. Abstract classes also typically declare fields, as shown in the preceding Course class example. These fields could be available to all derived classes of the abstract class.

Abstract Classes and Instantiation

There is one caveat with respect to abstract classes: *they can't be instantiated*. That is, if we define Course to be an abstract class in the SRS, we can't ever instantiate Course objects in our application. This makes intuitive sense because if we *could* create an object of type Course, it would then be expected to know how to respond to a method call to establish a course schedule (because the Course class declares a method header for the EstablishCourseSchedule behavior). But because there is no code behind that method, the Course object in question wouldn't know *how* to behave in response to such a method call.

The compiler comes to our assistance by preventing us from even writing code to instantiate an abstract class in the first place; suppose that we were to try to compile the following code snippet:

```
Course c = new Course();  // Impossible!  The compiler will generate
                          // an error on this line of code.
// details omitted...

c.EstablishCourseSchedule(dateTimeStart, dateTimeEnd);  // Behavior undefined!
```

We'd get the following compilation error on the first line of code:

```
error: cannot create an instance of the abstract class or interface 'Course'
```

While we're indeed prevented from instantiating an abstract class, we're nonetheless permitted to *declare reference variables* to be of an abstract type:

```
Course x;  // This is OK.
```

Why would we ever want to declare reference variables of type Course if we can't instantiate objects of type Course? The answer has to do with facilitating polymorphism; you'll learn the importance of being able to define reference variables of an abstract type when we talk about iterating through generic C# collections in more depth in Chapter 13.

Overriding Abstract Methods

When we derive a class from an abstract base class, the derived class will inherit all the base class's members, including all its abstract method headers. The derived class may replace an inherited abstract method with a concrete version using the override keyword, as illustrated in the following code:

```
// The abstract base class.
public abstract class Course
{
  private string courseName;
  // etc.

  // Other details omitted.

  public abstract void EstablishCourseSchedule (DateTime startDate,
                                                 DateTime endDate);
}
```

```
// Deriving a class from an abstract base class.
public class LectureCourse : Course
{
  // Details omitted.

  // Replace the abstract method with a concrete method.
  public override void EstablishCourseSchedule(DateTime startDate,
DateTime endDate) {
    // Logic specific to the business rules for a LectureCourse...
    // details omitted.
  }
}
```

We used the override keyword in similar fashion in Chapter 5, when it was used to override a virtual method declared in a base class. Note that in the preceding example, we've dropped the abstract keyword off of the overridden EstablishCourseSchedule method in the LectureCourse derived class because the method is no longer abstract; we provided a concrete method body.

Unless a derived class provides a concrete implementation for *all* the abstract methods that it inherits from an abstract base class, the derived class will automatically be rendered abstract, as well. In such a situation, the derived class, of course, can't be instantiated, either. Therefore, somewhere in the derivation hierarchy, a class derived from an abstract class must have concrete implementations for all its ancestors' abstract methods if it wants to "break the spell of abstractness" (that is, if we want to instantiate objects of that derived type—see Figure 7-2).

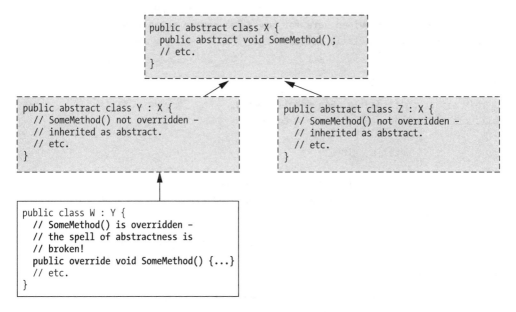

Figure 7-2. *"Breaking the spell" of abstractness by overriding abstract methods*

Breaking the Spell of Abstractness

Let's look at a detailed example. Having intentionally designed Course as an abstract class ear-lier to serve as a common template for all the various course types we envision needing for the SRS, we later decide to derive classes LectureCourse, LabCourse, and IndependentStudyCourse. In the following code snippet, we show these three derived classes of Course; of these, only two—LectureCourse and LabCourse—provide implementations for the abstract Establish-CourseSchedule method, and so the third derived class—IndependentStudyCourse—remains abstract and can't be instantiated.

```
public class LectureCourse : Course
{
  // Other class details omitted.

  public override void EstablishCourseSchedule (DateTime startDate,
                                                DateTime endDate) {
    // Logic would be provided here for how a lecture course
    // establishes a course schedule; details omitted...
  }
}

public class LabCourse : Course
{
  // Other class details ommitted.

  public override void EstablishCourseSchedule (DateTime startDate,
                                                DateTime endDate) {
    // Logic would be provided here for how a lab course establishes a
    // course schedule; details omitted...
  }
}

//  This class won't compile. See details below…
public class IndependentStudyCourse : Course
{
  // Other class details ommitted.

  // We are purposely choosing NOT to implement the
  // EstablishCourseSchedule method in this derived class.
}
```

If we were to try to compile the preceding code, the C# compiler would force us to flag the IndependentStudyCourse class with the abstract keyword; that is, we'd get the following com-pilation error:

```
error:  'IndependentStudyCourse' does not implement inherited
abstract member 'Course.EstablishCourseSchedule(DateTime, DateTime)'
```

Unless we go back and amend the IndependentStudyCourse class declaration to reflect it as being abstract:

```
public abstract class IndependentStudyCourse : Course
{
  // details omitted...
}
```

We just hit upon how abstract methods serve to enforce implementation requirements! Declaring an abstract method in a base class ultimately *constrains* all derived classes to provide type-specific implementations of all inherited abstract methods; otherwise, the derived classes themselves can't be instantiated.

Note that having allowed IndependentStudyCourse to remain an abstract class isn't necessarily a mistake; the only error was subsequently trying to instantiate it. We may plan on deriving another "generation" of classes from IndependentStudyCourse—perhaps IndependentStudyGraduateCourse and IndependentStudyUndergraduateCourse—making *them* concrete in lieu of making IndependentStudyCourse concrete. It's perfectly acceptable to have multiple layers of abstract classes in an inheritance hierarchy; we simply need a terminal/leaf class to be concrete in order for it to be useful in creating objects.

In addition to abstract methods, properties can also be declared to be abstract. This feature can be useful if you want all derived classes to provide their own implementation of computing a property value (a student's GPA, for instance). When an abstract property is declared, only the get and set keywords are included in the declaration without any bodies to the get and set accessors.

```
public abstract string Gpa { get; set; }
```

Interfaces

Recall that a class, as a type, is an abstraction of a real-world object from which some of the unessential details have been omitted. We can therefore see that an abstract class is more of an abstraction than a concrete class because with an abstract class we omitted the details for how one or more particular behaviors are to be performed.

Now, let's take the notion of abstractness one step further. With an abstract class, we can avoid programming the bodies of methods that are declared to be abstract. But what about the *fields* declared in an abstract a class? In our Course example, we went ahead and prescribed the data structure (fields) that we thought would be needed generally by all types of courses:

```
private string courseName;
private string courseNumber;
private int creditValue;
private Collection enrolledStudents;
private Professor instructor;
```

But, what if we only wanted to specify common *behaviors*, and not even bother with declaring *fields*? Fields are, after all, typically declared to be private; we simply might not want to mandate what data structure a future derived class must use in order to achieve the desired public behaviors, instead leaving it up to the designer of that class to ultimately decide.

Say, for example, that we want to define what it means to teach at a university. Perhaps, in order to teach, an object would need to be able to perform the following actions:

- Agree to teach a particular course.

- Designate a textbook to be used for the course.

- Define a syllabus for the course.

- Approve the enrollment of a particular student in the course.

Each of these behaviors could be formalized by specifying a method header, representing how an object that is *capable of teaching* would be asked to perform each behavior:

```
public bool AgreeToTeach(Course c)
public TextBook DesignateTextbook(Course c)
public Syllabus DefineSyllabus(Course c)
public bool ApproveEnrollment(Student s, Course c)
```

A set of method headers such as these, which collectively define what it means to assume a certain *role* within an application (such as teaching) is known as an *interface*. Interfaces, like classes, are given names; so, let's call this the ITeacher interface. (The .NET Framework convention is for interface names to use the Pascal capitalization style; names are prefixed with the letter I to indicate that the type is an interface versus a class.)

To declare an interface, we enclose the method headers that we defined for the interface, each ending with a semicolon (;), in a set of braces, with the keywords public interface and the name of the interface preceding the opening brace, as illustrated here:

```
public interface ITeacher {
    bool AgreeToTeach(Course c);
    TextBook DesignateTextbook(Course c);
    Syllabus DefineSyllabus(Course c);
    bool ApproveEnrollment(Student s, Course c);
}
```

An interface can be given public or internal access, but is typically either declared to be public or given no access modifier at all. An interface given private access won't compile. As with classes, each public interface typically goes into its own source code file, whose name matches the name of the interface contained within (for example, the ITeacher interface would go into a file named ITeacher.cs).

All of an interface's method headers are implicitly public and abstract, so we needn't specify either of those two keywords when declaring them; in fact, if we *were* to explicitly try to assign public access to an interface method header, as follows:

```
public interface ITeacher {
    public bool AgreeToTeach(Course c);
    // etc.
```

the compiler would generate an error:

```
error: the modifier 'public' is not valid for this item
```

A similar compiler error is generated if the `abstract` keyword is applied to an interface method header by mistake.

Implementing an Interface

After we defined an interface such as `ITeacher`, we can set about designating various classes as being teachers—for example, `Professors`, or `Students`, or general `Person` objects—simply by declaring that the class of interest *implements* the `ITeacher` interface using the syntax shown here:

```
// Implementing an interface...
public class Professor : ITeacher
{
  // details omitted...
}
```

Note that the syntax for declaring that a class is implementing an interface is the same as the syntax that indicates inheritance—a colon followed by the interface/base class name:

```
// Extending a class via inheritance...
public class Professor : Person
{
  // details omitted...
}
```

■Note The only way to differentiate an interface (`ITeacher`) from a class (`Person`) when inspecting the derived/implementing class's code (`Professor`) is the fact that an interface name typically begins with an I, followed by another capital letter; for example, `IFoo` or `IBar` would be interfaces, whereas `IceCream` or `Igloo` would be class names. However, if a class inherits from a base class and implements one or more interfaces, the base class must appear first after the colon, followed by the interfaces.

After a class declares that it is implementing an interface, as follows, the implementing class *must* provide concrete versions of *all* the (implicitly abstract) methods declared by the interface in question in order to satisfy the compiler:

```
public class Professor : ITeacher {...
```

As an example, let's say that we were to code the `Professor` class, as shown in the following code, implementing three of the four methods called for by the `ITeacher` interface but neglecting to code the fourth method:

```
//  Note: This class won't compile.
public class Professor : ITeacher
{
  private string name;
  private string employeeId;
  // etc.
```

```
// Properties defined; details omitted.

// We implement three of the four methods called for by the
// ITeacher interface, to provide method bodies.

public bool AgreeToTeach(Course c) {
  // Logic for the method body goes here; details omitted.
}

public void DesignateTextbook(TextBook b, Course c) {
  // Logic for the method body goes here; details omitted.
}

public Syllabus DefineSyllabus(Course c) {
  // Logic for the method body goes here; details omitted.
}

// Note that we've failed to provide an implementation of the
// ApproveEnrollment method...
}
```

If we were to try to compile this class as shown previously, we'd get the following compiler error:

```
error: 'Professor' does not implement interface
member 'ITeacher.ApproveEnrollment(Student, Course)'
```

Another Form of "Is A" Relationship

You learned in Chapter 5 that inheritance is thought of as the "is a" relationship. As it turns out, implementing an interface is another form of an "is a" relationship:

- If the Professor class *extends* the Person *class*, a professor *is a* person.

- If the Professor class *implements* the ITeacher *interface*, a professor *is a* teacher.

Also, when a class A implements an interface X, all the classes that are derived from A can also be said to implement that same interface. For example, if we derive a class called AdjunctProfessor from Professor, then if Professor implements the ITeacher interface, an adjunct professor is a teacher.

```
public class Professor : ITeacher
{
  // All methods required by ITeacher will be implemented by this class...
  // details omitted.
}

public class AdjunctProfessor : Professor
{
```

```
// All methods required by ITeacher will be, at a minimum, inherited
// from Professor...details omitted.
}
```

This makes intuitive sense because AdjunctProfessor will either inherit all the methods called for by the ITeacher interface from Professor or will override them; but, either way, an AdjunctProfessor will be "equipped" to perform all the operations required of an (I)Teacher.

Abstract Classes versus Interfaces

Implementing an interface is conceptually similar to having to "flesh out" abstract methods when extending an abstract class. What are the differences, then, between implementing an interface versus extending an abstract class? Why might we want to use one approach over the other when designing an application?

- With an interface, we specify abstract behaviors only, whereas an abstract class often specifies a "concrete" data structure (fields) as well as a mixture of abstract and concrete behaviors. So, in terms of the "abstractness spectrum," an interface is more abstract than an abstract class (which is in turn more abstract than a concrete class) because an interface leaves even more details to the imagination.

■**Note** An abstract class can be merely a set of abstract method headers if we want to design it as such. For example:

```
public abstract class Person

{
  // We are purposely declaring NO FIELDS for this class...

  //...and ALL of our methods are abstract.
  public abstract void Print();
  public abstract double ComputeSalary();
  // etc.
}
```

However, in such a situation, the preferred approach would be to simply declare an interface instead.

- When a nonabstract class is derived from an abstract class, the derived class provides a concrete implementation of abstract methods declared in the abstract class by overriding them. The derived class method headers therefore must include the override keyword.

- When a class implements an interface, the implementing class must once again provide a concrete implementation of all the methods declared in the interface. However, the implementing class doesn't override them. Instead, we're defining the methods for the first time from scratch, so the override keyword is not included in the implementing class method headers. (If we were to try to apply the override keyword, the compiler would inform us that it has "found no suitable method to override.")

- The syntactical differences in these two approaches are compared side-by-side here:

Example Using an Abstract Class	Example Using an Interface
Declaring the Teacher Type as an Abstract Class:	Declaring the Teacher Type as an Interface:

```
public abstract class Teacher
{
  // Abstract classes may declare
  // fields.
  private string name;
  private string employed;
  // etc.

  // We declare abstract methods using
  // the "abstract" keyword.
  public abstract void AgreeToTeach(
    Course c);
  public abstract void DesignateTextbook(
    TextBook b, Course c);

  // etc.

  // Abstract classes may declare concrete
  // methods.
  public void Print() {
    Console.WriteLine(name);
    // etc.
  }
}
```

```
public interface ITeacher
{
  // Interfaces cannot declare
  // fields.

  // We can't use the "public" or
  // "abstract" keywords.
  void AgreeToTeach(Course c);

  void DesignateTextbook(
    TextBook b, Course c);

  // etc.

  // Interfaces cannot declare concrete
  // methods.
}
```

Deriving Professor from Teacher:	Professor Implements ITeacher:

`public class Professor : Teacher`
`{`
  `// Professor inherits fields, if any,`
  `// from parent class, and optionally`
  `// adds additional fields; details`
  `// omitted.`
 	
  `// We override abstract methods inherited`
  `// from the Teacher class.`
 	
  `public override void AgreeToTeach(`
    `Course c) {`
    `// Logic for the method body goes here;`
    `// details omitted.`
  `}`
 	
  `// etc. for other abstract methods.`
 	
  `// Additional methods may be added;`
  `// details omitted.`
`}`
	`public class Professor : ITeacher`
	`{`
	  `// Class must provide its own data`
	  `// structure, as an interface`
	  `// cannot provide any.`
	  `private string name;`
	  `private string employeeid;`
	  `// etc.`
	
	  `// We implement the methods from the`
	  `// ITeacher interface without using`
	  `// the override keyword.`
	
	  `public void AgreeToTeach(Course c) {`
	    `// Logic for the method body goes here;`
	    `// details omitted.`
	  `}`
	
	  `// etc. for other abstract methods.`
	
	  `// Additional methods may be added;`
	  `// details omitted.`
	`}`

- A class that is derived from an abstract class needn't override all the abstract methods it inherits with concrete versions; if one or more of the abstract methods is inherited as is, the derived class must also be declared abstract.

- In contrast, a class that implements an interface must provide concrete versions of all abstract methods required of the interface; implementing an interface is an "all or nothing" proposition.

- Another important distinction between extending an abstract class versus implementing an interface is that although a given class can be derived from only one immediate base class, a class can implement as many interfaces as desired. Because this is such a powerful language feature, we'll illustrate it with an example in the next section.

Implementing Multiple Interfaces

As an example, suppose that we invent a second interface called IAdministrator, which in turn specifies the following method headers:

```
public interface IAdministrator
{
  bool ApproveNewCourse(Course c);
  bool HireProfessor(Professor p);
}
```

We could then declare that a class such as Professor implements *both* the ITeacher and IAdministrator interfaces, in which case the class would need to implement all the methods declared by *both* of these interfaces collectively:

```
public class Professor : ITeacher, IAdministrator
{
  // The Professor class must implement all of the methods called for
  // by the ITeacher interface...details omitted.

  // The Professor class must implement all of the methods called for
  // by the IAdministrator interface...details omitted.
}
```

When a class implements more than one interface, its objects are capable of assuming multiple identities or roles in an application; such objects can therefore be "handled" by various types of reference variables. Based on the preceding definition of a Professor as both an ITeacher and an IAdministrator, the following client code would be possible (as illustrated conceptually in Figure 7-3):

```
// Instantiate a Professor object, and associate it with a reference
// variable of type Professor.
Professor p = new Professor();

// We then declare reference variables of the two types of interfaces that the
// Professor class implements.
ITeacher t;
IAdministrator a;

t = p;  // Assign the Professor object to a reference variable of
        // type ITeacher; this is possible because a professor IS A teacher!

a = p;  // Assign the Professor object to a reference variable of
        // type IAdministrator; this is possible because a professor IS AN
        // administrator!
```

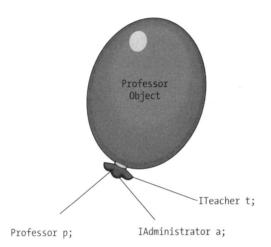

ITeacher t;

Professor p;   IAdministrator a;

A Professor object can be "handled" by Professor,
ITeacher, and IAdministrator references, because a Professor
is a Teacher, and a Professor is an Administrator!

Figure 7-3. *The Professor object has three different identities.*

This is conceptually the same thing as you, as a person, being viewed as having different roles by different people: you're viewed as an employee by your manager, as a son or daughter by your parents, perhaps as a parent by your children, and so forth. Here, IAdministrator represents the things you would do as an administrator while the ITeacher defines things you would do as a teacher. The interfaces define roles that the objects play, not attributes pertaining to the objects.

We may then command the *same* object as either a Professor . . .

```
// Department is a property defined for the Professor class...
p.Department = "Computer Science";
```

or as a ITeacher . . .

```
// AgreeToTeach is a method defined for the ITeacher interface...
t.AgreeToTeach(c);   // Note that p.AgreeToTeach(c); also works...
```

or as an IAdministrator . . .

```
// ApproveNewCourse is a method defined for the IAdministrator interface...
a.ApproveNewCourse(c);  // Note that p.ApproveNewCourse(c); also works…
```

Because it's all three, rolled into one!

■**Note** Not all OOPLs embrace the notion of interfaces. For example, both C# and Java do, but C++ does not. C++ does, however, support multiple inheritance; C#'s provision for a class to be able to implement multiple interfaces enabled the C# language designers to avoid multiple inheritance, as we discussed in Chapter 5.

A class may simultaneously extend a single base class and implement one or more interfaces, as follows:

```
public class Professor : Person, ITeacher, IAdministrator {...}
```

Under such circumstances, the name of the base class must always come first in the list, followed by the names of all interfaces to be implemented. As we discussed in Chapter 5, C# does not support multiple inheritance of classes, so it isn't possible to list more than one class name after the colon; assuming that Professor and Student are both classes, the following wouldn't compile:

```
// This would not compile.
public class StudentTeacher : Professor, Student, ITeacher
{
  // details omitted
}
```

The preceding code would produce the following compilation error:

```
error: Class 'StudentTeacher' cannot have multiple base classes:
 'Professor' and 'Student'
```

In other words, the compiler will consider only the first entry after the colon as a base class, and everything else in the list is assumed to be an interface.

Interfaces and Instantiation

Interfaces can't be instantiated. That is, if we define ITeacher to be an interface, we can't try to instantiate it directly:

```
ITeacher t = new ITeacher();  // Impossible!  The compiler will
                              // generate an error.
```

We'd get the following compilation error on the preceding line of code:

```
error: Cannot create an instance of the abstract class or
interface 'ITeacher'
```

Although we're indeed prevented from instantiating an interface, we're nonetheless permitted to declare reference variables to be of an interface type, as you saw earlier:

```
ITeacher t;  // This is OK.
```

We could, therefore, do the following:

```
ITeacher t = new Professor();
```

Why is this permitted? The compiler allows assignments to occur if the type of the expression to the right of the equal sign (=) is a type that is compatible with the variable to the left of the equal sign. Because Professor implements ITeacher, a professor *is a* teacher, and so this assignment is permitted.

The Importance of Interfaces

Interfaces are some of the most poorly understood, and hence underutilized, features of the OOPLs that support them. This is quite unfortunate because interfaces are extremely powerful if utilized properly.

Whenever possible/feasible, design the public aspects of your classes using interface types instead of specific class types to allow for greater flexibility/utility of your methods, to include the following:

- Formal parameters to methods

- Method return types

Let's use two different examples to illustrate the power of interfaces.

Example #1

In this example, assume that

- `Professor` implements the `ITeacher` interface.

- `StudentTeacher` also implements the `ITeacher` interface.

- `Professor` and `StudentTeacher` are sibling classes—neither derives from the other.

We'll start by designing a class called `Course` with a private field of type `Professor` called `teachingAssistant` and a property for accessing the value of this field:

```
public class Course
{
  private Professor teachingAssistant;

  // Other members omitted...

  public Professor TeachingAssistant {
    get {
      return teachingAssistant;
    }
    set {
      teachingAssistant = value;
    }
  }

  // Other members omitted...
}
```

Then we'd perhaps utilize this class from client code as follows:

```
// Client code.
Course c = new Course("Math 101");
Professor p = new Professor("John Smith");
c.TeachingAssistant = p;
```

If, later on we prefer to change the type of the private teachingAssistant field from Professor to StudentTeacher, we'd also have to change the type of the public Teaching-Assistant property to match:

```
public class Course
{
  private StudentTeacher teachingAssistant;

  public StudentTeacher TeachingAssistant {
    // Details omitted...
  }

  // etc.
}
```

Our client code as originally written would no longer work—the highlighted line in the following code will no longer compile—because the TeachingAssistant property as modified is expecting to be assigned a StudentTeacher reference now, and a Professor is not a Student-Teacher:

```
// Client code.
Course c = new Course("Math 101");
Professor p = new Professor("John Smith");
c.TeachingAssistant = p;  // This line of code would no longer compile.
```

Now, let's look at an alteration to our original Course class design. Let's say that we originally took advantage of the fact that the Professor class implements the ITeacher interface to declare the TeachingAssistant property to be of type ITeacher from the outset:

```
public class Course
{
  private ITeacher teachingAssistant;
  // details omitted...

  public ITeacher TeachingAssistant {
    // details omitted...
  }

  // etc.
}
```

We're thus opening up more possibilities for client code; we can assign a Professor as a teaching assistant:

```
// Client code
Course c = new Course("Math 101");
Professor p = new Professor("John Smith");
c.TeachingAssistant = p;
```

or a StudentTeacher as a teaching assistant:

```
// Client code
Course c = new Course("Math 101");
StudentTeacher s = new StudentTeacher("George Jones");
c.TeachingAssistant = s;
```

or a reference to any other type of object that implements the ITeacher interface.

Example #2

An example of a commonly used *predefined* interface from the Framework Class Library (FCL) is the generic ICollection<T> interface. The ICollection<T> interface enforces implementation of the following method headers:

```
void Add(T item)
void Clear()
bool Contains(T item)
void CopyTo(T[] array, int arrayIndex)
IEnumerator<T> GetEnumerator()
bool Remove(T item)
```

The T syntax in the ICollection<T> method headers reflects the fact that ICollection<T> objects are generic collections and are declared to hold references of a given type. The type of item added to an ICollection<T> object, for example, will depend on what the collection was declared to hold. The ICollection<T> interface is implemented by several of the predefined C# generic collection types, including the List and Dictionary classes.

If we write a method that is to operate on a collection so that it accepts an ICollection reference versus a specific type of collection—say, a List—the method is much more versatile; client code is free to pass in whatever collection type it wants:

```
public class SomeClass
{
  // details omitted...

  public void SomeMethod(ICollection<sometype> list) {
    // Within this method, we can manipulate the list argument with
    // any of the methods defined by the IList interface...
  }
}
```

Static Members

Up until this point, all the methods, fields, and properties that we've discussed have been associated with an instance of a class. Every object has its own copy of the member and can manipulate it independently of what other objects are doing. But there might be times when you'll want to make a member common to all instances of a class. In other words, instead of having each object have its own copy of a field, there might be a field whose value will be shared by all objects of a given class. A common field, for example, can be useful to keep track of how many objects of a given type have been instantiated in an application. The C# language satisfies this need through *static* members that are associated with classes as a whole instead of with individual objects.

Static Fields

You learned previously that whenever we create an object, we're creating an instance of the appropriate class whose fields subsequently get "filled" with values specific to that object (see Figure 7-4).

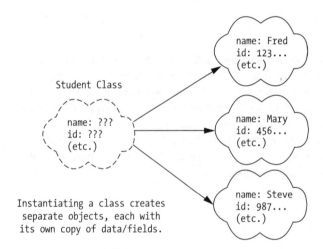

Figure 7-4. *Objects "fill in" their individual field values.*

Suppose that there were some piece of general information—say, the count of the total number of students enrolled at the university—that we wanted *all* Student objects to have shared access to. We could implement this as a simple field of the Student class, int totalStudents, along with code for manipulating the field (as shown here):

```
using System;

public class Student
{
  private int totalStudents;
  // etc.
```

```
  // Property.
  public int TotalStudents {
    // accessor details omitted...
  }

  public int ReportTotalEnrollment() {
    Console.WriteLine("Total Enrollment:  " + TotalStudents);
  }

  public void IncrementEnrollment() {
    TotalStudents = TotalStudents + 1;
  }

  // etc.
}
```

This would be inefficient for two reasons:

- First of all, each object would be duplicating the same information. Although an int(eger) doesn't take up a lot of memory, this is still, in principle, a waste of storage. And, storage space aside, one of our "quests" in adopting object technology is to avoid redundancy of data and/or code whenever possible.

- Secondly, and perhaps more significantly, it would be cumbersome to have to call the IncrementEnrollment method on every Student object in the system each time a new Student were to be created, to ensure that all Student objects were in agreement on the total student count.

Fortunately, there is a simple solution! We can designate totalStudents to be what is known as a *static field* of the Student class through use of the static keyword:

```
public class Student
{
  // totalStudents is declared to be a static field.
  private static int totalStudents;

  // details omitted...

  public int ReportTotalEnrollment() {
    Console.WriteLine("Total Enrollment:  " + TotalStudents);
  }

  public void IncrementEnrollment() {
    totalStudents = totalStudents + 1;
  }
}
```

A static field is one whose value is shared by all instances of a class; its value conceptually belongs to the class as a whole instead of belonging to any one instance/object of that class (see Figure 7-5).

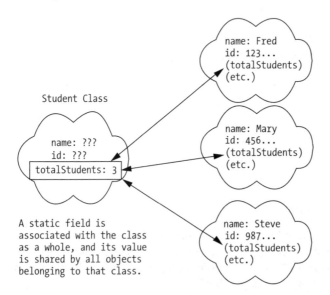

Figure 7-5. *The value of a static field conceptually belongs to the class as a whole.*

Each Student object can access and modify the shared totalStudents field just as if it were a nonstatic field; in our earlier code example, the ReportTotalEnrollment and Increment-Enrollment methods look no different from any other Student method in terms of how they manipulate the totalStudents field. The difference is that the value of a static field is shared, so if we were to execute the following client code:

```
Student s1 = new Student();
s1.Name = "Fred";
s1.IncrementEnrollment();

Student s2 = new Student();
s2.Name = "Mary";
s2.IncrementEnrollment();

Student s3 = new Student();
s3.Name = "Steve";
s3.IncrementEnrollment();
```

the resultant value of totalStudents would be affected as follows (assuming that it starts with a value of 0):

- When s1 is passed the method call s1.IncrementEnrollment(), the shared value of totalStudents is incremented by 1 (from 0 to 1).

- When s2 is passed the method call s2.IncrementEnrollment(), the shared value of totalStudents is incremented by 1 (from 1 to 2).

- When s3 is passed the method call s3.IncrementEnrollment(), the shared value of totalStudents is incremented by 1 (from 2 to 3).

At any time thereafter, if any one of the objects accesses the value of totalStudents, it will be equal to 3. That is, if we were to invoke the ReportTotalEnrollment method on s1, s2, or s3, the result would be the same: the information printed by the method call would be the same in every case. Expanding upon our previous example:

```
Student s1 = new Student();
s1.Name = "Fred";
s1.IncrementEnrollment();

Student s2 = new Student();
s2.Name = "Mary";
s2.IncrementEnrollment();

Student s3 = new Student();
s3.Name = "Steve";
s3.IncrementEnrollment();
s1.ReportTotalEnrollment());
s2.ReportTotalEnrollment());
s3.ReportTotalEnrollment());
```

Here's the output for the preceding code:

```
Total Enrollment:  3
Total Enrollment:  3
Total Enrollment:  3
```

Static Properties

We would most likely declare the static totalStudents field to be private (like virtually all fields), in which case we'd perhaps want to code public accessors for it. The preferred way to access the value of a static field in C# is to declare a *static property*. Other than the obvious use of the static keyword, a static property is syntactically indistinguishable from a nonstatic property:

```
public class Student
{
  private static int totalStudents;

  // Other details omitted.

  // We've declared a public static property to access our static field.
  public static int TotalStudents {
    get {
      return totalStudents;
    }
```

```
  set {
    totalStudents = value;
  }
}

// Details omitted.

public void IncrementEnrollment() {
  // We're now taking advantage of our get/set accessors (note use
  // of captial "T" in the following code.
  TotalStudents = TotalStudents + 1;
}
}
```

The get and set accessors for a static property are defined in the same manner as they are for a nonstatic property: the return type of the get accessor is implicitly the same as the property type, and the set accessor implicitly has a return type of void and is passed a parameter named value.

Static properties can't be invoked on an individual object, but are instead invoked on a class as a whole using dot notation:

```
Console.WriteLine("Total Enrollment = " + Student.TotalStudents);
```

If we were to try to invoke a static property on an object by mistake:

```
Student s1 = new Student();
Console.WriteLine("Total Enrollment = " + s1.TotalStudents);
```

the compiler would generate the following error:

```
Error: Member 'Student.TotalStudents' cannot be accessed
with an instance reference; qualify it with a type name instead
```

Let's rework the client code from the previous example to make use of the static property:

```
Student s1 = new Student();
s1.Name = "Fred";
s1.IncrementEnrollment();

Student s2 = new Student();
s2.Name = "Mary";
s2.IncrementEnrollment();

Student s3 = new Student();
s3.Name = "Steve";
s3.IncrementEnrollment();
Console.WriteLine("Total Enrollment = " + Student.TotalStudents);
```

This code results in the following output:

```
Total Enrollment = 3
```

Static Methods

Just as static fields/properties are associated with a class as a whole versus relating to a specific individual object, *static methods* are in turn methods that can be invoked on a class as a whole. Static methods are useful for implementing general-purpose functionality— mathematical evaluations, for example—that can be used by any number of classes.

Let's declare both the IncrementEnrollment and ReportTotalEnrollment methods to be static:

```
public class Student
{
  private static int totalStudents;

  // Other details omitted.

  public static int TotalStudents {
    get {
      return totalStudents;
    }
    set {
      totalStudents = value;
    }
  }

  // These two methods are now static methods.

  public static void IncrementEnrollment() {
    // The method body is unchanged from when this was a nonstatic method.
    TotalStudents = TotalStudents + 1;
  }

  public static int ReportTotalEnrollment() {
    // Ditto!
    Console.WriteLine("Total Enrollment:  " + TotalStudents);
  }

  // etc.
}
```

As with static properties, static methods can *only* be invoked on a class as a whole:

```
Student.IncrementEnrollment();
```

We can't invoke static methods on individual object references; if we were to attempt to invoke the IncrementEnrollement method on a Student object by mistake, as follows:

```
Student s1 = new Student();
s1.IncrementEnrollment(); // This won't compile; IncrementEnrollment is static
```

the compiler would produce the following error message:

```
Error:  Member 'Student.IncrementEnrollment()' cannot be
accessed with an instance reference; qualify it with a type name instead
```

Reworking our client code example yet again to take into account the fact that Increment-Enrollment and ReportTotalEnrollment methods are now static methods, we'd have the following:

```
Student s1 = new Student();
s1.Name = "Fred";
Student.IncrementEnrollment();

Student s2 = new Student();
s2.Name = "Mary";
Student.IncrementEnrollment();

Student s3 = new Student();
s3.Name = "Steve";
Student.IncrementEnrollment();

Student.ReportEnrollment();
```

Here's the output that we'd get:

```
Total Enrollment = 3
```

Restrictions on Static Methods and Properties

Note that there is an important restriction on static methods with respect to how they can access fields of the class in which they are declared: namely, they can't access *nonstatic* members of that class. If we were to attempt to write a static method such as Print, as in the following code example, that tried to access the value of a nonstatic field such as name, the compiler would prevent us from doing so:

```
public class Student
{
  // Two fields-- one static, one nonstatic.
  private string name;
  private static int totalStudents;
  // etc.

  // Assume that public properties Name and TotalStudents have been defined for
  // both fields (details omitted).

  public static void Print() {
    // A static method may NOT access NON-static members
    // such as 'Name' -- the following line won't compile.
    Console.WriteLine(Name + " is one of " + TotalStudents +
                "students.");
  }
}
```

The compiler would generate the following error message regarding the `WriteLine` statement:

```
error: An object reference is required for the non-static field,
method, or property 'Student.Name.get'
```

Why is this? As you learned in Chapter 3, classes are empty templates as far as nonstatic fields are concerned; it's not until we instantiate an object that its (nonstatic) field values get filled in (see Figures 7-6 and 7-7).

The class defines a template...

Field Name	Data Type	Value
name	string	To be determined
studentId	string	To be determined
birthdate	DateTime	To be determined
address	string	To be determined
major	string	To be determined
gpa	float	To be determined
advisor	???	To be determined
courseLoad	???	To be determined
transcript	???	To be determined

Figure 7-6. *A class serves as a template for creating objects.*

...and each object subsequently
fills in its own unique field values.

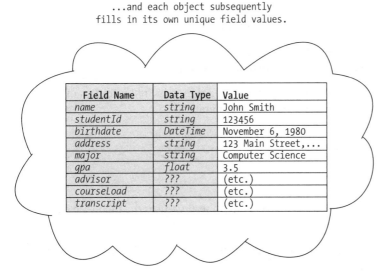

Field Name	Data Type	Value
name	string	John Smith
studentId	string	123456
birthdate	DateTime	November 6, 1980
address	string	123 Main Street,...
major	string	Computer Science
gpa	float	3.5
advisor	???	(etc.)
courseLoad	???	(etc.)
transcript	???	(etc.)

Figure 7-7. *Objects then fill in the values of their nonstatic fields.*

If a static method is invoked on a class as a whole, and that method were in turn to try to access the value of a nonstatic field, the value of that field would be undefined for the class. Because the name field pertains to individual objects, which name should the static method try to access? This situation is illustrated conceptually in Figure 7-8.

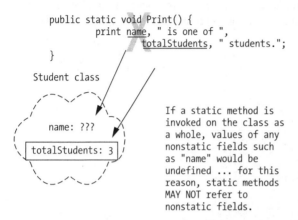

```
public static void Print() {
        print name, " is one of ",
                totalStudents, " students.";
}
```
Student class

name: ???

totalStudents: 3

If a static method is invoked on the class as a whole, values of any nonstatic fields such as "name" would be undefined ... for this reason, static methods MAY NOT refer to nonstatic fields.

Figure 7-8. *Nonstatic member values are undefined in the class context.*

Two other restrictions on static methods:

- They can't be overridden by derived classes, so the virtual keyword can't be applied to a static method when it is declared:

```
// This won't compile.
public virtual static void IncrementEnrollment() {
  // details omitted...
}
```

- Static methods may not be declared to be abstract, either:

```
// This won't compile either.
public abstract static void IncrementEnrollment();
```

If we were to try to compile either of the previous code snippets in the context of the Student class, the following compiler error would be generated:

```
error: A static member 'Student.IncrementEnrollment' cannot be
marked as override, virtual, or abstract
```

C#-Specific Terminology

To differentiate between static, nonstatic, and local members, C# uses the following alternative (preferred) terminology:

- The term *instance variable* refers to a nonstatic field because such a field has value or meaning for an *instance*, or object.

- The term *static variable* refers to a static field.

- The term *local variable* refers to a variable that is declared inside of a method, so is locally scoped relative to that method. Local variables are neither static nor instance variables.

- Just as there are static and instance variables, there are static and instance properties and methods with the same distinctions between them.

Here is a code snippet that illustrates all three types of fields:

```
public class Student
{
  // Fields.
  private string name;                 // an instance variable
  private static int totalStudentCount; // a static variable

  // Methods.
  public void SomeMethod(int x) {    //  x is a local variable
    bool y;                          //  as is y
    // etc.
  }

  // etc.
}
```

Utility Classes

As we've just seen, static methods are used to provide general functionality that is independent of any particular object. For example, we've been using the following syntax throughout the book to display messages to the console:

```
Console.WriteLine(string expression);
```

As it turns out, Console is a class predefined in the .NET FCL (in the System namespace), and WriteLine is a static method on that class. We therefore needn't ever instantiate a Console object to print messages to the screen; we simply call the WriteLine method on the Console class as a whole.

Another example of a predefined class that is comprised wholly of static methods and public static fields is the Math class (also in the System namespace):

- The Math class declares a variety of static methods to compute trigonometric, exponential, logarithmic, and power functions, to round numeric values, and to generate random numbers. For example, one such method—Math.Sqrt—computes the square root of a number.

```
squareRoot[i] = Math.Sqrt(i);
```

- The mathematical constants e and π are declared as public static fields of the Math class, named Math.E and Math.PI, respectively:

```
Console.WriteLine("The value of pi = " + Math.PI);
```

We informally refer to such classes as *utility classes*. Classes that contain only static members can be declared to be static themselves. A static class object is never created; instead the class is made available automatically by the .NET Framework when the program that contains the class is loaded. An example of a static class in the FCL is the System.Math class:

```
public static class Math
```

User-Defined Utility Classes

We can use this same technique to create our own *custom* utility classes. For example, suppose that we have a frequent need to do temperature conversions from degrees Fahrenheit to degrees Centigrade and vice versa. We could invent a static utility class as follows:

```
// A utility class to provide F=>C and C=>F conversions.

public static class Temperature {
  public static double FahrenheitToCentigrade(double tempF) {
    double tempC = (tempF - 32.0) * (5.0/9.0);
    return tempC;
  }

  public static double CentigradeToFahrenheit(double tempC) {
    double tempF = tempC * (9.0/5.0) + 32.0;
    return tempF;
  }
}
```

To use this class, we simply write client code as follows:

```
double temp1 = 212.0;  // Boiling point on the Fahrenheit scale

// Calling our own static method.
double temp2 = Temperature.FahrenheitToCentigrade(temp1);
Console.WriteLine("" + temp1 + " degrees F = " + temp2 + " degrees C");
```

This would give us the following output:

```
212.0 degrees F = 100.0 degrees C
```

We might even want to include some commonly used constants—say, the boiling and freezing points of water in both F and C terms—as public static fields in our utility class:

```
// A utility class to provide F=>C and C=>F conversions.

public static class Temperature {
  // We've added some public static fields.
  public static double FahrenheitFreezing = 32.0;
  public static double CentigradeFreezing = 0.0;
  public static double FahrenheitBoiling = 212.0;
  public static double CentigradeBoiling = 100.0;
```

```
public static double FahrenheitToCentigrade(double tempF) {
  double tempC = (tempF - 32.0) * (5.0/9.0);
  return tempC;
}

public static double CentigradeToFahrenheit(double tempC) {
  double tempF = tempC * (9.0/5.0) + 32.0;
  return tempF;
}
}
```

We could then take advantage of these constants in our client code, as well:

```
double soupTemperature;
// The value of soupTemperature is established...details omitted.
if (soupTemperature >= Temperature.FahrenheitBoiling) {...}
```

There is only one minor problem: we want these "constant" values to *truly be* constants, but as we've declared them previously—as public (static) fields—there is nothing to prevent client code from altering their values:

```
Temperature.FahrenheitBoiling = 98.6;  // Whoops!
```

Fortunately, we can take advantage of a special type of variable known as a *constant* to remedy this problem.

Constants

As shown in the previous example, sometimes we might want a field to be publicly accessible but want to make sure that its value isn't changed. Physical constants such as the boiling temperature of water are examples of this type of situation. In .NET, a *constant* is a variable whose value can't be changed once it has been given an initial value. We declare a constant with the const keyword, as follows:

```
public const double FahrenheitFreezing = 32.0;
```

- Constants are implicitly static, so the static keyword shouldn't be used in declaring them; to do so would cause a compilation error as follows:

  ```
  // The following line won't compile.
  public static const double FahrenheitFreezing = 32.0;
  ```

  Compilation error:

```
error: The constant 'Temperature.FahrenheitFreezing' cannot be marked static
```

- Constants must be given a value when they are declared; that is, we can't declare a const in one part of a program and assign it a value somewhere else. Suppose we try to declare an uninitialized const:

  ```
  public const double FahrenheitFreezing;
  ```

The compiler will generate the following error:

```
error: a const field requires a value to be provided
```

- When naming constants, the convention is to use the Pascal capitalization style.

Let's retrofit our Temperature class with constant fields:

```
// A utility class to provide F=>C and C=>F conversions.

public static class Temperature
{
  // We've added the const keyword to these declarations.
  public const double FahrenheitFreezing = 32.0;
  public const double CentigradeFreezing = 0.0;
  public const double FahrenheitBoiling = 212.0;
  public const double CentigradeBoiling = 100.0;

  public static double FahrenheitToCentigrade(double tempF) {
    double tempC = (tempF - 32.0) * (5.0/9.0);
    return tempC;
  }

  public static double CentigradeToFahrenheit(double tempC) {
    double tempF = tempC * (9.0/5.0) + 32.0;
    return tempF;
  }
}
```

If we attempt to alter the value of one of these *truly constant* constants from client code:

```
Temperature.FahrenheitBoiling = 98.6;  // This won't compile!
```

we get the following (admittedly somewhat cryptic) compilation error:

```
error: The left-hand side of an assignment must be a variable,
property, or indexer
```

Of course, even within our Temperature class, this same prohibition exists: after the first assignment of a value to any const variable, that value is unchangeable.

Other facts about consts:

- The initial value assigned to a const must be an expression that is known at *compile* time:

```
public class MyUtilityClass
{
  // This will compile...
  public const int ImportantConstant = 123 + 456;
  // This will NOT...
  public const double AnotherConstant = Math.Sqrt(2.0);
```

In the preceding snippet, the second `const` declaration won't compile, because `Math.Sqrt` is a *method* and hence can only be invoked at *run time*.

- The type of a `const` can only be one of the predefined numerical types (`char`, `int`, `double`, `byte`, and so on) or a `string`.

- We may declare `const`s locally to a method, as well:

```
public class SomeClass
{
  // Details omitted.

  public void SomeMethod() {
    int x;
    const int y = 7;
    // etc.
  }
}
```

Read-Only Fields

Another way to ensure that the value of a field is fixed after it is assigned a value is to declare the field to be read-only using the `readonly` keyword:

```
public readonly double someValue;
```

Read-only fields are similar in some ways to constant fields but different in other ways:

- Constant fields are always static. Read-only fields can be either instance or static.

- Constant fields must be initialized when they are declared. Read-only fields can be initialized when they are declared or they can be assigned a value in a constructor.

- Constant fields can be used as local variables.

Between the two of them, `const` fields and `readonly` fields should take care of all of your "publicly accessible but fixed value" variable needs.

Summary

Hooray—you did it! You made it through all of the major OO technology concepts that you'll need to know for the rest of the book, learning a great deal of C# syntax in the process.

Please make sure that you're comfortable with these concepts before proceeding to Part Two because they will form the foundation of the rest of your object learning experience:

- These same concepts will be reinforced when you learn how to model a problem in Part Two.

- They will be reinforced yet again when you learn how to render a model as C# code in Part Three.

In this chapter, you learned the following:

- Different objects can respond to the same exact method call in different class-specific ways, thanks to an OOPL feature known as *polymorphism*.

- Abstract classes are useful if we want to prescribe common behaviors among a group of (derived) classes. We specify the "*what*" that an object must do (the messages that an object must be able to respond to, also known as method signatures) without specifying the "*how*" (the method bodies) in the base class.

- Interfaces are an even more abstract way to prescribe behaviors; in essence, interfaces define roles that objects can play.

- Static fields/properties can be used to enable an entire class of objects to share data, and static methods enable us to provide capabilities that are available to the application through a class as a whole.

- How to take advantage of static members along with constant fields to create custom utility classes.

The first part of this book has given you all the programming tools you'll need in your toolbox to build powerful C# applications. But you still need to learn how to lay out a blueprint for using them effectively in building an application—we'll teach you how to do so in Part Two!

Exercises

1. Test yourself: run through the following list of OO terms—some formal, some informal—and see whether you can define each term in your own words without referring to the text:

Abstract class	Class	Derived class
Abstract method	Class hierarchy	Dictionary
Abstraction	Class variable	Encapsulation
Accessor (of a property)	Classification	Field
Accessor method	Client (object)	Generalization
Aggregation	Client code	Generic class
Ancestor class	Collection class	Get accessor
Association	Composite class	Get method
Base class	Constant	Getter
Behavioral relationship	Constructor	Information hiding
Binary association	Delegation	Inheritance

Instance	Operation	Set method
Instance variable	Ordered list	Setter
Instantiation	Overloading	Sibling class
Interface	Overriding	Simple type
Local variable	Parent class	Sorted ordered list
Leaf node	Polymorphism	Specialization
Link	Predefined type	State
Member	Private accessibility	Static field
Method	Public accessibility	Static method
Method header	Reference	Static variable
Method signature	Reference variable	Structural relationship
Modeling	Reflexive association	Supplier (object)
Multiple inheritance	Root (of a class hierarchy)	Unary association
Multiplicity	Set (collection)	User-defined type
Object (in the software sense)	Set accessor	

2. Which fields, belonging to which SRS classes, might be well suited to being declared as static?

3. It has been argued that the capability to declare and implement interfaces in the C# language eliminates the need for derived classes to inherit from multiple base classes. Do you agree or disagree? Why? Can you think of any ways in which implementing multiple interfaces "falls short" as compared with true multiple inheritance?

4. The following client code scenarios would each cause compilation errors—can you explain why this is so in each case? Be as precise as possible as to the reasons—they might not be as obvious as first meets the eye!

Assume that Professor and StudentTeacher are both classes that implement the ITeacher interface.

Scenario #1:

```
Professor p;
StudentTeacher s = new StudentTeacher();
ITeacher t;

t = s;
p = t;
```

Scenario #2:

```
Professor p = new Professor();
StudentTeacher s;
ITeacher t = new StudentTeacher();

s = t;
```

Scenario #3:

```
Professor p = new Professor();
StudentTeacher s = new StudentTeacher();
ITeacher t;

p = t;
```

Object Modeling 101

CHAPTER 8

■■■

The Object Modeling Process in a Nutshell

Let's look in on the homebuilder you met in the introduction to this book. He just returned from a seminar titled "Blue Stars: A Builder's Dream Come True." He now knows all about the unique properties of blue stars and appreciates why they are superior construction materials—just as you learned about the unique properties of software objects as application "construction materials" earlier in the book. But he is still inexperienced with actually *using* blue stars in a construction project; in particular, he doesn't yet know how to develop a blueprint suitable for a home that is to be built from blue stars. And, we still need to discuss how to develop a blueprint for a software system that is to be constructed from objects, which is the focus of Part Two of this book.

Some readers (not you of course, but some other readers) might be tempted to conclude that "I know about classes and other elements of the C# language; I'm ready to write some code." You should resist this impulse until you finish reading Part Two of this book because nothing wastes more time in a programmer's life than having to rewrite a program because it was based on a poorly designed object model. Being able to come up with an effective, efficient, flexible object model before you start writing code will make your life much easier—and you'll become a stronger programmer as well.

In this chapter, you'll learn the following:

- The goals and philosophy behind object modeling

- How much flexibility we have in terms of selecting or devising a modeling methodology

- The pros and cons of object modeling software tools

The "Big Picture" Goal of Object Modeling

Our goal in object modeling is to render a precise, concise, understandable object-oriented (OO) model, or *blueprint*, of the system to be automated. This model will serve as an important tool for communication:

- To the future users of the system that we are about to build, an object model communicates part of the understanding of the system requirements (along with screen mock-ups, architecture diagrams, infrastructure design, and so on). Having the users review and "bless" the model will ensure that we get off on the right foot with a project because a mistake in judgment at the requirements analysis stage can prove much more costly to fix—by orders of magnitude—than if such a misunderstanding is found and corrected when the system is still just a "gleam in the user's eye."

- To the software development team, an object model communicates the structure and function of the software that needs to be built in order to satisfy those requirements. The object model bridges the semantic gap between users and developers. It facilitates communication between the two groups to help enable the folks responsible for quality assurance, testing, and documentation to identify potential problems early on in the development process (they would know exactly what the program was supposed to do and how it was designed to do it).

- Long after the application is operational, an object model lives on as a *schematic diagram* to help the myriad folks responsible for supporting and maintaining an application understand its structure and function.

Note Of course, this last point is true only if the object model accurately reflects the system as it was actually built, not just as it was originally conceived. The design of complex systems invariably changes during their construction, so care should be taken to keep the object model up to date as the system is built.

Modeling Methodology = Process + Notation + Tool

According to Webster's dictionary, a *methodology* is

> *A set of systematic procedures used by a discipline [to achieve a particular desired outcome].*

A modeling methodology, OO or otherwise, ideally involves three components:

- A *process:* The how-to steps for gathering the requirements and determining the abstraction to be modeled

- A *notation*: A graphical language for communicating the model

- A *tool:* An automated way of rendering the notation, typically in drag-and-drop fashion

Although they constitute the ideal components of a modeling methodology, they are not all of equal importance. Adhering to a sound *process* is certainly critical. However, we can sometimes get by with a narrative text description of an abstraction without having to resort to portraying it with formal graphical *notation*. When we do choose to depict an abstraction formally via a graphical notation, it isn't mandatory that we use a specialized *tool* for doing so.

In other words, following an organized process is the most critical aspect of object modeling; using a particular notation is important, but less so; and our choice of a particular tool for rendering the model is the least important aspect of the three (see Figure 8-1).

```
Process + Notation + Tool
```

Figure 8-1. *Of the three aspects of a methodology, a sound process is by far the most important.*

Many important contributions in the form of new processes, notations, and tools have been made in the OO methodology arena over the years by numerous well-known methodologists. In some sense, you're fortunate if you're just getting into objects for the first time now because you managed to avoid the "methodology wars" that raged for many years as methodologists and their followers argued about what were in some cases seemingly esoteric details.

Here is a partial list of contributions made in the object methodology arena over the past few decades (the list is in no particular order):

- James Rumbaugh et al.: The Object Modeling Technique (OMT)

- Grady Booch: The Booch Method

- Ivar Jacobson: Use cases as a means of formalizing requirements

- Erich Gamma, Richard Helm, Ralph Johnson, John Vlissides (the "Gang of Four"): Design pattern reuse

- Sally Shlaer and Stephen Mellor: Emphasis on state diagrams

- Rebecca Wirfs-Brock et al.: Responsibility-driven design; "Classes—Responsibilities—Collaborations" (CRC) cards

- Bertrand Meyer: The Eiffel programming language; the notion of programming by contract

- James Martin/James Odell: Retooling of their functional decomposition methodologies for use with OO systems

- Peter Coad/Edward Yourdon: As in the preceding entry

- Derek Coleman et al. (HP): The Fusion Method

- Martin Fowler: Enterprise patterns and architecture

Some years ago there was a major push in the industry to meld the best ideas of competing methodologies into a single approach, with particular emphasis being placed on coming up with a universal modeling notation. The resultant notation, known as the Unified Modeling Language (UML), represents the collaborative efforts of three of the leaders in the OO methodology field—James Rumbaugh, Grady Booch, and Ivar Jacobson—and has become the industry standard object modeling notation. (A brief introduction to UML is provided in Chapters 10 and 11.)

Along with the UML, these three gentlemen—known affectionately in the industry as the "Three Amigos"—have also contributed heavily to the evolution of an overall methodology known as the Rational Unified Process (RUP), a full-blown software development methodology encompassing modeling, project management, and configuration management workflows. But we aren't going to dwell on the details of this particular methodology in this book because it isn't our intention to teach you any one specific methodology in great detail. By learning a sound, *generic* process for object modeling, you'll be armed with the knowledge you need to read about, evaluate, and select a specific methodology such as RUP; or to craft your own hybrid approach by mixing and matching the processes, notation, and tool(s) from various methodologies that make the most sense for your organization.

As for modeling tools, you don't need one, strictly speaking, to appreciate the material presented in this book. But we anticipated that you'll likely want to get your hands dirty with a modeling tool, so we include a general discussion of tool pros and cons a bit later in this chapter.

It's important to keep in mind that a methodology is but a means to an end, and it's the *end*—a usable, flexible, maintainable, reliable, and functionally correct software system, along with thorough, clear supporting documentation—that we care most about when all is said and done.

To help illustrate this point, let's use a simple analogy. Say that our goal is to cheer people up. We decide to hand draw (process) a smiley face (an abstraction of the desired behavior, rendered with a graphical notation) with a pencil (tool), as shown in Figure 8-2.

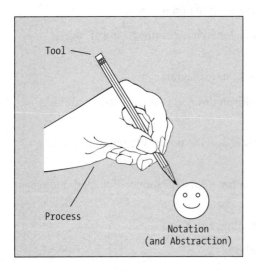

Figure 8-2. *A methodology encompasses process, notation, and tools.*

After we're done, we put our pencil away, hang our smiley face picture on the wall, and go about our business. A few days go by, and we note that people are indeed cheered up by our picture, so our original goal has been achieved. In hindsight, we could have accomplished this same goal using the following:

- A variety of different processes: hand drawing, rubber stamping, or cutting pictures from a magazine

- A variety of different notations: the graphical notation of a smiley face, a cartoon, or the narrative text of a joke or sign

- A variety of different tools: a pen, a pencil, a paintbrush, or a crayon

Now back to our homebuilding analogy. Long after the architect and construction crew have left a building site, taking their equipment and tools with them, the house that they have built will remain standing as a testimonial to the quality of the materials they used, how sound a construction approach was employed, and how elegant a blueprint they had to start with. The blueprint will come in handy later on when the time comes to remodel or maintain the home, so we certainly won't throw it away, but the livability and ease/affordability of maintaining the home will be the primary measure of success.

The same is true for software development: the real legacy of a software development project is the resultant software system, which is, after all, the reason for using a methodology to produce a model in the first place. We must take care to avoid getting so caught up in debating the relative merits of one methodology versus another that we fail to produce useful software; as you can see in Figure 8-3, there are *many* paths to the same destination.

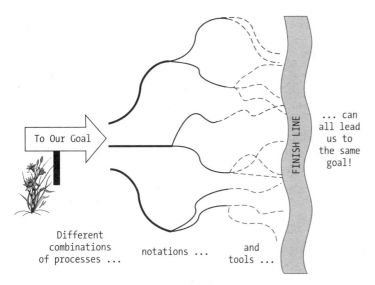

Figure 8-3. *Many different approaches can serve us well when building software.*

Our Object Modeling Process in a Nutshell

We present here a basic preview of the modeling process that we advocate and will illustrate in depth throughout the remainder of Part Two of the book:

- Begin by obtaining or writing a narrative problem statement, similar to the Student Registration System (SRS) problem statement presented in the introduction. Think about the different categories of users that will be interacting with the system, and the various situations in which each will use it, to make sure that you uncover any not-so-obvious requirements that might have been missed. (We'll discuss a technique for doing this—known as *use case modeling*—in Chapter 9.)

- Handle the data side of the application by identifying the different classes of real-world objects that your application will need to be concerned with and determine how they interrelate. (We'll illustrate the process of creating a *class diagram* in Chapter 10.)

- Handle the functional side of the application by studying how objects need to collaborate to accomplish the system's mission, determining what behaviors/responsibilities will be required of each class. (We'll illustrate the process of modeling the *behavioral aspects* of an OO system in Chapter 11.) The emphasis of code development should usually be on behavior-driven design. After the desired behaviors are identified, many of the required classes will appear as a byproduct.

- Test the model to ensure that it does indeed meet all the original requirements. (We'll discuss testing in Chapter 12.)

You'll see plenty of examples of each of these techniques in the chapters to follow and will get an opportunity to practice these techniques based on the hands-on exercises suggested at the end of each chapter. Armed with a solid model of the SRS, you'll then be ready to render the model into C# code, which is the subject of Part Three of the book.

Note that these process steps need not be performed in strictly sequential fashion. In fact, as you become comfortable with each of the steps, you might find yourself carrying some of them out in parallel, or in *shuffled* order. For example, contemplating the behavioral aspects of a model might bring to light new data requirements. In fact, for all but the most trivial models, it's commonplace to iterate through these steps multiple times, dialing in increased levels of understanding (hence more detail in the model and supporting documentation) with each iteration.

It's also important to note that the formality of the process should be adjusted to the size of the project team and the complexity of the requirements. If we separate the *form* of using a methodology from the *substance* of what that methodology produces in the way of *artifacts*—models, documentation, code, and so on—a good rule of thumb is that a project team should spend no more than 10 to 20 percent of its time on form and 80 to 90 percent on substance. If the team finds itself spending so much time on form that little or no progress is being made on substance, it's time to reevaluate the methodology and its various components to see where simplifying adjustments or improvements to efficiency can be made.

Thoughts Regarding Object Modeling Software Tools

It's worthwhile to spend a little bit of time talking about the pros and cons of using an object modeling software tool. For purposes of learning how to produce models, a generic drawing tool such as Microsoft Paint, Visio, or Eclipse can be good enough; for that matter, you might simply want to sketch your models using paper and pencil. But, getting some hands-on experience with using a tool specifically designed for object modeling will better prepare you for your first "industrial-strength" project, so you might wish to acquire one before embarking upon the next chapter. You'll find information about various object modeling software tools, including links to free or evaluation copies of software, at http://objectstart.com.

Object modeling tools fall under the general heading of Computer-Aided Software Engineering (CASE) tools, which afford us with many advantages, but aren't without their drawbacks.

The Advantages of Using CASE Tools

There are many arguments in favor of using CASE tools; several of the more compelling are as follows.

Ease of Use

CASE tools provide a quick drag-and-drop way to create visual models. Instead of trying to render a given notation with a generic drawing tool, in which your basic drawing components are simple lines, arrows, text, boxes, and other geometric shapes, CASE tools provide one or more palettes of prefabricated graphical components specific to the supported notation. For example, you can drag and drop the graphical representation for a class instead of having to painstakingly fabricate it from simpler drawing components.

Added Information Content

CASE tools produce "intelligent" drawings that enforce the syntax rules of a particular notation. This is in contrast to a generic drawing package, which lets you draw almost anything you like, regardless of whether it adheres to the notational syntax or not.

The controls imposed by a CASE tool can be a mixed blessing: on the plus side, they prevent you from making syntactic errors, but (as we discuss a little later) they might also prevent you from making desired adjustments to the notation.

Also, information about the classes reflected in a diagram—their names, attributes, methods, and relationships—is typically stored in a repository that underlies the diagram. Most CASE tools provide documentation-generation features based upon this repository, enabling you to automatically generate project documentation such as a data dictionary report, a type of report that we'll discuss in Chapter 10. Some tools even allow you to tap into this repository programmatically if you find a need to do so.

Consistency Checking

CASE tools can identify discrepancies between various design diagrams, such as a class in a sequence diagram that's missing from the class diagram.

Automated Code Generation

Most CASE tools provide code-generation capabilities, enabling you to transition from a diagram to skeletal C# (or other) code with the push of a button. You might or might not want to avail yourself of this feature, however, because the code that is generated might not meet team/corporate standards (depending on how much control the CASE tool gives you as to the structure that the generated code takes).

When you're first learning a language, it's sometimes better to write your code from scratch. You'll learn more about a given programming language and come up to speed on it faster if you do. Using a CASE tool or other integrated development environment (IDE) is a bit like riding a bike with training wheels. It's easier at first, but you don't really know how to ride a bike (or write code) until you take the training wheels off and do it yourself. It's the author's experience that you gain a lot by writing it yourself, particularly when it comes to processes such as learning how to debug code.

Project Management Aids

Many CASE tools provide some sort of version control, enabling you to maintain different generations of the same model. If you make a change to your model, but then decide that you prefer to return to the way things were previously after reviewing the change with your users, it's easy to do if version control is in place.

CASE tools also often provide configuration management/team collaboration capabilities to enable a group of modelers to easily share in the creation of a single model.

Some Drawbacks of CASE Tools

CASE tools aren't without their drawbacks, however:

- CASE tools can be expensive; it's not unusual for a high-end CASE tool to cost hundreds or even thousands of dollars per "seat."

- CASE tools can sometimes be inflexible—we talk about adapting processes, notations, and tools to suit your own needs throughout Part Two of the book, but tools don't always cooperate! We'll point out in upcoming chapters some specific examples of situations in which you might want to bend the notation a little bit if your CASE tool will accommodate it.

- You run the risk of getting "locked into" a particular vendor's product if the CASE tool in question can't export your model in a vendor-neutral fashion (as XML, for example).

- It's easy to get caught up with form over substance! This is true of any automated tool—even a word processor tends to lure people into spending more time on the cosmetics of a document than is warranted, long after the substantive content is rock solid.

Generally speaking, however, the pros of using an OO CASE tool significantly outweigh the cons—consider the cons as words to the wise on how to successfully apply a tool to your modeling efforts.

A Reminder

Although we said it several times already in this book, it's important to remind you that the process of object modeling is language neutral. We presented C# syntax in Part One of the book because our ultimate goal is to make you comfortable with both object modeling and C# programming. In Part Two of the book, however, we'll drift away from C# temporarily because you truly are at a point where the concepts you'll be learning are just as applicable to C# as they are to Java , or C++, or any other OO programming language. But, never fear—we'll return to C# "big time" in Part Three!

Summary

By far, the most important lesson to take away from this chapter is the following:

Don't get caught up in form over substance! The model that you produce is only a means to an end . . . and the process, notation, and tools that you use to produce the model are but a *means* to the means to this end. If you get too hung up on which notation to use, or which process to use, or which tool to use, you might wind up spinning your wheels in "analysis paralysis." Don't lose sight of your ultimate goal: *to build usable, flexible, maintainable, reliable, functionally correct software systems.*

Exercises

1. Briefly describe the methodology—process, notation, and tool(s)—that you used on a recent software development project. Which aspects of this methodology worked well for you and your teammates, and which, in hindsight, do you think could have been approached more effectively?

2. Research one of the object modeling technologies/techniques mentioned in the "Modeling Methodology = Process + Notation + Tool" section earlier in this chapter (UML is a good choice) and report briefly on the process, notation, and tools involved.

CHAPTER 9

■ ■ ■

Formalizing Requirements Through Use Cases

When you get ready to leave on a vacation, you might run through a mental or written checklist. Did you pack everything you need to take? Did you pack too much? Did you arrange to have the appropriate services (newspaper, mail delivery, and so on) stopped? Did you arrange for someone to water the plants and feed your pet rat? Once you depart on your trip, you want to enjoy yourself and know that when you arrive home again, you won't find any disasters waiting for you.

This isn't unlike a software development project. We need to organize a checklist of the things that must be provided for by the system before we embark on its development, so that the project runs smoothly and we don't create a disaster (in the form of unmet requirements and dissatisfied customers/users) when the system is delivered.

The art and science of requirements analysis—for it truly is both!—is so extensive a topic that we could devote an entire book to this subject alone. There is one technique in particular for discovering and rounding out requirements known as *use case modeling* that warrants your consideration. Use cases aren't strictly an artifact of object-oriented (OO) methodologies; they can be prepared for any software system, regardless of the development methodology to be used. However, they made their debut within the software development community in the context of object systems, and have gained widespread popularity in that context.

In this chapter, you'll learn the following:

- How we must anticipate all of the different roles that users will play when interacting with our future system

- That we must assume each of their viewpoints in describing the services that a software application as a whole is to provide

- How to prepare use cases as a means of documenting all the preceding requirements

We'll also give you enough general background about requirements analysis to provide an appropriate context for use case modeling.

What Are Use Cases?

When determining what the desired functionality of a system is to be, we must seek answers to the following questions:

- *Who* will want to use the system?

- What *capabilities* will the system need to provide to be of value to them?

- When users interact with the system for a particular purpose, what is their expectation as to the *desired outcome?*

Use cases are a natural way to express the answers to these questions. Each use case is a simple statement, narrative or graphical in fashion, that describes a particular goal or outcome of the system, and by whom that outcome is expected. For example, a goal of the Student Registration System (SRS) could be to "enable a student user to register for a course" or to "allow a professor to agree to teach a course." Thus we've just expressed our first use cases! Yes, use cases really are that straightforward initially. In fact, we *need* for them to be that straightforward, so that they are understandable by the users/sponsors of the system, as we'll discuss further in a moment.

Functional versus Technical Requirements

The purpose of thinking through all the use cases for a system is to explore the system's functional requirements thoroughly to make sure that a particular category of user, or potential purpose for the system, isn't overlooked. We differentiate between functional requirements and technical requirements in the following sections.

Functional requirements are those behaviors of a system that have to do with how it is to operate or function from the perspective of someone using the system. Functional requirements might in turn be subdivided into the following:

- *Goal-oriented functional requirements*: These requirements provide a statement of a system's purpose without regard to how the requirement will "play out" from the user's vantage point—for example, "The system must be able to produce customized reports." Avoid discussing implementation details when specifying goal-oriented requirements—for example, "The system must be able to produce customized reports using CrystalReports." We emphasize goal-oriented functional requirements when preparing use cases.

- *Look and feel requirements*: These requirements get a bit more specific in terms of what users expect the system to look like externally (for example, how the graphical user interface [GUI] will be presented) and how they expect it to behave, again from their perspective. For example, we might have as a requirement "The user will click a button on the main GUI, and a confirmation message will appear. . ." A good practice is to write a *concept of operations* document to serve as a "paper prototype" that describes how you envision the future system will look and behave, to stimulate discussion with intended users of the as-yet-to-be-built system before you even begin modeling.

CHAPTER 9 ■ FORMALIZING REQUIREMENTS THROUGH USE CASES   251

Note We present a sample concept of operations for the SRS application in Chapter 16.

Technical requirements, on the other hand, have more to do with *how* a system is to be built internally in order to meet the functional requirements; for instance: "The system must be compatible with the TCP/IP protocol . . . " You can think of these requirements as fixed constraints on technology, in contrast with functional requirements, which are a statement of what the problem to be tackled actually is. Technical requirements such as these don't play a role in use case analysis.

Although it's certainly conceivable that the users of our system might be technically sophisticated, it's best to express functional requirements so that even a user who knows nothing about the inner workings of a computer will understand them. This helps to ensure that technical requirements don't creep into the functional requirements statement, a common mistake made by many inexperienced software developers. When we allow technical requirements to color the functional requirements, they artificially constrain the solution to a problem too early in the development life cycle.

Involving the Users

Users are the ultimate experts in what they need the system to do, so it's absolutely essential that they be involved in the use case definition process. If the intended users haven't (as individuals) been specifically defined or recruited, as with a software product that is to be sold commercially, their anticipated needs nonetheless need to be taken into account by identifying people with comparable experience to serve as "user surrogates." Ideally, the users or user surrogates (the human ones, anyway) will write some or all of the use cases themselves; at a minimum, you'll interview such people, write the use cases on their behalf, and then get their confirmation that what you've written is indeed accurate.

Use cases are some of the first deliverables/artifacts to emerge in a software development project's life cycle. They turn out to be quite useful as a basis for writing testing scripts, to ensure that all functional threads are exercised during system and user acceptance testing. They also lend themselves to the preparation of a *requirements traceability matrix* (that is, a final checklist against which the users can verify that all of their initial requirements have indeed been met when the system is delivered). Of course, a requirements traceability matrix must take into account all of the requirements for a system—functional as well as technical— of which use cases represent only a subset. An example of a requirements traceability matrix created inside an Excel workbook is shown in Figure 9-1.

Requirement #	Requirement Statement	Source	Test Specification	Test Case #	Verification	Modification
SRS1.1	Adherence to W3C and related standards	System adminstrato	Developer unit tes	1.1.2	Verified	None
SRS1.2	Can be linked with ADO.NET database	Dean of College	System integration	1.2.0	Pending	None

Figure 9-1. *A sample requirements traceability matrix*

Returning to the questions that we posed at the outset of this section, let's answer the first question ("Who will want to use our system?"), which is known as *identifying actors* in use case nomenclature.

Actors

Actors represent anybody or anything that will interact with the system after it's built; actors' needs are the basis for use cases. Actors generally fall into two broad categories:

- Human users

- Other computer systems

When actors interact with the system, they generally want to achieve some result, but actors can also simply provide/contribute information to the system and/or receive/consume information from the system.

By *providing* information, we mean whether or not the actor inputs substantive information that adds to the residual data stored by the system; for example, a department chairperson defining a new course offering or a student registering his or her plan of study. This doesn't include the relatively trivial information that users have to provide to look things up; for example, typing in a student ID to request their transcript.

By *consuming* information, we mean whether or not the actor uses the system to obtain information; for example, a faculty user printing out a student roster for a course that he or she will be teaching, or a student viewing his or her course schedule online.

Identifying Actors and Determining Their Roles

We must create an actor for every different role that will be assumed by various categories of user relative to the system. To identify such roles, we typically turn first to the *narrative requirements specification*, if one exists, which is a statement of the functional requirements, such as the SRS specification. The only category of user explicitly mentioned by that specification is a student user. So, we would definitely consider a student to be one of the actor types for the SRS.

If we think beyond the specification, however, it isn't difficult to come up with other potential categories of user who might also benefit from using the SRS:

- Faculty might want to get a head count of how many students are registered for one of the upcoming classes that they will be teaching or might use the system to post final grades, which in turn are reflected by a student's transcript.

- Department chairs might want to see how popular various courses are or conversely, whether or not a course ought to be cancelled due to lack of interest on the part of the student body.

- Personnel in the Registrar's Office might want to use the SRS to verify that a particular student is projected to have met the requirements to graduate in a given semester.

- Alumni might want to use the SRS to request copies of their transcripts.

- Prospective students—those who are thinking about applying for admission but who haven't yet done so—might want to browse the courses that are going to be offered in an upcoming semester to help them determine whether or not the university has a curriculum that meets their interests.

Similarly, because we said that other computer systems can be actors, we might have to build interfaces between the SRS and other existing automated systems at the university, such as the following:

- The Billing System, so that students can be billed accurately based on their current course load

- The Classroom Scheduling System, to ensure that classes to be taught are assigned to rooms of adequate capacity based on the student head count

- The Admissions System, so that the SRS can be notified when a new student has been admitted and is eligible to register for courses

Of course, we have to make a decision early on as to what the scope of the system we're going to build should be, to avoid "requirements inflation" or "mission creep." To try and accommodate all the actors hypothesized earlier would result in a massive undertaking that might simply be too costly for the sponsors of the system. For example, does it make sense to provide for potential students to use the SRS to preview what the university offers in the way of courses, or is there a different system—say, an online course catalog of some sort—that is better suited to this purpose? Through in-depth interviews with representatives of all the intended user groups, the scope of the system can be appropriately bounded, and some of the actors that we conceived of might be eliminated as a result.

In our particular case, we'll assume that the sponsors of the SRS have decided that we needn't accommodate the needs of alumni or prospective students in building the system; that is, that we needn't recognize alumni or prospective students as actors. A key point here is that the sponsors decide such things, *not the programmers*! One responsibility of a software engineer is indeed to identify requirements, and certainly part of that responsibility might include suggesting functional enhancements that the software engineer feels will be of benefit to the user. But, the sponsors of the system rightfully have the final say in what actually gets built.

Tip Many software engineers get into trouble because they assume that they know better than their clients what users really need. You might indeed have a brilliant idea to suggest, but think of it simply as that—a suggestion—and consider your task as one of either convincing the sponsors/users of its merit, or of graciously accepting their decision to decline your suggestion.

Note that the same user might interact with the system on different occasions in different roles. That is, a professor who chairs a department might assume the role of a Department Chair actor when he or she is trying to determine whether a course should be cancelled. Alternatively, the same professor might assume the role of a Faculty user when he or she wants to query the SRS for the student head count for a particular course that he or she is teaching.

Diagramming a System and Its Actors

After we settle on the actors for our system, we might want to diagram them. Unified Modeling Language (UML) notation calls for representing all actors—whether a human user or a computer system—as stick figures and then connecting them via straight lines to a rectangle representing the system, as shown in Figure 9-2.

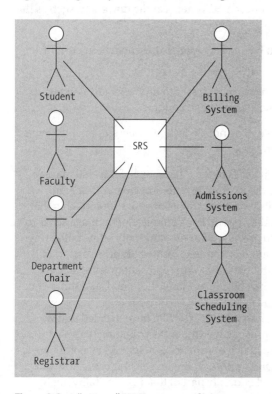

Figure 9-2. *A "proper" UML use case diagram*

This figure appears rather simplistic, yet it is a legitimate diagram that might be produced for a project such as the SRS development effort.

We prefer to use a slightly modified version of the UML notation, as follows:

- We'll use rectangles to represent not only the core system but also all actors that are external systems instead of representing the latter as human stick figures.

- We find that using arrowheads to reflect a directional flow of information—whether an actor provides or consumes information—is a bit more communicative. For example, in our amended version of the notation we represent a Student as both providing and consuming information, whereas a Registrar only consumes information.

Note The Registrar does indeed provide information, but not to the SRS directly. He or she provides information to the Admissions System about which Students are registered at the university; this information then gets fed into the SRS by the Admissions System. So the Admissions System is shown as providing information as an actor to the SRS, but from the standpoint of the SRS, the Registrar is but a consumer.

With these slight changes in notation, as reflected in Figure 9-3, the UML diagram becomes a more communicative instrument.

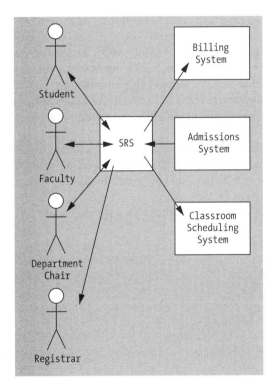

Figure 9-3. *Our customized version of use case notation*

Of course, if you do decide to deviate from a widely understood notational standard such as UML, you need to follow these steps:

1. Reach consensus among your fellow software developers, to ensure that the team as a whole is speaking the same language.

2. Document and communicate such deviations (along with the notation as a whole) to your customers/users, so that they, too, understand your particular "dialect."

3. Make sure that such documentation is incorporated into the full documentation set for the project, so that future reviewers of the documentation will immediately understand your notational "embellishments."

If you make these enhancements intuitive enough, however, they might just speak for themselves! Of course, as we pointed out in Chapter 8, you'll also need to consider whether the Computer-Aided Software Engineering (CASE) tool you're using, if any, will support such alterations.

Time and again throughout Part Two of this book, we'll remind you that it's perfectly acceptable to adapt or extend any process, notation, or tool that you care to adopt to best suit your company's or project's purposes; none of these methodology components is sacred.

Specifying Use Cases

Having made a first cut at what the SRS actors are, we'll next enumerate in what ways the system will be used by these actors: in other words, the use cases themselves.

A use case represents a logical *thread*, or a series of cause-and-effect events, beginning with an actor's first contact with the system and ending with the achievement of that actor's goal for using the system in the first place. Note that an actor always initiates a use case; actions initiated by a system on its own behalf don't warrant the development of a use case (although they do warrant expression as either a functional or technical requirement, as defined earlier in the chapter).

Use cases emphasize *what* the system is to do—functional requirements—without concern for *how* such things will be accomplished internally, and aren't unlike method signatures in this regard. In fact, you can think of a use case as a "behavioral signature" for the system as a whole.

Some example high-level use cases for the Student actor might be the following:

- Register for a course.
- Drop a course.
- Choose a faculty advisor.
- Establish a plan of study.
- View the schedule of classes.
- Request a transcript.
- Determine a student's eligibility for graduation.

Some high-level use cases for the Faculty actor might include the following:

- Determine a student's course load.
- View the schedule of classes.
- Request a student roster for a given course.
- Request a transcript for a given student.
- Maintain course information (for example, change the course description, reflect a different instructor for the course, and so on).
- Post final semester grades for a given course.

Looking at the sample use cases, sometimes different actors will share the same use cases. Both students and faculty might, for example, need to check the schedule of classes. Remember that a use case is initiated by an actor, which is why we didn't list other functionality called out by the SRS requirements specification, such as "Notify student by email," as use cases.

We might decompose any one of the use cases into steps, each step representing a more detailed use case; for example, "Register for a course " might be decomposed into these steps:

1. Verify that a student has met the prerequisites.

2. Check student's plan of study to ensure that this course is required.

3. Check for availability of a seat in the course.

4. (Optionally) Place student on a wait list.

Use cases might be interrelated in parent-child fashion, with more detailed use cases being shared by more than one general use case. For example, the "Request a student roster " and "Post final semester grades" general use cases might both involve the more detailed "Verify that professor is teaching the course in question" use case.

Unfortunately, as is true of all requirements analysis, there is no magical formula to apply to determine whether you identified all the important use cases or all of the actors, and/or whether you've gone into sufficient depth in terms of sub use cases. The process of use case development is iterative; when subsequent iterations fail to yield substantial changes, you're probably finished! Copious interviews and reviews with users, observing (or tracking) prospective users in their daily tasks, and periodic team walkthroughs of the use case set as a whole go a long way to ensure that nothing important has been missed.

Matching Up Use Cases with Actors

Another important step is to match up use cases with actors. The relationship between actors and use cases is potentially many-to-many, in that the same actor might initiate many different use cases, and a single use case might be relevant to many different actors. By cross-referencing actors with use cases, we ensure the following:

- We didn't identify an actor who, in the final analysis, really has no use for the system after all.

- Conversely, that we didn't specify a use case that nobody really cares about after all.

- And most important of all, it enables each actor to focus on the individual part of the system when they are reviewing the use case diagram to make sure that an important requirement the actor might have hasn't been left out of the model.

For each use case–actor combination, it's useful to determine whether the actor consumes information and/or provides information. Another way to view this aspect of a system is whether actors need write access to the system's information resources (providing) versus having read-only access (consuming).

If the number of actors and/or use cases isn't prohibitive, a simple table such as Table 9-1 can be used to summarize all the preceding.

Table 9-1. *A Simple Actor/Use Case Cross-Referencing Technique*

Initiating Actor ➤ Use Cases	Student	Faculty	Billing System	Etc.
Register for a course	Provides info	N/A	N/A	
Post final grades	Consumes info	Provides info	N/A	
Request a transcript	Consumes info	Consumes info	N/A	
Determine a student's course load	Consumes info	Consumes info	Consumes info	
Etc.				

To Diagram or Not to Diagram?

The use case concept is fairly straightforward, and hence simple narrative text as we've seen thus far in the chapter is often sufficient for expressing use cases. The UML does, however, provide a formal means for diagramming use cases and their interactions with actors. As mentioned earlier:

- Actors who are people are represented as stick figures;

- The core system and all actors that are external systems are represented with rectangles.

Now we'll add the following:

- Use cases are represented as ovals labeled underneath with a brief phrase describing the use case

- The boxes surrounding the oval(s) represent the system boundaries.

Figure 9-4 shows a sample UML use case diagram; here, we depict three actors—Student, Faculty, and Registrar—as having occasion to participate individually in the Request Transcript use case.

When deciding whether to go to the trouble of diagramming your use cases instead of merely expressing them in narrative form, think back to the rationale for producing use cases in the first place: to think through and to then communicate the software development team's understanding of the system requirements to the users/sponsors in order to obtain their concurrence. It's up to you, your project team, and your users/sponsors to determine whether diagrams enhance this process or not. If they do, use them; if they don't, go with narrative use case documentation, such as the "SRS Requirements Specification" shown at the end of the Introduction section of this book instead.

Once you've documented a system's actors and use cases, whether in text alone or with accompanying diagrams, they become part of the core documentation set defining the problem to be automated. In the next chapter, we'll examine how to use such documentation as a starting point for determining what classes we'll need to create and instantiate as our system building blocks.

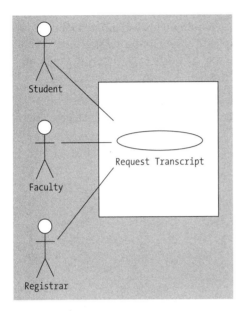

Figure 9-4. *A sample UML use case diagram*

The UML spells out some additional conventions with regard to use case modeling; for more details on use case diagrams, including advanced diagramming techniques, please see our recommended reading list in Chapter 17.

Summary

In this chapter, you learned the following:

- Use case analysis is a simple yet powerful technique for specifying the functional requirements for a system more precisely and completely.

- Use cases are based upon the goal-oriented functional requirements for a system.

- Use cases are used to describe:

  - The desired behavior/functionality of the system to be built

  - The external users or systems (known as actors) who avail themselves of these services

  - The interactions between the two

- The elements that don't belong in a use case (for example, technical requirements).

Exercises

1. For the problem area whose requirements you defined for exercise 3 in Chapter 2, determine what the appropriate actors might be.

2. Based on the context of the problem area whose requirements you defined for exercise 3 in Chapter 2, list (a) the use cases that are explicitly called for by the specification and (b) any additional use cases that you suspect might be worth exploring with the future users of the system.

3. Create a table mapping the actors you identified in exercise 1 to the use cases you listed in exercise 2, indicating whether a particular actor's participation in a use case is as an information provider or consumer.

CHAPTER 10

■ ■ ■

Modeling the Static/Data Aspects of the System

Having employed use case analysis techniques in Chapter 9 to round out the Student Registration System (SRS) requirements specification, we're ready to tackle the next stage of modeling, which is determining how we can meet those requirements in an object-oriented (OO) fashion. It's important when undertaking any code development project to spend time analyzing and designing the application before starting to write the actual code—and that's what we'll do with the SRS in this chapter. Writing code without proper planning is like driving somewhere new without looking at a map or using a GPS. You might get where you want to go, but not without a lot of wrong turns and backtracking.

You saw in Part One of the book that objects form the building blocks of an OO system, and classes are the templates used to define and instantiate objects. An OO model, then, must specify the following:

- *What types of objects we'll need to define and instantiate in order to represent the proper abstraction.* In particular, the fields, properties, and methods the classes will declare; and their structural relationships with one another. Because these elements of an OO system, once established, are fairly static—in the same way that a house, once built, has a specific layout, a given number of rooms, a particular roofline, and so forth—we often refer to this process as preparing the *static model*.

  We can certainly change the static structure of a house over time by undertaking remodeling projects, just as we can change the static structure of an OO software system as new requirements emerge by deriving new subclasses, inventing new methods for existing classes, and so forth. However, if a structure—whether a home or a software system—is properly designed from the outset, the need for such changes should arise relatively infrequently over its lifetime and shouldn't be overly difficult to accommodate.

- *How these objects will need to collaborate in carrying out the overall requirements, or "mission," of the system.* The ways in which objects interact can change literally from one moment to the next based upon the circumstances that are in effect. One moment, a Course object might be registering a Student object, and the next, it might be responding to a query by a Professor object as to the current student head count. We refer to the process of detailing object collaborations as preparing the *dynamic model*. Think of this as all of the different day-to-day activities that go on in a home: same structure, different functions.

The static and dynamic models are simply two different sides of the same coin: they jointly comprise the OO "blueprint" that we'll work from in implementing an OO SRS application in Part Three of the book.

In this chapter, we'll focus on building the static model for the SRS, leaving a discussion of the dynamic model for Chapter 11. You'll learn the following:

- A technique for identifying the appropriate classes and their fields

- How to determine the structural relationships that exist among these classes

- How to graphically portray this information as a *class diagram* using Unified Modeling Language (UML) notation

Identifying Appropriate Classes

Our first challenge in object modeling is to determine what classes we'll need as our system building blocks. Unfortunately, the process of class identification is rather "fuzzy"; it relies heavily on intuition, prior modeling experience, and familiarity with the subject area, or *domain*, of the system to be developed. So, how does an object-modeling novice ever get started? One tried and true (but somewhat tedious) procedure for identifying candidate classes is to use the "hunt and gather" method: that is, to hunt for and gather a list of all nouns and noun phrases from the project documentation set and to then use a process of elimination to whittle this list down into a set of appropriate classes.

In the case of the SRS, our documentation set thus far consists of the following:

- The requirements specification

- The use case model that we prepared in Chapter 9

Noun Phrase Analysis

Let's perform noun phrase analysis on the SRS requirements specification first, which was originally presented in the Introduction. Alternatively, the noun phrase analysis can be performed on the SRS use case descriptions from Chapter 9. As shown in the following sidebar, the noun phrases in the SRS specification have been highlighted.

HIGHLIGHTING NOUN PHRASES IN THE SRS SPECIFICATION

We have been asked to develop an **automated Student Registration System (SRS)** for the **university**. This **system** will enable **students** to register online for **courses** each **semester**, as well as track their **progress** toward **completion** of their **degree**.

When a **student** first enrolls at the **university**, he/she uses the **SRS** to set forth a **plan of study** as to which **courses** he/she plans on taking to satisfy a particular **degree program**, and chooses a **faculty advisor**. The **SRS** will verify whether or not the proposed **plan of study** satisfies the **requirements of the degree** that the **student** is seeking.

Once a **plan of study** has been established, then, during the **registration period** preceding each **semester, students** are able to view the **schedule of classes** online, and choose whichever **classes** they wish to attend, indicating the **preferred section (day of the week** and **time of day)** if the **class** is offered by more than one **professor.** The **SRS** will verify whether or not the **student** has satisfied the necessary **prerequisites** for each **requested course** by referring to the **student's** online **transcript** of **courses completed** and **grades received** (the **student** can review his/her **transcript** online at any time).

Assuming that (a) the **prerequisites** for the **requested course(s)** are satisfied, (b) the **course(s)** meet(s) one of the **student's plan of study requirements,** and (c) there is **room** available in each of the **class(es),** the **student** is enrolled in the **class(es).**

If (a) and (b) are satisfied, but (c) is not, the **student** is placed on a **first-come, first-served wait list.** If a **class/section that he/she was previously waitlisted for** becomes available (either because some other **student** has dropped the **class** or because the **seating capacity** for the **class** has been increased), the **student** is automatically enrolled in the **waitlisted class,** and an **email message** to that effect is sent to the **student.** It is his/her **responsibility** to drop the **class** if it is no longer desired; otherwise, he/she will be billed for the **course.**

Students can drop a **class** up to the **end** of the **first week of the semester in which the class is being taught.**

A simple spreadsheet serves as an ideal tool for recording our initial findings; just enter noun phrases as a single-column list in the order in which they occur in the specification. Don't worry about trying to eliminate duplicates or consolidating synonyms just yet; we'll do that in a moment. The resultant spreadsheet is shown in part in Figure 10-1.

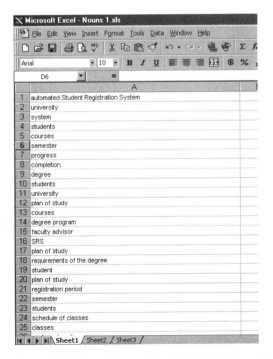

Figure 10-1. *Noun phrases found in the SRS specification*

We're working with a very concise requirements specification (approximately 350 words long), and yet this process is already proving to be very tedious! It would be impossible to carry out an exhaustive noun phrase analysis for anything but a trivially simple specification. If you're faced with a voluminous requirements specification, start by writing an "executive summary" of no more than a few pages to paraphrase the system's mission, and then use your summary version of the specification as the starting point for your noun survey. Paraphrasing a specification in this fashion provides the added benefit of ensuring that you have read through the system requirements and understand the big picture. Of course, you'll need to review your summary narrative with your customers/users to ensure that you've accurately captured all key points.

After you type all the nouns/noun phrases into the spreadsheet, sort the spreadsheet and eliminate duplicates; this includes eliminating plural forms of singular terms (for example, eliminate "students" in favor of "student"). We want all our class names to be singular in the final analysis, so if any plural forms remain in the list after eliminating duplicates (for example, "prerequisites"), make them singular as well. In so doing, our SRS list shrinks to 38 items in length, as shown in Figure 10-2.

	A
1	automated Student Registration System
2	class
3	class that he/she was previously waitlisted for
4	completion
5	course
6	courses completed
7	day of the week
8	degree
9	degree program
10	email message
11	end
12	faculty advisor
13	first week of the semester in which the class is being taught
14	first-come, first-served wait list
15	grades received
16	plan of study
17	plan of study requirements
18	preferred section
19	prerequisites
20	professor
21	progress
22	registration period
23	requested course
24	requirements of the degree
25	responsibility
26	room
27	schedule of classes
28	seating capacity
29	section
30	section that he/she was previously waitlisted for
31	semester
32	SRS
33	student
34	system
35	time of day
36	transcript
37	university
38	waitlisted class

Sheet1 / Sheet2 / Sheet3 /

Figure 10-2. *Removing duplicates streamlines the noun phrase list.*

Remember that we're trying to identify both physical and conceptual objects; as stated in Chapter 3, *"something mental or physical toward which thought, feeling, or action is directed."* Let's now make another pass to eliminate the following:

- References to the system itself ("automated Student Registration System," "SRS," "system").

- References to the university. Because we're building the SRS within the context of a single university, the university in some senses "sits outside" and "surrounds" the SRS; we don't need to manipulate information about the university within the SRS, and so we can eliminate the term "university" from our candidate class list.

  Note, however, that if we were building a system that needed to span multiple universities—say, a system that compared graduate programs of study in information technology across the top 100 universities in the country—then we would indeed need to model each university as a separate object, in which case we'd keep "university" on our candidate class list.

- Other miscellaneous terms that don't seem to fit the definition of an object are "completion," "end," "progress," "responsibility," "registration period," and "requirements of the degree." Admittedly, some of these are debatable, particularly the last two; to play it safe, you might wish to create a list of rejected terms to be revisited later on in the modeling life cycle.

The list shrinks to 27 items as a result, as shown in Figure 10-3—it's starting to get manageable now!

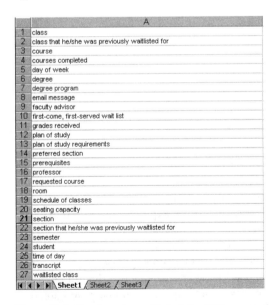

	A
1	class
2	class that he/she was previously waitlisted for
3	course
4	courses completed
5	day of week
6	degree
7	degree program
8	email message
9	faculty advisor
10	first-come, first-served wait list
11	grades received
12	plan of study
13	plan of study requirements
14	preferred section
15	prerequisites
16	professor
17	requested course
18	room
19	schedule of classes
20	seating capacity
21	section
22	section that he/she was previously waitlisted for
23	semester
24	student
25	time of day
26	transcript
27	waitlisted class

◄◄ ◄ ► ►◄ \ **Sheet1** ⟨ Sheet2 ⟨ Sheet3 ⟨

Figure 10-3. *Further streamlining the SRS noun phrase list*

The next pass is a bit trickier. We need to group apparent synonyms, to choose the one designation from among each group of synonyms that is best suited to serve as a class name. Having a subject matter expert on your modeling team is important for this step because determining the subtle shades of meaning of some of these terms so as to group them properly isn't always easy.

We've grouped together terms that seem to be synonyms in Figure 10-4, bolding the term in each synonym group that we're inclined to choose above the rest. The gray shading in the figure is used to highlight individual synonym groups. Words that are *italicized* represent those terms for which no synonyms have been identified.

	A
1	**class**
2	**course**
3	waitlisted class
4	class that he/she was previously waitlisted for
5	section that he/she was previously waitlisted for
6	preferred section
7	requested course
8	**section**
9	prerequisites
10	courses completed
11	grades received
12	**transcript**
13	*day of week*
14	**degree**
15	degree program
16	*email message*
17	faculty advisor
18	**professor**
19	*first-come, first-served wait list*
20	**plan of study**
21	plan of study requirements
22	*room*
23	*schedule of classes*
24	*seating capacity*
25	*semester*
26	*student*
27	*time of day*

Figure 10-4. *Grouping synonyms*

Let's now review the rationale for our choices.

We choose the shorter form of similar expressions whenever possible—"degree" instead of "degree program" and "plan of study" instead of "plan of study requirements"—to make our model more concise.

Although they aren't synonyms as such, the notion of a *transcript* implies a record of "courses completed" and "grades received," so we'll opt to drop the latter two noun phrases for now.

When choosing candidate class names, we should avoid choosing nouns that imply *roles* between objects. As you learned in Chapter 5, a role is something that an object belonging to class A possesses by virtue of its relationship to/association with an object belonging to class B. For example, a professor holds the role of "faculty advisor" when that professor is associated with a student via an *advises* association. Even if a professor were to lose all of his or her advisees, thus losing the role of faculty advisor, he or she would still be a professor by virtue of being employed by the university—it's intrinsic in the person's nature relative to the SRS.

Note If a professor were to lose his or her job with the university, one might argue that he or she is no longer a professor; but then, this person would have no dealings with the SRS, either, so it's a moot point.

For this reason, we prefer "Professor" to "Faculty Advisor" as a candidate class name, but make a mental note to ourselves that faculty advisor would make a good potential association when we get to considering such things later on.

Regarding the notion of a course, we see that we've collected numerous noun phrases that all refer to a course in one form or another: "class," "course," "preferred section," "requested course," "section," "prerequisite," "waitlisted class," "class that they were previously waitlisted for," "section that they were previously waitlisted for." Within this grouping, several roles are implied:

- "Waitlisted class" in its several different forms implies a role in an association between a Student and a Course.

- "Prerequisite" implies a role in an association between two Courses.

- "Requested course" implies a role in an association between a Student and a Course.

- "Preferred section" implies a role in an association between a Student and a Course.

Eliminating all these role designations, we're left with only three terms: "class," "course," and "section." Before we hastily eliminate all but one of these as synonyms, let's think carefully about what real-world concepts we're trying to represent.

- The notion that we typically associate with the term "course" is that of a semester-long series of lectures, assignments, exams, and so on that all relate to a particular subject area. It is a unit of education toward earning a degree. For example, Beginning Math is a course.

- The terms "class" and "section," on the other hand, generally refer to the offering of a *particular* course in a *given* semester on a given day of the week and at a given time of day. For example, the course Math 101 is being offered this coming Spring semester as three classes/sections:

  - Section 1, which meets Tuesdays from 4 to 6 p.m.

  - Section 2, which meets Wednesdays from 6 to 8 p.m.

  - Section 3, which meets Thursdays from 3 to 5 p.m.

- There is thus a one-to-many association between Course and Class/Section. The same course is offered potentially many times in a given semester and over many semesters during the "lifetime" of the course.

Therefore, "course" and "class/section" truly represent different abstractions, and we'll keep both concepts in our candidate class list. Because "class" and "section" appear to be synonyms, however, we need to choose one term and discard the other. Our initial inclination would be to keep "class" and discard "section," but in order to avoid confusion when referring to a class named Class (!), we'll opt for "section" instead.

Refining the Candidate Class List

A list of candidate classes has begun to emerge from the fog! Here is our remaining short list (please disregard the trailing symbols [*, +] for the moment—we'll explain their significance shortly):

- Course
- Day of week*
- Degree*
- Email message+
- Plan of study
- Professor
- Room*
- Schedule of classes+
- Seating capacity*
- Section
- Semester*
- Student
- Time of day*
- Transcript
- (First-come, first-served) Wait list

Not all of these will necessarily survive to the final model, however, because we'll scrutinize each one very closely before deeming it worthy of implementation as a class. One classic test for determining whether or not an item can stand on its own as a class is to ask these questions:

- Can we think of any *fields* for this class?
- Can we think of any *capabilities* that would be expected of objects belonging to this class?

One example is the term "room." We could invent a Room class as follows:

```
public class Room {
  // Fields.
  int roomNo;
  string building;
  int seatingCapacity;
  // etc.
}
```

Or we could simply represent a room location as a `string` field of the `Section` class:

```
public class Section {
  // Fields.
  Course offeringOf;
  string semester;
  string dayOfWeek;  // "Mon", "Tue", "Wed", "Thu", "Fri"
  string timeOfDay;
  string classroomLocation; // building name and room name:  e.g.,
                            // "Government Hall Room 105"
  // etc.
}
```

Which approach to representing a room is preferred? It all depends on whether or not a room needs to be a focal point of our application. If the SRS were meant to also do "double duty" as a Classroom Scheduling System, then we might indeed wish to instantiate Room objects to be able to ask them to perform such duties as printing out their weekly usage schedules or telling us their seating capacities. However, because these capabilities weren't mentioned as requirements in the SRS specification, we'll opt for making a room designation a simple `string` field of the `Section` class. We reserve the right, however, to change our minds about this later on; it's not unusual for some items to "flip flop" over the life cycle of a modeling exercise between being classes on their own versus being represented as simple fields of other classes.

Following a similar train of thought for all of the items marked with an asterisk (*) in the preceding candidate class list, we'll opt to treat them all as fields rather than making them classes of their own:

- "Day of week" will be incorporated as either a `string` or `char` field of the `Section` class.

- "Degree" will be incorporated as a `string` field of the `Student` class.

- "Seating capacity" will be incorporated as an `int` field of the `Section` class.

- "Semester" will be incorporated as a `string` field of the `Section` class.

- "Time of day" will be incorporated as a `string` or `DateTime` field of the `Section` class.

When we're first modeling an application, we want to focus exclusively on functional requirements to the exclusion of technical requirements, as defined in Chapter 9; this means that we need to avoid getting into the technical details of how the system is going to function behind the scenes. Ideally, we want to focus solely on what are known as *domain classes*—that is, abstractions that an end user will recognize, and which represent "real-world" entities—and to avoid introducing any extra classes that are used solely as behind-the-scenes "scaffolding" to hold the application together, known alternatively as *implementation classes* or *solution space classes*. Examples of the latter would be the creation of a collection object to organize and maintain references to all of the `Professor` objects in the system, or the use of a dictionary to provide a way to quickly find a particular `Student` object based on the associated student ID number. We'll talk more about solution space objects in Part Three of the book; for the time being, the items flagged with a plus sign (+) in the candidate class list earlier—"email message" and "schedule of classes"—seem arguably more like implementation classes than domain classes.

- An email message is typically a *transient* piece of data, not unlike a pop-up message that appears on the screen while using an application: it gets sent *out* of the SRS system, and after it's read by the recipient, we have no control over whether the email is retained or deleted. It's unlikely that the SRS is going to archive copies of all email messages that have been sent—there certainly was no requirement to do so—so we won't worry about modeling them as objects at this stage in our analysis.

  Email messages will resurface in Chapter 11, when we talk about the behaviors of the SRS application, because *sending* an email message is definitely an important *behavior;* but, emails don't constitute an important *structural* piece of the application, so we don't want to introduce a class for them at this stage in the modeling process. When we actually get to programming the system, we might indeed create an `EmailMessage` class in C#, but it needn't be modeled as a domain class. (If, on the other hand, we were modeling an email messaging system in anticipation of building one, then `EmailMessage` would indeed be a key domain class in our model.). The email could alternatively be included as a technical requirement of the SRS (as discussed in Chapter 9).

- We could go either way with the schedule of classes—include it as a candidate class or drop it from our list. The schedule of classes, as a single object, might not be something that the user will manipulate directly, but there will be some notion behind the scenes of a schedule of classes *collection* controlling which `Section` objects should be presented to the user as a graphical user interface (GUI) pick list when he or she registers in a given semester. We'll omit `ScheduleOfClasses` from our candidate class list for now, but we can certainly revisit our decision as the model evolves.

Determining whether or not a class constitutes a domain class instead of an implementation class is admittedly a gray area, and either of the preceding candidate class "rejects" could be successfully argued into or out of the list of core domain classes for the SRS. In fact, this entire exercise of identifying classes hopefully illustrates a concept that was first introduced in Chapter 2; because of its importance, we'll repeat it again in the following sidebar.

OBJECT MODELING ISN'T EASY!

Developing an appropriate model for a software system is perhaps the most difficult aspect of software engineering, because there is an unlimited number of possibilities. Abstraction is to a certain extent in the eye of the beholder: several different observers working independently are almost guaranteed to arrive at different models. Whose is the best? Passionate arguments have ensued!

To further complicate matters, there is virtually never only one "best" or "correct" model, only "better" or "worse" models relative to the problem to be solved. The same situation can be modeled in a variety of different, equally valid ways. There is no "acid test" to determine whether a model has adequately captured all of a user's requirements.

As we continue along with our SRS modeling exercise, and particularly as we move from modeling to implementation in Part Three of the book, we'll have many opportunities to rethink the decisions that we made here. The key point to remember is that the model isn't "cast in stone" until we actually begin programming. Even then, if we've used objects wisely,

CHAPTER 10 ■ MODELING THE STATIC/DATA ASPECTS OF THE SYSTEM   **271**

the model can be fairly painlessly modified to handle most new requirements. Think of a model as being formed out of modeling clay: we'll continue to reshape it over the course of the analysis and design phases of our project until we're satisfied with the result.

Meanwhile, back to the task of coming up with a list of candidate classes for the SRS. The terms that have survived our latest round of scrutiny are as follows:

- `Course`
- `PlanOfStudy`
- `Professor`
- `Section`
- `Student`
- `Transcript`
- `WaitList`

Let's examine `WaitList` one last time. There is indeed a requirement for the SRS to maintain a student's position on a first-come, first-served wait list. But, it turns out that this requirement can actually be handled through a combination of an association between the `Student` and `Section` classes, plus something known as an *association class*, which you'll learn about later in this chapter. This would not be immediately obvious to a beginning modeler, and so we'd fully expect that the `WaitList` class might make the final cut as a suggested SRS class. But we'll assume that we have an experienced object modeler on the team, who convinces us to eliminate the class; we'll see that this was a suitable move when we complete the SRS class diagram at the end of the chapter.

So, we'll settle on the following list of classes, based on our noun phrase analysis of the SRS specification:

- `Course`
- `PlanOfStudy`
- `Professor`
- `Section`
- `Student`
- `Transcript`

The results of the noun phrase analysis we just performed for the SRS might seem pretty obvious. You might think you could have arrived at the final list yourself without going through the whole noun phrase analysis process. That might be true for the SRS, which is a fairly simple system, but for more complex applications the final classes needed might not be obvious at all. In these situations, a systematic approach is critical for narrowing down the potential classes to the ones that you will model.

Revisiting the Use Cases

One more thing that we need to do before we deem our class list good to go is to revisit our use cases—in particular, the actors—to see whether any of them ought to be added as classes. You might recall that we identified seven potential actors for the SRS in Chapter 9:

- Student

- Faculty

- Department Chair

- Registrar

- Billing System

- Admissions System

- Classroom Scheduling System

Do any of them deserve to be modeled as classes in the SRS? Here's how to make that determination: if any user associated with any actor type A is going to need to manipulate (access or modify/produce or consume) information concerning an actor type B when A is logged onto the SRS, then B needs to be included as a class in our model. This is best illustrated with a few examples.

- When a student logs on to the SRS, might he or she need to access information about faculty? Yes; when a student selects an advisor, for example, he or she might need to view information about a variety of faculty members in order to choose an appropriate advisor. So, the Faculty actor role must be represented as a class in the SRS; indeed, we have already designated a Professor class, so we're covered there. But, student users are not concerned with department chairs per se.

- Following the same logic, we'd need to represent the Student actor role as a class because when professors log on to the SRS, they will be manipulating Student objects when printing out a course roster or assigning grades to students, for example. Because Student already appears in our candidate class list, we're covered there, as well.

- When any of the actors—Faculty, Students, the Registrar, the Billing System, the Admissions System, or the Classroom Scheduling System—access the SRS, will there be a need for any of them to manipulate information about the registrar? No; at least not according to the SRS requirements that we've seen so far. Therefore, we needn't model the Registrar actor role as a class.

- The same holds true for the Billing, Admissions, and Classroom Scheduling Systems: they require behind the scenes access to information managed by the SRS, but nobody logging on to the SRS expects to be able to manipulate any of these three systems directly, so they needn't be represented by domain classes in the SRS.

Note Again, when we get to implementing the SRS in code, we might indeed find it appropriate to create "solution space" C# classes to represent interfaces to these other automated systems; but such classes don't belong in a domain model of the SRS.

Therefore, our proposed candidate class list remains unchanged after revisiting all actor roles:

- Course

- PlanOfStudy

- Professor

- Section

- Student

- Transcript

Is this a perfect list? No—there is no such thing! In fact, before all is said and done, the list might—and in fact probably will—evolve in the following ways:

- We might add classes later on: terms we eliminated from the specification, or terms that don't even appear in the specification, but which we'll unearth through continued investigation.

- We might see an opportunity to generalize—that is, we might see enough commonality between two or more classes' respective fields, methods, or relationships with other classes to warrant the creation of a common base class.

- In addition, as mentioned earlier, we might rethink our decisions about representing some concepts as simple fields (semester, room, and so on) instead of as full-blown classes, and vice versa.

The development of a candidate class list is fraught with uncertainty. For this reason, it's important to have someone experienced with object modeling available to your team when embarking on your first object modeling effort. Most experienced modelers don't use the rote method of noun phrase analysis to derive a candidate class list; such folks can pretty much review a specification and directly pick out significant classes, in the same way that a professional jeweler can easily choose a genuine diamond from among a pile of fake gemstones. Nevertheless, what does "significant" really mean? That's where the "fuzziness" comes in! It's impossible to define precisely what makes one concept significant and another less so. We've tried to illustrate some procedural rules of thumb by working through the SRS example, but you ultimately need a qualified mentor to guide you until you develop—and trust—your own intuitive sense for such things.

The bottom line, however, is that even expert modelers can't really confirm the appropriateness of a given candidate class until they see its proposed use in the full context of a class diagram that also reflects associations, fields, and methods, which we'll explore later in this chapter as well as in Chapter 11.

Producing a Data Dictionary

Early on in our analysis efforts, it's important that we clarify and begin to document our use of terminology. A *data dictionary* is ideal for this purpose. For each candidate class, the data dictionary should include a simple definition of what this item means in the context of the model/system as a whole; include an example if it helps to illustrate the definition.

The following sidebar shows our complete SRS data dictionary so far.

THE SRS DATA DICTIONARY, TAKE 1: CLASS DEFINITIONS

Course: A semester-long series of lectures, assignments, exams, and so on that all relate to a particular subject area, and are typically associated with a particular number of credit hours; a unit of study toward a degree. For example, Beginning Objects is a required **course** for the Master of Science degree in Information Systems Technology.

PlanOfStudy: A list of the **courses** that a student intends to take to fulfill the **course** requirements for a particular degree.

Professor: A member of the faculty who teaches **sections** or advises **students**.

Section: The offering of a particular **course** during a particular semester on a particular day of the week and at a particular time of day (for example, the Beginning Objects **course**, as taught in the Spring 2009 semester on Mondays from 1:00 to 3:00 p.m.).

Student: A person who is currently enrolled at the university and who is eligible to register for one or more **sections**.

Transcript: A record of all of the **courses** taken to date by a particular **student** at this university, including which semester each **course** was taken in, the grade received, and the credits granted for the **course,** as well as a reflection of an overall total number of credits earned and the **student's** grade point average (GPA).

Note that it's permissible, and in fact encouraged, for the definition of one term to include one or more of the other terms; when we do so, we highlight the latter in **bold text**. These terms might give us insight into the associations that might exist between the various classes.

The data dictionary joins the set of other SRS narrative documents as a subsequent source of information about the model. As our model evolves, we'll expand the dictionary to include definitions of fields, associations, and methods.

■**Tip** It's a good idea to also include the dictionary definition of a class as a header comment in the C# code representing that class. Make sure to keep this inline documentation in sync with the external dictionary definition, however.

Determining Associations Between Classes

Once we've settled on an initial candidate class list, the next step is to determine how these classes are interrelated. To do this, we go back to our narrative documentation set (which has grown to consist of the SRS requirements specification, use case descriptions, and data dictionary) and study *verb* phrases this time. These verb phrases indicate the capabilities or functions that the classes will have to implement. Our goal in looking at verb phrases is to choose those that suggest structural relationships, as were defined in Chapter 5—associations, aggregations, and inheritance—but to eliminate or ignore those that represent (transient) actions or behaviors. (We'll focus on behaviors, but from the standpoint of use cases, in Chapter 11.)

For example, the specification states that a student "chooses a faculty advisor." This is indeed an action, and the result of this action is a lasting structural relationship between a professor and a student, which can be modeled via the association "a professor *advises* a student."

On the other hand, as a student's advisor, a professor also meets with the student, answers the student's questions, recommends courses for the student to take, approves his or her plan of study, and so on—these are behaviors on the part of a professor acting in the role of an advisor, but don't directly result in any new relationships being formed between objects.

Let's try the verb phrase analysis approach on the requirements specification. We've highlighted all relevant verb phrases in the sidebar that follows (note that we omitted such obviously irrelevant verb phrases as "We've been asked to develop an automated SRS . . .").

HIGHLIGHTING VERB PHRASES IN THE SRS SPECIFICATION

We have been asked to develop an automated Student Registration System (SRS) for the university. This system will **enable students to register online for courses** each semester, as well as **track their progress toward completion of their degree**.

When a student first **enrolls at the university**, he/she uses the SRS to **set forth a plan of study** as to which **courses he/she plans on taking** to **satisfy a particular degree program**, and **chooses a faculty advisor**. The SRS will **verify whether or not the proposed plan of study satisfies the requirements of the degree that the student is seeking**.

Once a **plan of study has been established,** then, during the registration period preceding each semester, students are able to **view the schedule of classes** online, and **choose whichever classes he/she wishes to attend, indicating the preferred section** (day of the week and time of day) if the **class is offered by more than one professor**. The SRS will **verify whether or not the student has satisfied the necessary prerequisites** for each requested course by **referring to the student's online transcript** of courses completed and grades received (the **student can review his/her transcript** online at any time).

Assuming that (a) the **prerequisites for the requested course(s) are satisfied**, (b) the **course(s) meet(s) one of the student's plan of study requirements**, and (c) **there is room available** in each of the class(es), the **student is enrolled in the class(es)**.

If (a) and (b) are satisfied, but (c) is not, the **student is placed on a first-come, first-served wait list**. If a **class/section that he/she was previously waitlisted for becomes available** (either because some other **student has dropped the class** or because the **seating capacity for the class has been increased**), the **student is automatically enrolled in the waitlisted class,** and an **email message** to that effect **is sent** to the student. It is his/her responsibility to **drop the class** if it is no longer desired; otherwise, **he/she will be billed for the course**.

Students can drop a class up to the end of the first week of the semester in which the **class is being taught**.

Let's scrutinize a few of these:

- *"Students [. . .] register [. . .] for courses"*: Although the act of registering is a behavior, the end result is that a static relationship is created between a Student and a Section, as represented by the association "a Student *registers* for a Section." (Note that the specification mentions registering for "courses," not "sections," but as we stated in our data dictionary, a Student registers for concrete Sections as specific types of Courses.) Keep in mind when reviewing a specification that natural language is often imprecise, and that as a result we have to read between the lines as to what the author really meant in every case. (If we're going to be the ones to write the specification, here is an incentive to keep the language as clear and concise as possible!)

- *"[Students track] their progress toward completion of their degree"*: Again, this is a behavior, but it nonetheless implies a structural relationship between a Student and a Degree. However, recall that we didn't elect to represent Degree as a class—we opted to reflect it as a simple string field of the Student class—and so this suggested relationship is immaterial with respect to the candidate class list that we've developed.

- *"Student first enrolls at the university"*: This is a behavior that results in a static relationship between a Student and the University; but we deemed the notion of "university" to be external to the SRS system and so chose not to create a University class in our model. So, we disregard this verb phrase, as well.

- *"[Student] sets forth a plan of study"*: This is a behavior that results in the static relationship "a Student pursues/follows a Plan of Study."

- *"Students are able to view the schedule of classes online"*: This is strictly a transient behavior of the SRS; no lasting relationship results from this action, so we disregard this verb phrase.

Association Matrices

Another complementary technique for both determining and recording what the relationships between classes should be is to create a two-dimensional *association matrix*, where the rows and columns of the matrix are labeled with the candidate classes that we identified, as shown in Table 10-1.

Table 10-1. *An "Empty" Association Matrix for the SRS*

	Section	Course	PlanOfStudy	Professor	Student	Transcript
Section						
Course						
PlanOfStudy						
Professor						
Student						
Transcript						

To complete the matrix, list all the associations in each cell that you can identify between the class named at the head of the row and the class named at the head of the column. For example, in the cell highlighted in Table 10-2 at the intersection of the Student row and the Section column, we have listed three potential associations:

- A Student *is waitlisted for* a Section.

- A Student *is registered for* a Section (this could be alternatively phrased as "a Student *is currently attending* a Section").

- A Student *has previously taken* a Section: This third association is important if we plan to maintain a history of all the classes a student has ever taken in his or her career as a student, which we must do if we are to prepare a student's transcript online. (As it turns out, we'll be able to get by with a single association that does "double duty" for the latter two of these—as you'll see later on in this chapter.)

Mark a cell with an X if there are no known relationships between the classes in question or if the potential relationships between the classes are irrelevant. For example, we marked the cells representing the intersection between Professor and Course with an X, even though there is an association possible—a Professor *is qualified to teach* a Course—because it isn't relevant to the mission of the SRS.

We mentioned in Chapter 4 that all associations are inherently bidirectional. This implies that if a cell in row *j*, column *k* indicates one or more associations, then the cell in row *k*, column *j* should reflect the reciprocal of these relationships. For example, because the intersection of the PlanOfStudy row and the Course column indicates that a PlanOfStudy *calls for* a Course, the intersection of the Course row and the PlanOfStudy column must indicate that a Course *is called for by* a PlanOfStudy.

It's not always practical to state the reciprocal of an association; for example, our association matrix shows that a Student *plans to take* a Course, but trying to state its reciprocal—a Course *is planned to be taken by* a Student—is quite awkward. In such cases where a reciprocal association would be awkward to phrase, simply indicate its presence with the check mark symbol.

Table 10-2. *Our Completed Association Matrix*

	Section	Course	PlanOfStudy	Professor	Student	Transcript
Section	✕	*example of*	✕	*is taught by*	✔	*included in*
Course	✔	*prerequisite for*	*is called for by*	✕	✔	✕
PlanOfStudy	✕	*calls for*	✕	✕	*observed by*	✕
Professor	*teaches*	✕	✕	✕	*advises; teaches*	✕
Student	*waitlisted for; registered for; has previously taken*	*plans to take*	*follows*	*is advised by; studies under*	✕	*owns*
Transcript	*includes*	✕	✕	✕	*belongs to*	✕

We'll be portraying these associations in graphical form shortly! For now, we'd want to go back and extend our data dictionary to explain what each of these associations means; the following is one such example.

ADDITIONS TO THE SRS DATA DICTIONARY

Calls for (a Plan of Study calls for a Course): In order to demonstrate that a **student** will satisfy the requirements for his or her chosen degree program, the **student** must formulate a **plan of study**. This **plan of study** lays out all of the **courses** that a **student** intends to take, and possibly specifies in which semester the **student** hopes to complete each **course**.

Identifying Fields

To determine what the fields for each of our domain classes should be, we make yet another pass through the requirements specification looking for clues. We already stumbled upon a few fields earlier, when we weeded out some nouns/noun phrases from our candidate class list:

- For the Section class, we identified "day of week", "room", "seating capacity", "semester", and "time of day" as nouns or noun phrases that would be represented as fields in the Section class.

- For the Student class, we identified "degree" as noun that should become a field of the class.

We can also bring any prior knowledge that we have about the domain into play when assigning fields to classes. Our knowledge of the way universities operate, for example, suggests that all students will need some sort of student ID number as a field, even though this isn't mentioned anywhere in the SRS specification. We can't be sure whether this particular university assigns an arbitrary student ID number, or whether the policy is to use a student's social security number (SSN) as his or her ID; these are details that we'd have to go back to our end users for clarification on. Steps would also have to be taken to ensure the security of sensitive information such as a student's ID.

Finally, we can also look at how similar information has been represented in existing legacy systems for clues as to what a class's fields should be. For example, if a Student Billing System already exists at the university based on a relational database design, we might wish to study the structure of the relational database table housing student information. The columns that have been provided in that table—name, address, birth date, and so on—are logical field choices. Keep in mind when thinking about the data modeling of classes that behavior modeling is just as (or more) important than the data modeling. We'll go into behavior modeling in detail in Chapter 11.

UML Notation: Modeling the Static Aspects of an Abstraction

Now that we have a much better understanding about the static aspects of our model, we're ready to portray these in graphical fashion to complement the narrative documentation that we've developed for the SRS. We'll be using UML to produce a class diagram. These next few sections will give you a brief introduction to UML diagramming but won't provide a comprehensive tutorial. For more details on UML, look to the references listed in Chapter 17. Here are the rules for how various aspects of the model are to be portrayed.

Classes, Fields, and Operations

We represent classes as rectangles. When we first conceive of a class—before we know what any of its fields or methods are going to be—we simply place the class name in the rectangle, as illustrated in Figure 10-5.

Figure 10-5. *UML depiction of the* Student *class*

An *abstract* class is denoted by presenting the class name in *italics*.

When we're ready to define the fields and operations of a class, we divide the class rectangle into three *compartments*—the class name compartment, the fields compartment, and the operations compartment—as shown in Figure 10-6. Note that the UML favors the nomenclature of *operations* instead of *methods* to reinforce the notion that the diagram is intended to be programming language independent.

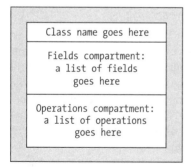

Figure 10-6. *Class rectangles are divided into three compartments.*

As we begin to identify what the fields and/or operations need to be for a particular class, we can add them to the diagram in as much or as little detail as we care to. We might choose simply to list field names, or we might specify their names along with their types (see Figure 10-7). For the Student we identified in the noun phrase analysis of the SRS, we might think to define fields that represent the name, ID, birth date, and grade point average (GPA) of a student as well as the total number of students enrolled in the university, as shown in Figure 10-7. Static fields are identified as such by underlining their names.

Figure 10-7. *Sometimes both field names and types are shown.*

We might choose simply to list operation names in the operations compartment of a class rectangle, or we might optionally choose to use an expanded form of operation definition as we have for the RegisterForCourse operation in Figure 10-8, in which the input parameter (Course x) and return type (bool) for the method are included.

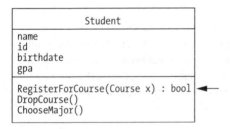

Figure 10-8. *Sometimes argument signatures and return types are also defined.*

It's often impractical to show all the fields and operations of every class in a class diagram because the diagram will get so cluttered that it will lose its "punch" as a communications tool. Consider the data dictionary to be the official, complete source of information concerning the model, and only reflect in the diagram those fields and operations that are particularly important in describing the mission of each class. In particular, "get" and "set" operations (whether implemented through methods or, in the case of C#, accessed as properties) are implied for all fields during the design stage and shouldn't be explicitly shown.

Also, just because the field or operation compartment of a class is empty, don't assume that there are no features of that type associated with a class; it usually simply means that the model is still evolving.

Relationships Between Classes

In Chapter 4, we defined several different types of structural relationships that can exist between classes—associations, aggregations (a specific type of association), and inheritance. Let's explore how each of these relationship types is represented graphically.

Binary associations—in other words, relationships between two different classes—are indicated by drawing a line between the rectangles representing the participating classes, and labeling the line with the name of the association. Role names can be reflected at either end of the association line if they add value to the model, but should otherwise be omitted.

We also mark each end of the line with the appropriate *multiplicity designator*, to indicate whether the relationship is one-to-one, one-to-many, or many-to-many (see Figure 10-9); we'll talk about how to do this a bit later in the chapter.

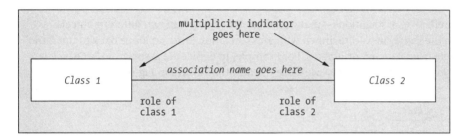

Figure 10-9. *Representing associations between classes*

All associations are assumed to be bidirectional at this stage in the modeling effort, and it doesn't matter in which order the participating classes are arranged in a class diagram. So to depict the association "a Professor *advises* a Student," the graphical notations in Figure 10-10 are all considered equivalent.

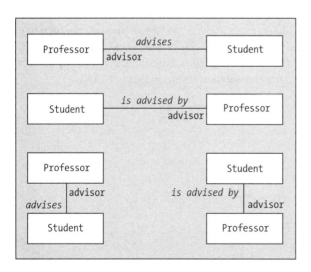

Figure 10-10. *Equivalent depictions of the advises association between the* Professor *and* Student *classes*

UML uses the simple convention of a small arrowhead (▶) to reflect the direction in which the association name is to be interpreted, giving us a lot more freedom in how we place our class rectangles in a diagram, as shown in Figure 10-11.

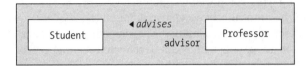

Figure 10-11. *Using an arrowhead to indicate the direction of an association label*

With the UML, no matter how the preceding two rectangles are situated, we can still always label the association *advises*.

Unary (reflexive) associations—that is, relationships between two different objects belonging to the same class—are drawn with an association line that loops back to the same class rectangle from which it originates. For example, to depict the association "a Course *is a prerequisite for* a (different) Course," we'd use the notation shown in Figure 10-12.

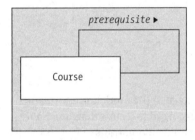

Figure 10-12. *A reflexive association involving the* Course *class*

Aggregation, which (as you learned in Chapter 5) is a specialized form of association that happens to imply containment, is differentiated from a "normal" association by placing a diamond at the end of the association line that touches the "containing" class. For example, to portray the fact that a faculty is composed of professors we'd use the notation shown in Figure 10-13.

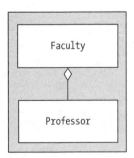

Figure 10-13. *Indicating aggregation with a diamond*

As we mentioned when we first introduced aggregation in Chapter 5, however, you can get by without ever using aggregation! To represent the preceding concept, we could have just created a simple association between the University and School classes, and labeled it *is composed of*, as shown in Figure 10-14.

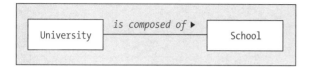

Figure 10-14. *A simple association as an alternative to an aggregation*

The decision of whether to use aggregation versus plain association is subtle because it turns out that both can be rendered in C# code in essentially the same way, as you'll see in Part Three of the book.

Unlike association lines, which should always be labeled with the name of the association that they represent, aggregation lines are typically not labeled because an aggregation by definition implies containment. However, if you wish to optionally label an aggregation line with a phrase such as *consists of, is composed of, contains,* and so on, it is permissible to do so.

When two or more different classes represent "parts" of some other "whole," each "part" is involved in a separate aggregation with the "whole," as shown in Figure 10-15.

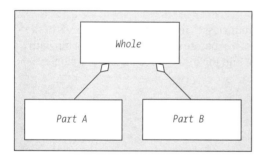

Figure 10-15. *Two aggregations, drawn using two diamonds*

However, we often join such aggregation lines into a single structure that looks something like an organization chart, as shown in Figure 10-16.

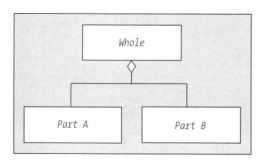

Figure 10-16. *Two aggregations involving the same "whole" class, drawn using a single diamond*

Doing so is not meant to imply anything about the relationship of Part A to Part B; it's simply a way to clean up the diagram.

Inheritance (generalization/specialization) is illustrated by connecting a derived class to its base class with a line, and then marking the line with a triangle that touches the base class (see Figure 10-17).

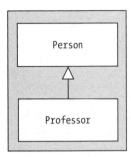

Figure 10-17. *Inheritance is indicated with a triangle.*

As with aggregation, the classes involved in an inheritance relationship can be portrayed with any orientation, as long as the triangle points to the base class.

Unlike association lines, which must always be labeled, and aggregation lines, which needn't be labeled (but can be if you desire), inheritance lines should *not* be labeled, as they unambiguously represent the "is a" relationship.

As with aggregation, when two or more different classes represent derived classes of the same parent class, each derived class is involved in a separate inheritance relationship with the parent, as shown in Figure 10-18, but we often join the inheritance lines into a single structure, as illustrated in Figure 10-19.

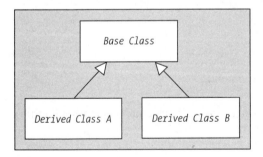

Figure 10-18. *Depicting two derived classes with two different triangles*

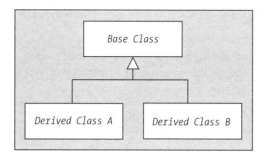

Figure 10-19. *Depicting two derived classes with a single triangle*

Doing so isn't meant to imply anything different about the relationship of derived class A to derived class B as compared with the previous depiction—these classes are considered to be sibling classes with a common parent class in both cases. It's simply a way to clean up the diagram.

Indicating Multiplicity

You learned in Chapter 5 that for a given association type X between classes A and B, the term *multiplicity* refers to the number of instances of objects of type A that must/might be associated with a given instance of type B, and vice versa. When preparing a class diagram, we mark each end of an association line to indicate what its multiplicity should be from the perspective of an object belonging to the class at the other end of the line; in other words:

- We mark the number of instances of B that can relate to a single instance of A at B's end of the line.

- We mark the number of instances of A that can relate to a single instance of B at A's end of the line.

This is depicted in Figure 10-20.

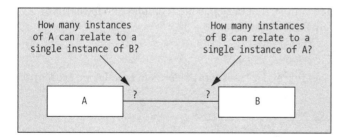

Figure 10-20. *Indicating multiplicity between classes*

By way of review, given a single object belonging to class A, there are four different scenarios for how object(s) of type B can be related to it:

- The A type object can be related to *exactly one* instance of a B type object, as in the situation "a Student (A) *has* a Transcript (B)." Here, the existence of an instance of B for every instance of A is *mandatory*.

- The A type object can be related to *at most one* instance of a B type object, as in the situation "a Professor (A) *chairs* a Department (B)." Here, the existence of an instance of B for every instance of A is *optional*.

- The A type object can be related to *one or more* instances of a B type object, as in the situation "a Department (A) *employs many* Professors (B)." Here, the existence of at least one instance of B for every instance of A is *mandatory*.

- The A type object can be related to *zero or more* instances of a B type object, as in the situation "a Student (A) *is attending many* Sections (B)." (A Student can take 0 Sections because at our hypothetical university, a Student is permitted to take a semester off.) Here, the existence of at least one instance of B for every instance of A is *optional*.

With UML notation, multiplicity symbols are as follows:

- "Exactly one" is represented by the notation "1".

- "At most one" is represented by the notation "0..1", which is alternatively read as "zero or one."

- "One or more" is represented by the notation "1..*".

- "Zero or more" is represented by the notation "0..*".

- We use the notation * when we know that the multiplicity should be "many" but we aren't certain (or we don't care to specify) whether it should be "zero or more" or "one or more."

- It's even possible to represent an arbitrary range of explicit numerical values *x..y*, such as using "3..7" to indicate, for example, that "a Department employs no fewer than three, and no more than seven, Professors."

Here are some UML examples:

"A Student *has* exactly one Transcript, and a Transcript *belongs to* exactly one Student." (See Figure 10-21.)

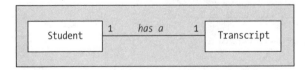

Figure 10-21. *An example of mandatory one-to-one multiplicity*

"A Professor *works for* exactly one Department, but a Department *has* many (one or more) Professors as employees." (See Figure 10-22.)

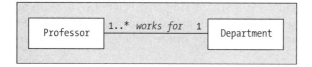

Figure 10-22. *An example of mandatory one-to-many multiplicity*

"A Professor optionally *chairs* at most one Department, while a Department *has* exactly one Professor in the role of chairman." (See Figure 10-23.)

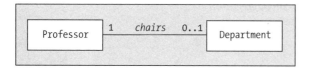

Figure 10-23. *An example of optional one-to-many multiplicity*

"A Student *attends* many (zero or more) Sections, and a Section *is attended by* many (zero or more) Students." (See Figure 10-24.)

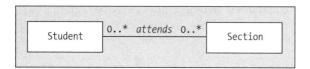

Figure 10-24. *An example of optional many-to-many multiplicity*

■**Note** A Section that continues to have zero Students signed up to attend will most likely be cancelled; nonetheless, there is a period of time after a Section is first made available for enrollment via the SRS that it will have zero Students enrolled.

"A Course *is a prerequisite for* many (zero or more) Courses, and a Course *can have* many (zero or more) *prerequisite* Courses." (See Figure 10-25.)

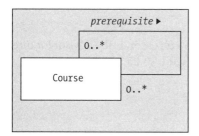

Figure 10-25. *An example of optional many-to-many multiplicity on a reflexive association*

We reflect multiplicity on aggregations as well as on simple associations. For example, the UML notation shown in Figure 10-26 would be interpreted as follows: "A (Student's) Plan of Study *is composed of* many Courses; any given Course *can be included in* many different (Students') Plans of Study."

Figure 10-26. *Reflecting multiplicity on an aggregation*

Object Diagrams

When describing how objects can interact, we sometimes find it helpful to sketch out a scenario of specific objects and their linkages, and for that we create an *object diagram*. An instance, or object, looks much the same as a class in UML notation, the main differences being that the following:

- We typically provide both the name of the object and its type, separated by a colon. We underline the text to emphasize that this is an object, not a class (see Figure 10-27).

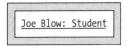

Figure 10-27. *Representing an object*

- The object's name can be omitted if we want to refer to a "generic" object of a given type; such an object is known as an *anonymous object*. Note that we must precede the class name with a colon (:) in such a situation (see Figure 10-28).

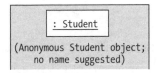

Figure 10-28. *Representing an anonymous object*

Therefore, if we wanted to indicate that Dr. Brown, a Professor, is the advisor for three Students, we could create the object diagram shown in Figure 10-29.

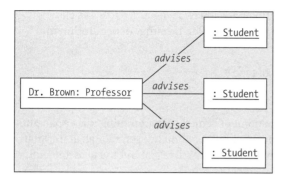

Figure 10-29. *Dr. Brown advises three students.*

Associations As Fields

Given Figure 10-30, which shows the association "a Course *is offered as* a Section," we see that a Course object can be related to many different Section objects, but that any one Section object can only be related to a single Course object.

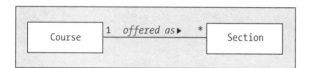

Figure 10-30. *A one-to-many association between the Course and Section classes*

By way of review, what does it mean for two objects to be related? It means that they maintain object references on one another so that they can easily find one another to communicate and collaborate, a concept that we talked about with the balloon strings metaphor in Chapter 4. If we were to sketch out the fields of the Course and Section classes based solely on the diagram in Figure 10-30, we'd need to allow for these object references as reference variables, as follows:

```
public class Section {
  // Fields.
  private Course course;    // A reference to a single Course
                            // object

  // etc.
}

public class Course {
  // Fields.
  private Collection sectionsOffered;    // A collection of Section
                                         // object references.
  // etc.
}
```

So we see that the presence of an association between two classes A and B in a class diagram implies that class A *potentially* has a field declared to be either depending on the multiplicity involved, and vice versa:

- A reference to a *single* instance/object of type B

- A *collection* of references to *many* objects of type B

We say *potentially* because when we get to the point of actually programming this application, we might or might not wish to code this relationship bidirectionally, even though at the analysis stage all associations are presumed to be bidirectional. We'll talk about the pros and cons of using bidirectional relationships in Chapter 14.

Because the presence of an association line implies fields as object references in both related classes, it's inappropriate to additionally list such fields in the field compartment of the respective classes (see Figure 10-31).

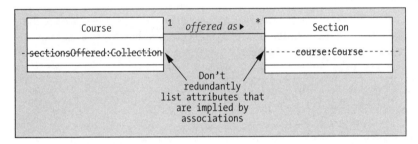

Figure 10-31. *Redundantly reflecting references as fields is incorrect; the presence of an association implies these.*

■**Note** This is a mistake commonly made by beginners. The biggest resultant problem with doing so arises when using the code generation capability of a Computer-Aided Software Engineering (CASE) tool: if the field is listed explicitly in a class's fields compartment, and also implied by an association, it can appear in the generated code twice, as shown in the following snippet representing code that might be generated from the erroneous UML diagram shown in Figure 10-31:

```
public class Course {
  Collection sectionsOffered;   // by virtue of an explicit field
  Collection offeredAs;         // by virtue of the association
  // etc.
}
```

Information "Flows" Along the Association "Pipeline"

Beginning modelers also tend to make the mistake of introducing undesired redundancy when it comes to fields in general. In the association portrayed in Figure 10-32, we see that the name field of the Professor class is inappropriately mirrored by the chairmanName field of the Department class.

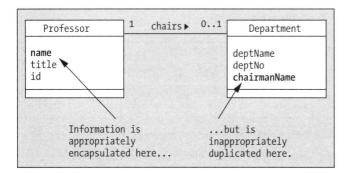

Figure 10-32. *The* name *and* chairmanName *fields are redundant.*

Although it's true that a Department object needs to know the name of the Professor object that chairs that Department, it's inappropriate to explicitly create a chairmanName field to hold this information. Because the Department object maintains a reference to its associated Professor object as a field, the Department has ready access to this information any time it needs it, simply by invoking the Professor object's GetName method (or accessing the Name property, in the case of C#). This piece of information is rightfully encapsulated in the Professor class, where it belongs, and shouldn't be duplicated by declaring the string field chairmanName in the Department class. A corrected version of the preceding diagram is shown in Figure 10-33, with the redundancy eliminated.

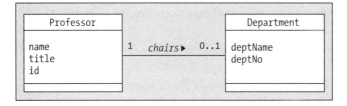

Figure 10-33. *The redundancy of Figure 10-32 has been eliminated.*

In essence, whenever we see an association/aggregation line in a diagram, we can think of this as a conceptual "pipeline" across which information can "flow" between related objects as needed.

Note At the analysis stage, we don't worry about the accessibility (public, private) of fields, or of the directionality of associations; we'll assume that the values of all of the fields reflected in a diagram are obtainable by calling the appropriate "get" methods on an object, or by alternatively accessing C# properties.

Sometimes, this "pipeline" extends across *multiple* objects, as illustrated by the next example.

Figure 10-34 shows a diagram involving three classes.

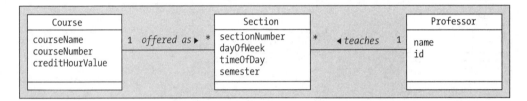

Figure 10-34. *An association "pipeline" between the* Course, Section, *and* Professor *classes*

Many university courses, especially the beginning-level courses, can be taught by more than one professor. Let's say that someone wishes to obtain a list of all of the Professors who have ever taught the Course titled "Beginning Objects." Because each Course object maintains a reference to all its Section objects, past and present, the Course object representing Beginning Objects can ask each of its Section objects the name of the Professor who previously taught, or is currently teaching, that Section. The Section objects, in turn, each maintain a reference to the Professor object who taught/teaches the Section, and can use the Professor object's GetName method (or can access the Name property, in the case of C#) to retrieve the name. So information flows along the association "pipeline" from the Professor objects to their associated Section objects and from there back to the Course object that we started with.

Tip You'll learn a formal, UML-appropriate way to analyze and depict such "object conversations" in Chapter 11.

We modeled these three classes' fields in the code that follows, highlighting all the association-driven fields:

```
public class Course {
  // Fields.
  // Pseudocode.
  private Collection sectionsOffered;  // a collection of Section
                                       // object references
  private string courseName;
  private int courseNumber;
  private double creditHourValue;
```

```
  // etc.
}

public class Section {
  // Fields.
  private Course course;    // a reference to the related Course
                           // object
  private int sectionNumber;
  private string dayOfWeek;
  private string timeOfDay;
  private string semester;
  private Professor professor;  // a reference to the related
                               // Professor object

  // etc.
}

public class Professor {
  // Pseudocode.
  private Collection sectionsTaught; // a collection of Section
                                    // object references
  private string name;
  private string id;

  // etc.
}
```

If we knew that the Course class regularly needed to know who all the Professors were that had ever taught the Course, we might decide to introduce the redundant association "a Professor *has taught* a Course" into our diagram, as illustrated in Figure 10-35.

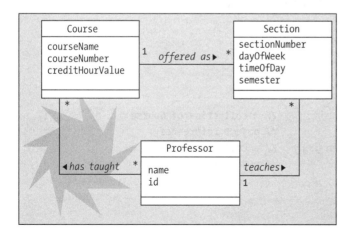

Figure 10-35. *We add redundant associations when objects frequently need a more direct "pipeline" for communication.*

This has the advantage of improving the speed with which a Course object can determine who has ever taught it: with the addition of the redundant association in Figure 10-35, Course objects can now talk *directly* to Professor objects without using Section objects as go-betweens—but the cost of this performance improvement is that we've just introduced additional complexity to our application, reflected by the highlighted additions to the following code:

```
public class Course {
  // Fields.
  // Pseudocode.
  private Collection sectionsOffered;   // a collection of Section
                                        // object references
  private string courseName;
  private int courseNumber;
  private float creditHourValue;
  // Pseudocode.
  private Collection professors;        // a collection of Professor
                                        // object references
  // etc.
}

public class Section {
  // Fields.
  private Course course;    // a reference to the related Course
                            // object
  private int sectionNumber;
  private string dayOfWeek;
  private string timeOfDay;
  private string semester;
  private Professor professor;   // a reference to the related
                                 // Professor object

  // etc.
}

public class Professor {
  // Pseudocode.
  private Collection coursesTaught;     // a collection of Course
                                        // object references
  private Collection sectionsTaught;    // a collection of Section
                                        // object references
  private string name;
  private string id;

  // etc.
}
```

By adding the redundant association, we now have extra work to do in terms of maintaining referential integrity. That is, if a different Professor is assigned to teach a particular Section, we have two links to update rather than one: the link between the Professor and the Section, and the link between the Professor and the related Course.

We'll talk more in Part Three of the book about the implications, from a coding standpoint, of making such trade-offs. The bottom line, however, is that deciding which associations to include, and which to eliminate as derivable from others, is similar to the decision of which web pages you might want to create a bookmark for in your web browser. You bookmark those that you visit frequently and type out the URL longhand, or alternatively traverse a chain of links, for those that you only occasionally need to access. The same is true for object linkages: the decisions of which to implement in code depends on which "communication pathways" through the application we're going to want to use most frequently. We'll get a much better sense of what these communication patterns are when we move on to modeling behaviors in Chapter 11.

"Mixing and Matching" Relationship Notations

It's possible to intertwine the various relationship types in some rather sophisticated ways. To appreciate this fact, let's study the model in Figure 10-36 to see what it's telling us. Note that the UML model shown in Figure 10-36 is a bit more complicated than the SRS model in that it includes University, School, and Department classes that won't be part of the SRS.

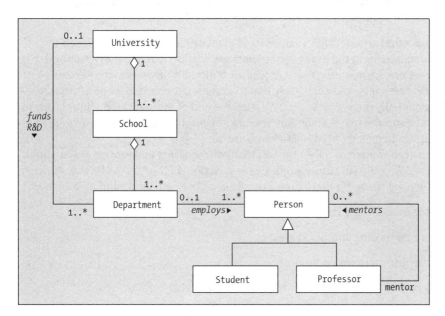

Figure 10-36. *A sample UML model*

First of all, we see some familiar uses of aggregation and inheritance.

The use of aggregation in the upper-left corner of the diagram—a two-tier aggregation—communicates the facts that a University is composed of one or more Schools, and that a School is composed of one or more Departments, but that any one Department is only associated with a single School, and any one School is only associated with a single University.

The use of inheritance in the lower-right corner of the diagram indicates that Person is the common base class for both Student and Professor. Alternatively, stated another way: a Student *is a* Person, and a Professor *is a* Person.

The first interesting use of the notation that we observe is that an association can be used to relate classes at differing levels in an aggregation, as in the use of the *funds R&D (Research & Development)* association used to relate the University and Department classes. This indicates that the University funds one or more Departments for research and development purposes, but that a given Department might or might not be funded for R&D.

Next, we note the use of the *employs* association to relate the Department and Person classes, indicating that a Department *employs* one or more Persons, but that a given Person *can work for* only one Department, if indeed they work for *any* Department at all.

Because Person is a base class of both the Student and Professor derived classes, then by virtue of the "is a" relationship, anything we can say about a Person must also be true of its derived classes. Therefore:

- Associations/aggregations that a base class participates in are inherited by its derived classes. (This makes sense because we now know that associations are really rendered as fields.) Thus, a given Student can optionally *work for* one Department, perhaps as a teaching assistant, and a given Professor can optionally *work for* one Department.

- Also, because we can deduce (via the aggregation relationship) which School and University a given Department belongs to, the fact that a Person *works for* a given Department also implies which School and University the Person *works for*.

Finally, we note that an association can be used to relate classes at differing levels in an inheritance hierarchy, as in the use of the *mentors* association to relate the Person and Professor classes. Here, we're stating that a Professor optionally *mentors* many Persons— Students and/or Professors—and conversely that a Person—either a Student or a Professor— is mentored by optionally many Professors. We label the end of the association line closest to the Professor class with the role designation "mentor" to emphasize that Professors are mentors , but that Persons in general (that is, Students) are not.

What if we instead wanted to reflect the fact that both Students and Professors can hold the role of mentor? We could substitute a reflexive association on the Person class, as shown in Figure 10-37, which, by virtue of inheritance, actually implies four relationship possibilities:

- A Professor mentoring a Student

- A Professor mentoring another Professor

- A Student mentoring another Student

- A Student mentoring a Professor (which is not very likely!)

If we want to reflect that only the first three of these are possible, we have to resort to the rather more complex version shown in Figure 10-38, in which the three relationships of interest are all reflected as separate association lines (two reflexive, one binary).

As cumbersome as it is to change the diagram to reflect these refinements in our understanding, it would be orders of magnitude more painful to change the software once the application has been coded. An alternative approach to avoid some of the issues we just discussed would be to define a "policy" class that encapsulated the rules for mentoring.

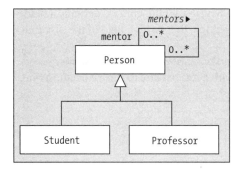

Figure 10-37. *Various possible "mentorship" associations are implied.*

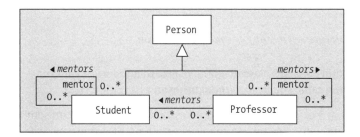

Figure 10-38. *Specific mentor associations are deliniated.*

Association Classes

We sometimes find ourselves in a situation in which we identify a field that is critical to our model, but doesn't seem to fit nicely into any one class. As an example, let's revisit the association "a Student *attends* a Section," as shown in Figure 10-39. (Note that we're using the "generic" *many* multiplicity symbol this time: a single asterisk [*] at each end of the association line.)

Figure 10-39. *A many-to-many association between* Student *and* Section

At the end of every semester, a student receives a letter grade for every section that he or she attended during that semester. We decide that the grade should be represented as a string field (for example, A-, C+). However, where does the "grade" field belong?

- It's not a field of the Student class because a student doesn't get a single overall grade for all of his or her coursework, but rather a different grade for each course attended.

- It's not a field of the Section class, either, because not all students attending a section typically receive the same letter grade.

If we think about this situation for a moment, we realize that the grade is actually a field of the *pairing* of a given Student object with a given Section; that is, it's a field of the *link* that exists between these two objects.

With UML, we create a separate class, known as an *association class*, to house field(s) belonging to the link between objects, and attach it with a *dashed* line to the association line, as shown in Figure 10-40.

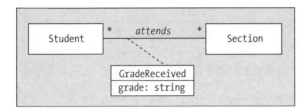

Figure 10-40. *Placing an association class on a many-to-many association*

Any time you see an association class in a class diagram, realize that there is an alternative equivalent way to represent the same situation *without* using an association class.

- In the case of a *many-to-many association* involving an association class, you can split the many-to-many association into two one-to-many associations, inserting what was formerly the association class as a "normal" class between the other two classes. Doing this for the preceding *attends* association, we wind up with the alternative equivalent representation in Figure 10-41.

  One important point to note is that the "many" ends of these two new associations reside with the newly inserted class, because a Student *receives* many grades and a Section *issues* many grades.

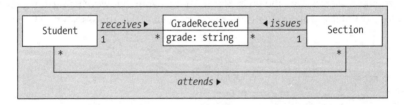

Figure 10-41. *An alternative representation for Figure 10-40*

- If we happen to have an association class for a *one-to-many association*, as in the *works for* association between Professor and Department in Figure 10-42, then the association class's field(s) can, in theory, be "folded into" the class at the "many" end of the association instead, and we can do away with the association class completely, as shown in Figure 10-43.

- With a *one-to-one association*, we can fold the association class's fields into either class.

That being said, this practice of folding in association class fields into one end of a one-to-many or one-to-one association is discouraged, however, because it reduces the amount of information communicated by the model. In the preceding example, the only reason that a

Professor has a salary field is because he or she *works for* a Department; knowledge of this cause-and-effect connection between employment and salary is lost if the association class is eliminated as such from the model.

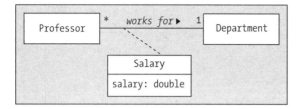

Figure 10-42. *Placing an association class on a one-to-many association*

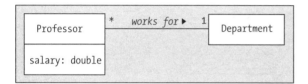

Figure 10-43. *An alternative representation for Figure 10-42*

Our Completed Student Registration System Class Diagram

Applying all that we've learned in this chapter about static modeling, we've produced the UML class diagram for the SRS shown in Figure 10-44. Of course, as we've said repeatedly, this isn't the only correct way to model the requirements, nor is it necessarily the "best" model that we could have produced; but it is an accurate, concise, and correct model of the static aspects of the problem to be automated.

We opted to use the "generic" *many* notation (* for UML) instead of specifying 0..* or 1..*; this is often adequate during the initial modeling stages of a project.

Note that we've reflected two separate many-to-many associations between the Student and Section classes: *waitlisted for* and *attends*. A given Student might be waitlisted for many different Sections, and he or she might be registered for/attending many *other* Sections. What this model doesn't reflect is the fact that a Student is *not* permitted to simultaneously be attending and waitlisted for the *same* Section. Constraints such as these can be reflected as textual notes on the diagram, enclosed in curly braces, or can be omitted from the diagram but spelled out in the data dictionary.

As mentioned earlier in this chapter, we can get by with a single *attends* association to handle the Sections that a Student is currently attending, as well as those that he or she has attended in the past. The date of attendance—past or present—is reflected by the "semester" field of the Section class; also, for any courses that are currently in progress, the value of the "grade" field of the TranscriptEntry association class would be as of yet undetermined.

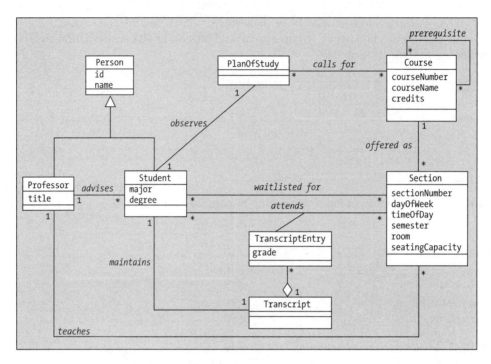

Figure 10-44. *Our completed SRS class diagram*

We could have also defined an association class on the *waitlisted for* association representing a given Student's position in the wait list for a particular Section, and then could have gone on to model the notion of a WaitList as an aggregation of WaitListEntry objects.

We also renamed the association class for the *attends* relationship; it was introduced earlier in this chapter as GradeReceived, but is now called TranscriptEntry. It's important to choose meaningful class names that are easily understood by user representatives when they review the class diagram. We also introduced an aggregation relationship between the TranscriptEntry class and another new class called Transcript (see Figure 10-44).

Let's explore how the proposed Transcript and TranscriptEntry classes evolved.

When we first introduced the *attends* association earlier in this chapter, we portrayed it as shown in Figure 10-45.

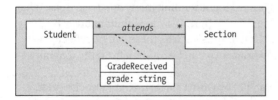

Figure 10-45. *Initial portrayal of the attends association*

We then learned that it could equivalently be represented as a pair of one-to-many associations *issues* and *receives* (see Figure 10-46). The information can be passed between the objects using the get and set accessors of associated properties.

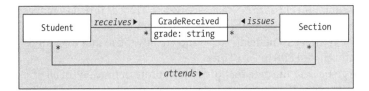

Figure 10-46. *The attends association can be portrayed alternatively as issues and receives.*

In the alternative form shown in Figure 10-47, it's clear that any individual GradeReceived object maintains one reference to a Student object and another reference to a Section object, and can ask either of them for information whenever necessary. The Section object, in turn, maintains a reference to the Course object that it represents by virtue of an *offered as* association. It's a trivial matter, therefore, for the GradeReceived object to request the values of fields semester, courseNumber, courseName, and credits from the Section object (which would in turn have to ask its associated Course object for the last three of these four values); this is illustrated conceptually in Figure 10-47.

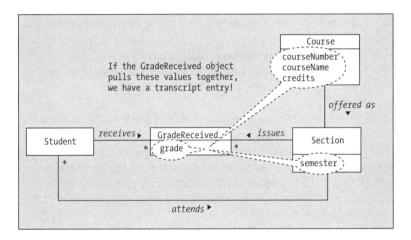

Figure 10-47. GradeReceived *has access to all of the makings of a* TranscriptEntry.

If the GradeReceived object pulls these values together, we have everything that we need for a line item entry on a student's transcript, as shown in Figure 10-48.

```
Transcript For: Joe Blow                          Semester: Spring 2009


Course No.      Credits       Course Name       Grade Received      Credits Earned*
MATH 101          3           Beginning Math          B                   9
OBJECTS 101       3           Intro to Objects        A                  12
ART 200           3           Clay Modeling           A                  12

* 'Credits Earned' is computed by multiplying the credit value of a course-
  say 3 by 4 if student earned an A grade, 3 if he/she earned a B, and so forth.
```

Figure 10-48. *A sample transcript report*

Therefore, renaming the association class from GradeReceived to TranscriptEntry makes good sense. It was then a natural step to aggregate them into a Transcript class.

Our SRS diagram is a little light in terms of fields; we've shown only those that we'll minimally need when we build an automated SRS in Part Three.

Of course, we now need to go back to the data dictionary to capture definitions of all of the new fields, relationships, and classes that we identified in putting together this model. The following sidebar shows our revised SRS data dictionary.

THE REVISED SRS DATA DICTIONARY

Classes

Course: A semester-long series of lectures, assignments, exams, and so on that all relate to a particular subject area, and which are typically associated with a particular number of credit hours; a unit of study toward a degree. For example, Beginning Objects is a required **course** for the Master of Science degree in Information Systems Technology.

Person: A human being associated with the university.

PlanOfStudy: A list of the **courses** that a student intends to take to fulfill the **course** requirements for a particular degree.

Professor: A member of the faculty who teaches **sections** or advises **students**.

Section: The offering of a particular **course** during a particular semester on a particular day of the week and at a particular time of day. (For example, **course** Beginning Objects is taught in the Spring 2009 semester on Mondays from 1:00 to 3:00 p.m.).

Student: A person who is currently enrolled at the university and who is eligible to register for one or more **sections**.

Transcript: A record of all the **courses** taken to date by a particular **student** at this university, including which semester each **course** was taken in, the grade received, and the credits granted for the **course,** as well as reflecting an overall total number of credits earned and the **student's** grade point average (GPA).

TranscriptEntry: One-line item entry from a **transcript**, reflecting the **course** number and name, semester taken, value in credit hours, and grade received.

Relationships

Advises: a professor advises a student: A professor is assigned to oversee a student's academic pursuits for the student's entire academic career, leading up to his or her attainment of a degree. An advisor counsels his or her advisees regarding course selection, professional opportunities, and any academic problems the student might be having.

Attends: a student attends a section: A student registers for a section, attends class meetings for a semester, and participates in all assignments and examinations, culminating in the award of a letter grade representing the student's mastery of the subject matter.

Calls for: a plan of study calls for a course: A student can take a course only if it's called out by his or her plan of study. The plan of study can be amended with a student's advisor's approval.

Owns: a student owns a transcript: Each time a student completes a course, a record of the course and the grade received is added to the student's transcript.

Follows: a student follows a plan of study: See notes for the *calls for* association.

Offered as: a course is offered as a section: The same course can be taught numerous times in a given semester and over numerous semesters for the "lifetime" of a course—that is, until such time as the subject matter is no longer considered to be of value to the student body or there is no qualified faculty to teach the course.

Prerequisite: a course is a prerequisite for another course: If it's determined that the subject matter of a course A is necessary background to understanding the subject matter of a course B, then course A is said to be a prerequisite of course B. A student typically can't take course B unless he or she has either successfully completed course A, or can otherwise demonstrate mastery of the subject matter of course A.

Teaches: a professor teaches a section: A professor is responsible for delivering lectures, assigning thoughtful homework assignments, examining students, and otherwise ensuring that a quality treatment of the subject matter of a course is made available to students.

Waitlisted for: a student is waitlisted for a section: If a section is "full"—for example, the maximum number of students have signed up for the course based on either the classroom capacity or the student group size deemed effective for teaching—then interested students can be placed on a wait list, to be given consideration should seats in the course subsequently become available.

(aggregation between Transcript and TranscriptEntry)

(specialization of Person as Professor)

(specialization of Person as Student)

Fields

Person.id: The unique identification number assigned to an individual.

Person.name: The person's name.

Professor.title: The rank attained by the professor; for example, Adjunct Professor.

Student.major: A reflection of the department in which a student's primary studies lie—for example, Mathematics. (We assume that a student can only designate a single major.)

Student.degree: The degree that a student is pursuing; for example, Master of Science degree.

TranscriptEntry.grade: A letter grade of A, B, C, D, or F, with an optional +/- suffix, such as A+ or C-.

Course.courseNunber: A unique ID assigned to a course, consisting of the department designation plus a unique numeric ID within the department.

Course.courseName: A full name describing the subject matter of a course; for example, Beginning Objects.

Course.credits: The number of units or credit hours a course roughly equates to the number of hours spent in the classroom in a single week (typically, three credits for a full semester lecture course).

Section.sectionNumber: A unique number assigned to distinguish one section/offering of a particular course from another offering of the same course in the same semester, for example, MATH 101 section no. 1.

Section.dayOfWeek: The day of the week on which the lecture course meets.

Section.timeOfDay: The time (range) during which the course meets, for example 2–4 p.m.

Section.semester: An indication of the scholastic semester in which a section is offered—for example, Spring 2009.

Section.room: The building and room number where the section will be meeting—for example, Government Hall, Room 105.

Section.seatingCapacity: The maximum number of students permitted to register for a section.

Keep in mind that the fields might very well change during the behavioral design process.

Inheritance or Association?

One question that is often raised by beginning modelers is why we don't use an inheritance relationship to relate the Course and Section classes instead of using a simple association, as we've chosen to do. On the surface, it does indeed seem tempting to want Section to be a derived class of Course because all the fields listed for a Course—courseNumber, courseName, and credits—also pertain to a Section; so, why wouldn't we want Section to inherit them in the same way that Student and Professor inherit all the fields of Person? A simple example should quickly illustrate why inheritance isn't appropriate.

Let's say that because Beginning Object Concepts is such a popular course, the university is offering three sections of the course for the Spring 2009 semester. So we instantiate one Course object and three Section objects. If Section were a derived class of Course, all four objects would carry courseNumber, courseName, and credits fields. Filling in the field values for these four objects, as shown in Table 10-3, you see that there is quite a bit of repetition in the field values across these four objects: we repeated the same courseName, courseNumber, and creditValue field values four times! That's because the information contained within a Course object is common to, and hence describes, numerous Section objects.

Table 10-3. *Duplication of Data Across Four Object Instances*

Field Name	Field Values for the Course Object
courseName	Beginning Object Concepts
courseNumber	OBJECTS 101
creditValue	3

Field Name	Field Values for Section Object #1	Field Values for Section Object #2	Field Values for Section Object #3
courseName	Beginning Object Concepts	Beginning Object Concepts	Beginning Object Concepts
courseNumber	OBJECTS 101	OBJECTS 101	OBJECTS 101
creditValue	3	3	3
studentsRegistered	(To be determined)	(To be determined)	(To be determined)
instructor	Reference to professor X	Reference to professor Y	Reference to professor Z
semesterOffered	Spring 2009	Spring 2009	Spring 2009
dayOfWeek	Monday	Tuesday	Thursday
timeOfDay	7:00 p.m.	4:00 p.m.	6:00 p.m.
classroom	Hall A, Room 123	Hall B, Room 234	Hall A, Room 345

To reduce redundancy and to promote encapsulation, we should eliminate inheritance of these fields, and instead create only one instance of a Course object for *n* instances of its related Section objects. We can then have each Section object maintain a reference to the common Course object to retrieve these shared values whenever necessary. This is precisely what we've modeled via the one-to-many *offered as* association.

Summary

Our object model has started to take shape! We have a good idea of what the static structure needs to be for the SRS—the classes, and their fields and relationships with one another—and can communicate this knowledge in a concise, graphical form. There are many more embellishments to the UML notation that we haven't covered in this chapter, but we've presented the core concepts that will suffice for most industrial-strength modeling projects. Once you've mastered these, you can explore the "Recommended Reading" section in Chapter 17 of the book if you'd like to learn more about these notations.

There is an obvious hole in our class diagram, however: all classes have empty operations compartments. We'll address this deficiency by learning some complementary modeling techniques for determining the dynamic behavior of our intended system in Chapter 11.

In this chapter, you learned the following:

- The noun phrase analysis technique for identifying candidate domain classes

- The verb phrase analysis technique for determining potential relationships among these classes

- That coming up with candidate classes is a bit subjective, so we have to remain flexible and willing to revisit our model, through many iterations, until we—and our users—are satisfied with the outcome

- The importance of producing a data dictionary as part of a project's documentation set

- How to graphically portray the static structure of our model as a class diagram using UML

- How important it is to have an experienced object modeling mentor available to a project team and at the beginning of the move from design to code.

Exercises

1. Devise a list of candidate classes for the problem area whose requirements you defined for exercise 3 in Chapter 2, as well as an association matrix.

2. Develop a class diagram for the problem area whose requirements you defined for exercise 3 in Chapter 2, using UML notation. Reflect all significant fields and relationships among classes, including the appropriate multiplicity. Ideally, you should use an object modeling software tool if you have one available to you.

3. Prepare a data dictionary for the problem area whose requirements you defined for exercise 3 in Chapter 2 to include definitions of all classes, fields, and associations.

CHAPTER 11

■■■

Modeling the Dynamic/ Behavioral Aspects of the System

Thus far, we've been focused on the *static structure* of the problem being modeled—the blueprint for our custom home, as it were. As you learned in Chapter 10, this static structure is communicated via a class diagram plus supporting documentation. The building blocks of a class diagram are as follows:

- Classes

- Associations/aggregations

- Fields

- Generalization/specialization hierarchies (also known as inheritance relationships)

- Operations/methods

■Note Operations/methods are conspicuously absent from our class diagram at the moment. Why? Because they aren't part of the static structure, so we haven't discussed how to determine them yet (this is the focus of this chapter).

As discussed many times already, an object-oriented (OO) software system is a set of collaborating objects, each with a life of its own. If each object went about its own business without regard to what any other object needed it to do, however, utter chaos would reign! The only way that objects can collaborate to perform some overall system mission, such as registering a student for a course, is if each class defines the appropriate methods—*operations*—that will enable its instances to fulfill their respective roles in the collaboration.

In order to determine what these methods/operations must be, we must complement our knowledge of the static structure of the system to be built by also modeling the *dynamic* aspects of the situation; that is, the ways in which concurrently active objects interact over time and how these interactions affect each object's state. Producing a dynamic model to complement the static model will not only enable us to determine the methods required for each class but also give us new insights into ways to improve upon the static structure. In this chapter, you'll learn about the building blocks of a dynamic model and how to use this knowledge to identify the methods/operations needed to complete the class diagram:

- Events

- Scenarios

- Sequence diagrams

- Collaboration diagrams

How Behavior Affects State

Back in Chapter 3, we defined the *state* of an object as the collective set of all the object's field values at a given point in time, including the following:

- The values of all the "simple" fields for that object—in other words, fields that don't represent other domain objects

- The values of all the reference variable fields representing links to other domain objects

Table 11-1 repeats the list of the Student class fields from Chapter 6, adding a column to indicate which category each field falls into.

Table 11-1. Student *Class Fields*

Field Name	Data Type	Represents Link(s) to an SRS Domain Object?
name	string	No
studentID	string	No
birthdate	DateTime	No
address	string	No
major	string	No
gpa	double	No
advisor	Professor	Yes
courseLoad	Collection of Section objects	Yes
transcript	Collection of TranscriptEntry objects, or Transcript	Yes

In Chapter 10, you learned about Unified Modeling Language (UML) object diagrams as a way of portraying a "snapshot" of the links between specific individual objects. Let's use an object diagram to reflect the state of a few hypothetical objects within the Student Registration System (SRS) domain.

In Figure 11-1, Dr. Smith (a Professor) works for the Math Department, Dr. Green (another Professor) works for the Science Department, and Bill and Mary, both Students, are majoring in Math and Science, respectively.

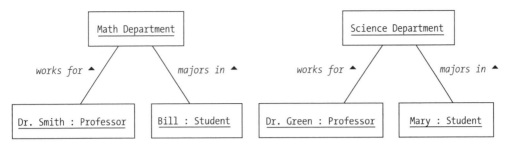

Figure 11-1. *The state of an object includes the links it maintains with other objects.*

Bill is dissatisfied with his choice of majors, and calls Dr. Green, a professor whom he admires, to make an appointment. Bill wants to discuss the possibility of transferring to the Science Department. After meeting with Dr. Green and discussing his situation, Bill indeed decides to switch majors. We've informally reflected these object interactions using arrows on the object diagram in Figure 11-2; as this chapter progresses, you'll learn the official way to portray object interactions in UML notation.

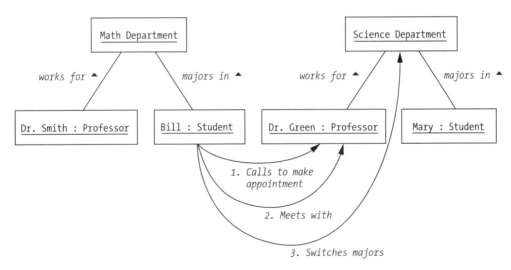

Figure 11-2. *Objects' interactions can affect their state.*

When the dust settles from all this activity, the resultant state of the system has changed, as reflected in the revised object diagram "snapshot" in Figure 11-3. In particular, the following events have occurred:

- Bill's state has changed because his link to the Math Department object has been replaced with a link to the Science Department object.

- The Math Department object's state has changed because it no longer has a link to Bill.

- The Science Department's state has changed because it now has an additional link (to Bill) that wasn't previously there.

■**Note** Although Dr. Green collaborated with Bill in helping him to make his decision to switch majors, the state of the Dr. Green (Professor) object has *not* changed as a result of the collaboration.

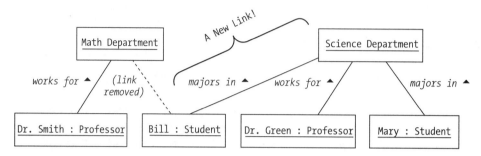

Figure 11-3. *Some interacting objects experience a change of state, others don't.*

So you now see the following:

- Objects' dynamic activities can result in changes to the *static structure of a system*—that is, the states of all of its objects taken collectively.

- However, such activities needn't affect the state of *all* objects involved in a collaboration.

Events

You saw in Chapter 4 that object collaborations are triggered by events. By way of review, an *event* is an external stimulus to an object, signaled to the object in the form of a *message* (method call). An event can be any of the following:

- *User initiated*: For example, the result of clicking a "button" on a graphical user interface (GUI)

- *Initiated by another computer system*: For example, the arrival of information being transferred from the Student Billing System to the SRS

- *Initiated by another object within the same system*: For example, a Section object requesting some method of a Transcript object

When an object receives notification of an event via a method call, it can react in one or more of the following ways:

- An object can change its state.

- An object can direct an event (message) toward another object.

- An object can return a value.

- An object can react with the external boundaries of its system.

- An object can seemingly ignore an event.

Let's discuss these five types of reaction in detail, one by one.

An Object Can Change Its State

An object can change its state (the values of its "simple" fields and/or links to other objects), as in the case of a Professor object receiving a message to take on a new Student advisee, illustrated by the following code snippet:

```
Professor p = new Professor();
Student s = new Student();
// details omitted
p.AddAdvisee(s);
```

Let's look at the code for the Professor class's AddAdvisee method to see how the Professor will respond to this message. We see that the Professor object is inserting the reference to Student object s that it is being handed as an argument into a Collection of Student object references called advisees:

```
public class Professor {
  // Fields.
  // (pseudocode)
  Collection advisees;  // Holds Student object references.

  // Other details omitted.

  public void AddAdvisee(Student s) {
    // Insert s into the advisees collection.
    // (pseudocode)
    advisees.Insert(s);
  }
}
```

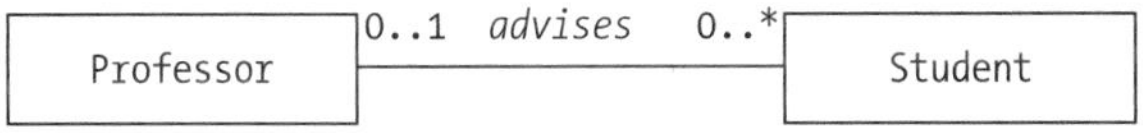

Figure 11-4. *Revisiting the UML diagram for the advises association.*

An Object Can Direct an Event (Message) Toward Another Object

An object can direct an event (message) toward another object (including, perhaps, the sender of the original message), as in the case of a Section object receiving a message to register a Student, illustrated by the following code snippet:

```
Section x = new Section();
Student s = new Student();
// details omitted
x.Register(s);
```

If you next look at the method code for the Section class's Register method to see how it will respond to this message, you see that the Section object in turn sends a message to the Student to be enrolled, to verify that the Student has completed a necessary prerequisite course:

```
public class Section {
  // details omitted

  bool Register(Student s) {
    // Verify that the student has completed a necessary
    // prerequisite course. (We are delegating part
    // of the work to another object, Student s.)
    // (pseudocode)
    bool completed = s.SuccessfullyCompleted(some prerequisite);
    if (completed) {
      register the student and return a value of true;
    }
    else {
      return a value of false to signal that the registration
        request has been rejected;
    }
  }
}
```

This happens to be an example of *delegation*, which we discussed in Chapter 4; namely, another object (a Student, in this case) helping to fulfill an operation request originally made of the Section object.

An Object Can Return a Value

An object can return a value; the returned value can be one of the following:

- The value of one of the object's fields

- Some computed value (that is, a *pseudofield*), as discussed in Chapter 4)

- A value that was obtained from some *other* object through delegation

- A status code (as in true/false responses, signaling success or failure of Boolean methods)

Typical "get" methods fall into this category of event response.

An Object Can React with the External Boundaries of a System

An object can react with the external boundaries of a system; that is, it might display some information on a GUI or cause information to be printed to a printer. As you'll learn in Chapters 15 and 16, however, what appears to be an external system boundary is often implemented in C# as yet another class.

An Object Can Seemingly Ignore an Event

Finally, an object might seemingly ignore an event, as would be the case if a Professor object received the message to add an advisee, but determined that the Student whom it was being asked to take on as an advisee was *already* an advisee:

```
public class Professor {
  // (pseudocode)
  Collection advisees;  // Holds Student object references.
  // details omitted

  public void AddAdvisee(Student s) {
    // ONLY insert s into the 'advisees' collection IF IT
    // ISN'T ALREADY IN THERE.
    // (pseudocode)
    if (s is already in collection)
        return;  // do nothing
    else
        advisees.Insert(s);
  }
}
```

Actually, to say that the Professor object is doing nothing is an oversimplification; at a minimum, the object is executing the appropriate method code, which is performing some internal state checks ("Is this student already one of my advisees?"). When the dust settles, the Professor object has neither changed state nor fired off any messages to other objects, so it *appears* as if nothing has happened.

Scenarios

Events originating externally to a system occur randomly; we can't predict, for example, when a user will click a button on a GUI. For a system to perform useful functions, however, the *internal* events that arise in *response* to these external events—in other words, the messages that objects exchange in carrying out some system function—can't be left to occur randomly. Instead, they must be orchestrated in such as way as to lead, in a cause-and-effect fashion, to some desired result. In the same way that a musical score indicates which notes must be played by various instruments to produce a melody, a *scenario* prescribes the sequence of internal messages (events) that must occur in carrying out some system function from beginning to end.

We introduced use cases in Chapter 9 as a way to specify all the goals for a system from the standpoint of external actors—users or other computer systems. *Merriam-Webster's Collegiate Dictionary, Eleventh Edition* defines the term scenario as follows (which is precisely how the term is used in the object modeling sense):

A sequence of events especially when imagined; especially an account or synopsis of a possible course of action or events.

A scenario is one hypothetical instance of how a particular use case might play out. Just as an object is an instance of a class, and a link is an instance of an association, a scenario might be thought of as an instance of a use case. Or, stated another way, just as a class is a template for creating objects, and an association is a template for creating links, a use case is a template for creating scenarios. A single use case thus inspires many different scenarios, in the same way that planning a driving trip from one city to another can involve many different routes.

We describe scenarios in narrative fashion, as a series of steps observed from the standpoint of a hypothetical observer who can see not only what is happening outwardly as the system carries out a particular request but also what is going on behind the scenes, internally to the system.

Note Even though we're now concerned with internal system processes, we're still interested only in *functional* requirements (as defined in Chapter 9), not in the technical requirements of how the computer works.

The following is a sample scenario representing the "Register for a Section" use case, one of several use cases identified for the SRS in Chapter 9.

Scenario #1 for the "Register for a Section" Use Case

In this first scenario, a student named Fred successfully registers for a section of a course. The specific sequence of events is as follows:

1. Fred, a student, logs on to the SRS.

2. He views the schedule of classes for the current semester to determine which section(s) he wants to register for.

3. Fred requests a seat in a particular section of a course titled "Beginning Computer Technology," course number CMP101, section 1.

4. Fred's plan of study is checked to ensure that the requested course is appropriate for his overall degree goals. (We assume that students are not permitted to take courses outside of their plans of study.)

5. His transcript is checked to ensure that he has satisfied all the prerequisites for the requested course, if there are any.

6. Seating availability in the section is confirmed.

7. The section is added to Fred's current course load.

From Fred's vantage point (sitting in front of a computer screen!), here's what he perceives to be occurring: after logging on to the SRS, he indicates that he wants to register for CMP101, section 1 by choosing it from the available course list, and then clicks the Add button (see Figure 11-5).

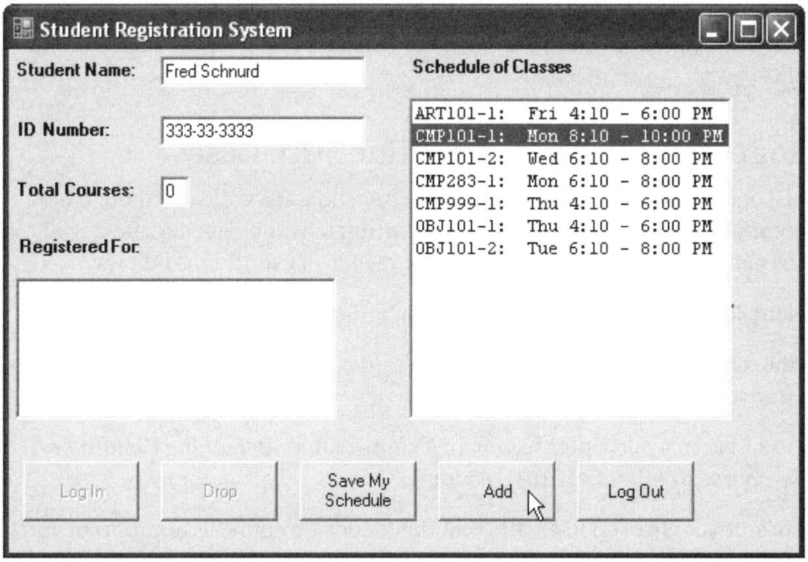

Figure 11-5. *Fred's view of things, part 1*

A few moments later, Fred receives a confirmation message, as shown in Figure 11-6.

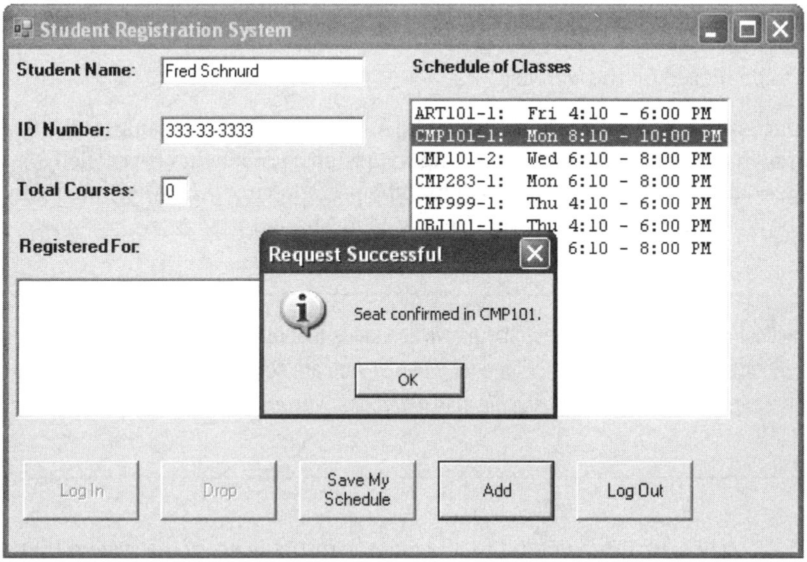

Figure 11-6. *Fred's view of things, part 2*

Fred is unaware (for the most part) of all the behind-the-scenes processing steps that are taking place on his behalf!

The preceding scenario represents a best-case scenario, in which everything goes smoothly, and Fred ends up being successfully registered for the requested course. But as we know all too well, things don't always work out this smoothly, as evidenced by the following alternative scenario for the *same* use case. Everything is the same between Scenarios #1 and #2 except for the steps shown in *italic*.

Scenario #2 for the "Register for a Section" Use Case

In this scenario, Fred once again attempts to register for a section of a course; although he meets all the requirements, the requested section is unfortunately full. The SRS offers Fred the option of putting his name on a wait list. The specific sequence of events is as follows:

1. Fred, a student, logs on to the SRS.

2. Fred views the schedule of classes for the current semester to determine which section(s) he wants to register for.

3. Fred requests a seat in a particular section of a course titled "Beginning Computer Technology," course number CMP101, section 1.

4. Fred's plan of study is checked to ensure that the requested course is appropriate for his overall degree goals.

5. His transcript is checked to ensure that he has satisfied all the prerequisites for the requested course, if any.

6. Seating availability in the section is checked, but the section is found to be full.

7. Fred is asked if he wants to be put on a first come, first served wait list.

8. Fred elects to be placed on the wait list.

With a little imagination, you can undoubtedly think of numerous other scenarios for this use case, involving such circumstances as Fred having requested a course that isn't called for by his plan of study, or a course for which he hasn't met the prerequisites. And, there are many other use cases to be considered, as well, as were discussed in Chapter 9.

Note Are there practical limits to the number of alternative scenarios that one should consider for a given use case? As with all requirements analysis, the criteria for when to stop are somewhat subjective; we stop when it appears that we can no longer generate *significantly different scenarios*; trivial variations are to be avoided.

When devising scenarios, it's often helpful to imagine the future users of the system that we're modeling as they go about performing the same business functions today. In the case of current student registration, for example, what manual or automated steps does a student have to go through to register for a course? What steps does the university take before deeming a student eligible to register? Whether the registration process is 100 percent manual at present or is based on an automated system that you'll be replacing or augmenting, observing the steps that are involved today in carrying out a particular business goal can serve as the basis for one or more useful scenarios.

Scenarios, once written, should be added to our project's use case documentation; generally, we pair all scenarios with their associated use cases in that document.

Why are scenarios so important? Because they are the means by which we start to gain insight into the *behaviors* that will be required of our objects. We'll need a way to formalize these scenarios so that the actual methods needed for each of our classes become apparent; UML *sequence diagrams* are the means by which we do so, so let's now discuss how to prepare these.

Sequence Diagrams

Sequence diagrams are one of two types of UML *interaction diagrams* (we'll explore the second type, *collaboration diagrams*, a bit later in this chapter). Sequence diagrams are a way of graphically portraying how messages should flow from one object to another in carrying out a given scenario.

We'll illustrate the process of creating a sequence diagram by creating one for Scenario #1 of the "Register for a Course" use case, which was presented in Chapter 9.

Determining Objects and External Actors for Scenario #1

To prepare a sequence diagram, we must first determine the following:

- Which classes of objects (from among those that we specified in the static model [class diagram] in Chapter 10) are involved in carrying out a particular scenario

- Which external actors are involved

Looking back at Scenario #1 for the "Register for a Course" use case, we determine that the following objects are involved:

- One Student object (representing Fred)

- One Section object (representing the course titled "Beginning Computer Technology," course number CMP101, section 1)

- One PlanOfStudy object, belonging to Fred

- One Transcript object, also belonging to Fred

The scenario also mentions that the student "views the schedule of classes for the current semester to determine which section(s) he wants to register for." You might recall that when we were determining what our candidate classes should be back in Chapter 10, we debated whether or not to add ScheduleOfClasses as a candidate class to our model, and elected to leave it out at that time. To fully represent the details of Scenario #1, we'll reverse that decision and retrofit ScheduleOfClasses into our UML class diagram now as follows:

- We'll show ScheduleOfClasses participating in a one-to-many aggregation with the Section class because one ScheduleOfClasses object will be instantiated per semester to represent all the sections that are being taught that semester. (It's an abstraction of the paper booklet or online schedule that students look at in choosing which classes they want to register for in a given semester.)

- We'll also transfer the semester field from the Section class to ScheduleOfClasses. Because each Section object will now be maintaining a reference to its associated ScheduleOfClasses object by virtue of the aggregation relationship between them, a Section object will be able to request semester information whenever it is needed.

The results of these changes to the class diagram are highlighted in Figure 11-7.

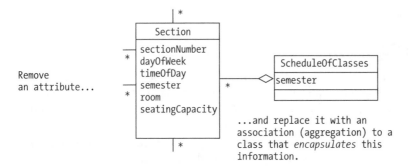

Figure 11-7. *Fine-tuning the UML diagram*

Representing ScheduleOfClasses as a class in our model allows us to now reference a ScheduleOfClasses object in our sequence diagram, as you'll see in a moment. Scenarios often unearth new classes, fields, and relationships, thus contributing to our structural "picture" of the system; this is a common occurrence and is a desirable side effect of dynamic modeling.

Of course, we must remember to add a definition of ScheduleOfClasses to our data dictionary!

Note What is the schedule of classes? It is a list of all course sections that are being offered for a particular semester; students review the schedule of classes to determine which sections they want to register for.

Finally, because the scenario explicitly mentions interactions between the student user and the system, we'll represent Fred the *actor* separately from Fred the *object*. Doing so will allow us to represent the SRS interacting with the user, as well as showing the system's internal object-to-object interactions. We refer to an object that represents an abstraction of an actor as an instance of a *boundary class*.

Our adjusted list of object/actor participants is now as follows:

- One Student object (representing Fred)

- One Section object (representing the course titled "Beginning Objects," course number CMP101, section number 1)

- One PlanOfStudy object, belonging to Fred

- One Transcript object, also belonging to Fred

- One ScheduleOfClasses object

- One Student actor (Fred again!)

Preparing the Sequence Diagram

To prepare a sequence diagram for Scenario #1, we do the following:

- We draw vertical dashed lines, one per object or actor that participates in the scenario; these are referred to as the objects' *lifelines*. Note that the objects/actors can be listed in any order from left to right in a diagram, although it's common practice to place the external user/actor at the far left.

- At the top of each lifeline, as appropriate, we place either an *instance icon*—that is, a box containing the (optional) name and class of an object participant—or a stick figure symbol to designate an actor. (For rules governing how an instance icon is to be formed, please refer to the section on creating object diagrams in Chapter 10.)

- Then, for each event called out by our scenario, we reflect its corresponding message as a horizontal solid-line arrow drawn from the lifeline of the sender to the lifeline of the receiver.

- Responses back from messages (in other words, return values from methods, or simple `return;` statements in the case of methods declared to have a `void` return type) are shown as horizontal dashed-line arrows drawn from the lifeline of the *receiver* of the original message back to the lifeline for the *sender* of the message.

- Message arrows appear in chronological order from top to bottom in the diagram.

The completed sequence diagram for Scenario #1 is shown in Figure 11-8.

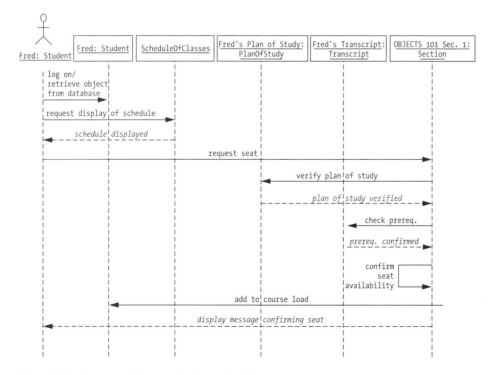

Figure 11-8. *Sequence diagram for Scenario #1*

Let's step through the diagram to make sure that we understand all the activities that are reflected in the diagram.

1. When Fred logs on to the system, his "alter ego" as an object is activated (see Figure 11-9).

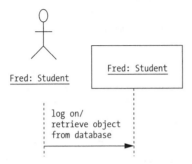

Figure 11-9. *When Fred logs on, a* Student *object is created.*

■**Note** Presumably, information representing each Student—in other words, the Student object's field values—is maintained offline in persistent storage, such as a database management system (DBMS) or file, until such time as he or she logs on, at which time the information is used to instantiate a Student object in memory, mirroring the user who has just logged on. We'll talk about reconstituting objects from persistent storage in Chapter 15.

---

2. When Fred the user/actor requests that the semester class schedule be displayed, we reflect the message "request display of schedule" being sent to an anonymous ScheduleOfClasses object. The dashed-line arrow response from the ScheduleOfClasses object indicates that the schedule is being displayed to the user, strictly speaking, via a GUI (see Figure 11-10).

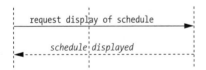

Figure 11-10. *As requested, a schedule of classes is displayed.*

3. The next message shown in our diagram is a message from the user to the Section object, requesting a seat in the class.

■**Note** This message is shown originating from the user; in reality, it originates from a GUI component object of the SRS GUI, but we aren't worrying about such implementation details at this stage in the analysis effort. We'll talk about the OO aspects of GUI design and event processing in depth in Chapter 16.

---

4. Note that there is no immediate reply to this message; that's because the Section object has a few other objects that it needs to consult with before it can grant a seat to this student, namely the following:

- The Section sends a message to the object representing Fred's plan of study, asking that object to confirm that Fred is permitted to take the course.

- The Section next sends a message to the object representing Fred's transcript, asking that object to confirm that a prerequisite course—say OBJ 001—has been satisfactorily completed by this student.

Assuming that both of these other objects respond favorably, as they are expected to do by virtue of how this scenario was written, the Section object then performs some internal processing to verify that there is indeed room for Fred in this section. We reflect internal processing within a single object as an arrow that loops back to the same lifeline that it starts with, as shown in Figure 11-11.

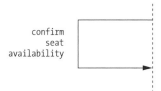

Figure 11-11. *Availability of the requested section is confirmed.*

Of course, if we were to reflect all the internal processing that is performed by every one of the objects in our sequence diagram, it would be *flooded* with such loops! The only reason that we chose to show this particular loop is because it's explicitly called out as a step in Scenario #1; if we had omitted it from our diagram, it might appear that we had accidentally overlooked this step.

5. Finally, with all checks having been satisfied, the Section object has two remaining responsibilities:

- First, it sends a new message to the Fred Student object, requesting that the Student object add this Section object to Fred's course load.

- Next, the Section object sends a response back to Fred the user/actor (via the GUI) confirming his seat in the section. This is the response to the original "request seat" message that was sent by the user toward the beginning of the scenario! All the extra behind-the-scenes processing necessary to fulfill the request—involving a Section object collaborating with a PlanOfStudy object, a Transcript object, and a Student object—is invisible to the user. As you saw earlier in the chapter, Fred merely selected a section from the schedule of classes that was displayed on the SRS GUI, clicked the Add button, and saw a confirmation message appear on his screen a few moments later.

Of course, as with all modeling, this particular sequence diagram isn't necessarily the best or only way to portray the selected scenario. And for that matter, one can argue the relative merits of one scenario as compared with another. It's important to keep in mind that preparing sequence diagrams is but a means to an end: namely, discovering the dynamic aspects of the system to be built—that is, the methods—to complement our static/structural knowledge of the system.

Recall that our ultimate goal for Part Two of the book is to produce an OO blueprint that we can use as the basis for coding the SRS as a C# application in Part Three. But, as we've already pointed out, the class diagram that we created in Chapter 10 had a noticeable deficiency: all of its classes' operations compartments were empty. Fortunately, sequence diagrams provide us with the missing pieces of information.

Using Sequence Diagrams to Determine Methods

Now that we've prepared a sequence diagram, how do we put the information that it contains to good use? In particular, how do we extract information from such diagrams concerning the methods that the various classes need to implement?

The process is actually quite simple. We step through the diagram, one lifeline at a time, and study all arrows pointing into that line.

- Arrows representing a new request being made of an object—solid-line arrows—signal methods that the receiving object must be able to perform. For example, we see a solid-line arrow labeled "check prerequisite" pointing into the lifeline representing a Transcript object. This tells us that the Transcript class needs to define a method that will allow some client object to pass in a particular course object reference, and receive back a response indicating whether or not the Transcript contains evidence that the course was successfully completed.

  We're free to name our methods in whatever intuitive way makes the most sense, consistent with the method naming conventions discussed in Chapter 4. We're using the method in this particular scenario to check completion of a prerequisite course, so we could declare the method as follows:

  ```
  bool CheckPrerequisite(Course c)
  ```

  But this name is unnecessarily restrictive; what we're really doing with this method is checking the successful completion of some Course c; the fact that it happens to be a prerequisite of some other course is immaterial to how this method will perform. So, by naming the method instead, as follows, we'll be able to use it anywhere in our application that we need to verify successful completion of a course—for example, when we check whether a student has met all the course requirements necessary to graduate:

  ```
  bool VerifyCompletion(Course c)
  ```

Tip Of course, we could have still used the method in this fashion even if it had been named CheckPrerequisite, but then our code would be less transparent to readers.

- Arrows representing responses from an operation that some other object has performed —dashed-line arrows—don't get modeled as methods/operations. These do, however, hint at the return type of the method from which this response is being issued. For example, because the response to the "verify plan of study" message is "plan of study verified," this would imply that the method is returning a bool result, hence we'd declare a method header as follows:

  ```
  bool VerifyPlan(Course c)
  ```

- Loops also represent method calls, performed by an object on itself; these might either represent private "housekeeping" methods or public methods that other client objects can avail themselves of.

In looking at the sequence diagram for Scenario #1 from a few pages back, note the arrows in Table 11-2.

Table 11-2. *Determining the Methods Implied by Scenario #1*

Arrow Labeled	Drawn Pointing into Class X	A New Request or a Response to a Previous Request?	Method to Be Added to Class X
log on	Student	Request	A method to reconstitute this object from persistent storage, such as a file or database; perhaps a special form of constructor—we'll discuss this in Part Three of the book.
request display	ScheduleOfClasses	Request	void Display() of schedule.
schedule displayed	Student (Actor)	Response	N/A.
request seat	Section	Request	bool Enroll(Student s).
verify plan	PlanOfStudy	Request	bool VerifyPlan(Course c) of study.
plan of study verified	Section	Response	N/A.
check prerequisite	Transcript	Request	bool VerifyCompletion(Course c).
prerequisite confirmed	Section	Response	N/A.
confirm seat availability	Section	Request	bool ConfirmSeatAvailability() (perhaps a private housekeeping method).
add to course load	Student	Request	void AddSection(Section s).
display message confirming seat	(actor/user)	Response	N/A. Will eventually involve calling upon some method of a user interface object—we'll worry about this in Part Three of the book.

Thus we have identified six new "standard" methods plus one constructor that will need to be added to our class diagram; we'll do so shortly.

Repeating this process of sequence diagram production and analysis for various other use case/scenario combinations will flush out most of the methods that we'll need to implement for the SRS. Despite our best efforts, however, a few methods might not surface until we've begun to program our classes; this is to be expected.

Collaboration Diagrams

The UML notation introduced a second type of interaction diagram, called a *collaboration diagram*, as an alternative to sequence diagrams; both types of diagram present more or less the same information, but portrayed in a different manner.

In a collaboration diagram, we eliminate the lifelines used to portray objects and actors. Rather, we lay out instance icons representing objects and stick figures representing actors in whatever configuration is most visually appealing. We then use lines and arrows to represent the flow of messages and responses back and forth between these objects/actors. Because we lose the top-to-bottom chronological sense of message flow that we had with the sequence diagrams, we compensate by numbering the arrows in the order that they would occur during execution of a particular scenario.

The collaboration diagram in Figure 11-12 is equivalent to the sequence diagram that we produced for Scenario #1.

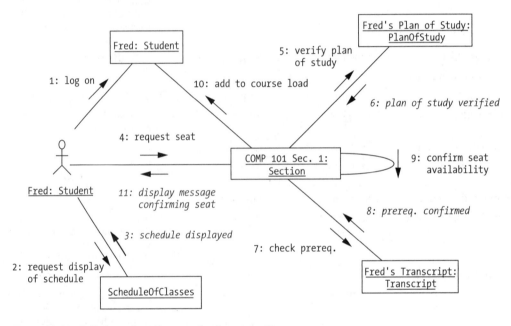

Figure 11-12. *Collaboration diagram for Scenario #1*

Again, from Fred's vantage point, he observes only a few of these actions, as shown in Figure 11-13.

Tip Because the sequence and collaboration diagrams reflect essentially the same information, many object modeling software tools automatically enable us to produce one diagram from the other with the push of a button. There is no right or wrong way; use whatever diagram type works best for you.

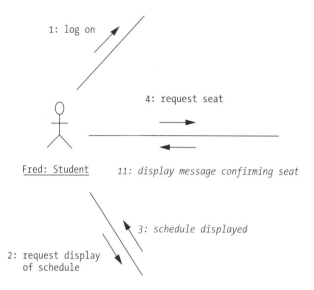

Figure 11-13. *Fred sees only a small subset of the SRS collaborations.*

Revised SRS Class Diagram

Going back to the SRS class diagram that we produced in Chapter 10, let's reflect all the new insights—some behavioral, some structural—that we gained from analyzing one scenario/sequence diagram (see Figure 11-14).

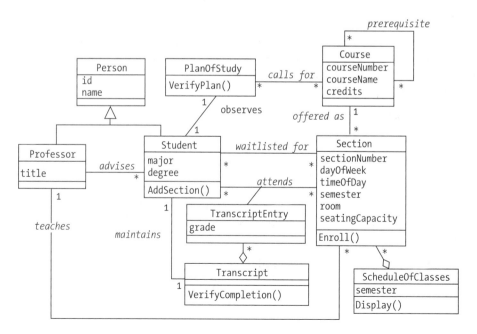

Figure 11-14. *Revised SRS class diagram*

Note that we decided not to reflect the `ConfirmSeatAvailability()` "housekeeping" method at this time because we suspect that it will be a private method and therefore don't want to clutter our diagram. The decision of whether to reflect private methods on a class diagram—or to reflect *any* member of a class—is up to the modeler because the purpose of the diagram is to communicate, and too much detail can actually lessen a diagram's effectiveness in this regard.

UML also provides notation to indicate the access (public/protected/private) given to each member of a class by placing a symbol to the left of the member name. A + symbol indicates public access, a – symbol means private access, and a # symbol indicates protected access. Because we haven't yet mapped out what the access of the SRS class members will be, we'll omit this notation for now.

We must remember to update the SRS data dictionary any time we add classes, fields, relationships, or methods to our model. Here's a suggested format for how we might want to describe a method in the dictionary:

Method: `Enroll`

Defined for class: `Section`

Header: `bool Enroll(Student s)`

Description: This method enrolls the designated person in the section, unless (a) the section is already full, (b) the student's plan of study doesn't call for this course, or (c) the student hasn't met the prerequisites. It returns a `bool` value to indicate success (`true`) or failure (`false`) of the enrollment.

Summary

In this chapter, you saw how the process of dynamic modeling is a complementary technique to static modeling that enriches our overall understanding of the problem to be automated, hence enabling us to improve our object blueprint, also known as a class diagram. In particular, you saw the following:

- How events trigger state changes

- How to develop scenarios, based on use cases

- How to represent these as UML interaction diagrams: sequence diagrams or, alternatively, collaboration diagrams

- How to extract information from sequence diagrams concerning the behaviors expected of objects—that is, the methods that our classes will need to implement—to round out our class diagram

- How sequence diagrams can also yield additional knowledge about the structural aspects of a system

Exercises

1. Prepare a sequence diagram for Scenario #2, as presented earlier in this chapter.

2. Prepare a sequence diagram to represent a Scenario #3 for the SRS use case:

   • Mary, a student, logs on to the SRS.

   • She indicates that she wants to drop ART 222, Section 1.

   • ART 222, Section 1 is removed from Mary's course load.

   • The system determines that Joe, another student, is waitlisted for this section.

   • The section is added to Joe's current course load.

   • An email is sent to Joe notifying him that ART 222 has been added to his course load.

3. Provide a list of all the method headers that you would add to each of your classes based on the sequence diagram that you prepared for exercise 2. Also, note any new classes, fields, or relationships that would be needed.

4. Prepare a second sequence diagram for the SRS case study, representing a scenario of your own choosing based upon any of the SRS use cases identified in Chapter 9. This scenario should be significantly different from those presented in this chapter and from the scenario in exercise 2. You must also narrate the scenario as was done for exercise 2.

5. Provide a list of all the method headers that you would add to each of your classes based on the sequence diagram that you prepared for exercise 4. Also, note any new classes, fields, or relationships that would be needed.

6. Devise an "interesting" scenario and prepare the corresponding sequence diagram for the problem area whose requirements you defined for exercise 3 in Chapter 2.

7. Provide a list of all the method headers that you would add to each of your classes based on the sequence diagram that you prepared for exercise 6. Also, note any new classes, fields, or relationships that would be needed.

CHAPTER 12

■ ■ ■

Wrapping Up Our Modeling Efforts

Having used the techniques for static and dynamic modeling presented in Chapters 10 and 11, respectively, we've arrived at a fairly thorough object model of the Student Registration System (SRS)—or so it seems! Before we embark upon implementing our class diagram as C# code in Part Three of the book, we need to make sure that our model is as accurate and representative of the goal system as possible.

In this chapter, we'll do the following:

- Explore some simple techniques for testing our model.

- Talk about the notion of reusing models.

Testing Your Model

Testing a model doesn't involve rocket science; instead, it calls for some common-sense measures designed to identify errors and/or omissions:

- First of all, revisit all requirements-related project documentation—the original problem statement and the supporting use cases—to ensure that no requirements were overlooked. You'll do so for our SRS model in a moment.

- Conduct a minimum of two separate formal walk-throughs of the model: one with the development team members, and a second with the future users of the system. A formal walk-through should involve, at least, the items in the following list. Make sure to distribute copies of the following documentation to each of the participants far enough in advance to allow them adequate time to review them if they so desire (but be prepared to discuss significant aspects of these at the meeting in case they haven't reviewed them):

  - "Executive summary" problem statement, if available

  - Class diagram

  - Data dictionary

  - Use case documentation

  - Significant scenarios and corresponding object collaboration diagrams

By this stage in the project, you'll have hopefully already educated your users on how to read UML diagrams, and they'll have informally seen numerous iterations of the evolving models. If any of the participants in the upcoming walk-throughs aren't familiar with any of the notation, however, take time in advance to tutor them in this regard.

Note The information contained in Chapters 10 and 11 of this book should be more than adequate as the basis for such a tutorial.

When conducting the walk-through, designate someone to be the narrator and discussion leader, and a different person to be responsible for recording significant discussion content, particularly changes that need to be made. Having one person trying to do both is too distracting, and important notes might be missed as a result. If appropriate, you might even arrange to tape record the discussion.

Remain open-minded throughout the review process. It's human nature to want to defend something that we've worked hard to put together, but remember that it's far better to find and correct shortcomings now, when the SRS is still a paper skeleton, than after it has been rendered into code.

Revisiting Requirements

In revisiting the SRS case study problem statement, we find that we indeed *missed* one requirement:

> *"The SRS will verify whether or not the proposed plan of study satisfies the requirements of the degree that the student is seeking."*

We didn't model Degree as a class—recall that we debated whether or not to do so back in Chapter 10, and ultimately decided against it. Nor, for that matter, do we reflect the requirements of a particular degree program in our model. As an example of revisiting requirements, let's look at what it would take to model a degree as a class properly.

Researching the way in which our university specifies degree program requirements, we learn the following:

- Every degree program specifies five core courses—that is, courses that a student *must* take. For example, for the degree of Master of Science in Information Technology (MSIT), students are required to complete the following five core courses:

  - Analysis of Algorithms

  - Application Programming Design

  - Computer Systems Architecture

  - Data Structures

  - Information Systems Project Management

- Students are expected to select an area of specialization within their degree program known as a *concentration*. For the MSIT degree, the university offers three different concentrations:

  - Object Technology

  - Database Management Systems

  - Networking and Communications

- Each concentration in turn specifies three mandatory, concentration-specific courses; for the MSIT degree with a concentration in Object Technology, the following courses are required:

  - Object Methods for Software Development

  - Advanced C# Programming

  - Object Database Management Systems

- Finally, the student must take two additional electives to bring the course total to 10.

Whew! To model all these interdependencies would require a fairly complex class diagram structure, as shown in Figure 12-1. The numbers of the associations indicate the multiplicity; for example, a DegreeProgram has precisely five courses as core requirements.

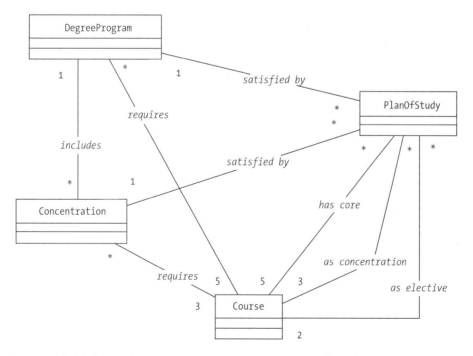

Figure 12-1. *Modeling degree program requirements prove to be rather complicated.*

We go back to our project sponsors—the future users of the SRS—and break the news to them that we've just uncovered a previously missed requirement that will significantly increase the complexity and cost of our automation effort. The sponsors decide that having the SRS verify the correctness of a student's plan of study is too ambitious a goal; they instead decide that a student will use the SRS to submit a *proposed* plan of study, but the advisor will then be responsible for *manually* verifying and approving it. To correct the SRS class diagram as last presented, add one field to the PlanOfStudy class, reflecting the date on which it was approved, and a new *approves* association connecting the Professor class to the PlanOfStudy class, and it's good to go!

Note that we don't need to add an ApprovePlan method to the PlanOfStudy class because (as discussed in Chapter 10) we might assume the presence of "set" methods or properties for all fields; the DateApproved property would suffice for marking a plan as approved. And the *approves* association between the PlanOfStudy and Professor classes (see the diagram excerpt in Figure 12-2) ensures that each PlanOfStudy object will maintain a reference to the Professor object that actually approved the plan on the date indicated.

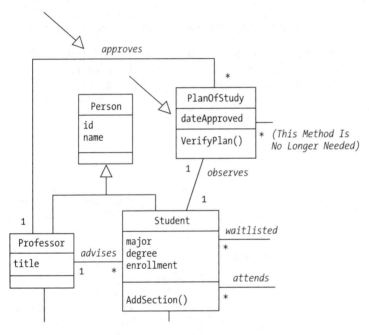

Figure 12-2. *Making minor adjustments to the SRS class diagram*

Reusing Models: A Word About Design Patterns

As discussed in Chapter 2, when learning about something new, we automatically search our "mental archive" for other abstractions/models that we previously built and mastered to look for similarities to build on. This technique of comparing features to find an abstraction that is similar enough to be reused effectively is known as *pattern reuse*. As it turns out, pattern reuse is an important technique for object-oriented (OO) software development.

Let's say that after we finish up our SRS class diagram, we're called upon to model a reservation system for a bed-and-breakfast (B&B) in Costa Rica. In keeping with the Internet age, the B&B wants to allow its customers to view the rooms and grounds, check availability, select special package deals, link to local attractions, and make reservations via the B&B website. Because there are a limited number of rooms, if clients can't get confirmed reservations for the desired dates, they can place themselves on a first-come, first-served wait list.

To keep track of clients' overall experience during their stay, the B&B plans on following up with each client after a trip to conduct a satisfaction survey. It will ask the client to rate the experience for that trip on a scale of 1 to 10, with 10 being outstanding. By doing so, the B&B can determine which packages and local attractions are the most popular to give them more visibility on the web site (the less-popular ones can also be eliminated). The B&B can also make more-informed recommendations for future trips that a given client is likely to enjoy by studying that client's travel satisfaction history.

In reflecting on the requirements for this system, we experience déjà vu! We recognize that many aspects of the B&B system requirements are similar to those of the SRS. In fact, we can reuse the overall structure, or *pattern*, of the SRS object model by making the following class substitutions:

- Substitute `TravelPackage` for `Course`

- Substitute `Trip` for `Section`

- Substitute `Client` for `Student`

- Substitute `TripRecord` for `TranscriptEntry`

- Substitute `TravelHistory` for `Transcript`

Note that all of the relationships among these classes—their names, types, and even their multiplicities—remain unchanged from the SRS class diagram (see Figure 12-3).

■Note Such an exact match is exceptionally rare when reusing design patterns; don't hesitate to change some things (eliminate classes or associations, change multiplicities, and so forth) to facilitate reuse. Keep in mind that pattern reuse is usually on a much smaller scale. You typically won't be able to reuse the entire class diagram, but perhaps two or three classes that fulfill a particular aspect of tricky functionality might be useful in another application design.

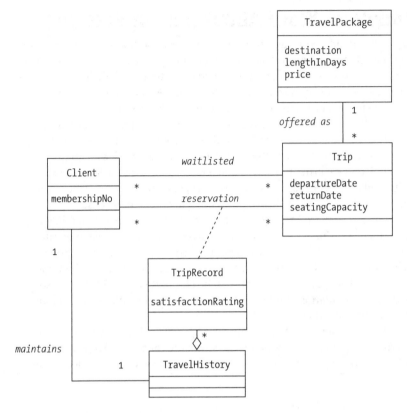

Figure 12-3. *Reusing the SRS design pattern for the Costa Rica B&B*

Having recognized the similarities between these two designs, we're poised to take advantage of quite a bit of reuse with regard to the code of these two systems. In fact, if we worked for a company whose product was to design reservation systems for multiple clients, we could have taken steps up front to develop a *generic* pattern that could have been used as the starting point for any future reservation systems we might be called upon to model, as illustrated in Figure 12-4.

Many useful, reusable patterns have been studied and documented; before embarking on a new object modeling project, it's worth exploring whether any of these might be a suitable starting point.

Tip Our "Recommended Reading" section in Chapter 17 suggests some references that you might want to explore on this topic.

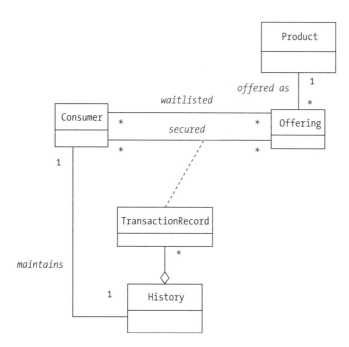

Figure 12-4. *A general-purpose class diagram for a partial reservation system*

Summary

Learning to model a problem from the perspective of objects is a bit like learning to ride a bicycle. You can read all the books ever published on the subject of successful bicycle riding, but until you actually sit on the seat, grab the handlebars, and start pedaling, you won't get a real sense of what it means to ride. The same is true of object modeling: at first it will seem hard. Developing your object models will seem to take more time than it should. You will make mistakes and then have to backtrack and rework sections of your model. With practice, however, you'll get an intuitive feel for what makes a good candidate class, a useful scenario, and so on. Eventually, you'll be able to conceptualize an effective object model in your mind soon after you read the problem description.

In this chapter, we did the following:

- Discussed techniques for verifying the accuracy and completeness of a class diagram

- Looked at how object models can be reused/adapted to other problems with similar requirements

Exercises

1. Conduct a walk-through of the class diagram that you prepared as an exercise for Chapter 10—the problem area whose requirements you defined for exercise 3 in Chapter 2—with a classmate or coworker. Report on any insights that you gained as a result of doing so.

2. Think of two other problem areas in which the reservation pattern identified for the Costa Rica B&B might also apply. What adjustments, if any, would you need to make to the reservation pattern to use it in those situations?

■ ■ ■

PART THREE

Translating a UML "Blueprint" into C# Code

CHAPTER 13

A Deeper Look at C#

We're almost ready to develop the Student Registration System (SRS) application in C#, based on the UML model that we created in Part Two. Before we dive into the specifics of coding the SRS, however, there are a number of additional C# language features that we want to cover, many of which we'll put to use in building the SRS.

Realize that we can't do justice to all of the remaining features of the C# language in just one chapter; C# is an extremely rich language, and most good C# references are many hundreds of pages long. Our goal isn't to duplicate the hard work that has gone into existing C# reference books, but instead to complement them by showing you how to bridge the gap between producing an object model and turning it into C# code—something that few, if any, other books do.

With that in mind, we'll be selective in terms of which aspects of the C# language we introduce in this chapter: namely, those that are most critical to understanding the SRS coding examples that follow in Chapters 14 through 16. Nonetheless, you'll have gone from "concept to code" and will acquire a very respectable working knowledge of C# by the time that we've finished.

■Tip Even if you've already been programming in C# for a while, and thus feel that you have a fairly good grasp of the language syntax, we encourage you to at least skim this chapter before moving on to Chapter 14 because we'll mention a few things along the way with regard to how we'll be approaching the SRS.

In this chapter, you'll learn about the following:

- The C# notion of *namespaces*—how to define them and why we use them

- The object nature of a `string`, and some of the methods/properties provided to manipulate them

- The `Object` class, a predefined class that is the ultimate base class of every C# type

- Using a special keyword, `this`, to "self-reference" an object from within one of its own methods

- The object nature of arrays and some of the methods/properties provided to manipulate them

- The `List` and `Dictionary` classes, two of the .NET Framework generic collection classes

- The nature of object identities in C#, how to discover the true class that an object belongs to, and how to test the equality of two C# objects

- Important variants on the `Main` method and the `base` keyword

- How auto-implemented properties can be used to simplify code listings

- How dynamically created objects are deleted to recycle their memory and the role that the common language runtime (CLR) *garbage collector* plays in this recycling

- A .NET Framework language construct called an attribute

We'll also revisit some of the topics that we introduced in earlier chapters to provide you with additional insights.

Namespaces

Throughout the examples in Parts One and Two of this book, and in most of the examples to follow, we've commonly placed a `using` statement (more formally referred to as a `using` directive) at the top of our programs to allow us to access the elements of a particular *namespace* by their *simple names*. By way of review, a namespace is a logical grouping of related programming elements, as was briefly discussed in Chapter 1; the .NET Framework libraries are so vast that namespaces are used to divide the libraries up into more manageable sublibraries.

A simple name is the name of the class as it appears in the class declaration; for example:

```
// This class has the simple name "Student".
public class Student {
  // Details omitted.
}
```

When a class is placed inside a namespace, its name "changes" in that it acquires its namespace as part of its *fully qualified name*. For example, as discussed earlier in the book, because the `String` class is contained in the `System` namespace, the fully qualified name of the class is `System.String`; the simple name of the class remains `String`.

It's conceivable that two classes that belong to two different namespaces A and B could be given the same simple name X, just as, by way of analogy, it's possible to create two different Microsoft Word documents with the same name (for example, `xyz.doc`) as long as they are located in different Windows folders (for example, `C:\MyDocs` and `D:\Stuff`). When we fully qualify the names of such like-named classes—`A.X` and `B.X`—these names are guaranteed to be unique, just as in the Word document analogy, the two like-named documents in our example would have different fully qualified file names; for example, `C:\MyDocs\xyz.doc` and `D:\Stuff\xyz.doc`.

To be absolutely certain that the compiler knows which class we want to use in any given situation, we could always use fully qualified class names in our program:

```
// Note that we've provided no "using" directives
// with this program.

public class SimpleProgram3
{
```

```
  static void Main() {
    System.String name = "Jackson";
    System.Console.WriteLine("The name is " + name);
  }
}
```

Having to type the fully qualified name of every namespace member that we're using in a program is cumbersome, however, and makes for less readable code. Fortunately, the C# language provides the using directive to afford us the convenience of accessing the members of a namespace using the members' simple names.

As we've seen numerous times before, a using directive is placed at the top of a source code file for every namespace whose members are to be accessed within that file; we're then free to refer to the classes of interest by their simple names throughout the code in this source file:

```
// We plan on using the "Console" class from the System namespace.
using System;

// We plan on using the "Foo" class from a DIFFERENT namespace
// named "BarStuff".
using BarStuff;

public class SimpleProgram3
{
  static void Main() {
    // We may now refer to Foo and Console by their simple names.
    Foo x = new Foo();
    Console.WriteLine("A Foo is born every minute!");
  }
}
```

The compiler will search each of the specified namespaces in turn to ensure that it can find declarations of Console and Foo in one or the other of them.

A small problem arises if a class name that we're referring to in our code exists in *more than one* of the namespaces that we specified in using directives. As an example, let's assume that we want to use two different versions of a class called Course in the same program: one that is defined by the SRS namespace and another that is defined by the ObjectStart namespace. Even if we were to provide using directives for these two namespaces, we would still have to fully qualify each use of the Course class names to disambiguate the situation:

```
// Example.cs

using ObjectStart;
using SRS;

public class Example
{
  static void Main() {
    // Use the SRS version of Course here...
```

```
    SRS.Course math = new SRS.Course();

    //...and the ObjectStart version here.
    ObjectStart.Course english = new ObjectStart.Course();
    // etc.
  }
}
```

Thus, there is no point in providing using directives for namespaces SRS or ObjectStart in this particular case.

Of course, if we wanted to use additional *uniquely named* classes from either the SRS or ObjectStart namespaces that we weren't planning on fully qualifying, such using directives would be helpful. Say, for example, that we were not only using the two versions of Course, as discussed previously, but also using a class named Student that exists in the SRS namespace but not in ObjectStart; and conversely, a class named Professor that exists in the ObjectStart namespace but not in SRS, as illustrated in Figure 13-1.

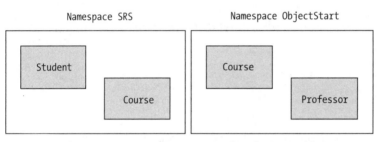

Both namespaces contain versions of a class named Course, but Student exists only in SRS, and Professor exists only in ObjectStart.

Figure 13-1. Course *exists in two namespaces;* Professor *and* Student *do not.*

We'll need to fully qualify references to the name Course once again, but won't have to fully qualify Student or Professor if we include using directives in our program, as illustrated in the following code:

```
using SRS;
using ObjectStart;
using System;

public class Example
{
  static void Main() {
    // We are still qualifying Course wherever we use it in
    // this program...
    SRS.Course math = new SRS.Course();
    ObjectStart.Course english = new ObjectStart.Course();

    //...but simple name string is OK because of the using
```

```
    // directive at the top of the code listing.
    string name = "Dinesh Prabhu";
    math.Professor = name;

    // Ditto for Student.
    Student s = new Student();

    // etc.
  }
}
```

We'll use predefined classes from five of the .NET Framework namespaces in developing the SRS application in Chapters 14 through 16:

- The `System` namespace, which includes the `String`, `Console`, and `Array` classes

- The `System.Collections.Generic` namespace, which includes the `List` and `Dictionary` collection classes

- The `System.IO` namespace, which includes the `FileStream`, `StreamReader`, and `StreamWriter` classes that we'll use to save and restore the data used by the SRS to/from files in Chapter 15

- The `System.Windows.Forms` and `System.Drawing` namespaces, which include the GUI classes and support classes that we'll use in creating a GUI front-end for the SRS in Chapter 16

Programmer-Defined Namespaces

The C# language also gives us the ability to create our own namespaces. The reasons we might want to do so are the same reasons used by Microsoft in creating/designing the .NET Framework:

- *To logically partition our classes to facilitate their reuse.* For example, a rocket scientist might want to put all the classes she designed relating to planets into a `Planets` namespace for reuse by astronomers and all the classes she designed relating to rocket design in a `Rockets` namespace for reuse by rocket manufacturers.

- *To ensure unique fully qualified names for our user-defined classes.* For example, if we want to design a class with the same simple name as a class found in one of the .NET namespaces (perhaps a class called `Console`) then by putting it into a namespace of our own creation (say, perhaps `ObjectStart`), we'd facilitate use of both the `System.Console` and `ObjectStart.Console` classes in the same program.

To assign a particular programming element (for example, a class or interface) to a namespace, we place the `namespace` keyword followed by the name that we're inventing for the namespace (observing Pascal casing conventions) at the top of the code listing, followed by a pair of braces {...} enclosing the declarations of one or more classes, interfaces, or other elements that are to be included in that particular namespace.

For example, if we were designing an application to manage the inventory of a pet store, we might want to create a namespace called PetStore that is to include classes representing different types of pets. To include a class representing a pet rat as part of the namespace, we might create a source code file named PetRat.cs as follows:

```
// PetRat.cs

// "using" directives for any OTHER namespaces required by the
// code that follows are inserted here. In this example, we are
// using two such classes -- Console and Seed -- which come from
// the System and AnimalFood namespaces, respectively.
using System;        // a standard .NET Framework namespace
using AnimalFood;    // a different user-defined namespace,
                     // defined elsewhere

// Simply by using "PetStore" in a namespace declaration,
// the PetStore namespace is born!
namespace PetStore
{
  // Everything declared within this namespace code
  // block becomes part of the PetStore namespace.

  // The PetRat class now becomes part of the PetStore namespace;
  // its fully qualified name is PetStore.PetRat.
  public class PetRat
  {
    // Fields.
    private string name;
    private string coatColor;

    // Seed is a class in the AnimalFood namespace, but since
    // we've included a "using AnimalFood" directive above, we
    // may reference the Seed class by its simple name.
    Seed favoriteSeedType;

    public void DisplayRatInfo() {
      // The "using System" directive above enables us to refer to
      // the Console class by its simple name.
      Console.WriteLine("Rat's Name:  " + name);
      Console.WriteLine("Coat Color:  " + coatColor);
      Console.WriteLine("Favorite Seed Type:  " +
          FavoriteSeedType.Name);
      // etc.
    }
  }

  // Other classes/interfaces to be inserted into PetStore could
  // be defined here, if desired, or in separate source files
```

```
// (preferred).
} // end of namespace declaration
```

The PetRat class would thus be assigned to the PetStore namespace.

Then, if we had a second class—say, Tarantula—that we also wanted to include in the same PetStore namespace, we could do so in the same file. However, it is much more common for namespaces to span (be defined in) multiple files. For example, we might want to add a class representing a tarantula to the PetStore namespace. The class is implemented in a separate file named Tarantula.cs, as shown here:

```
// Tarantula.cs

// "using" directives for any OTHER namespaces required by the
// Tarantula class code are inserted here; details omitted.

// We're inserting the Tarantula class into the SAME namespace
// as the PetRat class.
namespace PetStore
{
  // The Tarantula class now becomes part of the PetStore
  // namespace; it's fully qualified name is "PetStore.Tarantula".
  public class Tarantula
  {
    // Details omitted.
  }
}
```

Then, if we want to access either the PetRat or Tarantula class by its simple name from client code, we'd insert a using PetStore; directive at the top of that code:

```
// NamespaceDemo.cs

using PetStore;
// Any other using directives required by the Example program
// would be inserted here, as well...

public class NamespaceDemo
{
  static void Main() {
    // We're able to use the simple name "PetRat" here...
    PetRat r = new PetRat();
    r.Name = "Baby Grode";

    //...and the simple name "Tarantula" here.
    Tarantula t = new Tarantula();
    t.Name = "Fuzzy";

    // etc.
  }
}
```

The compile commands don't change for source files that include a namespace definition. For example, if the NamespaceDemo.cs, PetRat.cs, and Tarantula.cs files were in the same directory, the application could be compiled using the following command:

```
csc NamespaceDemo.cs PetRat.cs Tarantula.cs
```

When dealing with applications that require a large amount of source files or that reuse files from an existing namespace, it is common practice to place the source files in separate folders or directories. If the PetRat.cs and Tarantula.cs files were placed in a folder named PetStore that existed in the folder that contained the NamespaceDemo.cs file, the compile command would be the following:

```
csc NamespaceDemo.cs PetStore\PetRat.cs PetStore\Tarantula.cs
```

The Global Namespace

One final point about namespaces is that if we don't include an explicit namespace directive in a source file, the class or interface that we're defining in that source file will be assigned to the "nameless" *global namespace*. If two classes A and B reside in the global namespace:

- A can make references to B using B's simple name.

- B can make references to A using A's simple name.

- *Both* classes will compile properly.

All without either class having to include a using directive to find the other because they both reside in the global namespace. To simplify things a bit when we start writing the SRS-related classes in Chapter 14, we won't make use of a user-defined namespace to house the SRS classes. Instead, we'll place them in the (default) global namespace. Thus, all the SRS classes will "know" each other, enabling us to write code such as the following without having to include using directives to qualify the simple names Student and Course for the compiler:

```csharp
public class SRS
{
  static void Main() {
    Student s = new Student();    // Using a simple name.
    Course c = new Course();      // Ditto.
    // etc.
  }
}
```

Strings As Objects

In Chapter 1, we introduced a number of predefined C# types, including the string type. What we hinted at, but didn't make explicitly clear at the time, is that strings are objects. We went over some of the basics of creating and using strings in Chapter 1; we'll now review some of what we discussed before, as well as provide additional insights about strings' object nature in this section.

The "string" Alias

The keyword string is really an alias for the String class defined in the System namespace. When we declare a string variable and assign it a value, as follows:

```
string name = "Jackson";
```

we're actually instantiating an object/instance of the System.String class and initializing the object with the string literal "Jackson".

- The expressions string and System.String are syntactically equivalent as far as the C# compiler is concerned; a string object has access to the methods, properties, and constructors declared in the System.String class.

- Despite the fact that we don't see the use of the new operator to explicitly invoke a constructor of the System.String class, we're doing so nonetheless in "shorthand" fashion.

To reference the string type in our programs, we thus have several choices:

- We can refer to the simple name of the class, String (uppercase S), if we include a using System; directive at the top of the program:

```
using System;

public class Foo
{
  static void Main() {
    String s = "Whee!";
  }
}
```

- The fully qualified name System.String can be used, in which case it isn't necessary to provide the using System; directive at the top of the program:

```
// No "using" directive needed!

public class Foo
{
  static void Main() {
    System.String s = "Whee!";
  }
}
```

Note Of course, the using System; directive is still necessary if we want to access other System namespace elements, such as the Console class, by their simple names.

- The preferred method in C# is to use the alias string (lowercase s). It provides a simpler syntax than System.String, but again enables us to omit a using System; directive at the top of the program:

```
// No "using" directive needed!

public class Foo
{
  static void Main() {
    string s = "Whee!";
  }
}
```

Given the convenience of the string alias, we virtually never use either the simple or fully qualified capitalized forms of String in a C# application.

Note As it turns out, all the predefined simple types discussed in Chapter 1—bool, float, int, double, long, char, and so on—are in actuality aliases for types defined in the System namespace.

Creating String Instances

As you learned in Chapter 1, we create a string instance by declaring a reference variable of type string, and it can be initialized with any valid string expression as a value:

```
string name = "Chen";
```

or

```
string name = student.Name;
```

or

```
string name = department.FindChairperson().Name;
```

A string can also be created using one of the overloaded String class constructors in conjunction with the new operator; the headers for some of the more commonly used String constructors are as follows:

```
public String(char[] characters)
public String(char c, int count)
public String(char[] characters, int start, int length)
```

As an example of using one of the String class constructors, we could do the following:

```
char[] chars = { 'C', 'h', 'e', 'n' };
string name = new String(chars);
```

The @ Character

You learned in Chapter 1 that certain *escape characters* can be used to represent special characters such as tabs (\t), newlines (\n), or backslashes (\\) within a string literal. For example, suppose we want to define the path to a file:

```
C:\MyFolder\MySubFolder\NewFile.txt
```

We can do so through the use of \\ (backslash) escape characters as follows:

```
string filePath = C:\\MyFolder\\MySubFolder\\NewFile.txt";
```

C# provides us with an alternative way of declaring such string literals without having to resort to the use of escape characters. If we precede the opening double quote mark of a string literal with @, the literal will be read verbatim from the source code file, allowing the literal to span multiple lines and leaving all newlines, tabs, backslashes, and so on intact.

Using the @ character, the previous code example could be rewritten exactly as follows:

```
string filePath = @"C:\MyFolder\MySubFolder\NewFile.txt";
```

Special String Operators

As you learned in Chapter 1, the plus sign operator (+) concatenates string values:

```
string x = "foo";
string y = "bar";
string z = x + y + "!";  // z now has the value "foobar!"
```

The String class also provides specially defined versions of the == and != operators that can be used to compare the values of two strings for equality or inequality, respectively. The following code snippet demonstrates how these operators can be used:

```
string name = "Mary Jones";
if (name == "Cynthia Coleman") {
  Console.WriteLine("This is Cynthia Coleman");
}
else {
  Console.WriteLine("Hey!  What happened to Cynthia?");
}
```

The previous code snippet would generate the following output:

```
Hey!  What happened to Cynthia?
```

■**Tip** You'll discover a bit later in this chapter that when we use the == and != operators to compare object references in general, the outcome is somewhat different.

String Properties

The String class also defines two useful properties.

The Length property returns the number of characters in the associated String, including white space characters:

```
string sentence = "How long am I?";
Console.WriteLine("Length = " + sentence.Length);
```

The output for the previous code snippet would be as follows:

```
Length = 14
```

Another useful feature of the String class is a special property called the Chars property that acts as an indexer, allowing the individual characters of a String to be accessed according to a character's position, or *index*, in the String. The use of the Chars property is indicated by placing a pair of square brackets around the desired index, similar to the syntax for accessing an element of an array:

```
String str = "Tom Servo";
Console.WriteLine("The first character is " + str[0]);
```

This code snippet would generate the following output:

```
The first character is Ts
```

String Methods

In addition to the operators and properties discussed so far, every string object has access to the methods declared by the String class. We'll discuss a few of the more useful methods in this section; for a complete description of all of the methods defined by the String class, please consult the .NET Framework Class Library Reference on the MSDN web site.

- public bool StartsWith(string str): Returns true if the string to which this method is applied starts with the value of the string expression provided as an argument; returns false otherwise:

  ```
  string string1 = "foobar";
  string string2 = "foo";

  // This will evaluate to true.
  if (string1.StartsWith(string2))...
  ```

- public bool EndsWith(string str): Returns true if the string to which this method is applied ends with the value of the string expression provided as an argument; false otherwise.

  ```
  string string1 = "foobar";

  // This will evaluate to true.
  if (string1.EndsWith("bar"))...
  ```

- `public int IndexOf(string str)`: Returns a nonnegative integer indicating the starting character position (counting from 0) at which the value of the string expression provided as an argument is found within the string on which this method is called (or –1 if the string argument isn't found):

```
string string1 = "foobar";
int i = string1.IndexOf("bar");  // i will equal 3

string string2 = "cat";
int j = string1.IndexOf(string2);  // j will be -1, because the
                                   // value of the argument "cat"
                                   // is not found in "foobar".
```

- `public string Replace(char old, char new)`: Creates a new `string` object in which all instances of the old character are replaced with the new character—the original string remains unaffected:

```
string string1 = "o1o2o3o4";
// Note use of single quotes around character literals.
string p = string1.Replace('o', 'x');  // p now equals "x1x2x3x4",
                                        // while string1 remains "o1o2o3o4"
```

- `public string Replace(string old, string new)`: An overloaded version of the `Replace` method that allows us to replace one substring with another substring; note that the substrings need not be of equal length:

```
string string1 = "foobar";
string p = string1.Replace("foo", "candy"); // p becomes "candybar"
```

- `public string Substring(int startIndex)`: Creates a new string whose value is based on a substring of an existing string, starting at the position in the existing string indicated by the `int` expression passed as an argument (counting from 0) and continuing through the end of the existing string:

```
string string1 = "foobar";
int i = 3;
string p = string1.Substring(i); // p now equals "bar"
```

- `public string Substring(int startIndex, int length)`: An overloaded form of the `Substring` method that creates a new string by taking a substring of an existing string, starting at the position indicated by the *first* `int` expression passed as an argument and continuing for `length` additional characters; again, we begin counting with 0 as the first character position:

```
string string1 = "foobar";
string p = string1.Substring(1, 4);  // p now equals "ooba"
```

- `public string ToLower()`: Returns a copy of the string on which this method is applied, changing all the characters to lowercase:

```
string string1 = "Jose Cruz";
string p = string1.ToLower();    // p now equals "jose cruz"
```

- public string ToUpper(): Returns a copy of the string on which this method is applied, changing all the characters to uppercase:

```
string string1 = "Jose Cruz";
string p = string1.ToUpper();     //  p now equals "JOSE CRUZ"
```

Object Class

In addition to the String class, there are several other classes that deserve special mention in the C# language—one such class is the Object class. The Object class is at the very root of the .NET class hierarchy. Every other .NET type, from the simple predefined value types, to strings, to arrays, to predefined reference types, to user-defined types, ultimately derives from the Object class.

Inheritance from the Object class is implicit; there is no need to include the syntax in a class definition:

```
: Object
```

That is, the class definition syntax

```
public class Student {...}
```

is equivalent to the more explicit

```
public class Student : Object {...}
```

The Object class is contained in the System namespace, but as with the String class there is an alias for the Object class—the keyword object (all lowercase)—which allows us to declare Object references without having to insert a using System; directive at the top of our program; the following two lines of code are thus equivalent:

```
System.Object x = y;
```

and

```
object x = y;
```

The Object class declares seven public methods that are inherited by, and hence available to, any object of any type. We'll discuss the two most commonly used Object methods in detail in the following sections: Equals and ToString.

Equals Method

The Equals method determines whether two object references are "equal." If the method is used to compare reference-type objects (for example, class instances or arrays), the Equals method determines whether the two references are referring to the exact same object in memory. If the method is applied to value-type objects (for example, primitive types such as int or float), Equals performs a bitwise comparison of the values of the objects. There are two versions of this method:

- public virtual bool Equals(Object obj): This method can be called on any object, passing in a second object as an argument: if (x.Equals(y)) {...}.

- public static bool Equals(Object objA, Object objB): This static method is called on the Object class, and the two references to be compared are both passed in as arguments to the method: if (Object.Equals(x, y)) {...}.

For example, let's create a Student object and maintain two references to it:

```
Student s1 = new Student("Fred");
Student s2 = s1;
```

Reference variables s1 and s2 thus reference the same object in memory. Now, let's create a second Student object with the same data values as the first:

```
Student s3 = new Student("Fred");
```

Using the "object as helium balloon" analogy, we created the situation portrayed in Figure 13-2.

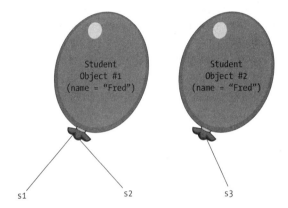

Figure 13-2. *Object #2 has the same data values as Object #1 but is a separate, distinct object in memory.*

If we test for equality of s1 and s2 using the Equals method:

```
if (s1.Equals(s2)) {  // or, equivalently: Object.Equals(s1, s2);
  Console.WriteLine("s1 equals s2");
}
else {
  Console.WriteLine("s1 does not equal s2");
}
```

the output of this code would be as follows:

```
s1 equals s2
```

because s1 and s2 are indeed referencing the same object, whereas testing s1 and s3 for equality:

```
if (s1.Equals(s3)) {  // or, equivalently: Object.Equals(s1, s3);
  Console.WriteLine("s1 equals s3");
}
```

```
else {
  Console.WriteLine("s1 does not equal s3");
}
```

would generate the following output:

```
s1 does not equal s3
```

because despite the fact that s1 and s3 have the same data values (name is "Fred" in both cases), they are nonetheless references to *distinct* objects.

Overriding the Equals Method

The nonstatic version of the Object class's Equals method is declared to be virtual, allowing us to override its behavior in a derived class. We often override the Equals method to define a different interpretation of what it means for two objects to be equal: for example, in the Student class, we might want to deem two *physically distinct* Student objects as nonetheless being "equal" if they have the same value for their respective student ID numbers. To achieve this end, the Student class overrides the Equals method:

```
using System;

public class Student
{
  // Field.
  private string id;

  // Property.
  public string Id {
    // Accessor details omitted.
  }

  // Overriding the Equals method.
  public override bool Equals(object obj) {
    // Initialize a flag.
    bool isEqual = false;

    //  Use the as operator to try to cast the object
    //  argument into a Student object. This operator
    //  returns null if the cast was unsuccessful
    Student s = obj as Student;

    //  If the cast Student object reference is not null
    //  and if it has the same Id property value
    //  as the current Student object, set the isEqual
    //  flag to be true
    if ( s != null && s.Id == this.Id ) {
      isEqual = true;
    }
```

```
      return isEqual;
  }
}
```

The overridden Equals method first uses the as operator to try to cast the object argument to the method into a Student. If the cast is unsuccessful, the operator returns null. If the cast Student object isn't null, and if the value of its Id property is equal to that of the current Student object, the isEqual flag is set to be true.

Let's put our new overridden method to work in our client code:

```
public class Example
{
  static void Main() {
    Professor p = new Professor();

    Student s1 = new Student(); // first object...
    s1.Id = "123-45-6789";

    Student s2 = new Student(); // second object...
    s2.Id = "123-45-6789"; // same ID as s1

    Student s3 = new Student(); // third object!
    s3.Id = "987-65-4321"; // different ID as s1 and s2

    Console.WriteLine("Is s1 equal to s2?  " + s1.Equals(s2));
    Console.WriteLine("Is s1 equal to s3?  " + s1.Equals(s3));
    Console.WriteLine("Is s1 equal to p?  " + s1.Equals(p));
  }
}
```

The preceding code would generate the following output:

```
Is s1 equal to s2?  True
Is s1 equal to s3?  False
Is s1 equal to p?  False
```

Note that when we instead use the == operator to test two references for equality

```
  if (x == y) {...}
```

the nature of the equality test is again class-dependent; if x and y are reference-type object references, then == tests to see if the two references are referring to the same physical object in memory. If x and y are value types, then == tests to see whether the two variables have the same values. For string objects, the == operator compares the values of the strings, even though strings are objects.

For a user-defined class such as Student that has overridden the Equals method, there is also a way to override the == operator, but the means of doing so is beyond the scope of this book to address.

ToString Method

The most commonly used (and most commonly overridden) Object class method is ToString. It's used to return a string representation of the object on which the method is called, and has the following header:

```
public virtual string ToString()
```

The Object class implementation of ToString simply returns the fully qualified name of the type of the object on which it's called. For example, if the Student class belongs in the SRS namespace and we were to call the ToString method on a Student object as it's inherited from the Object class:

```
Student s = new Student();
s.Name = "Dianne Bolden";
s.Id = "999999";
Console.WriteLine(s.ToString());
```

the following output would result:

```
SRS.Student
```

However, simply printing out the name of the class that an object belongs to isn't very informative. Fortunately, as was the case with the Equals method, the Object class version of the ToString method is declared to be virtual, which enables us to override its behavior for a derived class.

Overriding the ToString Method

In the preceding example, we'd prefer that the ToString method for a Student return a more informative result, such as perhaps the label "Student:" followed by a given student's name and student ID number, formatted as shown here:

```
Student:  Dianne Bolden [999999]
```

To achieve this result, we'd simply need to override the ToString method in the Student class as follows:

```
public class Student {
  // Fields.
  private string name;
  private string id;
  // Other details omitted...

  public override string ToString() {
    return "Student:   " + Name + " [" + Id + "]";
  }
}
```

Now, the snippet shown earlier:

```
Student s = new Student();
s.Name = "Dianne Bolden";
s.Id = "999999";
Console.WriteLine(s.ToString());
```

would output the desired result when executed by virtue of our overridden ToString method:

```
Student:  Dianne Bolden [999999]
```

"Behind the Scenes" Use of ToString

As it turns out, the ToString method is often called behind the scenes—for example, by the Console.WriteLine method. The Console.WriteLine method, which we normally think of as accepting string arguments, is overloaded so that an arbitrary object reference can be passed as an argument to the method. It's therefore perfectly acceptable to write code as follows:

```
Student s = new Student();
s.Name = "Cheryl Richter";
s.Id = "123456";
Console.WriteLine(s);
```

When an arbitrary object reference is passed to the WriteLine method, the WriteLine method automatically calls the object's ToString method to obtain its class-specific string representation, which is then printed to the console. Given the way in which we'd overridden the ToString method for the Student class earlier, the result of running the preceding code snippet would produce the following output:

```
Student:  Cheryl Richter [123456]
```

Many of the predefined classes in the .NET Framework libraries have overridden the ToString method. What's more, it's a good idea to get into the habit of overriding the ToString method for all user-defined classes, to ensure that whenever ToString is called behind the scenes on an instance of such a class, a meaningful result is returned.

Object Self-Referencing with "this"

In client code, such as the Main method of a program, we declare reference variables with which to store references to objects:

```
Student s = new Student(); // a reference variable of type Student
```

and can then conveniently access the objects that these reference variables refer to by manipulating the reference variables themselves:

```
s.Name = "Fred";
```

When we're executing the code that comprises the body of one of an object's own methods, we sometimes need the object to be able to refer to itself—that is, to *self-reference*—as in this next bit of code:

```
public class Student
{
  Professor facultyAdvisor;
  // other details omitted
```

```
public void SelectAdvisor(Professor p) {
    // We're down in the "bowels" of the SelectAdvisor() method,
    // executing this method for a particular Student object.

    // We save the reference to the advisor as one of our fields.
    facultyAdvisor = p;

    //...and now we want to turn around and tell this Professor
    // object to add us as one of its (Student) advisees.
    // The Professor class has a method with signature:
    //
    //          public void AddAdvisee(Student s);
    //
    // so, all we need to do is call this method on our advisor
    // object and pass in a reference to ourselves; but who the
    // heck are we? That is, how do we refer to ourself?
    p.AddAdvisee(???);
  }
}
```

Within the body of a method, when we need a way to refer to the object whose method we're executing, we use the reserved word this to "self-reference." So, in our preceding example, the following line of code would do the trick:

```
p.AddAdvisee(this);
```

Specifically, it would pass a reference to *this* Student—the Student object whose method we're executing at this very moment—as an argument of the AddAdvisee method, to Professor p.

We mentioned back in Chapter 4 that we can invoke one member of a class from within another method of the *same* class without using dot notation:

```
public class Student
{
  // details omitted

  public void MethodA() {
    // We can call MethodB from within MethodA without
    // using dot notation.
    MethodB();
    // other details omitted...
  }

  public void MethodB() {
    // details omitted...
  }
}
```

As it turns out, this is shorthand for the following equivalent dot notation:

```
public void MethodA() {
  // Calling MethodB from within MethodA.
  this.MethodB();
  // other details omitted...
}
```

Because the this. prefix is implied, we needn't include it, but are free to do so if we want.

You'll see yet another use for the this keyword, having to do with constructors, later in this chapter.

C#'s Collection Classes

Back in Chapter 6, we discussed the need for a convenient way to collect references to objects as we create them, so that we can iterate over them, retrieve a particular object on demand, and so forth. We learned that the way to do so in an object-oriented programming language (OOPL) is to create a special type of object called a *collection,* and that one of the simplest collection types in C# is the fixed-size array. When we introduced arrays in Chapter 6, we alluded to the fact that they are objects in the C# language; as it turns out, the System.Array class is the basis for all arrays. We'll revisit arrays in this section to learn about some of the more interesting features of the System.Array class.

As we discussed in Chapter 6, it's often impossible to anticipate how many of a given object type we'll have to create as an application is running, and so using fixed-size arrays to store varying numbers of objects is often inefficient. The System.Collections and System. Collections.Generic namespaces of the .NET Framework Class Library (FCL) defines a number of alternative collection classes that can be used to store object collections. In this section, we'll discuss two of the collection classes that we plan to use when building the SRS: the List and Dictionary classes.

■**Note** The System.Array class isn't part of the System.Collections namespace. However, like the System.Collections classes, the System.Array class implements the ICollection interface, which is defined in the System.Collections namespace, and hence the Array class shares a common set of behaviors with other collection classes.

Arrays, Revisited

The System.Array class defines a variety of useful methods and properties that can be used to do such things as search, sort, modify, and determine the length of arrays.

Array Length Property

One of the most commonly used Array property is the Length property. It's of type int and represents the total number of elements in an array across all its dimensions. The following snippet shows the Length property in use for a one-dimensional array:

```
int[] x = new int[20];

// details of array content initialization omitted...

// Step through the array.
// Stop BEFORE i equals x.Length!!!!
for (int i = 0; i < x.Length; i++) {
  Console.WriteLine(x[i]);
}
```

Because arrays are zero-based, we always need to stop just one short of the length when using it as an upper bound in a for loop, as the preceding example illustrates.

Note that the length of an array doesn't reflect how many elements have been explicitly assigned values because, technically speaking, even if nothing is stored explicitly in an array, its elements will be automatically filled with zero-equivalent values suitable for the array's type (as was discussed in Chapter 6). Instead, the length of an array simply represents the total size of the array in terms of the total number of slots in the array; the size is fixed when an array is first declared and can't be changed thereafter.

■**Note** It turns out there is a method declared in the Array class that can be used to resize a one-dimensional array. You'll learn about that method in the next section.

The Length property can be applied to multidimensional arrays as well. In the following example, the Length property is used to determine the number of rows in a two-dimensional, jagged array as well as the number of columns in each row:

```
// Create a two-dimensional array with 3 rows and a different
// number of columns for each row.
double[][] values = new double[3][];
    values[0] = new double[4];
    values[1] = new double[2];
    values[2] = new double[3];

    Console.WriteLine("Number of rows = "+values.Length);
    for(int i=0; i<values.Length; ++i) {
      Console.WriteLine("Number of columns in row "+i+
                    " is "+values[i].Length);
    }
```

```
Number of rows = 3
Number of columns in row 0 is 4
Number of columns in row 1 is 2
Number of columns in row 2 is 3
```

Array Methods

The Array class declares a variety of useful static and instance methods that can be used to examine or manipulate arrays; we'll discuss a few of the more commonly used methods here. A complete description of all of the Array class methods can be found in the FCL Reference on the MSDN web site.

The methods discussed here are static methods, meaning that they must be invoked on the Array class as a whole, passing in the array instance to be affected as an argument:

- `public static void Clear(Array array, int startIndex, int length)`: Resets the contents of all or part of an array to zero-equivalent values. The arguments include the array to be cleared, the starting index (counting from 0), and the number of elements to clear:

  ```
  // Create an array named x and fill the array with values

  // Clear the entire array.
  Array.Clear(x, 0, x.Length);
  ```

- `public static void Reverse(Array array)`: Reverses the order of the elements of a one-dimensional array:

  ```
  int[] x = {1, 2, 3};
  Array.Reverse(x);
  // x now contains the values: {3, 2, 1}
  ```

  There is also an overloaded version of this method in which the starting index and number of elements to reverse can be specified:

  ```
  public static void Reverse(Array array, int startIndex, int length)
  ```

- `public static void Sort(Array array)`: Sorts the elements of a one-dimensional array. The default sorting criterion is alphabetically for string elements and smallest-to-largest for numerical elements.

  ```
  string[] names = {"Vijay", "Tiger", "Phil"};
  Array.Sort(names);
  // the order of the elements is now "Phil", "Tiger", "Vijay"
  ```

  There is also an overloaded version of this method in which the starting index and number of elements to sort can be specified:

  ```
  public static void Sort(Array array, int startIndex, int length)
  ```

Note Other versions of the Sort method enable user-defined sorting criteria to be specified for arbitrary object types, but this topic is beyond the scope of this book to address.

- public static void Resize<T>(ref T[] array, int newSize): This method is used to resize a one-dimensional array. Strictly speaking, what takes place is a new array is created with the specified size, the elements of the old array are copied into the new one, and the old array is replaced with the new one.

There are a couple of new features with the parameter list of this method. The ref keyword allows the method to change the reference to the array variable. In other words, when the array is resized, a new array is created, and the variable reference is changed to point to the new resized array. The T[] syntax indicates that Resize is a generic method and will work with arrays containing any value or reference type.

```
double[] data = new double[10];  // Initial size is 10
                                 //elements

int numData = 13;
for(int i=0; i<numData; ++i) {  //  oh, oh, we're going to
                                // overflow the array

    //  Resize the array if needed.
    if ( i == data.Length ) {
        Array.Resize(ref data, data.Length+5);
    }
    data[i] = 1.0;
}

Console.WriteLine("Array size = "+data.Length);

// Use Resize to reduce array size to match amount of data
Array.Resize(ref data, numData);

Console.WriteLine("New array size = "+data.Length);
```

Here is the output:

```
Array size = 15
New array size = 13
```

There are a lot more Array class methods that can be used to manipulate arrays. Consult the FCL Reference on the MSDN web site for a description of these methods.

List Class

You first learned about the List class in Chapter 6. It represents a generic, dynamically resizable, one-dimensional ordered list that allows us to store a varying number of elements without having to worry about properly sizing the container in advance. It's the logical equivalent of a one-dimensional Array, but one whose size is automatically increased or decreased as needed.

The List class is the generic equivalent of the ArrayList class. Recall the following about ArrayList collections:

- Can store elements of any type.

- Store their elements as type Object.

- Any type of element can be added to an existing ArrayList. There is no type-checking, and it's possible to mix and match types within an ArrayList.

- The programmer must keep track of what elements have been added to an ArrayList.

- Elements extracted from an ArrayList are always returned as Object types and must be cast into their "proper" type.

In contrast, the following are true about generic List collections:

- Are assigned to hold elements of a specific type when the List is declared.

- Only elements of the declared type are allowed to be added to a List.

- Elements extracted from a List are returned as the type that the List is declared to hold. There is no need to cast the extracted elements from type Object.

Because of their inherent type-safety and because they generally offer better performance, List collections are preferred over ArrayList collections, and we will make use of the List class when we write the code for the SRS in Chapter 14.

The List class is defined within the System.Collections.Generic namespace. To refer to the List class by its simple name, a using directive can be included at the top of the code:

```
using System.Collections.Generic;
```

or a List can be referred to by its fully qualified name:

```
System.Collections.Generic.List
```

Creating a List

A List object can be instantiated by using one of three constructors provided by the List class:

- The simplest form of constructor is the parameterless constructor. For example, to create a List that will hold a collection of Course objects:

```
List<Course> coursesTaken = new List<Course>();
```

This constructor will create an empty List with an initial default capacity of 0. When the first item is added to the List, the capacity is set to 4. When the number of elements in the List subsequently reaches the current capacity of the List, its capacity is doubled.

- The second form of List constructor takes an integer argument representing the initial capacity (that is, reserved space) of the List; for example:

```
List<Student> students = new List<Student>(400);
```

We might use this form of constructor if we knew that we would be adding a large number of object references to the List. Starting with a larger capacity can increase performance by reducing the number of times the List would need to resize itself as it grows.

- The third constructor initializes the List with the elements of a collection, specifically a collection that implements the generic IEnumerable interface defined in the System. Collections.Generic namespace. For example, a List can be initialized with the contents of a one-dimensional array of Course objects:

```
// Create an array of Course objects...
Course[] courses = new Course[3];
courses[0] = new Course("Math 101");
courses[1] = new Course("Management 283");
courses[2] = new Course("Physics 250");

//...and, later in the program, use it to initialize
// an List.
List<Course> coursesTaken = new List<Course>(courses);
```

In the previous code snippet, the length of the List is 3, and it contains references to all of the Course objects in the array; note that both collections are now referencing the same objects, as illustrated conceptually in Figure 13-3.

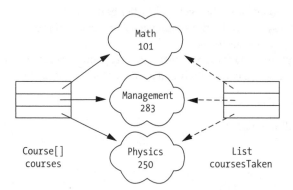

Figure 13-3. *A* List *can be initialized with the contents of another collection.*

List Properties

The List class declares a number of properties that return information about the List:

- The Capacity property is used to get or set the capacity of the List. (If we programmatically attempt to resize the capacity of a List to be smaller than the number of items it holds at any given time, an ArgumentOutOfRangeException is thrown.)

- The Count property returns the current number of elements actually contained in the List.

- To access an element stored inside a List, the List class defines a special indexer Item property that allows us to get or set an element of a List just as we would access an element of a standard array—with an integer expression representing the desired index, surrounded by square brackets.

Here is an example illustrating all these properties:

```
// Not Shown: A List collection is initialized with a number of
//   Course objects.

// Access the Capacity and Count properties.
Console.WriteLine("capacity = " + coursesTaken.Capacity);
Console.WriteLine("no. of elements = " + coursesTaken.Count);

// Let's now pull the List elements back out, again
// using the indexer.
for (int i = 0; i < coursesTaken.Count; i++) {

  Course c = coursesTaken[i];

  // We now can invoke the properties and methods on Course c.
  Console.WriteLine(c.Name);
}
```

List Methods

Some of the more commonly used List class methods are as follows:

- public void Add(T item): Adds an element to the end of the List, automatically expanding the List if need be to accommodate the reference. One of the key benefits of generic collections is that compiler will check that the item being added to the List is compatible with the type that the List was declared to be. For example, an attempt to add a string object to a List that was declared to hold Course objects will generate the following compiler error:

```
Error: The best overloaded method match for
'List<Course>.Add(Course)' has some invalid arguments.
Cannot convert from 'string' to 'Course'.
```

- public void Insert(int index, T item): Inserts the specified item into the List at the specified location. The existing elements are shifted forward to make room for the new item.

- public void AddRange(IEnumerable<T> collection): Appends the contents of the specified collection to the end of the List.

- `public int IndexOf(T item)`: Searches the `List` for the existence of a specific object and, if found, returns an integer indicating the (first) index location at which this reference was found (counting from 0). If the specified object isn't found, the value –1 is returned.

- `public bool Contains(T item)`: Searches the `List` for existence of the object in question and, if found, returns the value `true`, otherwise `false`.

- `public void RemoveAt(int index)`: Takes out the element at the specified index and closes up/collapses the resultant "hole." The value of the `Count` property decreases by one, but the `Capacity` remains the same. An `ArgumentOutOfRangeException` is thrown if the specified index exceeds the `Count` or is less than zero.

- `public bool Remove(T item)`: Searches for existence of a specific object in question and, if found, removes the (first) occurrence of that object from the `List`, again closing up the hole. The `Count` decreases by one, but the `Capacity` remains the same. The return value is `true` if the item was successfully removed; it is `false` if the item wasn't found in the `List` or if the removal was unsuccessful for some other reason. If the specified object isn't found, the `List` is unchanged. To remove all instances of `item`, use a combination of the `Contains` and `Remove` methods in conjunction with a `while` loop:

```
while (list.Contains(x)) {
   list.Remove(x)
}
```

- `public void Sort()`: Sorts the elements of the `List`. The default is to sort `string` elements alphabetically and numerical elements smallest-to-largest.

■**Note** Other versions of this method enable us to customize the sorting algorithm for arbitrary object types, but discussing user-defined sorting algorithms is beyond the scope of this book.

- `public void Clear()`: Empties out the `List`. The `Count` property is set to zero. The `Capacity` is unchanged.

- `public T[] ToArray()`: Creates an instance of an array, and copies the elements of the `List` into the array. The type of elements in the array will coincide with the type of elements contained in the `List`.

And there are more! Please consult the FCL Reference on the MSDN web site for a complete description of all of the `List` methods.

Dictionary Class

The `Dictionary` class provides us with another way to manage collections of elements in C#. A `Dictionary` is a bit more sophisticated than a `List` because it gives us direct access to a given object based on a unique key value; it's an implementation of the dictionary collection type that we defined in Chapter 6. Like the `List` class, the `Dictionary` class represents a generic collection. The type of both the key and the value are specified when the Dictionary is instantiated; keys are often, but not always, strings.

Like the List class, the Dictionary class can be found in the System.Collections.Generic namespace. To refer to a Dictionary by its simple name, a using System.Collections.Generic; directive can be placed at the top of a source code file, or a Dictionary can be referred to by its fully qualified name: System.Collections.Generic.Dictionary.

Creating a Dictionary

A Dictionary object can be created using any one of the various constructors declared by the Dictionary class. The simplest way to instantiate a Dictionary is with the parameterless constructor, which creates an empty Dictionary. We then insert objects as desired using the Add method, whose header is as follows:

```
public void Add(TKey key, TValue value)
```

Note that we must specify a key for each value as we add it to the Dictionary, to be used to retrieve the value later on; we'll use simple string objects for the keys in this example—in particular, the students' ID numbers:

```
// Create a Dictionary instance.
Dictionary<string, Student> students = new Dictionary<string, Student>();

// Create several Student objects
Student s1 = new Student("123-45-6789", "David Chen");
Student s2 = new Student("987-65-4321", "Mary Jones");
Student s3 = new Student("654-32-1987", "Gerson Lopez");

// Store the Student objects in the Dictionary, using the value of
// the Id property (which happens to be declared as type string)
// as the key for each.
students.Add(s1.Id, s1);
students.Add(s2.Id, s2);
students.Add(s3.Id, s3);
```

The Dictionary class defines an indexer that can be used to get or set an element of the Dictionary. As with the List class, the indexer is denoted by a pair of square brackets; with Dictionary objects, however, the brackets surround the key value of the element to be accessed:

```
// Retrieve a Student object based on its key.
Student s = students["123-45-6789"];   // retrieves the object
                                        // reference representing
                                        // Student David Chen
Console.WriteLine("name is " + s.Name);
```

Dictionary Properties

In addition to Count and indexer properties, which work the same for a Dictionary as they do for a List, the Dictionary class declares a number of other properties to return information about the Dictionary. Here are details on two of the properties:

- The Keys property returns a Dictionary(TKey, TValue).KeyCollection object whose elements are the keys contained in the Dictionary.

- The Values property returns a Dictionary(TKey, TValue).ValueColletion object whose elements are the values contained in the Dictionary.

For a complete list of all Dictionary properties, consult the FCL reference on the MSDN web site.

Dictionary Methods

Some of the more commonly used methods from the Dictionary class are as follows:

- public void Add(TKey key, TValue value): As already discussed, this method inserts a value into the Dictionary that can be retrieved using the specified key. This method will throw an ArgumentException if there already was a previously stored object at that key location, so it's important to first verify that the key we're about to use isn't already in use in the table, using the ContainsKey method discussed next. The compiler will perform type-checking and an error will result if the type of the key and value don't match those that were declared for the Dictionary.

- public bool ContainsKey(TKey key): Returns true if an entry with the designated key value is found in the Dictionary; otherwise returns false.

  Here's how we'd use the ContainsKey method in concert with the Add method to make sure we weren't trying to overwrite an existing entry in the Dictionary:

  ```
  Student s = new Student("111-11-1111", "Arnold Brown");
  if (students.ContainsKey(s.Id)) {
    // Whoops! This is a duplicate; we need to decide what to do!
    // details omitted...
  }
  else {
    students.Add(s.Id, s);  // OK, because no duplicate was detected.
  }
  ```

- public bool ContainsValue(TValue value): Looks for the designated *value* without the aid of its associated key, and returns true if the value is found, otherwise returns false.

- public bool Remove(TKey key): Attempts to remove the value corresponding to the given key from the Dictionary. The method returns true if the removal was successful; and returns false if the key doesn't exist in the Dictionary or if the removal was unsuccessful for some other reason.

- public void Clear(): Empties out the Dictionary, as if it had just been newly instantiated. The Count property is set to zero.

There are more `Dictionary` class methods than those that were just described. For complete details on all of the `Dictionary` methods, consult the FCL Reference on the MSDN web site.

Stepping Through Collections Using the foreach Loop

The `foreach` loop is a C# flow of control structure beyond those that we discussed in Chapter 1. A `foreach` loop provides a way to iterate through the elements of a C# collection.

The general syntax of the `foreach` loop is as follows:

```
foreach (type variable_name in collection_name) {
  // code to be executed
}
```

Inside the parentheses following the `foreach` keyword, we find the following:

- The type of items in the collection being processed—items retrieved from the collection being processed are automatically cast to this type

- A local reference variable that refers one by one to each of the items in the collection in turn

- The name of the collection to be searched, preceded by the keyword `in`

Here is an example of using a `foreach` loop to iterate through a generic `List` collection that stores `Student` objects:

```
List<Student> students = new List<Student>();

// Details on filling List collection omitted.

// Use foreach loop to iterate through the List.
foreach ( Student student in students ) {
  Console.WriteLine(student.Name);
}
```

The block of code provided as part of the `foreach` statement is executed every time another element of the specified type is retrieved by the `foreach` loop.

Note that once we begin iterating within a `foreach` block, we can't change where the `foreach` reference variable is "pointing" by attempting to assign a new value to the variable; that is, the following won't compile:

```
foreach (Student s in studentBody) {
  // This will not compile!  Reference s is read-only.
  s = studentBody[0];
}
```

```
error: cannot assign to 's' because it is a 'foreach' iteration variable
```

Of course, the iteration variable s that refers to the current element of the collection is accessible/modifiable the same way that any object is once we have a reference to it:

```
foreach (Student s in studentBody) {
  // This is perfectly OK to do.
  s.Name = "?";
}
```

There are more options when using foreach loops to iterate through the elements of a Dictionary collection. A Dictionary stores one or more key-value pairs. The Keys property of the Dictionary class can be used to obtain a reference to a Dictionary.KeyCollection object that contains the keys of the Dictionary. A foreach loop can then be used to iterate through the keys:

```
Dictionary<string, Student> students =
                new Dictionary<string, Student>();

// Details on adding key-value pairs to Dictionary omitted.

foreach( string key in students.Keys ) {
    Console.WriteLine("key name is "+key);
}
```

In a similar fashion, the Values property of the Dictionary class can be used to obtain a reference to a Dictionary.ValueCollection object that contains the values stored by the Dictionary. A foreach loop can then be used to iterate through the values:

```
Dictionary<string, Student> students =
                new Dictionary<string, Student>();

// Details on adding key-value pairs to Dictionary omitted.

foreach( Student s in students.Values ) {
    Console.WriteLine("Student name is "+s.Name);
}
```

A foreach loop can also be applied to the Dictionary object directly to obtain the keys and values stored by the Dictionary at the same time. In this case, the elements are retrieved as KeyValuePair objects. The Key and Value properties of the KeyValuePair class can then be used to obtain references to the keys and values in the Dictionary.

```
Dictionary<string, Student> students =
                new Dictionary<string, Student>();

// Details on adding key-value pairs to Dictionary omitted.

foreach( KeyValuePair<string, Student> kv in students ) {
    Student s = kv.Value;
    Console.WriteLine("key is "+kv.Key+
                    " Student name is "+s.Name);
}
```

More on Fields

Now that we've gone into more detail on some of the generic collection classes available in the FCL, let's talk a little more about fields. Previous chapters of this book discussed fields, which are values or objects responsible for storing the data specific to a given object. In the earlier chapters, we glossed over some of the finer points. Let's now take a little time to flesh out a couple of the finer points about fields.

Initialization of Variables Revisited

We said back in Chapter 1 that trying to access local variables without explicitly initializing them will result in a compilation error. For example, this next bit of code

```
public class Example
{
  static void Main() {
      // Declare several local variables within the Main() method.
      int i;  // not automatically initialized
      int j;  // ditto
      j = i;  // compilation error!
    }
}
```

was shown to produce the following compilation error on the line that is highlighted in the snippet:

```
error: Use of unassigned local variable 'i'
```

We also stated in Chapter 3 that variables are implicitly assigned their zero-equivalent value in some situations, if we haven't explicitly assigned them a value. Both of these statements regarding initialization of variables were a bit oversimplified, however, and we want to correct the oversimplification now.

To properly understand the notion of initialization in C#, we must differentiate between *local variables*—that is, variables declared *within a method,* and whose scope is therefore limited to that method (recall our discussion of the scope of a variable in Chapter 1)—and *fields* of a class (whether instance or static variables), which are declared at the class scope level. As it turns out:

- All local variables, of any type, are considered by the compiler to be uninitialized until they have been explicitly initialized within a program.

- All fields, on the other hand, of any type, are automatically initialized to their zero-equivalent values—that is, bools are initialized to false, numerics to either 0 or 0.0, reference types to null, and so forth.

Here is an example illustrating all these points:

```
public class Student
{
  // Fields ARE automatically initialized.
  private int age;                    // initialized to 0
```

```
        private double gpa;              // initialized to 0.0
        private bool isHonorsStudent;    // initialized to false
        private Professor myAdvisor;     // initialized to null
        // This includes STATIC variables.
        private static int studentCount;   // initialized to 0
        // etc.

        // Methods.
        public void UpdateGPA() {
          // Local variables are NOT automatically initialized.
          double val;   // NOT initialized - value is undefined.
          Course c;     // NOT initialized - value is undefined.
          // etc.
        }
    }
```

Implicitly Typed Local Variables

Local variables, those declared inside a method body, can be given the implicit type of var instead of an explicit type. The implicitly typed local variable must be initialized when it is declared, and the compiler infers what the variable type is based on the value to which it is initialized. Implicitly typed local variables can be used in for and foreach statements. Consider the following examples:

```
using System;
using System.Collections.Generic;

// This simple program shows some var syntax

public class VarDemo
{
  static void Main() {
    //  name is compiled as a string
    var name = "Lisa";

    //  names is compiled as a List<string>
    var names = new List<string>();

    // Use var in foreach statement
    foreach(var item in names ) {  //  var assumed to be a string
      //  Do something with item
    }
  }
}
```

The var keyword can only be applied to local variables and can't be used on fields declared at the class level. Implicitly typed local variables can't be used with the array initializer. The following examples of var won't compile:

```
public class VarDemo
{
  // This won't compile; it's a class variable
  private var id = "111-11-111.dat";

  static void Main() {

    // Can't use var with array initializer
    var names = { "Math 101", "Ballroom 262", "Physics 245" };
  }
}
```

Note that overuse of var can make your code hard to read. It's often a good idea to explicitly declare the type of a variable. The main use of var in C# is when working with Language-Integrated Query (LINQ) features—a subject beyond the scope of this book to discuss in detail.

More About the Main Method

In Chapter 1, we introduced the Main method as the initial point of execution for a C# program. We'd now like to go into a little more detail on some features and nuances of the Main method.

Main Method Variants

It turns out that there are actually four variations of the Main method header:

- The first is the version we introduced in Chapter 1—a parameterless method with a return type of void:

  ```
  static void Main()
  ```

- The next version returns a result of type int instead:

  ```
  static int Main()
  ```

  Returning an int value is a way to signal to the execution environment (operating system) the status of how the program terminated:

  ```
  public class Foo
  {
    static int Main() {
      if (something goes awry) {
        return -1;
      }
      else {
        // All is well!
  ```

```
        return 0;
      }
    }
}
```

A return value of 0 is typically used to indicate that the program executed normally. Having the Main method return a value is sometimes used when running programs in batch mode. The return value can be tested and/or examined in the batch file.

- The other two forms of Main take an array of strings as an argument, representing command-line arguments that can be passed in to the Main method when the program is invoked. Note that the name given to this array, typically args, can in actuality be any valid array name:

```
static void Main(string[] args)
static int Main(string[] args)
```

We'll talk about passing command-line arguments into a C# program in more detail when we build the command-line driven version of the SRS in Chapter 14.

Note that none of the four Main method headers includes an access modifier (for example, public). If we include one, the runtime will ignore it. The C# convention is to omit the access modifier from the Main method.

Static Main

Why must the Main method of an application be declared to be static? At the moment that the .NET runtime launches an application by calling its Main method, no objects exist yet because it's the Main method that will start the process of instantiating our application's objects. Thus, we're faced with a "chicken vs. egg" dilemma: how can we invoke the Main method to initiate object creation if we don't have an initial object to invoke it on?

As we learned in Chapter 7, a static method is a type of method that can be invoked on a class as a whole, even if we don't have an instance of that class handy. So before any objects were created, the best option for the designers of C# was to mandate that the Main method be designed as a static method, so that it could be called on the class that serves as the "wrapper" for that method.

Printing to the Screen, Revisited

As we saw in Chapter 1, we invoke one of two methods—Console.WriteLine() or Console.Write()—to print text messages to the command-line window as follows:

```
Console.WriteLine(expression to be printed);
Console.Write(expression to be printed);
```

We glossed over the syntax of this particular operation when this capability was first introduced; now that you know much more about objects, let's revisit this syntax in more depth.

Console is a class provided by the CLR Base Class Library (part of the FCL) within the System namespace. The Console class defines numerous overloaded static Write and WriteLine methods; the various versions each accept a different argument type: string, the various predefined value types, or arbitrary object references:

```
public static void WriteLine(string s)
public static void WriteLine(int i)
public static void WriteLine(double d)
public static void WriteLine(bool b)
public static void WriteLine(object obj)
```

And so forth (the same is true for Write).

The Write and WriteLine methods can accept expressions of arbitrary complexity and do their best to ultimately render them into a single string value, which then gets displayed to the standard output window (that is, the command-line window from which we invoked the program). This is accomplished by calling the ToString method behind the scenes on *non-string* arguments to render a string representation of the argument, as discussed earlier in this chapter.

The following code snippet illustrates several complex invocations of Console.Write. The expression being passed in as an argument to the first call to Write ultimately evaluates to a string value, and the expression being passed in as an argument to the second call to Write evaluates to a double value; thus, two different (overloaded) versions of the Write method are being called in this example:

```
Professor p = new Professor();
// Details omitted.
Console.Write("Professor " + p.Name + " has an advisee named " +
              p.Advisee.Name + " with a GPA of ");
Console.Write(p.Advisee.ComputeGPA());
Console.WriteLine(".");
```

Here's some simulated output:

```
Professor Jacquie Barker has an advisee named Sandy Tucker with a GPA of 4.0.
```

Formatted Printing

We have been using the + operator to concatenate different strings in the arguments for the Write and WriteLine methods. The .NET Framework also provides the capability for defining formatted strings that allow greater flexibility in specifying how output will appear on the screen or written to a file. The simplest way to declare a formatted string is to place integer markers inside curly braces inside the string. The integers correspond to parameters that are included after the string. For instance, the string in the previous example could have been rewritten as a formatted string:

```
Console.WriteLine(
  "Professor {0} has an advisee name {1} with a GPA of {2}.",
  p.Name, p.Advisee.Name, p.Advisee.ComputeGPA());
```

Using parameter indices inside curly braces is the simplest way to use formatted printing. You can also specify things such as the width and justification of a printed value as well as the format that will be used to display the value (for example, decimal, exponential, percent, and so on). See the MSDN documentation pages for further details on formatted printing.

Constructors, Revisited

As we get deeper into some of the features of C# we've been passing over until now, we'll need to take another look at constructors. We learned in Chapter 4 that when we instantiate a brand-new object with the new operator, we're creating a "bare bones" object with essentially empty fields (each field will be initialized to 0, null, or whatever is appropriate for a given field type, as discussed earlier). You also learned that if you want to create an object in a more intelligent fashion—that is, to do more elaborate things when the object is first created—you need to declare a constructor.

By way of review, a constructor

- Has the same name as the class

- Has no explicit return type because it really has a *default* return type matching the class that it's defined for—a constructor returns a brand-new object/instance of that type

- Can take any number or variety of arguments

Here's one simple example of a constructor for the Student class:

```
public class Student
{
  // Fields.
  private string name;
  // other details omitted

  // A constructor. (Note: no return type!)
  // This constructor receives a string value representing the
  // name that is to be assigned to the Student object when it is
  // first instantiated.
  public Student(string name) {
    this.name = name;
  }

  // etc.
}
```

In the previous example, the this keyword appeared in the constructor because there was a naming conflict in that the parameter in the constructor argument list had the same name (name) as a field declared in the class. The this.name syntax tells the compiler that we are referring to the field instead of the parameter.

We'll now provide some new insights regarding constructors.

Constructor Overloading

We can create many different constructors for the same class that take different combinations of arguments—this is known as *overloading*, a concept that we discussed in Chapter 5. As long as each constructor has a different argument signature, it's considered to be a different constructor:

```
// One argument, a string.
public Student(string name) {
  // details omitted...
}

// Two string arguments; this is OK!
public Student(string name, string id) {
  // details omitted...
}

// One int, one string; this is also OK!
public Student(string name, int id) {
  // details omitted...
}
```

If we tried to add the following fourth constructor to the Student class, it would be rejected by the compiler because there is already another constructor with two string arguments—the fact that the parameter names are different is immaterial.

```
public Student(string firstName, string lastName) {
  // details omitted...
}
```

Replacing the Default Parameterless Constructor

We learned in Chapter 4 that if we don't declare any constructors for a class, a default parameterless constructor is provided by the system that will initialize any fields to their zero-equivalent values. There is one very important caveat about default constructors in C#: if we invent any of our own constructors for a class, with any argument signature, then the default parameterless constructor is not automatically provided. This is by design because it's assumed that if we've gone to the trouble to program any constructors whatsoever, we must have some special initialization requirements for our class that the C# default constructor couldn't possibly anticipate.

If we want or need a parameterless constructor for a particular class along with other versions of constructors that do take arguments, we must explicitly program a parameterless constructor ourselves.

Here is another version of a Student class, this time with multiple constructors provided; note that here we're indeed replacing the "lost" parameterless constructor (please read in-line comments):

```
// Student.cs

using System;

public class Student
{
  private string name;
  private string id;
  private Professor facultyAdvisor;
```

```
// Constructors.

// This constructor takes three arguments.
public Student(string n, string id, Professor p) {
  name = n;
  this.id = id;
  facultyAdvisor = p;
}

// This constructor takes two arguments.
public Student(string n, string id) {
  name = n;
  this.id = id;

  // Since we aren't getting a Professor object handed in to us
  // in this version, we set the facultyAdvisor field to null
  // for the time being.  (Strictly speaking, this isn't
  // necessary, as it will automatically be initialized to null,
  // but this makes it clear to anyone reading the code.)
  facultyAdvisor = null;
}

// We provide a parameterless constructor.
public Student() {
  // Note here that we've decided to invent some "placeholder"
  // values for the name and id fields in the case where
  // specific values are not being passed in.

  name = "???";
  id = "???-??-????";
  facultyAdvisor = null;
}

public string Name {
  // Accessor details omitted.
}

// etc. for other properties

public string GetFacultyAdvisorName() {
  // Note: since some of our constructors initialize
  // facultyAdvisor with a Professor object, and others do not,
  // we cannot assume that the field has been initialized with a
  // Professor reference when this method is invoked. We
  // check to make sure that the facultyAdvisor field
  // is NOT null before proceeding.
  if (facultyAdvisor != null) {
```

```
      return facultyAdvisor.Name;
    }
    else {
      return "TBD";
    }
  }
}
```

Here is a simplistic version of a Professor class to use in testing:

```
// Professor.cs

public class Professor {
  private string name;

  public string Name {
    get {
      return name;
    }
    set {
      name = value;
    }
  }
}
```

And here is a main program that exercises the various forms of constructor:

```
public class MyProgram
{
  static void Main() {
    Student[] students = new Student[3];
    Professor p;

    p = new Professor();
    p.Name = "Dr. Oompah";

    // We'll try out the various Student constructor signatures.
    students[0] = new Student("Joe", "123-45-6789", p);
    students[1] = new Student("Bob", "987-65-4321");
    students[2] = new Student();

    Console.WriteLine("Advisor Information\n");
    foreach( Student s in students ) {
      Console.WriteLine("Name: {0}\tAdvisor: {1} ",
          s.Name, s.GetFacultyAdvisorName());
    }
  }
}
```

The preceding program produces the following output when run at the command line:

```
Advisor Information

Name:  Joe    Advisor:  Dr. Oompah
Name:  Bob    Advisor:  TBD
Name:  ???    Advisor:  TBD
```

There are some additional complexities that you need to be aware of when it comes to constructors of derived classes and inheritance—we'll discuss these later in this chapter, in the section titled "More About Inheritance and C#."

Reusing Constructor Code Within a Class

We talked about the use of the this keyword for object self-referencing earlier in this chapter; another use of the this keyword has to do with reusing constructor code.

If we have a class that declares more than one form of constructor and we want to reuse the code from one constructor in the body of another constructor, we can use the this keyword in the declaration of a constructor as a shorthand way of running one constructor from within another:

```
: this(optional arguments)
```

This is best illustrated by a short example:

```
// Student.cs

using System;

public class Student
{
  private string name;
  private string id;
  private Transcript transcript;

  // Constructors.

  // This version takes one argument.
  public Student(string n) {
    name = n;
    transcript = new Transcript();
    // do some other complicated things...
  }

  // This version takes two arguments.  We want to reuse the logic
  // from the preceding constructor without having to repeat the
  // same code in both constructors. We can invoke the
  // one-argument constructor from this two-argument version by
  // using the "this" keyword in the manner shown below:
  public Student(string n, string id) : this(n) {
```

```
        // Now, we can go on to do other "extra" things that this
        // version of the constructor needs to take care of.
        this.id = id;
    }

    // etc.
}
```

By using the syntax : this(n) in this fashion, it's as if we've written the code for the second constructor as follows—but *without* having to duplicate code from the first constructor:

```
public Student(string n, string id) {
    // Duplicate the code from the first constructor...
    name = n;
    transcript = new Transcript();
    // do some other complicated things...

    //...then go on to do other "extra" things that this version
    // of the constructor needs to take care of.
    this.id = id;
}
```

Thus, by using the : this(...) syntax to reuse constructor code from one version to another, if the logic of the first constructor changes down the road, the second constructor will also benefit.

Because each overloaded version of a constructor in a class is guaranteed to have a unique parameter list, the argument signature being passed into the this(...) expression will unambiguously select the alternative constructor that is to be invoked.

Note that if constructor version 1 invokes constructor version 2 in this manner, the invocation of constructor version 2 is the *first* operation performed when the constructor version 1 is invoked. That is, by the time the first explicit line of code of constructor 1 is executed, all the code of constructor 2 might be assumed to have already executed, as illustrated here:

```
public Student(string n, string id) : this(n) {
    // The single argument constructor has already run
    // by the time we reach this next line of code...
    this.id = id;
}
```

More About Inheritance and C#

From our discussion of inheritance in Chapter 5, we learned that

- Inheritance is used to derive a new class definition from an existing class when the new class is perceived to be a special case of the existing class.

- The derived class automatically inherits the data structure and behaviors of the base class.

- C# uses a colon followed by a class name in a class declaration to signal that one class is derived from another:

```
public class Person
{
  private string name;

  public string Name {
    get {
      return name;
    }
    set {
      name = value;
    }
  }
}
```

```
// We derive the Student class from Person.
public class Student : Person
{
  // If we define nothing in the body of this class, it will still
  // have one field, name, and one property, Name, because these
  // are inherited from Person. (Actually, we have more members
  // than that, because Person in turn inherits members from
  // Object!)
}
```

Although we introduced the basics of inheritance in Chapter 5, it turns out that there are a lot of important subtleties about inheritance in C# that we haven't yet discussed; we'll do so now.

Accessibility of Inherited Components

By virtue of inheritance, everything defined in a base class is automatically present in a derived class—inheritance is an all-or-nothing proposition. However, some inherited members (fields, methods, properties, and so on) might not be directly accessible by the derived class, depending on their access permissions as assigned in the base class.

Consider the following base class:

```
public class Person
{
  // Field.
  Accessibility_modifier int age;

  // Other details of this class omitted.
}
```

Accessibility for a member, as you learned in Chapter 4, can be one of the following:

- private

- public

- protected

- internal

- protected internal

- Unspecified (which for fields, methods, and properties defaults to private)

You learned in Chapter 4 about public and private accessibility; a member given protected accessibility is in scope and hence publicly available to the class it's declared in as well as derived classes, but private to everything else. The other two accessibilities, internal and protected internal, are less frequently used, and a discussion of them is beyond the scope of this book.

Suppose that we derive the Student class from Person as follows:

```
public class Student : Person
{
  // The age field is inherited from the base class...
  // here, we add a method that directly manipulates this field
  // by name.
  public bool IsOver65( ) {
    if (age > 65) {
      return true;
    }
    else {
      return false;
    }
  }
}
```

What will happen when we try to compile the Student class? The answer to this question depends on how access has been defined for the age field of Person:

- If we declared age to be either protected or public in Person, the age field is both inherited and directly accessible to the Student class by its simple name, and the Student class shown earlier will compile without error.

- If, on the other hand, age is declared to be private in Person, we'll get a compilation error on the following line of Student code:

```
if (age > 65) {
```

The error message will be the following:

```
error: 'Person.age' is inaccessible due to its protection level
```

That's because the age field is indeed inherited—it's part of the data structure comprising a Student object—but it's nonetheless "invisible" to the Student class! It's analogous to an internal organ in our body; for example, our heart is part of our physical body, but we can't see or access it directly.

If our inclination is to make all fields private, how can a subclass ever manipulate its privately inherited fields? The answer is quite simple: through the public (or protected) accessor methods or properties that it has also inherited from its parent class. We've revised the previous example program to illustrate this technique.

First, we declare a public Age property in the Person class:

```
public class Person
{
  private int age;
  // details omitted

  // We provide a property for subclasses to inherit.
  // (The property could be given protected access if
  // we ONLY want subclasses to access it.)
  public int Age {
    get {
      return age;
    }
    set {
      age = value;
    }
  }
}
```

Then, we use the *inherited* Age property from within the Student's IsOver65 method, and we're back in business: Student compiles without error.

```
public class Student : Person
{
  // other details omitted.

  public bool IsOver65( ) {
    // Even though the age field per se is inaccessible,
    // the Age property that we inherit from Person
    // allows us to access the value of the age field.
    if (Age > 65) return true;
    else return false;
  }
}
```

Because the Age property was given public access, it is accessible to all other classes. If we wanted to permit access only to derived classes (in addition to the Person class), the Age property could have been given protected access. As we mentioned back in Chapter 4, it's generally considered good practice to always use properties to access the values of fields, even from within a class's own methods, to take advantage of any special processing that the property accessors might provide relative to that field.

Reusing Base Class Behaviors: The "base" Keyword

As you learned in Chapter 5, if we provide a method in a derived class whose signature matches that of a base class method (identical method name and parameter list), we're said to have *overridden* the base class method (the base class method signature would include the virtual keyword). When would we want/need to do this? When the derived class needs to do something slightly more specialized in response to a method call than its base class did, as in the following example:

```
public class Person
{
  private string name;
  private string id;

  public string Name {
    // Accessor details omitted.
  }

  // etc. for Id

  // Have a Person object describe itself.
  // e.g., "John Doe (123-45-6789)"
  public virtual string GetDescription() {
    return Name + " (" + Id + ")";
  }
}

public class Student : Person
{
  private string major;

  public string Major {
    // Accessor details omitted.
  }

  // We want a Student object to return a description of itself
  // differently from the way its parent class (Person) does so.
  // So, we equip this subclass with a method having the exact
  // same signature as was defined for its parent class; this
  // version of the method overrides (masks) the inherited
  // version.
  // This method adds information about a student's major
  public override string GetDescription() {
    return Name + " (" + Id + ") [" + Major + "]";
  }
}
```

As you learned in Chapter 5, a derived class method can call a base class version of the same method using the base keyword. This feature allows us to reduce code redundancy because we can reuse the work done by the base class method and then add in whatever additional code the derived class method needs.

Let's streamline the GetDescription method of the Student class so that it first calls the Person class version of the same method:

```
public class Student : Person
{
  private string major;

  // etc.

  // Exact same method signature as was defined for Person -- so,
  // this method overrides (masks) the inherited version.
  // Notice, however, that we are now calling the parent class's
  // version of the method so as to reuse that code.
  public override string GetDescription() {
    return base.GetDescription() + " [" + Major + "]";
  }
}
```

Just as the this keyword is used to generically refer to an object from within one of its methods, base is used when we want to generically refer to the parent class's version of a member from within one of its methods.

Another important use of the base keyword has to do with constructors and inheritance, which we'll discuss next.

Inheritance and Constructors

Constructors aren't inherited in the same manner that methods and properties are. This raises some interesting complications that are best illustrated via an example.

Let's start by declaring a constructor for the Person class that takes two arguments:

```
public class Person
{
  private string name;
  private string id;

  // Public properties Name and Id are declared; details omitted.

  // Only one constructor is explicitly declared.
  public Person(string n, string id) {
    Name = n;
    Id = id;
  }

  // etc.
}
```

We know from an earlier discussion that the Person class now recognizes only one con-structor signature—one that takes two arguments—because the default parameterless constructor for Person has been eliminated.

Now, suppose that we derive the Student class from Person and that we want the Student class to define two constructors—one that takes two arguments and one that takes three argu-ments. Because constructors aren't inherited, we won't automatically benefit from the fact that the Person class has already gone to the trouble to define a constructor that takes two argu-ments; we have to recode one explicitly for Student, as follows:

```
public class Student : Person
{
  private string major;

  // Major property provided; details omitted.

  // Constructor that takes two arguments.
  public Student(string n, string id) {
    // Note the redundancy of logic between this constructor and
    // the parent constructor -- we'll come back and fix this in a
    // moment.
    Name = n;  // redundant
    Id = id;   // redundant
    Major = null;
  }

  // Constructor that takes three arguments.
  public Student(string n, string id, string m) {
    // MORE redundancy!
    Name = n;  // redundant
    Id = id;  // redundant
    Major = m;
  }

  // No other constructors are explicitly declared.
}
```

In addition to having a lot of redundancies, the preceding code won't even compile. A derived constructor will always call a base constructor as its first task—and by default it will try to call the no-argument base constructor. If the base class doesn't have a no-argument constructor (the Person class does not), the result will be a compile error.

Fortunately, there is a way to reuse a parent class's constructor code without having to duplicate its logic in the derived class's constructor(s). We accomplish this via the same base keyword we discussed a moment ago for the reuse of methods. To explicitly reuse a particular parent class's constructor, we refer to it as : base(optional arguments) and pass in whatever arguments it needs, as the following revised version of the Student class illustrates:

```
public class Student : Person
{
  private string major;
```

```
  // Major property provided; details omitted.

  // Constructor that takes two arguments.
  // We'll explicitly invoke the Person constructor with two
  // arguments, passing in the values of n and id.
  public Student(string n, string id) : base(n, id) {
    // We can now concentrate on only those things that need be
    // done uniquely for a Student.
    Major = null;
  }

  // Constructor that takes three arguments.
  // See above comments.
  public Student(string n, string id, string m) : base(n, id) {
    Major = m;
  }
}
```

Similar to the situation in which we used the syntax : this(...) to reuse constructor code within the same class, if a derived class constructor calls a base class constructor, that call is the first operation performed when the derived class constructor is invoked.

Implied Invocations of base( )

Whether we explicitly invoke a base class constructor from a derived class constructor using the : base(...) syntax or not, C# will always attempt to execute constructors for all the ancestor classes for a given class, from most general to most specific in the class hierarchy, before launching into a given class's constructor code.

For example, when we create a Student object, in reality we're simultaneously creating three "layers" of the Student object. First, the Object-part is initialized using the Object constructor, then the members of the Person class are initialized via the Person constructor, and finally the Student members are initialized with the Student constructor. So a Student can be thought of as an Object and a Person, as well as a Student. When we invoke a Student constructor, an Object constructor will be executed first, followed by a Person constructor, and then followed by a Student constructor. So, if we were to write a Student constructor without taking advantage of the base(...) syntax, as shown here:

```
public class Student : Person
{
  private string major;

  // Constructor that takes two arguments.
  // Here, we're not calling any particular base constructor.
  public Student(string n, string id) {
    // We can now concentrate on only those things that need be
    // done uniquely for a Student.
    major = null;
  }
```

It's as if we've written the following code instead (note **bolding**), thereby explicitly calling the parameterless Person constructor:

```
public class Student : Person
{
  private string major;

  // Constructor that takes two arguments.
  public Student(string n, string id) : base() {
    // We can now concentrate on only those things that need be
    // done uniquely for a Student.
    major = null;
  }
}
```

This makes intuitive sense because we said that inheritance represents the "is a" relationship—a Student is a Person, and a Person is an Object—so whatever we have to do when we create an Object and a Person will also be required when we create a Student. But which base class constructor will be called if we've defined more than one?

There are several different scenarios that we must explore to answer this question.

Case #1: A Derived Class Declares No Constructors of Its Own

We already know that if we derive a class such as Student, but don't bother to define any constructors for the derived class, then C# will attempt to provide us with a default parameterless constructor for that derived class. When we create a new object of the derived class, the default constructor in the derived class will implicitly invoke the parameterless constructor in the base class.

The following example won't compile (we'll explain why in a moment):

```
public class Person
{
  private string name;

  // A constructor that takes one argument - by having created
  // this, we've lost Person's default (parameterless)
  // constructor.
  public Person(string n) {
    Name = n;
  }

  // The parameterless constructor is not being replaced in this
  // example.
}

public class Student : Person
{
  private string major;

  // NO constructors are explicitly defined for Student!  So, all
```

```
        // we get for Student is the default parameterless constructor.
    }
```

When we try to compile Student, we'll get the following (rather cryptic) error message:

```
error: 'Person' does not contain a constructor that takes '0' arguments
```

This is because the C# compiler is trying to create a default constructor that takes no arguments for the Student class. To do so, it knows that it will need to be able to call a parameterless constructor for a Person from within the Student default constructor—but no such constructor for Person exists! The compiler is, in essence, trying to generate the following default constructor for Student:

```
public Student() : base() {
    // Initialize a "bare bones" Student -- details omitted.
}
```

The only way around this dilemma is to do either of the following:

- Explicitly program a parameterless constructor for the Person class to replace the lost default Person constructor, for the compiler to take advantage of when creating a default Student class constructor (this is the preferred approach).

- Always use a constructor for the Student class that explicitly invokes a particular version of Person constructor through use of the base keyword.

This latter option is explored in the next case.

Case #2: The Derived Class Explicitly Declares One or More Constructors

This case can actually be split into two subcases:

Subcase #2A: Derived Class Constructor Does Not Explicitly Invoke a Base Class Constructor

If a base class constructor isn't explicitly called from the derived class constructor via the base : (...) construct, a base class parameterless constructor will still be called, as in Case #1. The following code won't compile, for the same reasons cited earlier:

```
public class Person
{
    // Details omitted.

    // A constructor that takes one argument - by having created
    // this, we've lost Person's default parameterless constructor.
    public Person(string n) {
        Name = n;
    }
}

public class Student : Person {
    // Details omitted.
```

```
  // We declare a Student constructor, but don't explicitly invoke
  // a particular Person constructor from within it.
  public Student(string n, string m) {
    Name = n;
    Major = m;
  }
}
```

When we try to compile Student, we'll get the following compiler error message:

```
No constructor matching Person() found in class Person
```

Subcase #2B: Derived Class Constructor Does Explicitly Invoke a Base Class Constructor

Let's repair the problem in Subcase #2A by having the derived class constructor explicitly call a particular parent class constructor that we know to exist via the base(. . .) construct:

```
public class Person
{
  private string name;

  // A constructor that takes one argument - by having created
  // it, we've lost Person's default parameterless constructor.
  public Person(string n) {
    name = n;
  }

  // No additional constructors are provided for Person.
}

public class Student : Person
{
  private string major;

  // Constructor.
  // We'll explicitly invoke the Person constructor with one
  // argument, passing through the value of n.
  public Student(string n, string m) : base(n) {
    major = m;
  }
}
```

All is well when this code is compiled!

Object Initializers

Up to this point, we have been using constructors to provide the initial values to the fields of an object. The *object initializer* syntax is an alternative way to assign values to fields and properties of an object without having to invoke a parameterized constructor (it will still call the no-argument constructor). The values for the fields and/or properties are separated by commas and placed inside braces. As an example, consider a Person class listing that defines two fields: name and age.

```
public class Person
{
    private string name;
    private int age;

    //  constructors
    public Person() {
        Name = "??";
        Age = 0;
    }

    public Person(string n, int age) {
        Name = n;
        Age = age;
    }

    //  properties
    public string Name {
        get {
            return name;
        }
        set {
            name = value;
        }
    }

    public int Age {
        get {
            return age;
        }
        set {
            age = value;
        }
    }

    //  Other Person class members omitted.
}
```

The object initializer syntax could be used to create a Person object while assigning values to the Name and Age properties using the following syntax:

```
Person p = new Person{ Name="Emile Sanchez", Age=21 };
```

Note that the object initializer syntax is different from calling a constructor in that braces are used to surround property assignment statements. In other words, both the name of the property and its initial value are provided. Only accessible fields and properties can be assigned values with the object initializer. The `name` and `age` fields, for example, have `private` access, and an attempt to assign values to them in the object initializer:

```
Person p = new Person{ name="Emile Sanchez", age=21 };
```

would generate a compiler error:

```
Error: 'Person.name' is inaccessible due to its protection level
```

One of the things object initializers are useful for is to initialize objects that contain auto-implemented properties—a topic discussed later in this chapter.

More on Methods

We've discussed methods in a fair amount of detail in this chapter and in Part One of this book. Now it's time to round out the discussion with a few more important observations about methods.

Message Chaining

In OOPLs such as C#, it's quite commonplace to form complex expressions by concatenating one method call onto another via dot notation, a mechanism known as *message chaining*. Here's one hypothetical example:

```
Student s = new Student();
s.Name = "Fred";

Professor p = new Professor();
p.Name = "John";

Course c = new Course();
c.Name = "Math";

s.setFacultyAdvisor(p);
p.setCourseTaught(c);

Course c2 = new Course();

// A message "chain".
c2.Name = "Beginning " + (s.GetFacultyAdvisor().GetCourseTaught().Name);
```

As you saw in Chapter 1, we evaluate expressions from innermost to outermost parentheses, left to right, so let's evaluate the expression in the last line of this snippet:

1. Looking for the deepest level of nested parentheses, we see that part of the expression is two sets of parentheses deep, so we evaluate the leftmost deepest subexpression first—where the `GetFacultyAdviser` method is called on the `Student` reference s, which returns a reference to `Professor` p:

   ```
   s.GetFacultyAdvisor()
   ```

   2. Next, the GetCourseTaught() method is called on the Professor reference p, which
   returns a reference to Course c:

   ```
   p.GetCourseTaught()
   ```

   3. Next, we access the Name property of the Course object, which returns the string value
   "Math":

   ```
   c.Name
   ```

   4. We've now completed evaluating the expression enclosed within the innermost set of
   parentheses, effectively giving us this equivalent expression:

   ```
   c2.Name = "Beginning " + "Math";
   ```

So, we see in the final analysis that the outcome of the complex expression is to assign the
name "Beginning Math" to the Name property of the Course object c2.

Method Hiding

In Chapter 5, you learned that a derived class can override a method that has been declared as
virtual in a base class: the derived class declares a new version of the base class method with
the same signature and includes the override keyword in the method declaration.

There is also a second way to replace the logic of a base class method, even one that hasn't
been declared virtual in the base class, via a technique known as *method hiding*.

To "hide" a base class method, the derived class must define a method with the same signature using the new keyword in the method declaration in lieu of the override keyword. Here
is a simple example in which the derived Student class hides the PrintDescription method
first declared by the Person base class:

```
public class Person
{
  // details omitted

  // Note:  no virtual keyword -- no provision for overriding was
  // made by the designers of the Person class.
  public void PrintDescription() {
    // details omitted
  }
}

public class Student : Person
{
  // The Student class HIDES the PrintDescription()
  // method from the Person class via the use of the
  // new keyword.
  public new void PrintDescription() {
    // details omitted
  }
}
```

Any base class method—whether virtual or not—can be hidden; thus, we have a work-around (of sorts) if we find ourselves in a position of wanting to modify the behavior of a method derived from a base class that wasn't "prepped" for overriding by the original designer of the base class via the inclusion of the virtual keyword in the base class's method signature. Note, however, that hiding a nonvirtual base class method differs from truly overriding a virtual base class method in one very significant way, having to do with the notion of polymorphism that we discussed in Chapter 7. Let's explore this issue.

Method Hiding and Polymorphism

We learned in Chapter 7 that *polymorphism* refers to the ability of different objects belonging to different classes to respond to the same method call in different, class-specific ways. For example, assuming that ChooseMajor is a virtual method in the Student class that has been over-ridden by both the GraduateStudent- and UndergraduateStudent-derived classes, the version of ChooseMajor invoked on s in the following code will depend on what type of Student s is:

```
// Iterating through a List of Students.
List<Student> students = new List<Student>;

// Other List details omitted.

foreach( Student s in students ) {

  // This next line of code is said to be polymorphic:
  // If s refers to a GraduateStudent at run time, the
  // GraduateStudent version of the ChooseMajor method will be
  // executed; and, if s refers to an UndergraduateStudent at run
  // time, the UndergraduateStudent version of ChooseMajor will be
  // executed.
  s.ChooseMajor();
}
```

By contrast, the version of a *hidden* method that is run for a given object is "locked in" at compile time. Let's now assume that ChooseMajor is a nonvirtual method in the Student class, and is hidden (not overridden) by both the GraduateStudent- and UndergraduateStudent-derived classes. While the following two invocations of ChooseMajor will indeed be of the derived classes' respective versions because we're invoking that method on reference variables explicitly declared to be a GraduateStudent and an UndergraduateStudent, respectively:

```
GraduateStudent g = new GraduateStudent();
g.ChooseMajor(); // GraduateStudent version of this method will execute

UndergraduateStudent s = new UndergraduateStudent();
s.ChooseMajor(); // UndergraduateStudent version of this method will execute
```

polymorphism will not be enabled in the next example—the Student base class's version of the ChooseMajor method will be invoked for both GraduateStudents and UndergraduateStudents because s is declared to be of type Student at compile time:

```
// Iterating through a List of Students.
foreach( Student s in students ) {

    // This next line of code is NOT polymorphic:
    // Regardless of whether s refers to a GraduateStudent at run
    // time or to an Undergraduate student, the Student version of
    // the ChooseMajor method will be executed.
    s.ChooseMajor();
}
```

We mentioned earlier that any method, virtual or not, can be hidden. Why might we want to hide a virtual base class method vs. overriding it if we lose the benefit of polymorphism? Because hidden methods yield better performance (they run faster) than virtual methods.

Final Notes Regarding Method Hiding

A few final points:

- The original base class version of a hidden method can be called from within the "new" derived/hidden method using the base keyword, just as when overriding.

- A derived class's "hidden" method can have a different return type than the base class version it is hiding.

- An abstract method can't be hidden.

More on Properties

Chapter 4 introduced properties as a way to get or set the value of fields that have been given private access. Properties are used as if they were public data members, but behind the scenes they make use of a special type of method called accessors. In this section we will explore a few of the nuances of properties that make them even handier and more powerful.

Asymmetric Accessibility

By default, the get and set accessors of a property will have the same access as was given to the property itself. For example, the following property might be defined to access the id field of the Student class:

```
public string Id {
    get {
        return id;
    }
    set {
        id = value;
    }
}
```

In the previous example, the Id property is declared to be public, so by default the get and set accessors are given public access as well. This situation might not be desirable. For example, you might want to restrict access to the set accessor (that changes the value of the id field) to only the Student class and its derived classes.

Using a concept called *asymmetric accessibility* it is possible to give a different access to one of the two accessors of a property. Typically, the get accessor is given public access, and a different accessibility is assigned to the set accessor. To change the previous example so that only the Student class and its derived classes could change the value of the id field, the set accessor could be given protected access.

```
public string Id {
    get {
        return id;
    }
    protected set {
        id = value;
    }
}
```

Asymmetric accessibility can be used only if both get and set accessors are defined for a property and only one of the accessors can be given a different access than the property itself.

Auto-Implemented Properties

The get and set accessors of a property are methods and, if desired, complicated programming logic can be built into the accessors. Many times, however, properties are used simply to access or change the value of a field. For example, the Person class might declare a field representing the person's name and a property that is used to access or change the value of the name field:

```
public class Person
{
    private string name;

    // constructor
    public Person (string name) {
        Name = name;
    }

    // property for accessing the name field
    public string Name {
        get {
            return name;
        }
        set {
            name = value;
        }
    }
}
```

```
    //  Other Person class members omitted.
}
```

Suppose the following code were executed:

```
Person p = new Person("Jackson");
Console.WriteLine("Name is "+p.Name);
```

The output would be as follows:

```
Name is Jackson
```

If no other logic is built into the accessors other than to access the value of a field, the property syntax can be simplified by using what is called an *auto-implemented property*. The bodies of the accessors are omitted, and only the get and set keywords are used.

```
public class Person
{
    //  The name field has been eliminated!

    //  constructor
    public Person (string name) {
        Name = name;
    }

    //  auto-implemented property
    public string Name { get; set; }

    //  Other Person class members omitted.
}
```

Suppose we try to run the same client code:

```
Person p = new Person("Jackson");
Console.WriteLine("Name is "+p.Name);
```

The output is the same as before:

```
Name is Jackson
```

In looking at the two versions of the Person class, one key difference is that when auto-implemented properties are used to store and access the person's name, there is no declaration of a name field. The reason for this change is that auto-implemented properties are implicitly tied to a private, anonymous (that is, hidden) backing field of the same type. The value of the private hidden field is accessed through the property's get and set accessors.

It turns out that the Person constructor can be done away with entirely, and a Person object can be created using the object initializer syntax:

```
Person p = new Person { Name="Jackson" };
```

If the constructor is removed, the Person class code listing becomes quite simple indeed:

```
public class Person
{
    // auto-implemented property
    public string Name { get; set; }
}
```

One final note about auto-implemented properties is that they must define both a get and set accessor. To make the property read-only, the set accessor can be given private access:

```
// Name property is read-only
 public string Name { get; private set; }
```

We will use auto-implemented properties when we write the code for the SRS classes starting in Chapter 14.

Overriding and Abstract Classes, Revisited

You learned in Chapter 7 that a class derived from an abstract class can be made concrete by providing *nonabstract* implementations of all the abstract methods declared by the abstract base class. As it turns out, it's also possible to go the other direction as well: that is, a derived class can override a nonabstract method declared in a base class with an abstract method. Let's look at an example using predefined C# classes.

We know that every C# class implicitly derives from the Object class of the System namespace. One of the methods declared by the Object class is ToString, a nonabstract, virtual method that we discussed earlier in this chapter. It's perfectly acceptable to define a Person class that implicitly derives from Object (as all classes do), but which overrides the nonabstract ToString method it inherits from Object with an abstract version:

```
// Derives from Object implicitly.
public abstract class Person
{
  // We're overriding the nonabstract Object class's ToString
  // method with an ABSTRACT version.
  public abstract override string ToString();

  // Other Person class details omitted.
}
```

There are several things to note about the Person class:

- As discussed earlier in this chapter, derivation from the Object class is implicit, so we don't need the syntax : Object in the Person class declaration.

- Second, because the ToString method as defined in the Person class is abstract, the Person class itself is declared to be abstract.

- Finally, because the Person's ToString method is overriding the Object class's version of that method, the override keyword is used in the method declaration.

Why might we want to override a nonabstract method with an abstract one? The answer is to force derived classes of Person to implement their own class-specific versions of the ToString method. That is, we don't want any of the future classes derived from Person to be "lazy" by simply inheriting the default behavior of the Object class's ToString method—we want to effectively "erase" the details of how this behavior is carried out. We'll in fact do this very thing when we create the Person class in Chapter 14 that will be used in conjunction with the SRS application. The Person class will declare an abstract ToString method that will be overridden by its derived classes.

Object Identities

In an earlier example, GraduateStudent and UndergraduateStudent objects were stored in a List collection that had been declared to hold Student objects. An element extracted from the List will be returned as a Student object. The extracted object hasn't "forgotten" what class to which it belongs. An object always retains its class identity; it's simply that we can refer to an object with various different reference variables, which might be declared to be of different types, and it's this phenomenon that affects which messages the compiler believes that an object is capable of responding to. To help illustrate this point, let's use an example.

A Derived Class Object Is a Base Class Object, Too

If we instantiate a Professor object, which is a type of Person, and therefore, as we saw earlier, is also a type of Object, we can think of the Professor object as being allocated in memory, as demonstrated in Figure 13-4.

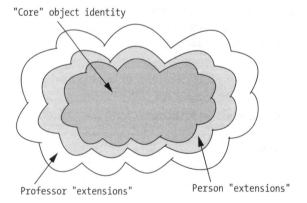

Figure 13-4. *A Professor object is simultaneously a* Person *object and an* Object *object, all rolled into one!*

We can then create reference variables of varying types (any of the types in this object's derivation chain) to store references to this Object/Person/Professor; each reference refers to a different "rendition" of the object:

```
// Create a Professor object, and maintain three references to it
// of varying types.
```

```
Professor pr = new Professor();
Person p = pr;
object obj = pr;
```

If we refer to this Professor object by its object reference obj, as far as the compiler is concerned, the only aspects of the object that exist are its Object "core": the "Person-ness" and "Professor-ness" of the object is in question (see Figure 13-5).

Only the "Core" object
identity is available
from the compiler's
standpoint.

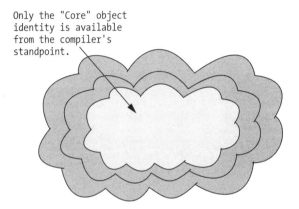

Figure 13-5. *The compiler only knows about this* Professor *object's* "Object-ness."

So, the compiler will reject any attempts to access the Professor- or Person-defined members of obj:

```
// The compiler would reject this attempt to invoke the
// AddAdvisee() method, declared for the Professor class, on this
// object, because even though WE know from the code above that it
// is really a Professor whose handle is
// stored as an object, the compiler cannot be certain of this.
obj.AddAdvisee();  // compiler error
```

```
// However, we can invoke any of the methods that this Professor
// inherited from the Object class:
obj.ToString();
```

If we instead refer to the Professor object by its Person reference p, as far as the compiler is concerned, the only aspects of the object that exist are its Object "core" and its Person "extensions." The "Professor-ness" of the object is in question (see Figure 13-6):

```
// The compiler would again reject this attempt to invoke the
// AddAdvisee() method, declared for the Professor class, on this
// object, because even though WE know from the code above that it
// is really a Professor whose reference is stored as a Person at
// run time, the compiler cannot be certain of this at COMPILE
// time.
p.AddAdvisee();  // compiler error
```

```
// However, we can invoke any of the methods that this Professor
// inherited from EITHER the Object class...
p.ToString();

//...OR the Person class:
p.Name;
```

The compiler now
recognizes both the "core"
object identity of this
Professor object ...

... as well as its
Person features.

Figure 13-6. *The compiler now recognizes this* Professor *object's "Object-ness" and "Person-ness."*

Only if we refer to the object by its Professor reference, pr, will the compiler allow us to access Professor-specific members of the object.

Determining the Class That an Object Belongs To

There are several ways to ask an object what class it belongs to at run time; we can take advantage of the following:

- The GetType method defined by the Object class

- The typeof operator

- The is keyword

The GetType Method

As mentioned earlier, by virtue of being derived from the Object class, every object inherits a method with the header:

```
public Type GetType()
```

When invoked on an object, this method returns an object of type Type, representing the type of the object on which the GetType method has been invoked. For example, if the Person class is defined to belong to the SRS namespace, then the following invocation of GetType would yield a Type object representing the class SRS.Person:

```
Person p = new Person();
Type t = p.GetType();
```

The Type class, in turn, defines a string property named FullName that can be used to access the fully qualified name of the type:

```
Person p = new Person();
Type t = p.GetType();
String s = t.FullName; // s now equals "SRS.Person".
```

Chaining the method call and property invocation together, we can ask any object reference to identify which class the object it refers to belongs to, as follows:

reference.GetType().FullName;

For example:

```
using System;
using System.Collections;

public class CastingExample
{
  static void Main() {
    Student s = new Student();
    Professor p = new Professor();

    ArrayList list = new ArrayList();
    list.Add(s);
    list.Add(p);

    for (int i = 0; i < list.Count; i++) {
      // Note that we are not casting the objects here!
      // We're pulling them out as generic objects.
      object o = list[i];
      Console.WriteLine(o.GetType().FullName);
    }
  }
}
```

This program produces as output (assuming that neither Student nor Professor belongs to a named namespace):

```
Student
Professor
```

This demonstrates that the objects themselves really do remember their roots!

The typeof Operator

Another way to test whether a given object reference belongs to a particular class is via the typeof operator. This operator takes as its argument the name of a type (note: the type name is not quoted) and returns the corresponding Type object. Here is a simple code snippet to illustrate how the typeof operator can be used to see whether a reference is of a certain type. (The == operator works in this case because there is only one System.Type object for each type in the C# language, whether user-defined or predefined.)

```
Student s = new Student();

// Determine if the type of the s reference variable is
// is equal to the Student type.
if (s.GetType() == typeof(Student)) {
  Console.WriteLine("s is a Student");
}
```

The preceding code would produce the following as output:

```
s is a Student
```

Note that if we want to refer to the name of a class that belongs to an explicitly named namespace, and we haven't included the appropriate using statement with our code, we must fully qualify the class name when using typeof:

```
// Assume that Bar is a class in the Foo namespace.
if (x.GetType() == typeOf(Foo.Bar) {...}
```

■**Note** Although the use of parentheses to surround the name of a class—typeof(Student)—makes it look as if typeof is a method, it's indeed an *operator*.

The is Operator

A third way to determine whether an object is of a certain type is by using the is operator, which typically generates cleaner code than the typeof operator. For instance, here is the previous example using the is operator:

```
Student s = new Student();

// Determine if the type of the s reference variable is
// is equal to the Student type.
if (s is Student) {
  Console.WriteLine("s is a Student");
}
```

Object Deletion and Garbage Collection

In the C++ language, there is a delete operator that allows the programmer to explicitly control when a dynamically allocated object is no longer needed, and its memory can therefore be recycled. This is both a blessing and a curse! It's a blessing because it gives a C++ programmer very tight control over his/her memory resources in a program. But if a C++ programmer forgets to recycle his/her objects, the program can literally run out of memory—this is known as a *memory leak.*

With C#, however, there is no delete operator: anything dynamically created—all reference types as opposed to value types—is a candidate for C# garbage collection when all references to it (handles) have been eliminated. Like the "object as a helium balloon" example discussed in Chapter 3, when we let go of all strings on a balloon, it essentially floats away. Garbage collection is an automatic function performed by the .NET common language runtime (CLR); when an object is garbage collected, the memory that was allocated to that object is recycled and added back to the pool of memory that is available to the runtime for new object creation.

By way of review, there are several ways to release handles on objects in C# so as to make them candidates for garbage collection, as the following example illustrates:

```
// Declare two reference variables to hold on to future
// (as of yet to be created) Student objects.
Student s1;
Student s2;

// Create a Student object, and store a reference to this object
// as the variable s1.
s1 = new Student();

// Copy the handle into s2, so that we now have two handles on the same object.
s2 = s1;

// Let's now look at two different ways to "drop" an object reference.

// We can reset a variable previously holding a handle to the value null...
s1 = null;  // (We still have one of two references left on the
            // object.)

//...or we can hand a variable some OTHER object's handle,
// causing it to drop the first handle. Here, by creating a
// second Student object and handing it to s2, s2 drops the
// only remaining handle on the first Student object.
s2 = new Student( );  // No more handles on the original student
                      //remain!
```

We eliminated all obvious references to the original instance of a Student; if there are no remaining references to an object, it becomes a candidate for garbage collection. We emphasize the word *candidate* in the previous sentence, however, because the garbage collector doesn't immediately recycle the object. Rather, the garbage collector runs whenever the runtime determines that there is a need for some recycling to be done; that is, when the application is getting low on free memory necessary to allocate new objects. So for some period of time, the "orphaned" Student object will still exist in memory—we merely won't have any handles with which to reach it.

The inclusion of garbage collection in C# has virtually eliminated memory leaks. Note that it's still possible for the runtime to run out of memory, however, if too many handles are maintained on too many objects; so a C# programmer can't be totally oblivious to memory management—but it's far less error-prone than with C/C++.

Attributes

Some object-oriented texts use the word *attribute* to represent a data member in a class. We've been using the term *field* because attribute has a very specific meaning in .NET. Although we don't make use of this .NET attribute in building the SRS, we want to at least provide a brief description of a .NET attribute.

A .NET attribute is a reference type that derives from the System.Attribute class and is used to assign *metadata tags* to other programming elements—that is, descriptive information about such elements.

An attribute can be applied to any code element (class, constructor, delegate, method, field, and so on) by placing the name of the attribute in brackets before the code element. For example, the System.Array class has an associated attribute named SerializableAttribute, as shown here:

```
[Serializable()]
public abstract class Array : ICloneable, IList, ICollection, IEnumerable {...}
```

The application of this attribute to the Array class indicates that Array objects are *serializable*, meaning that they can be stored to or restored from disk in binary form.

As programmers, we could certainly determine that Arrays are serializable from inspecting the C# language documentation. So what does an attribute buy us? The "knowledge" that is imparted through the application of an attribute can be programmatically "discovered" at run time through a mechanism known as *reflection*. (Going into the full details of how reflection works is beyond the scope of a beginning-level book such as this to address.)

We can apply any of the predefined attributes provided by the FCL to our own code. For example, we can place the predefined ObsoleteAttribute attribute before the header of a method that we want to flag as obsolete, to indicate that this method is perhaps going to be phased out at some later date to discourage its use:

```
public class MyClass
{
  // We're adding an attribute to Foo().
  [Obsolete()]
  public void Foo() {
    // Method details omitted...
```

```
    }

    // Other details omitted.
}
```

Suppose that a client code subsequently attempts to invoke the Foo method on an instance of MyClass:

```
public class AttrDemo {
  static void Main() {
    MyClass x = new MyClass();

    // We're trying to call a method that has been
    // tagged as obsolete.
    x.Foo();
  }
}
```

When the AttrDemo class is compiled, the compiler will detect that a method that has been tagged as obsolete is being called on an object and will generate the following warning:

```
warning CS0612:  'MyClass.Foo()' is obsolete
```

The program can still be executed, but the programmer has been "warned" that using the Foo method might not be advisable.

■**Note** We can also create user-defined attributes for whatever specific metadata needs we might have (for debugging, for example), but this topic is beyond the scope of this book to address.

Summary

We've just been on a whirlwind tour of the C# language! Although there is much more that can be said about C#, you've been armed with all the essential information that you'll need in order to understand—and experiment with—the sample SRS application that we'll build in the remaining chapters of the book.

In particular, we discussed the following:

- The C# notion of namespaces and how they are used to divide classes and interfaces into logical units

- The object nature of strings and some of the methods provided to manipulate them

- The parent of all C# types: the Object class

- The object nature of Arrays in a bit more depth

- How to use two of C#'s collection classes, List and Dictionary, and the use of a foreach loop to iterate through the contents of a collection

- Some subtleties of variable initialization

- Additional insights regarding the Main method

- Using constructors to initialize an object's fields at the time that the object first comes into being and how to use object initializer syntax to do the same thing

- How auto-implemented properties can simplify code listings

- Inheritance in the C# language; in particular, how the visibility of a member affects the way in which a derived class can utilize that member, how to reuse base class behaviors via the base keyword, and complexities concerning constructors and inheritance

- The nature of object identities in C#, how to discover the true class that an object belongs to, and how to test the equality of two C# objects

- How we delete dynamically created objects to recycle their memory at run time and the role that the C# garbage collector plays in this recycling

With all this C# knowledge at our fingertips, we're now ready to proceed to building the SRS application.

■**Tip** This is a great time to download the code associated with the remaining chapters from the Apress web site, if you haven't already done so! Please see Appendix B for instructions.

Exercises

1. Follow the instructions included in Appendix A to get the latest version of Microsoft's .NET Framework running on your computer.

2. Write a C# program that will print out the integers from 1 to 10 in reverse order.

3. Rewrite the code in the "Overriding the Equals Method" section using auto-implemented properties. Change the test code to instantiate the Student object using object initializer syntax.

4. Write a simple program that creates a generic List collection and fill the collection with a random series of strings. Use a method (you decide which one) from the List class to sort the strings alphabetically. Use a foreach loop to cycle through and write the sorted names out.

CHAPTER 14

■■■

Transforming Our UML Model into C# Code

It's now time to turn our attention back to the class diagram that we produced in Part Two of the book in order to develop a C# application based on that object-oriented (OO) blueprint. We'll step through all of the C# code necessary to automate a simple command-line version of the Student Registration System (SRS) application first, so that we may focus solely on what it takes to accurately model the SRS domain information in an OO programming language. Then, in the next two chapters, we'll round out our application by adding a means of persisting data from one session to another and a graphical user interface, respectively.

In this chapter, when we create the SRS domain classes, we'll translate into C# code the OO constructs you've learned about in the previous chapters of this book. In this chapter, you'll learn about the following:

- Abstract classes, when we create the Person class as the base class for all of our "people" classes

- Associations of varying multiplicities (one-to-one, one-to-many, and many-to-many), including aggregations; most of the SRS classes make use of associations

- Inheritance relationships, when we derive the Student and Professor classes from the Person base class

- Association classes, when we create the TranscriptEntry class

- Reflexive associations, when we include class prerequisites to the Course class

- Metadata, when we incorporate information relevant to different Section objects into the Course class

- Static fields and methods, when we implement functionality into the TranscriptEntry class

In addition, we'll provide practical guidelines as to when to use these various constructs. We'll also cover a technique for testing your core classes via a command line–driven application.

Getting the Maximum Value Out of This and Subsequent Chapters

Our primary goal for this book is to show you how to take the same SRS case study through a complete object life cycle, from requirements definition via use cases, to object modeling, and from there into C# code as a working application. To do so, however, required us to develop a nontrivial application that was complex enough to be able to demonstrate as many "real-world" issues surrounding OO development as was possible within the scope of a single book.

The code that we've written for the SRS application is sizeable; to have included the full listings for each and every C# class intact in every chapter would have been difficult for you to read. So, to make this as effective a learning experience as possible for you, we've chosen to feature just those portions of code in each chapter that are particularly critical to your understanding of object concepts as they translate into the C# language.

Of course, we realize that you'll need access to the complete source code to round out your understanding of the SRS application as we've implemented it, so we're making an electronic softcopy of the SRS source code files available for download from the Apress web site, `http://www.apress.com/book/download.html`.

One of the best ways to master a language is to start with code that works and to experiment with it. We'd like you to get some hands-on experience with C# by actually compiling and running the SRS application; studying it, so as to familiarize yourself with the techniques that we've used; and finally, modifying it yourself. Exercises provided at the end of each chapter provide specific suggestions for experiments that you may wish to try. Therefore, before you dive into this chapter, we encourage you to download the C# source code for this chapter from the Apress web site if you haven't already done so; instructions for doing so are included in Appendix B. You'll also want to install Microsoft's free .NET Framework if you haven't already done so; please see Appendix A for details. For those of you who want to run the examples using an IDE, Microsoft's Visual Studio is an excellent choice.

Developing Command Line–Driven Applications

We occasionally have a need to develop a command line–driven application—i.e., an application that doesn't have a formal GUI front-end for either soliciting input from the user or for displaying output to the user. Running a program from the command line is also useful during code development, because debugging messages can be written to appear on the console window. When building command line–driven applications, we need to be able to

- Accept input, either by

  - Reading data from the command line, in the form of command-line arguments, or

  - Accepting keyboard input as typed by the user

- Display textual messages to the user, including both prompts for input as well as feedback on operations that have been performed

Reading Command-Line Arguments

As mentioned earlier, as a "driver" method for the program, the Main method can accept command-line arguments. Such arguments are typically used to either pass in small amounts of data or control some aspect of the program's execution.

Command-line arguments can be included as part of the command to execute a C# application, following the name of the class that contains the Main method that will serve as the entry point for the program on the command line. For example, if we wanted to provide an executable named SimpleProgram.exe with the command-line arguments Jackson, ABC, and 123, we would type the following command to run the program:

```
SimpleProgram Jackson ABC 123
```

Such data gets passed to the Main method of the C# program as a string array called args (or whatever else we wish to name it, as indicated by the Main method's parameter list). To accept command-line arguments, therefore, a program must use one of the two forms of the Main method that takes a string array as a parameter:

```
static void Main(string[] args)
static int Main(string[] args)
```

The args array is automatically sized to hold however many arguments are provided on the command line when the program is invoked. In the previous SimpleProgram invocation, the args array would contain three entries: the string "Jackson" would be placed as the first element of the args array (args[0]), the string "ABC" would be the next element of args, and the string "123" would be the last element. Command-line arguments surrounded by double quotes are taken literally. For example, if the following command were executed:

```
SimpleProgram "Zachary Palmer"
```

the first command-line argument, args[0], would have the value "Zachary Palmer".

Inside the Main method, we can do with args whatever we'd do with any other array—for example, determine its length, manipulate individual string items within the array, and so forth. The program that follows illustrates some of the things that we might wish to do with command-line arguments:

```
// FruitExample.cs

// This program is intended to illustrate command-line argument
// passing.

using System;

public class FruitExample {
    // The args[] array is automatically initialized when the
    // program is run from the command prompt with whatever
    // (space-separated) values ('arguments') we've typed on the
    // command line after the program name.
    //
```

```
static void Main(string[] args) {
  // Let's print out a few things.
  Console.WriteLine("The args array contains " + args.Length +
                    " entries." );

  // Only execute this next block of code if the array isn't
  // empty. The Length property returns the number of elements
  // in the array.
  if (args.Length > 0) {
    int last = args.Length - 1;
    Console.WriteLine("The last array entry is: " + args[last]);

    // Every string has a Length property, as well, that
    // contains the number of characters in the string.
    Console.WriteLine("The last array entry is " +
                      args[last].Length +" characters long.");
  }
  else {
    Console.WriteLine("No command line arguments detected.");
  }
 }
}
```

When this program is run from the command line as follows:

```
FruitExample apple banana cherry
```

it produces the following output:

```
The args array contains 3 entries.
The last array entry is: cherry
The last array entry is 6 characters long.
```

Accepting Keyboard Input

Most applications receive information either directly from users via an application's graphical user interface or by reading information from a file or database. But, until you've learned how to program such things in C# in Chapters 15 and 16, it's handy to know how to prompt for textual input from the command-line window.

To read keyboard input, we'll turn once again to the Console class from the System namespace. The Console class declares a ReadLine method that can be used to read keyboard input.

```
public static string ReadLine()
```

Data is read character by character but is buffered internally by this method until the Enter key is pressed, at which point an entire line of input is returned by the method as a string.

The ReadLine method reads data from the standard input/output (I/O) stream, which in most cases is associated with the keyboard. The ReadLine method can generate an IOException, so calls to the method should be enclosed in a try block.

Here is a simple example that illustrates reading data from the keyboard using the ReadLine method; we'll present the program in its entirety first, then narrate it in step-by-step fashion.

```
using System;
using System.IO;

public class KeyboardDemo
{
  static void Main() {
    string name = "";

    try {
      // Prompt the user for input; note the use of
      // Write() vs. WriteLine(), so that the prompt will
      // be displayed on the same line as the text entered
      // by the user.
      Console.Write("Enter your name: ");

      // Read their response from the keyboard.
      name = Console.ReadLine();
    }
    catch (IOException ioe) {
      Console.WriteLine("IO Exception occurred: " + ioe);
    }

    // Display the input back as a test.
    Console.WriteLine("Name entered was " + name);
  }
}
```

Stepping through the code:

- When the KeyboardDemo program is run, the user is prompted to enter his or her name via a call to the Console.Write method:

```
Console.Write("Enter your name: ");
```

  Note our use of Write vs. WriteLine, so that the prompt will be displayed on the same line as the text entered by the user.

- The value of a local string variable called name is set to the string value returned by the ReadLine method:

```
name = Console.ReadLine();
```

  This operation is performed inside a try block.

- A catch clause is provided to catch IOExceptions. We'll cover exception handling in detail in Chapter 15, but for now just consider the catch clause as a safety net that lets the program keep running if something goes wrong with one of the I/O operations.

Running this program would produce the following results (**bold text** reflects input by the user):

```
Enter your name: Jackie Chan
Name entered was Jackie Chan
```

The SRS Class Diagram, Revisited

Now that you've learned a little bit about creating command line–driven applications, let's turn our attention back to the SRS class diagram that we produced in Part Two of the book. In speaking with our sponsors for the SRS system, we learn that they've decided to cut back on a few features in the interest of reducing development costs:

- First of all, they've decided not to automate students' plans of study via the SRS. Instead, it will be up to each student to make sure that the courses that he or she registers for are appropriate for the degree that he or she is seeking.

- Since automated plans of study are being eliminated, there will no longer be a need to track whom a student's faculty advisor is. The only reason for modeling the *advises* relationship between the Professor and Student classes in the first place was so that a student's advisor could be called upon to approve a tentative plan of study when a student had first posted it via the SRS.

- Finally, our sponsors have decided that maintaining a wait list for a section once it becomes full is a luxury that they can live without, since most students, upon learning that a section is full, immediately choose an alternative course anyway.

Therefore, we've pared down the SRS class diagram accordingly to eliminate these unnecessary features; also, to keep the diagram from getting too cluttered, we didn't reflect field types or full method headers. The resultant diagram is shown in Figure 14-1.

Fortunately for us, the resultant model still provides examples of all of the key OO/C# elements that we need to learn how to program, as listed in Table 14-1.

Table 14-1. *OO/C# Features Illustrated by the SRS Class Diagram*

OO/C# Feature	Embodied in the SRS Class Diagram As Follows
Inheritance	The Person class serves as the base class for the Student and Professor classes.
Aggregation	We have two examples of this: the Transcript class represents an aggregation of TranscriptEntry objects, and the ScheduleOfClasses class represents an aggregation of Section objects.
One-to-one association	The *maintains* association is between the Student and Transcript classes.
One-to-many association	The *teaches* association is between Professor and Section; the *offered as* association is between Course and Section.
Many-to-many association	The *attends* association is between Student and Section; the *prerequisite* (reflexive) association is between instances of the Course class.
Association class	The TranscriptEntry class is affiliated with the *attends* association.

OO/C# Feature	Embodied in the SRS Class Diagram As Follows
Reflexive association	The *prerequisite* association between instances of the Course class is a reflexive association, because it refers to associations between objects of the same class.
Multiplicity	A student can attend more than one section, so Section has multiplicity with regards to Student.
Abstract class	The Person class is implemented as an abstract class.
Metadata	Each Course object embodies information that is relevant to multiple Section objects.
Properties	Properties are used throughout the SRS to access or change the values of the instance variables of the SRS classes.
Static fields	Although not specifically illustrated in the class diagram, we'll take advantage of static fields when we code the Section class.
Static methods	Although not specifically illustrated in the class diagram, we'll take advantage of static methods when we code the TranscriptEntry class.

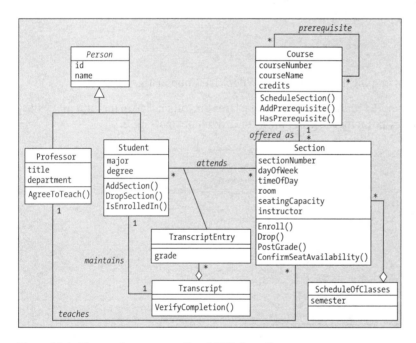

Figure 14-1. *The resultant streamlined SRS class diagram*

As mentioned earlier, we're going to implement a command line–driven version of the SRS in this chapter; in particular, we're going to code the eight classes illustrated in the class diagram along with a ninth "driver" class that will be used to launch the command line–driven version of the SRS. The driver class will declare the Main method that serves as the entry point when the code is run.

The SRS Plan of Attack

When we develop the SRS, we'll create one source code file for every class that we create. Specifically,

- We'll create one .cs file for each of the domain classes that we defined in our object model; for the SRS application, for example, we'll have eight:

```
Course.cs
Person.cs
Professor.cs
ScheduleOfClasses.cs
Section.cs
Student.cs
Transcript.cs
TranscriptEntry.cs
```

- We'll also typically have a separate .cs file for each of the primary windows comprising the graphical user interface of our application, if any. For the SRS application, we'll eventually create two such classes:

```
MainForm.cs
PasswordForm.cs
```

(We'll talk about graphical user interfaces in depth in Chapter 16.)

- We'll typically have a separate .cs file that declares the "official" Main method that will serve as the entry point for the program, as illustrated in Figure 14-2.

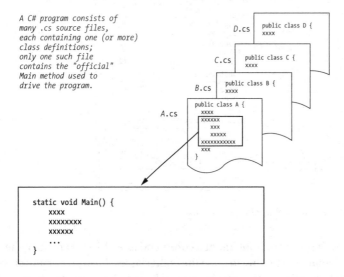

Figure 14-2. One "official" Main method will drive the SRS.

- One of the primary responsibilities of this driver class's Main method is to instantiate the core objects needed to fulfill a system's mission. Actions taken by these objects, as well as by users as they interact with the application, will cause additional objects to be instantiated as the application executes.

- The Main method is also responsible for displaying the startup window of the graphical user interface of an application, if any.

We'll name the driver class for our SRS application SRS, contained in the file SRS.cs.

- Finally, we often create other "helper" classes necessary for behind-the-scenes application support; with the SRS, we'll have a need for two such classes:

```
CourseCatalog.cs
Faculty.cs
```

All told, by the time we reach the end of Chapter 16, we'll have programmed a total of 13 classes, integrating them into a single SRS application with a GUI front-end and a way to persist data from one SRS application session to the next.

The Person Class (Specifying Abstract Classes)

The Person class will be the abstract base class for all of the "people" represented by the SRS. The Student and Professor classes, for example, will be derived from the Person class. Figure 14-3 shows the class diagram for the Person class. The first thing that you'll notice in the class diagram is that the name of the class is *italicized*, which you learned in Chapter 10 means that Person is to be implemented as an abstract class.

Figure 14-3. *The* Person *class*

The source code for the Person class will be placed in a file named Person.cs. We will be using the System.Console class in this class, so we'll include a using directive at the top of the code.

```
using System;
```

The next part of the code listing is the class declaration header. By including the keyword abstract in the class declaration, we prevent the Person class from ever being instantiated directly.

```
// We are making this class abstract because we do not wish for it
// to be instantiated.

public abstract class Person {
```

```
// Person members...see following sections.

}
```

Person Fields

The Person class will maintain two data elements: a string representing the person's name, and a string corresponding to the person's identification (ID) number. One way to implement these data elements would be to declare private fields of type string and then declare standard properties to access or change the value of the fields. However, for the Person class, we're going to use simple get and set accessors. We're not going to perform value checking, for instance, so to simplify the code listing, we're going to use auto-implemented properties to access the name and ID data. Since auto-implemented properties make use of implied (i.e., not included in the code listing) private fields, the Person class won't declare any fields.

Person Constructors

We'll provide a constructor for the Person class that accepts two arguments, so as to initialize the Name and Id property values.

```
//----------------
// Constructor(s).
//----------------

// Initialize the auto-implemented property values using the set
// accessor.

public Person(string name, string id) {
  Name = name;
  Id = id;
}
```

The constructor is used to initialize the value of the Name and Id properties using the set accessor. If this initialization weren't performed, the Name and Id properties would have initially had the value of null.

And, because the creation of any constructor for a class suppresses the automatic generation of that class's default parameterless constructor, as we discussed in Chapter 13, we'll program a parameterless constructor to replace it.

```
// We're replacing the default parameterless constructor that
// got "wiped out" as a result of having created a constructor
// previously. We reuse the two-argument constructor with dummy
// values.

public Person() : this("?", "???-??-????")  {
  // Because this constructor needn't do anything more than what
  // the first constructor is going to do, the body of this
  // constructor is empty.
}
```

This parameterless constructor takes advantage of the : this(...) construct to reuse the code from the first constructor.

Person Properties

The name and ID number data elements of the Person object are accessed using auto-implemented properties. Note how compact the auto-implemented property syntax is compared to a standard property. Because we don't want to give client code the ability to change a Person object's name or ID number, we're going to make use of asymmetric accessibility to give protected access to the set accessor of the properties. With protected access, only the Person class and classes that are derived from Person can change the value of the name and ID number.

```
//------------------------------
// Auto-implemented properties.
//------------------------------

public string Name { get; protected set; }
public string Id { get; protected set; }
```

ToString Method

We'd like for all derived classes of the Person class to implement a ToString method, but we don't want to bother coding the details of such a method for Person; we'd prefer to let each derived class handle the details of how the ToString method will work in its own class-appropriate way. The best way to enforce the requirement for a ToString method is to declare ToString as an *abstract method* in Person, as we discussed in Chapters 7 and 13. The override keyword is required because the Object class (the base class of our Person class) also declares a ToString method.

```
//------------------------------
// Miscellaneous other methods.
//------------------------------

// We'll let each derived class implement how it wishes to be
// represented as a String value.

public abstract override string ToString();
```

■**Note** The ToString method is declared in the Object class as a nonabstract, virtual method. We're overriding that method in the Person class with an abstract method, but it's perfectly acceptable to do so, as we discussed in Chapter 13; making the Person ToString method abstract forces derived classes of Person to implement their own ToString logic.

Display Method

We also want all derived classes of Person to implement a Display method, to be used for printing the values of all of an object's fields to the command-line window. We'll be using the

Display method solely for testing our application, to verify that an object's property values have been properly initialized. But, rather than making this method abstract as well, we'll go ahead and actually program the body of this method, since we know how we'd like the data of Person to be displayed when these are inherited, at a minimum.

```
// Used for testing purposes.

public virtual void Display() {
  Console.WriteLine("Person Information:");
  Console.WriteLine("\tName:  " + this.Name);
  Console.WriteLine("\tID number:  " + this.Id);
}
```

By declaring the Display method to be virtual, we're enabling derived classes to override the Person class's Display method for their own purposes. Derived classes can use the base keyword to make use of the Person class's Display method logic in their own Display methods.

That's all there is to programming the Person class—pretty straightforward! We'll tackle the Student and Professor classes derived from Person next.

The Student Class (Reuse Through Inheritance, Extending Abstract Classes, and Delegation)

The Student class serves as a representation of a student in the SRS, and is derived from the abstract Person class. To be able to instantiate Student objects within the SRS, we must implement all of Person's abstract methods concretely within the Student class, thus breaking the spell of abstractness, as we discussed in Chapter 7.

We indicate that Student is a derived class of Person in the section of the UML diagram shown in Figure 14-4.

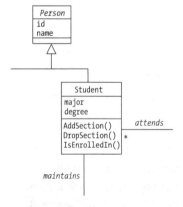

Figure 14-4. *The* Student *class*

The Student class code listing is placed in a file named Student.cs. The class makes use of language elements from the System.Collections.Generic and System namespaces, so using statements to these namespaces are placed at the top of the code listing. Following the using statements is the header for the Student class.

```csharp
using System;
using System.Collections.Generic;

public class Student : Person {

  //  Student class code listing here

}
```

Student Data Elements

Two data elements are indicated for the Student class in our class diagram—strings representing a student's major and degree. We could implement these data elements as private fields with associated properties, but since we aren't going to do anything fancy with the data, it's simpler to use auto-implemented properties. This is a widely used approach as of C# 3.5.

In addition to auto-implemented properties to store the student's major and degree, you learned in Chapter 10 that you must also encode associations. A Student object participates in two associations:

- *attends*, a many-to-many association with the Section class

- *maintains*, a one-to-one association with the Transcript class

You must allow for each Student to maintain object references to *one* Transcript object and on *many* Section objects. This data element is also modeled using an auto-implemented property, so the Student class declares three such properties The set accessor of the properties is given protected access (the concept of asymmetric accessibility) so that only Student and Student-derived objects are able to change the values.

```csharp
//------------------------------
// Auto-implemented properties.
//------------------------------

public string Major { get; protected set; }
public string Degree { get; protected set; }
public Transcript Transcript { get; protected set; }
```

The third auto-implemented property is named Transcript and stores a reference to a Transcript object. Declaring a property to have the same name as a class is a perfectly acceptable thing to do in C#. If we were to try to access the property with the following client code snippet:

```csharp
Student s1 = new Student("Gerson Lopez", "123456789");
Transcipt t = new Transcript();
s1.Transcript = t;
```

the runtime would understand that the third line of code is accessing the get accessor of the Transcript property on the s1 Student object.

The attends association requires a collection to store the (possible) multiple sections that a student might attend. Of the C# collection types that you learned about in Chapters 6 and 13—Array, List, and Dictionary—a List declared to hold Section references seems like the best choice for managing multiple Section object references:

- An Array is too rigid; we'd have to size the Array in advance to be large enough to accommodate references to all of the Sections that a Student will ever attend over the course of his or her studies at the university. A List, on the other hand, can start out small and automatically grow in size as needed.

- The decision of whether to use a List vs. a Dictionary to manage a collection comes down to whether or not we'll need to retrieve an object reference from the collection based on some key value. We don't anticipate the need for such a look-up capability as it pertains to the Sections that a Student has attended; we'll need the ability to verify if a Student has taken a particular Section or not, but this can be accomplished by using the List class's Contains method. That is, if attends is declared to be of type List, then we can use the statement

```
if (attends.Contains(someSection)) {...}
```

For most other uses of the attends collection, we'll need to step through the entire collection anyway, as when printing out the Student's course schedule. So, a List should serve our purposes just fine.

We have the same decision to make with the attends collection as we did with the other data elements in the Student class. We could implement the attends collection using an auto-implemented property, or we could declare attends as a private field with a standard property associated with it. Both approaches will work, but in order to demonstrate the approach of using a standard property in the SRS, the attends List will be implemented as a private field and an associated standard property.

```
//------------
// Field.
//------------

private List<Section> attends; // of Sections

//----------------------------
// Standard property for List.
//----------------------------

public List<Section> Attends {
  get {
    return attends;
  }
  set {
    attends = value;
  }
}
```

We can use the Attends property to return a reference to the entire attends collection. We'll also provide the methods AddSection and DropSection to add and remove Section objects from the List; we'll talk about these methods momentarily.

Student Constructors

The Student class declares two constructors for initializing the field and property values of a Student object. The first constructor takes arguments representing the name, ID number, major, and degree of the Student. The name and ID arguments are sent to the Person constructor using the base keyword to initialize the data elements inherited from the Person class. The attends List is initially created to be empty, because a Student object may (and most likely will) come into existence before we know which Sections the student will be attending.

```
// Reuse the code of the parent's constructor using the base
// keyword.

public Student(string name, string id,
               string major, string degree) : base(name, id) {

  Major = major;
  Degree = degree;
  Transcript = new Transcript(this);

  // We create an empty List.

  attends = new List<Section>();
}
```

In the preceding code, note that we create a brand-new Transcript object on the fly by calling the Transcript constructor, passing a reference to *this* Student as the lone argument to the constructor. Since we haven't discussed the structure of the Transcript class yet, the signature of its constructor may seem a bit puzzling to you but will make sense once we get a chance to review the Transcript class in its entirety later in this chapter.

We choose to overload the Student constructor by providing a second constructor signature, to be used if we wish to create a Student object for whom we don't yet know the major field of study or degree sought. We once again take advantage of the this keyword (introduced in Chapter 13) to reuse the code from the first constructor, passing in the String value "TBD" to serve as a temporary value for both the major and degree data elements.

```
// A second form of constructor, used when a Student has not yet
// declared a major or degree.
// Reuse the code of the other Student constructor.

public Student(string name, string id) : this(name, id, "TBD", "TBD") {
  // Because this constructor needn't do anything more than what
  // the other Student constructor is going to do, the body of
  // this constructor is empty.
}
```

Display Method

As we did for Person, we choose to provide a Display method for Student for use in testing our command-line version of the SRS. Because Student is a derived class of Person, we'll override the Display method from the Person class, using the override keyword, to print out information about the Student class data elements. Information about the data elements declared in the Person class will be obtained by calling the Person class's Display method using the base keyword.

```
public override void Display() {
    // First, let's display the Person class data elements.

    base.Display();

    // Then, display Student-specific info.

    Console.WriteLine("Student-Specific Information:");
    Console.WriteLine("\tMajor:   " + Major);
    Console.WriteLine("\tDegree:   " + Degree);
    DisplayCourseSchedule();
    Transcript.Display();
}
```

The last line of the Display method is a straightforward example of delegation: we use the get accessor of the Student's Transcript property to retrieve a reference to the (implicit) Transcript field associated with the auto-implemented property, and then invoke the Display method on that Transcript object.

The Display method also calls one of the Student class's other methods, DisplayCourseSchedule. We chose to program this functionality as a separate method vs. incorporating its code into the body of the Display method to keep the Display method from getting too cluttered.

DisplayCourseSchedule Method

The DisplayCourseSchedule method is a more complex example of delegation; we'll defer a discussion of this method until we've discussed a few more of the SRS classes.

ToString Method

The Student class is a derived class of the abstract Person class. Therefore, for the Student class to be nonabstract (which we want), it must provide a concrete implementation for all of the abstract methods declared in the Person class. In this case, there is one such method, ToString, that we must implement in the Student class.

```
// We are forced to program this method because it is specified
// as an abstract method in our parent class (Person); failing
// to do so would render the Student class abstract, as well.
//
```

```
// For a Student, we wish to return a String as follows:
//    Jackson Palmer (123-45-6789) [Master of Science - Math]

public override string ToString() {
  return Name + " (" + Id + ") [" + Degree +" - " + Major + "]";
}
```

Note that the Student class's ToString method is accessing the values of the Name and Id properties that were declared in the Person class. This operation is permitted because the get accessors for those properties were given protected access, and Student is a derived class of Person.

AddSection Method

The AddSection method is called when a Student enrolls in a Section. It simply adds a reference to the Section to the end of the attends List collection.

```
public void AddSection(Section s) {
  attends.Add(s);
}
```

DropSection Method

The DropSection method is called when a Student withdraws from a Section. It simply removes the specified section from the attends List.

```
public void DropSection(Section s) {
  attends.Remove(s);
}
```

IsEnrolledIn Method

The IsEnrolledIn method is used to determine whether a Student is already enrolled in a particular Section—that is, whether that Student is already maintaining an object reference to the Section in question—by taking advantage of the List class's Contains method.

```
public bool IsEnrolledIn(Section s) {
  return attends.Contains(s);
}
```

IsCurrentlyEnrolledInSimilar Method

Although not specified by our model, we've added another version of the IsEnrolledIn method called IsCurrentlyEnrolledInSimilar, because we found a need for such a method when we coded the Section class (coming up later in this chapter). No matter how much thought you put into object modeling, you'll inevitably determine the need for additional fields, properties, and methods for your classes once coding is under way, because coding causes you to think at a much more finely grained level of detail about the mechanics of your application.

Because this method is so complex, we'll show the method code in its entirety first, followed by an in-depth explanation.

```csharp
// Determine whether the Student is already enrolled in ANOTHER
// Section of this SAME Course.

public bool IsCurrentlyEnrolledInSimilar(Section s1) {
  bool foundMatch = false;
  Course c1 = s1.RepresentedCourse;

  foreach( Section s2 in attends ) {
    Course c2 = s2.RepresentedCourse;
    if (c1 == c2) {
      // There is indeed a Section in the attends
      // List representing the same Course.
      // Check to see if the Student is CURRENTLY
      // ENROLLED (i.e., whether or not he/she has
      // yet received a grade). If there is no
      // grade, he/she is currently enrolled; if
      // there is a grade, then he/she completed
      // the course some time in the past.
      if ( s2.GetGrade(this) == null ) {
        // No grade was assigned! This means
        // that the Student is currently
        // enrolled in a Section of this
        // same Course.
        foundMatch = true;
        break;
      }
    }
  }

  return foundMatch;
}
```

In coding the Enroll method of the Section class, we realized that we needed a way to determine whether a particular Student is enrolled in any Section of a given Course. That is, if a Student is attempting to enroll for Math 101 Section *1*, we want to reject this request if he or she is already enrolled in Math 101 Section *2*. Although we could have alternatively declared the argument to this method to be a Course reference, we chose to pass in a reference to a Section object to the method.

```csharp
// Determine whether the Student is already enrolled in another
// Section of this same Course.

public bool IsCurrentlyEnrolledInSimilar(Section s1) {
```

We initialize a flag to false, with the intention of resetting it to true later on if we do indeed discover that the Student is currently enrolled in a Section of the same Course.

```
bool foundMatch = false;
```

We obtain a reference to the Course object that the Section of interest represents, and then use a foreach loop to step through all of the Sections that this Student is either currently enrolled in or has previously enrolled in, using the variable s2 to maintain a temporary object reference to each such Section one by one.

```
Course c1 = s1.RepresentedCourse;
foreach( Section s2 in attends ) {
```

We obtain a reference to a second Course object—the Course object that Section s2 is a Section of—and test the equality of the two Course objects. Even if we find a match, we're not quite done yet, because the attends List for a Student holds onto all Sections that the Student has ever taken. To determine if Section s2 is truly a Section that the Student is currently enrolled in, we must check to see if a grade has been issued for this Section; a missing grade—that is, a grade value of null—will indicate that the Section is currently in progress. As soon as we've found the first such situation, we can break out of the enclosing while loop and return a value of true to the caller.

```
    Course c2 = s2.RepresentedCourse;
    if (c1 == c2) {
      // There is indeed a Section in the attends
      // List representing the same Course.
      // Check to see if the Student is CURRENTLY
      // ENROLLED (i.e., whether or not he has
      // yet received a grade).  If there is no
      // grade, he/she is currently enrolled; if
      // there is a grade, then he/she completed
      // the course some time in the past.
      if ( s2.GetGrade(this) == null ) {
        // No grade was assigned!  This means
        // that the Student is currently
        // enrolled in a Section of this
        // same Course.
        foundMatch = true;
        break;
      }
    }
  }
}

  return foundMatch;
}// end of method
```

Next, we'll turn our attention to the Professor class.

The Professor Class (Bidirectionality of Relationships)

As seen in Figure 14-5, the Professor class is a derived class of Person that serves as an abstraction of a college professor. Because the code that is necessary to implement the Professor class is so similar to that of Student, we'll only comment on those features of Professor that are particularly noteworthy. We encourage you to look at the full code of the Professor class as downloaded from the Apress web site, to reinforce your ability to read and interpret C# syntax.

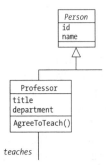

Figure 14-5. *The* Professor *class*

The Professor class is implemented in a file named Professor.cs. The class makes use of language elements from the System.Collections.Generic and System namespaces, so using statements for these namespaces are placed at the top of the code listing. Following the using statements is the header for the Professor class.

```
using System;
using System.Collections.Generic;

public class Professor : Person {
  // Professor class code listing here
}
```

Professor Data Elements

The Professor class introduces two data elements: strings representing the Professor's title and the department that the Professor is a part of. As was done with the Student class, these data elements are modeled using auto-implemented properties.

The Professor class is involved in one association—the one-to-many *teaches* association with the Section class—so we must provide a means for a Professor object to maintain multiple Section object references. The List collection type is a good way to store these references. To simplify the Professor class code listing, we'll use an auto-implemented property to store and access this List. The Professor class declares three auto-implemented properties.

```
//------------------------------
// Auto-implemented properties.
//------------------------------
```

```
public string Title { get; set; }
public string Department { get; set; }
public List<Section> Teaches { get; set; }
```

Professor Constructor

The Professor class declares one constructor, which is similar in form and function to one of the Student constructors. The Professor constructor first calls the Person constructor using the base keyword to initialize the values for the name and ID data elements declared in the Person class. It then assigns values to the Title and Department properties and creates an empty List collection to store references to the Sections that the Professor will teach.

```
public Professor(string name, string id,
                 string title, string dept) : base(name, id) {

    Title = title;
    Department = dept;

    // Create an empty List.
    Teaches = new List<Section>();
}
```

AgreeToTeach Method

Our class diagram calls for us to implement an AgreeToTeach method. This method accepts a Section object reference as an argument, and begins by storing this object reference in the List accessed through the Teaches property.

```
public void AgreeToTeach(Section s) {
    Teaches.Add(s);
```

Associations, as modeled in a class diagram, are assumed to be bidirectional. When implementing associations in code, however, we must think about whether or not bidirectionality is important.

- *Can we think of any situations in which a* Professor *object would need to know which* Sections *it's responsible for teaching?* Yes—for example, when we ask a Professor object to print out its teaching assignments.

- *How about the reverse—that is, can we think of any situations in which a* Section *object would need to know who is teaching it?* Yes—for example, when we print out a Student's course schedule, the Section accesses its Instructor property (which refers to a Professor object).

So, not only must we store a reference to the Section object in the Professor's Teaches List, but we must also make sure that the Section object is somehow notified that this Professor is going to be its instructor. We accomplish this by accessing the Section object's Instructor property, passing it a reference to this Professor.

```
public void AgreeToTeach(Section s) {
    Teaches.Add(s);
```

```
    // We need to link this bidirectionally.
    s.Instructor = this;
}
```

We'll explore the implications of bidirectionality and the various options for implementing bidirectional relationships in more depth a bit later in this chapter.

We'll turn our attention next to the Course class.

The Course Class (Reflexive and Unidirectional Relationships)

The Course class, shown in Figure 14-6, represents an abstraction of a college course. Note that Course participates in the only reflexive association found in our UML diagram.

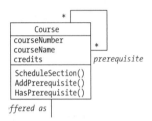

Figure 14-6. *The* Course *class*

The Course class listing is contained in a file named Course.cs. As with the previous classes, it starts with using statements for the System and System.Collections.Generic namespaces followed by the class header.

```
using System;
using System.Collections.Generic;

public class Course {

    // Course class listing

}
```

Course Data Elements

The Course class has three simple data elements: strings that represent the course name and number, and a double value that represents the number of credits awarded for completing the course successfully. These elements are implemented using auto-implemented properties.

```
// Auto-implemented properties.

public string CourseNumber { get; set; }
public string CourseName { get; set; }
public double Credits { get; set; }
```

A Course object also participates in two associations:

- *offered as*, a one-to-many association with the Section class

- *prerequisite*, a many-to-many reflexive association

We implement the two associations using auto-implemented properties that access List collection objects.

```
public List<Section> OfferedAsSection { get; set; }
public List<Course> Prerequisites { get; set; }
```

Note that a reflexive association is handled in exactly the same way that any other association is handled: we provide the Course class with access to a List that stores Course references so that a given Course object can maintain references to other Course objects. We've chosen not to encode this reflexive association bidirectionally. That is, a given Course object X knows which other Course objects A, B, C, and so on serve as its prerequisites, but it doesn't know which Course objects L, M, N, and so on consider X to be one of *their* prerequisites (see Figure 14-7).

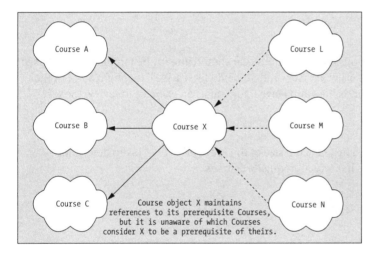

Figure 14-7. *The prerequisite association isn't implemented bidirectionally.*

Had we wanted this association to be bidirectional, we would have had to include a second List as an auto-implemented property in the Course class.

```
public List<Course> Prerequisites { get; set; }
public List<Course> PrerequisitesOf { get; set; }
```

This way, Course object X could hold onto this latter group of Course objects separately.

Course Constructor

The Course class declares a single constructor that initializes the value of the CourseNumber, CourseName, and Credits properties and creates two empty List objects.

```
public Course(string cNo, string cName, double credits) {

    //  Initialize property values.

    CourseNumber = cNo;
    CourseName = cName;
    Credits = credits;

    // Create two empty Lists.

    OfferedAsSection = new List<Section>();
    Prerequisites = new List<Course>();
}
```

Course Methods

Most of the Course class methods use techniques that should already be familiar to you, based on our discussions of the Person, Professor, and Student classes. We'll highlight a few of the more interesting Course methods here and leave it for you as an exercise to review the rest.

HasPrerequisites Method

The HasPrerequisites method inspects the size of the Prerequisites List to determine whether or not a given Course has any prerequisite Courses.

```
public bool HasPrerequisites() {
    if (Prerequisites.Count > 0) {
        return true;
    }
    else {
        return false;
    }
}
```

ScheduleSection Method

The ScheduleSection method illustrates several interesting techniques. First, note that this method creates a new Section object on the fly. The reference is first stored in the OfferedAsSection List and then is returned to the client code.

```
public Section ScheduleSection(string day, string time, string room,
                        int capacity) {
    // Create a new Section (note the creative way in
    // which we are assigning a section number)...
```

```
Section s = new Section(OfferedAsSection.Count + 1,
                        day, time, this, room, capacity);

// ...and then add it to the List
OfferedAsSection.Add(s);

//  Return the Section to the caller.
return s;
}
```

Second, we're generating the first argument to the Section constructor—representing the Section number to be created—as a "one up" number by adding 1 to the number of elements in the OfferedAsSection List. The first time that we invoke the ScheduleSection method for a given Course object, the List will be empty, and so the expression

```
OfferedAsSection.Count + 1
```

will evaluate to 1; hence, we'll be creating Section number 1. The second time that this method is invoked for the same Course object, the List will already contain a reference to the first Section object that was created, and so the expression

```
OfferedAsSection.Count + 1
```

will evaluate to 2; hence, we'll be creating Section number 2, and so forth.

There is one flaw to this approach: if we were to create and then delete Section objects, the size of the List would expand and contract, and we could wind up with duplicate Section numbers. We'll remedy this flaw in Chapter 15.

Now, let's turn our attention to the Section class.

The Section Class (Representing Association Classes and Public Constant Fields)

The Section class represents an abstraction of a particular section of a college course as offered in a given semester, and is illustrated in Figure 14-8.

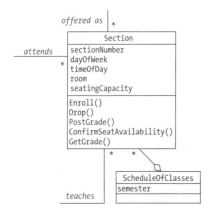

Figure 14-8. *The* Section *class*

The Section class listing is contained in a file named Section.cs. It starts with using statements for the System and System.Collections.Generic namespaces, followed by the class header.

```
using System;
using System.Collections.Generic;

public class Section {

  //  Section class code listing

}
```

Section Data Elements

The Section class maintains a number of data elements that define the state of a Section object. These data elements are implemented as auto-implemented properties.

```
//-------------------------------
// Auto-implemented properties.
//-------------------------------

public int SectionNumber { get; set; }
public string DayOfWeek { get; set; }
public string TimeOfDay { get; set; }
public string Room { get; set; }
public int SeatingCapacity { get; set; }
```

In addition, the Section class participates in numerous relationships with other classes:

- *offered as*, a one-to-many association with Course

- An unnamed, one-to-many aggregation with ScheduleOfClasses

- *teaches*, a one-to-many association with Professor

- *attends*, a many-to-many association with Student

The *attends* association is in turn affiliated with an association class, TranscriptEntry. You learned in Chapter 10 that an association class can alternatively be depicted in a class diagram as having direct relationships with the classes at either end of the association, so we'll encode a fifth relationship for the Section class, namely

- *assigns grade*, a one-to-many association with the TranscriptEntry class

(You may be wondering whether we should now go back and adjust the Student class to reflect the *earns grade* association with the TranscriptEntry class as a Student class field. The decision of whether or not to implement a particular relationship in code depends in part on what we anticipate our usage patterns to be, as we discussed in Chapter 10. We'll defer the decision of what to do with *earns grade* until we talk about the TranscriptEntry class in a bit more depth later in this chapter.)

We'll represent three of these five relationships in terms of auto-implemented properties declared in the Section class as follows.

A Section object need only maintain a reference to one other object for those one-to-many relationships in which Section occupies the "many" end, namely

```
public Course RepresentedCourse { get; set; }
public ScheduleOfClasses OfferedIn { get; set; }
public Professor Instructor { get; set; }
```

For the two situations in which Section needs to maintain references to *collections* of objects—Students and TranscriptEntries—we're going to employ Dictionary objects instead of List objects this time. We do so because it's conceivable that we'll have a frequent need to "pluck" a given item from the collection directly, and the Dictionary class provides a key-based look-up mechanism that is ideal for this purpose. These Dictionary objects will be accessed in the Section class using auto-implemented properties.

For the Dictionary of Student object references, we'll use a string representing the Student's identification number as a key for looking up a Student.

```
// The EnrolledStudents Dictionary stores Student object
// references using each Student's ID as a String key.

public Dictionary<string, Student> EnrolledStudents {get; set;}
```

For the Dictionary of TranscriptEntry object references, on the other hand, we'll use a Student object as a whole as a key for looking up that particular Student's TranscriptEntry, as issued by this Section.

```
// The assignedGrades Dictionary stores TranscriptEntry object
// references, using a reference to the Student to whom it
// belongs as the key.

public Dictionary<Student, TranscriptEntry> AssignedGrades {get; set;}
```

Section Constructor

The Section class declares one constructor that assigns values to the auto-implemented properties and creates two empty Dictionary objects.

```
public Section(int sNo, string day, string time, Course course,
               string room, int capacity) {
    SectionNumber = sNo;
    DayOfWeek = day;
    TimeOfDay = time;
    RepresentedCourse = course;
    Room = room;
    SeatingCapacity = capacity;

    // A Professor has not yet been identified.
```

```
    Instructor = null;

    // Create empty Dictionary objects.

    EnrolledStudents = new Dictionary<string, Student>();
    AssignedGrades = new Dictionary<Student, TranscriptEntry>();
  }
```

Public Constant Fields and Enumerations

In the Section class, we encounter our first use of const fields, which as we learned in Chapter 13 are a means of defining constant values. In this particular situation, we could define some status codes that the Section class can use when signaling the outcome of an enrollment attempt.

```
public const int SUCCESSFULLY_ENROLLED = 0;
public const int SECTION_FULL = 1;
public const int PREREQ_NOT_SATISFIED = 2;
public const int PREVIOUSLY_ENROLLED = 3;
```

An alternative approach would have been to use a language construct called an *enumeration*, which defines a set of name-value pairs.

```
public enum EnrollFlags
{
  SUCCESSFULLY_ENROLLED = 0,
  SECTION_FULL = 1,
  PREREQ_NOT_SATISFIED = 2,
  PREVIOUSLY_ENROLLED = 3
}
```

By default, the elements of the enum are of type int, but we can specify other types as well. The SRS uses an enumeration to define the status codes from an attempted enrollment. The EnrollFlags enumeration is contained in a file named EnrollFlags.cs. Now let's look how it is put to use by studying the Enroll method of Section.

Enroll Method

The Enroll method is complex; we'll present the code in its entirety first without discussing it and then proceed to dissect it afterward.

```
public EnrollFlags Enroll(Student s) {
    // First, make sure that this Student is not already
    // enrolled for this Section, has not already enrolled
    // in another section of this class, and has
    // NEVER taken and passed the course before.

    Transcript transcript = s.Transcript;

    if (s.IsEnrolledIn(this) ||
```

```
      s.IsCurrentlyEnrolledInSimilar(this) ||
      transcript.VerifyCompletion(RepresentedCourse)) {
    return EnrollFlags.PREVIOUSLY_ENROLLED;
  }

  // If there are any prerequisites for this course,
  // check to ensure that the Student has completed them.

  Course c = RepresentedCourse;
  if (c.HasPrerequisites()) {

    foreach ( Course pre in c.Prerequisites ) {

      // See if the Student's Transcript reflects
      // successful completion of the prerequisite.

      if (!transcript.VerifyCompletion(pre)) {
        return EnrollFlags.PREREQ_NOT_SATISFIED;
      }
    }
  }

  // If the total enrollment is already at
  // the capacity for this Section, we reject this
  // enrollment request.

  if (!ConfirmSeatAvailability()) {
    return EnrollFlags.SECTION_FULL;
  }

  // If we made it to here in the code, we're ready to
  // officially enroll the Student.

  // Note bidirectionality: this Section holds
  // onto the Student via the Dictionary, and then
  // the Student is given an object reference to this Section.

  EnrolledStudents.Add(s.Id, s);
  s.AddSection(this);
  return EnrollFlags.SUCCESSFULLY_ENROLLED;
}
```

We begin by verifying that the Student seeking enrollment (represented by argument s) hasn't already enrolled for this Section, and furthermore that he or she has never taken and successfully completed this Course (any Section of it) in the past. To do so, we must obtain an object reference to the Student's transcript; we store it in a locally declared reference variable called transcript, because we're going to need to consult with the Transcript object twice in this method.

```
public EnrollFlags Enroll(Student s) {
  // First, make sure that this Student is not already
  // enrolled for this Section, has not already enrolled
  // in another section of this class, and has
  // NEVER taken and passed the course before.
```

Transcript transcript = s.Transcript;

We then use an if statement to test for either of two conditions: (a) is the Student currently enrolled in *this* Section or *another* Section of the *same* Course, and/or (b) does his or her Transcript indicate successful *prior* completion of the Course that is represented by this Section? Because we only need to use this Course object once in this method, we don't bother to save the object reference returned to us by the RepresentedCourse property in a local variable; we just nest the invocation of this method within the call to VerifyCompletion, so that the Course object can be retrieved by the former and immediately passed along as an argument to the latter.

```
if (s.IsEnrolledIn(this) ||
    s.IsCurrentlyEnrolledInSimilar(this) ||
    transcript.VerifyCompletion(RepresentedCourse)) {
  return EnrollFlags.PREVIOUSLY_ENROLLED;
}
```

Whenever we encounter a return statement midway through a method as we have here, the method will immediately terminate execution without running to completion.

Note our use of PREVIOUSLY_ENROLLED—one of the EnrollFlags enumeration values—as a return value. Declaring and using such standardized values is a great way to communicate status back to client code, as this sample pseudocode invocation of the Enroll method illustrates:

```
// Client code (pseudocode).

Section sec = new Section(...);
Student s = new Student(...);
// ...
int status = sec1.Enroll(s1);
if (status == EnrollFlags.PREVIOUSLY_ENROLLED) {
  // Pseudocode.
  take appropriate action
}
else if (status == EnrollFlags.PREREQ_NOT_SATISFIED) {
  // Pseudocode.
  take appropriate action
}
else if (status == EnrollFlags.SECTION_FULL) {
  // Pseudocode.
  take appropriate action
}
// etc.
```

Thus, both the client code and the Section object's method code are using the same symbolic names to communicate.

Next, we check to see if the Student has satisfied the prerequisites for this Section, if there are any. We use the Section's RepresentedCourse property to obtain a reference to the Course object that this Section represents, and then invoke the HasPrerequisites method on that Course object; if the result returned is true, then we know that there are prerequisites to be checked.

```
// If there are any prerequisites for this course,
// check to ensure that the Student has completed them.

Course c = RepresentedCourse;
if (c.HasPrerequisites()) {
```

If there are indeed prerequisites for this Course, we use a foreach loop to cycle through all (or any) prerequisite Courses.

```
    foreach ( Course pre in c.Prerequisites ) {
```

For each Course object reference pre that we extract from the Prerequisites List, we invoke the VerifyCompletion method on the Student's Transcript object, passing in the prerequisite Course object reference pre. We haven't taken a look at the inner workings of the Transcript class yet, so for now, all we need to know about VerifyCompletion is that it will return a value of true if the Student has indeed successfully taken and passed the Course in question, or a value of false otherwise. We want to take action in situations where a prerequisite was *not* satisfied, so we use the unary negation operator (!) in front of the expression to indicate that we want the if test to succeed if the method call returns a value of false.

```
    // See if the Student's Transcript reflects
    // successful completion of the prerequisite.

    if (!transcript.VerifyCompletion(pre)) {
      return EnrollFlags.PREREQ_NOT_SATISFIED;
    }
  } // end if
```

If we make it through the prerequisite check without triggering the return statement, the next step in this method is to verify that there is still available seating in the Section; we return the status value SECTION_FULL value if there is not.

```
// If the total enrollment is already at the
// capacity for this Section, we reject this
// enrollment request.

if (!ConfirmSeatAvailability()) {
  return EnrollFlags.SECTION_FULL;
}
```

Finally, if we've made it through both of the preceding tests unscathed, we're ready to officially enroll the Student. We use the Add method to insert the Student reference into the EnrolledStudents Dictionary, accessing the Id property on the Student to retrieve the string value of its id field, which we pass in as the key value. To achieve bidirectionality of the link between a Student and a Section, we then turn around and invoke the AddSection method on the Student object reference, passing it an object reference to this Section.

```
  // Note bidirectionality: this Section holds
  // onto the Student via the Hashtable, and then
  // the Student is given an object reference to this Section.

  EnrolledStudents.Add(s.Id, s);
  s.AddSection(this);
  return EnrollFlags.SUCCESSFULLY_ENROLLED;
}
```

Drop Method

The Drop method of Section performs the reverse operation of the Enroll method. We start by verifying that the Student in question is indeed enrolled in this Section, since we can't drop a Student who isn't enrolled in the first place.

```
public bool Drop(Student s) {
  // We may only drop a student if he/she is enrolled.

  if (!s.IsEnrolledIn(this)) {
    return false;
  }
```

If he or she truly is enrolled, then we use the Remove method to locate and delete the Student reference from the Dictionary, again via its Id property. In the interest of bidirectionality, we invoke the DropSection method on the Student, as well, to get rid of the object references at both ends of the link.

```
  else {
    // Find the student in our Dictionary, and remove it.

    EnrolledStudents.Remove(s.Id);

    // Note bidirectionality.

    s.DropSection(this);
    return true;
  }
}
```

PostGrade Method

The PostGrade method is used to assign a grade to a Student by creating a TranscriptEntry object to link the two. To ensure that we aren't inadvertently trying to assign a grade to a given Student more than once, we first invoke the ContainsKey method on the AssignedGrades

Dictionary to see if it already contains an entry for this Student. If the Dictionary contains the Student as a key, then we know a grade has already been posted for this Student, and we terminate execution of the method.

```csharp
public bool PostGrade(Student s, string grade) {

  // Make sure that we haven't previously assigned a
  // grade to this Student by looking in the Dictionary
  // for an entry using this Student as the key. If
  // we discover that a grade has already been assigned,
  // we return a value of false to indicate that
  // we are at risk of overwriting an existing grade.
  // (A different method, EraseGrade(), can then be written
  // to allow a Professor to change his/her mind.)

  if ( AssignedGrades.ContainsKey(s) == true ) {
    return false;
  }
```

Assuming that a grade wasn't previously assigned, we create a new TranscriptEntry object. As we'll see when we study the inner workings of the TranscriptEntry class, this object will maintain references to both the Student to whom a grade has been assigned and on the Section for which the grade was assigned. To enable this latter link to be bidirectional, we also store a reference to the TranscriptEntry object in the AssignedGrades Dictionary for this purpose.

```csharp
  // First, we create a new TranscriptEntry object. Note
  // that we are passing in a reference to THIS Section,
  // because we want the TranscriptEntry object,
  // as an association class..., to maintain object
  // references on the Section as well as on the Student.
  // (We'll let the TranscriptEntry constructor take care of
  // "hooking" this T.E. to the correct Transcript.)

  TranscriptEntry te = new TranscriptEntry(s, grade, this);

  // Then, we add the TranscriptEntry and its associated
  // Student to the AssignedGrades Dictionary.

  AssignedGrades.Add(s, te);

  return true;
}
```

ConfirmSeatAvailability Method

The ConfirmSeatAvailability method called from within Enroll is an internal housekeeping method; by declaring it to have private vs. public visibility, we restrict its use so that only other methods of the Section class may invoke it.

```
private bool ConfirmSeatAvailability() {
  if ( EnrolledStudents.Count < SeatingCapacity ) {
    return true;
  }
  else {
    return false;
  }
}
```

Delegation, Revisited

In discussing the Student class, we briefly mentioned the DisplayCourseSchedule method as a complex example of delegation, and promised to come back and discuss it further.

What are the raw materials—data—available for an object to use when one of its methods has been invoked? By way of review, an object might have at its disposal the following data sources:

- Simple data and/or object references defined as fields or auto-implemented properties within the object itself

- Simple data and/or object references that are passed in as arguments in the method signature

- Data that is made available globally to the application—for example, as public static fields of some other class

- Data that can be requested from any of the objects that this object has a reference to—a process that, as we learned in Chapter 3, is known as *delegation*

It's this last source of data—data available by collaborating with other objects and delegating part of a task to them—that is going to play a particularly significant role in implementing the DisplayCourseSchedule method for the Student class.

Let's say we want the DisplayCourseSchedule method to display the following information for each Section that a Student is currently enrolled in:

```
Course No.:
Section No.:
Course Name:
Meeting Day and Time:
Room Location:
Professor's Name:
```

For example:

```
Course Schedule for Fred Schnurd
  Course No.:  CMP101
  Section No.:  2
  Course Name:  Beginning Computer Technology
  Meeting Day and Time Held:  W - 6:10 - 8:00 PM
  Room Location:  GOVT202
  Professor's Name:  John Carson
  -----
  Course No.:  ART101
  Section No.:  1
  Course Name:  Beginning Basketweaving
  Meeting Day and Time Held:  M - 4:10 - 6:00 PM
  Room Location:  ARTS25
  Professor's Name:  Marc Chagall
  -----
```

Let's start by looking at the fields/properties of the Student class, to see which of this information is readily available to us. Student inherits from Person

```
public string Name { get; protected set; }
public string Id { get; protected set; }
```

and adds

```
public string Major { get; protected set; }
public string Degree { get; protected set; }
public Transcript Transcript { get; protected set; }
private List<Section> attends; // Generic List of Sections
```

Let's begin to write the DisplayCourseSchedule method from the Student class; by stepping through the attends List, we can gain access to Section objects one by one.

```
  public void DisplayCourseSchedule() {
    // Display a title first.

    Console.WriteLine("Course Schedule for " + this.Name);

    // Step through the List of Section objects,
    // processing these one by one.

    foreach ( Section s in attends ) {

      // Now what goes here????
      // We must create the rest of the method...
    }
  }
```

Now that we have the beginnings of the method, let's determine how to fill in the gap (highlighted) in the preceding code.

Looking at all of the property headers declared for the Section class as evidence of the services that a Section object can perform, we see that several of these can immediately provide us with useful pieces of information relative to our mission of displaying a Student's course schedule.

```
public int SectionNumber { get; set; }
public string DayOfWeek { get; set; }
public string TimeOfDay { get; set; }
public Professor Instructor { get; set; }
public Course RepresentedCourse { get; set; }
public string Room { get; set; }
public int SeatingCapacity { get; set; }
public ScheduleOfClasses OfferedIn { get; set; }
```

Let's put the four highlighted Section class properties to use, and where we can't yet fill the gap completely, we'll insert ??? as a placeholder:

```
public void DisplayCourseSchedule() {
  // Display a title first.

  Console.WriteLine("Course Schedule for " + this.Name);

  // Step through the List of Section objects,
  // processing these one by one.

  foreach ( Section s in attends ) {

    // Since the attends List contains Sections that the
    // Student took in the past as well as those for which
    // the Student is currently enrolled, we only want to
    // report on those for which a grade has not yet been
    // assigned.

    if (s.GetGrade(this) == null) {
      Console.WriteLine("\tCourse No.:  " + ???);
      Console.WriteLine("\tSection No.:  " + s.SectionNumber);
      Console.WriteLine("\tCourse Name:  " + ???);
      Console.WriteLine("\tMeeting Day and Time Held:  " +
             s.DayOfWeek + " - " + s.TimeOfDay);
      Console.WriteLine("\tRoom Location:  " + s.Room);
      Console.WriteLine("\tProfessor's Name:  " + ???);
      Console.WriteLine("\t-----");
    }
  }
}
```

Now what about the remaining holes?

The following two Section class properties:

```
public Professor Instructor { get; set; }
public Course RepresentedCourse { get; set; }
```

each hand us yet another object that we can "talk to": the Professor who teaches this Section, and the Course that this Section represents. Let's now look at what these objects can provide us in the way of information.

A Professor object provides the following properties (those marked with an asterisk comment [// *] are inherited from Person):

```
public string Name(get; protected set;)       // *
public string Id(get; protected set;)         // *
public string Title { get; set; }
public string Department { get; set; }
```

And a Course object provides the following properties:

```
public string CourseNumber { get; set; }
public string CourseName { get; set; }
public double Credits { get; set; }
```

If we bring all of the highlighted properties to bear, we can wrap up the DisplayCourseSchedule method of the Student class as follows:

```
public void DisplayCourseSchedule() {
  // Display a title first.

  Console.WriteLine("Course Schedule for " + this.Name);

  // Step through the List of Section objects,
  // processing these one by one.

  foreach ( Section s in attends ) {

    // Since the attends List contains Sections that the
    // Student took in the past as well as those for which
    // the Student is currently enrolled, we only want to
    // report on those for which a grade has not yet been
    // assigned.

    if (s.GetGrade(this) == null) {
      Console.WriteLine("\tCourse No.:   " +
                        s.RepresentedCourse.CourseNumber);
      Console.WriteLine("\tSection No.:  " + s.SectionNumber);
      Console.WriteLine("\tCourse Name:  " +
                        s.RepresentedCourse.CourseName);
      Console.WriteLine("\tMeeting Day and Time Held:   " +
                        s.DayOfWeek + " - " +
                        s.TimeOfDay);
```

```
        Console.WriteLine("\tRoom Location:   " + s.Room);
        Console.WriteLine("\tProfessor's Name:   " +
                          s.Instructor.Name);
        Console.WriteLine("\t-----");
      }
    }
  }
```

This method is a classic example of delegation:

- We start out asking a Student object to do something for us—namely, to display the Student's course schedule.

- The Student object in turn has to talk to the Section objects representing sections that the student is enrolled in, asking each of them to perform some of their services (methods).

- The Student object also has to ask those Section objects to hand over references to the Professor and Course objects that the Section objects know about, in turn asking *those* objects to perform some of *their* services.

This multitiered collaboration is depicted conceptually in Figure 14-9.

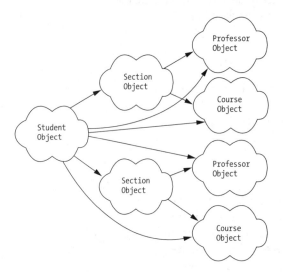

Figure 14-9. *Many objects collaborate to accomplish a single method.*

The ScheduleOfClasses Class

The ScheduleOfClasses class is a fairly simple class that serves as an example of how we can encapsulate a standard collection object within another class (see Figure 14-10)—a design technique that we discussed in Chapter 6.

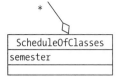

Figure 14-10. *The* ScheduleOfClasses *class*

The ScheduleOfClasses class listing is contained in a file named ScheduleOfClasses.cs. It starts with using statements for the System and System.Collections.Generic namespaces, followed by the class header.

```
using System;
using System.Collections.Generic;

public class ScheduleOfClasses {

//  ScheduleOfClasses code listing

}
```

ScheduleOfClasses Data Elements

The ScheduleOfClasses class has two data elements: a string representing the name of the current semester (e.g. "SP2009") and a Dictionary used to maintain object references to all of the Sections that are being offered that semester. Both of these data elements are implemented using auto-implemented properties.

```
    //-------------------------------
    // Auto-implemented properties.
    //-------------------------------

    public string Semester { get; set; }

    // This Dictionary stores Section object references, using
    // a String concatenation of course no. and section no. as the
    // key, e.g., "MATH101 - 1".

    public Dictionary<string, Section> SectionsOffered { get; set; }
```

ScheduleOfClasses Constructor

The ScheduleOfClasses class declares one constructor that initializes the value of the Semester property and creates an empty Dictionary.

```
    public ScheduleOfClasses(string semester) {
      Semester = semester;
```

```
// Create a new Dictionary.

SectionsOffered = new Dictionary<string, Section>();
}
```

AddSection Method

Aside from a simple constructor and a Display method, the only other feature that this class provides is a method for adding a Section object to the Dictionary, and then bidirectionally connecting the ScheduleOfClasses object back to the Section.

```
public void AddSection(Section s) {
    // We formulate a key by concatenating the course no.
    // and section no., separated by a hyphen.

    string key = s.RepresentedCourse.CourseNumber+
                " - "+s.SectionNumber;
    SectionsOffered.Add(key, s);

    // Bidirectionally connect the ScheduleOfClasses back to the
    // Section.

    s.OfferedIn = this;
}
```

The TranscriptEntry Association Class (Static Methods)

As we discussed in Chapter 6, the TranscriptEntry class represents a single line item on a student's transcript (see Figure 14-11).

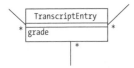

Figure 14-11. *The* TranscriptEntry *class*

This class is implemented in a file named TranscriptEntry.cs. At the top of the code listing is a using statement to access the System namespace and the class header.

```
using System;

public class TranscriptEntry {

    //  TranscriptEntry code listing

}
```

TranscriptEntry Data Elements

As we saw earlier in this chapter, the TranscriptEntry class has a string data element that represents a letter grade, which is implemented using an auto-implemented property. The TranscriptEntry class maintains associations with two other classes:

- *earns grade*, a one-to-many association with Student

- *assigns grade*, a one-to-many association with Section

The *earns grade* and *assigns grade* associations are between the TranscriptEntry, Student, and Section classes, as shown in Figure 14-12.

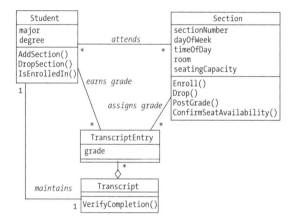

Figure 14-12. *The* TranscriptEntry *class has relationships with other SRS classes.*

TranscriptEntry is at the *many* end of both of these associations, and so it only needs to maintain a single reference to each type of object; no collection fields are required. The associations are all modeled using auto-implemented properties.

```
public Student Student { get; set; }
public Section Section { get; set; }
public string Grade { get; set; }
```

TranscriptEntry Constructor

The constructor for this class does most of the work of maintaining all of these relationships.

```
public TranscriptEntry(Student s, string grade, Section se) {
    Student = s;
    Section = se;
    Grade = grade;

    // Add the TranscriptEntry to the Student's Transcript.

    s.Transcript.AddTranscriptEntry(this);
}
```

Note that we've provided no code in either this or the Student class to provide the Student object with a reference to this TranscriptEntry object. We've made this decision based upon the fact that we don't expect a Student to ever have to manipulate TranscriptEntry objects directly. Every Student object has an indirect means of reaching all of its TranscriptEntry objects, via the reference that a Student object maintains on its Transcript object, and the references that the Transcript object in turn maintains on its TranscriptEntry objects. One might think that giving a Student object the ability to directly pull a given TranscriptEntry might be useful when wishing to determine the grade that the Student earned for a particular Section, but we've provided an alternative means of doing so, via the Section class's GetGrade method.

Even though it may not appear so, we are maintaining the *assigns grade* association with Section bidirectionally. We only see half of the "handshake" in the TranscriptEntry constructor.

```
Section = se;
```

However, recall that when we looked at the PostGrade method of the Section class, we discussed the fact that Section was responsible for maintaining the bidirectionality of this association. When the Section's PostGrade method creates a new TranscriptEntry object, the Section object keeps hold of a reference to the new TranscriptEntry object. So, we only need to worry about the second half of this handshake in TranscriptEntry.

ValidateGrade and PassingGrade Methods

The TranscriptEntry class provides our first SRS example of public static methods: it declares two methods, ValidateGrade and PassingGrade, which may be invoked as utility methods on the TranscriptEntry class from anywhere in the SRS application.

The first method is used to validate whether or not a particular string—say, "B+"—is formatted properly to represent a grade: namely, whether it starts with a capital letter "A," "B," "C," "D," "F," or "I" (for "Incomplete"), followed by an optional + or - character:

```
public static bool ValidateGrade(string grade) {
  bool outcome = false;

  string[] possibleGrades = {"A+", "A", "A-", "B+", "B", "B-",
                             "C+","C", "C-", "D+", "D", "D-",
                             "F", "I" };

  foreach ( string g in possibleGrades ) {
    if ( grade.Equals(g) ) {
      outcome = true;
      break;
    }
  }

  return outcome;
}
```

The second method is used to determine whether or not a particular string—say "D+"—represents a passing grade.

```
public static bool PassingGrade(string grade) {
  // First, make sure it is a valid grade.

  if (!ValidateGrade(grade)) {
    return false;
  }

  // Next, make sure that the grade is a D- or better.

  if (grade.StartsWith("A") || grade.StartsWith("B") ||
      grade.StartsWith("C") || grade.StartsWith("D")) {
    return true;
  }
  else {
    return false;
  }
}
```

As we discussed in Chapters 7 and 13, public static methods are invoked on the hosting class as a whole—in other words, an object needn't be instantiated in order to use these methods.

We'll see actual use of the PassingGrade method in a moment, when we discuss the Transcript class.

The Transcript Class

The Transcript class, shown in Figure 14-13, serves as an abstraction of a student's transcript (i.e., a collection of TranscriptEntry references).

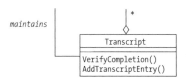

Figure 14-13. *The* Transcript *class*

The Transcript class is implemented in a file named Transcript.cs. At the top of the code listing is a using statement to access the System.Collections.Generic and System namespaces and the class header.

```
using System;
using System.Collections.Generic;

public class Transcript {
```

```
//  Transcript class code listing

}
```

Transcript Data Elements

The Transcript class participates in two relationships:

- *maintains*, a one-to-one association with Student

- An unnamed, one-to-many aggregation with TranscriptEntry

    The first of these relationships is implemented using an auto-implemented property.

```
public Student StudentOwner { get; set; }
```

    We use a List collection to store the TranscriptEntry object references implemented as an auto-implemented property.

```
public List<TranscriptEntry> TranscriptEntries { get; set; }
```

Transcript Constructor

The Transcript class declares one constructor that assigns a value to the StudentOwner property and creates an empty List that stores TranscriptEntry references.

```
public Transcript(Student s) {
  StudentOwner = s;

  // Create an empty List.

  TranscriptEntries = new List<TranscriptEntry>();
}
```

VerifyCompletion Method

The Transcript class has one particularly interesting method, VerifyCompletion, which is used to determine whether or not the Transcript contains evidence that a particular Course requirement has been satisfied. This method steps through the List of TranscriptEntries maintained by the Transcript object.

```
public bool VerifyCompletion(Course c) {
  bool outcome = false;

  // Step through all TranscriptEntries, looking for one
  // that reflects a Section of the Course of interest.
  foreach ( TranscriptEntry te in TranscriptEntries ) {
```

    For each entry, the method obtains a reference to the Section object represented by this entry, and then invokes the IsSectionOf method on that object to determine whether or not that Section represents the Course of interest.

```
    Section s = te.Section;

    if (s.IsSectionOf(c)) {
```

Assuming that the Section is indeed relevant, the method next uses the static PassingGrade method of the TranscriptEntry class to determine whether the grade earned in this Section was a passing grade or not. If it was a passing grade, we can terminate the loop immediately, since we only need to find one example of a passing grade for the Course of interest in order to ensure that the student whose Transcript we are inspecting contains evidence of successful course completion.

```
      // Ensure that the grade was high enough.

      if (TranscriptEntry.PassingGrade(te.Grade)) {
        outcome = true;

        // We've found one, so we can afford to
        // terminate the loop now.

        break;
      }
    }
  }

  return outcome;
}
```

Display Method

The Display method implemented by the Transcript class cycles through the TranscriptEntry references stored in the List and prints out information about them. This method is called from the PrintTranscript method of the Student class.

```
public void Display() {
  Console.WriteLine("Transcript for:   " +
                    this.StudentOwner.ToString());

  if ( TranscriptEntries.Count == 0 ) {
    Console.WriteLine("\t(no entries)");
  }
  else {
    foreach ( TranscriptEntry te in TranscriptEntries ) {
      Section sec = te.Section;
      Course c = sec.RepresentedCourse;
      ScheduleOfClasses soc = sec.OfferedIn;

      Console.WriteLine("\tSemester:      "+soc.Semester);
      Console.WriteLine("\tCourse No.:    "+c.CourseNumber);
      Console.WriteLine("\tCredits:       "+c.Credits);
```

```
            Console.WriteLine("\tGrade Received:  "+te.Grade);
            Console.WriteLine("\t-----");
        }
      }
    }
```

The SRS Driver Program

Now that we've coded all of the classes called for by our model of the SRS, we need a way
to test these. We could wait to put our application through its paces until we've built a GUI
front-end; however, it would be nice to know sooner rather than later that our core classes are
working properly. One helpful technique for doing so is to write a command line–driven program to instantiate objects of varying types and to invoke their critical methods, displaying
the results to the command-line window for us to inspect.

    We've developed just such a program by creating a class called SRS with a Main method
that serves as our test driver. Its basic template is as follows:

```
public class SRS {

  static void Main() {

    //  Body of Main method here.

  }
}
```

Public Static Fields

We're going to instantiate some Professor, Student, Course, and Section objects in this program, so we need a way to organize references to these objects; we'll create collection objects
as fields of the SRS class to hold each of these different object types. While we're at it, we'll
declare them to be public static fields, which means that we're making these main object
collections globally available to the entire application.

```
  // We can effectively create "global" data by declaring
  // public static fields in the main class.

  // Entry points/"roots" for getting at objects.

  public static ScheduleOfClasses scheduleOfClasses =
    new ScheduleOfClasses("SP2009");
  public static List<Professor> faculty;    // List of Professors
  public static List<Student> studentBody;  // List of Students
  public static List<Course> courseCatalog; // List of Courses
```

    The SRS ScheduleOfClasses class serves as a collection point for Section objects; for the
other types of objects, we use simple Lists, although we could go ahead and design classes
comparable to ScheduleOfClasses to serve as encapsulated collections, perhaps named
Faculty, StudentBody, and CourseCatalog, respectively. (In fact, we'll actually do so in

Chapter 15, for reasons that will become clear at that time.) We don't need a collection for Transcript objects—we'll get to these via the references that Student objects maintain—nor do we need one for TranscriptEntry objects—we'll get to these via the Transcript objects themselves.

Main Method

We'll now dive into the Main method for the SRS class. We'll start by declaring reference variables for each of the four main object types.

```
static void Main(string[] args) {
  Professor p1, p2, p3;
  Student s1, s2, s3;
  Course c1, c2, c3, c4, c5;
  Section sec1, sec2, sec3, sec4, sec5, sec6, sec7;
```

We'll then use their various constructors to fabricate object instances, storing references in the appropriate collections. (In Chapter 15, we'll explore how we can instantiate objects by reading data from a file instead of hard-coding literal field values as we have here.)

```
// -----------
// Professors.
// -----------

p1 = new Professor("Jacquie Barker", "123-45-6789",
                   "Adjunct Professor", "Information Technology");
p2 = new Professor("John Carson", "567-81-2345",
                   "Full Professor", "Information Technology");
p3 = new Professor("Jackie Chan", "987-65-4321",
                   "Full Professor", "Information Technology");

// Add these to the appropriate List.

faculty = new List<Professor>();
faculty.Add(p1);
faculty.Add(p2);
faculty.Add(p3);

// ---------
// Students.
// ---------

s1 = new Student("Zachary Palmer", "111-11-1111", "Math", "M.S.");
s2 = new Student("Gerson Lopez", "222-22-2222",
                 "Information Technology", "Ph. D.");
s3 = new Student("Mannat Durgapal", "333-33-3333", "Physics", "B.S.");

// Add these to the appropriate List.
```

```
studentBody = new List<Student>();
studentBody.Add(s1);
studentBody.Add(s2);
studentBody.Add(s3);

// ---------
// Courses.
// ---------

c1 = new Course("CMP101","Beginning Computer Technology", 3.0);
c2 = new Course("OBJ101","Object Methods for Software Development", 3.0);
c3 = new Course("CMP283","Higher Level Languages (C#)", 3.0);
c4 = new Course("CMP999","Living Brain Computers", 3.0);
c5 = new Course("ART101","Beginning Basketweaving", 3.0);

// Add these to the appropriate List.

courseCatalog = new List<Course>();
courseCatalog.Add(c1);
courseCatalog.Add(c2);
courseCatalog.Add(c3);
courseCatalog.Add(c4);
courseCatalog.Add(c5);
```

We use the AddPrerequisite method of the Course class to interrelate some of the Courses, so that c1 is a prerequisite for c2, c2 for c3, and c3 for c4. The only Courses that we don't specify prerequisites for in our test case are c1 and c5.

```
// Establish some prerequisites (c1 => c2 => c3 => c4).

c2.AddPrerequisite(c1);
c3.AddPrerequisite(c2);
c4.AddPrerequisite(c3);
```

To create Section objects, we take advantage of the Course class's ScheduleSection method, which, as you may recall, creates a Section object as part of its duties. Each invocation of ScheduleSection returns a reference to a newly created Section object, which we store in the appropriate collection.

```
// ---------
// Sections.
// ---------

// Schedule sections of each Course by calling the
// ScheduleSection method of Course (which internally
// invokes the Section constructor).

sec1 = c1.ScheduleSection("M", "8:10 - 10:00 PM","GOVT101", 30);
sec2 = c1.ScheduleSection("W", "6:10 - 8:00 PM", "GOVT202", 30);
```

```
sec3 = c2.ScheduleSection("Th", "4:10 - 6:00 PM","GOVT105", 25);
sec4 = c2.ScheduleSection("Tu", "6:10 - 8:00 PM", "SCI330", 25);
sec5 = c3.ScheduleSection("M", "6:10 - 8:00 PM", "GOVT101", 20);
sec6 = c4.ScheduleSection("Th", "4:10 - 6:00 PM", "SCI241", 15);
sec7 = c5.ScheduleSection("F", "4:10 - 6:00 PM", "ARTS25", 40);

// Add these to the Schedule of Classes.

scheduleOfClasses.AddSection(sec1);
scheduleOfClasses.AddSection(sec2);
scheduleOfClasses.AddSection(sec3);
scheduleOfClasses.AddSection(sec4);
scheduleOfClasses.AddSection(sec5);
scheduleOfClasses.AddSection(sec6);
scheduleOfClasses.AddSection(sec7);
```

Next, we use the AgreeToTeach method declared for the Professor class to assign Professor objects to Section objects.

```
// Recruit a professor to teach each of the sections.

p3.AgreeToTeach(sec1);
p2.AgreeToTeach(sec2);
p1.AgreeToTeach(sec3);
p3.AgreeToTeach(sec4);
p1.AgreeToTeach(sec5);
p2.AgreeToTeach(sec6);
p3.AgreeToTeach(sec7);
```

We then simulate student registration by having Students enroll in the various Sections using the Enroll method. Recall that this method returns one of a set of predefined status values—either SUCCESSFULLY_ENROLLED, SECTION_FULL, PREREQ_NOT_SATISFIED, or PREVIOUSLY_ENROLLED from the EnrollFlags enumeration—so in order to display which status is returned in each case, we created a ReportStatus method solely for the purpose of formatting an informational message (the ReportStatus method is discussed separately a bit later):

```
Console.WriteLine("Student registration has begun!");
Console.WriteLine("");

// Students drop/add courses.

Console.WriteLine("Student " + s1.Name +
    " is attempting to enroll in " + sec1.ToString());

// The Enroll method returns one of the EnrollFlags enumeration values.
EnrollFlags status = sec1.Enroll(s1);

// Note the use of a special method to interpret
// and display the outcome of this enrollment request.
```

```
// (We could have included the code inline here, but
// since (a) it is rather complex and (b) it will need
// to be repeated for all subsequent enrollment requests
// below, it made sense to turn it into a reusable method
// instead.)

ReportStatus(status);

Console.WriteLine("Student " + s1.Name +
    " is attempting to enroll in " + sec2.ToString());
status = sec2.Enroll(s1);
ReportStatus(status);

Console.WriteLine("Student " + s2.Name +
    " is attempting to enroll in " + sec2.ToString());
status = sec2.Enroll(s2);
ReportStatus(status);

Console.WriteLine("Student " + s2.Name +
    " is attempting to enroll in " + sec3.ToString());
status = sec3.Enroll(s2);
ReportStatus(status);

Console.WriteLine("Student " + s2.Name +
    " is attempting to enroll in " + sec7.ToString());
status = sec7.Enroll(s2);
ReportStatus(status);

Console.WriteLine("Student " + s3.Name +
    " is attempting to enroll in " + sec1.ToString());
status = sec1.Enroll(s3);
ReportStatus(status);

Console.WriteLine("Student " + s3.Name +
    " is attempting to enroll in " + sec5.ToString());
status = sec5.Enroll(s3);
ReportStatus(status);

// Output a blank line.
Console.WriteLine("");

// When the dust settles, here's what folks wound up
// being registered for:
//    Section sec1:  Students s1, s3
//    Section sec2:  Student s2
//    Section sec7:  Student s2
```

In some cases, the students weren't successful in signing up for a section either because they hadn't met the course prerequisites or because they were already enrolled in a section of the course.

Next, we simulate the assignment of grades at the end of the semester by invoking the postGrade method for each Student-Section combination.

```
// Semester is finished (boy, that was quick!).
// Professors assign grades.

sec1.PostGrade(s1, "C+");
sec1.PostGrade(s3, "A");
sec2.PostGrade(s2, "B+");
sec7.PostGrade(s2, "A-");
```

Finally, we put our various Display methods to good use by displaying the internal state of the various objects that we created—in essence, a data dump.

```
// Let's see if everything got set up properly
// by calling various display methods!

Console.WriteLine("====================");
Console.WriteLine("Schedule of Classes:");
Console.WriteLine("====================");
Console.WriteLine("");
scheduleOfClasses.Display();

Console.WriteLine("======================");
Console.WriteLine("Professor Information:");
Console.WriteLine("======================");
Console.WriteLine("");
p1.Display();
Console.WriteLine("");
p2.Display();
Console.WriteLine("");
p3.Display();
Console.WriteLine("");

Console.WriteLine("====================");
Console.WriteLine("Student Information:");
Console.WriteLine("====================");
Console.WriteLine("");
s1.Display();
Console.WriteLine("");
s2.Display();
Console.WriteLine("");
s3.Display();
}
```

Here is the ReportStatus housekeeping method that we mentioned earlier; it simply translates the various EnrollFlags constant int values into a printed string message:

```
public static void ReportStatus(EnrollFlags status) {
  if (status == EnrollFlags.SUCCESSFULLY_ENROLLED) {
    Console.WriteLine("outcome:  SUCCESSFULLY_ENROLLED");
  } else if (status == EnrollFlags.PREREQ_NOT_SATISFIED) {
    Console.WriteLine("outcome:  PREREQ_NOT_SATISFIED");
  } else if (status == EnrollFlags.PREVIOUSLY_ENROLLED) {
    Console.WriteLine("outcome:  PREVIOUSLY_ENROLLED");
  } else if (status == EnrollFlags.SECTION_FULL) {
    Console.WriteLine("outcome:  SECTION_FULL");
  }
}
```

Compiling the SRS

Now that we've written the initial version of the SRS, we can compile it. The simplest way to compile the source code is with the following command:

```
csc *.cs
```

However, if the code is compiled in this manner, the result will be an executable named Course.exe, because as we discussed in Chapter 13, an executable is by default named after the first source code file that is compiled. A file named Course.exe would indeed serve just fine as the SRS application's executable, but it would be more intuitive if the executable were named SRS.exe. To achieve this end, we can either rename the Course.exe file after the fact, or we can use the /out option when the source code is compiled, as follows:

```
csc /out:SRS.exe *.cs
```

As discussed in Chapter 13, the /out option is used to designate an output file name—in this case, SRS.exe.

We then execute the SRS program simply by typing

```
SRS
```

at the command line.

When compiled and run, the SRS program produces the following command-line window output:

```
Student registration has begun!

Student Zachary Palmer is attempting to enroll in CMP101 - 1 - M - 8:10 - 10:00 PM
outcome:  SUCCESSFULLY_ENROLLED
Student Zachary Palmer is attempting to enroll in CMP101 - 2 - W - 6:10 - 8:00 PM
outcome:  PREVIOUSLY_ENROLLED
Student Gerson Lopez is attempting to enroll in CMP101 - 2 - W - 6:10 - 8:00 PM
outcome:  SUCCESSFULLY_ENROLLED
Student Gerson Lopez is attempting to enroll in OBJ101 - 1 - Th - 4:10 - 6:00 PM
outcome:  PREREQ_NOT_SATISFIED
```

Student Gerson Lopez is attempting to enroll in ART101 - 1 - F - 4:10 - 6:00 PM
outcome: SUCCESSFULLY_ENROLLED
Student Mannat Durgapal is attempting to enroll in CMP101 - 1 - M - 8:10 - 10:00 PM
outcome: SUCCESSFULLY_ENROLLED
Student Mannat Durgapal is attempting to enroll in CMP283 - 1 - M - 6:10 - 8:00 PM
outcome: PREREQ_NOT_SATISFIED

====================
Schedule of Classes:
====================

Schedule of Classes for SP2009

Section Information:
     Semester: SP2009
     Course No.: CMP101
     Section No: 1
     Offered: M at 8:10 - 10:00 PM
     In Room: GOVT101
     Professor: Jackie Chan
     Total of 2 students enrolled, as follows:
          Zachary Palmer
          Mannat Durgapal

Section Information:
     Semester: SP2009
     Course No.: CMP101
     Section No: 2
     Offered: W at 6:10 - 8:00 PM
     In Room: GOVT202
     Professor: John Carson
     Total of 1 students enrolled, as follows:
          Gerson Lopez

Section Information:
     Semester: SP2009
     Course No.: OBJ101
     Section No: 1
     Offered: Th at 4:10 - 6:00 PM
     In Room: GOVT105
     Professor: Jacquie Barker
     Total of 0 students enrolled.

Section Information:
     Semester: SP2009
     Course No.: OBJ101
     Section No: 2

```
     Offered:  Tu at 6:10 - 8:00 PM
     In Room:  SCI330
     Professor:  Jackie Chan
     Total of 0 students enrolled.

Section Information:
     Semester:  SP2009
     Course No.:  CMP283
     Section No:  1
     Offered:  M at 6:10 - 8:00 PM
     In Room:  GOVT101
     Professor:  Jacquie Barker
     Total of 0 students enrolled.

Section Information:
     Semester:  SP2009
     Course No.:  CMP999
     Section No:  1
     Offered:  Th at 4:10 - 6:00 PM
     In Room:  SCI241
     Professor:  John Carson
     Total of 0 students enrolled.

Section Information:
     Semester:  SP2009
     Course No.:  ART101
     Section No:  1
     Offered:  F at 4:10 - 6:00 PM
     In Room:  ARTS25
     Professor:  Jackie Chan
     Total of 1 students enrolled, as follows:
          Gerson Lopez


=======================
Professor Information:
=======================


Person Information:
     Name:  Jacquie Barker
     ID number:  123-45-6789
Professor-Specific Information:
     Title:  Adjunct Professor
     Teaches for Dept.:  Information Technology
Teaching Assignments for Jacquie Barker:
     Course No.:  OBJ101
     Section No.:  1
     Course Name:  Object Methods for Software Development
```

```
      Day and Time:  Th - 4:10 - 6:00 PM
      -----
      Course No.:  CMP283
      Section No.:  1
      Course Name:  Higher Level Languages (C#)
      Day and Time:  M - 6:10 - 8:00 PM
      -----


Person Information:
      Name:  John Carson
      ID number:  567-81-2345
Professor-Specific Information:
      Title:  Full Professor
      Teaches for Dept.:  Chemistry
Teaching Assignments for John Carson:
      Course No.:  CMP101
      Section No.:  2
      Course Name:  Beginning Computer Technology
      Day and Time:  W - 6:10 - 8:00 PM
      -----
      Course No.:  CMP999
      Section No.:  1
      Course Name:  Living Brain Computers
      Day and Time:  Th - 4:10 - 6:00 PM
      -----


Person Information:
      Name:  Jackie Chan
      ID number:  987-65-4321
Professor-Specific Information:
      Title:  Full Professor
      Teaches for Dept.:  Physical Education
Teaching Assignments for Jackie Chan:
      Course No.:  CMP101
      Section No.:  1
      Course Name:  Beginning Computer Technology
      Day and Time:  M - 8:10 - 10:00 PM
      -----
      Course No.:  OBJ101
      Section No.:  2
      Course Name:  Object Methods for Software Development
      Day and Time:  Tu - 6:10 - 8:00 PM
      -----
      Course No.:  ART101
      Section No.:  1
      Course Name:  Beginning Basketweaving
      Day and Time:  F - 4:10 - 6:00 PM
```

```
     -----


====================
Student Information:
====================


Person Information:
     Name:  Zachary Palmer
     ID number:  111-11-1111
Student-Specific Information:
     Major:  Math
     Degree:  M.S.
Course Schedule for Zachary Palmer
Transcript for:  Zachary Palmer (111-11-1111) [M.S. - Math]
     Semester:        SP2009
     Course No.:      CMP101
     Credits:         3
     Grade Received:  C+
     -----


Person Information:
     Name:  Gerson Lopez
     ID number:  222-22-2222
Student-Specific Information:
     Major:  Information Technology
     Degree:  Ph. D.
Course Schedule for Gerson Lopez
Transcript for:  Gerson Lopez (222-22-2222) [Ph. D. - Information Technology]
     Semester:        SP2009
     Course No.:      CMP101
     Credits:         3
     Grade Received:  B+
     -----
     Semester:        SP2009
     Course No.:      ART101
     Credits:         3
     Grade Received:  A-
     -----


Person Information:
     Name:  Mannat Durgapal
     ID number:  333-33-3333
Student-Specific Information:
     Major:  Physics
     Degree:  B.S.
Course Schedule for Mannat Durgapal
Transcript for:  Mannat Durgapal (333-33-3333) [B.S. - Physics]
```

```
Semester:       SP2009
Course No.:     CMP101
Credits:        3
Grade Received: A
-----  -----
```

The preceding output demonstrates that the SRS is working properly! Of course, the SRS driver program could be extended to test various other scenarios; some of the exercises at the end of this chapter suggest ways that you might wish to try doing so.

Summary

You've now seen C# in action! We've built a command line–driven version of the SRS application; although this isn't typically how most applications are invoked—most industrial-strength applications have GUI front-ends—developing such a version is a crucial step in testing your core classes to ensure that all methods are working properly. And, aside from the various Display methods that we encoded for testing purposes, most of the code that we've written for the command-line version of the application will carry forward intact when we round out the application in the next two chapters.

Exercises

All of the following exercises involve making modifications/extensions to the SRS code presented in this chapter. If you haven't already done so, please download the code from the Apress web site in preparation for these exercises; see Appendix B for details.

1. Expand the SRS.cs class's Main method to represent a second semester's worth of course registrations. (Hint: this will require a second instantiation of the ScheduleOfClasses class.)

   Change the grades received by some Students in the first semester to failing grades, then attempt to register a Student for a course in the second semester requiring successful completion in a previous semester.

   Try registering a Student for a course in the second semester that he or she has already successfully completed in the first semester.

2. Improve the logic of the AddPrerequisite method of the Course class to ensure that a Course can't accidentally be assigned as its own prerequisite.

3. Improve the logic of the AgreeToTeach method of the Professor class so that a Professor can't accidentally agree to teach two different Sections that meet at the same day/time.

4. Implement a CancelSection method for the Course class, and then correct the erroneous logic of the ScheduleSection method having to do with the manner in which Section numbers are assigned. (Hint: introduce a static field to the Course class for this purpose and increment it every time a new Section is created, so there is no possibility of duplicate session numbers if a Section is cancelled later on.)

5. The Enroll method of the Section class doesn't take into account the fact that a Student may simultaneously be registered for a course and its prerequisite. Modify this method to allow for this possibility.

6. The PostGrade method of the Section class makes mention of the need for an EraseGrade method, in the event that a Professor wishes to change his or her mind about the grade that has been issued to a Student; create the EraseGrade method.

7. *Advanced exercise*: Modify the ScheduleSection method of the Course class to prevent two Sections from being scheduled for the same classroom at the same day/time.

8. *Advanced exercise*: The Display method of the ScheduleOfClasses class doesn't presently list Sections in alphabetically sorted order by course name; make whatever changes are necessary to do so.

CHAPTER 15

■■■

Rounding Out Our Application, Part 1: Adding File Persistence

In Chapter 14, we built our first version of the Student Registration System (SRS) as a command line–driven application that focused on the domain classes called out by our model: Person, Professor, Student, Course, Section, ScheduleOfClasses, Transcript, and TranscriptEntry. The Main method of the SRS driver class was written simply to instantiate objects of the various types and to put them through their paces, as a means of testing that we've implemented the logic of their methods correctly. But, the SRS application as written isn't useful as an industrial-strength application yet because

- It uses string and numerical literals declared in the Main method of the driver code to initialize all of its objects/data.

- It provides no means of saving the state of the objects from one invocation of the application to the next—a process known as *persisting data*.

- Most industrial-strength information systems requiring significant user interaction rely on a graphical user interface (GUI) for such interaction.

In essence, we've developed the core of our application by creating the classes that represent the domain model. In this chapter, we're going to revise our SRS application to provide a means for reading/writing data to/from files so that we can remedy the first two of these shortcomings; then, in Chapter 16, we'll remedy the third deficiency by adding a GUI front-end, as shown in Figure 15-1.

In this chapter, you'll get to apply much of what you've learned about C# in Chapter 13 and actually see it in action in the SRS. You'll also learn the following:

- How we approach file input/output (I/O) in C#

- An approach for parsing tab-delimited ASCII records to initialize an object's state or to initialize a collection of objects

- A means of persisting an object's state in a simple ASCII file

- How to prepare a "test scaffold" Main method for testing isolated classes, similar to what we did in Chapter 14

- How proper encapsulation streamlines client code (for example, the SRS Main method)

- A little bit about the differences between character- and binary-based I/O

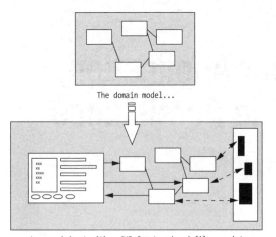

The domain model...

...gets rounded out with a GUI front end and file persistence.

Figure 15-1. *Adding file persistence and a GUI front end to the SRS*

What Is Persistence?

Whenever we run a program such as our SRS application, any objects (or value types, for that matter) that we declare and instantiate live in memory. When the program terminates, all of the memory allocated to the program is released back to the operating system, and the internal states of all of the objects created by the application are lost unless they have been saved—*persisted*—in some fashion.

Using various built-in I/O classes in the .NET Framework Class Library (FCL), C# provides a wealth of options with regard to persisting data.

- The programming elements found in the System.Data, System.Data.Odbc, System.Data.OleDb, System.Data.SqlClient, and System.Data.Oracle namespaces allow us to save data to an Open Database Connectivity (ODBC) database, an Object Linking and Embedding Database (OLE DB), or an Oracle database.

- We can output whole objects in a special binary form known as a C# *serialized object*, ideal for distributing objects over a network.

- We can also save information in a fairly straightforward, human-readable ASCII data format, as either of the following:

  - Hierarchically arranged data, such as with the Extensible Markup Language (XML) standard, in which we intersperse information—*content*—with *custom tags* that describe how the information is to be interpreted. For example, this simple example illustrates a Professor object with two Student advisees:

    ```
    <Professor>
      <name>Dr. Irving Smith</name>
      <id>123-45-6789</id>
      <title>Associate Professor</title>
      <advisee>
    ```

```
      <type>Student</type>
      <sname>Gerson Lopez</sname>
      <sid>987-65-4321</sid>
    </advisee>
    <advisee>
      <type>Student</type>
      <sname>Mary Jones</sname>
      <sid>999-88-7777</sid>
    </advisee>
  </Professor>
```

- Simple tab- or comma-delimited record-oriented data, like this:

```
222-22-2222  Gerson Lopez  Information Technology  Ph. D.  ART101-1
```

We'll be illustrating the most basic form of data persistence—*record-oriented ASCII file persistence*—in our SRS application code. However, many of the same design issues are applicable to the other forms of persistence as well, such as

- *Hiding the details of how we persist an object*: By encapsulating the details within an object's methods, the client code doesn't have to get bogged down with the details.

- *Ensuring that whatever approach we take to persisting an object today is flexible*: This allows us to swap out one approach and swap in another without making dramatic changes to our entire application.

- *Providing exception handling when something goes amiss*: Since persistence involves interacting with an external file system, database management system, and/or network, there are a lot of potential points of failure that are outside of the immediate program's control.

Before we discuss the two "sides" to the file-persistence "coin"—writing an object's state out to a file, and reading it back in again later—let's talk briefly about C# exception handling, which is an important (and necessary) part of writing code to read and write data.

C# Exception Handling

Exceptions are a way for the .NET runtime to signal that something has gone wrong during program execution—that something could potentially cause a program to abort. One such situation would be trying to access a nonexistent object, as in the following example:

```
Student s1 = new Student();
Student s2 = null;

s1.Name = "Fred";  // this line is fine
s2.Name = "Mary";  // this line throws an exception
```

Let's explore what is happening in the preceding code.

We declare two Student object references but only instantiate *one* Student object; s2 is assigned the value null, indicating that it isn't presently holding onto any object.

```
Student s1 = new Student();
Student s2 = null;
```

When we subsequently attempt to assign a value to the Name property of s1, all is well.

```
s1.Name = "Fred";  // this line is fine
```

However, this next line of code throws a NullReferenceException at run time, because we are trying to access a property of a nonexistent object:

```
s2.Name = "Mary"; // throws an exception
```

Exception handling enables a programmer to gracefully anticipate and handle such exceptions by providing a way for a program to automatically transfer control from within the block of code where the exception arose—known as a try block—to a special error-handling code block known as a catch block.

The Mechanics of Exception Handling

The mechanics of exception handling are as follows:

- We place code that is likely to throw an exception inside of a pair of braces {...}, then place the keyword try just ahead of the opening brace for that block to signal the fact that we intend to catch exceptions thrown within that block.

  ```
  try {
    code likely to cause problems goes in here...
  }
  ```

  This is known as a try block.

- A try block must also be accompanied by either: (a) one (or more) catch blocks, (b) a finally block, or (c) a combination of (a) and (b).

- Each catch block begins with a catch clause of the form

  ```
  catch (exception_type variable_name)
  ```

  that declares which category of exception it will catch, along with a reference variable name to represent the exception object being thrown so that we may manipulate the exception object from within the catch block if desired. The contents of the catch block represent the "recovery" code that is to be automatically executed upon occurrence of that exception.

  ```
  try {
    code likely to cause problems goes in here...
  }
  catch (exception_type_1 variable_name_1) {
    recovery code for the first exception type goes here...
  }
  catch (exception_type_2 variable_name_2) {
  ```

```
    recovery code for the second exception type goes here...
}
// etc.
```

- We can also optionally specify a block of code that will *always* execute regardless of whether an exception has occurred in the try block or not. Known as a finally block, this block of code is preceded by the finally keyword and follows the last catch block (if any are present). A finally block is typically used to perform any necessary cleanup operations, such as perhaps closing either a file or a connection to a database.

```
try {
    code likely to cause problems goes in here...
}
catch (exception_type_1 variable_name) {
    recovery code for the first exception type goes here...
}
catch (exception_type_2 variable_name) {
    recovery code for the second exception type goes here...
}
finally {
    perform cleanup operations...
}
```

Alternative paths through a try-catch block *without* an optional finally block are illustrated in Figure 15-2. When an exception occurs inside the try block, the runtime compares the exception type against the exception types that are declared in the catch clauses. If a match is found, the code inside the corresponding catch block will be executed, and the code will jump to the next line of code following the last catch block. If a matching catch clause is not found, the code execution will transfer directly to the next line of code following the last catch block without executing the code in *any* of the catch blocks.

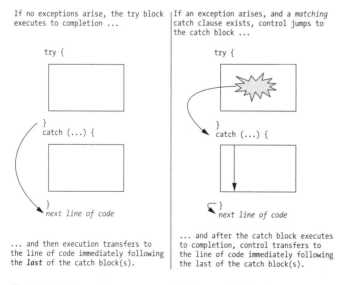

Figure 15-2. *Execution sequence for* try-catch *blocks*

Alternative paths through a try-catch block *with* an optional finally block are illustrated in Figure 15-3. The initial execution is the same as before: the runtime compares the type of exception thrown in the try block against those declared in the catch clauses and executes code inside the corresponding catch block if a match is found. The difference here is that the code inside the finally block is always executed whether or not a matching catch clause is found.

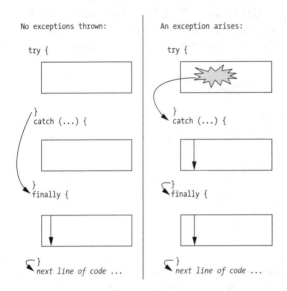

Figure 15-3. *Execution sequence for* try-catch-finally *blocks*

If none of the catch blocks match when an exception is thrown, the current method will exit after the try or finally block has executed, and control will pass back to the calling method to see if it has a suitable catch block (see Figure 15-4).

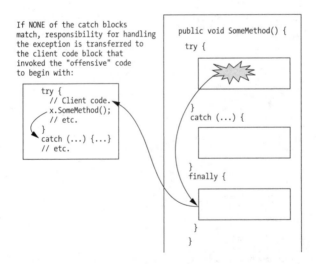

Figure 15-4. *If no* catch *blocks match, the exception is thrown to the calling method.*

Going back to our previous example involving Student objects, here's an enhanced version of the code that employs exception handling:

```
// We declare two Student object references, but only instantiate
// one Student object; s2 is given a value of null, indicating
// that it isn't presently holding onto any object.
Student s1 = new Student();
Student s2 = null;

// Exception handling is now in place.
try {
  Console.WriteLine("Initializing students...");

  // This line executes without throwing an exception.
  s1.Name = "Fred";

  // This next line of code throws a NullReferenceException at run
  // time because s2 was never initialized to refer to an actual
  // Student object...
  s2.Name = "Mary";

  // ...and as soon as the exception is detected by the runtime,
  // execution jumps out of the try block -- none of the remaining
  // code in this try block will be executed -- and into the first
  // catch block below that is found to match a
  // NullReferenceException, if any.

  s1.Major = "MATH";
  s2.Major = "SCIENCE";

  Console.WriteLine("Initialization successfully completed.");
} // end of try block
// Pseudocode.
catch (UnrelatedExceptionType e1) {
  // exception handling code for this type of (hypothetical)
  // exception goes here...but, since our example doesn't
  // involve throwing this particular type of exception at run
  // time, this catch block will be skipped over without
  // being executed.
  Console.WriteLine("UnrelatedExceptionType was detected...");
}
catch (NullReferenceException e2) {
  // Here's where we place the code for what the program should do
  // if a null reference was detected at run time.
  Console.WriteLine("Oops -- we forgot to initialize all of the students!");
}
finally {
  // This code gets executed whether or not an exception occurred:
```

```
    // that is whether we made it through the try block without any
    // exceptions being thrown, or whether one of the catch blocks
    // was triggered.
    Console.WriteLine("Finally!!!");
}

// After the finally block executes, control transfers to the
// line of code immediately following the finally block.
Console.WriteLine("Continuing along our merry way...");
```

When the previous code is executed, the following output results:

```
Initializing students...
Whoops -- we forgot to initialize all of the students!
Finally!!!
Continuing along our merry way...
```

because both the second catch block and the finally block will have executed. The previous example is intended to show basic exception-handling syntax. In reality, because exception handling requires the runtime to expend a lot of energy, performance would be better if an if-test were performed to determine if a reference were null to preempt the possibility of an exception being thrown.

```
if ( s2 != null ) {
  s2.Major = "SCIENCE";
}
```

Note that nothing needs to be done from a programming perspective to *explicitly* transfer control from the try block to the appropriate catch block—that is, there is no "jump" type statement required; the runtime handles this transfer automatically as needed.

■**Note** Much of the code in this section of the chapter is shown as snippets rather than full code listings, but you can download full, working versions of the example code from the Apress web site (http://www.apress.com) so you can look at and test the examples yourself.

The Exception Class Hierarchy

The System.Exception class is the base class of all exceptions in the C# language. For example, the System.IO.IOException class is derived from System.Exception and collectively represents any of the things that can go wrong when performing IO operations; the System.IO.FileNotFoundException class is in turn a derived class of System.IO.IOException, and represents a specific IO problem.

By virtue of the "is a" nature of inheritance, a FileNotFoundException is also both an IOException and a generic Exception, all rolled into one, so we can catch it as any one of these three exception types.

Sequential Evaluation of catch Clauses

The catch clauses for a given try block are examined in order from top to bottom. The run-time compares the type of exception that has been thrown with the exception type declared to be caught for each catch clause until it finds a match—either an exact match or a match with a base class of the exception type—and then executes the code enclosed in the braces immediately following the matching catch clause; note that only the *first* such match is executed.

```
try {
  // File IO operations are being performed here...details omitted.
}
catch (FileNotFoundException e1) {
  Console.WriteLine("FileNotFoundException detected!");

  // Pseudocode.
  recovery code would go here...
}
catch (IOException e2) {
  Console.WriteLine("IOException detected!");

  // Pseudocode.
  recovery code would go here...
}
catch (Exception e3) {
  // Note: "Exception" is the base class for all exception types,
  // and hence a "catch (Exception e)" block is a "catch-all" for
  // any exceptions that weren't a match for any of the preceding
  // catch clauses.
  Console.WriteLine("Exception detected!");

  // Pseudocode.
  recovery code would go here...
}
```

Let's examine the output that would occur if various types of exceptions were to arise while the try block of this example is executing:

- If a FileNotFoundException is thrown, this code would print this output:

  FileNotFoundException detected!

- If some other type of IOException is thrown while the try block is executing, this code would print this output:

  IOException detected!

  Of course, catching an IOException could in theory take care of any FileNotFoundExceptions that arise, except for the fact that this catch clause occurs *after* an explicit catch of FileNotFoundException.

- And if any type of exception other than an IOException were to be thrown—say, a NullReferenceException—then the output would be

Exception detected!

The generic Exception type can be used in the last catch block of a try block (as shown in the preceding code) to literally serve as a "catch-all" if desired.

Proper Ordering of catch Blocks

The preceding example illustrates the fact that catch blocks for derived types must precede catch blocks for base types; otherwise, a compiler error will occur. The following code snippet wouldn't even compile:

```
try {
  // File IO operations are being performed here...details omitted.
}
catch (IOException e2) {
  // This block will catch all types of IOExceptions, INCLUDING
  // FileNotFoundExceptions specifically.

  //Pseudocode.
  recovery code for handling IOExceptions generally...
}
catch (FileNotFoundException e1) {
  // This block will never be executed because
  // FileNotFoundException is a derived class of IOException.

  //Pseudocode.
  recovery code for handling FileNotFoundExceptions specifically...
}
```

Referencing the Thrown Exception Object

Exception classes are like any other classes in that they define properties and methods with which to manipulate exception objects. As we've previously seen, a reference to the exception object being caught is included in the declaration of a catch clause. This reference is locally scoped to/available inside of the catch block, and provides us with a reference with which to call methods on or invoke properties of the exception object. For example, we may wish to access an exception's type-specific message via the Message property.

```
catch (IOException e) {
  Console.WriteLine(e.Message);
}
```

In the preceding code snippet, an instance of the IOException class named e is declared in a catch clause. Inside the catch block, the Message property is invoked on reference variable e to write a message to the console explaining the nature of the exception; an example of such a message is

Could not find file "C:\MyDocs\default.dat"

▓**Note** Another useful Exception class property is the Source property, used to determine the application or object that triggered the exception. For a complete listing of methods/properties available for each of the derived exception types, please consult the FCL Reference on the MSDN web site.

User-Defined Exceptions

In addition to the exception classes provided by the FCL, it's also possible in C# to declare user-defined, application-specific exception types by extending the System.Exception class or any of its derived classes. We then may explicitly instantiate and throw such exceptions to signal problems when they arise. Defining and then subsequently throwing custom exception types is a popular technique for signaling that an application-specific problem has taken place.

As an example of creating a user-defined exception, let's define a class called InvalidStudentIdException, derived from the Exception class, to signal a problem when an attempt is made to instantiate a Student object with an invalid student ID. The InvalidStudentIdException class simply declares two constructors that call the one-parameter Exception constructor and change the default value of the Message property of the Exception class.

```
using System;

public class InvalidStudentIdException : Exception {

  //  This message will be assigned to the Message property
  //  of the InvalidStudentIdException. It's declared to be
  //  a const (and therefore static) string.
  const string baseMessage = "Error: Invalid student ID: ";

  // The constructors call the Exception constructor,
  // changing the default Message property of the
  // Exception class.

  //  Zero-parameter constructor assigns baseMessage to Message
  public InvalidStudentIdException() : base(baseMessage) {
  }

  //  One-parameter constructor adds the invalid Student ID.
  public InvalidStudentIdException(string id) : base(baseMessage+id) {
  }
}
```

Next, we'll take advantage of our user-defined exception in the constructor of the Student class to enforce the fact that we want a student's ID to be 11 characters long. (There are most likely other considerations that we'd also check, such as ensuring that the ID consists of only numeric characters and hyphens arranged in a certain sequence, but for this simple example, we'll only test for the number of characters.) If the number of characters in the string passed as an argument to the Student constructor doesn't equal 11, we'll want the Student constructor to send up a signal flare (i.e., to throw a new instance of an InvalidStudentIdException object using the throw keyword).

Here is the code listing of the Student class; once again, we've kept this example simple by having the Student class declare a single auto-implemented property named Id and a single constructor to assign an initial value to the property:

```
public class Student {

  // Constructor
  public Student(string id) {
    // Test to see if the string passed to the constructor
    // has 11 characters. If the string doesn't, it doesn't
    // represent a proper student ID and an
    // InvalidStudentIdException is thrown.
    if ( id.Length != 11 ) {
      throw new InvalidStudentIdException(id);
    }

    // If the string passed to the constructor has 11
    // characters, assign the Id property to it.
    Id = id;
  }

  // Declare an auto-implemented property representing a student ID.
  public string Id { get; set; }
}
```

We must now add the necessary exception-handling logic to our application to detect such exceptions. Because the Student constructor can now throw an InvalidStudentIdException, we place all client code logic for instantiating Student objects inside a try-catch block; the catch clause will specify the InvalidStudentIdException type.

In this first example, a valid 11-character string is passed to the Student constructor:

```
using System;

public class ExceptionDemo
{
  public static void Main() {
    Student s;

    try {
      //  This is a valid student ID
      s = new Student("123-45-6789");

    }
    catch (InvalidStudentIdException ex) {
      Console.WriteLine(ex.Message);
      s = new Student("???-??-????");
```

```
        }

      // Write out the student ID
      Console.WriteLine("Student ID = "+s.Id);
    }
  }
```

When this code snippet is run, an InvalidStudentIdException is *not* thrown, and so the output will be as follows:

```
Student ID = 123-45-6789
```

However, if we change the code snippet such that an invalid student ID is passed as an argument to the Student constructor

```
using System;

public class ExceptionDemo
{
  public static void Main() {
    Student s;

    try {

      //  This is an invalid student ID
      s = new Student("123-45-67");
    }
    catch (InvalidStudentIdException ex) {
      Console.WriteLine(ex.Message);
      s = new Student("???-??-????");
    }

    // Write out the student ID
    Console.WriteLine("Student ID = "+s.Id);
  }
}
```

an InvalidStudentIdException *is* thrown, the catch block is executed, and the output is instead as follows:

```
Error: Invalid student ID: 123-45-67
Student ID = ???-??-????
```

■**Note** While we chose not to take advantage of user-defined exceptions in building the SRS, this is nonetheless an important technique to be aware of. User-defined exceptions are valuable any time you want to get more information about an application-specific exception than is provided by the .NET FCL exception classes' default exceptions.

Compiler-Mandated Exception Handling

Many programming languages support the notion of exception handling. In some of these languages—Java, for example—the compiler will mandate try statements in certain situations. That is, in Java, if we were to try to write the following logic without an enclosing try statement:

```
// Pseudocode.
string filename = the name of a file provided by a user via a GUI;
attempt to open the filename file;
```

the Java compiler would generate an error message, forcing us to deal with the potential for an exception in some fashion.

In contrast, the C# compiler doesn't mandate exception handling; if we choose to write code such as that just shown in C#, it will indeed compile, but of course if an IOException arises at run time that we haven't provided recovery code for, the runtime will abruptly terminate the program's execution. So, while the use of try statements for code that can throw exceptions isn't mandatory in C#, inclusion of explicit exception-handling code is nonetheless highly desirable because it's the only mechanism with which to gracefully anticipate and handle certain run-time issues.

Reading Data from or Writing Data to a File

Now that we've finished introducing exception handling, we're ready to dive into how to read data from or write data to a file using the I/O classes provided by the .NET FCL. We accomplish the I/O functionality in .NET using the concept of data streams. An input stream is opened to a data source (a file, for example), and the input data is pulled into the input stream, where we can read it inside a program. Similarly, we can place data from the program into an output stream, where it can flow (e.g., be written) to an output destination such as a file. When we provide the I/O functionality for the final version of the SRS, we'll be using the FileStream class extensively to read data from or write data to files.

The FileStream Class

The FileStream class is part of the System.IO namespace. A FileStream object is a type of C# object that knows how to open a file and either read data from the file or write data to the file, one byte at a time. The FileStream class defines a number of constructors. One of the simpler constructors has the following header:

```
public FileStream(string filename, int mode)
```

An example of using this constructor to create a FileStream object is as follows:

```
FileStream fileStream = new FileStream("data.dat", FileMode.Open);
```

where mode is one of several constants defined by the FileMode enumeration:

- FileMode.Open opens an existing file for either reading or writing; if the file in question doesn't exist, a FileNotFoundException will be thrown.

- FileMode.Create creates a new file. If the file already exists, it will be overwritten. If the file can't be created for some reason—e.g., if the target directory is write-protected— then an IOException will be thrown.

- `FileMode.Append` opens an existing file and moves the stream location to the end of the file; if the specified file isn't found, a new file will be created.

- `FileMode.CreateNew` creates a new file. If the file already exists, an `IOException` will be thrown.

- `FileMode.OpenOrCreate` will open a file if it exists or will create a new file if the file does not exist.

- `FileMode.Truncate` opens an existing file and truncates the data in the file so the file size is 0 bytes. Attempting to read from a file opened with `Truncate` causes an exception to be thrown.

Reading from a File

The basic C# approach that we're going to use for reading records one by one from an ASCII file involves *two* types C# objects—a `FileStream` object and a `StreamReader` object (see Figure 15-5).

1. First, we create an object of type `FileStream`, which as we've already mentioned knows how to open a file and read data from the file one byte at a time in a stream, which is written to a physical memory register—hence, the name `FileStream`.

2. Next, we pass a reference to that `FileStream` object as an argument to the constructor for a `StreamReader`, a more sophisticated type of object that is effectively "wrapped around" the `FileStream` by passing a reference to the `FileStream` object to the `StreamReader` constructor. The `StreamReader`'s `ReadLine` method knows how to internally collect up, or *buffer*, individual characters as read by the `FileStream` until an end-of-line character is detected, at which point the `StreamReader` hands back a complete line/record of data to the client code. In other words, the `StreamReader` class allows data to be read from an ASCII input file one line at a time.

The `StreamReader` class is also defined in the `System.IO` namespace.

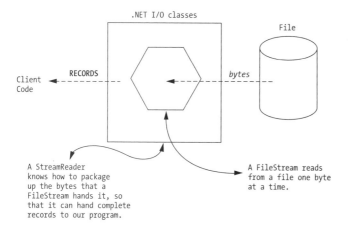

Figure 15-5. *Reading character data from a file, C# style*

Here is an example to illustrate the general process of reading from a file; we've left out some details, but you'll see this process carried out in earnest in the various SRS classes that we'll be reviewing later on in this chapter. We'll present the example in its entirety first, and then we'll highlight some noteworthy points afterward.

```
using System.IO;

public class IOExample
{
  static void Main() {
    // Declare references to the objects that we'll need
    // in order to read from a file.
    FileStream fileStream;
    StreamReader reader;

    // Read operations should be placed in a try-catch block.
    try {
      // Create a FileStream...
      fileStream = new FileStream("data.dat", FileMode.Open);

      // ...and a StreamReader based on that FileStream.
      reader = new StreamReader(fileStream);

      // Read the first line from the file.
      string line = reader.ReadLine();

      // As long as the line isn't null, keep going!
      while (line != null) {
        // Pseudocode.
        // process the most recently read line

        // Read another line (will be set to null when
        // the file has been exhausted).
        line = reader.ReadLine();
      }
    }
    catch (IOException ioe) {
      // Perform exception handling...details omitted.
    }
    finally {
      // Close the StreamReader, which causes the FileStream to
      // also be closed.
      if ( reader != null ) {
        reader.Close();
      }
    }
  }
}
```

Narrating our example:

- Because so many things can potentially go wrong when attempting to perform file I/O—a file that we're trying to open may not exist, a file that we want to write data to may have read-only protection, and so forth—we must place our code within a try block, and provide code to catch and respond to potential IOExceptions.

- We want to read data from an existing file, and so the FileMode.Open parameter is being passed to the FileStream constructor:

  ```
  fileStream = new FileStream("data.dat", FileMode.Open);
  ```

- We then "wrap" a StreamReader around the FileStream by passing a reference to the FileStream object to the StreamReader constructor to allow us to read data from the file a line at a time using the ReadLine method of the StreamReader class:

  ```
  reader = new StreamReader(fileStream);
  ```

  To make the code more compact, we could have combined the previous two statements into a single line.

  ```
  reader = new StreamReader(new FileStream("data.dat", FileMode.Open));
  ```

- We use the StreamReader's ReadLine method to read one line/record's worth of data at a time.

  ```
  string line = reader.ReadLine();
  ```

  As long as this method doesn't return a value of null—null signals that the end of file has been reached—then we know that we've read in a legitimate record from the file.

  ```
  // As long as the line isn't null, keep going!
  while (line != null) {...}
  ```

- We must remember to read another record's worth of data from within the while loop so that we don't wind up creating an infinite loop:

  ```
  line = reader.ReadLine();
  ```

- Finally, we must remember to close the StreamReader, which also closes the FileStream. This is performed inside a finally block, so the stream closes whether an exception is thrown or not.

  ```
  reader.Close();
  ```

  It's important to remember to close a StreamReader when we're finished with a file for several reasons:

  - So that the file won't remain open/locked to subsequent access

  - So that the application as a whole won't exceed the (platform-dependent) maximum allowable open-file limit

  - For the general good of freeing up unused objects so that the memory allocated to them will be subject to garbage collection

Writing to a File

The basic C# approach that we'll be using for writing records to an ASCII file is similar to what we've used to read character data from a file: we use a FileStream object to open the file to which the data will be written. We write the character data to the file using the StreamWriter class, which is derived from the TextWriter class. You can find both the StreamWriter and TextWriter classes in the System.IO namespace. Figure 15-6 depicts the general process for writing character data to a file.

1. We again create an object of type FileStream; by specifying the appropriate mode to the FileStream constructor, we can use the FileStream to overwrite an existing file (FileMode.Open), append data to an existing file (FileMode.Append), create a new file (FileMode.Create), or combine the previous two approaches (FileMode.OpenOrCreate).

2. We pass that FileStream object as an argument to the constructor for a StreamWriter, a more sophisticated type of object that is "wrapped around" the FileStream. The StreamWriter's WriteLine method knows how to pass an entire record/line's worth of data, one character at a time, to its encapsulated FileStream object, which then outputs the data one byte at a time to the file.

The StreamWriter class inherits the WriteLine method from the TextWriter class. The method works in a similar fashion to the Console.WriteLine method that you're already familiar with, the only difference being that the former causes text to be written to a file or output stream, whereas the latter causes text to be displayed in the command-line window. StreamWriter also defines a Write method, which works exactly like the Console.Write method.

We'll see this carried out in earnest in the Student class, which we'll be reviewing in detail later in this chapter, but for now, here's the general approach; because this code is so similar to the previous IOExample, we'll present it without narration here—please refer to the in-line comments:

```
using System.IO;

public class IOExample2
{
  static void Main() {
    FileStream fileStream;
    StreamWriter writer;

    // Write operations should be placed in a try-catch block.
    try {
      // Create a FileStream...
      fileStream = new FileStream("data.dat", FileMode.OpenOrCreate);

      // ...and a StreamWriter based on that FileStream.
      writer = new StreamWriter(fileStream);

      // Pseudocode.
      while (still want to print more) {
```

```
      writer.WriteLine(whatever string data we wish to output);
    }
  }
  catch (IOException ioe) {
    // perform some exception handling
  }
    finally {
      // Close the StreamWriter, which causes the FileStream to
      // also be closed.
      if ( writer != null ) {
        writer.Close();
      }
    }
  }
}
```

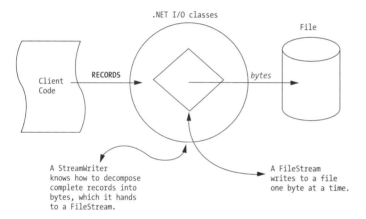

Figure 15-6. *Writing character data to a file, C# style*

We'll follow this basic approach of using FileStream, StreamReader, and StreamWriter objects inside try-catch-finally blocks when we persist the results of a student registration session to a file; we'll discuss this in detail later in the chapter.

Populating the Main SRS Collections

In Chapter 14, we introduced the ScheduleOfClasses class as a means of encapsulating a collection of Section objects, but all of the work necessary to populate this collection was performed in the Main method of the SRS class. By way of review, we first instantiated a ScheduleOfClasses object.

```
ScheduleOfClasses scheduleOfClasses =
  new ScheduleOfClasses("SP2009");
```

Next, we called the ScheduleSection method on various Course objects named c1 through c5 from the SRS Main method to instantiate seven Section objects named sec1 through sec7, using hard-coded field values.

```
sec1 = c1.ScheduleSection("M", "8:10 - 10:00 PM", "GOVT101", 30);
sec2 = c1.ScheduleSection("W", "6:10 - 8:00 PM", "GOVT202", 30);
sec3 = c2.ScheduleSection("Th", "4:10 - 6:00 PM", "GOVT105", 25);
sec4 = c2.ScheduleSection("Tu", "6:10 - 8:00 PM", "SCI330", 25);
sec5 = c3.ScheduleSection("M", "6:10 - 8:00 PM", "GOVT101", 20);
sec6 = c4.ScheduleSection("Th", "4:10 - 6:00 PM", "SCI241", 15);
sec7 = c5.ScheduleSection("F", "4:10 - 6:00 PM", "ARTS25", 40);
```

We then invoked the AddSection method on the scheduleOfClasses object numerous times to add these Sections to its encapsulated collection.

```
// Add these to the Schedule of Classes.

scheduleOfClasses.AddSection(sec1);
scheduleOfClasses.AddSection(sec2);
scheduleOfClasses.AddSection(sec3);
scheduleOfClasses.AddSection(sec4);
scheduleOfClasses.AddSection(sec5);
scheduleOfClasses.AddSection(sec6);
scheduleOfClasses.AddSection(sec7);
```

Rather than hard-coding the information about these Sections in the Main method of the SRS class, we're now going to acquire this information dynamically from an ASCII file. In fact, while we're at it, we're going to acquire *all* of the data needed to initialize the SRS application's primary object collections from ASCII files. This includes

- The schedule of classes itself

- The course catalog—that is, a list of courses on which the schedule of classes is based, along with information about which course is a prerequisite of which other(s)

- The faculty roster, along with information regarding which professor is scheduled to teach which section(s)

These latter two collections haven't appeared in our object model before, because they weren't necessary for fulfilling the use cases that we came up with for the SRS back in Chapter 9. These collections represent what we've spoken of before as *implementation classes* and are used as conveniences to make the application implementation easier; looking ahead, we know that we're going to need these when the time comes to build our SRS user interface, so we'll go ahead and implement them now. (We're not worrying about creating a StudentBody collection to house Student objects, for reasons that will become apparent later.)

We'll define five data files to "feed" these three collections, as follows:

- CourseCatalog.dat: This file contains records consisting of three tab-delimited fields: a course number, a course title, and the number of credits that the course is worth, represented as a floating point number.

In other words, this file represents the data needed to initialize a Course object in our domain model. It will "feed" the CourseCatalog collection.

Here are the test data contents of the file that we'll use for all of the work that we'll do in this chapter; \t represents the presence of an otherwise invisible tab character:

```
CMP101 \t Beginning Computer Technology \t 3.0
OBJ101 \t Object Methods for Software Development \t 3.0
CMP283 \t Higher Level Languages (C#) \t 3.0
CMP999 \t Living Brain Computers \t 3.0
ART101 \t Beginning Basketweaving \t 3.0
```

- Faculty.dat: This file contains records consisting of four tab-delimited fields, representing a professor's name, ID, title, and the department that he or she works for.

In other words, this file represents the data needed to initialize a Professor object in our domain model. It will "feed" the Faculty collection.

Here is the test data that we'll use:

```
Jacquie Barker \t 123-45-6789 \t Asst. Professor \t Info. Technology
John Carson \t 567-81-2345 \t Full Professor \t Info. Technology
Jackie Chan \t 987-65-4321 \t Full Professor \t Info. Technology
```

- SoC_SP2009.dat: This file contains the Schedule of Classes (SoC) information for the Spring 2009 (SP2009) semester; each tab-delimited record consists of six fields representing the course number, section number, day of the week, time of day, room, and seating capacity for the section in question.

This file represents data needed to initialize a Section object, combined with the courseNumber field of Course, which the Section class is able to "pull" by virtue of its one-to-many association with Course (recall our discussion of "data flowing along an association line" from Chapter 10). In other words, it simultaneously represents Section objects as a whole as well as links that Section objects maintain to Course objects. Here is the test data that we'll use:

```
CMP101 \t 1 \t M  \t 8:10 - 10:00 PM \t GOVT101 \t 30
CMP101 \t 2 \t W  \t 6:10 - 8:00 PM  \t GOVT202 \t 30
OBJ101 \t 1 \t Th \t 4:10 - 6:00 PM  \t GOVT105 \t 25
OBJ101 \t 2 \t T  \t 6:10 - 8:00 PM  \t SCI330 \t 25
CMP283 \t 1 \t M  \t 6:10 - 8:00 PM  \t GOVT101 \t 20
CMP999 \t 1 \t Th \t 4:10 - 6:00 PM  \t SCI241 \t 15
ART101 \t 1 \t M  \t 4:10 - 6:00 PM  \t ARTS25 \t 40
```

- Prerequisites.dat: This file contains information about which Course, listed in the first column, is a prerequisite for which other Course, listed in the second column.

In other words, this file represents the reflexive *prerequisite* association that exists on the Course class, and the records themselves represent links between specific Course objects.

Here is the test data that we'll use:

```
CMP101 \t OBJ101
OBJ101 \t CMP283
CMP283 \t CMP999
```

- TeachingAssignments.dat: This file pairs up a Professor (whose id is reflected in the first column) with the Course/Section number that the professor is going to be teaching (listed in the second column).

  In other words, this file represents the *teaches* association between a Professor and a Section.

  Here is our test data:

```
987-65-4321 \t CMP101 - 1
567-81-2345 \t CMP101 - 2
123-45-6789 \t OBJ101 - 1
987-65-4321 \t OBJ101 - 2
123-45-6789 \t CMP283 - 1
567-81-2345 \t CMP999 - 1
987-65-4321 \t ART101 - 1
```

Note All five of these data files are provided with the accompanying SRS code for download from the Apress web site (http://www.apress.com).

Persisting Student Data

One key difference between the way that we plan on handling Student data as compared with data for the other classes mentioned previously is that we're going to store each Student object's data in its own separate file rather than lump all of the data about all Students into a single StudentBody.dat file. This will enable us to retrieve the information for just one student at a time—namely, whichever student is currently logged on to the SRS—and to easily save any changes that occur to that Student object's information during his or her SRS session when he or she logs off. (We'll see how a student logs on in Chapter 16, when we add a GUI to our application.)

- The name of the student's data file is added as a field of the Student class. The name of the file is the Student's ID with a .dat extension—for example, 111-11-1111.dat.

- At a minimum, a student's data file will contain a single *primary* record, comprised of four tab-delimited fields representing the student's ID, name, major department, and degree sought. In other words, this record represents data needed to initialize a Student object in our object model.

- If the student has already registered for one or more sections in a previous SRS session, then the student's data file will also contain one or more *secondary* records, each consisting of a single field representing the full section number (that is, the course number followed by a hyphen, followed by the section number as an integer) of a section that the student is currently enrolled in. In other words, a secondary record represents the *attends* association in our object model, and any one record implies a link between this Student and a Section object.

We'll simulate three students in this fashion:

- 111-11-1111.dat: This student will be simulated as already having enrolled in two sections; the contents of this data file are as follows:

```
111-11-1111 \t Zachary Palmer \t Math \t M.S.
CMP101 - 1
ART101 - 1
```

- 222-22-2222.dat: This student will be simulated as not yet having enrolled in any sections; the contents of this data file are as follows:

```
222-22-2222 \t Gerson Lopez \t Information Technology \t Ph. D.
```

- 333-33-3333.dat: This student will also be simulated as not yet having enrolled in any sections; the contents of this data file are as follows:

```
333-33-3333 \t Mary Smith \t Physics \t B.S.
```

■**Note** As with the previous data files, all three of these are provided with the accompanying SRS code for download from the Apress web site.

Why Aren't We Going to Persist Other Object Types?

We're not worried about persisting information about any other object type besides Student, because we assume that the rest of the data is read-only during a particular login session; for example, the user won't be able to alter Professor or Course information. All the student user will be able to do is to choose classes (sections) from the ScheduleOfClasses to register for, and/or to drop classes (sections); this merely changes the status of the *links* between a Student and various Section objects, which are stored as *secondary* records in the student's data file. In fact, we aren't even giving student users the ability to change their own *primary* information—name, id, etc.—via this application.

Keep in mind that a real-world university would have to take steps to make sure that student data—if it were stored in ASCII files—couldn't be accessed or changed by unauthorized users. A discussion of computer security measures is beyond the scope of this book, so we'll keep it pretty simple as far as accessing the student data files.

General I/O Approach for the SRS Classes

Just as with almost every other aspect of programming, you can take more than one approach when installing an I/O capability into a program. You could, for example, define a single class that would define general I/O functions that are applicable to every conceivable class in the

SRS, and you could write the SRS classes as subclasses of this super-IO class. This approach would maximize code reuse, but would result in fairly complicated and less readable code.

One of the oldest and most valuable bits of programming advice is "Keep It Simple, Stupid" (KISS). True, it's a bit insulting, but it's excellent advice nonetheless. When faced with two or more possible approaches to a programming problem, it's almost always better to go with the simplest approach, and that's what we're going to do to install file persistence in the SRS.

Instead of trying to come up with a super-IO class that will handle file persistence for any conceivable SRS class (now and in the future), we're going to have each class that needs to read and/or write data to implement its own I/O functionality. At the expense of some code duplication, this approach will result in simpler, more readable code. Because the I/O functionality of each class is self-contained within the class, changes to any other class (the super-IO class, specifically) won't filter down and possibly break any downstream classes.

Now that we have decided on the approach we'll use, let's see how to implement it in the various SRS classes.

CourseCatalog

We'll start with the CourseCatalog class. This is a new class to the SRS implementation that stores Course object references in a Dictionary collection using the course numbers as the keys. In addition to the Dictionary, the CourseCatalog class maintains two string data elements that contain the names of the files that store the course catalog and course prerequisite data. The three data elements are implemented using auto-implemented properties.

```
using System;
using System.Collections.Generic;
using System.IO;

public class CourseCatalog {

    //-------------------------------
    // Auto-implemented properties.
    //-------------------------------

    public string CourseCatalogFile { get; set; }
    public string PrerequisitesFile { get; set; }
    public Dictionary<string, Course> Courses { get; set; }
```

Constructor

The constructor for this class takes two arguments that represent the names of the course catalog and the course prerequisites data files. In addition to creating an empty Dictionary, the values of auto-implemented properties are initialized with the file names.

```
    public CourseCatalog(string courseCatalogFile, string prerequisitesFile) {

        // Initialize auto-implemented property values
        CourseCatalogFile = courseCatalogFile;
        PrerequisitesFile = prerequisitesFile;
```

```
    // Create a new Dictionary.
    Courses = new Dictionary<string, Course>();
}
```

Display Method

We create a Display method for testing purposes, which uses a foreach loop to step through the Course object references stored in the Dictionary—a technique that we discussed in Chapter 13.

```
public void Display() {
  Console.WriteLine("Course Catalog:");
  Console.WriteLine("");

  // Use a foreach statement to step through the Dictionary.
  foreach ( KeyValuePair<string, Course> kv in Courses ) {
    Course c = kv.Value;
    c.Display();
    Console.WriteLine("");
  }
}
```

AddCourse Method

We also create an AddCourse "housekeeping" method, which we use to insert a Course object reference into the encapsulated collection using the course number as the key.

```
public void AddCourse(Course c) {
  Courses.Add(c.CourseNumber, c);
}
```

FindCourse Method

We also provide a convenience method, FindCourse, to enable client code to easily retrieve a particular Course object from this collection based on its course number. If the requested course number (the Dictionary key) isn't found, a KeyNotFoundException will be thrown.

```
public Course FindCourse(string courseNumber) {
  return Courses[courseNumber];
}
```

Providing such a method hides the fact that the collection is implemented as a Dictionary: client code simply invokes the method and gets handed back a Course object, without any idea as to what is happening behind the scenes, as simulated by the following hypothetical client code snippet:

```
// Sample client code.
CourseCatalog courseCatalog = new CourseCatalog();
// ...
Course c = courseCatalog.FindCourse("ART101");
```

ReadCourseCatalogData Method

Now we're ready to talk about adding the I/O functionality to the `CourseCatalog` class. One of the files we need to read contains course catalog data. The file contains tab-delimited records that represent the course number, course name, and number of credits. We'll use this data to create and initialize `Course` objects and add them to the `Dictionary`. The first thing the method does is declare a `StreamReader` variable and set it initially to `null`.

```
public void ReadCourseCatalogData() {
    // We're going to parse tab-delimited records into
    // three elements -- courseNumber, courseName, and credits --
    // and then create a new Course object using these values.

    StreamReader reader = null;
```

The next section of the method opens an input stream and connects it to the file that contains the course catalog data. The data is then read from the file line by line, values are extracted, and a `Course` object is created based on the data. Because a lot can go wrong when dealing with I/O, the code used to read from the file is placed inside a try-catch block.

```
try {
    // Open the file.
    reader = new StreamReader(new FileStream(CourseCatalogFile, FileMode.Open));

    //  Read first line from input file.
    string line = reader.ReadLine();

    //  Keep reading lines until there aren't any more.
    while (line != null) {

        // We'll use the Split() method of the String class to
        // split the line we read from the file into substrings
        // using tabs as the delimiter.

        string[] strings = line.Split('\t');

        // Now assign the value of the fields to the appropriate
        // substring

        string courseNumber = strings[0];
        string courseName = strings[1];
        string creditValue = strings[2];

        // We have to convert the last value into a number,
        // using a static method on the Double class to do so.

        double credits = Convert.ToDouble(creditValue);

        // Create a Course object, and store it in the
```

```
    // Dictionary.

    Course c = new Course(courseNumber, courseName, credits);
    AddCourse(c);

    //  Read the next line of data (if any)
    line = reader.ReadLine();
  }
} //  end of try block
```

Let's look the code inside the try block in more detail. We use the ReadLine method to read the first line of data from the data file.

```
//  Read first line from input file.
line = reader.ReadLine();
```

The ReadLine method returns the line of data read as a string or null if the end of file has been reached. A while loop keeps reading lines from the file until there aren't any more lines to read. Inside the while loop, the Split method splits the most recently read line into substrings using tabs as the delimiter.

```
//  Keep reading lines until there aren't any more.
while (line != null) {

    // We'll use the Split() method of the String class to
    // split the line we read from the file into substrings
    // using tabs as the delimiter.

    string[] strings = line.Split('\t');
```

Next, we assign the values of the substrings to fields representing the course number, course name, and number of credits for the course.

```
// Now assign the value of the fields to the appropriate
// substring

string courseNumber = strings[0];
string courseName = strings[1];
string creditValue = strings[2];
```

However, there's one little problem: when we use this information to initialize a Course object, the Course constructor needs the number of credits expressed as a double value rather than a string. This conversion is easy to perform using the static ToDouble method from the Convert class.

```
// We have to convert the last value into a number,
// using a static method on the Double class to do so.

double credits = Convert.ToDouble(creditValue);
```

Now that we have all the information that we need, we can use it to initialize a Course object and add it to the Dictionary.

```
// Create a Course object, and store it in the
// Dictionary.

Course c = new Course(courseNumber, courseName, credits);
AddCourse(c);
```

The current line of data from the input file has been processed, the next line of data (if any) is read, and the process repeats.

```
//  Read the next line of data (if any)
line = reader.ReadLine();
  }
} //  end of try block
```

Following the try block are catch blocks to catch exceptions that might be thrown during the read operation and a finally block to close the input stream.

```
catch (FileNotFoundException f) {
  Console.WriteLine(f);
}
catch (IOException i) {
  Console.WriteLine(i);
}
finally {
  // Close the input stream.
  if ( reader != null ) {
    reader.Close();
  }
}

return;
}
```

ReadPrerequisitesData Method

The CourseCatalog class also needs to read data on the course prerequisites. This data is found in an ASCII file that contains two columns of tab-delimited course number data. The courses in the left-hand column are prerequisites for the courses in the right-hand column. The ReadPrerequisitesData method follows a pattern similar to the ReadCourseCatalogData method. At the top of the method, a StreamReader reference is declared.

```
public void ReadPrerequisitesData() {

  // We're going to parse tab-delimited records into
  // two values, representing the courseNo "A" of
  // a course that serves as a prerequisite for
```

```
// courseNo "B".
```

```
StreamReader reader = null;
```

The code to read data from the prerequisites file is placed inside a try block. Lines are read one-by-one from the file. The lines are split into substrings using tabs as the delimiter. We use the previously described FindCourse method to return a reference to the Course object corresponding to the course numbers read from the file. If the Course references aren't null, we'll add the second Course as a prerequisite to the first.

```
try {
  // Open the file.
  reader = new StreamReader(new FileStream(PrerequisitesFile, FileMode.Open));

  // Read first line from input file.
  string line = reader.ReadLine();

  // Keep reading lines until there aren't any more.
  while (line != null) {

    // Once again we'll make use of the Split() method to split
    // the line into substrings using tabs as the delimiter

    string[] strings = line.Split('\t');

    // Now assign the value of the fields to the appropriate
    // substring

    string courseNoA = strings[0];
    string courseNoB = strings[1];

    // Look these two courses up in the CourseCatalog.

    Course a = FindCourse(courseNoA);
    Course b = FindCourse(courseNoB);
    if (a != null && b != null) {
      b.AddPrerequisite(a);
    }

    line = reader.ReadLine();
  }
} // end of try block
```

After the try block come catch blocks to handle any exceptions that might be thrown, and a finally block to close the input stream.

```
catch (FileNotFoundException f) {
  Console.WriteLine(f);
}
```

```
catch (IOException i) {
  Console.WriteLine(i);
}
finally {
  // Close the input stream.
  if ( reader != null ) {
    reader.Close();
  }
}

return;

}
```

Adding a "Test Scaffold" Main Method

In Chapter 13, we discussed the fact that the C# runtime environment looks for a method with a particular header (e.g., static void Main()) when we start up the application. As an example, to run the SRS application we developed in Chapter 14, we'd type the command SRS, and the C# runtime environment would invoke the Main method declared within the SRS.cs file.

As we've discussed previously in the book, it's permissible to have more than one Main method sprinkled throughout an application's classes; however, only one of these will serve as the official main method for purposes of driving the application. Why would we ever want to declare extra Main methods? That is, what would we use the other Main methods for? We'd use them as test drivers, or *scaffolds*, for putting a single class through its paces. As an example, perhaps after we finish coding the CourseCatalog class, we wish to test it to ensure that it

- Properly parses the CourseCatalog.dat and Prerequisites.dat files

- Instantiates all Course objects correctly

- Links prerequisites appropriately

- Stores them all in the Dictionary that is encapsulated within the CourseCatalog class

We could run the full-blown SRS application to test this class. However, we'd have to jump ahead and modify the SRS class's Main method to take advantage of the CourseCatalog class and all of its various methods in order to do this. A simpler approach is to provide the CourseCatalog class with its own Main method, for use in testing the class in isolation, as follows:

```
// Test scaffold (a Main() method INSIDE OF the CourseCatalog class!).

static void Main() {

  // We create a CourseCatalog object...

  CourseCatalog catalog =
    new CourseCatalog("CourseCatalog.dat", "Prerequisites.dat");
```

```
   //  Read data from input files...

   catalog.ReadCourseCatalogData();
   catalog.ReadPrerequisitesData();

   // ...and use its Display() method to demonstrate the
   // results!

   catalog.Display();
}
```

With the addition of this `Main` method to the `CourseCatalog` class, we can now compile the application from the command line using the following command:

`csc /out:CourseCatalog.exe *.cs /main:CourseCatalog`

As we've discussed previously, the `/out` compiler option tells the compiler to name the resulting executable file `CourseCatalog.exe`. The `/main` option signifies that the `Main` method defined in the `CourseCatalog` class will be used to drive the program. If the `CourseCatalog.exe` file were run, the following output would be produced:

```
Course Catalog:

Course Information:
     Course No.:  CMP101
     Course Name:  Beginning Computer Technology
     Credits:  3
     Prerequisite Courses:
     Offered As Section(s):

Course Information:
     Course No.:  OBJ101
     Course Name:  Object Methods for Software Development
     Credits:  3
     Prerequisite Courses:
         CMP101:  Beginning Computer Technology
     Offered As Section(s):

Course Information:
     Course No.:  CMP283
     Course Name:  Higher Level Languages (C#)
     Credits:  3
     Prerequisite Courses:
         OBJ101:  Object Methods for Software Development
     Offered As Section(s):

Course Information:
     Course No.:  CMP999
     Course Name:  Living Brain Computers
```

```
    Credits:  3
    Prerequisite Courses:
        CMP283:  Higher Level Languages (C#)
    Offered As Section(s):

Course Information:
    Course No.:  ART101
    Course Name:  Beginning Basketweaving
    Credits:  3
    Prerequisite Courses:
    Offered As Section(s):
```

thus demonstrating that our code does indeed work!

Note that there is no harm in leaving this Main method in the CourseCatalog class even after our testing is finished—in fact, it's a handy thing to keep around in case we change the details of how any of these methods work later on, and want to retest it.

Changes to ScheduleOfClasses

Next, we'll retrofit the ScheduleOfClasses class that we developed in Chapter 14 with this same ability to "self-initialize" from an ASCII file. We'll add an additional data element to the class: a string that contains the name of the file that holds the SoC data. We'll implement this data element as an auto-implemented property.

```
using System;
using System.Collections.Generic;
using System.IO;

public class ScheduleOfClasses {

  //-------------------------------
  // Auto-implemented properties.
  //-------------------------------

  public string Semester { get; set; }
  public string ScheduleFile { get; set; }

  // This Dictionary stores Section object references using
  // a String concatenation of course no. and section no. as the
  // key (e.g., "MATH101 - 1").

  public Dictionary<string, Section> SectionsOffered { get; set; }
```

Constructor Changes

We'll also declare a second two-parameter constructor where the second parameter is a string containing the name of the SoC data file. The previous one-parameter constructor is modified to call the new two-parameter constructor with a dummy file name.

```
// Modify the one-parameter constructor so it calls the new
// two-parameter constructor with a dummy ScheduleFile values.
public ScheduleOfClasses(string semester) : this("", semester) {
}

public ScheduleOfClasses(string scheduleFile, string semester) {
  ScheduleFile = scheduleFile;
  Semester = semester;

  // Instantiate a new Dictionary.

  SectionsOffered = new Dictionary<string, Section>();
}
```

FindSection Method

We use the FindSection method to obtain a Section from the Dictionary that we access through the SectionsOffered property. The string representing a section number passed to the method is the key used to search for the Section.

```
// The full section number is a concatenation of the
// course no. and section no., separated by a hyphen;
// e.g., "ART101 - 1".

public Section FindSection(string fullSectionNumber) {
  return SectionsOffered[fullSectionNumber];
}
```

ReadScheduleData Method

We use the ReadScheduleData method to read SoC data from a file. It is similar to the ReadCourseCatalogData method from the CourseCatalog class with one important difference: it takes a reference to a CourseCatalog object as an input parameter. The first thing the method does is declare a reference to a StreamReader that we'll use to read data from the file.

```
public void ReadScheduleData(CourseCatalog courseCatalog) {
  // We're going to parse tab-delimited records into
  // six fields: courseNumber, sectionNumber, dayOfWeek,
  // timeOfDay, room, and capacity. We'll use courseNumber to
  // look up the appropriate Course object, and then
  // call the ScheduleSection() method to fabricate a
  // new Section object.

  StreamReader reader = null;
```

As was the case with the CourseCatalog I/O methods, the code used to read data from the SoC file is placed inside a try block. Data is read from the file line by line, the lines are split into substrings, and variable values are assigned based on the substrings.

```
try {
  // Open the file.
  reader = new StreamReader(new FileStream(ScheduleFile, FileMode.Open));

  // Read first line from input file.
  string line = reader.ReadLine();

  // Keep reading lines until there aren't any more.
  while (line != null) {

    // We'll use the Split() method of the String class to
    // split the line we read from the file into substrings
    // using tabs as the delimiter.

    string[] strings = line.Split('\t');

    // Now assign the value of the fields to the appropriate
    // substring

    string courseNumber = strings[0];
    string sectionValue = strings[1];
    string dayOfWeek = strings[2];
    string timeOfDay = strings[3];
    string room = strings[4];
    string capacityValue = strings[5];

    // We need to convert the sectionNumber and capacityValue
    // Strings to ints

    int sectionNumber = Convert.ToInt32(sectionValue);
    int capacity = Convert.ToInt32(capacityValue);
```

The SoC data file contains course numbers. To schedule a section of a course, we need a reference to the corresponding Course object. We can achieve this goal by using the FindCourse method of the CourseCatalog class. A reference to CourseCatalog object is passed to this method as an input parameter.

```
    // Look up the Course object in the Course Catalog.
    Course c = courseCatalog.FindCourse(courseNumber);
```

Once we have a reference to the proper Course object, we call the ScheduleSection method on it and add the resulting Section reference to the Dictionary.

```
    // Schedule the Section and add it to the Dictionary.
```

```
    Section s = c.ScheduleSection(sectionNumber, dayOfWeek,
                        timeOfDay, room, capacity);
    AddSection(s);

    line = reader.ReadLine();
  }
} // End of try block
```

Because we are now creating a section based on a section number read from a file, we need to change the ScheduleSection method of the Course class so that it takes an integer section number as its first parameter. We'll look at the updated ScheduleSection method a little later in the chapter.

To finish off the ReadScheduleData method, we'll add a couple of catch blocks for exception handling and a finally block to close the input stream.

```
catch (FileNotFoundException f) {
  Console.WriteLine(f);
}
catch (IOException i) {
  Console.WriteLine(i);
}
catch (Exception e) {
  Console.WriteLine(e);
}
finally {
  // Close the input stream.
  if ( reader != null ) {
    reader.Close();
  }
}

  return;
}
```

Testing the Revised ScheduleOfClasses Class

As we did with the CourseCatalog class, we'll include a Main method in the revised ScheduleOfClasses class to test out the updated class. The new wrinkle here is that because the ReadScheduleData method requires a reference to a CourseCatalog object, we need to create one in the Main method to test out the ScheduleOfClasses class.

```
static void Main() {

  // We need a CourseCatalog object to test the ScheduleOfClasses
  CourseCatalog catalog =
    new CourseCatalog("CourseCatalog.dat", "Prerequisites.dat");
  catalog.ReadCourseCatalogData();
  catalog.ReadPrerequisitesData();
```

```
// Create a ScheduleOfClasses object...
ScheduleOfClasses schedule =
    new ScheduleOfClasses("SoC_SP2009.dat", "SP2009");

//  Read data from the input file...
schedule.ReadScheduleData(catalog);

// ...and use its Display() method to list the
// ScheduleOfClasses results!

schedule.Display();
}
```

To compile and run this example properly, we have to modify the ScheduleSection method of the Course class, as explained previously. Here is the output when the Main method is run:

```
Schedule of Classes for SP2009

Section Information:
    Semester:  SP2009
    Course No.:  CMP101
    Section No:  1
    Offered:  M at 8:10 - 10:00 PM
    In Room:  GOVT101
    Total of 0 students enrolled.

Section Information:
    Semester:  SP2009
    Course No.:  CMP101
    Section No:  2
    Offered:  W at 6:10 - 8:00 PM
    In Room:  GOVT202
    Total of 0 students enrolled.

Section Information:
    Semester:  SP2009
    Course No.:  OBJ101
    Section No:  1
    Offered:  R at 4:10 - 6:00 PM
    In Room:  GOVT105
    Total of 0 students enrolled.

Section Information:
    Semester:  SP2009
    Course No.:  OBJ101
    Section No:  2
    Offered:  T at 6:10 - 8:00 PM
    In Room:  SCI330
    Total of 0 students enrolled.
```

```
Section Information:
    Semester:  SP2009
    Course No.:  CMP283
    Section No:  1
    Offered:  M at 6:10 - 8:00 PM
    In Room:  GOVT101
    Total of 0 students enrolled.

Section Information:
    Semester:  SP2009
    Course No.:  CMP999
    Section No:  1
    Offered:  R at 4:10 - 6:00 PM
    In Room:  SCI241
    Total of 0 students enrolled.

Section Information:
    Semester:  SP2009
    Course No.:  ART101
    Section No:  1
    Offered:  M at 4:10 - 6:00 PM
    In Room:  ARTS25
    Total of 0 students enrolled.
```

Faculty

Next, we'll create the Faculty class, which is a new class to the SRS used to populate a
Dictionary with Professor object references by reading their pertinent information from
two data files:

- Faculty.dat, the primary file used as the basis for creating the Professors

- TeachingAssignments.dat, a secondary file used for linking Professor objects to the
  Section objects that they are assigned to teach, and vice versa

Since the structure and behaviors of the Faculty class are so similar to those of
CourseCatalog, we won't explain the Faculty class in detail, but will discuss the FindProfessor
method and point out one interesting nuance regarding the ReadAssignmentData method.

FindProfessor Method

The FindProfessor method searches for a reference to a Professor object in the Dictionary
accessed through the Professors property. The search is conducted based on a string passed
to the method that represents an ID for a professor.

```
public Professor FindProfessor(string id) {
    return Professors[id];
}
```

ReadAssignmentData Method

The ReadAssignmentData method reads data from one of the two input files used by the Faculty class. The method takes a reference to a ScheduleOfClasses object as an argument. You'll see in just a minute why the method needs this parameter. The top portion of the method declares a reference to a StreamReader object.

```
public void ReadAssignmentData(ScheduleOfClasses scheduleOfClasses) {

    StreamReader reader = null;
```

The next part of the ReadAssignmentData method of the Faculty class is similar to the logic that was used in the ReadCourseCatalogData and ReadPrerequisitesData methods from the CourseCatalog class: a line of text is read from a file and split into substrings using the Split method.

```
    try {
      // Open the file.
      reader = new StreamReader(new FileStream(AssignmentsFile, FileMode.Open));

      string line = reader.ReadLine();
      while (line != null) {

        // Once again we'll make use of the Split() method to split
        // the line into substrings using tabs as the delimiter

        string[] strings = line.Split('\t');

        // Now assign the value of the fields to the appropriate
        // substring

        string id = strings[0];

        // The full section number is a concatenation of the
        // course no. and section no., separated by a hyphen;
        // e.g., "ART101 - 1".

        string fullSectionNumber = strings[1];
```

Just as we did in the ReadPrerequisitesData method of CourseCatalog, we're linking together two objects here, so we need to first verify that both objects do indeed exist and then obtain references to them. However, unlike the ReadPrerequisitesData method of CourseCatalog, where both objects were Courses and hence both objects were stored in the Dictionary internal to the CourseCatalog class, here we have a situation where one of the objects (a Professor) is stored in the Dictionary that is part of the Faculty class, but the other object (a Section) is stored in a collection elsewhere in our application: namely, in the ScheduleOfClasses object. However, we have access to the required ScheduleOfClasses object because it has been passed as an argument to the method. The ScheduleOfClasses object is used to get a reference to the Section that the Professor agrees to teach.

```
        // Look these two objects up in the appropriate
        // collections using the ScheduleOfClasses reference that
        // was passed to this method.

        Professor p = FindProfessor(id);
        Section s =
            scheduleOfClasses.FindSection(fullSectionNumber);
        if (p != null && s != null) {
          p.AgreeToTeach(s);
        }

        line = reader.ReadLine();
      }
    } // end of try block
```

Adding a "Test Scaffold" Main Method

Just as we did for the previous classes in this chapter, we also provide a test scaffold Main method for the Faculty class. Because the ReadAssignmentData method of the Faculty class requires a ScheduleOfClasses argument, in order to test the Faculty class we also must instantiate a ScheduleOfClasses object. The ScheduleOfClasses class, in turn, needs a reference to a CourseCatalog object, which we also create in the Main method.

```
static void Main() {
  // We need a CourseCatalog object to test the Faculty class

  CourseCatalog catalog =
    new CourseCatalog("CourseCatalog.dat", "Prerequisites.dat");
  catalog.ReadCourseCatalogData();
  catalog.ReadPrerequisitesData();

  // We also need a ScheduleOfClasses object.

  ScheduleOfClasses schedule =
    new ScheduleOfClasses("SoC_SP2009.dat", "SP2009");
  schedule.ReadScheduleData(catalog);

  // Create a Faculty object.

  Faculty faculty =
      new Faculty("Faculty.dat", "TeachingAssignments.dat");

  // Read Faculty data from input file.

  faculty.ReadFacultyData();
  faculty.ReadAssignmentData(schedule);

  // Display information about the faculty.
```

```
        faculty.Display();
    }
```

Here is the output from the Main method of the Faculty class:

```
Faculty:

Person Information:
     Name:  Jacquie Barker
     ID number:  123-45-6789
Professor-Specific Information:
     Title:  Adjunct Professor
     Teaches for Dept.:  Information Technology
Teaching Assignments for Jacquie Barker:
     Course No.:  OBJ101
     Section No.:  1
     Course Name:  Object Methods for Software Development
     Day and Time:  R - 4:10 - 6:00 PM
     -----
     Course No.:  CMP283
     Section No.:  1
     Course Name:  Higher Level Languages (C#)
     Day and Time:  M - 6:10 - 8:00 PM
     -----

Person Information:
     Name:  John Carson
     ID number:  567-81-2345
Professor-Specific Information:
     Title:  Full Professor
     Teaches for Dept.:  Information Technology
Teaching Assignments for John Carson:
     Course No.:  CMP101
     Section No.:  2
     Course Name:  Beginning Computer Technology
     Day and Time:  W - 6:10 - 8:00 PM
     -----
     Course No.:  CMP999
     Section No.:  1
     Course Name:  Living Brain Computers
     Day and Time:  R - 4:10 - 6:00 PM
     -----

Person Information:
     Name:  Jackie Chan
     ID number:  987-65-4321
```

```
Professor-Specific Information:
    Title:  Full Professor
    Teaches for Dept.:  Physical Education
Teaching Assignments for Jackie Chan:
    Course No.:  CMP101
    Section No.:  1
    Course Name:  Beginning Computer Technology
    Day and Time:  M - 8:10 - 10:00 PM
    -----
    Course No.:  OBJ101
    Section No.:  2
    Course Name:  Object Methods for Software Development
    Day and Time:  T - 6:10 - 8:00 PM
    -----
    Course No.:  ART101
    Section No.:  1
    Course Name:  Beginning Basketweaving
    Day and Time:  M - 4:10 - 6:00 PM
    -----
```

Course Modifications

There is only one minor change to be made to the Course class from the way that it was presented in Chapter 14, to accommodate our new file persistence scheme.

Because we're now reading in a *predetermined* section number from the SoC_SP2009.dat file, we must modify the ScheduleSection method of the Course class so that it no longer automatically assigns a "one-up" section number to each Section.

Here is the original code for the ScheduleSection method from Chapter 14; the highlighted code shows that we were automatically determining how many sections had already been created and stored in the offeredAsSection collection (a field of Course), and bumping that up by one to create a section number on the fly:

```
public Section ScheduleSection(string day, string time,
                               string room, int capacity) {
    // Create a new Section (note the creative way in
    // which we are assigning a section number)...
    Section s = new Section(OfferedAsSection.Count + 1,
                            day, time, this, room, capacity);

    // ...and then add it to the List
    OfferedAsSection.Add(s);

    return s;
}
```

In our new, modified version of this method, shown in the following code, we've added an argument, secNumber, to enable us to simply hand in the section number as read in from the data file:

```
public Section ScheduleSection(int secNumber, string day,
                   string time, string room, int capacity) {
  // Create a new Section...
  Section s =
     new Section(secNumber, day, time, this, room, capacity);

  // ...and then remember it!
  OfferedAsSection.Add(s);

  return s;
}
```

The Student Class (Dynamic Data Retrieval; Persisting Object State)

Aside from making a minor change to the ScheduleSection method of the Course class that we just discussed, and "refurbishing" the ScheduleOfClasses class that we previously discussed, the only other domain class that we wish to enhance among those that we created in Chapter 14 is the Student class. To demonstrate the techniques of dynamic data retrieval and data persistence, we're going to

- Declare a ReadStudentData method that will read Student data from a file.

- Add a WriteStudentData method that can be called from the SRS Main method when a student logs off, to persist the student's state by writing the current data back to his or her data file.

Much of the Student class's code remains unchanged from the way that it was presented in Chapter 14, so we'll only touch upon the significant changes that we've made to the class here.

Changes to the Student Constructors

There is one change to the Student class data structure: the name of the file containing the Student data is stored as an auto-implemented property of the Student class. The file name is passed to the constructor as a string.

```
public Student(string studentFile, string name, string id,
              string major, string degree) : base(name, id) {

  // Assign auto-implemented property values
  Major = major;
  Degree = degree;
  StudentFile = studentFile;
```

```
  Transcript = new Transcript(this);

  // Create an empty List.

  attends = new List<Section>();
}

// A second form of constructor, used when a Student has not yet
// declared a major or degree.
// Reuse the code of the other Student constructor.

public Student(string studentFile, string name, string id) :
  this(studentFile, name, id, "TBD", "TBD"){
}

// A third form of constructor, used when the only information
// about a Student is his/her Student data file name.

public Student(string studentFile) :
    this(studentFile, "TBD", "TBD", "TBD", "TBD"){
}
```

ReadStudentData Method

The ReadStudentData method reads information from a student data file, assigns the values of
the data read to the Student object, and enrolls the student based on the section information
read from the file. A ScheduleOfClasses object is needed to properly enroll the student, so a
reference to a ScheduleOfClasses object is passed to the method as an input parameter.

```
public void ReadStudentData(ScheduleOfClasses schedule) {
  // We're going to parse tab-delimited records into
  // four attributes -- id, name, major, and degree.

  StreamReader reader = null;
```

The read operations are placed inside a try block. The first line of the student data file
contains the identification number, name, major, and degree of the Student. The line is read
from the file using a StreamReader, split into substrings, and the substring values are assigned
to the auto-implemented properties of the class.

```
  try {
    // Open the file.
    reader = new StreamReader(new FileStream(StudentFile, FileMode.Open));

    //  Read first line from input file.

    string line = reader.ReadLine();

    // We'll use the Split() method of the String class to split
```

```
  // the line we read from the file into substrings using tabs
  // as the delimiter.

  string[] strings = line.Split('\t');

  // Now assign the value of the auto-implemented properties
  // to the appropriate substring

  Id = strings[0];
  Name = strings[1];
  Major = strings[2];
  Degree = strings[3];
```

Subsequent lines of the input file (if any) contain the numbers of the sections in which the student is currently enrolled. The ScheduleOfClasses object reference passed to the method is used to return a reference to the Section object corresponding to the section number that was read. The Enroll method is called on the Section object to enroll the Student in the Section.

```
  //  Keep reading lines to get section info.
  while (line != null) {

    // The full section number is a concatenation of the
    // course no. and section no., separated by a hyphen;
    // e.g., "ART101 - 1".

    string fullSectionNumber = line.Trim();
    Section s = schedule.FindSection(fullSectionNumber);

    // Note that we are using the Section class's enroll()
    // method to ensure that bidirectionality is established
    // between the Student and the Section.
    s.Enroll(this);

    line = reader.ReadLine();
  }
} // end of try block
catch (FileNotFoundException f) {
  Console.WriteLine(f);
}
catch (IOException i) {
  Console.WriteLine(i);
}
finally {
  // Close the input stream.
  if ( reader != null ) {
    reader.Close();
  }
```

```
  }

  return;
}
```

Persisting the State of a Student

During the course of an SRS session, the student will presumably be registering for sections and/or dropping sections. The state of the Student object representing that student—namely, the data values of the Student object and all links maintained by that Student object with other objects (in particular, with Section objects in which the student is enrolled)—is thus likely to change.

We must provide a way for the SRS to remember these changes from one logon session to the next; otherwise, the SRS system will be of no practical value. So, we're going to provide a method to persist a Student object's state whenever the student logs off: specifically, we're going to write information about this Student back out to the same data file that we originally used to initialize the Student object's state in the constructor.

The output operations are performed in a method named WriteStudentData. As discussed earlier in the chapter, we use a combination of FileStream and StreamWriter objects to write to the student's data file. The first line of the method declares a reference to a StreamWriter object.

```
public void WriteStudentData() {
  StreamWriter writer = null;
```

The writing operations are placed inside a try block. A FileStream object that is connected to the Student data file is passed as an argument to the StreamWriter constructor. The StreamWriter is then used to write the student's personal and section information to the file.

```
try {
  // Attempt to create the Student data file. Note that
  // it will overwrite one if it already exists, which
  // is what we want to have happen.

  writer = new StreamWriter(new FileStream(StudentFile, FileMode.OpenOrCreate));

  // First, we output the header record as a tab-delimited
  // record.

  writer.WriteLine(Id + "\t" + Name + "\t" +
                   Major + "\t" + Degree);

  // Then, we output one record for every Section that
  // the Student is enrolled in.

  foreach( Section s in attends ) {
    writer.WriteLine(s.GetFullSectionNumber());
  }
```

```
  }  //  end of try block
```

A catch block is provided to handle any I/O exceptions that might occur, and the output stream is closed inside a finally block.

```
catch (IOException e) {
  // Signal that an error has occurred.
  Console.WriteLine(e);
}
finally {
  //  Close the output stream.
  if ( writer != null ) {
    writer.Close();
  }
}

return;
}
```

Binary I/O

Up to this point, we have been discussing and implementing character-based (or ASCII) I/O. The data files we have been working with contain readable character data, which was read from or written to the file a line at a time. Another option when dealing with data persistence is to use what is known as binary I/O, where the data is read from or written to files as individual bytes of data. The advantages of binary I/O include smaller data files, more efficient I/O operations at run time, and files that are "safer" in a sense because they are not human-readable. The disadvantages of binary I/O are that it is somewhat awkward reading character data with binary I/O, and binary files can be platform dependent, making them difficult to integrate with other applications in your organization. We won't go into binary I/O in detail in this book, but as always, you can look to the MSDN documentation pages for more information.

Revisiting the SRS Class

Having encapsulated so much functionality into the Student, ScheduleOfCourses, CourseCatalog, and Faculty classes allows us to *dramatically* simplify the Main method for the SRS "driver" class; let's revisit that class to see how it should be changed to accommodate all that we've done in this chapter.

The first part of the method creates CourseCatalog, ScheduleOfClasses, and Faculty objects in a process identical to what was done in the "test scaffolding" Main methods of the individual classes. The order that the objects are created is important, because a ScheduleOfClasses object needs a reference to a CourseCatalog, and a Faculty object needs a reference to a ScheduleOfClasses.

```
// Create CourseCatalog, ScheduleOfClasses, and Faculty
// objects. The order of creation is important because a
// ScheduleOfClasses needs a CourseCatalog object to properly
```

```
//  initialize, and a Faculty object needs a ScheduleOfClasses
//  object.

//  Create a CourseCatalog object and read data from input
//  files.

CourseCatalog catalog =
  new CourseCatalog("CourseCatalog.dat", "Prerequisites.dat");
catalog.ReadCourseCatalogData();
catalog.ReadPrerequisitesData();

//  Create a ScheduleOfClasses object and read data from the
//  input file.

ScheduleOfClasses schedule =
    new ScheduleOfClasses("SoC_SP2009.dat", "SP2009");
schedule.ReadScheduleData(catalog);

//  Create a Faculty object and read data from input files.

Faculty faculty =
    new Faculty("Faculty.dat", "TeachingAssignments.dat");
faculty.ReadFacultyData();
faculty.ReadAssignmentData(schedule);
```

We'll handle the students differently: that is, rather than loading them all in at application outset, we'll pull in the data that we need just for one Student when that Student logs on, as we saw when we reviewed the "new and improved" Student class constructor earlier in this chapter. Because we don't yet have a mechanism to allow a user to log on—we'll provide that in Chapter 16—we'll temporarily create a few Student objects by hard-coding calls to the Student constructor, to simulate students logging on to the SRS. This enables us to exercise and test the enhanced Student class constructor. Note that only the first of these Students has preregistered for courses based on the content of their student data file, as discussed earlier.

```
// Let's temporarily create Students this way as a test,
// to simulate Students logging on. Note that only the
// first Student has preregistered for courses based
// on the content of his/her id.dat file (see Student.cs
// for details).

Student s1 = new Student("111-11-1111.dat");
s1.ReadStudentData(schedule);

Student s2 = new Student("222-22-2222.dat");
s2.ReadStudentData(schedule);

Student s3 = new Student("333-33-3333.dat");
s3.ReadStudentData(schedule);
```

Now, we'll simulate having Student s2 enroll in a Section, so that we may exercise and test the WriteStudentData method. We use the FindSection convenience method of the ScheduleOfClasses class to obtain a reference to a Section object based on a particular course and section number, and we then use the Enroll method of the Section class to bidirectionally enroll Student s2 in that Section.

```
// Let's have one Student try enrolling in something, so
// that we can simulate their logging off and persisting
// the enrollment data in the id.dat file (see Student.cs
// for details).

Section sec = scheduleOfClasses.FindSection("ART101 - 1");
sec.Enroll(s2);
```

Now, we invoke the WriteStudentData method on Student object s2.

```
s2.WriteStudentData();
```

Before running the SRS application, the contents of the 222-22-2222.dat file consisted of a single record as follows:

```
222-22-2222  Gerson Lopez   Information Technology  Ph. D.
```

because this student wasn't enrolled in any sections. After running the SRS application, if we inspect the contents of the 222-22-2222.dat file, we'll find that a record has been added to persist the fact that this student is now enrolled in ART101 section 1:

```
222-22-2222  Gerson Lopez   Information Technology  Ph. D.
ART101 - 1
```

and so the WriteStudentData method is indeed working!

To round out our testing, we include a few calls to the Display methods of our various collection objects:

```
// Let's see if everything got initialized properly
// by calling various display methods!

Console.WriteLine("====================");
Console.WriteLine("Course Catalog:");
Console.WriteLine("====================");
Console.WriteLine("");
courseCatalog.Display();

Console.WriteLine("====================");
Console.WriteLine("Schedule of Classes:");
Console.WriteLine("====================");
Console.WriteLine("");
scheduleOfClasses.Display();

Console.WriteLine("======================");
Console.WriteLine("Professor Information:");
```

```
            Console.WriteLine("======================");
            Console.WriteLine("");
            faculty.Display();

            Console.WriteLine("====================");
            Console.WriteLine("Student Information:");
            Console.WriteLine("====================");
            Console.WriteLine("");
            s1.Display();
            Console.WriteLine("");
            s2.Display();
            Console.WriteLine("");
            s3.Display();
    }
}
```

Because several of the classes that make up the SRS have Main methods, we'll have to use the /main option when we compile the SRS application. The following command compiles the SRS and names the executable SRS.exe:

```
csc /out:SRS.exe *.cs /main:SRS
```

The output produced by running this program is as follows:

```
====================
Course Catalog:
====================

Course Catalog:

Course Information:
     Course No.:  CMP101
     Course Name:  Beginning Computer Technology
     Credits:  3
     Prerequisite Courses:
     Offered As Section(s):  1 2

Course Information:
     Course No.:  OBJ101
     Course Name:  Object Methods for Software Development
     Credits:  3
     Prerequisite Courses:
          CMP101:  Beginning Computer Technology
     Offered As Section(s):  1 2

Course Information:
     Course No.:  CMP283
     Course Name:  Higher Level Languages (C#)
     Credits:  3
```

```
    Prerequisite Courses:
        OBJ101:  Object Methods for Software Development
    Offered As Section(s):  1

Course Information:
    Course No.:  CMP999
    Course Name:  Living Brain Computers
    Credits:  3
    Prerequisite Courses:
        CMP283:  Higher Level Languages (C#)
    Offered As Section(s):  1

Course Information:
    Course No.:  ART101
    Course Name:  Beginning Basketweaving
    Credits:  3
    Prerequisite Courses:
    Offered As Section(s):  1


====================
Schedule of Classes:
====================

Schedule of Classes for SP2009

Section Information:
    Semester:  SP2009
    Course No.:  CMP101
    Section No:  1
    Offered:  M at 8:10 - 10:00 PM
    In Room:  GOVT101
    Professor:  Jackie Chan
    Total of 1 students enrolled, as follows:
        Zachary Palmer

Section Information:
    Semester:  SP2009
    Course No.:  CMP101
    Section No:  2
    Offered:  W at 6:10 - 8:00 PM
    In Room:  GOVT202
    Professor:  John Carson
    Total of 0 students enrolled.
```

```
Section Information:
    Semester:  SP2009
    Course No.:  OBJ101
    Section No:  1
    Offered:  R at 4:10 - 6:00 PM
    In Room:  GOVT105
    Professor:  Jacquie Barker
    Total of 0 students enrolled.

Section Information:
    Semester:  SP2009
    Course No.:  OBJ101
    Section No:  2
    Offered:  T at 6:10 - 8:00 PM
    In Room:  SCI330
    Professor:  Jackie Chan
    Total of 0 students enrolled.

Section Information:
    Semester:  SP2009
    Course No.:  CMP283
    Section No:  1
    Offered:  M at 6:10 - 8:00 PM
    In Room:  GOVT101
    Professor:  Jacquie Barker
    Total of 0 students enrolled.

Section Information:
    Semester:  SP2009
    Course No.:  CMP999
    Section No:  1
    Offered:  R at 4:10 - 6:00 PM
    In Room:  SCI241
    Professor:  John Carson
    Total of 0 students enrolled.

Section Information:
    Semester:  SP2009
    Course No.:  ART101
    Section No:  1
    Offered:  M at 4:10 - 6:00 PM
    In Room:  ARTS25
    Professor:  Jackie Chan
    Total of 2 students enrolled, as follows:
        Zachary Palmer
        Gerson Lopez
```

```
========================
Professor Information:
========================

Faculty:

Person Information:
    Name:  Jacquie Barker
    ID number:  123-45-6789
Professor-Specific Information:
    Title:  Adjunct Professor
    Teaches for Dept.:  Information Technology
Teaching Assignments for Jacquie Barker:
    Course No.:  OBJ101
    Section No.:  1
    Course Name:  Object Methods for Software Development
    Day and Time:  R - 4:10 - 6:00 PM
    -----
    Course No.:  CMP283
    Section No.:  1
    Course Name:  Higher Level Languages (C#)
    Day and Time:  M - 6:10 - 8:00 PM
    -----

Person Information:
    Name:  John Carson
    ID number:  567-81-2345
Professor-Specific Information:
    Title:  Full Professor
    Teaches for Dept.:  Information Technology
Teaching Assignments for John Carson:
    Course No.:  CMP101
    Section No.:  2
    Course Name:  Beginning Computer Technology
    Day and Time:  W - 6:10 - 8:00 PM
    -----
    Course No.:  CMP999
    Section No.:  1
    Course Name:  Living Brain Computers
    Day and Time:  R - 4:10 - 6:00 PM
    -----

Person Information:
    Name:  Jackie Chan
    ID number:  987-65-4321
Professor-Specific Information:
    Title:  Full Professor
```

```
     Teaches for Dept.:  Physical Education
Teaching Assignments for Jackie Chan:
     Course No.:  CMP101
     Section No.:  1
     Course Name:  Beginning Computer Technology
     Day and Time:  M - 8:10 - 10:00 PM
     -----
     Course No.:  OBJ101
     Section No.:  2
     Course Name:  Object Methods for Software Development
     Day and Time:  T - 6:10 - 8:00 PM
     -----
     Course No.:  ART101
     Section No.:  1
     Course Name:  Beginning Basketweaving
     Day and Time:  M - 4:10 - 6:00 PM
     -----


====================
Student Information:
====================


Person Information:
     Name:  Zachary Palmer
     ID number:  111-11-1111
Student-Specific Information:
     Major:  Math
     Degree:  M.S.
Course Schedule for Zachary Palmer
     Course No.:  CMP101
     Section No.:  1
     Course Name:  Beginning Computer Technology
     Meeting Day and Time Held:  M - 8:10 - 10:00 PM
     Room Location:  GOVT101
     Professor's Name:  Jackie Chan
     -----
     Course No.:  ART101
     Section No.:  1
     Course Name:  Beginning Basketweaving
     Meeting Day and Time Held:  M - 4:10 - 6:00 PM
     Room Location:  ARTS25
     Professor's Name:  Jackie Chan
     -----
Transcript for:  Zachary Palmer (111-11-1111) [M.S. - Math]
     (no entries)


Person Information:
```

```
    Name:  Gerson Lopez
    ID number:  222-22-2222
Student-Specific Information:
    Major:  Information Technology
    Degree:  Ph. D.
Course Schedule for Gerson Lopez
    Course No.:  ART101
    Section No.:  1
    Course Name:  Beginning Basketweaving
    Meeting Day and Time Held:  M - 4:10 - 6:00 PM
    Room Location:  ARTS25
    Professor's Name:  Jackie Chan
    -----
Transcript for:  Gerson Lopez (222-22-2222) [Ph. D. - Information Technology]
    (no entries)


Person Information:
    Name:  Mary Smith
    ID number:  333-33-3333
Student-Specific Information:
    Major:  Physics
    Degree:  B.S.
Course Schedule for Mary Smith
Transcript for:  Mary Smith (333-33-3333) [B.S. - Physics]
    (no entries)
```

In summary, Table 15-1 shows how we had to modify our Chapter 14 version of the SRS to achieve file persistence.

Table 15-1. *Modifications Made to Achieve File Persistence*

Class	Modifications?
CourseCatalog	(New class)
ScheduleOfClasses	Yes: it now reads data from a file, and we added a FindSection method.
Faculty	(New class)
Course	Yes: we changed the signature of the ScheduleSection method to accept an explicit section number as an argument, because we're now reading it from a file.
Student	Yes: we did a lot! We created a method to read student data from a file, and we created a method that writes the current state of a student's registration situation to a file when he or she logs off.
SRS	Yes: it was revamped—and streamlined!—to take advantage of all of the new collections that we've created.
Person	No
Professor	No
Section	No
Transcript	No
TranscriptEntry	No

This concludes the work that we're going to do with respect to persistence in the SRS application. We'll finish rounding out the SRS application by adding a GUI in Chapter 16.

Summary

In this chapter, you've learned

- How we approach file I/O in C#, using the `FileStream`, `StreamReader`, and `StreamWriter` classes of the `System.IO` namespace

- An approach for parsing tab-delimited ASCII records to initialize an object's state, or a collection of objects, using the `String.Split` method

- A means of persisting an object's state in an ASCII file

- How to prepare a "test scaffold" `Main` method for testing isolated classes

- How proper encapsulation streamlines client code (for example, the SRS `Main` method)

We're also getting quite an opportunity to apply the C# language skills that we covered in earlier chapters. We encourage you to work with the SRS code and to attempt some of the exercises that follow, to reinforce your learning experience.

Exercises

1. Review all of the code associated with the SRS as produced in this chapter, and cite all cases where error handling could be improved.

2. Use the test scaffold provided in the `CourseCatalog` class to test the `ReadCourseCatalogData` and `ReadPrerequisitesData` methods of that class against all of the following error situations in either the `CourseCatalog.dat` or `Prerequisites.dat` files. Edit these files to introduce the following problems one by one, and then run the code to see what happens:

   a. The course name is missing from one of the records in `CourseCatalog.dat` (i.e., the record only contains two fields instead of three).

   b. The value for credits (the third field in a record) in `CourseCatalog.dat` is a nonnumeric value, such as "X".

   c. The `Prerequisites.dat` file refers to a course that wasn't defined in the `CourseCatalog.dat` file.

   d. The `Prerequisites.dat` file is empty.

   e. The `Prerequisites.dat` file contains a record with only one field in it.

   Describe what happens in each case, and discuss what coding changes you'd have to make, if any, to handle each of the preceding situations gracefully.

3. Follow up exercise 2 by actually making the necessary changes to the `CourseCatalog.cs` file, and then retest. (Hint: this will involve exception handling.)

CHAPTER 16

■ ■ ■

Rounding Out Our Application, Part 2: Adding a Graphical User Interface

In Chapter 15, we greatly improved the usefulness of the Student Registration System (SRS) application by providing a means for persisting the state of Student objects—in particular, their enrollment status in various classes—from one SRS invocation to the next. However, we still haven't provided a means by which a student user can interact with the SRS. As it is currently implemented, we launch the application from the command line by running the SRS executable, and from then on the application runs to completion without any further user input, relying solely on ASCII files and/or hard-coded information as its "fuel" (data).

In this chapter, we'll enhance our latest version of the SRS application once again by retrofitting a graphical user interface (GUI) front-end. With the GUI that we add, we'll provide hypothetical student users with the capability to do the following:

- Log on to the SRS.

- View the schedule of sections available for registration in the current semester.

- View and modify their individual course load by dropping and adding sections of courses that they are eligible to attend.

- Save these changes to a file before logging off again.

In this chapter, you'll learn the following:

- The basics of C# GUI composition and event handling

- What the GUI classes in the System.Windows.Forms and System.Drawing namespaces have to offer

- Details about a number of Framework Class Library (FCL) GUI classes

- A recommended architecture for C# GUI applications

- The importance of developing an overall plan for how the GUI is to look, operate, and "flow," called a *concept of operations,* before any code is written

- How to retrofit a GUI to an existing application, using our SRS application from Chapter 15 as an example

When reading this chapter, note that it's meant to provide only an introduction to C# GUI development. Our goal is to teach you how to create a simple, yet completely functional GUI front-end for our SRS application. With this goal in mind, we'll cover only the subset of available GUI classes that we'll need for building the SRS GUI. Furthermore, we'll cover only those features of these classes that we'll be taking advantage of when building our GUI. Nonetheless, you'll gain valuable insights into the fundamentals of C# GUI building and event handling.

When you develop your own GUIs for job or school assignments, you will very likely use an integrated development environment (IDE) such as Visual Studio that will write a lot of the GUI code for you. In this chapter, however, we'll go through the process of writing a GUI front-end for an application from scratch. Although IDEs can improve productivity, it's our opinion that when an IDE does some of the work for you, there is a tendency to not pay as much attention to what is going on. You don't learn as much. On the other hand, when you write the GUI code (or any code), you (and only you) are responsible for getting the code to work. You'll really learn the ins and outs of how a program works and how to debug it when it doesn't.

With those caveats out of the way, let's dive into the world of C# GUIs.

C# GUIs: A Primer

The fundamental approach to GUI programming with virtually any programming language, C# or otherwise, is to assemble graphical building blocks generically called *components* (and, in C#, often referred to specifically as *controls*). We assemble them in specific ways to provide the look, or presentation, that we desire for an application, and then program their behind-the-scenes logic to enable them to do useful things. Users interact with GUI components—buttons, text fields, lists, and so on—to provide information to the system and/or to obtain information from the system to achieve some worthwhile goal: in other words, to fulfill the use cases that we identified in Chapter 9.

One of the many advantages of C# is that GUI development is supported by the FCL. Every aspect of our C# application—the domain classes/objects, persistence of the state of these objects to a file, GUI manipulation of these objects, and so on—can be conveniently programmed using FCL types. Therefore, the components that will make up the GUI are objects and can interact with the domain model objects from the SRS. In the case of the SRS GUI, for example, we'll be doing the following:

- *Instantiating objects*: For example, when a student user logs on to the system, we'll instantiate a Student object as an abstraction of that user.

- *Invoking their methods*: As we do when we invoke the soon-to-be-written ValidatePassword method on a Student object to ensure that the password a user has typed is valid.

- *Changing their states*: Modifying field values and/or creating new links between the objects; for example, when a student successfully enrolls in a course, we'll form a link between the appropriate Student and Section objects.

Because the GUI itself consists of objects, the GUI components

- Are described by classes

- Are instantiated via the new operator, using an appropriate constructor

- Have fields (which are typically private) and properties/methods (which are typically public) that we access via dot notation

- Communicate via method calls

- Participate in inheritance hierarchies

- Are referenced by reference variables, when we want to maintain named object references to them

- Maintain references to *other* objects—GUI objects as well as non-GUI objects

- Collaborate with other objects—GUI as well as non-GUI objects—to accomplish the mission of the overall system

Therefore, all the techniques that you've learned about creating and communicating with objects in general throughout this book will apply to GUI objects in particular. Through user interactions with the SRS GUI, the GUI's objects will be requested to perform functions, which in many cases lead them to collaborate behind the scenes with the domain objects—Students, Professors, Courses, Sections, and so on—to carry out a particular user-requested operation such as registering for a course.

Containers

Just as we often use collections to organize object references (e.g., a List to organize Student references), we assemble C# GUIs by organizing collections of components using a special type of GUI object known as a *container*. We may depict the relationship between containers, components, and objects via a UML diagram, as shown in Figure 16-1. A container is a component (by virtue of inheritance) just as all components and containers are objects because they derive from the Object class. However, every GUI component is not necessarily a container. Furthermore, because a container can contain components, and a container is a component, a container can contain other containers. In fact, this is the way that we build up complex GUIs—by embedding components in containers, a technique that we'll explore in depth in this chapter.

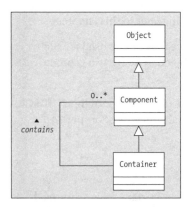

Figure 16-1. *Relationship of containers to components*

A container is like a directory on your computer system, and the objects placed in it are like items placed within that directory.

- Just as any one file has only one home directory, any one object can be placed in only one container.

- Conversely, a container can contain many objects—including other containers—just as a directory can contain many files and/or other directories.

Containers available in C# include the Form class of the System.Windows.Forms namespace, which we'll use as our top-level container when we construct our SRS GUI.

GUIs Are Event-Driven

The C# GUI model is an event-driven system, in which each visual object can generate a number of events based on a user's interaction with that object. For example, clicking a graphical button, pressing the Enter key on the keyboard after typing in a text field, or clicking an item within a list to select it all automatically generate events.

Events are the system's way of telling us that the user has interacted with the GUI in some fashion. Events are informational in nature; as application developers, we can choose to program a response to an event or to ignore it as we see fit. We'll discuss events and event handling in more detail later in this chapter.

System.Windows.Forms and System.Drawing Namespaces

The GUI classes and support classes that we'll discuss in this chapter can be found in the System.Windows.Forms and System.Drawing namespaces of the .NET FCL. These C# namespaces provide an extensive array of ready-made GUI classes:

- The System.Windows.Forms namespace contains predefined GUI classes that represent buttons, labels, menus, windows, panels, and many other things besides. We can extend the existing GUI classes to create our own custom GUI classes.

- The System.Windows.Forms namespace also contains a variety of delegate types. A *delegate* is a C# class that can be used to respond to events generated by a GUI object. We'll discuss delegates when we discuss C# event handling later in this chapter.

- The System.Drawing namespace contains support classes that can be used for such operations as changing a font, adding color to a GUI object, or defining a geometrical construct such as a point or a rectangle.

Before we dive into the details of the classes defined by the GUI libraries of the .NET FCL, however, let's take a step back and talk about some fundamental concepts of proper GUI design.

Separating the Model from the View

A technique known as *separating the model from the view* is an important design approach when developing a graphically oriented application. This concept relates to the Model-View-Controller (MVC) paradigm, which was popularized as a formal concept with the Smalltalk language, but is equally applicable to all object-oriented (OO) languages, including C#.

MVC is a way of thinking of an application as being subdivided into three parts: the model, the view, and the controller:

- The *model* embodies the abstract domain knowledge of the application; that is, the objects/classes that represent the real-world items/issues that the users of an application are familiar with, often referred to as the *business logic* or *domain* of the application. Up until this point in the book, we've been focusing almost exclusively on these so-called domain classes: Person, Student, Professor, Course, Section, and the like.

- The *view* is the way in which we present this knowledge to the user—typically, although not exclusively, via a GUI. Note that there can be many different views of the same model, in either the same or different applications. For example, with respect to the SRS GUI, we could represent the Students enrolled in a particular Section as a list of their names and student ID numbers; or as photographs; or in diagram form, as shown in Figures 16-2 through 16-4.

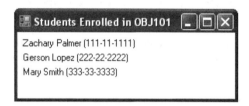

Figure 16-2. *Using a list to display* Student *information*

Figure 16-3. *Using photographs to display* Student *information*

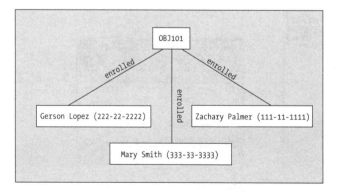

Figure 16-4. *Using a diagram to display* Student *information*

- The *controller* is the automatic mechanism by which the user interface is displayed, and by which events are communicated back and forth between the model and the view; changes to the model are reflected in the view, and user interactions with the view trigger changes to the model. In the case of C#, this is handled by the .NET runtime in conjunction with the underlying windowing mechanism of your particular computer system.

As OO developers, we must do the following

- Design and program the model, as we did throughout Part Two of the book and in Chapter 14, respectively.

- Design and program the view(s); in C#, this is accomplished through the use of the FCL GUI namespaces that provide the graphical user interface building blocks we'll focus our attention on for much of this chapter.

- Understand how the controller works in order to take advantage of the mechanism for connecting the model and view together. This involves learning the C# approach to event handling, (discussed later in this chapter).

When designing and programming an application, if we take care to separate the model and view elements by placing the code for those elements in different classes, it becomes much easier to accomplish the following:

- *Add or change a view, if need be, without disturbing the underlying model*: In essence, this is what we'll be doing when we add a GUI view to the SRS application later in this chapter. As you'll see, the domain classes that we've already programmed will remain virtually unchanged by our addition of a GUI; and, those changes that we do make to the domain classes will be to enhance their abstractions, not to introduce GUI features.

- *Provide multiple alternative views of the same underlying model*: Sometimes we provide different views for different categories of user; for example, a professor using the SRS might see different windows and options than a student would see.

- *Give a single user the ability to switch among multiple views*: A familiar example of this can be found within the Microsoft Windows operating system. With Windows, users can view the contents of a folder as icons, as a detailed list, as an HTML page, or even as a DOS directory listing, as shown in Figures 16-5 through 16-8.

Figure 16-5. *Viewing folder contents as icons*

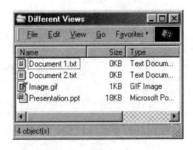

Figure 16-6. *Or viewing folder contents as a detailed list*

Figure 16-7. *Or viewing folder contents as an HTML page*

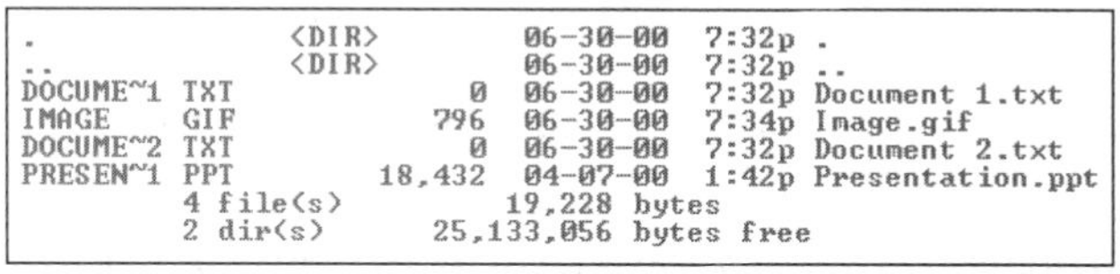

```
.                 <DIR>           06-30-00   7:32p .
..                <DIR>           06-30-00   7:32p ..
DOCUME~1 TXT              0       06-30-00   7:32p Document 1.txt
IMAGE    GIF           796        06-30-00   7:34p Image.gif
DOCUME~2 TXT              0       06-30-00   7:32p Document 2.txt
PRESEN~1 PPT        18,432        04-07-00   1:42p Presentation.ppt
         4 file(s)            19,228 bytes
         2 dir(s)         25,133,056 bytes free
```

Figure 16-8. *Or viewing folder contents as a DOS directory listing*

Regardless of the view chosen, however, the underlying model in our Windows example is the same: we have a directory titled Different Views on our file system, and it contains four files: two text documents, a GIF image, and a PowerPoint presentation, as reflected in the Unified Modeling Language (UML) diagram in Figure 16-9. The Windows File System Component in the figure would be implemented as an abstract class that represents either a `File` or a `Folder`, and would declare members common to both `File` and `Folder` objects (a name, a creation date, a read-only flag, and so on).

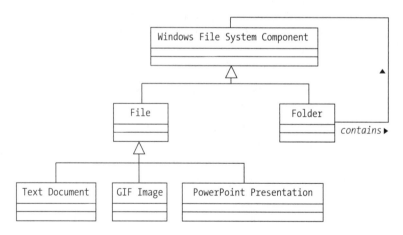

Figure 16-9. *The UML model underlying all Windows views*

Our model should, in essence, be unaffected by the current view; just as we can change the appearance of a sofa by adding a slipcover without changing its underlying structure or general functionality, so too should we be able to change the visual appearance of an application without changing its underlying structure.

One way to help ensure that the model and view are logically separated is to develop the model first, without regard for the view. In theory, if we do a proper job of developing the model, based on the analysis techniques of Part Two, virtually any view relevant to the original goals (use cases) set forth for the system should be attainable. We'll demonstrate this concept by retroactively adding a GUI to the model that we automated in Chapters 14 and 15.

Our Learning Roadmap

We'll learn about building C# GUIs in three stages:

- First, you'll learn how to describe the desired look and behavior of our GUI by preparing a *concept of operations* document.

- Second, you'll learn about the various classes and techniques used in producing the visual appearance of a GUI.

- Finally, you'll learn how to provide behavior to the GUI through event handling.

Stage 1: Preparing a Concept of Operations for the SRS GUI

Before we can decide which specific GUI classes will be needed in building the SRS GUI, we must consider what functionality the GUI is to provide. In particular, we must answer two questions: what information should the GUI present to the user? and what actions will the GUI allow a user to perform? Once we've answered these two questions, we can decide which classes are best suited to accomplishing the objectives of the GUI.

In a nutshell, the SRS GUI we'll create will function as follows:

1. When a student launches the SRS GUI, the list of available courses in the current semester's schedule of classes will be displayed.

2. To access current course information, the student logs in to the SRS GUI by typing in his or her student ID number and password.

3. Once a student has logged in, the student's name will be displayed, along with a list of the courses for which the student is already registered (the student's current course load/list).

4. After a student has logged in, the SRS GUI should allow a student to take any of the following actions:

   - Adding a course to his or her course list by selecting one from the schedule of classes

   - Dropping a course from his or her course list

   - Saving his or her current course schedule to a file

   - Logging off from the SRS

Sketching out the functional flow of a GUI through pictures and accompanying narrative—a technique informally known as *storyboarding*—is a great way to come to agreement with the future users of a system on how the application should look and behave before development begins. And if the application truly evolves as we envisioned that it would, the document that we've prepared to narrate the storyboard before developing the application, known as a *concept of operations document*, can be used as the basis for a user's guide and/or online tutorial after the application is finished. The story that is told by the concept of operations document is presented from the external viewpoint of a user; it is, in essence, a pictorial representation of how the various use cases for the application will be fulfilled. The concept of operations document is similar to (but less formal and extensive than) the use case documentation we developed for the SRS in Chapter 9.

In a real-life situation in which the concept of operations would be created before the GUI was developed, we'd likely start by informally sketching our ideas, perhaps with pen or paper or on a whiteboard, to test drive the concepts with future users of the system. Once we verify that we are on the right track, then, depending on what tools we have available, we might render our conceptualized GUI with a conventional drawing tool such as Microsoft PowerPoint, or even create a GUI shell using an IDE. Because the SRS GUI code itself was available to the authors when this chapter was written, we'll use some screenshots of the finished SRS as storyboards to demonstrate what a concept of operations might look like.

A Typical SRS Session

A concept of operations document helps us to think through and describe how the GUI should look and flow. To create the concept of operations for the SRS, we will follow the progress of a typical student named Zachary Palmer as he tries to sign up for a class using the SRS. When Zachary launches the SRS, the GUI that first appears, shown in Figure 16-10, presents a list, titled Schedule of Classes, of all sections offered this semester, along with a number of empty fields labeled Student Name, ID Number, and Total Courses. A number of buttons appear at the bottom of the window labeled Log In, Drop, Save My Schedule, Add, and Log Out, but all of them except the Log In button are initially grayed out to signal that they are disabled; until a user logs on, none of the functions provided by these buttons is valid.

Zachary logs on to the SRS by pressing the Log In button. A small dialog box appears (see Figure 16-11) and requests Zachary's student ID and password. As Zachary types in his password (which happens to be 111, the first three digits of his student ID number), asterisks (*) appear in place of the characters that he types to ensure his privacy.

After typing in his password, Zachary presses the Log In button. Unfortunately, he has mistyped his password, so the pop-up message shown in Figure 16-12 appears.

After Zachary clicks the OK button on this dialog box to dismiss it, he can try again by pressing the Log In button in the main SRS window. Assuming that he types his password correctly this time, he receives confirmation of a successful logon (see Figure 16-13).

After clicking OK, Zachary sees that his current registration information appears in the Student Name, ID Number, Total Courses, and Registered For fields in the main GUI window. (Although Zachary doesn't know it, this information was read in behind the scenes from a data file named 111-11-1111.dat.) Zachary previously used the SRS to register for section 1 of course number CMP101. Notice in Figure 16-14 that two of the buttons at the bottom of the GUI—Save My Schedule and Log Out—have now become enabled and clickable.

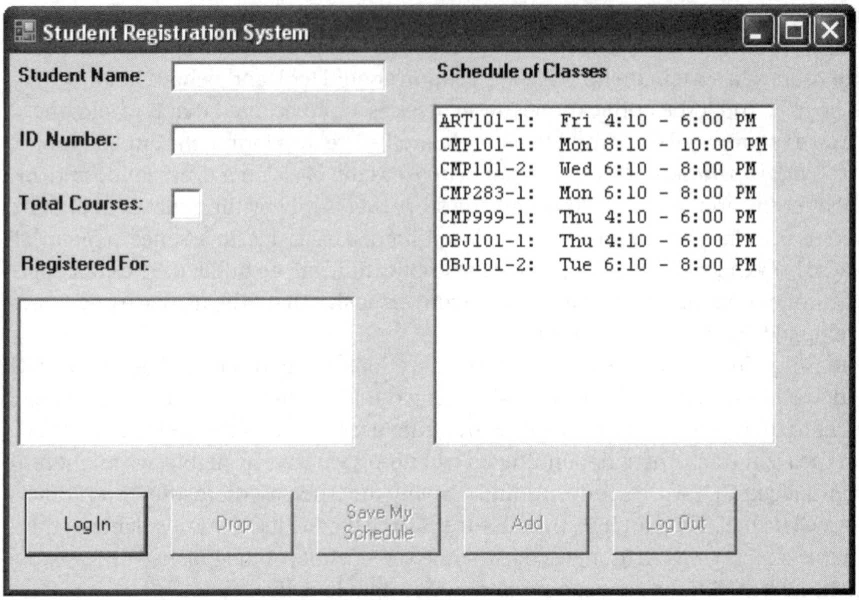

Figure 16-10. *The initial view of the SRS GUI*

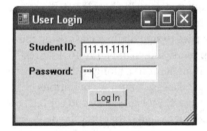

Figure 16-11. *Zachary types his student ID number and password into the dialog box.*

Figure 16-12. *If the password is invalid, a warning dialog box appears.*

Log In Succeeded
Log in succeeded for Zachary Palmer.
OK

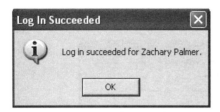

Figure 16-13. *Zachary has successfully logged on to the SRS.*

■Note There are three data files supplied with the SRS code download from Apress that support this application and represent three different students' data: `111-11-1111.dat`, `222-22-2222.dat`, and `333-33-3333.dat`.

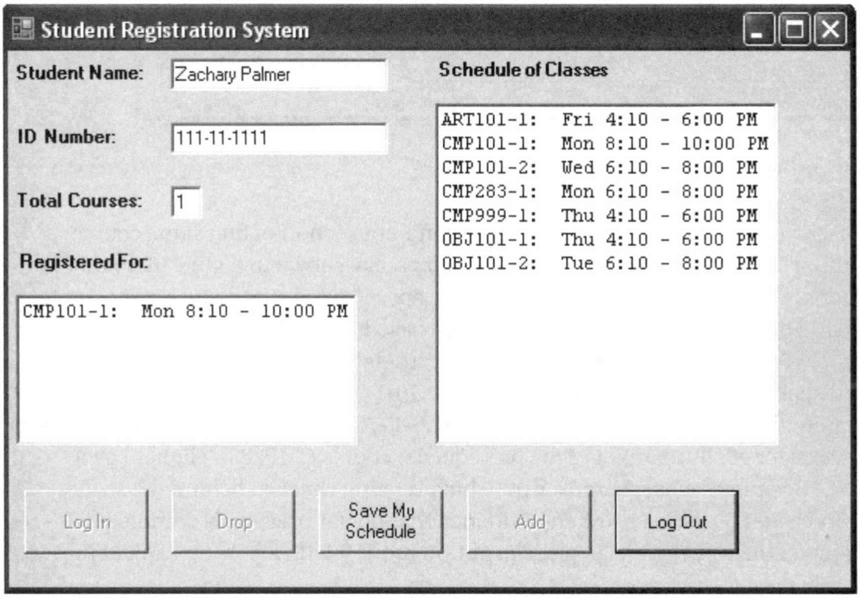

Student Registration System
Student Name:
Zachary Palmer
ID Number:
111-11-1111
Total Courses:
1
Registered For:
CMP101-1: Mon 8:10 - 10:00 PM
Schedule of Classes
ART101-1: Fri 4:10 - 6:00 PM
CMP101-1: Mon 8:10 - 10:00 PM
CMP101-2: Wed 6:10 - 8:00 PM
CMP283-1: Mon 6:10 - 8:00 PM
CMP999-1: Thu 4:10 - 6:00 PM
OBJ101-1: Thu 4:10 - 6:00 PM
OBJ101-2: Tue 6:10 - 8:00 PM
Log In
Drop
Save My Schedule
Add
Log Out

Figure 16-14. *Zachary's current registration data is displayed.*

Zachary decides to try to enroll in course CMP101–2. He selects this section from the `Schedule of Classes` list, which causes the `Add` button at the bottom of the screen to automatically become active. (Until he selected a section in the `Schedule of Classes` list, it made no sense for the `Add` button to be selectable.)

Zachary clicks the Add button, shown in Figure 16-15.

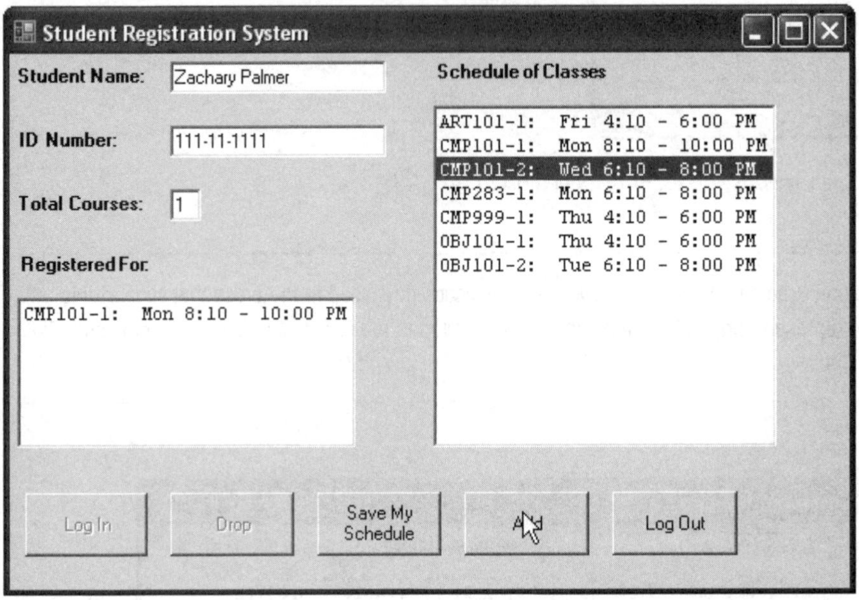

Figure 16-15. *Zachary tries to register for a course.*

But because Zachary is already registered for a different section of that same course (CMP101–1), the system notifies him via the pop-up message shown in Figure 16-16 that he may not register for CMP101–2. (Had Zachary's transcript reflected successful *prior* completion of any section of CMP101, his request would have also been rejected.)

Zachary clicks OK to dismiss the dialog box. He next selects CMP999–1 from the Schedule of Classes and again clicks the Add button (see Figure 16-17).

Unfortunately, this attempt also fails. Course CMP999, "Living Brain Computers," requires students to have successfully completed the prerequisite course CMP283, "Higher Level Languages (C#)." Because Zachary's transcript (which is being checked behind the scenes, unbeknownst to Zachary) doesn't show any evidence that he has previously completed CMP283, the system once again rejects his registration request with a pop-up explanation (see Figure 16-18).

After clicking OK to dismiss this pop-up dialog box, Zachary selects ART101–1 from the Schedule of Classes list, and clicks the Add button yet again (see Figure 16-19).

Figure 16-16. *Zachary has already enrolled in a different section of CMP101.*

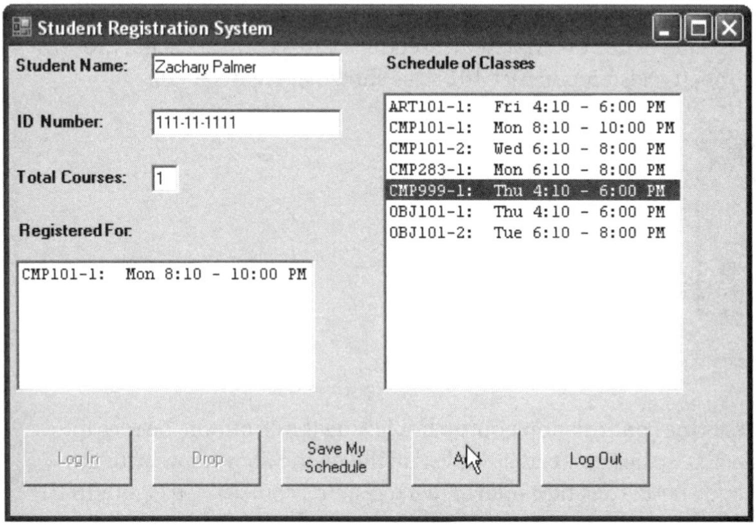

Figure 16-17. *Zachary attempts to register for CMP999.*

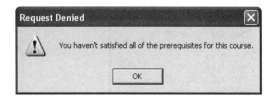

Figure 16-18. *Zachary hasn't satisfied the prerequisites for CMP999.*

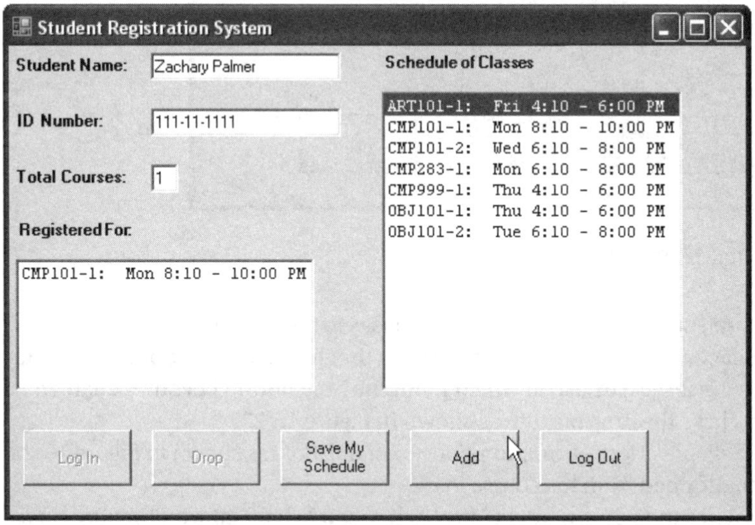

Figure 16-19. *Zachary tries to register for ART101.*

Success at last! ART101 has no prerequisites to satisfy, and Zachary is neither currently registered for (nor has ever successfully completed) a section of this course. Zachary receives confirmation that he has been registered in ART 101-1, as shown in Figure 16-20.

Figure 16-20. *Success at last!*

After Zachary dismisses the confirmation pop-up by clicking the OK button, he sees the newly added section reflected in the Registered For list on the main SRS window, with the Total Courses field reflecting his correct new total of two registered courses (see Figure 16-21).

Student Registration System	
Student Name: Zachary Palmer	**Schedule of Classes**
	ART101-1: Fri 4:10 - 6:00 PM
ID Number: 111-11-1111	CMP101-1: Mon 8:10 - 10:00 PM
	CMP101-2: Wed 6:10 - 8:00 PM
	CMP283-1: Mon 6:10 - 8:00 PM
Total Courses: 2	CMP999-1: Thu 4:10 - 6:00 PM
	OBJ101-1: Thu 4:10 - 6:00 PM
Registered For:	OBJ101-2: Tue 6:10 - 8:00 PM
CMP101-1: Mon 8:10 - 10:00 PM	
ART101-1: Fri 4:10 - 6:00 PM	

Log In | Drop | Save My Schedule | Add | Log Out

Figure 16-21. *Zachary is now registered for two courses.*

Note that Zachary's selection in the Schedule of Classes list has been cleared and that the Add button is no longer enabled. Next, Zachary decides that he wants to drop CMP101. He clicks that entry in his Registered For list, at which point the Drop button becomes enabled and selectable. Zachary clicks the Drop button, as shown in Figure 16-22.

In response, the SRS displays a confirmation pop-up dialog box, as shown in Figure 16-23, that the course has been dropped from his course load.

When Zachary dismisses the pop-up by clicking OK, his course load information has once again been properly updated and the Drop button has once again become disabled, as shown in Figure 16-24.

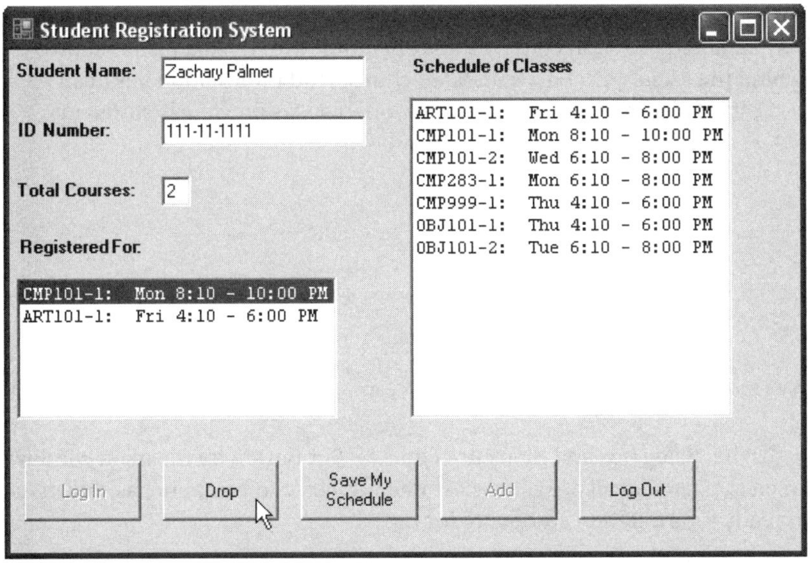

Figure 16-22. *Zachary drops CMP101.*

Figure 16-23. *The drop request is successful.*

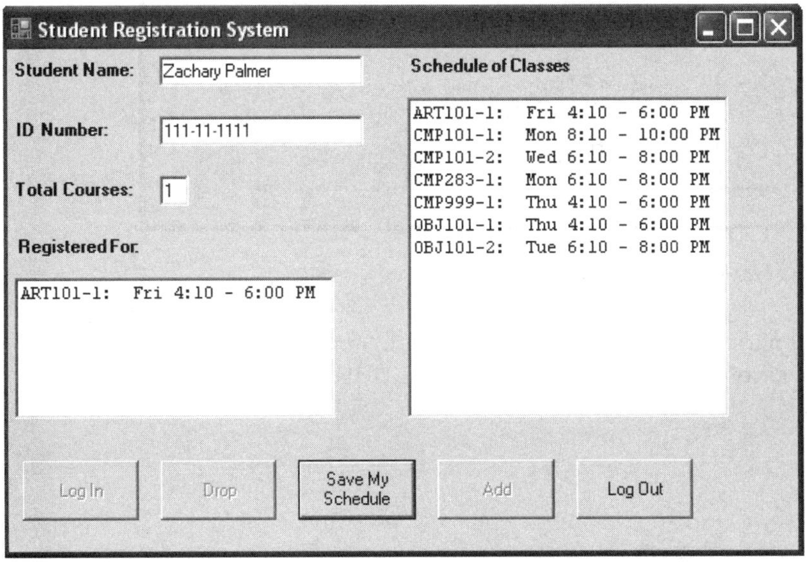

Figure 16-24. *Zachary is registered only for ART101 now.*

Satisfied with his new schedule, Zachary decides to save this information by clicking the Save My Schedule button, and the system confirms this operation with the dialog box shown in Figure 16-25. (Behind the scenes, Zachary's updated course load information has been persisted to file 111-11-1111.dat, replacing the information that was previously stored in that file.)

Figure 16-25. *Zachary's schedule is saved to a file.*

Zachary dismisses the dialog box and then clicks the Log Out button on the main window; in response, the screen is cleared of all of Zachary's student-specific information, as shown in Figure 16-26, and is ready for a different student to log on.

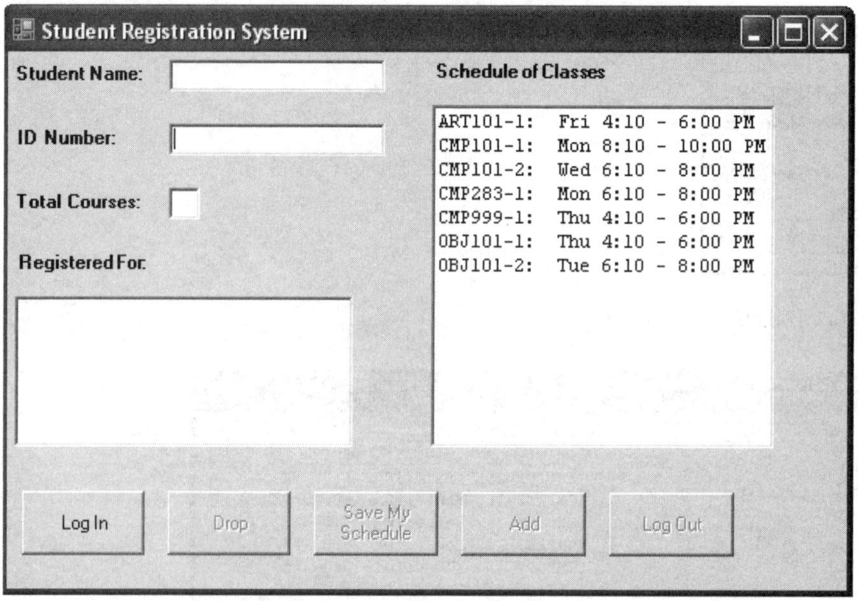

Figure 16-26. *Zachary has logged off of the SRS system.*

Now that we've narrated the concept of operations for our GUI, let's move on to stage 2: programming the look of the GUI through the use of FCL GUI classes.

Stage 2: Creating the Look of Our GUI

Let's look at each of the functional requirements of the GUI as specified by the concept of operations, and identify the GUI class best suited to each.

- To log in to the SRS, the student will need to type his or her identification number and password into a field. The C# TextBox class will suit this requirement nicely. We can also use noneditable TextBox objects to display the student's name, the identification number, and the number of courses for which he or she is registered.

- To display both the course catalog and the student's course list, we need an object that can display a multiline list of items. The object also has to allow the student to make a selection from the list and keep track of which item is selected. The ListBox class can fulfill all these requirements.

- One of the best ways to initiate an action is by having the user click a button. We'll use five Button objects to implement the Log In, Add, Drop, Save My Schedule, and Log Out functionality.

- The GUI would be somewhat confusing if we didn't include labels to describe what the various objects were to be used for. We'll use several instances of the Label class to achieve this goal.

- We'll need a container to organize all these objects into a main window for the GUI; we'll use the Form class for this purpose.

- Finally, we'll need a way to pop up various warning/confirmation messages; we'll use the MessageBox class to do so.

All these classes—Button, Form, Label, ListBox, MessageBox, and TextBox—are defined within the System.Windows.Forms namespace.

Now that we've proposed the objects that we'll use for the SRS GUI, we'll describe each of the chosen classes in more detail, creating the objects and adding them to our SRS GUI as we go. By the end of this section, we'll have completed building the look of the SRS GUI.

One thing to remember with GUI development is that there are multiple ways to achieve the same functional goals. That is, there is nothing "sacred" about the classes that we've chosen for the SRS GUI. We could have, for example, implemented the Log In, Add, Drop, Save My Schedule, and Log Out actions using menu items instead of buttons.

We'll be doing all the code development in a step-by-step, easy-to-follow manner. If you use an IDE such as Visual Studio to help create a GUI, the code structure might look different from what we'll develop here.

■**Note** The primary emphasis behind this chapter is to teach you how to create a working GUI that will provide the user front-end to our SRS program. We will focus on functionality—how to create the GUI components, how to place them on our Form, and how to make the components respond to user interaction. The emphasis of this chapter is not on how to create a GUI that will win visual design awards from *Spiffy GUI Monthly*. There are probably myriad ways that we could dress up our SRS GUI to make it look more visually stunning, but that subject is beyond the scope and intention of this book.

Form Class

Earlier in this chapter, we discussed how a container is used to organize, manage, and present other objects in a GUI. We can think of a top-level container as a surface onto which all the other GUI objects are arranged (see Figure 16-27).

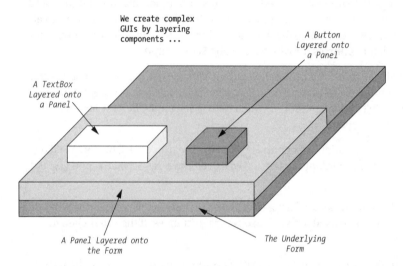

Figure 16-27. *GUI components are placed on a container.*

In building the SRS GUI, we'll use an instance of the Form class as our main container. A Form object serves as a stand-alone window; note that a Form can't be contained in/attached to any other type of GUI object.

A Form has a title bar and can optionally be equipped with a menu bar, toolbars, and status bars (we won't be using these elements for the SRS GUI as designed, however). A Form also automatically provides *window control buttons* in its upper-right corner; from left to right, the three window control buttons are used to minimize the size of, maximize the size of, or close the Form and optionally exit the application (see Figure 16-28). Users can also click the icon in the upper-left corner of the Form to move, resize, or close the window.

When building a C# GUI application, at least one main Form is created to hold the objects necessary to provide the desired GUI appearance and functionality. Nontrivial GUI applications typically consist of *multiple* separate windows—one main Form and multiple other Form/MessageBox/Dialog objects that can represent such things as transient pop-up windows. (We'll use MessageBox objects when we build the SRS GUI and will discuss them later in this chapter after we've explored event handling a bit.)

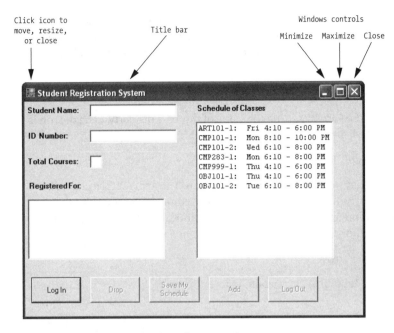

Figure 16-28. *Some of the built-in features of a* Form

Building a Simple Form

A Form object will serve as the primary container for the SRS GUI, but before we launch into actually building the SRS GUI, let's get our feet wet by building a simple Form.

First, we'll create a program/class called TestForm1 and will place using directives at the top of the program so we can refer to the appropriate GUI classes by their simple names. After those lines, we'll declare the class and Main method headers.

```
// TestForm1.cs

using System;
using System.Windows.Forms;

public class TestForm1
{
  static void Main() {
```

Within the Main method of this class, we'll perform the bare minimum steps necessary to create and display a Form; namely, we'll instantiate a Form object by using the Form class's lone, parameterless constructor, and will maintain a reference to the newly created Form object with a reference variable named simpleForm:

```
Form simpleForm = new Form();
```

Most of the characteristics that define the state of a Form can be manipulated through properties declared by the Form class. There are several properties that allow us to specify the size of a Form; in this example, we'll use the Height and Width properties.

The width and height of GUI objects is expressed in *pixels*; a pixel is the smallest address-able graphical unit on a display screen. The default size for a Form is 300 pixels high by 300 pixels wide. We'll set the size of our form to have a height of 200 pixels and a width of 200 pixels:

```
simpleForm.Height = 200;
simpleForm.Width = 200;
```

Next, we'll set a title to the Form by setting the value of the Text property. (The default is for a Form to be untitled.) We'll give our Form the title "Whee!!!":

```
simpleForm.Text = "Whee!!!";
```

We're now ready to display our simple Form on the screen. The Application class, also from the System.Windows.Forms namespace, defines static methods and properties that are used to manage an application, including methods to start and stop an application. We'll use the static Run method from the Application class to launch our Form:

```
Application.Run(simpleForm);
```

Here is the code for the TestForm1 class again, in its entirety:

```
// TestForm1.cs

using System;
using System.Windows.Forms;

public class TestForm1
{
  static void Main() {
    // Create a Form.
    Form simpleForm = new Form();

    // Set the size of the Form using the Height
    // and Width properties.
    simpleForm.Height = 200;
    simpleForm.Width = 200;

    // Set the title to the Form using the Text property.
    simpleForm.Text = "Whee!!!";

    // Use the Application class Run() method to launch
    // the Form.
    Application.Run(simpleForm);
  }
}
```

■Tip The complete code for all the examples in this chapter is available as a download from the Apress web site; see Appendix B for details.

When we subsequently compile, then run, the following program by typing the following commands we see the window (form) shown in Figure 16-29 appear in the upper-left region of the screen:

```
csc TestForm1.cs
TestForm1
```

Figure 16-29. *A simple* Form

Our form is blank because we haven't yet attached any objects (labels, buttons, and so on)—we'll do so in due time.

To dismiss this form and stop the TestForm1 program from executing, click the window close (X) button in the upper-right corner of the frame.

■**Note** C# programs can also be launched through other means; one of the most frequently used approaches is to create a Windows desktop shortcut. The shortcut should execute the same command that a user would have typed if launching the program from the command prompt.

In our simple Form example, we specified the height, width, and title of the Form by setting the value of the Height, Width, and Text properties. The Form class declares a large number of properties that can be used to define the appearance and behavior of a Form. We'll use another one of the Form properties in the next section to center our simple form on the screen.

Centering a Form on the Screen

By default, it's up to Windows to decide where a Form will appear on the computer screen; typically it's placed in the upper-left region of the screen. Alternatively, we might like to specify that a new Form will appear in the center of the screen when it first appears. To center a form, we need to set its StartPosition property value to the constant value FormStartPosition. CenterScreen, also defined by the Form class.

Let's rewrite the previous example to take advantage of the StartPosition property:

```
// TestForm2.cs

using System;
using System.Windows.Forms;
```

```
using System.Drawing;

public class TestForm2 {
  static void Main() {
    // Create a Form.
    Form simpleForm = new Form();

    // Set the size of the Form using the Height.
    // and Width properties
    simpleForm.Height = 300;
    simpleForm.Width = 300;

    // Set the title to the Form using the Text property.
    simpleForm.Text = "Whee!!!";

    // Center the Form on the Desktop.
    simpleForm.StartPosition = FormStartPosition.CenterScreen;

    // Use the Application class Run() method to launch
    // the Form
    Application.Run(simpleForm);
  }
}
```

The Form will now appear in the center of the computer screen, regardless of the size of the monitor in question (see Figure 16-30).

Frame is now automatically centered on the screen!

Figure 16-30. *A* Form *can be centered on the display using the* StartPosition *property.*

Application Architecture with GUIs

The simple GUI examples that we've seen thus far all involve a single class whose `Main` method instantiates and displays a `Form`; `TestForm1` and `TestForm2` were both designed in this fashion. This single-class methodology isn't an appropriate architecture for anything but trivial applications, however.

A better architecture for a GUI application is to create a minimum of two classes:

1. A class, derived from `Form`, that defines the appearance (and ultimately, the behavior) of the main GUI window:

   - The components that will be displayed in the GUI are declared to be *fields* of this class.

   - A constructor is declared that instantiates all the GUI components and positions them in the form.

2. A separate application driver class that does the following:

   - Creates an instance of the main window/`Form` in its `Main` method

   - Handles any other application initialization steps; for example, establishing database connectivity, perhaps with the help of a logon dialog box

   - Houses any constants or convenience methods (as public static methods) for the application as a whole

If more than one window is needed for the GUI (as will be the case for the SRS GUI), additional classes are created to define the appearance and behavior of the other key windows, each of which is derived from an appropriate predefined GUI container class (usually another `Form` or a different type of container, such as a `MessageBox`, which we'll discuss later in this chapter).

Let's take another look at the `TestForm2.cs` example, redesigned as previously suggested:

- First, we'll create a class called `TestForm3`, derived from the `Form` class, to represent the main window.

- Second, we'll create the driver class, `TestForm3Driver`, in a separate file called `TestForm3Driver.cs`.

Let's start with `TestForm3`; we'll show the complete code listing for `TestForm3.cs` first and will then comment on some of the differences between `TestForm3` and `TestForm2`:

```
// TestForm3.cs

using System;
using System.Windows.Forms;
using System.Drawing;

public class TestForm3 : Form {

  // (When we eventually attach components to the Form -
  // labels, buttons, and so forth -- they will be declared here,
```

```
// as FIELDS of the TestForm3 class.)

// Constructor: we "assemble" the GUI here
public TestForm3() {
   // Set the size of the Form using the Height
   // and Width properties.
   this.Height = 200;
   this.Width = 200;

   // Add a title to the Form using the Text property.
   this.Text = "Whee!!!";

   // Center the Form on the desktop.
   this.StartPosition = FormStartPosition.CenterScreen;
}

// Note that there is no longer a Main method in this class.
}
```

The Form's properties are set as before, except now we're doing so from within the TestForm3 class—specifically, inside its constructor—instead of setting them externally to the Form instance from within the Main method. Note the use of the this. prefix when setting the Form property values:

```
this.Height = 200;
this.Width = 200;
```

Strictly speaking, the this. prefix isn't necessary, but can optionally be used as a reminder that we're setting the value of the property on the current object: namely, *this* Form, which we're currently assembling.

Now, let's look at the code for the driver class, TestForm3Driver. For this example, the Main method of the driver class simply calls the Application.Run method, passing the method a newly created TestForm3 instance. The TestForm3 class constructor that we reviewed previously does all the work of assembling the GUI instance.

```
// TestForm3Driver.cs

using System;
using System.Windows.Forms;

public class TestForm3Driver {
   static void Main() {
      // The Main() method has become quite simple;
      // we simply call the Run() method to display
      // an (unnamed) instance of TestForm3.
      Application.Run(new TestForm3());
   }
}
```

The following is used to compile the TestForm3 example:

```
csc TestForm3Driver.cs TestForm3.cs
```

In the previous example, we created an unnamed TestForm3 object on the fly, nested inside of the Run method call:

```
Application.Run(new TestForm3());
```

We could have accomplished the same result as a two-step process:

```
TestForm3 form3 = new TestForm3();
Application.Run(form3);
```

However, because we have no reason to maintain a named reference to the TestForm3 object—once it's passed as an argument to the Run method, we have no further need to address it by name in this application—we collapsed what would have been two statements into one. This is a commonly used technique throughout the C# language, whenever an object A requires us to pass it an instance of a class B for its own private use.

The previous Form example is significant because the TestForm3 and TestForm3Driver classes will be the starting points for our SRS GUI—we'll rename them MainForm and SRS, respectively, as they evolve.

Now that we have our top-level container, you'll next learn about the various other objects needed to round out our GUI's main window (see Figure 16-31):

- Label

- Button

- ListBox

- TextBox

- MessageBox

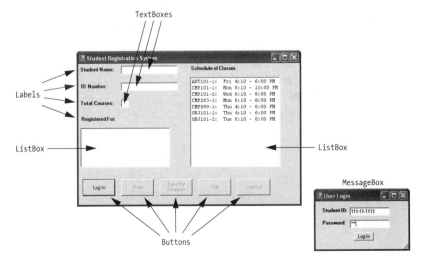

Figure 16-31. *The SRS GUI will showcase a variety of GUI objects.*

Tip While you read through the next several sections, it's helpful to look at the entire `MainForm.cs` and `PasswordForm.cs` code listings. This will give you a sense of the "big picture" of how the GUI objects are incorporated into their underlying Form. You can download the Chapter 16 source code from the Apress web site. Details are provided in Appendix B.

Label Class

A GUI wouldn't be very useful if it simply displayed an assortment of GUI objects with no explanation of what the objects were supposed to do or be used for. Virtually every GUI application uses labels to describe the purpose of the various GUI objects that it presents, as well as provide other instructions/status information to the user. We'll define a number of informational labels for the SRS GUI using instances of the `Label` class.

The `Label` class represents a simple GUI object that can be used to display a single line of text. (A `Label` can also be used to display an image, but we won't be using that capability in building the SRS GUI.) The `Label` class defines a single parameterless constructor:

```
public Label()
```

This constructor creates a blank `Label` with default properties. As with the `Form` class, the state and appearance of a `Label` can be specified through properties declared by the `Label` class. To create the labels for the SRS GUI, we'll make use of the following `Label` properties:

- `public virtual string Text`: The `Text` property is used to access the text that is displayed by the `Label`. The property defines both `get` and `set` accessors, so it can be used to retrieve or change `Label` text programmatically.

  ```
  Label name = new Label();
  name.Text = "Jackson";
  ```

  Note that `Label` values can't be modified directly by a user, only indirectly by our application in response to a user's actions on some other object; for example:

  ```
  Label status = new Label();  // Create a blank label.
  // Later in the application (pseudocode):
  if (user presses the Submit button) {
    // Programmatically set the text on this label.
    status.Text = "Process underway...please wait";
  }
  ```

- `public virtual Font Font`: The Font property is inherited from the `Control` class and is used to get or set the font used to display the text of the `Label` on the screen. It can also be used to specify whether the `Label` will be displayed using **bold** or *italic* font.

  The value of the Font property is set by assigning it an instance of the Font class (from the `System.Drawing` namespace). The Font class defines a wide variety of constructors; the constructor we'll use in building the SRS is used to create a new font style based on an already existing font:

  ```
  public Font(Font existingFont, FontStyle newStyle)
  ```

  For example, to change the style of the student's name `Label` font to **bold,** we would access the existing (default) Font for the name label and then set the Font property to a **bold** version as follows:

  ```
  name.Font = new Font(name.Font, FontStyle.Bold);
  ```

  We could similarly change the font style to *italic* by using the following:

  ```
  name.Font = new Font(name.Font, FontStyle.Italic);
  ```

  We can change the style to be both ***bold and italic*** in a single step using the | operator:

  ```
  name.Font = new Font(name.Font, FontStyle.Bold | FontStyle.Italic);
  ```

- `public override bool AutoSize`: If the AutoSize property is set to `true`, the width and height of the `Label` will be automatically set based on the textual content and font of the `Label`. The default value is `false`, meaning that the size of the `Label` will have to be explicitly changed using its `Width` and `Height` properties.

  ```
  // the name Label is automatically sized when the text of the Label is set.
  name.AutoSize = true;
  ```

- `public int Top`: The Top property is inherited from the `Control` class and is used to get or set the vertical position of the object inside its parent container. The value of the property is equal to the distance in pixels between the *top* edge of the `Label` and the *top* edge of its parent container.

  ```
  // The Label is positioned 200 pixels below the top of its container.
  name.Top = 200;
  ```

- `public int Left`: The Left property is inherited from the `Control` class and is used to get or set the horizontal position of the object inside its parent container. The value of the property is equal to the distance in pixels between the *left* edge of the `Label` and the *left* edge of its parent container.

  ```
  // The Label is positioned 200 pixels from the container's left edge.
  name.Left = 200;
  ```

■**Note** Many more `Label` properties allow us to customize the look and behavior of a `Label`. For a complete list and description of all of the `Label` class properties, please consult the .NET FCL reference on the MSDN web site.

Adding Labels to a Form

We'll use `Label` objects in the SRS GUI to describe the other `TextBox` and `ListBox` objects comprising the SRS GUI so that the user knows what their intended purposes are. The first set of `Label` objects we'll add to the SRS GUI will be those that describe the `TextBox` objects that will appear on the left side of the `Form`. We'll add `Label`s for the other GUI objects a little later in the chapter.

■**Note** In this section and the other sections that follow, we won't overwhelm you with the entire `MainForm` class listing. Instead, we'll show only excerpts of the code to highlight the particular GUI component that we're discussing. It's therefore important that you download the `MainForm.cs` source code in its entirety from the Apress web site before proceeding, if you haven't already done so, so that you can follow along as you read these sections.

To include `Label`s as part of the SRS GUI, we'll first declare reference variables for them as fields of the `MainForm` class:

```
// MainForm.cs

using System;
using System.Windows.Forms;
using System.Drawing;

public class MainForm : Form
{
  // The GUI objects that will be placed on the Form are declared as
  // fields of the MainForm class.
  private Label idLabel;
  private Label nameLabel;
  private Label totalCourseLabel;
  private Label registeredLabel;
```

The `Label` objects are then instantiated inside the `MainForm` constructor. The field names are chosen to be descriptive—you'll know exactly what component we're dealing with later in the GUI. We'll use the `Label` class properties we previously described to define the appearance of each `Label`. We'll set the text of each `Label` and set the font style to be bold, as well as use the autosize feature to allow the system to size our labels for us. We'll position each Label on the Form using the Top and Left properties. This is one instance in which an IDE such as Visual Studio can come in handy because it lets you instantly see what changes to Label properties will look like in the GUI.

```
// Constructor.
public MainForm() {
  // Create left-hand side labels.
  // All labels are offset five pixels from the left-hand edge of the form.
  int labelLeft = 5;
  // The vertical spacing between the top edges of adjacent vertical labels
  // will be 40 pixels.
  int labelVertSpace = 40;

  idLabel = new Label();
  idLabel.Text = "ID:";
  idLabel.Font = new Font(idLabel.Font, FontStyle.Bold);
  idLabel.AutoSize = true;
  idLabel.Top = 5;
  idLabel.Left = labelLeft;
  idLabel.TextAlign = ContentAlignment.MiddleCenter;
```

And so on for the remaining three labels.

Now that we've created our Label objects and defined their appearance, we're ready to add the Label objects to the Form. The way to add objects to a Form is through the Controls property of the Form class. The Controls property has the following header:

public Control.ControlCollection Controls

The Control.ControlCollection class is a nested class (a class declared inside another class) that represents a group of controls (GUI objects that accept input or display information) associated with a Form. To add a control to a Form, the Add method is called on the Control.ControlCollection object associated with the Form. It doesn't matter in which order the Label objects are added to the Form because their position is determined by the value assigned to their Top and Left properties.

```
// Add the controls to the form using the Controls property.
this.Controls.Add(idLabel);
this.Controls.Add(nameLabel);
this.Controls.Add(totalCourseLabel);
this.Controls.Add(registeredLabel);
```

Now it's time to size our Form and to make it visible on the screen. We'll specify the appearance of the SRS GUI form as a whole in a manner similar to that used in our previous TestForm examples, with one exception. When the various TestForm GUIs appeared on the screen, their size could be changed by grabbing one corner of the window and dragging the mouse inward or outward.

If the SRS GUI were to be resizable in this fashion, however—in particular, if users were able to *reduce* its size—some of the GUI objects might disappear from view, as illustrated in Figure 16-32.

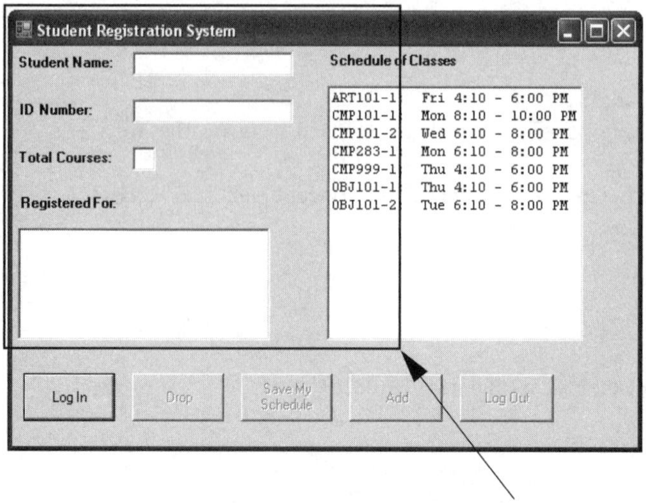

Figure 16-32. *If the SRS GUI is resized to be smaller, some of the components won't be visible.*

To prevent the user from "hiding" some of the controls if the Form is made smaller, we can set the MinimumSize property of the Form to be the initial size of the Form.

```
// Set some appearance properties for the Form.
this.Text = "Student Registration System";
this.Height = 370;
this.Width = 500;
this.MinimumSize = this.Size;
this.StartPosition = FormStartPosition.CenterScreen;
```

To launch the MainForm GUI, we will modify the TestForm3Driver class (now called SRS):

```
using System;
using System.Windows.Forms;

public class SRS {

  static void Main() {

    Application.Run(new MainForm());
  }
}
```

The compile command (which will remain the same for all of the SRS incarnations) is the following:

```
csc /out:SRS.exe *.cs /main:SRS
```

Figure 16-33 shows how the SRS GUI looks when the first four Label objects have been added to the Form.

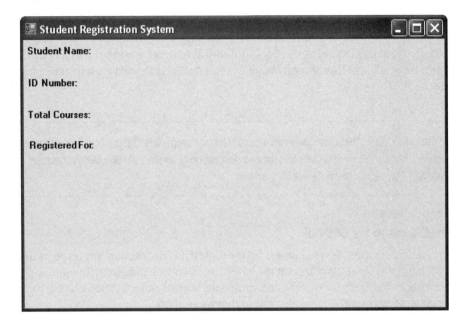

Figure 16-33. *We added four* Label *objects to the* Form.

TextBox Class

GUIs frequently need to provide components that enable the user to input a line of text. For example, in the case of the SRS GUI, a user has to enter his or her student identification number to log on to the SRS. A TextBox is a GUI object that is typically used to either accept as input, or display, a single line of text. It's also possible to create a multiline TextBox, but by default TextBox objects accommodate a single line of text.

In addition to the TextBox used to accept the user's ID number, the SRS GUI will also use read-only TextBox objects to display the student's name and the total number of courses in which the student is currently enrolled once he or she has logged on.

Similar to the Label class, the TextBox class declares only a single parameterless constructor:

```
public TextBox()
```

Once a TextBox object has been instantiated, its state can be defined by setting the value of various properties declared by the TextBox class. In addition to the Top, Left, and AutoSize properties you learned about previously when discussing Labels, we'll also make use of two other properties when we create the TextBox objects.

- public int Width: The value of the Width property represents the width of the TextBox in pixels. The AutoSize property works a little differently for TextBox objects than it does for Labels in that only the height of the TextBox is sized automatically based on the font used for the text; the width of a TextBox must be explicitly set through its Width property.

- public bool ReadOnly: The ReadOnly property controls whether a TextBox will accept user input. If the value of this property is set to true, the TextBox will be used for display purposes only.

■Note As with the Label class, there are many more TextBox class properties that allow us to customize the look and behavior of a TextBox. For a complete list and description of all the TextBox class properties, please consult the .NET FCL reference on the MSDN web site.

Adding TextBox Objects to the SRS GUI

The process for adding the three TextBox objects to the SRS GUI is similar in many respects to the process for adding the Labels. We'll revisit the MainForm.cs code, highlighting the significant additions made to the MainForm class to accommodate TextBox objects. The SRS.cs driver code needn't change at all from the previous version that we studied.

To include the TextBox objects as part of the SRS GUI, we'll first declare reference variables to them as fields of the MainForm class:

```
public class MainForm : Form
{
  // Label declarations go here (omitted from this code listing).

  // Declare three TextBox objects as fields of the MainForm class.
  private TextBox idTextBox;
  private TextBox nameTextBox;
  private TextBox totalTextBox;
```

The TextBox objects are created inside the MainForm class constructor. The state of each TextBox is specified by setting the value of some of the TextBox class properties. In our SRS code, we'll specify these property values. An IDE such as Visual Studio would remove some of these gritty details from the GUI component layout.

- The width of each TextBox is explicitly set through its Width property.

- The value of the AutoSize property is set to be true, so that the height of each TextBox will be set automatically.

- We want the left edges of each TextBox to be aligned with one another vertically, and so we set the value of the Left property for each of the TextBox objects to be the Right property of the corresponding Label.

- The position of the top edge of each TextBox is set to be the same as the top edge of its corresponding Label.

- These TextBox objects are meant for display purposes only, so the value of their ReadOnly property is set to true.

```
// Constructor.
public MainForm() {
  // Create left-hand side labels.
  // Details omitted...see code for previous example.

  // Create text box objects.
  nameTextBox = new TextBox();
  nameTextBox.Width = 140;
  nameTextBox.AutoSize = true;
  nameTextBox.Top = nameLabel.Top;
  nameTextBox.Left = nameLabel.Right;
  nameTextBox.ReadOnly = true;
  nameTextBox.BackColor = Color.White;

  idTextBox = new TextBox();
  idTextBox.Width = 140;
  idTextBox.AutoSize = true;
  idTextBox.Top = idLabel.Top;
  idTextBox.Left = idLabel.Right;
  idTextBox.ReadOnly = true;
  idTextBox.BackColor = Color.White;

  totalTextBox = new TextBox();
  totalTextBox.Width = 20;
  totalTextBox.AutoSize = true;
  totalTextBox.Top = totalCourseLabel.Top;
  totalTextBox.Left = totalCourseLabel.Right;
  totalTextBox.ReadOnly = true;
  totalTextBox.BackColor = Color.White;
```

The TextBox objects are then added to the GUI in the same manner that the Label objects were, by using the Add method on the Controls property of the Form:

```
this.Controls.Add(idTextBox);
this.Controls.Add(nameTextBox);
this.Controls.Add(totalTextBox);
```

Figure 16-34 shows how our SRS GUI looks now, with the TextBox objects added to the Form.

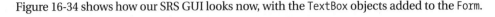

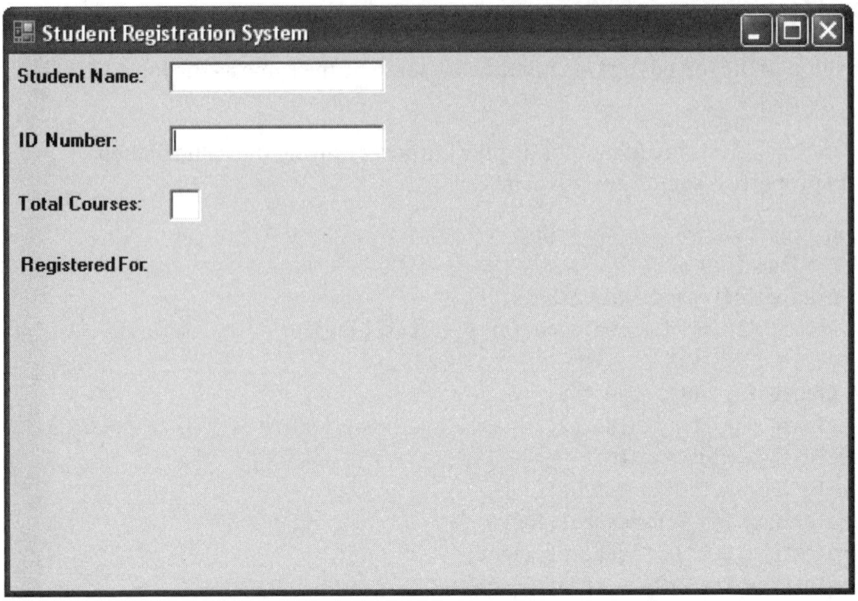

Figure 16-34. *Three* TextBox *objects are added to the SRS GUI.*

ListBox Class

The SRS GUI will need to display the schedule of classes for the semester and a list of the courses for which a given student is registered. We'll also want the user to be able to drop or add a class by selecting one of the classes in the appropriate list. An instance of the ListBox class will satisfy both of these requirements. A ListBox is a GUI object that displays a list of choices to the user; the user can select an item from the list by clicking it.

Elements of any type can be added to a ListBox. When the ListBox appears on the screen, the list elements are rendered visually as strings. In the case of the SRS GUI, Section object references will be added to both of the ListBox objects; the Section class's ToString method is used to render a string representation of each Section element. (We talked about overriding the ToString method to provide a meaningful, application-specific string representation of an object's data values in Chapter 13.)

To create a ListBox object, the ListBox class provides a single parameterless constructor:

```
public ListBox()
```

Once a ListBox object has been created, its state can be defined by setting the value of properties declared by the ListBox class. The only property we'll use that we haven't seen before for other GUI types is the Height property:

```
public int Height
```

A ListBox object inherits the AutoSize property from the Control class, but we can also explicitly set both the width and height of a ListBox. If the list of elements to be displayed by a ListBox is longer than the visible display area the ListBox can accommodate, a vertical scroll bar will automatically appear on the right side of the ListBox, allowing the user to scroll up or down to access the entire list. If the value of the ScrollAlwaysVisible property is set to be true, scroll bars will also be included with the ListBox.

Adding Elements to a ListBox

To add elements to a ListBox, we make use of the Items property of the ListBox class. This property is of type ListBox.ObjectCollection—a class that is used to store the elements contained in a ListBox.

To add an element to a ListBox, we use the Add method from the ListBox.ObjectCollection class, as illustrated in the following example:

```
ListBox aListBox = new ListBox();
aListBox.Items.Add("Sample Entry");
```

As you can see by the Add method header:

```
public int Add(object item)
```

any type of element can be added to a ListBox:

```
ListBox xBox = new ListBox();
Person p = new Person("Steve");
xBox.Items.Add(p); // the ToString method of the Person class will
                   // be used to render a string representation of p
```

In the SRS GUI, the Add method will be used to add Section objects to the ListBox.

Clearing the Elements of a ListBox

To clear all the elements stored by a ListBox, we again make use of the Items property, invoking the Clear method of the ListBox.ObjectCollection class:

```
public virtual void Clear()
```

For example:

```
ListBox xBox = new ListBox();
// Add items...details omitted.
xBox.Items.Clear();
```

We'll make use of the Clear method to refresh the SRS GUI display when a user logs off the SRS.

Adding ListBox Objects to the SRS GUI

We now have enough information to create the two ListBox objects we'll need and to add them to the SRS GUI. We'll also create an additional Label to describe the Schedule of Courses ListBox. As before, we won't display the entire MainForm class code listing, just the segments that we're adding in this iteration.

The first thing we'll do is to add references to the new ListBox and Label objects as private fields of the MainForm class:

```
public class MainForm : Form
{
    // Other GUI component declarations omitted from this example.

    // Declare the ListBox objects and a Label as private fields.
    private Label classScheduleLabel;
    private ListBox scheduleListBox;
    private ListBox registeredListBox;
```

The ListBox and Label objects are instantiated inside the MainForm constructor. The objects' states are defined by setting the value of selected properties. The properties for the classScheduleLabel object are set in similar fashion to the Label objects that we added earlier. The appearance of the ListBox objects is defined using properties from the ListBox class.

- The top edge of each ListBox object is positioned to be five pixels below the bottom edge of its corresponding Label.

- The value of the Width and Height properties are explicitly set. The Height of the registeredListBox is set so that the bottom edges of the two ListBox objects will align visually.

- The left edge of the registeredListBox is set to line up with the left side Labels. The left edge of the scheduleListBox is set to be 30 pixels to the right of the right edge of the Id TextBox.

- The font used in both ListBox objects is set to be Courier New font:

```
// Create class schedule ListBox object.
scheduleListBox = new ListBox();
scheduleListBox.Font = new Font(new FontFamily("Courier New"), 9.0f);
scheduleListBox.Width = 220;
scheduleListBox.Height = 225;
scheduleListBox.Top = classScheduleLabel.Bottom + 5;
scheduleListBox.Left = idTextBox.Right + 30;

// Create "Registered For" ListBox Object
registeredListBox = new ListBox();
registeredListBox.Font = new Font(new FontFamily("Courier New"), 9.0f);
registeredListBox.Width = 220;
registeredListBox.Top = registeredLabel.Bottom + 5;
registeredListBox.Height = scheduleListBox.Bottom-registeredListBox.Top+3;
registeredListBox.Left = labelLeft;
```

For now, we'll leave the ListBoxes empty, but will eventually populate them by reading in class schedule and student class list data from local files.

The Label and ListBox objects are then added to the Form:

```
this.Controls.Add(classScheduleLabel);
this.Controls.Add(scheduleListBox);
this.Controls.Add(registeredListBox);
```

The Form object's visual properties are then set as before.

With the ListBox objects included, the SRS Form now looks as shown in Figure 16-35.

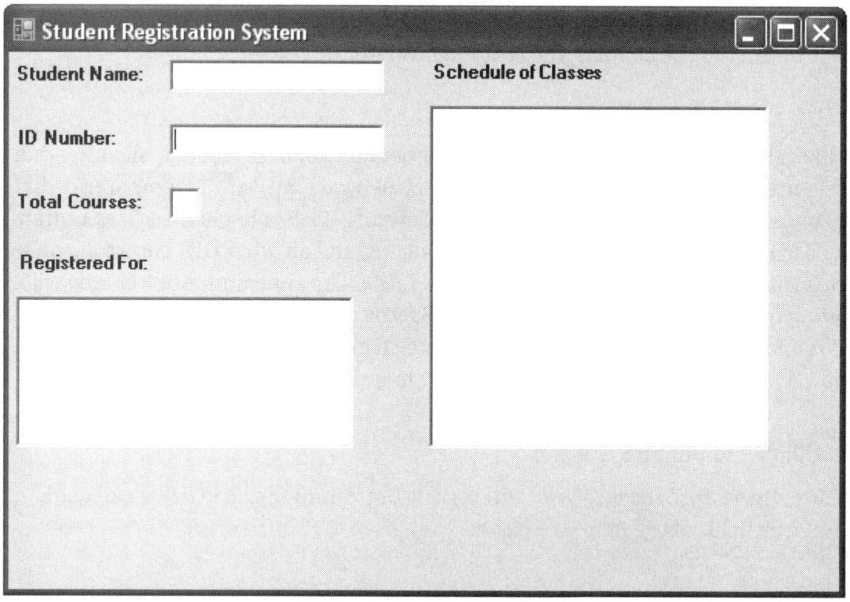

Figure 16-35. *Two* ListBox *objects are added to the SRS GUI.*

Our SRS GUI is really beginning to take shape! The only objects left to add are the buttons that will initiate the various actions of the GUI.

Button Class

A Button is a GUI object that allows a user to initiate an action by "clicking" what appears to be a three-dimensional button on the GUI. We have to program an event handler to define what we actually want the button to do when it's clicked (you'll learn about event handlers later in the chapter), but the button is inherently clickable just by virtue of creating it. A great thing about Button components, and all the other .NET GUI components for that matter, is that the details behind their visual behavior and appearance are already defined by the GUI classes in the FCL.

The Button class declares a single parameterless constructor:

```
public Button()
```

As with the other objects discussed in this chapter, the appearance of a Button can be specified by setting the value of properties declared by the Button class. We've already discussed most of the properties that we'll use for our Button objects before, in the context of other types of object.

- The Text property is used to set the text label that is displayed on the Button.

- The Width and Height properties are used to specify the dimensions of the Button as it will appear on the screen.

- The Top and Left properties are used to position the Button in its underlying container.

The Button class has one more property it inherits from the Control class that we'll take advantage of a little later in the chapter: the Enabled property:

```
public bool Enabled
```

A Button, like all other GUI controls, is enabled by default when it's created, meaning that it can respond to user input. There are times, however, when we may want to temporarily disable a Button. For example, it doesn't make sense to allow an SRS user to click the Drop button if that student hasn't yet registered for any classes. A Button (and all other GUI controls) can be *disabled* by setting the value of its Enabled property to false. The appearance of a Button will change, indicating that it's disabled, and clicking the Button will have no effect.

The TextBox and ListBox classes (and all other C# GUI classes, for that matter) also declare an Enabled property that functions in a similar manner.

Adding Button Objects to the SRS GUI

To add Log In, Drop, Save My Schedule, Add, and Log Out buttons to the SRS GUI, we declare references to them as fields of the MainForm class:

```
public class MainForm : Form
{
  // Other GUI component declarations omitted from this example.

  //  References to five Button objects are declared as private fields.
  private Button logInButton;
  private Button dropButton;
  private Button saveButton;
  private Button addButton;
  private Button logOutButton;
```

In the MainForm constructor, we create the Button objects and define their state by setting the value of some of the Button class properties:

- Each Button is given the same width and height.

- We want the five Button objects to appear aligned horizontally, so the value of the Top property for each Button is set to the same value.

- The left margin of the Log In Button is set to be 10 pixels from the left edge of the Form.

- The left margin of each subsequent Button in the row is set to be a certain distance from the right edge of the Button to its left.

```
// Create buttons; all will be of the same size, and at the same
// vertical distance from the top of the form.
int buttonHeight = 40;
int buttonWidth = 80;
int buttonTop = 275;

logInButton = new Button();
logInButton.Text = "Log In";
logInButton.Height = buttonHeight;
logInButton.Width = buttonWidth;
logInButton.Top = buttonTop;
logInButton.Left = 10;

//  Other Button declarations are similar … Details omitted.
```

The Button objects are then added to the Form:

```
this.Controls.Add(logInButton);
this.Controls.Add(dropButton);
this.Controls.Add(saveButton);
this.Controls.Add(addButton);
this.Controls.Add(logOutButton);
```

When the new code is compiled and the driver code executed, the GUI shown in Figure 16-36 will appear on the screen.

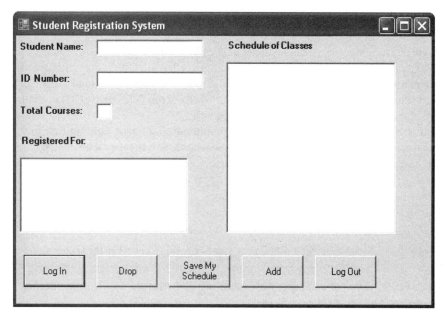

Figure 16-36. *The look of our SRS GUI is complete!*

Note that the four Button objects are initially enabled, in that each button label appears in black and each button is clickable. We'll want every Button except the Log In Button to initially be disabled until a user successfully logs on. When disabled, the button labels would appear to be grayed-out, as shown in Figure 16-37, and clicking them would have no effect. We'll add the logic for programmatically enabling/disabling the buttons a bit later in this chapter.

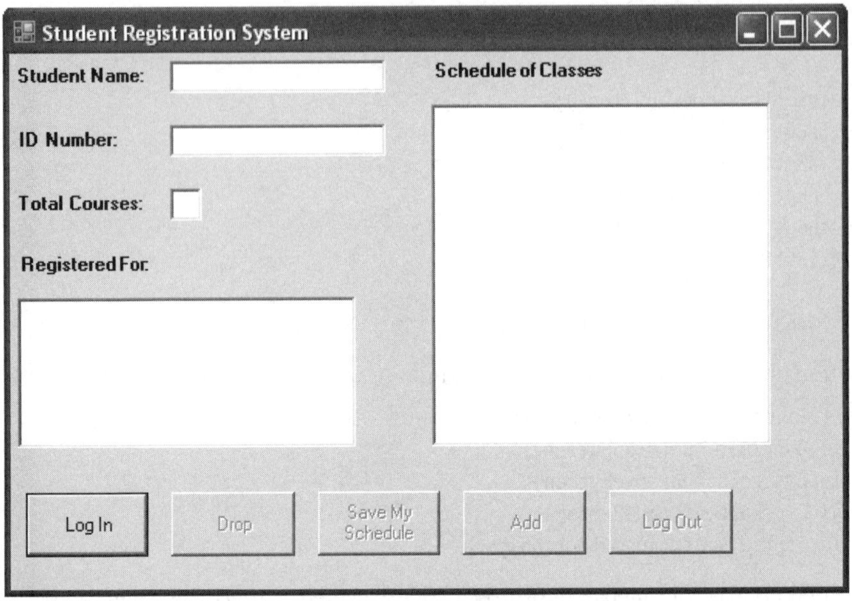

Figure 16-37. *The SRS GUI as it would appear with four of the* Button *objects disabled*

Creating Modal Message Dialog Boxes

The SRS GUI will use modal message dialog boxes at certain points in the SRS processing scenario to help guide the user along. The term *modal* means that any other interactions with the GUI are suspended until the message dialog box is dismissed by the user. That is, the user won't be able to click any of the other buttons or type into any of the fields of the GUI until he or she acknowledges and responds to the modal dialog box.

Recalling our SRS concept of operations from earlier in the chapter, one example of how we'll be using message dialog boxes with the SRS GUI will be to alert the user if he or she mistypes the password. In such a situation, a message dialog box will appear to inform the student what has happened; without displaying such a message, the GUI would seemingly just sit there, leaving the user to guess what went wrong.

■**Note** We could also simply display an error message in a read-only TextBox field on the main form. Message dialog boxes are a much better way to alert the user to a problem, however, because although a user can potentially ignore or overlook a message that appears in a field, he or she can't ignore a message dialog box because it must be closed before continuing.

Modal message dialog boxes are easily implemented in C# using the MessageBox class. A MessageBox is a dialog box that can have a title, display text along with an icon, and include one or more buttons used for responding to the dialog box. We can associate a MessageBox with another GUI object so that the MessageBox will appear automatically centered in front of its associated object.

There are no constructors declared by the MessageBox class. The way to create and display MessageBox objects is by invoking the static Show method on the MessageBox class as a whole. There are many overloaded versions of the Show method, used to create dialog boxes with different title, caption, and button combinations; the version of the Show method that we'll use with the SRS has the following header:

```
public static DialogResult Show(string text, string caption,
                          MessageBoxButtons buttons,
                          MessageBoxIcon icon)
```

- The return value of the Show method is one of eight DialogResult constants that indicate how the MessageBox was closed. By inspecting the returned value from a call to MessageBox.Show, we can ascertain how the user responded to any questions posed by the MessageBox. We won't do anything with the return value of this method for purposes of the SRS GUI.

- The text parameter is the text that will be displayed by the MessageBox.

- The caption serves as the title of the MessageBox.

- We can add one or more buttons to the MessageBox by specifying one of the MessageBoxButtons constants. The one we'll use is the following:

  MessageBoxButtons.OK

  Supplying this constant as an argument to the Show method results in a button marked OK being placed inside the MessageBox. When the OK button is subsequently clicked to indicate that the user has acknowledged the message being displayed, the MessageBox closes.

- We'll use two of the various MessageBoxIcon constants to define what icon will be displayed with a given MessageBox instance. The MessageBoxIcon.Information icon is a lowercase "i" inside a circle. It will be used to provide general information to the user. The MessageBoxIcon.Warning icon consists of an exclamation mark inside a triangle. It will be used to warn the user that an issue needs to be addressed.

As a simple example of using a MessageBox, the following code could be used to display an informational MessageBox with the text "You clicked the Drop button":

```
MessageBox.Show("You clicked the Drop button", "Button Clicked",
        MessageBoxButtons.OK, MessageBoxIcon.Information);
```

When the previous line of code is executed, the MessageBox shown in Figure 16-38 appears on the screen.

Figure 16-38. *A sample* MessageBox

Creating a Password Dialog Box

The first thing a student does when running the SRS application is to log on by clicking the Log In button. When this happens, we want a separate window to appear that will ask the student for his or her student ID number and password and will then "remember" the ID and password until we retrieve it a bit later in our application. The easiest way to accomplish this objective is to declare another class called PasswordForm, derived from Form, to serve as a password dialog box.

The PasswordForm class will be designed using many of the same features that we've already discussed for Forms in general. The PasswordForm class will collect the user's ID and password as it's typed, and will subsequently make them available to client code (specifically, to methods of the MainForm class in our application) through public Id and Password properties.

One new security feature will be added for the password dialog box. When a user types in a password, it is common practice to hide the characters that are being typed using an *echo character*—a character that will be shown instead of the characters that are actually typed. The TextBox class implements this feature via the PasswordChar property:

```
public char PasswordChar
```

Whatever character is assigned to the PasswordChar property will visibly replace the characters typed into the TextBox. The system will still know what the actual characters are, but passersby won't be able to see them on the computer screen.

Here is the code listing for the PasswordForm class. We'll defer building the event-handling capability of the PasswordForm class until a little later in the chapter.

```
// PasswordForm.cs

using System;
using System.Windows.Forms;
using System.Drawing;

public class PasswordForm : Form {

  private Button logInButton;
  private TextBox idTextBox;
  private TextBox passwordTextBox;
  private Label idLabel;
  private Label passwordLabel;
  private string id;
```

```
private string password;

public PasswordForm() {

  int componentTop = 15;

  // create label components
  idLabel = new Label();
  idLabel.Text = "Student ID:";
  idLabel.Top = componentTop;
  idLabel.Left = 15;
  idLabel.Width = 70;
  idLabel.Font = new Font(idLabel.Font, FontStyle.Bold);

  passwordLabel = new Label();
  passwordLabel.Text = "Password:";
  passwordLabel.Top = componentTop+30;
  passwordLabel.Left = 15;
  passwordLabel.Width = 70;
  passwordLabel.Font = new Font(passwordLabel.Font, FontStyle.Bold);

  // Create TextBox components
  idTextBox = new TextBox();
  idTextBox.Height = 40;
  idTextBox.Width = 100;
  idTextBox.Top = componentTop;
  idTextBox.Left = passwordLabel.Right;

  passwordTextBox = new TextBox();
  passwordTextBox.Height = 40;
  passwordTextBox.Width = 100;
  passwordTextBox.Top = componentTop+30;
  passwordTextBox.Left = passwordLabel.Right;
  passwordTextBox.PasswordChar = '*';

  logInButton = new Button();
  logInButton.Text = "Log In";
  logInButton.Height = 20;
  logInButton.Width = 50;
  logInButton.Top = componentTop+60;
  logInButton.Left = 95;

  // Assign event handler to the Button
  logInButton.Click += new EventHandler(LogInButtonClicked);

  // Add the GUI components to the form
  this.Controls.Add(idLabel);
```

```
      this.Controls.Add(idTextBox);
      this.Controls.Add(passwordLabel);
      this.Controls.Add(passwordTextBox);
      this.Controls.Add(logInButton);

      this.Text = "User Login";
      this.Height = 150;
      this.Width = 240;
      this.MinimumSize = this.Size;
      this.StartPosition = FormStartPosition.CenterScreen;
    }

    // Property
    public string Id {
      get {
        return id;
      }
    }

    public string Password {
      get {
        return password;
      }
    }
  }
}
```

The PasswordForm class is quite simple—it consists of two Label components, two TextBox components, and one Button component placed on a Form. Two private fields named id and password are declared that will store what was typed into the TextBox components after we implement event handling. The echo character for the password TextBox is set to be an asterisk character (note the use of single quotes: '*'). The get accessor of the Id and Password properties can be used to access the value of the id and password fields. The logInButton is pressed when the user has filled in the TextBox information and will send the program control back to the main SRS Form.

The View Is Complete

We're now finished with constructing the "view" of our SRS GUI. All the GUI objects we'll need to accomplish the functionality as described in the SRS concept of operations have been created and placed onto the underlying Form. There is still some work to be done, however, because although our SRS GUI looks as it should, it doesn't actually do anything useful yet. Users can click the buttons, but nothing useful will happen, at least as far as student registration is concerned.

To make our GUI fully functional, we need to engage the "controller" aspect of the MVC paradigm to connect our model and view classes together. Through a process known as event handling, we'll program the logic necessary to achieve the desired results for various user interactions with the GUI. In particular:

- We'll need to program the logic for what is to happen behind the scenes when each of the five buttons at the bottom of the GUI is clicked: `logInButton`, `addButton`, `dropButton`, `saveButton`, and `logOutButton`.

- We'll need the GUI to recognize when a user has clicked the `logInButton` of the `PasswordForm` as a signal that he or she wants to log in to the SRS.

- We'll need to recognize when a user has made a selection in either the `registeredListBox` or `scheduleListBox`.

We'll provide all these behaviors a bit later in this chapter, after we've touched on the other C# classes that these behaviors will be reliant upon.

Stage 3: Adding Functionality Through Event Handling

To introduce C# GUI event handling in a gentle, stepwise fashion, we'll do so in three phases:

- First, we'll talk about the C# event model in general.

- Second, we'll illustrate how to tackle event handling with a simple `Push Me` button example.

- Finally, we'll dive in and provide full-blown event handling for the SRS GUI.

The C# Event Model

GUI events are generated whenever a user interacts with an enabled object on the GUI—clicks a button, types in a field, and so on. As with virtually everything else in C#, events themselves are objects! There are many different types of events; we'll learn about several of these shortly.

When we create a GUI object, it automatically has the capability to generate one or more types of events whenever a user interacts with it (we don't need to do anything to get this phenomenon to occur). Some of the actions that can cause an event to occur include the following:

- Moving the mouse inside the SRS window

- Clicking a `Button`

- Typing a character into a `TextBox`

- Moving the mouse over a `Button`

- Adding an item to a `ListBox`

- Resizing the SRS window

- Selecting an item in a `ListBox`

And the list goes on and on. A veritable avalanche of events is generated every time someone uses the SRS GUI (or any GUI). Most of the events won't interest us, and they will be generated (and ignored) without us being aware of them. What we do need to explicitly deal with, however, is programming how the GUI should react to the subset of events that we're interested in (known as event handling).

The C# mechanism for "listening for" and responding to specific types of events on specific GUI objects takes advantage of the C# *delegation model*, and thus involves the use of a special C# type known as a *delegate*. Let's discuss the delegation model in general first, after which we'll return to a discussion of how the delegation model is used specifically in the case of C# GUI event handling.

C# Delegates and the Delegation Model

A .NET delegate is a reference type that defines a generic reference to a method with a specific return type and argument list (that is, a method signature). The delegate declaration gives no information about what the method actually does or even which class can implement it. You can create a delegate object that points to a specific method on a specific object. The method must have the correct signature to match the delegate type. When you're ready, you can invoke the method via the delegate object. Here's an example:

1. As shown in Figure 16-39, at compile time, a class X declares that it requires a delegate plug-in–a method with a header that is compatible with the delegate header in terms of its return type and argument signature; note that the plugged-in method needn't have the same name as the delegate, however.

```
At compile time, a class "X" declares
that it requires a delegate "plug-in" ...

public class X
{
// Features of the class are declared
// as always - details omitted.

delegate void Foo(int x);

// etc.
}
```

Figure 16-39. *Class X declares a requirement for a delegate plug-in.*

At run time, a method with a compatible header is associated with a particular object/instance of X, serving essentially as a plug-in for that object (see Figure 16-40).

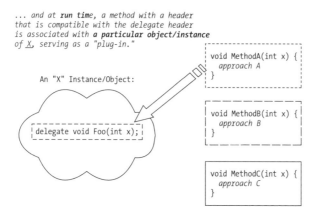

Figure 16-40. *An appropriate method is associated with an instance of* X *at run time.*

As long as the header of the method being handed into the object in question matches the prescribed header of the delegate in terms of its argument signature and return type, all is well. If the headers aren't compatible, the compiler will generate the following error:

```
error : Method <method_name> does not match delegate <delegate_name>
```

Note that each object/instance of X can be handed a different behavioral implementation at run time, if desired, as shown in Figure 16-41.

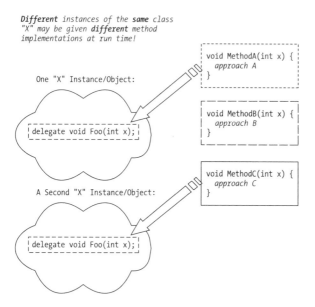

Figure 16-41. *Different instances of* X *can be associated with different methods.*

Of course, it's also possible to associate the same method with more than one object, if desired, as you can see in Figure 16-42.

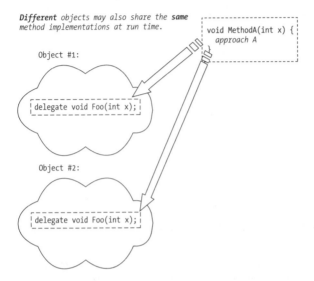

Figure 16-42. *The same method can be associated with more than one object.*

■**Note** For readers who are familiar with the C or C++ programming language, a delegate is conceptually similar in nature to a function pointer in those languages. However, C# delegates are far more sophisticated than C/C++ function pointers; delegates are true objects, they are instantiated at run time using the new keyword, and encapsulate both a method and a reference to the target object that the method is to operate upon.

The actual behind-the-scenes mechanism of delegates is much more complex than what we conceptualized here, but the net effect—having the ability at run time to plug in behavior for a given object—is all we need to understand conceptually about delegates to provide event handling for a GUI.

We'll be taking advantage of the delegation mechanism that is built in to the various C# GUI component classes to plug in behaviors for the various objects comprising the SRS GUI. For an in-depth discussion of how general-purpose delegates can be crafted and used for a variety of purposes beyond GUI event handling, please refer to the recommended reading list in Chapter 17.

Multicast Delegates

We can actually associate multiple behaviors to the same delegate if the delegate in question happens to be a special type of delegate known as a *multicast delegate*. As illustrated conceptually in Figure 16-43, a multicast delegate can accept multiple methods as plug-ins at run time, and will execute the logic of all of them in turn.

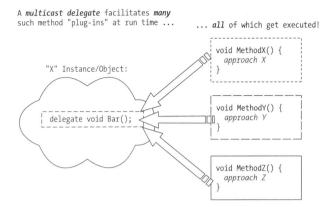

Figure 16-43. *More than one method can be associated with a single instance of a multicast delegate.*

Again, the actual mechanism of a multicast delegate is much more complex than what we've conceptualized here, but the net effect is the same: having the ability at run time to plug in multiple behaviors for a given object to perform.

GUI Event Handling Using Delegates

The C# language uses delegates as described previously to implement events and event handling. Events in C# are represented by instances of a special derived type of multicast delegate known as an *event delegate*. Every FCL GUI class declares or inherits one or more events as public members. Each such event represents a different type of event that a particular type of GUI object can generate in response to user interactions with the object. For example, here are some of the events declared as public members of the Button class:

- MouseDown: Occurs when the mouse pointer is over the Button and the mouse button is pressed.

- MouseUp: Occurs when the mouse pointer is over the Button and the mouse button is released.

- Click: Represents the user's click of a button, when the mouse pointer is over the Button and the mouse button is pressed and released. (Whenever a user clicks a button, therefore, all three of these event types—MouseDown, MouseUp, and Click—are generated.)

- BackColorChanged: Occurs when the background color of the Button is programmatically changed.

- SizeChanged: Is generated when the size of the Button is programmatically changed.

There are more; the Button class declares or inherits more than 50 events representing a wide variety of things that can happen to a Button. As always, look to the FCL reference on the MSDN site for complete details on the events that a given GUI component supports.

To provide event handling for a given object, there are three basic steps that programmers must take:

1. We must first decide which subset of available event types we're interested in handling for that given GUI object.

2. We must write event handler methods for every event type that is to be handled for that object, to define the logic that is to be performed when handling each event of interest. The return type and argument list of the event handling methods have to be the same as those declared by the event delegate.

3. We must provide the logic to "associate" the event handling method(s) to the object's appropriate event delegate(s) at run time.

Before we retrofit event handling into the SRS GUI, we'll use a simple example of a Push Me button to illustrate all three of these steps.

The PushMe GUI: The Initial Look

The look of our simple Push Me example is achieved via the following code—a Form with a single Button object attached to it—which should be self-explanatory, based on our earlier discussions of assembling the look of a GUI:

```
// PushMe.cs -- Take 1

using System;
using System.Windows.Forms;
using System.Drawing;

public class PushMe : Form
{
  Button pushMeButton;

  public PushMe() {
    // Create the Button.
    pushMeButton = new Button();
    pushMeButton.Text = "Push Me";
    pushMeButton.Height = 60;
    pushMeButton.Width = 80;
    pushMeButton.Top = 60;
    pushMeButton.Left = 60;

    // Add the Button to the Form.
    this.Controls.Add(pushMeButton);

    // Size the Form and make it visible.
    this.Height = 200;
    this.Width = 200;
    this.StartPosition = FormStartPosition.CenterScreen;
  }
```

```
  // For simplicity, we'll place a Main method inside of the PushMe.cs
  // file, to use as a "test scaffold" driver.
  static void Main() {
    Application.Run(new PushMe());
  }
}
```

When the PushMe.cs file is compiled and the resulting executable is run, the GUI in Figure 16-44 should appear on the screen.

Figure 16-44. *A* Form *with a single* Button

The concept of operations for our Push Me example is quite simple: the button will start out with a label that says "Push Me". When the button is first clicked, its label will change to read "Ouch!!!" When clicked a second time, the button's label will change back to "Push Me"; repeated clicks of the button will toggle its label back and forth.

As the application currently stands, however, we can indeed "click" the button, but although various types of events will automatically be generated in response to our clicks (Click events, MouseDown events, MouseUp events, and so on), nothing will change visually on our GUI as a result because we're not yet recognizing and responding to the Click events in particular.

Let's now add event handling to the Push Me button for Click events.

Writing Event Handler Methods for the PushMe GUI

First, let's write an event handler method that will change the label of the Button from "Push Me" to "Ouch!!!", or vice versa, when the Button is clicked. The precise header of an event handler method is mandated by the FCL based on the type of event that we want to handle; different types of events mandate different event handler signatures.

The Click event of the Button class requires a method with the following header wherein only the method name and parameter names are up to us to specify; the method must have a return type of void and an argument signature as shown:

```
public void MethodName(object source, EventArgs e)
```

Two arguments are passed into a method associated with an EventHandler delegate—an object reference representing the event source, and an instance of an EventArgs object, which will contain some additional information about the event, such as where on the screen the event occurred, how many mouse clicks caused the event, and so on.

Arguments are passed automatically by the C# runtime; we needn't concern ourselves with these, just as we didn't have to worry about how the reference to an Exception object gets "handed" to a catch block when performing exception handling.

As it turns out, the previous header pattern is known as the *generic* EventHandler header. Many event types, belonging to many different classes—for example, the Button class's Click, BackColorChanged, and SizeChanged event types, among many others—require this same header pattern when writing event handler methods. Other event types—for example, the MouseUp event type of the Button class—require slightly different header patterns; MouseUp, for example, requires a MouseEventHandler header pattern:

```
public void MethodName(object source, MouseEventArgs e)
```

■Tip An exhaustive discussion of all the various event types and their corresponding handler header syntax is beyond the scope of this book to address; once you've gotten a grasp on the general concepts of C# event handling, however, we encourage you to consult the .NET FCL reference on the MSDN web site to study the variations that event handling can take for various FCL GUI classes and event types.

An important consequence of the plug-in nature of the delegation event model used by C# is that an event handling method doesn't have to be declared within the class of the component that generates the event; for example, a method for handling a button click doesn't have to be declared within the Button class. This is fortunate because we wouldn't want to have to modify/extend the predefined Button class simply to include an event handling method! Event handling methods can be (and usually are) placed in a different class entirely; for the SRS GUI (as well as for our simple PushMe example), all the event handling methods will be placed in the main Form class to which a given component is attached.

Architecturally, we have several different options with respect to where we insert the event handling method code—in fact, event handlers can even be declared in a class by themselves. This facilitates reuse of the event handling logic across multiple forms in a given application and across multiple applications. The mechanics of doing so are beyond the scope of this book to address, however.

Here's a revised version of the PushMe class, expanded to include an appropriate event handler method (highlighted in the following code):

```
// PushMe.cs -- Take 2

using System;
using System.Windows.Forms;
using System.Drawing;

public class PushMe : Form
{
  Button pushMeButton;
```

```
public PushMe() {
  // Create the Button.
  pushMeButton = new Button();
  pushMeButton.Text = "Push Me";
  pushMeButton.Height = 60;
  pushMeButton.Width = 80;
  pushMeButton.Top = 60;
  pushMeButton.Left = 60;

  // Add the Button to the Form.
  this.Controls.Add(pushMeButton);

  // Size the Form and make it visible.
  this.Height = 200;
  this.Width = 200;
  this.StartPosition = FormStartPosition.CenterScreen;
}

// Event handling method for the "Push Me" button's Click events.
public void ButtonClicked(object source, EventArgs e) {
  // If the button label currently says "Push Me"...
  if (pushMeButton.Text == "Push Me") {
    //...switch the label to "Ouch!!!"...
    pushMeButton.Text = "Ouch!!!";
  }
  // Otherwise, do the reverse!
  else {
    pushMeButton.Text = "Push Me";
  }
}

// Test scaffold driver.
static void Main() {
  Application.Run(new PushMe());
}
}
```

Note that because the ButtonClicked method is declared at the class scope level of the PushMe class as a method, as is the reference variable pushMeButton as a field, we can refer to the Button object by reference as pushMeButton within the ButtonClicked method, thereby ignoring the availability of the source parameter that is being passed into the method:

```
// We're ignoring the "source" parameter in this method.
public void ButtonClicked(object source, EventArgs e) {
  // If the button label currently says "Push Me"...
  if (pushMeButton.Text == "Push Me") {
    // etc.
```

Alternatively, we can rewrite this method to take advantage of the source object reference as shown here:

```
public void ButtonClicked(object source, EventArgs e) {
  // We'll obtain a reference to the Button that generated the event by casting
  // the generic object reference "source" to a Button reference.
  Button b = (Button) source;

 // Everything else about the event handling method is the same, except
 // that we're now referring to "b" rather than "pushMeButton".
   if (b.Text == "Push Me") {
     b.Text = "Ouch!!!";
   }
   else {
     b.Text = "Push Me";
   }
}
```

While doing so certainly isn't necessary based on how we've crafted the PushMe class, if we were to use a different architectural approach to providing event handling methods (as discussed in an earlier background comment), such that the pushMeButton reference variable was not in scope, this would be the preferred means of referencing the source object. So we encourage you to get into the habit of using the second, more generic approach in all cases.

If we compile and run our Take 2 version of the program, we still won't see the button label change as we click it. Why not? Because it isn't sufficient to merely write an event handling method; we must also *associate* this event handling method with the PushMe button specifically, as described in the next section.

Associating an Event Handling Method with a GUI Object via a Delegate

All FCL GUI event delegates, including the Button class's Click delegate, are multicast delegates, which means that we can associate more than one event handling method with a given event type for a given component instance at run time. To associate a ButtonClicked event handling method with the Click multicast delegate for a particular Button reference, we therefore use the following syntax to add an event handler to the list of event handlers already acknowledged by the component:

```
// Associate an event handler method with a button.
// Pseudocode.
buttonReference.Click += new EventHandler(methodName);
```

If no such event handlers have previously been associated with the delegate in question, the one we're currently attaching becomes the *first* such event handler in the list.

Specifically, to associate our ButtonClicked event handling method with the Click multicast delegate for the pushMeButton, we use the following syntax in the PushMe class constructor:

```
// Associate an event handler method with the button.
pushMeButton.Click += new EventHandler(ButtonClicked);
```

As of C# 2.0, an equivalent shorthand notation was introduced without the new
EventHandler() syntax:

```
// Associate an event handler method with the button.
pushMeButton.Click += ButtonClicked;
```

Because event delegates are given public access as members of the associated class (Click
is a public member of the Button class), we can access an event delegate of a GUI object from
client code via dot notation, as shown earlier.

Our ButtonClicked method is now associated with Click type events for the pushMe
button. Whenever this button is clicked, the runtime will automatically invoke every event
handler method in the Click event's invocation list—in this case, our ButtonClicked method
will be called. All this activity happens automatically behind the scenes, without us having to
worry about any of the invocation details.

Here is the entire listing of the completed PushMe class, with the preceding logic placed in
context and highlighted:

```
// PushMe.cs -- Take 3

using System;
using System.Windows.Forms;
using System.Drawing;

public class PushMe : Form
{
  Button pushMeButton;

  public PushMe() {
    // Create a Button.
    pushMeButton = new Button();
    pushMeButton.Text = "Push Me";
    pushMeButton.Height = 60;
    pushMeButton.Width = 80;
    pushMeButton.Top = 60;
    pushMeButton.Left = 60;

    // Associate an event handler with the Button.
    pushMeButton.Click += ButtonClicked;

    // Add the Button to the Form.
    this.Controls.Add(pushMeButton);

    // Size the Form and make it visible
    this.Height = 200;
    this.Width = 200;
    this.StartPosition = FormStartPosition.CenterScreen;
  }
```

```
// Event handling method for the "Push Me" button.
public void ButtonClicked(object source, EventArgs e) {
  if (pushMeButton.Text == "Push Me") {
    pushMeButton.Text = " Ouch!!!";
  }
  else {
    pushMeButton.Text = "Push Me";
  }
}

static void Main() {
  Application.Run(new PushMe());
}
}
```

Now when the PushMe application is run, the text of the Button will indeed change from "Push Me" to "Ouch!!!" and back again every time the button is clicked.

An alternative way to associate an event handler to the Button is to declare an anonymous method as part of the assignment statement. The method body is included after the += syntax. Using this approach, the event handling method does not need to be named or declared in a separate section of the code:

```
// Assign an event handler to the Button using an anonymous method.
pushMeButton.Click += delegate(object source, EventArgs e) {
  if ( pushMeButton.Text == "Push Me" ) {
    pushMeButton.Text = "Ouch";
  }
  else {
    pushMeButton.Text = "Push Me";
  }
};  // Note the semi-colon after the brace.
```

Simple though it is, the PushMe example nonetheless illustrates how easy it is to take advantage of C# event handling. We'll use the exact same concepts and approach, with only slightly more complexity, in implementing event handling for the SRS GUI.

Adding Event Handling to the SRS GUI

We already created a GUI view—composed of the SRS MainForm and PasswordForm classes—of our model; that is, our domain objects Student, Professor, Course, Section, and so on. We're now ready to add event handling, the "controller" aspect, to our SRS GUI.

By way of review, we stated in the previous sections that we needed to provide listeners for each of the following GUI objects because they are the objects that the user will be interacting with:

- We'll need to program the logic for what is to happen behind the scenes when each of the five buttons at the bottom of the SRS GUI is clicked: logInButton, addButton, dropButton, saveButton, and logOutButton.

- We'll need the GUI to recognize when a user has clicked the logInButton of the PasswordForm as a signal that he or she wants to log on.

- We'll need to recognize when a user has made a selection in either the registeredListBox or scheduleListBox.

Because the MainForm.cs code listing has become so long (10+ pages!), we won't clutter up this chapter by repeating elements we covered earlier in the chapter, but once again we encourage you to download and print the entire file from the Apress web site. We'll provide editorial comments on those segments of code that are most unusual or complex, but please do take the time to read through all of the inline documentation as well.

Registering Event Handling Methods with Key GUI Objects

The first thing we'll do is to register event handling methods with various SRS GUI objects. We want to respond to events generated by various ListBox and Button components, so we'll associate an event handler with the public events of interest for each component using the += operator:

- For the ListBox objects, we'll provide event handling logic to react whenever the element selected by the user inside the ListBox changes. The SelectedIndexChanged event of the ListBox class will serve our purposes.

- For the Button objects, we want event handling to respond when a Button is clicked, so we'll associate event handling methods with the Click event of the Button class.

To associate event handling methods with the desired type of event as generated by each of our components, we'll add the following code to the MainForm class constructor:

```
// Add event handlers to the ListBox components
scheduleListBox.SelectedIndexChanged += ScheduleSelectionChanged;
registeredListBox.SelectedIndexChanged += RegisteredSelectionChanged;

// Assign event handlers to the Buttons
logInButton.Click += LogInButtonClicked;
addButton.Click += AddButtonClicked;
dropButton.Click += DropButtonClicked;
saveButton.Click += SaveButtonClicked;
logOutButton.Click += LogOutButtonClicked;
```

Note that we're using the shorthand notation to assign the event handling methods to the corresponding GUI component. We haven't written the event handler methods yet, but will do so shortly.

The logInButton object of the PasswordForm class will also implement event handling in a similar manner to the other Button components, in that we want to respond to the event that occurs when the Button is clicked. We'll enable our application to respond to Click events by adding the following code to the PasswordForm class constructor:

```
// Assign event handler to the Button
logInButton.Click += LogInButtonClicked;
```

Now that we've associated event handling methods with all GUI object events of interest, the next step is to implement those events.

The LogInButtonClicked Method

The LogInButtonClicked method is declared as a method in the MainForm class. This method is called whenever the Log In Button is clicked while it is enabled. The method's header syntax is prescribed by the EventHandler delegate that it's associated with, and is as follows:

```
// event handling method for "Log In" Button
public void LogInButtonClicked(object source, EventArgs e) {
```

The first thing the method does is invoke a private "housekeeping" method, ClearFields, which steps through the three objects on the GUI that represent student-specific information—nameTextBox, idTextBox, totalTextBox, and registeredListBox—clearing them of any information that is still being displayed for a previously logged-on student. You'll see the code for this method, along with the code for several other housekeeping methods, later in the chapter.

```
// First, clear the fields reflecting the
// previous student's information.
ClearFields();
```

A PasswordForm dialog box is then created and displayed for the user to type in his or her student ID number and password. This method waits until the user clicks the Log In button in the PasswordForm. The strings containing the user's ID number and password are obtained from the PasswordForm:

```
//  Display password dialog
passwordDialog = new PasswordForm();
passwordDialog.ShowDialog(this);

string password = passwordDialog.Password;
string id = passwordDialog.Id;
passwordDialog.Dispose();
```

At this point, the method attempts to create a valid Student object from the ID number and password information that the user supplied:

```
currentUser = new Student(id+".dat");
currentUser.ReadStudentData(schedule);
```

But it's not necessarily as simple as that. There are three possible outcomes when a user types an ID number and password, and we must account for all three:

- A user might type an invalid ID number.

- A user might type a valid ID number, but an invalid password.

- A user might type a valid ID number and a valid password.

The first possibility is that the user typed in an invalid ID number. To determine whether an ID number is valid, we use the StudentSuccessfullyInitialized method that was added to the Student class in Chapter 15:

```
// This method is declared in the Student class.

public bool StudentSuccessfullyInitialized() {
  if (Name.Equals("TBD")) {
    return false;
  }
  else {
    return true;
  }
}
```

This method simply checks the Name property of the Student. If its value is "TBD", the Student is assumed to be uninitialized, and the method returns false. Inside the LogInButtonClicked method, the StudentSuccessfullyInitialized method is called on the currentUser object. If the method returns false, the currentUser field of the MainForm class is set to null, and a warning message is displayed in a dialog box using the Show method of the MessageBox class, a technique discussed earlier in this chapter:

```
if (!currentUser.StudentSuccessfullyInitialized()) {
  // Drat!  The ID was invalid.
  currentUser = null;

  // Let the user know that login failed,
  string message = "Invalid student ID; please try again.";
  MessageBox.Show(message, "Invalid Student ID",
          MessageBoxButtons.OK, MessageBoxIcon.Warning);
}
```

If, on the other hand, the StudentSuccessfullyInitialized method returned a value of true, we know that the Student class's constructor successfully read in the contents of the student's data file, populating all the Student object's fields. So it's time to attempt to validate the password, and if the attempt succeeds, we display another MessageBox informing the user that the login succeeded. We then use another housekeeping method, SetFields, to populate the various objects on the GUI with this student's information so that he or she can see it. (You'll see that method code in a moment.)

```
else {
  // We have a valid Student.  Now, we need
  // to validate the password.

  if (currentUser.ValidatePassword(password)) {

    // Let the user know that the login succeeded.
    string message =
        "Log in succeeded for " + currentUser.Name + ".";
```

```
        MessageBox.Show(message, "Log In Succeeded",
                MessageBoxButtons.OK, MessageBoxIcon.Information);

        // Load the data for the current user into the TextBox and
        // ListBox components.
        SetFields(currentUser);
    }
```

If the password typed into the PasswordForm doesn't match the Student's password, the login operation is deemed to have failed, and we notify the user of this as follows:

```
    else {
        // The id was okay, but the password validation failed;
        // notify the user of this.
        currentUser = null;
        string message = "Invalid password; please try again.";
        MessageBox.Show(message, "Invalid Password",
                MessageBoxButtons.OK, MessageBoxIcon.Warning);
    }
}
```

The final thing the event handling method does is to use a third housekeeping method to enable/disable the buttons at the bottom of the screen, as appropriate. (We'll see the code for ResetButtons toward the end of our discussion of the MainForm class.)

```
    // Check states of the various buttons.
    ResetButtons();
}
```

AddButtonClicked Method

The addButton object is used to add a selected course to a student's registered course list, and the AddButtonClicked method will be called every time the addButton object is clicked to provide this functionality.

The method is declared in the MainForm class; the method's header syntax is prescribed by the EventHandler delegate that it's associated with, and is as follows:

```
// Event handling method for the "Add" Button.
public void AddButtonClicked(object source, EventArgs e) {
```

The first thing the method does is to pull the user-selected item from the scheduleListBox via the SelectedItem property. The get accessor of the SelectedItem property returns a reference to an object, so we must cast it back into a Section object; we maintain a reference to that Section object via the selected reference variable:

```
// Determine which section is selected (note that we must
// cast it, as it is returned as an object reference).
Section selected = (Section) scheduleListBox.SelectedItem;
```

The AddButtonClicked method now attempts to enroll the student in the selected Section. The return value of the Enroll method, which indicates the success or failure of the enrollment, is one of the elements of the EnrollFlags enumeration and is saved in a local variable called status:

```
// Attempt to enroll the student in the section, noting
// the status code that is returned.
EnrollFlags  status = selected.Enroll(currentUser);
```

There are four possible outcomes when a Section attempts to enroll a Student, as was discussed in Chapter 14, and we need to account for and respond to every possibility. The return value from the Enroll method will be one of the constant variables EnrollFlags.PREREQ_NOT_SATISFIED, EnrollFlags.PREVIOUSLY_ENROLLED, EnrollFlags.SUCCESSFULLY_ENROLLED, or EnrollFlags.SECTION_FULL. Based on which constant is returned, the appropriate dialog box message is formulated and displayed inside a MessageBox.

We'll start with the code for the three failure modes: a section was full, a prerequisite wasn't satisfied, or a student was already enrolled in the current or similar section:

```
// Report the status to the user.
if (status == EnrollFlags.SECTION_FULL) {
  MessageBox.Show("Sorry - that section is full.", "Request Denied",
         MessageBoxButtons.OK, MessageBoxIcon.Warning);
}
else if (status == EnrollFlags.PREREQ_NOT_SATISFIED) {
  string message = "You haven't satisfied all " +
             "of the prerequisites for this course.";
  MessageBox.Show(message, "Request Denied",
         MessageBoxButtons.OK, MessageBoxIcon.Warning);
}
else if (status == EnrollFlags.PREVIOUSLY_ENROLLED) {
  string message = "You are enrolled in or have successfully " +
             "completed a section of this course.";
  MessageBox.Show(message, "Request Denied",
         MessageBoxButtons.OK, MessageBoxIcon.Warning);
}
```

If we make it to this point in the code, we indeed succeeded in getting this student enrolled in the selected class!

```
else {  // success!
  string message = "Seat confirmed in " +
         selected.RepresentedCourse.CourseNumber + ".";
  MessageBox.Show(message, "Request Successful",
            MessageBoxButtons.OK, MessageBoxIcon.Information);
```

We must reflect the newly added section to the student's course list on the GUI; it's easy enough to just repopulate the entire list with all of the sections for which this student is enrolled presently. We also update the TextBox representing the total enrolled course count.

```
// Update the list of sections
// that this student is registered for.
registeredListBox.Items.Clear();

List<Section> enrolledSections = currentUser.Attends;
foreach( Section section in enrolledSections ) {
  registeredListBox.Items.Add(section);
}

// Update the field representing student's course total.
totalTextBox.Text = "" + currentUser.GetCourseTotal();
```

And, as a housekeeping measure, we clear out the user's "clicked" entry in the scheduleListBox, so that it's ready for another selection to be made:

```
    // Clear the selection in the schedule of classes list.
    scheduleListBox.SelectedItem = null;
  }
```

The ResetButtons method is a housekeeping method that we'll describe in more detail later in this chapter. It selectively enables and disables buttons based on the current state of the application, as affected by user input. For example, if there are no sections listed in the registeredListBox, the ResetButtons method will disable the DropButton because a user can't drop a section if he or she isn't registered for anything.

```
  // Check states of the various buttons.
  ResetButtons();
}
```

DropButtonClicked Method

The dropButton object is used by a student to drop a section of a course for which he or she is registered, and the DropButtonClicked method is called every time the dropButton object is clicked. The method is declared in the MainForm class, and its header is as follows:

```
public void DropButtonClicked(object source, EventArgs e)
```

The first thing the method does is determine which Section the user has selected in the registeredListBox:

```
public void DropButtonClicked(object source, EventArgs e) {

  // Determine which section is selected (note that we must
  // cast it, as it is returned as an Object reference).
  Section selected = (Section)registeredListBox.SelectedItem;
```

The Student is then dropped from the Section:

```
// Drop the Student from the Section.
selected.Drop(currentUser);
```

A confirmation message is shown to the user:

```
// Display a confirmation message.
string message = "Course " +
        selected.RepresentedCourse.CourseNumber + " dropped.";
MessageBox.Show(message, "Request Successful",
        MessageBoxButtons.OK, MessageBoxIcon.Information);
```

The method then refreshes the user-related information displayed on the screen and calls the ResetButton method:

```
// Update the list of sections that
// this student is registered for.
registeredListBox.Items.Clear();
List<Section> enrolledSections = currentUser.Attends;
foreach( Section section in enrolledSections ) {
  registeredListBox.Items.Add(section);
}

// Update the field representing student's course total.
totalTextBox.Text = "" + currentUser.GetCourseTotal();

// Check states of the various buttons.
ResetButtons();
}
```

SaveButtonClicked Method

The SaveButtonClicked method is invoked whenever the saveButton object is clicked. The method is a means of invoking the Student class's WriteStudentData method on the currentUser Student reference, a method that we studied in depth in Chapter 15. In a nutshell, this method saves all information about the student, including all sections in which he or she is enrolled, to a file by the name of <id>.dat, for example, 111-11-1111.dat. The SaveButtonClicked method is declared in the MainForm class, and its code is as follows:

```
// event handling method for the "Save" Button
public void SaveButtonClicked(object source, EventArgs e) {
  bool success = currentUser.WriteStudentData();
  if (success) {
    // Let the user know that his/her
    // schedule was successfully saved.
    MessageBox.Show("Schedule saved", "Schedule Saved",
        MessageBoxButtons.OK, MessageBoxIcon.Information);
  }
  else {
```

586 CHAPTER 16 ■ ROUNDING OUT OUR APPLICATION, PART 2: ADDING A GRAPHICAL USER INTERFACE

```
    // Let the user know that there was a problem.
    string message = "Problem saving your " +
                     "schedule; please contact " +
                     "SRS Support Staff for assistance.";
    MessageBox.Show(message, "Problem Saving Schedule",
            MessageBoxButtons.OK, MessageBoxIcon.Warning);
  }
}
```

LogOutButtonButtonClicked Method

This method is called whenever the logOutButton object is clicked, to clear out various
GUI objects and to reset the value of the currentUser Student reference to null. The
LogOutButtonClicked method is implemented in the MainForm class, and its code is as follows:

```
// event handling method for "Log Out" Button
public void LogOutButtonClicked(object source, EventArgs e) {
  ClearFields();
  idTextBox.Text = "";
  currentUser = null;

  // Clear the selection in the
  // schedule of classes list.
  scheduleListBox.SelectedItem = null;

  // Check states of the various buttons.
  ResetButtons();

}
```

RegisteredSelectionChanged and ScheduleSelectionChanged Methods

The RegisteredSelectionChanged and ScheduleSelectionChanged methods are called whenever the selected item in either the registeredListBox or scheduleListBox objects changes,
respectively. These two objects don't need much in the way of event handling:

- We want them to be mutually exclusive, so that when an element is selected in one of
  them, the selections in the other one are cleared.

- We also want to change the enabled state of some of the Buttons if an element is
  selected. For example, when a student selects a section in the scheduleListBox, the
  Add button should become enabled and the Drop button should be disabled. The
  ResetButtons method can be called to reset the enabled state of both buttons.

The ScheduleSelectionChanged and RegisteredSelectionChanged methods are declared in
the MainForm class. Their respective code listings are as follows:

```
// event handling method for the "Schedule of Classes" ListBox
public void ScheduleSelectionChanged(object source, EventArgs e) {
  // When an item is selected in this list,
```

```
  // we clear the selection in the other list.
  if (scheduleListBox.SelectedItem != null)  {
    registeredListBox.SelectedItem = null;
  }

  // reset the enabled state of the buttons
  ResetButtons();
}

// event handling method for the "Registered For:" ListBox
public void RegisteredSelectionChanged(object source, EventArgs e) {
  // When an item is selected in this list,
  // we clear the selection in the other list.
  if (registeredListBox.SelectedItem != null)  {
    scheduleListBox.SelectedItem = null;
  }

  // reset the enabled state of the buttons
  ResetButtons();
}
```

LogInButtonClicked Method of the PasswordForm Class

The PasswordForm class has its own Log In Button and declares its own LogInButtonClicked method to handle the event that occurs when the user clicks this Button. The method is quite simple. The first two lines are used to extract the values from the idTextBox and passwordTextBox components:

```
// event handling method for "Log In" Button of the PasswordForm class
public void LogInButtonClicked(object source, EventArgs e) {

    id = idTextBox.Text.Trim();
    password = passwordTextBox.Text.Trim();
    this.Visible = false;
}
```

The third line of the method sets the visibility of the PasswordForm to false, so that the password dialog box will "vanish" from the display without being garbage collected; we want to be able to communicate with the PasswordForm to retrieve what was typed inside the two TextBox components. When this method finishes executing, program execution returns to the MainForm class. The MainForm class calls the Dispose method on the PasswordForm object to recycle the memory associated with it.

Housekeeping Methods

As mentioned throughout this discussion, we outfitted the MainForm class with a few house-keeping methods; note that these are all declared to be private, meaning that they are only used within MainForm. The first housekeeping method is named ResetButtons. Because there are so many different situations in which one or more buttons need to be (de)activated, and because the logic is so complex, we centralize it here and then just call this method whenever we need to check the state of one or more of the buttons. It is a trade-off of code elegance for execution efficiency: we're doing a bit more work each time (because we don't need to reset all four buttons every time), but because the execution time is minimal, it seems like a reasonable trade-off.

```
private void ResetButtons() {
  // There are four conditions which collectively govern the
  // state of each button:
  //
  // 1:  Whether a user is logged on or not.
  bool isLoggedOn;
  if (currentUser != null) {
    isLoggedOn = true;
  }
  else {
    isLoggedOn = false;
  }


  // 2:  Whether the user is registered for at least one course.
  bool atLeastOne;
  if (currentUser != null && currentUser.GetCourseTotal() > 0) {
    atLeastOne = true;
  }
  else {
    atLeastOne = false;
  }



  // 3:  Whether a registered course has been selected.
  bool courseSelected;
  if (registeredListBox.SelectedItem == null) {
    courseSelected = false;
  }
  else {
    courseSelected = true;
  }

  // 4:  Whether an item is selected in the Schedule of Classes.
  bool catalogSelected;
  if (scheduleListBox.SelectedItem == null)  {
    catalogSelected = false;
  }
  else {
    catalogSelected = true;
  }

  // Now, verify the conditions on a button-by-button basis.
```

```
    // Log In button:
    if (isLoggedOn) {
      logInButton.Enabled = false;
    }
    else {
      logInButton.Enabled = true;
    }


    // Drop button:
    if (isLoggedOn && atLeastOne && courseSelected) {
      dropButton.Enabled = true;
    }
    else {
      dropButton.Enabled = false;
    }


    // Add button:
    if (isLoggedOn && catalogSelected) {
      addButton.Enabled = true;
    }
    else {
      addButton.Enabled = false;
    }


    // Save My Schedule button:
    if (isLoggedOn) {
      saveButton.Enabled = true;
    }
    else {
      saveButton.Enabled = false;
    }


    // Log Out button:
    if (isLoggedOn) {
      logOutButton.Enabled = true;
    }
    else {
      logOutButton.Enabled = false;
    }
  }
```

The second housekeeping method is used to clear the display of various TextBox and ListBox components:

```
  // Called whenever a user is logged off.
  private void ClearFields() {
    nameTextBox.Text = "";
    idTextBox.Text = "";
```

```
      totalTextBox.Text = "";
      registeredListBox.Items.Clear();
    }
```

The final housekeeping method is used to update the displays with information for the
Student currently logged in to the SRS:

```
    // Set the various fields, lists, etc. to reflect the information
    // associated with a particular student.  (Used when logging in.)
    private void SetFields(Student theStudent) {
      nameTextBox.Text = theStudent.Name;
      idTextBox.Text = theStudent.Id;
      int total = theStudent.GetCourseTotal();
      totalTextBox.Text = ""+total;

      // If the student is registered for any courses, list these, too.
      if (total > 0) {
        // Use the GetEnrolledSections() method to obtain a list
        // of the sections that the student is registered for and
        // add the sections to the registered ListBox

        List<Section> enrolledSections = currentUser.Attends;
        foreach( Section section in enrolledSections ) {
          registeredListBox.Items.Add(section);
        }
      }
    }
```

Revisiting Our SRS Model Classes

Many of the classes used in the Chapter 15 version of the SRS application remain unchanged in
the solution to Chapter 16—that's the beauty of separating the model from the view! Because the
model is, for the most part, blissfully ignorant that there even is a view (the view knows about
the model, but the model doesn't know about the view), the model classes needn't change to
accommodate it. So, the following classes (as presented in Chapter 15) are unaltered in the GUI
version of the SRS, so we won't revisit any of these classes' code in this chapter:

- Course.cs
- CourseCatalog.cs
- EnrollFlags.cs
- Faculty.cs
- Person.cs
- Professor.cs
- Transcript.cs
- TranscriptEntry.cs

The following classes have been modified from the versions used in Chapter 15 to add a method or two in support of the GUI; we'll study their code in detail one by one:

- `ScheduleOfClasses.cs`: We will add a single method, `GetSortedSections`, to support our use of `ListBox` objects.

- `Student.cs`: We will add a single field—`string password`—to handle the requirement for a user to log on to the SRS system and then made a few changes to the `Student` methods to recognize this new field. The field itself is implemented as an auto-implemented property. We'll also add a few other data-retrieval methods needed to support the GUI; we'll discuss all of these changes in depth shortly.

- `Section.cs`: We'll make only one minor change, which as it turns out wasn't related to the GUI at all, but rather is simply an improvement in the logic from that used in Chapter 15.

- And, of course, we'll significantly revamp the main `SRS.cs` "driver" code to accommodate the newly added GUI. As it turns out, we'll be able to significantly streamline the code of the SRS class, as you'll soon see.

Despite the fact that we will go back to make a few enhancements to the domain classes to accommodate the GUI, these enhancements involved business logic only and are made in such a way as to keep the model loosely coupled from the view. That is, we could easily swap out the SRS GUI that we're building and add a completely new GUI down the road, and our domain classes would remain intact. In the worst case, our domain classes would contain a few methods (those that we added for use by the first GUI) that would no longer get used.

As already discussed in this chapter, we added two new classes to the SRS application to take care of the GUI view:

- `MainForm.cs`: A type of `Form` used as our main application window.

- `PasswordForm.cs`: Provides a password dialog box used when logging a student on to the SRS.

We'll need to make some minor additional changes to these classes, as well.

■**Tip** If you haven't already done so, please consider downloading and printing a copy of all the SRS program files related to Chapter 16, so that you have them handy to refer to when following along with the discussion that follows. Download instructions are provided in Appendix B.

ScheduleOfClasses Class (Harnessing the Power of ListBox Objects)

The only change that we need to make to the `ScheduleOfClasses` class, as originally presented in Chapter 15, is related to our decision to use a `ListBox` to display the schedule of classes in our SRS GUI.

- You learned earlier in this chapter how to add elements to a `ListBox`. We want to add the schedule of classes to the `ListBox` in alphabetical order.

- However, as originally designed, the ScheduleOfClasses class maintains information on what sections are available for student registration as a Dictionary of Section objects. In Chapter 13, we learned how to use a foreach statement to step one by one through all the objects contained within a collection such as a List or a Dictionary. But the Section objects are stored in no particular order in the Dictionary—the nature of Dictionary objects doesn't guarantee sorted ordering—so stepping through the Dictionary with a foreach statement wouldn't necessarily yield an alphabetically sorted list of Sections. All things being equal, we would prefer to display the schedule of classes sorted in order by course number.

- By adding a single method, GetSortedSections, to return an alphabetically sorted List of Section objects based on this Dictionary, we can then use this method from within MainForm.cs to add an alphabetically sorted list of Section elements to the scheduleListBox.

First, we'll present the new GetSortedSections method in its entirety; then we'll review what the new method does in depth. (Because the code for the entire ScheduleOfClasses class is rather lengthy, and because you've seen much of the class code in previous chapters, we'll present only those chunks of code that are new as of the Chapter 16 version. Again, we encourage you to have a printed copy of the complete class available for comparison purposes.)

```
// Convert the contents of the SectionsOffered Dictionary
// into a List of Section objects that is sorted in
// alphabetical order

public List<Section> GetSortedSections() {
  List<string> sortedKeys = new List<string>();
  List<Section> sortedSections = new List<Section>();

  // Load the sortedKeys List with the keys from the Dictionary
  foreach ( KeyValuePair<string, Section> kv in SectionsOffered ) {
    string key = kv.Key;
    sortedKeys.Add(key);
  }

  // Sort the keys in the List alphabetically
  sortedKeys.Sort();

  // Load the value corresponding to the sorted keys into
  // the sortedSections List
  foreach( string key in sortedKeys ) {
    Section s = SectionsOffered[key];
    sortedSections.Add(s);
  }

  // Return the List containing the sorted Sections
  return sortedSections;
}
```

Let's step through the code for this new method. We begin by creating two empty generic List objects, which will be used to store the results of our sorting efforts:

```
public List<Section> GetSortedSections() {
  List<string> sortedKeys = new List<string>();
  List<Section> sortedSections = new List<Section>();
```

Using a foreach statement, we'll step through each key-value pair in the sectionsOffered Dictionary. The key (a string) is extracted for each element in the Dictionary, and this key is added to the sortedKeys List:

```
// Load the sortedKeys List with the keys from the Dictionary
foreach ( KeyValuePair<string, Section> kv in SectionsOffered ) {
  string key = kv.Key;
  sortedKeys.Add(key);
}
```

The keys are then sorted by calling the Sort method on the sortedKeys List. As we discussed in Chapter 13, the default behavior for the Sort method is to sort a collection of strings alphabetically:

```
sortedKeys.Sort();
```

Now that sortedKeys List contains all the keys in alphabetical order, we'll step through this List and use it to pull the Section objects themselves out of the Dictionary in sorted order! As we pull them out of the Dictionary, we'll stick them into a second List called sortedSections:

```
foreach( string key in sortedKeys ) {
  Section s = SectionsOffered[key];
  sortedSections.Add(s);
}
```

We now return a List containing all Sections that were originally in the Dictionary, but in alphabetically sorted order:

```
  return sortedSections;
}
```

Retrofitting the Student Class

When we first modeled the SRS in Part Two of the book, it didn't occur to us to allow for a Student to have a password field because this is more of a computer-related artifact than it is a real-world attribute of a student. But, as is frequently the case, we find that we often must expand the members of a class when the applications for it expand and new features are required. Such is the case with the password field of Student.

Because the Student class code is quite long, and because you've seen much of the Student class code in previous chapters, we'll present only those segments of code that are new as of the Chapter 16 version. Again, we encourage you to have a printed copy of the complete class available for comparison purposes.

First, we implement the `password` field as an auto-implemented property:

```
public string Password { get; protected set; }
```

Next, we acknowledge the existence of this new field by adding initialization code to the Student constructor. Most of the constructor code is unaltered from its Chapter 15 version; we repeated it all here, but highlighted only the changes that were necessary:

```
public Student(string studentFile, string name, string id, string major,
               string degree) : base(name, id) {

  // Assign auto-implemented property values
  Major = major;
  Degree = degree;
  StudentFile = studentFile;
  Transcript = new Transcript(this);

  // Create an empty List.

  attends = new List<Section>();

  // Initialize the password to be the first three digits
  // of the name of the student's data file.
  this.Password = this.StudentFile.Substring(0,3);  // added for GUI purposes

}
```

Keep in mind that a real-world application would most likely implement a more sophisticated (and secure) method for assigning a student's password.

We also added a method to the Student class that will be used to validate the password that a user types in when logging into the GUI against his or her "official" password. The argument `pw` represents the value that a user has typed in (we'll see how this is determined when we visit the event handling code of the PasswordForm class), and of course Password represents the "authentic" password for this student user.

```
public bool ValidatePassword(string pw) {

  if (pw == null) {
    return false;
  }
  if (pw.Equals(Password)) {
    return true;
  }
  else {
    return false;
  }
}
```

As it turns out, there is one more information retrieval method that we'll need in support of the GUI—a method to use in retrieving the total number of Sections that a Student is registered for, so that we may use this value to update the totalTextBox object on the GUI:

```
// This next method was added for use with the GUI.
public int GetCourseTotal() {
  return attends.Count;
}
```

Again, although we added new methods to the class, we won't have compromised our model-view separation in doing so because they essentially represent business logic only (for example, what it means for a password to be valid).

Redesigning the Section Class

The Section class for this chapter differs from the version that we presented in Chapter 15 in the way that a section enrolls a student. In the previous version of the SRS, we created a Section object and then called the Enroll method on the Section object, passing a reference to a Student object in as an argument. If all the "business logic" requirements for enrolling in the section were met, the Student was added to the EnrolledStudents Dictionary of the Section object using the value of the Student object's id field as the Dictionary key.

But now the access to the SRS is through the GUI that we developed in this chapter. When a student logs on to the SRS, a Student object is created with data read from the student's data file. The GUI will read the sections the student has enrolled in and will call the Enroll method of the corresponding Section object. However, there is a potential problem with this procedure. What happens if a student logs on to the SRS, logs off, and then changes his or her mind and logs on again without ever closing the SRS application? Every time the student logs on, the GUI will have the appropriate Section objects enroll the student. The upshot will be that the student will wind up being enrolled in all the sections twice! In fact, the student won't even get this far because an attempt to add a duplicate key to a C# Dictionary causes an exception to be thrown.

■Note This is an example of a bug that managed to make its way undetected through the testing that we performed via the command-line version of the SRS driver, as presented in Chapter 14. Despite our best efforts, some usage scenario problems will invariably escape detection when we're using a command line–driven application because we essentially have to try to simulate all possible permutations and combinations of user interactions as "hardwired" Main method code sequences, which is virtually impossible. Once we have a working GUI connected to the application, we can explore a much broader range of usage patterns. Nonetheless, the fact that we found only one such bug in our SRS model code after adding on the GUI speaks highly for the value in using a command line–driven application to flush out many bugs before GUI coding has begun.

Fortunately, the solution to this problem is quite simple. In the Enroll method of the Section class we need to check to see whether the Student object is already in the EnrolledStudents Dictionary. The ContainsKey method can be used to determine if a Dictionary contains a specified key. We need to change the original Enroll method syntax logic from the Chapter 15 code:

```
// If we made it to here in the code, we're ready to
// officially enroll the Student.

// Note bidirectionality:  this Section holds
// onto the Student via the Dictionary, and then
// the Student is given an object reference to this Section.

EnrolledStudents.Add(s.Id, s);
s.AddSection(this);
return EnrollFlags.SUCCESSFULLY_ENROLLED;
```

We'll change it to the following:

```
// When using the GUI, it's possible for a student to log
// on, log off, and then log on again while the SRS is
// still running. This prevents a student from being
// enrolled in the same class more than one time.

if ( !EnrolledStudents.ContainsKey(s.Id)) {
  EnrolledStudents.Add(s.Id, s);
}

s.AddSection(this);
return EnrollFlags.SUCCESSFULLY_ENROLLED;
```

Changes to the MainForm Class

Along with the changes we made to the ScheduleOfClasses and Student classes, several minor changes need to be made to the MainForm class. The first thing we need to add is a reference to the Student currently logged on to the SRS. This reference is declared as a field of the MainForm class.

```
// Maintain a reference to the Student who is logged in.
// (Whenever this is set to null, nobody is officially logged on.)
private Student currentUser;
```

We'll use this reference when we retrieve a student's list of registered courses to display them, as well as to save a student's data to a file.

Another new field of the MainForm class will be a reference to a PasswordForm object:

```
private PasswordForm passwordDialog;
```

When a user tries to log in to the SRS, the passwordDialog object will be displayed; we want to maintain a reference to this object so that we can "talk" to the dialog box to determine what was typed into the passwordDialog TextBox.

To display the courses being currently offered, a ScheduleOfClasses field is declared in the MainForm class:

```
private ScheduleOfClasses schedule;
```

The value of this field is initialized in the MainForm constructor using an argument passed to the constructor:

```
public MainForm(ScheduleOfClasses schedule) {

  currentUser = null;
  this.schedule = schedule;
```

The other change to the MainForm class is to load the course catalog into the scheduleListBox object when the SRS is launched. To list the course catalog alphabetically, we make use of GetSortedSections method described earlier in this chapter:

```
// Create "Schedule of Classes" ListBox Object.
scheduleListBox = new ListBox();
scheduleListBox.Width = 210;
scheduleListBox.Height = 225;
scheduleListBox.Top = classScheduleLabel.Bottom + 5;
scheduleListBox.Left = idTextBox.Right + 30;

// Display an alphabetically sorted course catalog list
// in the scheduleListBox component.
List<Section> sortedSections = schedule.GetSortedSections();
foreach( Section section in sortedSections) {
  scheduleListBox.Items.Add(section);
}
```

Once again, we're showing only snippets of the MainForm.cs code listing. Once you've downloaded the source file from the Apress web site, you can review the snippets within the context of the entire code listing.

SRS Driver Class—Significantly Streamlined

Now that we have a GUI to use in interacting with the SRS, many of the extra steps that we went through in the Chapter 15 version of the SRS driver class to initialize the application are now unnecessary. Let's run through the code segments of the SRS.cs file that we've been able to remove:

- We no longer need to create Student objects to simulate logins because we now have a GUI for this purpose, so we can remove the code that instantiates Students.

- We don't need to simulate a student enrolling in a section because we can perform that function via the GUI now, too.

- And because we can now verify the outcome of our interactions with the SRS simply by viewing the state of the GUI, we no longer need to use Console.WriteLine() calls to display the internal state of objects (although we may want to retain this code, and simply comment it out in our SRS program, to help us with debugging the application at a later date).

The only new logic that we've had to add to the SRS class was the code needed to create and display an instance of the main GUI window:

```
// Create and display an instance of the main GUI window.
Application.Run(new MainForm(schedule));
  }
}
```

The resulting streamlined SRS class is as follows:

```
// SRS.cs - Chapter 16 version.
// A main driver for the GUI version of the SRS.

using System;
using System.Windows.Forms;

public class SRS {

  static void Main() {

    //  Create CourseCatalog, ScheduleOfClasses, and Faculty objects.
    //  The order of creation is important because a ScheduleOfClasses
    //  needs a CourseCatalog object to properly initialize and a
    //  Faculty object needs a ScheduleOfClasses object.

    //  Create a CourseCatalog object and read data from input files.

    CourseCatalog catalog =
            new CourseCatalog("CourseCatalog.dat", "Prerequisites.dat");
    catalog.ReadCourseCatalogData();
    catalog.ReadPrerequisitesData();

    //  Create a ScheduleOfClasses object and read data from input file.

    ScheduleOfClasses schedule = new ScheduleOfClasses("SoC_SP2009.dat", "SP2009");
    schedule.ReadScheduleData(catalog);

    //  Create a Faculty object and read data from input files.

    Faculty faculty = new Faculty("Faculty.dat", "TeachingAssignments.dat");
    faculty.ReadFacultyData();
    faculty.ReadAssignmentData(schedule);
```

```
    // Create and display an instance of the main GUI window

    Application.Run(new MainForm(schedule));
  }
}
```

The SRS application is compiled as before with the following command:

```
csc /out:SRS.exe *.cs /main:SRS
```

This generates an executable file named SRS.exe that can be run from an MS-DOS prompt with the following command:

```
SRS
```

Summary

We covered a tremendous amount of ground in this chapter!

- We discussed the two primary FCL GUI namespaces: System.Windows.Forms and System.Drawing.

- We looked specifically at the following building blocks of GUIs:

  - A top-level container: the Form class.

  - Other GUI classes: Label, Button, ListBox, TextBox.

  - How to define the state of the GUI objects by setting property values.

  - How to position GUI objects inside a Form.

  - How to display model message dialog boxes using the MessageBox class.

- We covered the .NET event handling model; in particular, how delegates are used to associate event handling methods with an event source.

- We discussed the philosophy and advantages of model-view separation.

- We talked about the development of a concept of operations, or storyboard, as a means for getting sponsor/client/user buy-in before any code has been written, to ensure that the proposed look and flow of a GUI meets the use case requirements for the system.

- We discussed state retrieval methods as a data sharing technique.

And you saw the pièce de résistance: adding a GUI front-end to the SRS application! We've now come through the full life cycle of the SRS application, beginning with an expression of requirements via use cases in Chapter 9, to an object model in Chapters 10 and 11, to a command line–driven program in Chapter 14, a program with file persistence in Chapter 15, and a GUI-driven application in Chapter 16.

So pat yourself on the back. You've come a long way to get to this point in the book. Sixteen chapters ago you might have thought a class was the thing you were sitting in, and now you can use the word *GUI* and not be referring to the slug that you just stepped on. The world of C# and .NET is an exciting one, and you are now a part of it. Congratulations!

Exercises

1. For all the `catch` blocks located in the various SRS classes, introduce a `MessageBox` to report problems.

2. *Advanced exercise*: Research the .NET menu components using the FCL doc pages and replace the functionality of the five `Buttons` at the bottom of the SRS GUI using menu components instead of `Buttons`.

3. *Advanced exercise*: Modify the SRS application to provide the user with the capability for setting his or her password. This process will involve the following:

   - Displaying an appropriate error message to the user.

   - Adding a `Set Password` button on the `MainForm`.

   - Popping up a dialog box in response to a click of the `Set Password` button to request that the user enter the old and new password (consider creating a "clone" of the `PasswordForm` class).

   - Changing the structure of the `Student.dat` file to accommodate storing a student's password, which will in turn require changing the following methods of the `Student` class: `ReadStudentData`, `WriteStudentData`, and the `Student` constructor.

CHAPTER 17

■■■

Next Steps

Congratulations! You've made it through quite a learning curve, from object concepts, to object modeling, to C# programming. What you do next will depend on what your intentions were for learning this material in the first place:

- *If you're a software developer primarily interested in building C# applications*: You'll want to get some hands-on C# programming experience if you haven't already done so. A good first step is to tackle some of the exercises at the end of each chapter in Part Three of this book. If you've done so, you might be ready to try your hand at a full life cycle, object-oriented (OO) development project. See the next section in this chapter, "Our Tried-and-True Approach to Learning C# Properly," for a game plan on how to proceed and see the "Recommended Reading" section later in this chapter for other books in the Apress suite (and beyond) that might be appropriate next steps in your continued professional development.

- *If you're a systems analyst primarily interested in object modeling*: Be certain to attempt the exercises at the ends of the chapters in Part Two of the book if you haven't already done so. Then, seek out an opportunity to engage in an object modeling project within your organization, ideally with a senior object modeler to guide and mentor you.

- *If you're a manager whose goal is to become better versed in these technologies*: This may be an appropriate time to conduct a technology review of ongoing projects in your organization to learn how the techniques touched upon in this book are specifically being carried out.

- *If you're an instructor*: Please consider this book as the basis of a beginning object methods/C# curriculum in either an academic or corporate setting.

Whatever your focus, be sure to visit the Microsoft Developer's Network web site, `http://msdn.microsoft.com`, or Jacquie's web site, `http://objectstart.com`, for additional suggestions as well as links to related web sites that you might be interested in.

Our Tried-and-True Approach to Learning C# Properly

Here are our recommendations on how to advance through the C# learning curve as smoothly and effectively as possible.

1. Understand OO analysis and design—hopefully, our book has gone a long way toward helping you to accomplish this, and our recommended reading suggestions later in this chapter will help you to deepen this understanding.

2. Obtain a good reference book on C#—again, our book has hopefully given you a good jump start with the language, and our recommended reading suggestions later in this chapter will serve to complement this. Check the MSDN website for the current version of the .NET Framework and be sure to get a reference book that targets the current version.

3. Download and install a free copy of the latest release of the .NET Framework from the MSDN web site as described in Appendix A. You can also get the .NET Framework as part of the Visual Studio C# Express Edition download.

4. Compile and run a simple "Hello, World" program from the command line to ensure that all .NET components are installed and working properly.

5. Choose a *simple* first problem to automate: one that (a) you're very familiar with the requirements for—perhaps a small-scale application that you've already built in some other language, or an application based upon some hobby—and (b) only requires a handful of domain classes when modeled.

6. Produce a Unified Modeling Language (UML) class diagram for your application based on the object modeling techniques that you learned in Part Two of the book.

7. Write the code for your core model classes and get the application to work as a command-line application first, as we did for the Student Registration System (SRS) in Chapter 14. (This is your *model* without a graphical *view*.)

8. Learn more about C# graphical user interface (GUI) development beyond what we've introduced in Chapter 16, and buy a good reference book about this subject.

9. Add a GUI front-end onto the code that you produced in step 7, as we did for the SRS in Chapter 16. You'll learn more about the inner workings of GUI development if you write the GUI code from scratch the first time out. Once you feel comfortable with your competence, a drag-and-drop integrated development environment (IDE)/GUI building tool can be used to speed up GUI development time. Good IDE choices include Visual Studio 2008 or Sharp Develop.

10. Learn about the various C# database interface options offered as part of ADO.NET and buy a good reference book about this subject.

11. Acquire the appropriate .NET Framework data provider for your particular database management system (DBMS) if necessary and connect your application to a database back-end to persist your objects.

12. (Optional) If you're inclined to use an IDE, invest in a commercially available C# IDE such as Microsoft's Visual Studio .NET. The Visual Studio Express edition is free, and a free open source C# IDE known as SharpDevelop is also available at www.icsharpcode.net/OpenSource/SD.

13. (Optional) Join a C# special interest group, either online or in person. This is an invaluable way to get informal, ad hoc mentorship from colleagues who are more experienced with C#. One place to visit a variety of .NET forums and blogs is under the "Community" tab on the MSDN web site.

From this point forward, your options are open-ended! For example, you might want to expand beyond C#-specific matters to further explore the capabilities of the .NET Framework Class Library (FCL). Whichever direction you choose to take, you can rest assured that there will be plenty of new C#-related innovations in the months and years to come. And keep in mind there are plenty of real-world applications of C# that you might want to explore including game programming using Microsoft's XNA technology as well as VBA/VSTO/Microsoft Office programming, both of which make extensive use of C#.

Recommended Reading

Many fine books have been written and published on the subject of OO software development by a variety of publishers, and it would be virtually impossible to do justice to them all here. Consider this list to represent some of our personal recommendations (visit Jacquie's web site, http://objectstart.com, for more recommendations), but please do browse the titles available from your favorite technical bookseller because new titles are being released literally every day.

- Booch, Grady, James Rumbaugh, and Ivar Jacobson. *The Unified Modeling Language User Guide*, Addison-Wesley, 1998.

    A definitive reference on UML, written by its creators; definitely worth adding to your library if you're serious about object modeling.

- Rumbaugh, James, Ivar Jacobson, and Grady Booch. *The Unified Modeling Language Reference Manual*, Addison-Wesley, 1999.

    A second definitive reference by the same gentlemen; see our comments for the preceding title.

- Jacobson, Ivar, Grady Booch, and James Rumbaugh. *Unified Software Development Process*, Addison-Wesley, 1999.

    And a third!

- Quatrani, Terry. *Visual Modeling with Rational Rose and UML*, Addison-Wesley, 1998.

    A practical, step-by-step guide for how to use Rational Rose, one of the industry's leading object modeling Computer-Aided Software Engineering (CASE) tools, to prepare UML models.

- Eriksson, Hans and Magnus Penker. *UML Toolkit*, John Wiley & Sons, Inc., 1998.

- Shoemaker, Martin. *UML Applied: A .NET Perspective*, Apress, 2004.

- Rosenburg, Doug and Stephens, Matt. *Use Case Driven Object Modeling with UML Theory and Practice*, Apress 2007.

- Taylor, David A. *Object Technology: A Manager's Guide, Addison-Wesley, 1998.*

  A classic, high-level review of the direction in which the OO industry as a whole is headed.

- Gamma, Erich, Richard Helm, Ralph Johnson, and John Vlissides. *Design Patterns: Elements of Reusable Object-Oriented Software,* Addison-Wesley, 1994.

  An in-depth look at identifying and reusing common design patterns.

- Meyer, Bertrand. *Object-Oriented Software Construction,* Prentice Hall, 1988.

  Provides an introduction to the C# language and then moves to a discussion of key technical and architectural issues for .NET developers.

- Troelson, Andrew. *Pro C# 2008 and the .NET 3.5 Platform, Fourth Edition,* Apress, 2007.

  Covers the Windows Forms namespaces as well as a detailed discussion of good user-interface design principles.

- MacDonald, Matthew. *Pro .NET 2.0 Windows Forms and Custom Controls in C#*, Apress, 2005.

This list is by no means comprehensive. Check out the Apress website for other good C# or .NET references.

Your Comments, Please!

In the interest of making this book as useful as possible to our readers, we'd love to hear from you if you have suggestions for how this book could be improved! Please send Grant an e-mail at grantepalmer@gmail.com or visit Jacquie's web site at http://objectstart.com to contact her.

APPENDIX A

■ ■ ■

Installing .NET and Compiling C# Programs

This appendix explains how to get the .NET Framework up and running on your computer so that you can experiment with C# while reading our book. Specifically, this appendix covers the following:

- How to access the extensive online .NET Framework documentation

- How to download and install the .NET Framework on your computer

- How to troubleshoot any problems with the installation

- Details on how to compile C# programs

- Some behind-the-scenes tidbits on Microsoft Intermediate Language

The tips provided in this appendix aren't all-encompassing; they are simply provided as a professional courtesy, in the hope that you might find something useful among them. For full details on how to properly install and configure a given software tool, please consult the appropriate vendor's instructions.

Using the Online .NET Framework Documentation

Extensive documentation for the .NET Framework can be found at the MSDN web site. Because the URL for specific documentation can change as the MSDN web site is updated, the most dependable way to access the documentation is to go to the main MSDN web site and select the Library tab near the top of the page:

```
http://msdn.microsoft.com
```

The documentation includes tutorials, code examples, and a complete description of the contents of the .NET Framework libraries. Spend time getting familiar with the online C# documentation—it's tremendously useful!

Downloading the .NET Framework Software Development Kit

The .NET Framework is available as a free download from the Microsoft web site. The exact download URL changes from time to time, so the most dependable way to get to the download is to go to the MSDN home page:

`http://msdn.microsoft.com`

Near the top of the page, click the Downloads tab to go to the MSDN Download Center, from which you can find the necessary downloads. The .NET Framework download includes everything developers need to write, build, test, and deploy C# applications: documentation, samples, and command-line tools and compilers.

Among other things, the download comes with the following:

- A command-line C# compiler (`csc.exe`)

- The common language runtime (CLR)—the engine that runs compiled C# programs

- A wide variety of utility tools, including a runtime debugger

- Complete documentation for everything in the .NET Software Development Kit (SDK), including the contents of the .NET Framework Class Libraries

You must download two separate sets of software to get C# and .NET running on your machine:

- First, download and install the .NET Framework Redistributable package, which package contains the CLR and other .NET Framework components that are needed to run .NET Framework applications. It's best to download and install the latest version of the.NET Framework Redistributable package, but check the "Supported Operating Systems" information. You might have to go with an older version of the package if you are running an older operating system. You might also have to update your computer with one or more Service Packs in order to properly install and use the components.

- After the .NET Framework Redistributable package is installed on your machine, download and install the .NET Framework. Again, try to install the latest version, but make sure that your operating system is supported by the latest download. This download contains everything you will need to write, compile, test, and deploy C# applications, including documentation, libraries, compilers, and command-line tools.

Follow the instructions provided by Microsoft for installing both the Redistributable package and the .NET Framework on your particular system.

Odds and Ends Tips to Get C# to Work Properly

After you get the .NET Framework downloaded and installed per the instructions on Microsoft's web site, there are a few additional things you'll need to do to get C# up and running.

If You're Working Under Windows 2000 or Older Operating Systems

As of the time of publication of this book (fall 2008), the latest version of the .NET Framework is designed to work with Windows Vista, Windows XP, Windows Server 2003, and Windows Server 2008. If you're running on an older operating system (Windows 2000, Windows Me, and so on), you should seriously consider buying a new computer. If that's not practical, you can still install older versions of the .NET Framework on your computer, but you won't have access to more recently added features or language elements.

If You're Working Under UNIX (Solaris, Linux)

The .NET Framework isn't presently available for the UNIX operating system, although a Linux version is reportedly being considered at the time of publication of this book. Check the Microsoft web site periodically for developments in this regard.

Setting the Path Environment Variable

When the .NET Framework is installed, all associated files will be placed in a specific directory. To compile C# programs anywhere on your machine, you'll need to add the location of the folder that contains the C# compiler to the Path environment variable. The Path variable is a system variable that can be accessed through the System icon in the Control Panel. Edit the Path environment variable and add the path to the C# compiler to the end of the string, preceded by a semicolon. A typical C# compiler path looks like the following:

```
C:\WINDOWS\Microsoft.NET\Framework\v3.5
```

You should now be able to invoke the C# compiler from anywhere on your machine.

Note The manner in which these steps are accomplished might differ for other versions of Windows.

Once the .NET Framework Is Installed and the Path Variable Is Set

After you have successfully installed the .NET Framework and have set the Path environment variable, you are ready to start developing C# programs! Create a working directory in which you plan to store your various C# experiments and then download the example code for this book into that directory (see Appendix B for download instructions).

Caution Don't put any of your personal files or folders in the .NET Framework home directory or any of its subdirectories unless specifically instructed to do so.

Your C# environment should now be up and running. To give it a test drive, type, compile, and run the following trivially simple program:

```
using System;

public class Success
{
  static void Main() {
    Console.WriteLine("Hooray! It works!");
  }
}
```

You must first enter the preceding program text *exactly* as shown into a file. The file name can be anything, but the convention is to name the file Success.cs. You can use a variety of methods to enter a C# program into a file:

- Use the Windows Notepad editor.

- Use any other Windows-based text editor that you prefer.

- Use your favorite command-line text editor.

- Use an integrated development environment (IDE) of your choice; Visual Studio is the Microsoft standard.

Next, we'll attempt to compile and run this program from the command line. You can open a command prompt window in one of two ways:

- From the Start menu, choose Programs ➤ Accessories ➤ Command Prompt.

- From the Start menu, choose Run, and then type **cmd**.

Once the command prompt window opens, make sure to use the cd command to switch your working directory to be the directory in which your program resides (if you aren't already there), and then type the following command at the prompt to compile the program:

```
csc Success.cs
```

If the program compiles without any errors, an executable Success.exe file will be created in the same directory where the Success.cs file resides. Type the following command at the command prompt to run the program:

```
Success
```

If all goes well, the following should appear as output:

```
Hooray! It works!
```

Troubleshooting Your Installation

The following examples illustrate various problems that might arise when you try to compile a C# program:

- If you get the following error message when attempting to compile, the C# compiler could not be found:

```
C:\MyDir> csc Success.cs
'csc' is not recognized as an internal or external command, operable
program, or batch file.
```

  You either improperly installed the .NET Framework or did not properly update the Path environment variable.

- If you get the following error message when attempting to compile, the computer can't find your source code:

```
C:\MyDir> csc Success.cs
error: Source file 'Success.cs' could not be found
```

  Make sure that you're in the correct directory where the program source code file resides and that you're spelling the name of the file correctly.

- If you get any other compilation errors, such as the following, check to make sure that you've typed in the program exactly as shown previously:

```
C:\MyDir> csc Success.cs
Success.cs (5,23) error: Newline in constant Console.WriteLine("Hooray!);
```

  In this particular example, the double quote mark at the end of "Hooray!" is missing.

- If you get the following error message when attempting to run a successfully compiled program, it can mean one of several different things:

```
C:\MyDir> Success
'Success' is not a recognized internal or external command, operable
program, or batch file
```

  You might be spelling the name of the program incorrectly (again, pay attention to uppercase/lowercase), or the program didn't compile correctly, thus failing to produce a Success.exe file, or you're trying to run the program from the wrong directory.

Object Modeling Tools

At several points in this book, you have been subjected to our personal manifesto that it's better to write code from scratch using only a text editor when you're learning a programming language. When you write code from scratch, there's no IDE to hold your hand, so it's up to you to learn enough about the programming language to get your code to work. It's our experience that this approach gives a deeper understanding of the language—a better connection with it, if you will. You'll also be better prepared to deal with debugging situations when things don't go as planned.

That said, Microsoft has spent a lot of time and effort in developing its Visual Studio IDE and it has become the industry standard .NET Framework IDE. If you want to play around with Visual Studio, you can download a free trial version from the MSDN web site. To get to the free download, go to http://msdn.microsoft.com and click the Visual Studio Express link under the heading Developer Tools and Languages.

Compiling and Running C# Programs

As with all other programming languages, C# source code must be compiled before the program can be run. This section presents the basics of compiling and running C# programs.

C# Source Code Files

The C# language gives a fair amount of flexibility in naming C# source code files, but there are some conventions that are usually followed:

- Although it's not an absolute requirement, the recommended convention is to end source code file names with the extension .cs.

- It's also considered good practice for the name of a C# source file to match the name of the class or interface defined within that file.

- The code for two or more class or interface definitions can be placed in the same source file; we don't generally do so, however, because it's much easier to manage C# source code when there is a one-to-one correspondence between the external file name and the internal C# class name. You might forget, for example, that the Student class can be found in the file Course.cs.

The Simple Mechanics of C# Compilation

To illustrate the mechanics of compiling and running C# programs, we'll start with a very simple program. Assume that the following source code is stored in a file named

SimpleProgram.cs:

```
// SimpleProgram.cs

using System;

public class SimpleProgram
{
  static void Main() {
    Console.WriteLine("Hello");
  }
}
```

Assuming that the .NET Framework is properly installed, as discussed earlier in this appendix, we can compile the SimpleProgram.cs source code file by opening a command prompt window from within Windows, navigate to the directory in which the source code is located, and then type the following:

```
csc SimpleProgram.cs
```

This command invokes the C# compiler (its executable is named `csc.exe`). Assuming that the compiler is properly installed and that no compiler errors arise from our code, this command produces an *executable file* named `SimpleProgram.exe`. The executable file will by default be placed in the same directory from which the compiler was invoked (which, in this example, will cause it to be collocated with the `SimpleProgram.cs` source code file).

To execute our program, we then type the name of the executable file (the `.exe` suffix is optional) at the command line:

```
SimpleProgram
```

Compiling Multiclass Applications

There are several different ways to compile an application involving *multiple* source code files (multiple class/interface definitions):

- We can compile all of the source code (`.cs`) files simultaneously into an executable (`.exe`) file/application.

- We can compile individual source code (`.cs`) files into an intermediate form called a *dynamic-link library* (`.dll`) file for later inclusion into an application.

- We can combine the two preceding approaches.

We'll illustrate each of these scenarios in turn using the following simple multiclass application.

- First, we'll rewrite the `SimpleProgram` application so that it instantiates a `Person` object and accesses a property on this object. The source code for the revised `SimpleProgram2` class is contained in a file named `SimpleProgram2.cs`.

```
// SimpleProgram2.cs

using System;

public class SimpleProgram2
{
  static void Main() {
    Person p = new Person("Steve");
    Console.WriteLine("Our person's name is " + p.Name);
  }
}
```

- To support this program, we'll create a very simple `Person` class definition that has only one field, `name`; a constructor to initialize the `name` field; and a `Name` property with which to access the value of the field from client code. The source code for the `Person` class is contained in a separate file named `Person.cs`.

```
// Person.cs

public class Person
{
  // Field.
  private string name;
```

```
    // Constructor.
    public Person(string n) {
      name = n;
    }

    // Property.
    public string Name {
      get {
        return name;
      }
      set {
        name = value;
      }
    }
  }
```

Let's now explore various ways to produce an executable application (.exe file).

Scenario #1: Compiling from .cs to .exe Files Directly

Let's assume that neither the SimpleProgram2.cs nor the Person.cs file has previously been compiled. If we were to try to compile the SimpleProgram2 class by itself, using the following command:

```
csc SimpleProgram2.cs
```

the following compiler error message would arise:

```
error: The type or namespace name "Person" could not be found
```

This error arises because the C# compiler doesn't automatically search for other files that it needs in order to compile those that we've explicitly directed it to compile. Because Person isn't a predefined C# type, the compiler will complain that it doesn't recognize the name "Person".

One simple solution for this problem is to introduce the Person.cs source file into the syntax of the compilation command, thereby compiling the entire application in a single step to produce an executable file named SimpleProgram2.exe:

```
csc SimpleProgram2.cs Person.cs
```

(The default name for an .exe file matches the name of the *first* source (.cs) file specified by a compilation command.)

This command syntax can be extended to include any number of source files. Wildcards can also be used; for example, the following syntax will compile all the .cs files in the working directory:

```
csc *.cs
```

The previous compiler command:

```
csc SimpleProgram2.cs Person.cs
```

is actually shorthand for the following slightly more complex command:

```
csc /t:exe SimpleProgram2.cs Person.cs
```

The /t (or alternatively, /target) *compiler option* specifies what type of output the compilation will produce. /t:exe indicates that the target for the compilation is a *console application*; that is, one that will be run from the command line. As it turns out, /t:exe is a default compiler option and thus doesn't have to be specified.

To successfully compile one or more C# source code (.cs) files directly into an executable (.exe) application file, one of the source code files in the compile command must contain a class that defines a Main method. If none of the .cs files contains such a method, a compilation error will arise; for example, if we were to try to compile the Person.cs file by itself with the following command:

```
csc Person.cs
```

the compiler would generate the following error message:

```
error:  Program 'Person.exe' does not contain a static 'Main'
 method suitable for an entry point.
```

There is indeed a way to compile stand-alone class files incrementally, however, which brings us to scenario #2.

Scenario #2: Compiling from .cs to .dll Form

A source code file such as Person.cs can optionally be compiled into an intermediate, non-executable form known as a dynamic-link library file (.dll) This file is intended for use as a shared library file that can be dynamically linked into one or more applications by the .NET runtime.

We produce a .dll file using the /t:library compiler option. For example, the following compilation command will produce a file named Person.dll:

```
csc /t:library Person.cs
```

We can also use the wildcard character, *, to assemble all the local source code files into a single .dll file (in this case, the name of the resulting .dll file will match that of the first source file compiled):

```
csc /t:library *.cs
```

Compiling one or more source files into a .dll file form is useful when the classes and/ or interfaces in those source files will be used in multiple applications. We can compile the source files once as a .dll file and then link the file into as many applications as desired without having to recompile it over and over again. The process of integrating .dll files into an application is discussed as scenario #3 in the next section.

Another advantage of creating a .dll version of classes and/or interfaces is to protect proprietary source code. The .dll files can be shared with other programmers, who can in turn link them into their applications without being able to see how the code was written.

Scenario #3: Combining .cs and .dll Files in a Single Compilation

To make use of a previously compiled .dll file in the compilation of another C# program, the /r (or alternatively the /reference) compiler option can be specified. Returning to scenario #1, in which we ran into a roadblock because we were trying to compile the SimpleProgram2.cs file by itself. Let's now assume that the Person.cs file was previously compiled into a Person.dll file. We could then use the /r compiler option, as illustrated in the following command, to compile the SimpleProgram2 source file and the Person.dll DLL file into a single executable named SimpleProgram2.exe:

```
csc SimpleProgram2.cs /r:Person.dll
```

To incoporate multiple .dll files into an executable, the names of the files are separated with semicolons:

```
csc filename.cs /r:file1.dll;file2.dll;file3.dll
```

In the preceding compile statement, it is assumed that the Main method that serves as the entry point for the program is declared in filename.cs. The Main method shouldn't be declared in a source file that's part of a .dll file because the .dll file is intended to provide library behavior rather than entry-point behavior.

Naming the Resultant Executable

The /out compiler option is used to specify what the name of the resulting .exe or .dll file will be. For example, the following command would produce an executable file named MyApp.exe:

```
csc /out:MyApp.exe SimpleProgram2.cs Person.cs
```

If the /out option isn't used, the default .exe file name will match the name of the source (.cs) file that defines the Main method used by the application as its entry point.

Applications with Multiple Main Methods

We know that every application must define at least one Main method to serve as the entry point/driver for program execution. However, it's also possible for an application to contain more than one Main method if more than one class declares a Main method (for example, if we added a Main method to an arbitrary class so that we can test the features of that class in stand-alone fashion).

Let's modify the Person class introduced at the beginning of this section to include a Main method, as illustrated here:

```
// Person.cs

using System;

public class Person
{
  // Field.
  private string name;
```

```
  // Constructor.
  public Person(string n) {
    name = n;
  }

  // Property.
  public string Name {
    get {
      return name;
    }
    set {
      name = value;
    }
  }

  // We're providing the Person class with its own Main method so
  // that this class can be unit tested in isolation from the
  // application as a whole.
  static void Main() {
    // Create a Person object...
    Person p = new Person("Lisa");

    // ...and then display its name.
    Console.WriteLine("Name:  " + p.Name);
  }
}
```

We could now compile the Person.cs file by itself into an executable file named Person.exe using the following command:

```
csc Person.cs
```

It could in turn execute the Person class's Main method by typing the following:

```
Person
```

It would produce the following output:

```
Name:  Lisa
```

However, if we now try to compile the SimpleProgram2.cs and modified Person.cs source files together using the compile command:

```
csc SimpleProgram2.cs Person.cs
```

the compiler will generate the following error message:

```
error: Program 'SimpleProgram2.exe' has more than one entry
point defined.
```

We defined Main methods in both the SimpleProgram2 and Person classes, so the compiler doesn't know which one is intended to serve as the entry point for our application.

To solve this problem, we can use the /main compiler option to indicate which class is to serve as the application driver:

```
csc SimpleProgram2.cs Person.cs /main:SimpleProgram2
```

In this case, we indicated that the Main method in SimpleProgram2 is to be the entry point for the application. The resulting executable for this compilation will be named SimpleProgram2.exe.

We'll use the /main compiler option in Chapters 15 and 16 because the Student Registration System (SRS) application developed in those chapters will define more than one Main method to test the features of various individual classes.

Behind the Scenes: Microsoft Intermediate Language vs. Conventional Compilation

To appreciate how the behind the scenes mechanism for compiling and running C# programs differs from that of a programming language such as C++ or C, let's start with a review of the latter.

C or C++ Compilation

To execute a program written in a language such as C or C++, the source code of the program must first be compiled into an executable form known as *binary code* or *machine code*. Binary code, in essence, is a pattern of 1s and 0s understandable by the underlying hardware architecture of the computer on which the program is intended to run.

Even if the original (C, C++) source code is written to be *platform-independent* (the program doesn't take advantage of any operating system–specific language extensions), the resultant executable version will nonetheless still be tied to a particular hardware architecture, and can therefore only be run on that architecture. A version of a (C, C++) program compiled for Linux won't run on a Windows PC; a version compiled for Windows Vista won't run on a Mac; and so forth (see Figure A-1).

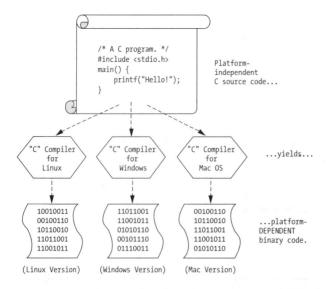

Figure A-1. *C or C++ compilation yields platform-dependent executable code.*

Microsoft Intermediate Language

The C# compiler doesn't produce machine code. Instead, C# programs are compiled into an intermediate form called *Microsoft Intermediate Language (MSIL)*, which is also referred to as *Common Intermediate Language*. MSIL is platform-independent code that contains instructions for a "virtual" processor. When a compiled C# program is actually executed, the .NET runtime environment converts the MSIL code just in time into machine code that is honed to the specific platform that the program is being run on and then executes that machine code (see Figure A-2). Thus, the *same* MSIL code can be executed on any platform that supports the common language runtime.

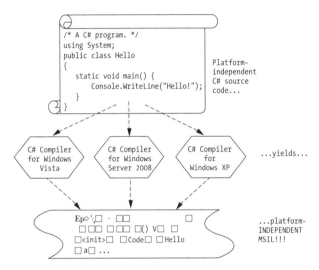

Figure A-2. *.NET compilation yields platform-independent MSIL code.*

The types of platforms that support the .NET CLR change as new versions of Windows and .NET are released. The best way to determine whether a current release of .NET is compatible with your operating system is to go the Downloads page at the MSDN web site and check the Supported Operating Systems information for the specific CLR version.

■ ■ ■

Downloading and Compiling the SRS Source Code

All the source code and supporting data files for the key example programs in this book are available for download from the Apress web site, www.apress.com/book/sourcecode, as a single file named 9781430210887.zip. To download the file, select the title of this book from the list, click the Submit button, and then click the Download Source Code File link. When downloaded and unzipped, this will create the directory structure shown in Figure B-1. At the top level of the file structure is a folder named Code, in which there are folders that correspond to the chapters of this book that have sample code.

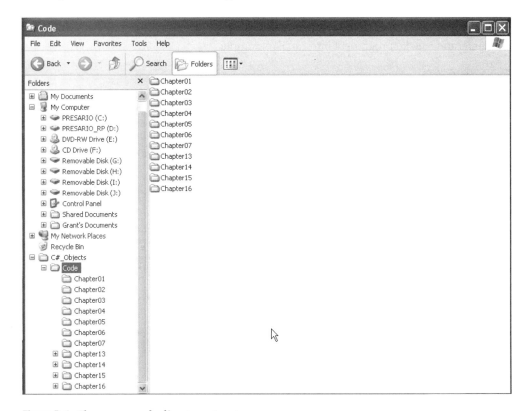

Figure B-1. *The source code directory structure*

For Chapters 14–16, the SRS-specific files will be located in a subdirectory called SRS—for example, *xxx*\Chapter14\SRS. For Chapters 14 and 16, small example programs unrelated to the SRS—for example, the TestForm examples from Chapter 16—will be located in the Chapter 14 and Chapter 16 "parent" subdirectories, respectively.

To compile the SRS code for a particular chapter, change your default working directory to the appropriate *xxx*\Chapter*nn*\SRS subdirectory (for example, *xxx*\Chapter14\SRS) and enter the appropriate compile command, which in many cases will simply be the following:

```
csc /out:SRS.exe *.cs
```

In other situations, the compilation command needs to be a bit more complicated (for selected code in Chapters 15 and 16, for example), so you'll be given specific instructions at that point in the chapter text.

Following the procedure that was outlined in Chapter 13, if the SRS source code for a given chapter has been compiled into a file named SRS.exe, the SRS application can be run by typing the command-prompt command:

```
SRS
```

To compile and run individual example files such as TestForm.cs, change your default working directory to the appropriate chapter subdirectory (*xxx*/Chapter14 or *xxx*/Chapter16), and type the following:

```
csc programName.cs
programName
```

to compile and run the program of interest. For example:

```
csc TestForm.cs
TestForm
```

Index

You Need the Companion eBook

Your purchase of this book entitles you to buy the companion PDF-version eBook for only $10. Take the weightless companion with you anywhere.

We believe this Apress title will prove so indispensable that you'll want to carry it with you everywhere, which is why we are offering the companion eBook (in PDF format) for $10 to customers who purchase this book now. Convenient and fully searchable, the PDF version of any content-rich, page-heavy Apress book makes a valuable addition to your programming library. You can easily find and copy code—or perform examples by quickly toggling between instructions and the application. Even simultaneously tackling a donut, diet soda, and complex code becomes simplified with hands-free eBooks!

Once you purchase your book, getting the $10 companion eBook is simple:

❶ Visit **www.apress.com/promo/tendollars/**.

❷ Complete a basic registration form to receive a randomly generated question about this title.

❸ Answer the question correctly in 60 seconds, and you will receive a promotional code to redeem for the $10.00 eBook.

THE EXPERT'S VOICE™

2855 TELEGRAPH AVENUE | SUITE 600 | BERKELEY, CA 94705

Offer valid through 4/09.